# UNIX® System V

## Programmer's Guide

UNIX® System V

Programmer's Guide

AT&T

Prentice-Hall, Inc., Englewood Cliffs, NJ 07632

Library of Congress Catalog Card Number: 87-60155

Editorial/production supervision: Karen S. Fortgang
Cover illustration: Jim Kinstry
Manufacturing buyer: S. Gordon Osbourne

Prentice-Hall International (UK) Limited, *London*
Prentice-Hall of Australia Pty. Limited, *Sydney*
Editora Prentice-Hall do Brasil, Ltda., *Rio de Janeiro*
Prentice-Hall of Canada Inc., *Toronto*
Prentice-Hall Hispanoamericana, S.A., *Mexico*
Prentice-Hall of India Private Limited, *New Delhi*
Prentice-Hall of Japan, Inc., *Tokyo*
Prentice-Hall of Southeast Asia Pte. Ltd., *Singapore*

# Table of Contents

# Part 2: Support Tools

# INTRODUCTION

## Purpose

This guide is designed to give you information about programming in a
UNIX system environment. It does not attempt to teach you how to write
programs. Rather, it is intended to supplement texts on programming
languages by concentrating on the other elements that are part of getting programs into operation.

## Audience and Prerequisite Knowledge

As the title suggests, we are addressing programmers, especially those
who have not worked extensively with the UNIX system. No special level of
programming involvement is assumed. We hope the book will be useful to
people who write only an occasional program as well as those who work on
or manage large application development projects.

Programmers in the expert class, or those engaged in developing system
software, may find this guide lacks the depth of information they need. For
them we recommend the *Programmer's Reference Manual* (P-H).

Knowledge of terminal use, of a UNIX system editor, and of the UNIX
system directory/file structure is assumed. If you feel shaky about your
mastery of these basic tools, you might want to look over the *User's Guide*
(P-H) before tackling this one.

## Organization

The material is organized into two parts and seventeen chapters, as follows:

- Part 1, Chapter 1 — Overview

  Identifies the special features of the UNIX system that make up the programming environment: the concept of building blocks, pipes, special
  files, shell programming, etc. As a framework for the material that follows, three different levels of programming in a UNIX system are
  defined: single-user, applications, and systems programming.

- Chapter 2 — Programming Basics

  Describes the most fundamental utilities needed to get programs running.

- Chapter 3 — Application Programming

  Enlarges on many of the topics covered in the previous chapter with particular emphasis on how things change as the project grows bigger. Describes tools for keeping programming projects organized.

- Part 2, Chapters 4 through 17 — Support Tools, Descriptions, and Tutorials

  Includes detailed information about the use of many of the UNIX system tools.

At the end of the text is an appendix on command packages for the AT&T 3B2 Computer, a glossary, and an index.

## The C Connection

The UNIX system supports many programming languages, and C compilers are available on many different operating systems. Nevertheless, the relationship between the UNIX operating system and C has always been and remains very close. Most of the code in the UNIX operating system is C, and over the years many organizations using the UNIX system have come to use C for an increasing portion of their application code. Thus, while this guide is intended to be useful to you no matter what language(s) you are using, you will find that, unless there is a specific language-dependent point to be made, the examples assume you are programming in C.

## Hardware/Software Dependencies

The text reflects the way things work on an AT&T 3B2 Computer running UNIX System V at the Release 3.0 level. If you find commands that work a little differently in your UNIX system environment, it may be because you are running under a different release of the software. If some commands just don't seem to exist at all, they may be members of packages not installed on your system. Appendix A describes the command packages available on the AT&T 3B2 Computer. If you do find yourself trying to execute a non-existent command, check Appendix A, then talk to the administrators of your system.

## Notation Conventions

Whenever the text includes examples of output from the computer and/or commands entered by you, we follow the standard notation scheme that is common throughout UNIX system documentation:

- Commands that you type in from your terminal are shown in **bold** type.

- Text that is printed on your terminal by the computer is shown in `constant width` type. Constant width type is also used for code samples because it allows the most accurate representation of spacing. Spacing is often a matter of coding style, but is sometimes critical.

- Comments added to a display to show that part of the display has been omitted are shown in *italic* type and are indented to separate them from the text that represents computer output or input. Comments that explain the input or output are shown in the same type font as the rest of the display.

  Italics are also used to show substitutable values, such as, *filename*, when the format of a command is shown.

- There is an implied RETURN at the end of each command and menu response you enter. Where you may be expected to enter only a RETURN (as in the case where you are accepting a menu default), the symbol <**CR**> is used.

- In cases where you are expected to enter a control character, it is shown as, for example, **CTRL-D**. This means that you press the **d** key on your keyboard while holding down the **CTRL** key.

- The dollar sign, **$**, and pound sign, **#**, symbols are the standard default prompt signs for an ordinary user and **root** respectively. **$** means you are logged in as an ordinary user. **#** means you are logged in as **root**.

- When the **#** prompt is used in an example, it means the command illustrated may be used only by **root**.

# Command References

When commands are mentioned in a section of the text for the first time, a reference to the manual section where the command is formally described is included in parentheses: **command**(section). The numbered sections are located in the following manuals:

Section (1)                 *User's Reference Manual* (P-H)

Sections (1, 1M), (7), (8)    *System Administrator's Reference Manual* (AT&T)

Sections (1), (2), (3), (4), (5)   *Programmer's Reference Manual* (P-H)

# Information in the Examples

While every effort has been made to present displays of information just as they appear on your terminal, it is possible that your system may produce slightly different output. Some displays depend on a particular machine configuration that may differ from yours. Changes between releases of the UNIX system software may cause small differences in what appears on your terminal.

Where complete code samples are shown, we have tried to make sure they compile and work as represented. Where code fragments are shown, while we can't say that they have been compiled, we have attempted to maintain the same standards of coding accuracy for them.

# CHAPTER 1: PROGRAMMING IN A UNIX SYSTEM ENVIRONMENT: AN OVERVIEW

## Introduction

The 1983 Turing Award of the Association for Computing Machinery was given jointly to Ken Thompson and Dennis Ritchie, the two men who first designed and developed the UNIX operating system. The award citation said, in part:

> "The success of the UNIX system stems from its tasteful selection of a few key ideas and their elegant implementation. The model of the UNIX system has led a generation of software designers to new ways of thinking about programming. The genius of the UNIX system is its framework which enables programmers to stand on the work of others."

As programmers working in a UNIX system environment, why should we care what Thompson and Ritchie did? Does it have any relevance for us today?

It does because if we understand the thinking behind the system design and the atmosphere in which it flowered, it can help us become productive UNIX system programmers more quickly.

## The Early Days

You may already have read about how Ken Thompson came across a DEC PDP-7 machine sitting unused in a hallway at AT&T Bell Laboratories, and how he and Dennis Ritchie and a few of their colleagues used that as the original machine for developing a new operating system that became UNIX.

The important thing to realize, however, is that what they were trying to do was fashion a pleasant computing environment for themselves. It was not, "Let's get together and build an operating system that will attract world-wide attention."

The sequence in which elements of the system fell into place is interesting. The first piece was the file system, followed quickly by its organization into a hierarchy of directories and files. The view of everything, data stores, programs, commands, directories, even devices, as files of one type or another was critical, as was the idea of a file as a one-dimensional array of bytes with no other structure implied. The cleanness and simplicity of this way of looking at files has been a major contributing factor to a computer environment that programmers and other users have found comfortable to work in.

The next element was the idea of processes, with one process being able to create another and communicate with it. This innovative way of looking at running programs as processes led easily to the practice (quintessentially UNIX) of reusing code by calling it from another process. With the addition of commands to manipulate files and an assembler to produce executable programs, the system was essentially able to function on its own.

The next major development was the acquisition of a DEC PDP-11 and the installation of the new system on it. This has been described by Ritchie as a stroke of good luck, in that the PDP-11 was to become a hugely successful machine, its success to some extent adding momentum to the acceptance of the system that began to be known by the name of UNIX.

By 1972 the innovative idea of pipes (connecting links between processes whereby the output of one becomes the input of the next) had been incorporated into the system, the operating system had been recoded in higher level languages (first B, then C), and had been dubbed with the name UNIX (coined by Brian Kernighan). By this point, the "pleasant computing environment" sought by Thompson and Ritchie was a reality; but some other things were going on that had a strong influence on the character of the product then and today.

It is worth pointing out that the UNIX system came out of an atmosphere that was totally different from that in which most commercially successful operating systems are produced. The more typical atmosphere is that described by Tracy Kidder in *The Soul of a New Machine*. In that case, dozens of talented programmers worked at white heat, in an atmosphere of extremely tight security, against murderous deadlines. By contrast, the UNIX system could be said to have had about a ten year gestation period. From the beginning it attracted the interest of a growing number of brilliant specialists, many of whom found in the UNIX system an environment that allowed them to pursue research and development interests of their own, but who in turn contributed additions to the body of tools available for succeeding ranks of UNIX programmers.

Beginning in 1971, the system began to be used for applications within AT&T Bell Laboratories, and shortly thereafter (1974) was made available at low cost and without support to colleges and universities. These versions, called research versions and identified with Arabic numbers up through 7, occasionally grew on their own and fed back to the main system additional innovative tools. The widely-used screen editor **vi**(1), for example, was added to the UNIX system by William Joy at the University of California, Berkeley. In 1979 acceding to commercial demand, AT&T began offering supported versions (called development versions) of the UNIX system. These are identified with Roman numerals and often have interim release numbers appended. The current development version, for example, is UNIX System V Release 3.0.

Versions of the UNIX system being offered now by AT&T are coming from an environment more closely related, perhaps, to the standard software factory. Features are being added to new releases in response to the expressed needs of the market place. The essential quality of the UNIX system, however, remains as the product of the innovative thinking of its originators and the collegial atmosphere in which they worked. This quality has on occasion been referred to as the UNIX philosophy, but what is meant is the way in which sophisticated programmers have come to work with the UNIX system.

## UNIX System Philosophy Simply Stated

For as long as you are writing programs on a UNIX system you should keep this motto hanging on your wall:

```
* * * * * * * * * * * * * * * * * * *
*                                   *
*      Build on the work of others  *
*                                   *
* * * * * * * * * * * * * * * * * * *
```

Unlike computer environments where each new project is like starting with a blank canvas, on a UNIX system a good percentage of any programming effort is lying there in **bin**s, and **lbin**s, and **/usr/bin**s, not to mention **etc**, waiting to be used.

The features of the UNIX system (pipes, processes, and the file system) contribute to this reusability, as does the history of sharing and contributing that extends back to 1969. You risk missing the essential nature of the UNIX system if you don't put this to work.

# UNIX System Tools and Where You Can Read About Them

The term "UNIX system tools" can stand some clarification. In the narrowest sense, it means an existing piece of software used as a component in a new task. In a broader context, the term is often used to refer to elements of the UNIX system that might also be called features, utilities, programs, filters, commands, languages, functions, and so on. It gets confusing because any of the things that might be called by one or more of these names can be, and often are, used in the narrow way as part of the solution to a programming problem.

## Tools Covered and Not Covered in this Guide

The *Programmer's Guide* is about tools used in the process of creating programs in a UNIX system environment, so let's take a minute to talk about which tools we mean, which ones are not going to be covered in this book, and where you might find information about those not covered here. Actually, the subject of things not covered in this guide might be even more important to you than the things that are. We couldn't possibly cover everything you ever need to know about UNIX system tools in this one volume.

Tools not covered in this text:

- the **login** procedure

- UNIX system editors and how to use them

- how the file system is organized and how you move around in it

- shell programming

Information about these subjects can be found in the *User's Guide* and a number of commercially available texts.

Tools covered here can be classified as follows:

- utilities for getting programs running

- utilities for organizing software development projects

- specialized languages

- debugging and analysis tools

- compiled language components that are not part of the language syntax, for example, standard libraries, systems calls, and functions

## The Shell as a Prototyping Tool

Any time you log in to a UNIX system machine you are using the shell. The shell is the interactive command interpreter that stands between you and the UNIX system kernel, but that's only part of the story. Because of its ability to start processes, direct the flow of control, field interrupts and redirect input and output it is a full-fledged programming language. Programs that use these capabilities are known as shell procedures or shell scripts.

Much innovative use of the shell involves stringing together commands to be run under the control of a shell script. The dozens and dozens of commands that can be used in this way are documented in the *User's Reference Manual*. Time spent with the *User's Reference Manual* can be rewarding. Look through it when you are trying to find a command with just the right option to handle a knotty programming problem. The more familiar you become with the commands described in the manual pages the more you will be able to take full advantage of the UNIX system environment.

It is not our purpose here to instruct you in shell programming. What we want to stress here is the important part that shell procedures can play in developing prototypes of full-scale applications. While understanding all the nuances of shell programming can be a fairly complex task, getting a shell procedure up and running is far less time-consuming than writing, compiling and debugging compiled code.

This ability to get a program into production quickly is what makes the shell a valuable tool for program development. Shell programming allows you to "build on the work of others" to the greatest possible degree, since it allows you to piece together major components simply and efficiently. Many times even large applications can be done using shell procedures. Even if the application is initially developed as a prototype system for testing purposes rather than being put into production, many months of work can be saved.

With a prototype for testing, the range of possible user errors can be determined—something that is not always easy to plan out when an application is being designed. The method of dealing with strange user input can be worked out inexpensively, avoiding large re-coding problems.

A common occurrence in the UNIX system environment is to find that an available UNIX system tool can accomplish with a couple of lines of instructions what might take a page and a half of compiled code. Shell procedures can intermix compiled modules and regular UNIX system commands to let you take advantage of work that has gone before.

# Three Programming Environments

We distinguish among three programming environments to emphasize that the information needs and the way in which UNIX system tools are used differ from one environment to another. We do not intend to imply a hierarchy of skill or experience. Highly-skilled programmers with years of experience can be found in the "single-user" category, and relative newcomers can be members of an application development or systems programming team.

## Single-User Programmer

Programmers in this environment are writing programs only to ease the performance of their primary job. The resulting programs might well be added to the stock of programs available to the community in which the programmer works. This is similar to the atmosphere in which the UNIX system thrived; someone develops a useful tool and shares it with the rest of the organization. Single-user programmers may not have externally imposed requirements, or co-authors, or project management concerns. The programming task itself drives the coding very directly. One advantage of a timesharing system such as UNIX is that people with programming skills can be set free to work on their own without having to go through formal project approval channels and perhaps wait for months for a programming department to solve their problems.

Single-user programmers need to know how to:

- select an appropriate language
- compile and run programs
- use system libraries
- analyze programs
- debug programs
- keep track of program versions

Most of the information to perform these functions at the single-user level can be found in Chapter 2.

## Application Programming

Programmers working in this environment are developing systems for the benefit of other, non-programming users. Most large commercial computer applications still involve a team of applications development programmers. They may be employees of the end-user organization or they may work for a software development firm. Some of the people working in this environment may be more in the project management area than working programmers.

Information needs of people in this environment include all the topics in Chapter 2, plus additional information on:

- software control systems

- file and record locking

- communication between processes

- shared memory

- advanced debugging techniques

These topics are discussed in Chapter 3.

## Systems Programmers

These are programmers engaged in writing software tools that are part of, or closely related to the operating system itself. The project may involve writing a new device driver, a data base management system or an enhancement to the UNIX system kernel. In addition to knowing their way around the operating system source code and how to make changes and enhancements to it, they need to be thoroughly familiar with all the topics covered in Chapters 2 and 3.

# Summary

In this overview chapter we have described the way that the UNIX system developed and the effect that has on the way programmers now work with it. We have described what is and is not to be found in the other chapters of this guide to help programmers. We have also suggested that in many cases programming problems may be easily solved by taking advantage of the UNIX system interactive command interpreter known as the shell. Finally, we identified three programming environments in the hope that it will help orient the reader to the organization of the text in the remaining chapters.

# CHAPTER 2: PROGRAMMING BASICS

## Introduction

The information in this chapter is for anyone just learning to write programs to run in a UNIX system environment. In Chapter 1 we identified one group of UNIX system users as single-user programmers. People in that category, particularly those who are not deeply interested in programming, may find this chapter (plus related reference manuals) tells them as much as they need to know about coding and running programs on a UNIX system computer.

Programmers whose interest does run deeper, who are part of an application development project, or who are producing programs on one UNIX system computer that are being ported to another, should view this chapter as a starter package.

# Choosing a Programming Language

How do you decide which programming language to use in a given situation? One answer could be, "I always code in HAIRBOL, because that's the language I know best." Actually, in some circumstances that's a legitimate answer. But assuming more than one programming language is available to you, that different programming languages have their strengths and weaknesses, and assuming that once you've learned to use one programming language it becomes relatively easy to learn to use another, you might approach the problem of language selection by asking yourself questions like the following:

- What is the nature of the task this program is to do?

  Does the task call for the development of a complex algorithm, or is this a simple procedure that has to be done on a lot of records?

- Does the programming task have many separate parts?

  Can the program be subdivided into separately compilable functions, or is it one module?

- How soon does the program have to be available?

  Is it needed right now, or do I have enough time to work out the most efficient process possible?

- What is the scope of its use?

  Am I the only person who will use this program, or is it going to be distributed to the whole world?

- Is there a possibility the program will be ported to other systems?

- What is the life-expectancy of the program?

  Is it going to be used just a few times, or will it still be going strong five years from now?

# Supported Languages in a UNIX System Environment

By "supported languages" we mean those offered by AT&T for use on an AT&T 3B2 Computer running UNIX System V Release 3.0. Since these are separately purchasable items, not all of them will necessarily be installed on your machine. On the other hand, you may have languages available on your machine that came from another source and are not mentioned in this discussion. Be that as it may, in this section and the one to follow we give brief descriptions of the nature of a) six full-scale programming languages, and b) a number of special purpose languages.

## C Language

C is intimately associated with the UNIX system since it was originally developed for use in recoding the UNIX system kernel. If you need to use a lot of UNIX system function calls for low-level I/O, memory or device management, or inter-process communication, C language is a logical first choice. Most programs, however, don't require such direct interfaces with the operating system so the decision to choose C might better be based on one or more of the following characteristics:

- a variety of data types: character, integer, long integer, float, and double

- low level constructs (most of the UNIX system kernel is written in C)

- derived data types such as arrays, functions, pointers, structures and unions

- multi-dimensional arrays

- scaled pointers, and the ability to do pointer arithmetic

- bit-wise operators

- a variety of flow-of-control statements: if, if-else, switch, while, do-while, and for

- a high degree of portability

C is a language that lends itself readily to structured programming. It is natural in C to think in terms of functions. The next logical step is to view each function as a separately compilable unit. This approach (coding a program in small pieces) eases the job of making changes and/or improvements.

If this begins to sound like the UNIX system philosophy of building new programs from existing tools, it's not just coincidence. As you create functions for one program you will surely find that many can be picked up, or quickly revised, for another program.

A difficulty with C is that it takes a fairly concentrated use of the language over a period of several months to reach your full potential as a C programmer. If you are a casual programmer, you might make life easier for yourself if you choose a less demanding language.

## FORTRAN

The oldest of the high-level programming languages, FORTRAN is still highly prized for its variety of mathematical functions. If you are writing a program for statistical analysis or other scientific applications, FORTRAN is a good choice. An original design objective was to produce a language with good operating efficiency. This has been achieved at the expense of some flexibility in the area of type definition and data abstraction. There is, for example, only a single form of the iteration statement. FORTRAN also requires using a somewhat rigid format for input of lines of source code. This shortcoming may be overcome by using one of the UNIX system tools designed to make FORTRAN more flexible.

## Pascal

Originally designed as a teaching tool for block structured programming, Pascal has gained quite a wide acceptance because of its straightforward style. Pascal is highly structured and allows system level calls (characteristics it shares with C). Since the intent of the developers, however, was to produce a language to teach people about programming it is perhaps best suited to small projects. Among its inconveniences are its lack of facilities for specifying initial values for variables and limited file processing capability.

## COBOL

Probably more programmers are familiar with COBOL than with any other single programming language. It is frequently used in business applications because its strengths lie in the management of input/output and in defining record layouts.

It is somewhat cumbersome to use COBOL for complex algorithms, but it works well in cases where many records have to be passed through a simple process; a payroll withholding tax calculation, for example. It is a rather tedious language to work with because each program requires a lengthy amount of text merely to describe record layouts, processing environment and variables used in the code. The COBOL language is wordy so the compilation process is often quite complex. Once written and put into production, COBOL programs have a way of staying in use for years, and what might be thought of by some as wordiness comes to be considered self-documentation. The investment in programmer time often makes them resistant to change.

## BASIC

The most commonly heard comment about BASIC is that it is easy to learn. With the spread of personal microcomputers many people have learned BASIC because it is simple to produce runnable programs in very little time. It is difficult, however, to use BASIC for large programming projects. It lacks the provision for structured flow-of-control, requires that every variable used be defined for the entire program and has no way of transferring values between functions and calling programs. Most versions of BASIC run as interpreted code rather than compiled. That makes for slower running programs. Despite its limitations, however, it is useful for getting simple procedures into operation quickly.

## Assembly Language

The closest approach to machine language, assembly language is specific to the particular computer on which your program is to run. High-level languages are translated into the assembly language for a specific processor as one step of the compilation. The most common need to work in assembly language arises when you want to do some task that is not within the scope of a high-level language. Since assembly language is machine-specific, programs written in it are not portable.

# Special Purpose Languages

In addition to the above formal programming languages, the UNIX system environment frequently offers one or more of the special purpose languages listed below.

 Since UNIX system utilities and commands are packaged in functional groupings, it is possible that not all the facilities mentioned will be available on all systems.

### awk

**awk** (its name is an acronym constructed from the initials of its developers) scans an input file for lines that match pattern(s) described in a specification file. On finding a line that matches a pattern, **awk** performs actions also described in the specification. It is not uncommon that an **awk** program can be written in a couple of lines to do functions that would take a couple of pages to describe in a programming language like FORTRAN or C. For example, consider a case where you have a set of records that consist of a key field and a second field that represents a quantity. You have sorted the records by the key field, and you now want to add the quantities for records with duplicate keys and output a file in which no keys are duplicated. The pseudo-code for such a program might look like this:

```
Read the first record into a hold area;
Read additional records until EOF;
  {
  If the key matches the key of the record in the hold area,
    add the quantity to the quantity field of the held record;
  If the key does not match the key of the held record,
    write the held record,
    move the new record to the hold area;
  }
At EOF, write out the last record from the hold area.
```

An **awk** program to accomplish this task would look like this:

```
        { qty[$1] += $2 }
END     { for (key in qty) print key, qty[key] }
```

This illustrates only one characteristic of **awk**; its ability to work with associative arrays. With **awk**, the input file does not have to be sorted, which is a requirement of the pseudo-program.

## lex

**lex** is a lexical analyzer that can be added to C or FORTRAN programs. A lexical analyzer is interested in the vocabulary of a language rather than its grammar, which is a system of rules defining the structure of a language. **lex** can produce C language subroutines that recognize regular expressions specified by the user, take some action when a regular expression is recognized and pass the output stream on to the next program.

## yacc

**yacc** (Yet Another Compiler Compiler) is a tool for describing an input language to a computer program. **yacc** produces a C language subroutine that parses an input stream according to rules laid down in a specification file. The **yacc** specification file establishes a set of grammar rules together with actions to be taken when tokens in the input match the rules. **lex** may be used with **yacc** to control the input process and pass tokens to the parser that applies the grammar rules.

## M4

**M4** is a macro processor that can be used as a preprocessor for assembly language, and C programs. It is described in Section (1) of the *Programmer's Reference Manual*.

## bc and dc

**bc** enables you to use a computer terminal as you would a programmable calculator. You can edit a file of mathematical computations and call **bc** to execute them. The **bc** program uses **dc**. You can use **dc** directly, if you want, but it takes a little getting used to since it works with reverse Polish notation. That means you enter numbers into a stack followed by the operator. **bc** and **dc** are described in Section (1) of the *User's Reference Manual*.

## curses

Actually a library of C functions, **curses** is included in this list because the set of functions just about amounts to a sub-language for dealing with terminal screens. If you are writing programs that include interactive user screens, you will want to become familiar with this group of functions.

In addition to all the foregoing, don't overlook the possibility of using shell procedures.

# After Your Code Is Written

The last two steps in most compilation systems in the UNIX system environment are the assembler and the link editor. The compilation system produces assembly language code. The assembler translates that code into the machine language of the computer the program is to run on. The link editor resolves all undefined references and makes the object module executable. With most languages on the UNIX system the assembler and link editor produce files in what is known as the Common Object File Format (COFF). A common format makes it easier for utilities that depend on information in the object file to work on different machines running different versions of the UNIX system.

In the Common Object File Format an object file contains:

- a file header

- optional secondary header

- a table of section headers

- data corresponding to the section header(s)

- relocation information

- line numbers

- a symbol table

- a string table

An object file is made up of sections. Usually, there are at least two: **.text**, and **.data**. Some object files contain a section called **.bss**. (**.bss** is an assembly language pseudo-op that originally stood for "block started by symbol.") **.bss**, when present, holds uninitialized data. Options of the compilers cause different items of information to be included in the Common Object File Format. For example, compiling a program with the **-g** option adds line numbers and other symbolic information that is needed for the **sdb** (Symbolic Debugger) command to be fully effective. You can spend many years programming without having to worry too much about the contents and organization of the Common Object File Format, so we are not going into any further depth of detail at this point. Detailed information is available in Chapter 11 of this guide.

# Compiling and Link Editing

The command used for compiling depends on the language used;

- for C programs, **cc** both compiles and link edits
- for FORTRAN programs, **f77** both compiles and link edits

## Compiling C Programs

To use the C compilation system you must have your source code in a file with a filename that ends in the characters **.c**, as in **mycode.c**. The command to invoke the compiler is:

> **cc mycode.c**

If the compilation is successful the process proceeds through the link edit stage and the result will be an executable file by the name of **a.out**.

Several options to the **cc** command are available to control its operation. The most used options are:

| | |
|---|---|
| **-c** | causes the compilation system to suppress the link edit phase. This produces an object file (**mycode.o**) that can be link edited at a later time with a **cc** command without the **-c** option. |
| **-g** | causes the compilation system to generate special information about variables and language statements used by the symbolic debugger **sdb**. If you are going through the stage of debugging your program, use this option. |
| **-O** | causes the inclusion of an additional optimization phase. This option is logically incompatible with the **-g** option. You would normally use **-O** after the program has been debugged, to reduce the size of the object file and increase execution speed. |
| **-p** | causes the compilation system to produce code that works in conjunction with the **prof**(1) command to produce a runtime profile of where the program is spending its time. Useful in identifying which routines are candidates for improved code. |

**-o** *outfile*        tells **cc** to tell the link editor to use the specified name for the executable file, rather than the default **a.out**.

Other options can be used with **cc**. Check the *Programmer's Reference Manual*.

If you enter the **cc** command using a file name that ends in **.s**, the compilation system treats it as assembly language source code and bypasses all the steps ahead of the assembly step.

## Compiling FORTRAN Programs

The **f77** command invokes the FORTRAN compilation system. The operation of the command is similar to that of the **cc** command, except the source code file(s) must have a **.f** suffix. The **f77** command compiles your source code and calls in the link editor to produce an executable file whose name is **a.out**.

The following command line options have the same meaning as they do for the **cc** command:

        **-c, -p, -O, -g,** and **-o** *outfile*

## Loading and Running BASIC Programs

BASIC programs can be invoked in two ways:

- With the command

  **basic bscpgm.b**

  where **bscpgm.b** is the name of the file that holds your BASIC statements. This tells the UNIX system to load and run the program. If the program includes a **run** statement naming another program, you will chain from one to the other. Variables specified in the first can be preserved for the second with the **common** statement.

- By setting up a shell script.

## Compiler Diagnostic Messages

The C compiler generates error messages for statements that don't compile. The messages are generally quite understandable, but in common with most language compilers they sometimes point several statements beyond where the actual error occurred. For example, if you inadvertently put an extra ; at the end of an if statement, a subsequent else will be flagged as a syntax error. In the case where a block of several statements follows the if, the line number of the syntax error caused by the else will start you looking for the error well past where it is. Unbalanced curly braces, { }, are another common producer of syntax errors.

## Link Editing

The **ld** command invokes the link editor directly. The typical user, however, seldom invokes **ld** directly. A more common practice is to use a language compilation control command (such as **cc**) that invokes **ld**. The link editor combines several object files into one, performs relocation, resolves external symbols, incorporates startup routines, and supports symbol table information used by **sdb**. You may, of course, start with a single object file rather than several. The resulting executable module is left in a file named **a.out**.

Any file named on the **ld** command line that is not an object file (typically, a name ending in **o**) is assumed to be an archive library or a file of link editor directives. The **ld** command has some 16 options. We are going to describe four of them. These options should be fed to the link editor by specifying them on the **cc** command line if you are doing both jobs with the single command, which is the usual case.

**-o** *outfile*  provides a name to be used to replace **a.out** as the name of the output file. Obviously, the name **a.out** is of only temporary usefulness. If you know the name you want use to invoke your program, you can provide it here. Of course, it may be equally convenient to do this:

**mv a.out progname**

when you want to give your program a less temporary name.

**-l**$x$  directs the link editor to search a library **lib**$x$**.a**, where $x$ is up to nine characters. For C programs, **libc.a** is automatically searched if the **cc** command is used. The **-l**$x$ option is used to bring in libraries not normally in the search path such as **libm.a**, the math library. The **-l**x option can occur more than once on a command line, with different values for the x. A library is searched when its name is encountered, so the placement of the option on the command line is important. The safest place to put it is at the end of the command line. The **-l**x option is related to the **-L** option.

**-L** *dir*     changes the **lib**x**.a** search sequence to search in the specified directory before looking in the default library directories, usually **/lib** or **/usr/lib**. This is useful if you have different versions of a library and you want to point the link editor to the correct one. It works on the assumption that once a library has been found no further searching for that library is necessary. Because **-L** diverts the search for the libraries specified by **-l**x options, it must precede such options on the command line.

**-u** *symname*     enters *symname* as an undefined symbol in the symbol table. This is useful if you are loading entirely from an archive library, because initially the symbol table is empty and needs an unresolved reference to force the loading of the first routine.

When the link editor is called through **cc**, a startup routine (typically **/lib/crt0.o** for C programs) is linked with your program. This routine calls **exit**(2) after execution of the main program.

The link editor accepts a file containing link editor directives. The details of the link editor command language can be found in Chapter 12.

# The Interface Between a Programming Language and the UNIX System

When a program is run in a computer it depends on the operating system for a variety of services. Some of the services such as bringing the program into main memory and starting the execution are completely transparent to the program. They are, in effect, arranged for in advance by the link editor when it marks an object module as executable. As a programmer you seldom need to be concerned about such matters.

Other services, however, such as input/output, file management, storage allocation do require work on the part of the programmer. These connections between a program and the UNIX operating system are what is meant by the term UNIX system/language interface. The topics included in this section are:

- How arguments are passed to a program

- System calls and subroutines

- Header files and libraries

- Input/Output

- Processes

- Error Handling, Signals, and Interrupts

## Why C Is Used to Illustrate the Interface

Throughout this section C programs are used to illustrate the interface between the UNIX system and programming languages because C programs make more use of the interface mechanisms than other high-level languages. What is really being covered in this section then is the UNIX system/C Language interface. The way that other languages deal with these topics is described in the user's guides for those languages.

## How Arguments Are Passed to a Program

Information or control data can be passed to a C program as arguments on the command line. When the program is run as a command, arguments on the command line are made available to the function **main** in two parameters, an argument count and an array of pointers to character strings. (Every C program is required to have an entry module by the name of **main**.) Since the argument count is always given, the program does not have to know in advance how many arguments to expect. The character strings pointed at by elements of the array of pointers contain the argument information.

The arguments are presented to the program traditionally as **argc** and **argv**, although any names you choose will work. **argc** is an integer that gives the count of the number of arguments. Since the command itself is considered to be the first argument, **argv[0]**, the count is always at least one. **argv** is an array of pointers to character strings (arrays of characters terminated by the null character \0).

If you plan to pass runtime parameters to your program, you need to include code to deal with the information. Two possible uses of runtime parameters are:

- as control data. Use the information to set internal flags that control the operation of the program.

- to provide a variable filename to the program.

Figures 2-1 and 2-2 show program fragments that illustrate these uses.

```
#include <stdio.h>

main(argc, argv)
  int argc;
  char *argv[];
{
                void exit();
                int oflag = FALSE;
                int pflag = FALSE;/* Function Flags */
                int rflag = FALSE;
                int ch;

                while ((ch = getopt(argc,argv, "opr")) != EOF)
                {
                  /* For options present, set flag to TRUE */
                  /* If no options present, print error message */
                switch (ch)
                {
                case 'o':
                oflag = 1;
                break;
                case 'p':
                pflag = 1;
                break;
                case 'r':
                rflag = 1;
                break;
                default:
                (void)fprintf(stderr,
                "Usage: %s [-opr]\n", argv[0]);
                exit(2);
                }
                }
                .
                .
                .
}
```

Figure 2-1: Using Command Line Arguments to Set Flags

```
#include <stdio.h>

main(argc, argv)
  int argc;
  char *argv[];
{
                   FILE *fopen(), *fin;
                   void perror(), exit();

                   if (argc > 1)
                   {
                   if ((fin = fopen(argv[1], "r")) == NULL)
                   {
                     /* First string (%s) is program name (argv[0]) */
                     /* Second string (%s) is name of file that could */
                     /* not be opened (argv[1]) */

                   (void)fprintf(stderr,
                     "%s: cannot open %s: ",
                     argv[0], argv[1]);
                   perror("");
                   exit(2);
                   }
                   }
                   .
                   .
                   .

}
```

Figure 2-2: Using **argv[n]** Pointers to Pass a Filename

The shell, which makes arguments available to your program, considers an argument to be any non-blank characters separated by blanks or tabs. Characters enclosed in double quotes ("abc def") are passed to the program as one argument even if blanks or tabs are among the characters. It goes without saying that you are responsible for error checking and otherwise making sure the argument received is what your program expects it to be.

A third argument is also present, in addition to **argc** and **argv**. The third argument, known as **envp**, is an array of pointers to environment variables. You can find more information on **envp** in the *Programmer's Reference Manual* under **exec**(2) and **environ**(5).

# System Calls and Subroutines

System calls are requests from a program for an action to be performed by the UNIX system kernel. Subroutines are precoded modules used to supplement the functionality of a programming language.

Both system calls and subroutines look like functions such as those you might code for the individual parts of your program. There are, however, differences between them:

- At link edit time, the code for subroutines is copied into the object file for your program; the code invoked by a system call remains in the kernel.

- At execution time, subroutine code is executed as if it was code you had written yourself; a system function call is executed by switching from your process area to the kernel.

This means that while subroutines make your executable object file larger, runtime overhead for context switching may be less and execution may be faster.

## Categories of System Calls and Subroutines

System calls divide fairly neatly into the following categories:

- file access
- file and directory manipulation
- process control
- environment control and status information

You can generally tell the category of a subroutine by the section of the *Programmer's Reference Manual* in which you find its manual page. However, the first part of Section 3 (3C and 3S) covers such a variety of subroutines it might be helpful to classify them further.

- The subroutines of sub-class 3S constitute the UNIX system/C
  Language standard I/O, an efficient I/O buffering scheme for C.

- The subroutines of sub-class 3C do a variety of tasks. They have in
  common the fact that their object code is stored in **libc.a**. They can be
  divided into the following categories:

  - string manipulation

  - character conversion

  - character classification

  - environment management

  - memory management

Figure 2-3 lists the functions that compose the standard I/O subroutines.
Frequently, one manual page describes several related functions. In Figure 2-3
the left hand column contains the name that appears at the top of the manual
page; the other names in the same row are related functions described on the
same manual page.

| Function Name(s) | | | | Purpose |
|---|---|---|---|---|
| **fclose** | **fflush** | | | close or flush a stream |
| **ferror** | **feof** | **clearerr** | **fileno** | stream status inquiries |
| **fopen** | **freopen** | **fdopen** | | open a stream |
| **fread** | **fwrite** | | | binary input/output |
| **fseek** | **rewind** | **ftell** | | reposition a file pointer in a stream |
| **getc** | **getchar** | **fgetc** | **getw** | get a character or word from a stream |
| **gets** | **fgets** | | | get a string from a stream |
| **popen** | **pclose** | | | begin or end a pipe to/from a process |
| **printf** | **fprintf** | **sprintf** | | print formatted output |

For all functions: #include <stdio.h>

The function name shown in **bold** gives the location in
the *Programmer's Reference Manual*, Section 3.

Figure 2-3: C Language Standard I/O Subroutines (sheet 1 of 2)

| Function Name(s) | | | | Purpose |
|---|---|---|---|---|
| **putc** | **putchar** | **fputc** | **putw** | put a character or word on a stream |
| **puts** | **fputs** | | | put a string on a stream |
| **scanf** | **fscanf** | **sscanf** | | convert formatted input |
| **setbuf** | **setvbuf** | | | assign buffering to a stream |
| **system** | | | | issue a command through the shell |
| **tmpfile** | | | | create a temporary file |
| **tmpnam** | **tempnam** | | | create a name for a temporary file |
| **ungetc** | | | | push character back into input stream |
| **vprintf** | **vfprintf** | **vsprintf** | | print formatted output of a varargs argument list |

For all functions: #include <stdio.h>

The function name shown in **bold** gives the location in
the *Programmer's Reference Manual*, Section 3.

Figure 2-3: C Language Standard I/O Subroutines (sheet 2 of 2)

Figure 2-4 lists string handling functions that are grouped under the
heading **string**(3C) in the *Programmer's Reference Manual*.

## String Operations

| | |
|---|---|
| **strcat(s1, s2)** | append a copy of s2 to the end of s1. |
| **strncat(s1, s2, n)** | append n characters from s2 to the end of s1. |
| **strcmp(s1, s2)** | compare two strings. Returns an integer less than, greater than or equal to 0 to show that s1 is lexicographically less than, greater than or equal to s2. |
| **strncmp(s1, s2, n)** | compare n characters from the two strings. Results are otherwise identical to strcmp. |
| **strcpy(s1, s2)** | copy s2 to s1, stopping after the null character (\0) has been copied. |
| **strncpy(s1, s2, n)** | copy n characters from s2 to s1. s2 will be truncated if it is longer than n, or padded with null characters if it is shorter than n. |
| **strdup(s)** | returns a pointer to a new string that is a duplicate of the string pointed to by s. |
| **strchr(s, c)** | returns a pointer to the first occurrence of character c in string s, or a NULL pointer if c is not in s. |
| **strrchr(s, c)** | returns a pointer to the last occurrence of character c in string s, or a NULL pointer if c is not in s. |

For all functions: #include <string.h>
**string.h** provides extern definitions of the string functions.

Figure 2-4: String Operations (sheet 1 of 2)

## String Operations

| | |
|---|---|
| **strlen(s)** | returns the number of characters in s up to the first null character. |
| **strpbrk(s1, s2)** | returns a pointer to the first occurrence in s1 of any character from s2, or a NULL pointer if no character from s2 occurs in s1. |
| **strspn(s1, s2)** | returns the length of the initial segment of s1, which consists entirely of characters from s2. |
| **strcspn(s1, s2)** | returns the length of the initial segment of s1, which consists entirely of characters not from s2. |
| **strtok(s1, s2)** | look for occurrences of s2 within s1. |

For all functions: #include <string.h>
**string.h** provides extern definitions of the string functions.

Figure 2-4: String Operations (sheet 2 of 2)

Figure 2-5 lists macros that classify ASCII character-coded integer values. These macros are described under the heading **ctype**(3C) in Section 3 of the *Programmer's Reference Manual*.

## Classify Characters

| | |
|---|---|
| **isalpha(c)** | is *c* a letter |
| **isupper(c)** | is *c* an upper-case letter |
| **islower(c)** | is *c* a lower-case letter |
| **isdigit(c)** | is *c* a digit [0-9] |
| **isxdigit(c)** | is *c* a hexadecimal digit [0-9], [A-F] or [a-f] |
| **isalnum(c)** | is *c* an alphanumeric (letter or digit) |
| **isspace(c)** | is *c* a space, tab, carriage return, new-line, vertical tab or form-feed |
| **ispunct(c)** | is *c* a punctuation character (neither control nor alphanumeric) |
| **isprint(c)** | is *c* a printing character, code 040 (space) through 0176 (tilde) |
| **isgraph(c)** | same as isprint except false for 040 (space) |
| **iscntrl(c)** | is *c* a control character (less than 040) or a delete character (0177) |
| **isascii(c)** | is *c* an ASCII character (code less than 0200) |

For all functions: #include <ctype.h>
Nonzero return == true; zero return == false

Figure 2-5: Classifying ASCII Character-Coded Integer Values

Figure 2-6 lists functions and macros that are used to convert characters, integers, or strings from one representation to another.

| Function Name(s) | | | Purpose |
|---|---|---|---|
| a64l | l64a | | convert between long integer and base-64 ASCII string |
| ecvt | fcvt | gcvt | convert floating-point number to string |
| l3tol | ltol3 | | convert between 3-byte integer and long integer |
| strtod | atof | | convert string to double-precision number |
| strtol | atol | atoi | convert string to integer |

| conv(3C): | Translate Characters |
|---|---|
| toupper | lower-case to upper-case |
| _toupper | macro version of toupper |
| tolower | upper-case to lower-case |
| _tolower | macro version of tolower |
| toascii | turn off all bits that are not part of a standard ASCII character; intended for compatibility with other systems |

For all **conv**(3C) macros: #include <ctype.h>

Figure 2-6: Conversion Functions and Macros

## Where the Manual Pages Can Be Found

System calls are listed alphabetically in Section 2 of the *Programmer's Reference Manual*. Subroutines are listed in Section 3. We have described above what is in the first subsection of Section 3. The remaining subsections of Section 3 are:

- 3M—functions that make up the Math Library, **libm**

- 3X—various specialized functions

- 3F—the FORTRAN intrinsic function library, **libF77**

- 3N—Networking Support Utilities

## How System Calls and Subroutines Are Used in C Programs

Information about the proper way to use system calls and subroutines is given on the manual page, but you have to know what you are looking for before it begins to make sense. To illustrate, a typical manual page (for **gets**(3S)) is shown in Figure 2-7.

# NAME

gets, fgets - get a string from a stream

# SYNOPSIS

#include <stdio.h>

char  *gets (s)
char  *s;

char  *fgets (s, n, stream)
char  *s;
int   n;
FILE  *stream;

# DESCRIPTION

*Gets* reads characters from the standard input stream, *stdin*, into the array pointed to by *s*, until a new-line character is read or an end-of-file condition is encountered. The new-line character is discarded and the string is terminated with a null character.

*Fgets* reads characters from the *stream* into the array pointed to by *s*, until *n*-1 characters are read, or a new-line character is read and transferred to *s*, or an end-of-file condition is encountered. The string is then terminated with a null character.

# SEE ALSO

ferror(3S),
fopen(3S),
fread(3S),
getc(3S),
scanf(3S).

# DIAGNOSTICS

If end-of-file is encountered and no characters have been read, no characters are transferred to *s* and a NULL pointer is returned. If a read error occurs, such as trying to use these functions on a file that has not been opened for reading, a NULL pointer is returned. Otherwise *s* is returned.

Figure 2-7: Manual Page for **gets**(3S)

As you can see from the illustration, two related functions are described on this page: **gets** and **fgets**. Each function gets a string from a stream in a slightly different way. The DESCRIPTION section tells how each operates.

It is the SYNOPSIS section, however, that contains the critical information about how the function (or macro) is used in your program. Notice in Figure 2-7 that the first line in the SYNOPSIS is

**#include <stdio.h>**

This means that to use **gets** or **fgets** you must bring the standard I/O header file into your program (generally right at the top of the file). There is something in **stdio.h** that is needed when you use the described functions. Figure 2-9 shows a version of **stdio.h**. Check it to see if you can understand what **gets** or **fgets** uses.

The next thing shown in the SYNOPSIS section of a manual page that documents system calls or subroutines is the formal declaration of the function. The formal declaration tells you:

- **the type of object returned by the function**

  In our example, both **gets** and **fgets** return a character pointer.

- **the object or objects the function expects to receive when called**

  These are the things enclosed in the parentheses of the function. **gets** expects a character pointer. (The DESCRIPTION section sheds light on what the tokens of the formal declaration stand for.)

- **how the function is going to treat those objects**

  The declaration

  ```
  char *s;
  ```

  in **gets** means that the token **s** enclosed in the parentheses will be considered to be a pointer to a character string. Bear in mind that in the C language, when passed as an argument, the name of an array is converted to a pointer to the beginning of the array.

We have chosen a simple example here in **gets**. If you want to test your-self on something a little more complex, try working out the meaning of the elements of the **fgets** declaration.

While we're on the subject of **fgets**, there is another piece of C esoterica that we'll explain. Notice that the third parameter in the **fgets** declaration is referred to as **stream**. A **stream**, in this context, is a file with its associated buffering. It is declared to be a pointer to a defined type FILE. Where is FILE defined? Right! In **stdio.h**.

To finish off this discussion of the way you use functions described in the *Programmer's Reference Manual* in your own code, in Figure 2-8 we show a program fragment in which **gets** is used.

```
#include <stdio.h>

main()
{
      char sarray[80];

      for(;;)
      {
            if (gets(sarray) != NULL)
            .
            .       /* Do something with the string */
            .

      }
}
```

Figure 2-8: How **gets** Is Used in a Program

You might ask, "Where is **gets** reading from?" The answer is, "From the standard input." That generally means from something being keyed in from the terminal where the command was entered to get the program running, or output from another command that was piped to **gets**. How do we know that? The DESCRIPTION section of the **gets** manual page says, "**gets** reads characters from the standard input...." Where is the standard input defined? In **stdio.h**.

```
#ifndef _NFILE
#define _NFILE 20

#define BUFSIZ 1024
#define _SBFSIZ 8

typedef struct {
            int         _cnt;
            unsigned char *_ptr;
            unsigned char *_base;
            char        _flag;
            char        _file;
} FILE;

#define _IOFBF          0000  /* _IOLBF means that a file's output  */
#define _IOREAD         0001  /* will be buffered line by line.     */
#define _IOWRT          0002  /* In addition to being flags, _IONBF,*/
#define _IONBF          0004  /* _IOLBF and IOFBF are possible      */
#define _IOMYBUF        0010  /* values for "type" in setvbuf.      */
#define _IOEOF          0020
#define _IOERR          0040
#define _IOLBF          0100
#define _IORW           0200

#ifndef NULL
#define NULL            0
#endif
#ifndef EOF
#define EOF             (-1)
#endif
```

Figure 2-9: A Version of **stdio.h** (sheet 1 of 2)

```
#define stdin                (&_iob[0])
#define stdout               (&_iob[1])
#define stderr               (&_iob[2])

#define _bufend(p)           _bufendtab[(p)->_file]
#define _bufsiz(p)           (_bufend(p) - (p)->_base)

#ifndef lint
#define getc(p)              (--(p)->_cnt < 0 ? _filbuf(p) : (int) *(p)->_ptr++)
#define putc(x, p)           (--(p)->_cnt < 0 ?
                             _flsbuf((unsigned char) (x), (p)) :
                             (int) (*(p)->_ptr++ = (unsigned char) (x)))
#define getchar()            getc(stdin)
#define putchar(x)           putc((x), stdout)
#define clearerr(p)          ((void) ((p)->_flag &= ~(_IOERR | _IOEOF)))
#define feof(p)              ((p)->_flag & _IOEOF)
#define ferror(p)            ((p)->_flag & _IOERR)
#define fileno(p)            (p)->_file
#endif

extern FILE    _iob[_NFILE];
extern FILE    *fopen(), *fdopen(), *freopen(), *popen(), *tmpfile();
extern long    ftell();
extern void    rewind(), setbuf();
extern char    *ctermid(), *cuserid(), *fgets(), *gets(), *tempnam(), *tmpnam();
extern unsigned char *_bufendtab[];

#define L_ctermid            9
#define L_cuserid            9
#define P_tmpdir             "/usr/tmp/"
#define L_tmpnam             (sizeof(P_tmpdir) + 15)
#endif
```

Figure 2-9: A Version of **stdio.h** (sheet 2 of 2)

# Header Files and Libraries

In the earlier parts of this chapter there have been frequent references to **stdio.h**, and a version of the file itself is shown in Figure 2-9. **stdio.h** is the most commonly used header file in the UNIX system/C environment, but there are many others.

Header files carry definitions and declarations that are used by more than one function. Header filenames traditionally have the suffix **.h**, and are brought into a program at compile time by the C-preprocessor. The preprocessor does this because it interprets the **#include** statement in your program as a directive; as indeed it is. All keywords preceded by a pound sign (#) at the beginning of the line, are treated as preprocessor directives. The two most commonly used directives are **#include** and **#define**. We have already seen that the **#include** directive is used to call in (and process) the contents of the named file. The **#define** directive is used to replace a name with a token-string. For example,

> **#define _NFILE    20**

sets to 20 the number of files a program can have open at one time. See **cpp**(1) for the complete list.

In the pages of the *Programmer's Reference Manual* there are about 45 different **.h** files named. The format of the **#include** statement for all these shows the file name enclosed in angle brackets (<>), as in

> **#include <stdio.h>**

The angle brackets tell the C preprocessor to look in the standard places for the file. In most systems the standard place is in the **/usr/include** directory. If you have some definitions or external declarations that you want to make available in several files, you can create a **.h** file with any editor, store it in a convenient directory and make it the subject of a **#include** statement such as the following:

> **#include "../defs/rec.h"**

It is necessary, in this case, to provide the relative pathname of the file and enclose it in quotation marks (""). Fully-qualified pathnames (those that begin with /) can create portability and organizational problems. An alternative to long or fully-qualified pathnames is to use the **-I***dir* preprocessor option when you compile the program. This option directs the preprocessor to search for **#include** files whose names are enclosed in "", first in the directory of the file being compiled, then in the directories named in the **-I** option(s), and finally in directories on the standard list. In addition, all **#include** files whose names are enclosed in angle brackets ( < > ) are first searched for in the list of directories named in the **-I** option and finally in the directories on the standard list.

## Object File Libraries

It is common practice in UNIX system computers to keep modules of compiled code (object files) in archives; by convention, designated by a **.a** suffix. System calls from Section 2, and the subroutines in Section 3, subsections 3C and 3S, of the *Programmer's Reference Manual* that are functions (as distinct from macros) are kept in an archive file by the name of **libc.a**. In most systems, **libc.a** is found in the directory **/lib**. Many systems also have a directory **/usr/lib**. Where both **/lib** and **/usr/lib** occur, **/usr/lib** is apt to be used to hold archives that are related to specific applications.

During the link edit phase of the compilation and link edit process, copies of some of the object modules in an archive file are loaded with your executable code. By default the **cc** command that invokes the C compilation system causes the link editor to search **libc.a**. If you need to point the link editor to other libraries that are not searched by default, you do it by naming them explicitly on the command line with the **-l** option. The format of the **-l** option is **-l**$x$ where $x$ is the library name, and can be up to nine characters. For example, if your program includes functions from the **curses** screen control package, the option

    **-lcurses**

will cause the link editor to search for **/lib/libcurses.a** or **/usr/lib/libcurses.a** and use the first one it finds to resolve references in your program.

In cases where you want to direct the order in which archive libraries are searched, you may use the **-L** *dir* option. Assuming the **-L** option appears on the command line ahead of the **-l** option, it directs the link editor to search the named directory for **lib**$x$**.a** before looking in **/lib** and **/usr/lib**. This is particularly useful if you are testing out a new version of a function that already exists in an archive in a standard directory. Its success is due to the fact that once having resolved a reference the link editor stops looking. That's why the **-L** option, if used, should appear on the command line ahead of any **-l** specification.

# Input/Output

We talked some about I/O earlier in this chapter in connection with system calls and subroutines. A whole set of subroutines constitutes the C language standard I/O package, and there are several system calls that deal with the same area. In this section we want to get into the subject in a little more detail and describe for you how to deal with input and output concerns in your C programs. First off, let's briefly define what the subject of I/O encompasses. It has to do with

- creating and sometimes removing files

- opening and closing files used by your program

- transferring information from a file to your program (reading)

- transferring information from your program to a file (writing)

In this section we will describe some of the subroutines you might choose for transferring information, but the heaviest emphasis will be on dealing with files.

## Three Files You Always Have

Programs are permitted to have several files open simultaneously. The number may vary from system to system; the most common maximum is 20. _NFILE in **stdio.h** specifies the number of standard I/O FILEs a program is permitted to have open.

Any program automatically starts off with three files. If you will look again at Figure 2-9, about midway through you will see that **stdio.h** contains three **#define** directives that equate **stdin**, **stdout**, and **stderr** to the address of _iob[0], _iob[1], and _iob[2], respectively. The array _iob holds information dealing with the way standard I/O handles streams. It is a representation of the open file table in the control block for your program. The position in the array is a digit that is also known as the file descriptor. The default in UNIX systems is to associate all three of these files with your terminal.

The real significance is that functions and macros that deal with **stdin** or **stdout** can be used in your program with no further need to open or close files. For example, **gets**, cited above, reads a string from **stdin**; **puts** writes a null-terminated string to **stdout**. There are others that do the same (in slightly different ways: character at a time, formatted, etc.). You can specify that output be directed to **stderr** by using a function such as **fprintf**. **fprintf** works the same as **printf** except that it delivers its formatted output to a named stream, such as **stderr**. You can use the shell's redirection feature on the command line to read from or write into a named file. If you want to separate error messages from ordinary output being sent to **stdout** and thence possibly piped by the shell to a succeeding program, you can do it by using one function to handle the ordinary output and a variation of the same function that names the stream, to handle error messages.

## Named Files

Any files other than **stdin**, **stdout**, and **stderr** that are to be used by your program must be explicitly connected by you before the file can be read from or written to. This can be done using the standard library routine **fopen**. **fopen** takes a pathname (which is the name by which the file is known to the UNIX file system), asks the system to keep track of the connection, and returns a pointer that you then use in functions that do the reads and writes.

A structure is defined in **stdio.h** with a type of FILE. In your program you need to have a declaration such as

```
FILE *fin;
```

The declaration says that **fin** is a pointer to a FILE. You can then assign the name of a particular file to the pointer with a statement in your program like this:

```
fin = fopen("filename", "r");
```

where **filename** is the pathname to open. The "f3r" means that the file is to be opened for reading. This argument is known as the **mode**. As you might suspect, there are modes for reading, writing, and both reading and writing. Actually, the file open function is often included in an if statement such as:

```
if ((fin = fopen("filename", "r")) == NULL)
    (void)fprintf(stderr,"%s: Unable to open input file %s\n",argv[0],"filename");
```

that takes advantage of the fact that **fopen** returns a NULL pointer if it can't open the file.

Once the file has been successfully opened, the pointer **fin** is used in functions (or macros) to refer to the file. For example:

```
int c;
c = getc(fin);
```

brings in a character at a time from the file into an integer variable called **c**. The variable **c** is declared as an integer even though we are reading characters because the function **getc()** returns an integer. Getting a character is often incorporated into some flow-of-control mechanism such as:

```
while ((c = getc(fin)) != EOF)
    .
    .
    .
```

that reads through the file until EOF is returned. EOF, NULL, and the macro **getc** are all defined in **stdio.h**. **getc** and others that make up the standard I/O package keep advancing a pointer through the buffer associated with the file; the UNIX system and the standard I/O subroutines are responsible for seeing that the buffer is refilled (or written to the output file if you are producing output) when the pointer reaches the end of the buffer. All these mechanics are mercifully invisible to the program and the programmer.

The function **fclose** is used to break the connection between the pointer in your program and the pathname. The pointer may then be associated with another file by another call to **fopen**. This re-use of a file descriptor for a different stream may be necessary if your program has many files to open. For output files it is good to issue an **fclose** call because the call makes sure that all output has been sent from the output buffer before disconnecting the file. The system call **exit** closes all open files for you. It also gets you completely out of your process, however, so it is safe to use only when you are sure you are completely finished.

### Low-level I/O and Why You Shouldn't Use It

The term low-level I/O is used to refer to the process of using system calls from Section 2 of the *Programmer's Reference Manual* rather than the functions and subroutines of the standard I/O package. We are going to postpone until Chapter 3 any discussion of when this might be advantageous. If you find as you go through the information in this chapter that it is a good fit with the objectives you have as a programmer, it is a safe assumption that you can work with C language programs in the UNIX system for a good many years without ever having a real need to use system calls to handle your I/O and file accessing problems. The reason low-level I/O is perilous is because it is more system-dependent. Your programs are less portable and probably no more efficient.

# System Calls for Environment or Status Information

Under some circumstances you might want to be able to monitor or control the environment in your computer. There are system calls that can be used for this purpose. Some of them are shown in Figure 2-10.

| Function Name(s) | | | Purpose |
|---|---|---|---|
| chdir | | | change working directory |
| chmod | | | change access permission of a file |
| chown | | | change owner and group of a file |
| getpid | getpgrp | getppid | get process IDs |
| getuid | geteuid | getgid | get user IDs |
| ioctl | | | control device |
| link | unlink | | add or remove a directory entry |
| mount | umount | | mount or unmount a file system |
| nice | | | change priority of a process |
| stat | fstat | | get file status |
| time | | | get time |
| ulimit | | | get and set user limits |
| uname | | | get name of current UNIX system |

Figure 2-10: Environment and Status System Calls

As you can see, many of the functions shown in Figure 2-10 have equivalent UNIX system shell commands. Shell commands can easily be incorporated into shell scripts to accomplish the monitoring and control tasks you may need to do. The functions are available, however, and may be used in C programs as part of the UNIX system/C Language interface. They are documented in Section 2 of the *Programmers' Reference Manual*.

# Processes

Whenever you execute a command in the UNIX system you are initiating a process that is numbered and tracked by the operating system. A flexible feature of the UNIX system is that processes can be generated by other processes. This happens more than you might ever be aware of. For example, when you log in to your system you are running a process, very probably the shell. If you then use an editor such as **vi**, take the option of invoking the shell from **vi**, and execute the **ps** command, you will see a display something like that in Figure 2-11 (which shows the results of a **ps -f** command):

| UID | PID | PPID | C | STIME | TTY | TIME | COMMAND |
|-----|-----|------|---|-------|-----|------|---------|
| abc | 24210 | 1 | 0 | 06:13:14 | tty29 | 0:05 | -sh |
| abc | 24631 | 24210 | 0 | 06:59:07 | tty29 | 0:13 | vi c2.uli |
| abc | 28441 | 28358 | 80 | 09:17:22 | tty29 | 0:01 | ps -f |
| abc | 28358 | 24631 | 2 | 09:15:14 | tty29 | 0:01 | sh -i |

Figure 2-11: Process Status

As you can see, user abc (who went through the steps described above) now has four processes active. It is an interesting exercise to trace the chain that is shown in the Process ID (PID) and Parent Process ID (PPID) columns. The shell that was started when user abc logged on is Process 24210; its parent is the initialization process (Process ID 1). Process 24210 is the parent of Process 24631, and so on.

The four processes in the example above are all UNIX system shell level commands, but you can spawn new processes from your own program. (Actually, when you issue the command from your terminal to execute a program you are asking the shell to start another process, the process being your executable object module with all the functions and subroutines that were made a part of it by the link editor.)

You might think, "Well, it's one thing to switch from one program to another when I'm at my terminal working interactively with the computer; but why would a program want to run other programs, and if one does, why wouldn't I just put everything together into one big executable module?"

Overlooking the case where your program is itself an interactive application with diverse choices for the user, your program may need to run one or more other programs based on conditions it encounters in its own processing. (If it's the end of the month, go do a trial balance, for example.) The usual reasons why it might not be practical to create one monster executable are:

- The load module may get too big to fit in the maximum process size for your system.

- You may not have control over the object code of all the other modules you want to include.

Suffice it to say, there are legitimate reasons why this creation of new processes might need to be done. There are three ways to do it:

- **system**(3S)—request the shell to execute a command

- **exec**(2)—stop this process and start another

- **fork**(2)—start an additional copy of this process

### system(3S)

The formal declaration of the **system** function looks like this:

```
#include <stdio.h>

int system(string)
char *string;
```

The function asks the shell to treat the string as a command line. The string can therefore be the name and arguments of any executable program or UNIX system shell command. If the exact arguments vary from one execution to the next, you may want to use **sprintf** to format the string before issuing the **system** command. When the command has finished running, **system** returns the shell exit status to your program. Execution of your program waits for the completion of the command initiated by **system** and then picks up again at the next executable statement.

## exec(2)

**exec** is the name of a family of functions that includes **execv**, **execle**, **execve**, **execlp**, and **execvp**. They all have the function of transforming the calling process into a new process. The reason for the variety is to provide different ways of pulling together and presenting the arguments of the function. An example of one version (**execl**) might be:

```
execl("/bin/prog2", "prog", progarg1, progarg2, (char *)0);
```

For **execl** the argument list is

**/bin/prog2**   path name of the new process file

**prog**         the name the new process gets in its argv[0]

**progarg1,**    arguments to *prog2* as char *'s
**progarg2**

**(char *)0**    a null char pointer to mark the end of the arguments

Check the manual page in the *Programmer's Reference Manual* for the rest of the details. The key point of the **exec** family is that there is no return from a successful execution: the calling process is finished, the new process overlays the old. The new process also takes over the Process ID and other attributes of the old process. If the call to **exec** is unsuccessful, control is returned to your program with a return value of -1. You can check **errno** (see below) to learn why it failed.

## fork(2)

The **fork** system call creates a new process that is an exact copy of the calling process. The new process is known as the child process; the caller is known as the parent process. The one major difference between the two processes is that the child gets its own unique process ID. When the **fork** process has completed successfully, it returns a 0 to the child process and the child's process ID to the parent. If the idea of having two identical processes seems a little funny, consider this:

- Because the return value is different between the child process and the parent, the program can contain the logic to determine different paths.

- The child process could say, "Okay, I'm the child. I'm supposed to issue an **exec** for an entirely different program."

- The parent process could say, "My child is going to be **exec**ing a new process. I'll issue a **wait** until I get word that that process is finished."

To take this out of the storybook world where programs talk like people and into the world of C programming (where people talk like programs), your code might include statements like this:

```
#include <errno.h>

int ch_stat, ch_pid, status;
char *progarg1;
char *progarg2;
void exit();
extern int errno;

    if ((ch_pid = fork()) < 0)
    {
        /* Could not fork...
           check errno
        */
    }
    else if (ch_pid == 0)                          /* child */
    {
        (void)execl("/bin/prog2","prog",progarg1,progarg2,(char *)0);
        exit(2);   /* execl() failed */
    }
    else            /* parent */
    {
        while ((status = wait(&ch_stat)) != ch_pid)
        {
            if (status < 0 && errno == ECHILD)
              break;
            errno = 0;
        }
    }
```

Figure 2-12: Example of **fork**

Because the child process ID is taken over by the new **exec**'d process, the parent knows the ID. What this boils down to is a way of leaving one program to run another, returning to the point in the first program where processing left off. This is exactly what the **system**(3S) function does. As a matter of fact, **system** accomplishes it through this same procedure of **fork**ing and **exec**ing, with a **wait** in the parent.

Keep in mind that the fragment of code above includes a minimum amount of checking for error conditions. There is also potential confusion about open files and which program is writing to a file. Leaving out the possibility of named files, the new process created by the **fork** or **exec** has the three standard files that are automatically opened: **stdin**, **stdout**, and **stderr**. If the parent has buffered output that should appear before output from the child, the buffers must be flushed before the fork. Also, if the parent and the child process both read input from a stream, whatever is read by one process will be lost to the other. That is, once something has been delivered from the input buffer to a process the pointer has moved on.

## Pipes

The idea of using pipes, a connection between the output of one program and the input of another, when working with commands executed by the shell is well established in the UNIX system environment. For example, to learn the number of archive files in your system you might enter a command like:

echo /lib/*.a /usr/lib/*.a | wc -w

that first echoes all the files in **/lib** and **/usr/lib** that end in **.a**, then pipes the results to the **wc** command, which counts their number.

A feature of the UNIX system/C Language interface is the ability to establish pipe connections between your process and a command to be executed by the shell, or between two cooperating processes. The first uses the **popen**(3S) subroutine that is part of the standard I/O package; the second requires the system call **pipe**(2).

**popen** is similar in concept to the **system** subroutine in that it causes the shell to execute a command. The difference is that once having invoked **popen** from your program, you have established an open line to a concurrently running process through a stream. You can send characters or strings to this stream with standard I/O subroutines just as you would to **stdout** or to a named file. The connection remains open until your program invokes the companion **pclose** subroutine. A common application of this technique might be a pipe to a printer spooler. For example:

```
#include <stdio.h>

main()
{
     FILE *pptr;
     char *outstring;

     if ((pptr = popen("lp","w")) != NULL)
     {
          for(;;)
          {    .
               .    /* Organize output */
               .
               (void)fprintf(pptr, "%s\n", outstring);
               .
               .
               .
          }
     .
     .
     .
     pclose(pptr);
     }
     .
     .
     .
}
```

Figure 2-13: Example of a **popen** pipe

# Error Handling

Within your C programs you must determine the appropriate level of checking for valid data and for acceptable return codes from functions and subroutines. If you use any of the system calls described in Section 2 of the *Programmer's Reference Manual*, you have a way in which you can find out the probable cause of a bad return value.

UNIX system calls that are not able to complete successfully almost always return a value of -1 to your program. (If you look through the system calls in Section 2, you will see that there are a few calls for which no return value is defined, but they are the exceptions.) In addition to the -1 that is returned to the program, the unsuccessful system call places an integer in an externally declared variable, **errno**. You can determine the value in **errno** if your program contains the statement

```
#include <errno.h>
```

The value in **errno** is not cleared on successful calls, so your program should check it only if the system call returned a -1. The errors are described in **intro**(2) of the *Programmer's Reference Manual*.

The subroutine **perror**(3C) can be used to print an error message (on **stderr**) based on the value of **errno**.

# Signals and Interrupts

Signals and interrupts are two words for the same thing. Both words refer to messages passed by the UNIX system to running processes. Generally, the effect is to cause the process to stop running. Some signals are generated if the process attempts to do something illegal; others can be initiated by a user against his or her own processes, or by the super-user against any process.

There is a system call, **kill**, that you can include in your program to send signals to other processes running under your user-id. The format for the **kill** call is:

```
kill(pid, sig)
```

where **pid** is the process number against which the call is directed, and **sig** is an integer from 1 to 19 that shows the intent of the message. The name "kill" is something of an overstatement; not all the messages have a "drop dead"

meaning. Some of the available signals are shown in Figure 2-14 as they are
defined in **<sys/signal.h>**.

```
#define     SIGHUP      1       /* hangup */
#define     SIGINT      2       /* interrupt (rubout) */
#define     SIGQUIT     3       /* quit (ASCII FS) */
#define     SIGILL      4       /* illegal instruction (not reset when caught)*/
#define     SIGTRAP     5       /* trace trap (not reset when caught) */
#define     SIGIOT      6       /* IOT instruction */
#define     SIGABRT     6       /* used by abort, replace SIGIOT in the future */
#define     SIGEMT      7       /* EMT instruction */
#define     SIGFPE      8       /* floating point exception */
#define     SIGKILL     9       /* kill (cannot be caught or ignored) */
#define     SIGBUS      10      /* bus error */
#define     SIGSEGV     11      /* segmentation violation */
#define     SIGSYS      12      /* bad argument to system call */
#define     SIGPIPE     13      /* write on a pipe with no one to read it */
#define     SIGALRM     14      /* alarm clock */
#define     SIGTERM     15      /* software termination signal from kill */
#define     SIGUSR1     16      /* user defined signal 1 */
#define     SIGUSR2     17      /* user defined signal 2 */
#define     SIGCLD      18      /* death of a child */
#define     SIGPWR      19      /* power-fail restart */

                                /* SIGWIND and SIGPHONE only used in UNIX/PC */
/*#define SIGWIND        20      */              /* window change */
/*#define SIGPHONE       21      */              /* handset, line status change */

#define     SIGPOLL 22  /* pollable event occurred */

#define     NSIG        23      /* The valid signal number is from 1 to NSIG-1 */
#define     MAXSIG      32      /* size of u_signal[], NSIG-1 <= MAXSIG*/
                                /* MAXSIG is larger than we need now. */
                                /* In the future, we can add more signal */
                                /* number without changing user.h */
```

Figure 2-14: Signal Numbers Defined in **/usr/include/sys/signal.h**

The **signal**(2) system call is designed to let you code methods of dealing with incoming signals. You have a three-way choice. You can a) accept whatever the default action is for the signal, b) have your program ignore the signal, or c) write a function of your own to deal with it.

# Analysis/Debugging

The UNIX system provides several commands designed to help you discover the causes of problems in programs and to learn about potential problems.

## Sample Program

To illustrate how these commands are used and the type of output they produce, we have constructed a sample program that opens and reads an input file and performs one to three subroutines according to options specified on the command line. This program does not do anything you couldn't do quite easily on your pocket calculator, but it does serve to illustrate some points. The source code is shown in Figure 2-15. The header file, **recdef.h**, is shown at the end of the source code.

The output produced by the various analysis and debugging tools illustrated in this section may vary slightly from one installation to another. The *Programmer's Reference Manual* is a good source of additional information about the contents of the reports.

```
                    /* Main module -- restate.c */

#include <stdio.h>
#include "recdef.h"

#define TRUE    1
#define FALSE   0

main(argc, argv)
int argc;
char *argv[];
{
     FILE *fopen(), *fin;
     void exit();
     int getopt();
     int oflag = FALSE;
     int pflag = FALSE;
     int rflag = FALSE;
     int ch;
     struct rec first;
     extern int opterr;
     extern float oppty(), pft(), rfe();

                /* restate.c is continued on the next page */
```

Figure 2-15: Source Code for Sample Program (sheet 1 of 4)

```
                    /* restate.c continued */

if (argc < 2)
{
    (void) fprintf(stderr, "%s: Must specify option\n",argv[0]);
    (void) fprintf(stderr, "Usage: %s -rpo\n", argv[0]);
    exit(2);
}

opterr = FALSE;
while ((ch = getopt(argc,argv,"opr")) != EOF)
{
    switch(ch)
    {
    case 'o':
        oflag = TRUE;
        break;
    case 'p':
        pflag = TRUE;
        break;
    case 'r':
        rflag = TRUE;
        break;
    default:
        (void) fprintf(stderr, "Usage: %s -rpo\n",argv[0]);
        exit(2);
    }
}
if ((fin = fopen("info","r")) == NULL)
{
(void) fprintf(stderr, "%s: cannot open input file %s\n",argv[0],"info");
exit(2);
}
```

Figure 2-15: Source Code for Sample Program (sheet 2 of 4)

```
                    /* restate.c continued */

        if (fscanf(fin, "%s %f %f %f %f %f %f",first.pname,&first.ppx,
        &first.dp,&first.i,&first.c,&first.t,&first.spx) != 7)
        {
          (void) fprintf(stderr,"%s: cannot read first record from %s\n",
             argv[0],"info");
          exit(2);
        }

        printf("Property: %s\n",first.pname);

        if(oflag)
             printf("Opportunity Cost: $%#5.2f\n",oppty(&first));

        if(pflag)
             printf("Anticipated Profit(loss): $%#7.2f\n",pft(&first));

        if(rflag)
             printf("Return on Funds Employed: %#3.2f%%\n",rfe(&first));
}
                   /* End of Main Module -- restate.c */

                   /* Opportunity Cost -- oppty.c */
#include "recdef.h"

float
oppty(ps)
struct rec *ps;
{
        return(ps->i/12 * ps->t * ps->dp);
}
```

Figure 2-15: Source Code for Sample Program (sheet 3 of 4)

```
                    /* Profit -- pft.c */

#include "recdef.h"

float
pft(ps)
struct rec *ps;
{
     return(ps->spx - ps->ppx + ps->c);
}

               /* Return on Funds Employed -- rfe.c */

#include "recdef.h"

float
rfe(ps)
struct rec *ps;
{
     return( 100 * (ps->spx - ps->c) / ps->spx);
}

               /* Header File -- recdef.h */

struct rec {            /* To hold input */
     char pname[25];
     float ppx;
     float dp;
     float i;
     float c;
     float t;
     float spx;
  } ;
```

Figure 2-15: Source Code for Sample Program (sheet 4 of 4)

# cflow

**cflow** produces a chart of the external references in C, **yacc**, **lex**, and assembly language files. Using the modules of our sample program, the command

    **cflow restate.c oppty.c pft.c rfe.c**

produces the output shown in Figure 2-16.

```
1     main: int(), <restate.c 11>
2          fprintf: <>
3          exit: <>
4          getopt: <>
5          fopen: <>
6          fscanf: <>
7          printf: <>
8          oppty: float(), <oppty.c 7>
9          pft: float(), <pft.c 7>
10         rfe: float(), <rfe.c 8>
```

Figure 2-16: **cflow** Output, No Options

The **-r** option looks at the caller:callee relationship from the other side. It produces the output shown in Figure 2-17.

```
 1    exit: <>
 2         main : <>
 3    fopen: <>
 4         main : 2
 5    fprintf: <>
 6         main : 2
 7    fscanf: <>
 8         main : 2
 9    getopt: <>
10         main : 2
11    main: int(), <restate.c 11>
12    oppty: float(), <oppty.c 7>
13         main : 2
14    pft: float(), <pft.c 7>
15         main : 2
16    printf: <>
17         main : 2
18    rfe: float(), <rfe.c 8>
19         main : 2
```

Figure 2-17: **cflow** Output, Using **-r** Option

The **-ix** option causes external and static data symbols to be included. Our sample program has only one such symbol, **opterr**. The output is shown in Figure 2-18.

```
1    main: int(), <restate.c 11>
2          fprintf: <>
3          exit: <>
4          opterr: <>
5          getopt: <>
6          fopen: <>
7          fscanf: <>
8          printf: <>
9          oppty: float(), <oppty.c 7>
10         pft: float(), <pft.c 7>
11         rfe: float(), <rfe.c 8>
```

Figure 2-18: **cflow** Output, Using **-ix** Option

Combining the **-r** and the **-ix** options produces the output shown in Figure 2-19.

```
1    exit: <>
2         main : <>
3    fopen: <>
4         main : 2
5    fprintf: <>
6         main : 2
7    fscanf: <>
8         main : 2
9    getopt: <>
10        main : 2
11   main: int(), <restate.c 11>
12   oppty: float(), <oppty.c 7>
13        main : 2
14   opterr: <>
15        main : 2
16   pft: float(), <pft.c 7>
17        main : 2
18   printf: <>
19        main : 2
20   rfe: float(), <rfe.c 8>
21        main : 2
```

Figure 2-19: **cflow** Output, Using **-r** and **-ix** Options

# ctrace

**ctrace** lets you follow the execution of a C program statement by statement. **ctrace** takes a **.c** file as input and inserts statements in the source code to print out variables as each program statement is executed. You must direct the output of this process to a temporary **.c** file. The temporary file is then used as input to **cc**. When the resulting **a.out** file is executed it produces output that can tell you a lot about what is going on in your program.

Options give you the ability to limit the number of times through loops. You can also include functions in your source file that turn the trace off and on so you can limit the output to portions of the program that are of particular interest.

**ctrace** accepts only one source code file as input. To use our sample program to illustrate, it is necessary to execute the following four commands:

> **ctrace restate.c > ct.main.c**
> **ctrace oppty.c > ct.op.c**
> **ctrace pft.c > ct.p.c**
> **ctrace rfe.c > ct.r.c**

The names of the output files are completely arbitrary. Use any names that are convenient for you. The names must end in **.c**, since the files are used as input to the C compilation system.

> **cc -o ct.run ct.main.c ct.op.c ct.p.c ct.r.c**

Now the command

> **ct.run -opr**

produces the output shown in Figure 2-20. The command above will cause the output to be directed to your terminal (**stdout**). It is probably a good idea to direct it to a file or to a printer so you can refer to it.

```
 8 main(argc, argv)
23  if (argc < 2)
    /* argc == 2 */
30  opterr = FALSE;
    /* FALSE == 0 */
    /* opterr == 0 */
31  while ((ch = getopt(argc,argv,"opr")) != EOF)
    /* argc == 2 */
    /* argv == 15729316 */
    /* ch == 111 or 'o' or "t" */
32  {
33      switch(ch)
        /* ch == 111 or 'o' or "t" */
35      case 'o':
36          oflag = TRUE;
            /* TRUE == 1 or "h" */
            /* oflag == 1 or "h" */
37          break;
48  }
31  while ((ch = getopt(argc,argv,"opr")) != EOF)
    /* argc == 2 */
    /* argv == 15729316 */
    /* ch == 112 or 'p' */
32  {
33      switch(ch)
        /* ch == 112 or 'p' */
38      case 'p':
39          pflag = TRUE;
            /* TRUE == 1 or "h" */
            /* pflag == 1 or "h" */
40          break;
48  }
```

Figure 2-20: **ctrace** Output (sheet 1 of 3)

```
31   while ((ch = getopt(argc,argv,"opr")) != EOF)
     /* argc == 2 */
     /* argv == 15729316 */
     /* ch == 114 or 'r' */
32   {
33       switch(ch)
         /* ch == 114 or 'r' */
41       case 'r':
42           rflag = TRUE;
             /* TRUE == 1 or "h" */
             /* rflag == 1 or "h" */
43           break;
48   }
31   while ((ch = getopt(argc,argv,"opr")) != EOF)
     /* argc == 2 */
     /* argv == 15729316 */
     /* ch == -1 */
49   if ((fin = fopen("info","r")) == NULL)
     /* fin == 140200 */
54   if (fscanf(fin, "%s %f %f %f %f %f %f",first.pname,&first.ppx,
         &first.dp,&first.i,&first.c,&first.t,&first.spx) != 7)
     /* fin == 140200 */
     /* first.pname == 15729528 */
61   printf("Property: %s0,first.pname);
     /* first.pname == 15729528 or "Linden_Place" */ Property: Linden_Place

63   if(oflag)
     /* oflag == 1 or "h" */
64       printf("Opportunity Cost: $%#5.2f0,oppty(&first));
 5 oppty(ps)
 8   return(ps->i/12 * ps->t * ps->dp);
     /* ps->i == 1069044203 */
     /* ps->t == 1076494336 */
     /* ps->dp == 1088765312 */ Opportunity Cost: $4476.87
```

Figure 2-20: **ctrace** Output (sheet 2 of 3)

```
 66   if(pflag)
      /* pflag == 1 or "h" */
 67        printf("Anticipated Profit(loss): $%#7.2f0,pft(&first));
  5 pft(ps)
  8   return(ps->spx - ps->ppx + ps->c);
      /* ps->spx == 1091649040 */
      /* ps->ppx == 1091178464 */
      /* ps->c == 1087409536 */  Anticipated Profit(loss): $85950.00

 69   if(rflag)
      /* rflag == 1 or "h" */
 70        printf("Return on Funds Employed: %#3.2f%%0,rfe(&first));
  6 rfe(ps)
  9   return( 100 * (ps->spx - ps->c) / ps->spx);
      /* ps->spx == 1091649040 */
      /* ps->c == 1087409536 */  Return on Funds Employed: 94.00%


      /* return */
```

Figure 2-20: **ctrace** Output (sheet 3 of 3)

Using a program that runs successfully is not the optimal way to demonstrate **ctrace**. It would be more helpful to have an error in the operation that could be detected by **ctrace**. It would seem that this utility might be most useful in cases where the program runs to completion, but the output is not as expected.

# cxref

**cxref** analyzes a group of C source code files and builds a cross-reference table of the automatic, static, and global symbols in each file.

The command

  **cxref -c -o cx.op restate.c oppty.c pft.c rfe.c**

produces the output shown in Figure 2-21 in a file named, in this case, **cx.op**.

The **-c** option causes the reports for the four **.c** files to be combined in one cross-reference file.

```
restate.c:

oppty.c:

pft.c:

rfe.c:

  SYMBOL              FILE                  FUNCTION      LINE

BUFSIZ            /usr/include/stdio.h        --        *9
EOF              /usr/include/stdio.h        --        49 *50
                 restate.c                   --        31
FALSE            restate.c                   --        *6   15   16   17   30
FILE             /usr/include/stdio.h        --        *29   73   74
                 restate.c                   main      12
L_ctermid        /usr/include/stdio.h        --        *80
L_cuserid        /usr/include/stdio.h        --        *81
L_tmpnam         /usr/include/stdio.h        --        *83
NULL             /usr/include/stdio.h        --        46 *47
                 restate.c                   --        49
P_tmpdir         /usr/include/stdio.h        --        *82
TRUE             restate.c                   --        *5   36   39   42
_IOEOF           /usr/include/stdio.h        --        *41
_IOERR           /usr/include/stdio.h        --        *42
_IOFBF           /usr/include/stdio.h        --        *36
_IOLBF           /usr/include/stdio.h        --        *43
_IOMYBUF         /usr/include/stdio.h        --        *40
_IONBF           /usr/include/stdio.h        --        *39
_IOREAD          /usr/include/stdio.h        --        *37
_IORW            /usr/include/stdio.h        --        *44
_IOWRT           /usr/include/stdio.h        --        *38
_NFILE           /usr/include/stdio.h        --        2 *3   73
_SBFSIZ          /usr/include/stdio.h        --        *16
```

Figure 2-21: **cxref** Output, Using **-c** Option (sheet 1 of 5)

| SYMBOL | FILE | FUNCTION | LINE |
|--------|------|----------|------|
| _base | /usr/include/stdio.h | -- | *26 |
| _bufend() | | | |
| | /usr/include/stdio.h | -- | *57 |
| _bufendtab | /usr/include/stdio.h | -- | *78 |
| _bufsiz() | | | |
| | /usr/include/stdio.h | -- | *58 |
| _cnt | /usr/include/stdio.h | -- | *20 |
| _file | /usr/include/stdio.h | -- | *28 |
| _flag | /usr/include/stdio.h | -- | *27 |
| _iob | /usr/include/stdio.h | -- | *73 |
| | restate.c | main | 25 26 45 51 57 |
| _ptr | /usr/include/stdio.h | -- | *21 |
| argc | restate.c | -- | 8 |
| | restate.c | main | *9  23  31 |
| argv | restate.c | -- | 8 |
| | restate.c | main | *10 25 26 31 45 51 57 |
| c | ./recdef.h | -- | *6 |
| | pft.c | pft | 8 |
| | restate.c | main | 55 |
| | rfe.c | rfe | 9 |
| ch | restate.c | main | *18  31  33 |
| clearerr() | | | |
| | /usr/include/stdio.h | -- | *67 |
| ctermid() | | | |
| | /usr/include/stdio.h | -- | *77 |
| cuserid() | | | |
| | /usr/include/stdio.h | -- | *77 |
| dp | ./recdef.h | | --*4 |
| | oppty.c | oppty | 8 |
| | restate.c | main | 55 |
| exit() | | | |
| | restate.c | main | *13  27  46  52  58 |
| fdopen() | | | |
| | /usr/include/stdio.h | -- | *74 |

Figure 2-21: **cxref** Output, Using **-c** Option (sheet 2 of 5)

| SYMBOL | FILE | FUNCTION | LINE |
|--------|------|----------|------|
| feof() | | | |
| | /usr/include/stdio.h | -- | *68 |
| ferror() | | | |
| | /usr/include/stdio.h | -- | *69 |
| fgets() | | | |
| | /usr/include/stdio.h | -- | *77 |
| fileno() | | | |
| | /usr/include/stdio.h | -- | *70 |
| fin | restate.c | main | *12  49  54 |
| first | restate.c | main | *19  54 55  61 64 67 70 |
| fopen() | | | |
| | /usr/include/stdio.h | -- | *74 |
| | restate.c | main | 12  49 |
| fprintf | restate.c | main | 25  26  45  51  57 |
| freopen() | | | |
| | /usr/include/stdio.h | -- | *74 |
| fscanf | restate.c | main | 54 |
| ftell() | | | |
| | /usr/include/stdio.h | -- | *75 |
| getc() | | | |
| | /usr/include/stdio.h | -- | *61 |
| getchar() | | | |
| | /usr/include/stdio.h | -- | *65 |
| getopt() | | | |
| | restate.c | main | *14  31 |
| gets() | | | |
| | /usr/include/stdio.h | -- | *77 |
| i | ./recdef.h | -- | *5 |
| | oppty.c | oppty | 8 |
| | restate.c | main | 55 |
| lint | /usr/include/stdio.h | -- | 60 |
| main() | | | |
| | restate.c | -- | *8 |

Figure 2-21: **cxref** Output, Using **-c** Option (sheet 3 of 5)

| SYMBOL | FILE | FUNCTION | LINE |
|---|---|---|---|
| oflag | restate.c | main | *15  36  63 |
| oppty() | | | |
| | oppty.c | -- | *5 |
| | restate.c | main | *21  64 |
| opterr | restate.c | main | *20  30 |
| p | /usr/include/stdio.h | -- | *57 *58 *61 62 |
| *62  63  64  67 *67  68 *68  69 *69  70 *70 | | | |
| pdp11 | /usr/include/stdio.h | -- | 11 |
| pflag | restate.c | main | *16  39  66 |
| pft() | | | |
| | pft.c | -- | *5 |
| | restate.c | main | *21  67 |
| pname | ./recdef.h | -- | *2 |
| | restate.c | main | 54  61 |
| popen() | | | |
| | /usr/include/stdio.h | -- | *74 |
| ppx | ./recdef.h | -- | *3 |
| | pft.c | pft | 8 |
| | restate.c | main | 54 |
| printf | restate.c | main | 61  64  67  70 |
| ps | oppty.c | -- | 5 |
| | oppty.c | oppty | *6  8 |
| | pft.c | -- | 5 |
| | pft.c | pft | *6  8 |
| | rfe.c | -- | 6 |
| | rfe.c | rfe | *7  9 |
| putc() | | | |
| | /usr/include/stdio.h | -- | *62 |
| putchar() | | | |
| | /usr/include/stdio.h | -- | *66 |
| rec | ./recdef.h | -- | *1 |
| | oppty.c | oppty | 6 |
| | pft.c | pft | 6 |
| | restate.c | main | 19 |
| | rfe.c | rfe | 7 |

Figure 2-21: **cxref** Output, Using **-c** Option (sheet 4 of 5)

| SYMBOL | FILE | FUNCTION | LINE |
|---|---|---|---|
| rewind() | | | |
| | /usr/include/stdio.h | -- | *76 |
| rfe() | | | |
| | restate.c | main | *21 70 |
| | rfe.c | -- | *6 |
| rflag | restate.c | main | *17 42 69 |
| setbuf() | | | |
| | /usr/include/stdio.h | -- | *76 |
| spx | ./recdef.h | -- | *8 |
| | pft.c | pft | 8 |
| | restate.c | main | 55 |
| | rfe.c | rfe | 9 |
| stderr | /usr/include/stdio.h | -- | *55 |
| | restate.c | -- | 25 26 45 51 57 |
| stdin | /usr/include/stdio.h | -- | *53 |
| stdout | /usr/include/stdio.h | -- | *54 |
| t | ./recdef.h | -- | *7 |
| | oppty.c | oppty | 8 |
| | restate.c | main | 55 |
| tempnam() | | | |
| | /usr/include/stdio.h | -- | *77 |
| tmpfile() | | | |
| | /usr/include/stdio.h | -- | *74 |
| tmpnam() | | | |
| | /usr/include/stdio.h | -- | *77 |
| u370 | /usr/include/stdio.h | -- | 5 |
| u3b | /usr/include/stdio.h | -- | 8 19 |
| u3b5 | /usr/include/stdio.h | -- | 8 19 |
| vax | /usr/include/stdio.h | -- | 8 19 |
| x | /usr/include/stdio.h | -- | *62 63 64 66 *66 |

Figure 2-21: **cxref** Output, Using **-c** Option (sheet 5 of 5)

# lint

**lint** looks for features in a C program that are apt to cause execution errors, that are wasteful of resources, or that create problems of portability.

The command

**lint restate.c oppty.c pft.c rfe.c**

produces the output shown in Figure 2-22.

```
restate.c:

restate.c
==============
(71)  warning: main() returns random value to invocation environment
oppty.c:
pft.c:
rfe.c:


==============
function returns value which is always ignored
    printf
```

Figure 2-22: **lint** Output

**lint** has options that will produce additional information. Check the *User's Reference Manual*. The error messages give you the line numbers of some items you may want to review.

# prof

**prof** produces a report on the amount of execution time spent in various portions of your program and the number of times each function is called. The program must be compiled with the **-p** option. When a program that was compiled with that option is run, a file called **mon.out** is produced. **mon.out** and **a.out** (or whatever name identifies your executable file) are input to the **prof** command.

The sequence of steps needed to produce a profile report for our sample program is as follows:

Step 1:    Compile the programs with the **-p** option:

      **cc -p restate.c oppty.c pft.c rfe.c**

Step 2:    Run the program to produce a file **mon.out**.

      **a.out -opr**

Step 3:    Execute the **prof** command:

      **prof a.out**

The example of the output of this last step is shown in Figure 2-23. The figures may vary from one run to another. You will also notice that programs of very small size, like that used in the example, produce statistics that are not overly helpful.

| %Time | Seconds | Cumsecs | #Calls | msec/call | Name |
|-------|---------|---------|--------|-----------|------|
| 50.0 | 0.03 | 0.03 | 3 | 8. | fcvt |
| 20.0 | 0.01 | 0.04 | 6 | 2. | atof |
| 20.0 | 0.01 | 0.05 | 5 | 2. | write |
| 10.0 | 0.00 | 0.05 | 1 | 5. | fwrite |
| 0.0 | 0.00 | 0.05 | 1 | 0. | monitor |
| 0.0 | 0.00 | 0.05 | 1 | 0. | creat |
| 0.0 | 0.00 | 0.05 | 4 | 0. | printf |
| 0.0 | 0.00 | 0.05 | 2 | 0. | profil |
| 0.0 | 0.00 | 0.05 | 1 | 0. | fscanf |
| 0.0 | 0.00 | 0.05 | 1 | 0. | _doscan |
| 0.0 | 0.00 | 0.05 | 1 | 0. | oppty |
| 0.0 | 0.00 | 0.05 | 1 | 0. | _filbuf |
| 0.0 | 0.00 | 0.05 | 3 | 0. | strchr |
| 0.0 | 0.00 | 0.05 | 1 | 0. | strcmp |
| 0.0 | 0.00 | 0.05 | 1 | 0. | ldexp |
| 0.0 | 0.00 | 0.05 | 1 | 0. | getenv |
| 0.0 | 0.00 | 0.05 | 1 | 0. | fopen |
| 0.0 | 0.00 | 0.05 | 1 | 0. | _findiop |
| 0.0 | 0.00 | 0.05 | 1 | 0. | open |
| 0.0 | 0.00 | 0.05 | 1 | 0. | main |
| 0.0 | 0.00 | 0.05 | 1 | 0. | read |
| 0.0 | 0.00 | 0.05 | 1 | 0. | strcpy |
| 0.0 | 0.00 | 0.05 | 14 | 0 | ungetc |
| 0.0 | 0.00 | 0.05 | 4 | 0. | _doprnt |
| 0.0 | 0.00 | 0.05 | 1 | 0. | pft |
| 0.0 | 0.00 | 0.05 | 1 | 0. | rfe |
| 0.0 | 0.00 | 0.05 | 4 | 0. | _xflsbuf |
| 0.0 | 0.00 | 0.05 | 1 | 0. | _wrtchk |
| 0.0 | 0.00 | 0.05 | 2 | 0. | _findbuf |
| 0.0 | 0.00 | 0.05 | 2 | 0. | isatty |
| 0.0 | 0.00 | 0.05 | 2 | 0. | ioctl |
| 0.0 | 0.00 | 0.05 | 1 | 0. | malloc |
| 0.0 | 0.00 | 0.05 | 1 | 0. | memchr |
| 0.0 | 0.00 | 0.05 | 1 | 0. | memcpy |
| 0.0 | 0.00 | 0.05 | 2 | 0. | sbrk |
| 0.0 | 0.00 | 0.05 | 4 | 0. | getopt |

Figure 2-23: **prof** Output

# size

size produces information on the number of bytes occupied by the three sections (text, data, and bss) of a common object file when the program is brought into main memory to be run. Here are the results of one invocation of the **size** command with our object file as an argument.

    11832 + 3872 + 2240 = 17944

Don't confuse this number with the number of characters in the object file that appears when you do an **ls -l** command. That figure includes the symbol table and other header information that is not used at run time.

# strip

strip removes the symbol and line number information from a common object file. When you issue this command the number of characters shown by the **ls -l** command approaches the figure shown by the **size** command, but still includes some header information that is not counted as part of the .text, .data, or .bss section. After the **strip** command has been executed, it is no longer possible to use the file with the **sdb** command.

# sdb

sdb stands for Symbolic Debugger, which means you can use the symbolic names in your program to pinpoint where a problem has occurred. You can use **sdb** to debug C, FORTRAN 77, or PASCAL programs. There are two basic ways to use **sdb**: by running your program under control of **sdb**, or by using **sdb** to rummage through a core image file left by a program that failed. The first way lets you see what the program is doing up to the point at which it fails (or to skip around the failure point and proceed with the run). The second method lets you check the status at the moment of failure, which may or may not disclose the reason the program failed.

Chapter 15 contains a tutorial on **sdb** that describes the interactive commands you can use to work your way through your program. For the time being we want to tell you just a couple of key things you need to do when using it.

1. Compile your program(s) with the **-g** option, which causes additional information to be generated for use by **sdb**.

2. Run your program under **sdb** with the command:

   **sdb myprog - srcdir**

   where **myprog** is the name of your executable file (**a.out** is the default), and **srcdir** is an optional list of the directories where source code for your modules may be found. The dash between the two arguments keeps **sdb** from looking for a core image file.

# Program Organizing Utilities

The following three utilities are helpful in keeping your programming work organized effectively.

## The make Command

When you have a program that is made up of more than one module of code you begin to run into problems of keeping track of which modules are up to date and which need to be recompiled when changes are made in another module. The **make** command is used to ensure that dependencies between modules are recorded so that changes in one module results in the re-compilation of dependent programs. Even control of a program as simple as the one shown in Figure 2-15 is made easier through the use of **make**.

The **make** utility requires a description file that you create with an editor. The description file (also referred to by its default name: **makefile**) contains the information used by **make** to keep a target file current. The target file is typically an executable program. A description file contains three types of information:

| | |
|---|---|
| dependency information | tells the **make** utility the relationship between the modules that comprise the target program. |
| executable commands | needed to generate the target program. **make** uses the dependency information to determine which executable commands should be passed to the shell for execution. |
| macro definitions | provide a shorthand notation within the description file to make maintenance easier. Macro definitions can be overridden by information from the command line when the **make** command is entered. |

The **make** command works by checking the "last changed" time of the modules named in the description file. When **make** finds a component that has been changed more recently than modules that depend on it, the specified commands (usually compilations) are passed to the shell for execution.

The **make** command takes three kinds of arguments: options, macro definitions, and target filenames. If no description filename is given as an option on the command line, **make** searches the current directory for a file named **makefile** or **Makefile**. Figure 2-24 shows a **makefile** for our sample program.

```
OBJECTS = restate.o oppty.o pft.o rfe.o
all: restate
restate: $(OBJECTS)
      $(CC) $(CFLAGS) $(LDFLAGS) $(OBJECTS) -o restate

$(OBJECTS): ./recdef.h

clean:
      rm -f $(OBJECTS)

clobber:   clean
      rm -f restate
```

Figure 2-24: **make** Description File

The following things are worth noticing in this description file:

- It identifies the target, **restate**, as being dependent on the four object modules. Each of the object modules in turn is defined as being dependent on the header file, **recdef.h**, and by default, on its corresponding source file.

- A macro, OBJECTS, is defined as a convenient shorthand for referring to all of the component modules.

Whenever testing or debugging results in a change to one of the components of **restate**, for example, a command such as the following should be entered:

    **make CFLAGS=-g restate**

This has been a very brief overview of the **make** utility. There is more on **make** in Chapter 3, and a detailed description of **make** can be found in Chapter 13.

## The Archive

The most common use of an archive file, although not the only one, is to hold object modules that make up a library. The library can be named on the link editor command line (or with a link editor option on the **cc** command line). This causes the link editor to search the symbol table of the archive file when attempting to resolve references.

The **ar** command is used to create an archive file, to manipulate its contents and to maintain its symbol table. The structure of the **ar** command is a little different from the normal UNIX system arrangement of command line options. When you enter the **ar** command you include a one-character key from the set **drqtpmx** that defines the type of action you intend. The key may be combined with one or more additional characters from the set **vuaibcls** that modify the way the requested operation is performed. The makeup of the command line is

**ar** -key [*posname*] *afile* [*name*]...

where *posname* is the name of a member of the archive and may be used with some optional key characters to make sure that the files in your archive are in a particular order. The *afile* argument is the name of your archive file. By convention, the suffix **.a** is used to indicate the named file is an archive file. (**libc.a**, for example, is the archive file that contains many of the object files of the standard C subroutines.) One or more *names* may be furnished. These identify files that are subjected to the action specified in the *key*.

We can make an archive file to contain the modules used in our sample program, **restate**. The command to do this is

**ar -rv rste.a restate.o oppty.o pft.o rfe.o**

If these are the only **.o** files in the current directory, you can use shell metacharacters as follows:

**ar -rv rste.a \*.o**

Either command will produce this feedback:

```
a - restate.o
a - oppty.o
a - pft.o
a - rfe.o
ar: creating rste.a
```

The **nm** command is used to get a variety of information from the symbol table of common object files. The object files can be, but don't have to be, in an archive file. Figure 2-25 shows the output of this command when executed with the **-f** (for full) option on the archive we just created. The object files were compiled with the **-g** option.

Symbols from rste.a[restate.o]

| Name | Value | Class | Type | Size | Line | Section |
|---|---|---|---|---|---|---|
| .0fake | | | strtag | struct | 16 | |
| restate.c | | file | | | | |
| _cnt | 0 | strmem | int | | | |
| _ptr | 4 | strmem | *Uchar | | | |
| _base | 8 | strmem | *Uchar | | | |
| _flag | 12 | strmem | char | | | |
| _file | 13 | strmem | char | | | |
| .eos | | endstr | | 16 | | |
| rec | | strtag | struct | 52 | | |
| pname | 0 | strmem | char[25] | 25 | | |
| ppx | 28 | strmem | float | | | |
| dp | 32 | strmem | float | | | |
| i | 36 | strmem | float | | | |
| c | 40 | strmem | float | | | |
| t | 44 | strmem | float | | | |
| spx | 48 | strmem | float | | | |
| .eos | | endstr | | 52 | | |
| main | 0 | extern | int( ) | 520 | | .text |
| .bf | 10 | fcn | | | 11 | .text |
| argc | 0 | argm't | int | | | |
| argv | 4 | argm't | **char | | | |
| fin | 0 | auto | *struct-.0fake | 16 | | |
| oflag | 4 | auto | int | | | |
| pflag | 8 | auto | int | | | |
| rflag | 12 | auto | int | | | |
| ch | 16 | auto | int | | | |

Figure 2-25: **nm** Output, with **-f** Option (sheet 1 of 5)

Symbols from rste.a[restate.o]

| Name | Value | Class | Type | Size | Line | Section |
|------|-------|-------|------|------|------|---------|
| first | 20 | auto | struct-rec | 52 | | |
| .ef | 518 | fcn | | | 61 | .text |
| FILE | | typdef | struct-.0fake | 16 | | |
| .text | 0 | static | | 31 | 39 | .text |
| .data | 520 | static | | | 4 | .data |
| .bss | 824 | static | | | | .bss |
| _iob | 0 | extern | | | | |
| fprintf | 0 | extern | | | | |
| exit | 0 | extern | | | | |
| opterr | 0 | extern | | | | |
| getopt | 0 | extern | | | | |
| fopen | 0 | extern | | | | |
| fscanf | 0 | extern | | | | |
| printf | 0 | extern | | | | |
| oppty | 0 | extern | | | | |
| pft | 0 | extern | | | | |
| rfe | 0 | extern | | | | |

Figure 2-25: **nm** Output, with **-f** Option (sheet 2 of 5)

Symbols from rste.a[oppty.o]

| Name | Value | Class | Type | Size | Line | Section |
|------|-------|-------|------|------|------|---------|
| oppty.c | | file | | | | |
| rec | | strtag | struct | 52 | | |
| pname | 0 | strmem | char[25] | 25 | | |
| ppx | 28 | strmem | float | | | |
| dp | 32 | strmem | float | | | |
| i | 36 | strmem | float | | | |
| c | 40 | strmem | float | | | |
| t | 44 | strmem | float | | | |
| spx | 48 | strmem | float | | | |
| .eos | | endstr | | 52 | | |
| oppty | 0 | extern | float() | 64 | | .text |
| .bf | 10 | fcn | | | 7 | .text |
| ps | 0 | argm't | *struct-rec | 52 | | |
| .ef | 62 | fcn | | | 3 | .text |
| .text | 0 | static | | 4 | 1 | .text |
| .data | 64 | static | | | | .data |
| .bss | 72 | static | | | | .bss |

Figure 2-25: **nm** Output, with **-f** Option (sheet 3 of 5)

Symbols from rste.a[pft.o]

| Name | Value | Class | Type | Size | Line | Section |
|------|-------|-------|------|------|------|---------|
| pft.c | | file | | | | |
| rec | | strtag | struct | 52 | | |
| pname | 0 | strmem | char[25] | 25 | | |
| ppx | 28 | strmem | float | | | |
| dp | 32 | strmem | float | | | |
| i | 36 | strmem | float | | | |
| c | 40 | strmem | float | | | |
| t | 44 | strmem | float | | | |
| spx | 48 | strmem | float | | | |
| ..eos | | endstr | | 52 | | |
| pft | 0 | extern | float() | 60 | | .text |
| ..bf | 10 | fcn | | | 7 | .text |
| ps | 0 | argm't | *struct-rec | 52 | | |
| ..ef | 58 | fcn | | | 3 | .text |
| ..text | 0 | static | | 4 | | .text |
| ..data | 60 | static | | | | .data |
| ..bss | 60 | static | | | | .bss |

Figure 2-25: **nm** Output, with **-f** Option (sheet 4 of 5)

Symbols from rste.a[rfe.o]

| Name | Value | Class | Type | Size | Line | Section |
|---|---|---|---|---|---|---|
| rfe.c | | file | | | | |
| rec | | strtag | struct | 52 | | |
| pname | 0 | strmem | char[25] | 25 | | |
| ppx | 28 | strmem | float | | | |
| dp | 32 | strmem | float | | | |
| i | 36 | strmem | float | | | |
| c | 40 | strmem | float | | | |
| t | 44 | strmem | float | | | |
| spx | 48 | strmem | float | | | |
| .eos | | endstr | | 52 | | |
| rfe | 0 | extern | float() | 68 | | .text |
| .bf | 10 | fcn | | | 8 | .text |
| ps | 0 | argm't | *struct-rec | 52 | | |
| .ef | 64 | fcn | | | 3 | .text |
| .text | 0 | static | | 4 | 1 | .text |
| .data | 68 | static | | | | .data |
| .bss | 76 | static | | | | .bss |

Figure 2-25: **nm** Output, with **-f** Option (sheet 5 of 5)

**For nm** to work on an archive file all of the contents of the archive have to be object modules. If you have stored other things in the archive, you will get the message:

```
nm: rste.a  bad magic
```

when you try to execute the command.

# Use of SCCS by Single-User Programmers

The UNIX system Source Code Control System (SCCS) is a set of programs designed to keep track of different versions of programs. When a program has been placed under control of SCCS, only a single copy of any one version of the code can be retrieved for editing at a given time. When program code is changed and the program returned to SCCS, only the changes are recorded. Each version of the code is identified by its SID, or **SCCS ID**entifying number. By specifying the SID when the code is extracted from the SCCS file, it is possible to return to an earlier version. If an early version is extracted with the intent of editing it and returning it to SCCS, a new branch of the development tree is started. The set of programs that make up SCCS appear as UNIX system commands. The commands are:

> **admin**
> **get**
> **delta**
> **prs**
> **rmdel**
> **cdc**
> **what**
> **sccsdiff**
> **comb**
> **val**

It is most common to think of SCCS as a tool for project control of large programming projects. It is, however, entirely possible for any individual user of the UNIX system to set up a private SCCS system. Chapter 14 is an SCCS user's guide.

# CHAPTER 3: APPLICATION PROGRAMMING

## Introduction

This chapter deals with programming where the objective is to produce sets of programs (applications) that will run on a UNIX system computer.

The chapter begins with a discussion of how the ground rules change as you move up the scale from writing programs that are essentially for your own private use (we have called this single-user programming), to working as a member of a programming team developing an application that is to be turned over to others to use.

There is a section on how the criteria for selecting appropriate programming languages may be influenced by the requirements of the application.

The next three sections of the chapter deal with a number of loosely-related topics that are of importance to programmers working in the application development environment. Most of these mirror topics that were discussed in Chapter 2, Programming Basics, but here we try to point out aspects of the subject that are particularly pertinent to application programming. They are covered under the following headings:

Advanced Programming    deals with such topics as File and Record Locking, Interprocess Communication, and programming terminal screens.

Support Tools    covers the Common Object File Format, link editor directives, shared libraries, SDB, and **lint**.

Project Control Tools    includes some discussion of **make** and SCCS.

The chapter concludes with a description of a sample application called **liber** that uses several of the components described in earlier portions of the chapter.

# Application Programming

The characteristics of the application programming environment that make it different from single-user programming have at their base the need for interaction and for sharing of information.

## Numbers

Perhaps the most obvious difference between application programming and single-user programming is in the quantities of the components. Not only are applications generally developed by teams of programmers, but the number of separate modules of code can grow into the hundreds on even a fairly simple application.

When more than one programmer works on a project, there is a need to share such information as:

- the operation of each function

- the number, identity and type of arguments expected by a function

- if pointers are passed to a function, are the objects being pointed to modified by the called function, and what is the lifetime of the pointed-to object

- the data type returned by a function

In an application, there is an odds-on possibility that the same function can be used in many different programs, by many different programmers. The object code needs to be kept in a library accessible to anyone on the project who needs it.

## Portability

When you are working on a program to be used on a single model of a computer, your concerns about portability are minimal. In application development, on the other hand, a desirable objective often is to produce code that will run on many different UNIX system computers. Some of the things that affect portability will be touched on later in this chapter.

## Documentation

A single-user program has modest needs for documentation. There should be enough to remind the program's creator how to use it, and what the intent was in portions of the code.

On an application development project there is a significant need for two types of internal documentation:

- comments throughout the source code that enable successor programmers to understand easily what is happening in the code. Applications can be expected to have a useful life of 5 or more years, and frequently need to be modified during that time. It is not realistic to expect that the same person who wrote the program will always be available to make modifications. Even if that does happen the comments will make the maintenance job a lot easier.

- hard-copy descriptions of functions should be available to all members of an application development team. Without them it is difficult to keep track of available modules, which can result in the same function being written over again.

Unless end-users have clear, readily-available instructions in how to install and use an application they either will not do it at all (if that is an option), or do it improperly.

The microcomputer software industry has become ever more keenly aware of the importance of good end-user documentation. There are cases on record where the success of a software package has been attributed in large part to the fact that it had exceptionally good documentation. There are also cases where a pretty good piece of software was not widely used due to the inaccessibility of its manuals. There appears to be no truth to the rumor that in one or two cases, end-users have thrown the software away and just read the manual.

## Project Management

Without effective project management, an application development project is in trouble. This subject will not be dealt with in this guide, except to mention the following three things that are vital functions of project management:

- tracking dependencies between modules of code
- dealing with change requests in a controlled way
- seeing that milestone dates are met

# Language Selection

In this section we talk about some of the considerations that influence the selection of programming languages, and describe two of the special purpose languages that are part of the UNIX system environment.

## Influences

In single-user programming the choice of language is often a matter of personal preference; a language is chosen because it is the one the programmer feels most comfortable with.

An additional set of considerations comes into play when making the same decision for an application development project.

Is there an existing standard within the organization that should be observed?

A firm may decide to emphasize one language because a good supply of programmers is available who are familiar with it.

Does one language have better facilities for handling the particular algorithm?

One would like to see all language selection based on such objective criteria, but it is often necessary to balance this against the skills of the organization.

Is there an inherent compatibility between the language and the UNIX operating system?

This is sometimes the impetus behind selecting C for programs destined for a UNIX system machine.

Are there existing tools that can be used?

If parsing of input lines is an important phase of the application, perhaps a parser generator such as **yacc** should be employed to develop what the application needs.

Does the application integrate other software into the whole package?

If, for example, a package is to be built around an existing data base management system, there may be constraints on the variety of languages the data base management system can accommodate.

# Special Purpose Languages

The UNIX system contains a number of tools that can be included in the category of special purpose languages. Three that are especially interesting are **awk**, **lex**, and **yacc**.

## What awk Is Like

The **awk** utility scans an ASCII input file record by record, looking for matches to specific patterns. When a match is found, an action is taken. Patterns and their accompanying actions are contained in a specification file referred to as the program. The program can be made up of a number of statements. However, since each statement has the potential for causing a complex action, most **awk** programs consist of only a few. The set of statements may include definitions of the pattern that separates one record from another (a newline character, for example), and what separates one field of a record from the next (white space, for example). It may also include actions to be performed before the first record of the input file is read, and other actions to be performed after the final record has been read. All statements in between are evaluated in order for each record in the input file. To paraphrase the action of a simple **awk** program, it would go something like this:

Look through the input file.
Every time you see this specific pattern, do this action.

A more complex **awk** program might be paraphrased like this:

First do some initialization.
Then, look through the input file.
Every time you see this specific pattern, do this action.
Every time you see this other pattern, do another action.
After all the records have been read, do these final things.

The directions for finding the patterns and for describing the actions can get pretty complicated, but the essential idea is as simple as the two sets of statements above.

One of the strong points of **awk** is that once you are familiar with the language syntax, programs can be written very quickly. They don't always run very fast, however, so they are seldom appropriate if you want to run the same program repeatedly on a large quantities of records. In such a case, it is likely to be better to translate the program to a compiled language.

## How awk Is Used

One typical use of **awk** would be to extract information from a file and print it out in a report. Another might be to pull fields from records in an input file, arrange them in a different order and pass the resulting rearranged data to a function that adds records to your data base. There is an example of a use of **awk** in the sample application at the end of this chapter.

## Where to Find More Information

The manual page for **awk** is in Section (1) of the *User's Reference Manual*. Chapter 4 in Part 2 of this guide contains a description of the **awk** syntax and a number of examples showing ways in which **awk** may be used.

## What lex and yacc Are Like

**lex** and **yacc** are often mentioned in the same breath because they perform complementary parts of what can be viewed as a single task: making sense out of input. The two utilities also share the common characteristic of producing source code for C language subroutines from specifications that appear on the surface to be quite similar.

Recognizing input is a recurring problem in programming. Input can be from various sources. In a language compiler, for example, the input is normally contained in a file of source language statements. The UNIX system shell language most often receives its input from a person keying in commands from a terminal. Frequently, information coming out of one program is fed into another where it must be evaluated.

The process of input recognition can be subdivided into two tasks: lexical analysis and parsing, and that's where **lex** and **yacc** come in. In both utilities, the specifications cause the generation of C language subroutines that deal with streams of characters; **lex** generates subroutines that do lexical analysis while **yacc** generates subroutines that do parsing.

To describe those two tasks in dictionary terms:

Lexical analysis has to do with identifying the words or vocabulary of a language as distinguished from its grammar or structure.

Parsing is the act of describing units of the language grammatically. Students in elementary school are often taught to do this with sentence diagrams.

Of course, the important thing to remember here is that in each case the rules for our lexical analysis or parsing are those we set down ourselves in the **lex** or **yacc** specifications. Because of this, the dividing line between lexical analysis and parsing sometimes becomes fuzzy.

The fact that **lex** and **yacc** produce C language source code means that these parts of what may be a large programming project can be separately maintained. The generated source code is processed by the C compiler to produce an object file. The object file can be link edited with others to produce programs that then perform whatever process follows from the recognition of the input.

## How lex Is Used

A **lex** subroutine scans a stream of input characters and waves a flag each time it identifies something that matches one or another of its rules. The waved flag is referred to as a token. The rules are stated in a format that closely resembles the one used by the UNIX system text editor for regular expressions. For example,

```
[ \t]+
```

describes a rule that recognizes a string of one or more blanks or tabs (without mentioning any action to be taken). A more complete statement of that rule might have this notation:

```
[ \t]+ ;
```

which, in effect, says to ignore white space. It carries this meaning because no action is specified when a string of one or more blanks or tabs is recognized. The semicolon marks the end of the statement. Another rule, one that does take some action, could be stated like this:

```
[0-9]+ {
        i = atoi(yytext);
        return(NBR);
        }
```

This rule depends on several things:

NBR must have been defined as a token in an earlier part of the **lex** source code called the declaration section. (It may be in a header file which is **#include**'d in the declaration section.)

**i** is declared as an **extern int** in the declaration section.

It is a characteristic of **lex** that things it finds are made available in a character string called **yytext**.

Actions can make use of standard C syntax. Here, the standard C subroutine, **atoi**, is used to convert the string to an integer.

What this rule boils down to is **lex** saying, "Hey, I found the kind of token we call NBR, and its value is now in **i**."

To review the steps of the process:

1.  The **lex** specification statements are processed by the **lex** utility to produce a file called **lex.yy.c**. (This is the standard name for a file generated by **lex**, just as **a.out** is the standard name for the executable file generated by the link editor.)

2.  **lex.yy.c** is transformed by the C compiler (with a −**c** option) into an object file called **lex.yy.o** that contains a subroutine called **yylex()**.

3.  **lex.yy.o** is link edited with other subroutines. Presumably one of those subroutines will call **yylex()** with a statement such as:

```
while((token = yylex()) != 0)
```

and other subroutines (or even **main**) will deal with what comes back.

## Where to Find More Information

The manual page for **lex** is in Section (1) of the *Programmer's Reference Manual.* A tutorial on **lex** is contained in Chapter 5 in Part 2 of this guide.

## How yacc Is Used

**yacc** subroutines are produced by pretty much the same series of steps as **lex**:

1.  The **yacc** specification is processed by the **yacc** utility to produce a file called **y.tab.c**.

2.  **y.tab.c** is compiled by the C compiler producing an object file, **y.tab.o**, that contains the subroutine **yyparse()**. A significant difference is that **yyparse()** calls a subroutine called **yylex()** to perform lexical analysis.

3.  The object file **y.tab.o** may be link edited with other subroutines, one of which will be called **yylex()**.

There are two things worth noting about this sequence:

1.  The parser generated by the **yacc** specifications calls a lexical analyzer to scan the input stream and return tokens.

2.  While the lexical analyzer is called by the same name as one produced by **lex**, it does not have to be the product of a **lex** specification. It can be any subroutine that does the lexical analysis.

What really differentiates these two utilities is the format for their rules. As noted above, **lex** rules are regular expressions like those used by UNIX system editors. **yacc** rules are chains of definitions and alternative definitions, written in Backus-Naur form, accompanied by actions. The rules may refer to other rules defined further down the specification. Actions are sequences of C language statements enclosed in braces. They frequently contain numbered variables that enable you to reference values associated with parts of the rules. An example might make that easier to understand:

```
%token   NUMBER
%%
expr     : numb                { $$ = $1; }
         | expr '+' expr       { $$ = $1 + $3; }
         | expr '-' expr       { $$ = $1 - $3; }
         | expr '*' expr       { $$ = $1 * $3; }
         | expr '/' expr       { $$ = $1 / $3; }
         | '(' expr ')'        { $$ = $2; }
         ;
numb     : NUMBER      { $$ = $1; }
         ;
```

This fragment of a **yacc** specification shows

- NUMBER identified as a token in the declaration section

- the start of the rules section indicated by the pair of percent signs

- a number of alternate definitions for *expr* separated by the | sign and terminated by the semicolon

- actions to be taken when a rule is matched

- within actions, numbered variables used to represent components of the rule:

  $$ means the value to be returned as the value of the whole rule

  $n means the value associated with the nth component of the rule, counting from the left

- *numb* defined as meaning the token NUMBER. This is a trivial example that illustrates that one rule can be referenced within another, as well as within itself.

As with **lex**, the compiled **yacc** object file will generally be link edited with other subroutines that handle processing that takes place after the parsing—or even ahead of it.

## Where to Find More Information

The manual page for **yacc** is in Section (1) of the *Programmer's Reference Manual.* A detailed description of **yacc** may be found in Chapter 6 of this guide.

# Advanced Programming Tools

In Chapter 2 we described the use of such basic elements of programming in the UNIX system environment as the standard I/O library, header files, system calls and subroutines. In this section we introduce tools that are more apt to be used by members of an application development team than by a single-user programmer. The section contains material on the following topics:

- memory management

- file and record locking

- interprocess communication

- programming terminal screens

## Memory Management

There are situations where a program needs to ask the operating system for blocks of memory. It may be, for example, that a number of records have been extracted from a data base and need to be held for some further processing. Rather than writing them out to a file on secondary storage and then reading them back in again, it is likely to be a great deal more efficient to hold them in memory for the duration of the process. (This is not to ignore the possibility that portions of memory may be paged out before the program is finished; but such an occurrence is not pertinent to this discussion.) There are two C language subroutines available for acquiring blocks of memory and they are both called **malloc**. One of them is **malloc**(3C), the other is **malloc**(3X). Each has several related commands that do specialized tasks in the same area. They are:

- **free**—to inform the system that space is being relinquished

- **realloc**—to change the size and possibly move the block

- **calloc**—to allocate space for an array and initialize it to zeros

In addition, **malloc**(3X) has a function, **mallopt**, that provides for control over the space allocation algorithm, and a structure, **mallinfo**, from which the program can get information about the usage of the allocated space.

**malloc**(3X) runs faster than the other version. It is loaded by specifying

**-lmalloc**

on the **cc**(1) or **ld**(1) command line to direct the link editor to the proper library. When you use **malloc**(3X) your program should contain the statement

    #include <malloc.h>

where the values for **mallopt** options are defined.

See the *Programmer's Reference Manual* for the formal definitions of the two **malloc**s.


# File and Record Locking

The provision for locking files, or portions of files, is primarily used to prevent the sort of error that can occur when two or more users of a file try to update information at the same time. The classic example is the airlines reservation system where two ticket agents each assign a passenger to Seat A, Row 5 on the 5 o'clock flight to Detroit. A locking mechanism is designed to prevent such mishaps by blocking Agent B from even seeing the seat assignment file until Agent A's transaction is complete.

File locking and record locking are really the same thing, except that file locking implies the whole file is affected; record locking means that only a specified portion of the file is locked. (Remember, in the UNIX system, file structure is undefined; a record is a concept of the programs that use the file.)

Two types of locks are available: read locks and write locks. If a process places a read lock on a file, other processes can also read the file but all are prevented from writing to it, that is, changing any of the data. If a process places a write lock on a file, no other processes can read or write in the file until the lock is removed. Write locks are also known as exclusive locks. The term shared lock is sometimes applied to read locks.

Another distinction needs to be made between mandatory and advisory locking. Mandatory locking means that the discipline is enforced automatically for the system calls that read, write or create files. This is done through a permission flag established by the file's owner (or the super-user). Advisory locking means that the processes that use the file take the responsibility for setting and removing locks as needed. Thus mandatory may sound like a simpler and better deal, but it isn't so. The mandatory locking capability is included in the system to comply with an agreement with */usr/group*, an organization that represents the interests of UNIX system users. The principal weakness in the mandatory method is that the lock is in place only while the single system call is being made. It is extremely common for a single transaction to require a series of reads and writes before it can be considered complete. In cases like this, the term atomic is used to describe a transaction that must be viewed as an indivisible unit. The preferred way to manage locking in such a circumstance is to make certain the lock is in place before any I/O starts, and that it is not removed until the transaction is done. That calls for locking of the advisory variety.

## How File and Record Locking Works

The system call for file and record locking is **fcntl**(2). Programs should include the line

```
#include <fcntl.h>
```

to bring in the header file shown in Figure 3-1.

```
/* Flag values accessible to open(2) and fcntl(2) */
/*  (The first three can only be set by open) */
#define     O_RDONLY    0
#define     O_WRONLY    1
#define     O_RDWR      2
#define     O_NDELAY    04          /* Non-blocking I/O */
#define     O_APPEND    010         /* append (writes guaranteed at the end) */
#define     O_SYNC                  020/* synchronous write option */
/* Flag values accessible only to open(2) */
#define     O_CREAT     00400       /* open with file create (uses third open arg)*/
#define     O_TRUNC     01000       /* open with truncation */
#define     O_EXCL      02000       /* exclusive open */
/* fcntl(2) requests */
#define     F_DUPFD     0           /* Duplicate fildes */
#define     F_GETFD     1           /* Get fildes flags */
#define     F_SETFD     2           /* Set fildes flags */
#define     F_GETFL     3           /* Get file flags */
#define     F_SETFL     4           /* Set file flags */
#define     F_GETLK     5           /* Get file lock */
#define     F_SETLK     6           /* Set file lock */
#define     F_SETLKW    7           /* Set file lock and wait */
#define     F_CHKFL     8           /* Check legality of file flag changes */
/* file segment locking set data type - information passed to system by user */
struct flock {
            short       l_type;
            short       l_whence;
            long        l_start;
            long        l_len;    /* len = 0 means until end of file */
            short       l_sysid;
            short       l_pid;
};
/* file segment locking types */
            /* Read lock */
#define     F_RDLCK     01
            /* Write lock */
#define     F_WRLCK     02
            /* Remove lock(s) */
#define     F_UNLCK     03
```

Figure 3-1: The **fcntl.h** Header File

The format of the **fcntl**(2) system call is

```
int fcntl(fildes, cmd, arg)
int fildes, cmd, arg;
```

*fildes* is the file descriptor returned by the **open** system call. In addition to defining tags that are used as the commands on **fcntl** system calls, **fcntl.h** includes the declaration for a *struct flock* that is used to pass values that control where locks are to be placed.

## lockf

A subroutine, **lockf**(3), can also be used to lock sections of a file or an entire file. The format of **lockf** is:

```
#include <unistd.h>

int lockf (fildes, function, size)
int fildes, function;
long size;
```

*fildes* is the file descriptor; *function* is one of four control values defined in **unistd.h** that let you lock, unlock, test and lock, or simply test to see if a lock is already in place. *size* is the number of contiguous bytes to be locked or unlocked. The section of contiguous bytes can be either forward or backward from the current offset in the file. (You can arrange to be somewhere in the middle of the file by using the **lseek**(2) system call.)

## Where to Find More Information

There is an example of file and record locking in the sample application at the end of this chapter. The manual pages that apply to this facility are **fcntl**(2), **fcntl**(5), **lockf**(3), and **chmod**(2) in the *Programmer's Reference Manual*. Chapter 7 in Part 2 of this guide is a detailed discussion of the subject with a number of examples.

# Interprocess Communications

In Chapter 2 we described **fork**ing and **exec**ing as methods of communicating between processes. Business applications running on a UNIX system computer often need more sophisticated methods. In applications, for example, where fast response is critical, a number of processes may be brought up at the start of a business day to be constantly available to handle transactions on demand. This cuts out initialization time that can add seconds to the time required to deal with the transaction. To go back to the ticket reservation example again for a moment, if a customer calls to reserve a seat on the 5 o'clock flight to Detroit, you don't want to have to say, "Yes, sir. Just hang on a minute while I start up the reservations program." In transaction driven systems, the normal mode of processing is to have all the components of the application standing by waiting for some sort of an indication that there is work to do.

To meet requirements of this type the UNIX system offers a set of nine system calls and their accompanying header files, all under the umbrella name of Interprocess Communications (IPC).

The IPC system calls come in sets of three; one set each for messages, semaphores, and shared memory. These three terms define three different styles of communication between processes:

messages          communication is in the form of data stored in a buffer. The buffer can be either sent or received.

semaphores      communication is in the form of positive integers with a value between 0 and 32,767. Semaphores may be contained in an array the size of which is determined by the system administrator. The default maximum size for the array is 25.

shared memory   communication takes place through a common area of main memory. One or more processes can attach a segment of memory and as a consequence can share whatever data is placed there.

The sets of IPC system calls are:

| | | |
|---|---|---|
| msgget | semget | shmget |
| msgctl | semctl | shmctl |
| msgop | semop | shmop |

## IPC get Calls

The **get** calls each return to the calling program an identifier for the type of IPC facility that is being requested.

## IPC ctl Calls

The **ctl** calls provide a variety of control operations that include obtaining (IPC_STAT), setting (IPC_SET) and removing (IPC_RMID), the values in data structures associated with the identifiers picked up by the **get** calls.

## IPC op Calls

The **op** manual pages describe calls that are used to perform the particular operations characteristic of the type of IPC facility being used. **msgop** has calls that send or receive messages. **semop** (the only one of the three that is actually the name of a system call) is used to increment or decrement the value of a semaphore, among other functions. **shmop** has calls that attach or detach shared memory segments.

## Where to Find More Information

An example of the use of some IPC features is included in the sample application at the end of this chapter. The system calls are all located in Section (2) of the **Programmer's Reference Manual**. Don't overlook **intro**(2). It includes descriptions of the data structures that are used by IPC facilities. A detailed description of IPC, with many code examples that use the IPC system calls, is contained in Chapter 9 in Part 2 of this guide.

# Programming Terminal Screens

The facility for setting up terminal screens to meet the needs of your application is provided by two parts of the UNIX system. The first of these, **terminfo**, is a data base of compiled entries that describe the capabilities of terminals and the way they perform various operations.

The **terminfo** data base normally begins at the directory **/usr/lib/terminfo**. The members of this directory are themselves directories, generally with single-character names that are the first character in the name of the terminal. The compiled files of operating characteristics are at the next level down the hierarchy. For example, the entry for a Teletype 5425 is located in both the file **/usr/lib/terminfo/5/5425** and the file **/usr/lib/terminfo/t/tty5425**.

Describing the capabilities of a terminal can be a painstaking task. Quite a good selection of terminal entries is included in the **terminfo** data base that comes with your 3B2 Computer. However, if you have a type of terminal that is not already described in the data base, the best way to proceed is to find a description of one that comes close to having the same capabilities as yours and building on that one. There is a routine (**setupterm**) in **curses**(3X) that can be used to print out descriptions from the data base. Once you have worked out the code that describes the capabilities of your terminal, the **tic**(1M) command is used to compile the entry and add it to the data base.

### curses

After you have made sure that the operating capabilities of your terminal are a part of the **terminfo** data base, you can then proceed to use the routines that make up the **curses**(3X) package to create and manage screens for your application.

The **curses** library includes functions to:

■ define portions of your terminal screen as windows

■ define pads that extend beyond the borders of your physical terminal screen and let you see portions of the pad on your terminal

■ read input from a terminal screen into a program

■ write output from a program to your terminal screen

■ manipulate the information in a window in a virtual screen area and then send it to your physical screen

## Where to Find More Information

In the sample application at the end of this chapter, we show how you might use **curses** routines. Chapter 10 in Part 2 of this guide contains a tutorial on the subject. The manual pages for **curses** are in Section (3X), and those for **terminfo** are in Section (4) of the *Programmer's Reference Manual*.

# Programming Support Tools

This section covers UNIX system components that are part of the programming environment, but that have a highly specialized use. We refer to such things as:

- link edit command language
- Common Object File Format
- libraries
- Symbolic Debugger
- **lint** as a portability tool

## Link Edit Command Language

The link editor command language is for use when the default arrangement of the **ld** output will not do the job. The default locations for the standard Common Object File Format sections are described in **a.out**(4) in the *Programmer's Reference Manual*. On a 3B2 Computer, when an **a.out** file is loaded into memory for execution, the text segment starts at location 0x80800000, and the data section starts at the next segment boundary after the end of the text. The stack begins at 0xC0020000 and grows to higher memory addresses.

The link editor command language provides directives for describing different arrangements. The two major types of link editor directives are MEMORY and SECTIONS. MEMORY directives can be used to define the boundaries of configured and unconfigured sections of memory within a machine, to name sections, and to assign specific attributes (read, write, execute, and initialize) to portions of memory. SECTIONS directives, among a lot of other functions, can be used to bind sections of the object file to specific addresses within the configured portions of memory.

Why would you want to be able to do those things? Well, the truth is that in the majority of cases you don't have to worry about it. The need to control the link editor output becomes more urgent under two, possibly related, sets of circumstances.

1. Your application is large and consists of a lot of object files.

2. The hardware your application is to run on is tight for space.

### Where to Find More Information

Chapter 12 in Part 2 of this guide gives a detailed description of the subject.

## Common Object File Format

The details of the Common Object File Format have never been looked on as stimulating reading. In fact, they have been recommended to hard-core insomniacs as preferred bedtime fare. However, if you're going to break into the ranks of really sophisticated UNIX system programmers, you're going to have to get a good grasp of COFF. A knowledge of COFF is fundamental to using the link editor command language. It is also good background knowledge for tasks such as:

- setting up archive libraries or shared libraries

- using the Symbolic Debugger

The following system header files contain definitions of data structures of parts of the Common Object File Format:

| | |
|---|---|
| <syms.h> | symbol table format |
| <linenum.h> | line number entries |
| <ldfcn.h> | COFF access routines |
| <filehdr.h> | file header for a common object file |
| <a.out.h> | common assembler and link editor output |
| <scnhdr.h> | section header for a common object file |
| <reloc.h> | relocation information for a common object file |
| <storclass.h> | storage classes for common object files |

The object file access routines are described below under the heading "The Object File Library."

### Where to Find More Information

Chapter 11 in Part 2 of this guide gives a detailed description of COFF.

# Libraries

A library is a collection of related object files and/or declarations that simplify programming effort. Programming groups involved in the development of applications often find it convenient to establish private libraries. For example, an application with a number of programs using a common data base can keep the I/O routines in a library that is searched at link edit time.

Prior to Release 3.0 of the UNIX System V the libraries, whether system supplied or application developed, were collections of common object format files stored in an archive (*filename*.**a**) file that was searched by the link editor to resolve references. Files in the archive that were needed to satisfy unresolved references became a part of the resulting executable.

Beginning with Release 3.0, shared libraries are supported. Shared libraries are similar to archive libraries in that they are collections of object files that are acted upon by the link editor. The difference, however, is that shared libraries perform a static linking between the file in the library and the executable that is the output of **ld**. The result is a saving of space, because all executables that need a file from the library share a single copy. We go into shared libraries later in this section.

In Chapter 2 we described many of the functions that are found in the standard C library, **libc.a**. The next two sections describe two other libraries, the object file library and the math library.

### The Object File Library

The object file library provides functions for the access and manipulation of object files. Some functions locate portions of an object file such as the symbol table, the file header, sections, and line number entries associated with a function. Other functions read these types of entries into memory. The need to work at this level of detail with object files occurs most often in the development of new tools that manipulate object files. For a description of the format of an object file, see "The Common Object File Format" in Chapter 11. This library consists of several portions. The functions reside in **/lib/libld.a** and are loaded during the compilation of a C language program by the **-l** command line option:

**cc** *file* **−lld**

which causes the link editor to search the object file library. The argument **-lld** must appear after all files that reference functions in **libld.a**.

The following header files must be included in the source code.

```
#include <stdio.h>
#include <a.out.h>
#include <ldfcn.h>
```

| Function | Reference | Brief Description |
|----------|-----------|-------------------|
| ldaclose | ldclose(3X) | Close object file being processed. |
| ldahread | ldahread(3X) | Read archive header. |
| ldaopen | ldopen(3X) | Open object file for reading. |
| ldclose | ldclose(3X) | Close object file being processed. |
| ldfhread | ldfhread(3X) | Read file header of object file being processed. |
| ldgetname | ldgetname(3X) | Retrieve the name of an object file symbol table entry. |
| ldlinit | ldlread(3X) | Prepare object file for reading line number entries via **ldlitem**. |
| ldlitem | ldlread(3X) | Read line number entry from object file after **ldlinit**. |
| ldlread | ldlread(3X) | Read line number entry from object file. |
| ldlseek | ldlseek(3X) | Seeks to the line number entries of the object file being processed. |
| ldnlseek | ldlseek(3X) | Seeks to the line number entries of the object file being processed given the name of a section. |

| Function | Reference | Brief Description |
|----------|-----------|-------------------|
| **ldnrseek** | **ldrseek**(3X) | Seeks to the relocation entries of the object file being processed given the name of a section. |
| **ldnshread** | **ldshread**(3X) | Read section header of the named section of the object file being processed. |
| **ldnsseek** | **ldsseek**(3X) | Seeks to the section of the object file being processed given the name of a section. |
| **ldohseek** | **ldohseek**(3X) | Seeks to the optional file header of the object file being processed. |
| **ldopen** | **ldopen**(3X) | Open object file for reading. |
| **ldrseek** | **ldrseek**(3X) | Seeks to the relocation entries of the object file being processed. |
| **ldshread** | **ldshread**(3X) | Read section header of an object file being processed. |
| **ldsseek** | **ldsseek**(3X) | Seeks to the section of the object file being processed. |

| Function | Reference | Brief Description |
|----------|-----------|-------------------|
| ldtbindex | ldtbindex(3X) | Returns the long index of the symbol table entry at the current position of the object file being processed. |
| ldtbread | ldtbread(3X) | Reads a specific symbol table entry of the object file being processed. |
| ldtbseek | ldtbseek(3X) | Seeks to the symbol table of the object file being processed. |
| sgetl | sputl(3X) | Access long integer data in a machine independent format. |
| sputl | sputl(3X) | Translate a long integer into a machine independent format. |

## Common Object File Interface Macros (ldfcn.h)

The interface between the calling program and the object file access routines is based on the defined type LDFILE, which is in the header file **ldfcn.h** (see **ldfcn**(4)). The primary purpose of this structure is to provide uniform access to both simple object files and to object files that are members of an archive file.

The function **ldopen**(3X) allocates and initializes the LDFILE structure and returns a pointer to the structure. The fields of the LDFILE structure may be accessed individually through the following macros:

- The TYPE macro returns the magic number of the file, which is used to distinguish between archive files and object files that are not part of an archive.

- The IOPTR macro returns the file pointer, which was opened by **ldopen**(3X) and is used by the input/output functions of the C library.

- The OFFSET macro returns the file address of the beginning of the object file. This value is non-zero only if the object file is a member of the archive file.

- The HEADER macro accesses the file header structure of the object file.

Additional macros are provided to access an object file. These macros parallel the input/output functions in the C library; each macro translates a reference to an LDFILE structure into a reference to its file descriptor field. The available macros are described in **ldfcn**(4) in the *Programmer's Reference Manual*.

## The Math Library

The math library package consists of functions and a header file. The functions are located and loaded during the compilation of a C language program by the −l option on a command line, as follows:

**cc** *file* **−lm**

This option causes the link editor to search the math library, **libm.a**. In addition to the request to load the functions, the header file of the math library should be included in the program being compiled. This is accomplished by including the line:

```
#include <math.h>
```

near the beginning of each file that uses the routines.

The functions are grouped into the following categories:

- trigonometric functions

- Bessel functions

- hyperbolic functions

- miscellaneous functions

### Trigonometric Functions

These functions are used to compute angles (in radian measure), sines, cosines, and tangents. All of these values are expressed in double-precision.

| Function | Reference | Brief Description |
|----------|-----------|-------------------|
| acos | **trig**(3M) | Return arc cosine. |
| asin | **trig**(3M) | Return arc sine. |
| atan | **trig**(3M) | Return arc tangent. |
| atan2 | **trig**(3M) | Return arc tangent of a ratio. |
| cos | **trig**(3M) | Return cosine. |
| sin | **trig**(3M) | Return sine. |
| tan | **trig**(3M) | Return tangent. |

### Bessel Functions

These functions calculate Bessel functions of the first and second kinds of several orders for real values. The Bessel functions are **j0**, **j1**, **jn**, **y0**, **y1**, and **yn**. The functions are located in section **bessel**(3M).

### Hyperbolic Functions

These functions are used to compute the hyperbolic sine, cosine, and tangent for real values.

| Function | Reference | Brief Description |
|----------|-----------|-------------------|
| cosh | **sinh**(3M) | Return hyperbolic cosine. |
| sinh | **sinh**(3M) | Return hyperbolic sine. |
| tanh | **sinh**(3M) | Return hyperbolic tangent. |

### Miscellaneous Functions

These functions cover a wide variety of operations, such as natural logarithm, exponential, and absolute value. In addition, several are provided to truncate the integer portion of double-precision numbers.

| Function | Reference | Brief Description |
|----------|-----------|-------------------|
| **ceil** | **floor**(3M) | Returns the smallest integer not less than a given value. |
| **exp** | **exp**(3M) | Returns the exponential function of a given value. |
| **fabs** | **floor**(3M) | Returns the absolute value of a given value. |
| **floor** | **floor**(3M) | Returns the largest integer not greater than a given value. |
| **fmod** | **floor**(3M) | Returns the remainder produced by the division of two given values. |
| **gamma** | **gamma**(3M) | Returns the natural log of the absolute value of the result of applying the gamma function to a given value. |
| **hypot** | **hypot**(3M) | Return the square root of the sum of the squares of two numbers. |

| Function | Reference | Brief Description |
|----------|-----------|-------------------|
| **log** | **exp**(3M) | Returns the natural logarithm of a given value. |
| **log10** | **exp**(3M) | Returns the logarithm base ten of a given value. |
| **matherr** | **matherr**(3M) | Error-handling function. |
| **pow** | **exp**(3M) | Returns the result of a given value raised to another given value. |
| **sqrt** | **exp**(3M) | Returns the square root of a given value. |

## Shared Libraries

As noted above, beginning with UNIX System V Release 3.0, shared libraries are supported. Not only are some system libraries (**libc** and the networking library) available in both archive and shared library form, but also applications have the option of creating private application shared libraries.

The reason why shared libraries are desirable is that they save space, both on disk and in memory. With an archive library, when the link editor goes to the archive to resolve a reference it takes a copy of the object file that it needs for the resolution and binds it into the **a.out** file. From that point on the copied file is a part of the executable, whether it is in memory to be run or sitting in secondary storage. If you have a lot of executables that use, say, **printf** (which just happens to require much of the standard I/O library) you can be talking about a sizeable amount of space.

With a shared library, the link editor does not copy code into the executable files. When the operating system starts a process that uses a shared library it maps the shared library contents into the address space of the process. Only one copy of the shared code exists, and many processes can use it at the same time.

This fundamental difference between archives and shared libraries has another significant aspect. When code in an archive library is modified, all existing executables are uneffected. They continue using the older version until they are re-link edited. When code in a shared library is modified, all programs that share that code use the new version the next time they are executed.

All this may sound like a really terrific deal, but as with most things in life there are complications. To begin with, in the paragraphs above we didn't give you quite all the facts. For example, each process that uses shared library code gets its own copy of the entire data region of the library. It is actually only the text region that is really shared. So the truth is that shared libraries can add space to executing **a.out**'s even though the chances are good that they will cause more shrinkage than expansion. What this means is that when there is a choice between using a shared library and an archive, you shouldn't use the shared library unless it saves space. If you were using a shared **libc** to access only **strcmp**, for example, you would pick up more in shared library data than you would save by sharing the text.

The answer to this problem, and to others that are somewhat more complex, is to assign the responsibility for shared libraries to a central person or group within the application. The shared library developer should be the one to resolve questions of when to use shared and when to use archive system libraries. If a private library is to be built for your application, one person or organization should be responsible for its development and maintenance.

### Where to Find More Information

The sample application at the end of this chapter includes an example of the use of a shared library. Chapter 8 in Part 2 of this guide describes how shared libraries are built and maintained.


## Symbolic Debugger

The use of **sdb** was mentioned briefly in Chapter 2. In this section we want to say a few words about **sdb** within the context of an application development project.

**sdb** works on a process, and enables a programmer to find errors in the code. It is a tool a programmer might use while coding and unit testing a program, to make sure it runs according to its design. **sdb** would normally be used prior to the time the program is turned over, along with the rest of the application, to testers. During this phase of the application development cycle programs are compiled with the **−g** option of **cc** to facilitate the use of the debugger. The symbol table should not be stripped from the object file. Once the programmer is satisfied that the program is error-free, **strip**(1) can be used to reduce the file storage overhead taken by the file.

If the application uses a private shared library, the possibility arises that a program bug may be located in a file that resides in the shared library. Dealing with a problem of this sort calls for coordination by the administrator of the shared library. Any change to an object file that is part of a shared library means the change effects all processes that use that file. One program's bug may be another program's feature.

### Where to Find More Information

Chapter 15 in Part 2 of this guide contains information on how to use **sdb**. The manual page is in Section (1) of the *Programmer's Reference Manual.*


# lint as a Portability Tool

It is a characteristic of the UNIX system that language compilation systems are somewhat permissive. Generally speaking it is a design objective that a compiler should run fast. Most C compilers, therefore, let some things go unflagged as long as the language syntax is observed statement by statement. This sometimes means that while your program may run, the output will have some surprises. It also sometimes means that while the program may run on the machine on which the compilation system runs, there may be real difficulties in running it on some other machine.

That's where **lint** comes in. **lint** produces comments about inconsistencies in the code. The types of anomalies flagged by **lint** are:

- cases of disagreement between the type of value expected from a called function and what the function actually returns

- disagreement between the types and number of arguments expected by functions and what the function receives

- inconsistencies that might prove to be bugs

- things that might cause portability problems

Here is an example of a portability problem that would be caught by **lint**.

Code such as this:

```
int i = lseek(fdes, offset, whence)
```

would get by most compilers. However, **lseek** returns a long integer representing the address of a location in the file. On a machine with a 16-bit integer and a bigger **long int**, it would produce incorrect results, because **i** would contain only the last 16 bits of the value returned.

Since it is reasonable to expect that an application written for a UNIX system machine will be able to run on a variety of computers, it is important that the use of **lint** be a regular part of the application development.

## Where to Find More Information

Chapter 16 in Part 2 of this guide contains a description of **lint** with examples of the kinds of conditions it uncovers. The manual page is in Section (1) of the *Programmer's Reference Manual*.

# Project Control Tools

Volumes have been written on the subject of project control. It is an item of top priority for the managers of any application development team. Two UNIX system tools that can play a role in this area are described in this section.

## make

**make** is extremely useful in an application development project for keeping track of what object files need to be recompiled as changes are made to source code files. One of the characteristics of programs in a UNIX system environment is that they are made up of many small pieces, each in its own object file, that are link edited together to form the executable file. Quite a few of the UNIX system tools are devoted to supporting that style of program architecture. For example, archive libraries, shared libraries and even the fact that the **cc** command accepts **.o** files as well as **.c** files, and that it can stop short of the **ld** step and produce **.o** files instead of an **a.out**, are all important elements of modular architecture. The two main advantages of this type of programming are that

- A file that performs one function can be re-used in any program that needs it.

- When one function is changed, the whole program does not have to be recompiled.

On the flip side, however, a consequence of the proliferation of object files is an increased difficulty in keeping track of what does need to be recompiled, and what doesn't. **make** is designed to help deal with this problem. You use **make** by describing in a specification file, called **makefile**, the relationship (that is, the dependencies) between the different files of your program. Once having done that, you conclude a session in which possibly a number of your source code files have been changed by running the **make** command. **make** takes care of generating a new **a.out** by comparing the time-last-changed of your source code files with the dependency rules you have given it.

**make** has the ability to work with files in archive libraries or under control of the Source Code Control System (SCCS).

## Where to Find More Information

The **make**(1) manual page is contained in the *Programmer's Reference Manual*. Chapter 13 in Part 2 of this guide gives a complete description of how to use **make**.

# SCCS

SCCS is an acronym for Source Code Control System. It consists of a set of 14 commands used to track evolving versions of files. Its use is not limited to source code; any text files can be handled, so an application's documentation can also be put under control of SCCS. SCCS can:

- store and retrieve files under its control

- allow no more than a single copy of a file to be edited at one time

- provide an audit trail of changes to files

- reconstruct any earlier version of a file that may be wanted

SCCS files are stored in a special coded format. Only through commands that are part of the SCCS package can files be made available in a user's directory for editing, compiling, etc. From the point at which a file is first placed under SCCS control, only changes to the original version are stored. For example, let's say that the program, **restate**, that was used in several examples in Chapter 2, was controlled by SCCS. One of the original pieces of that program is a file called **oppty.c** that looks like this:

```
                        /* Opportunity Cost -- oppty.c */
#include "recdef.h"

float
oppty(ps)
struct rec *ps;
{
                        return(ps->i/12 * ps->t * ps->dp);

}
```

If you decide to add a message to this funtion, you might change the file like this:

```
                        /* Opportunity Cost -- oppty.c */
#include "recdef.h"
#include <stdio.h>

float
oppty(ps)
struct rec *ps;
{
                (void) fprintf(stderr, "Opportunity calling\n");
                return(ps->i/12 * ps->t * ps->dp);
}
```

SCCS saves only the two new lines from the second version, with a coded notation that shows where in the text the two lines belong. It also includes a note of the version number, lines deleted, lines inserted, total lines in the file, the date and time of the change and the login id of the person making the change.

## Where to Find More Information

Chapter 14 in Part 2 of this guide is an SCCS user's guide. SCCS commands are in Section (1) of the *Programmer's Reference Manual.*

# liber, A Library System

To illustrate the use of UNIX system programming tools in the development of an application, we are going to pretend we are engaged in the development of a computer system for a library. The system is known as **liber**. The early stages of system development, we assume, have already been completed; feasibility studies have been done, the preliminary design is described in the coming paragraphs. We are going to stop short of producing a complete detailed design and module specifications for our system. You will have to accept that these exist. In using portions of the system for examples of the topics covered in this chapter, we will work from these virtual specifications.

We make no claim as to the efficacy of this design. It is the way it is only in order to provide some passably realistic examples of UNIX system programming tools in use.

**liber** is a system for keeping track of the books in a library. The hardware consists of a single computer with terminals throughout the library. One terminal is used for adding new books to the data base. Others are used for checking out books and as electronic card catalogs.

The design of the system calls for it to be brought up at the beginning of the day and remain running while the library is in operation. The system has one master index that contains the unique identifier of each title in the library. When the system is running the index resides in memory. Semaphores are used to control access to the index. In the pages that follow fragments of some of the system's programs are shown to illustrate the way they work together. The startup program performs the system initialization; opening the semaphores and shared memory; reading the index into the shared memory; and kicking off the other programs. The id numbers for the shared memory and semaphores (**shmid**, **wrtsem**, and **rdsem**) are read from a file during initialization. The programs all share the in-memory index. They attach it with the following code:

```
/* attach shared memory for index */
if ((int)(index = (INDEX *) shmat(shmid, NULL, 0)) == -1)
{
        (void) fprintf(stderr, "shmat failed: %d\n", errno);
        exit(1);
}
```

Of the programs shown, **add-books** is the only one that alters the index. The semaphores are used to ensure that no other programs will try to read the index while **add-books** is altering it. The checkout program locks the file record for the book, so that each copy being checked out is recorded separately and the book cannot be checked out at two different checkout stations at the same time.

The program fragments do not provide any details on the structure of the index or the book records in the data base.

```
                    /* liber.h - header file for the
                     *           library system.
                     */
typedef ... INDEX;   /* data structure for book file index */
typedef struct {     /* type of records in book file */
     char title[30];
     char author[30];
     .

     .

     .
} BOOK;
int shmid;
int wrtsem;
int rdsem;
INDEX *index;

int book_file;
BOOK book_buf;
```

*continued*

```
/*    startup program */

/*
 * 1. Open shared memory for file index and read it in.
 * 2. Open two semaphores for providing exclusive write access to index.
 * 3. Stash id's for shared memory segment and semaphores in a file
 *    where they can be accessed by the programs.
 * 4. Start programs:  add-books, card-catalog, and checkout running
 *    on the various terminals throughout the library.
 */

#include    <stdio.h>
#include    <sys/types.h>
#include    <sys/ipc.h>
#include    <sys/shm.h>
#include    <sys/sem.h>
#include    "liber.h"

void exit();
extern int errno;

key_t key;
int shmid;
int wrtsem;
int rdsem;
FILE *ipc_file;

main()
{
    .
    .
    .

    if ((shmid = shmget(key, sizeof(INDEX), IPC_CREAT | 0666)) == -1)
    {
        (void) fprintf(stderr, "startup: shmget failed: errno=%d\n", errno);
        exit(1);
    }
    if ((wrtsem = semget(key, 1, IPC_CREAT | 0666)) == -1)
    {
        (void) fprintf(stderr, "startup: semget failed: errno=%d\n", errno);
        exit(1);
    }
```

*continued*

```
    if ((rdsem = semget(key, 1, IPC_CREAT | 0666)) == -1)
    {
        (void) fprintf(stderr, "startup: semget failed: errno=%d\n", errno);
        exit(1);
    }
    (void) fprintf(ipc_file, "%d\n%d\n%d\n", shmid, wrtsem, rdsem);

    /*
     * Start the add-books program running on the terminal in the
     * basement.  Start the checkout and card-catalog programs
     * running on the various other terminals throughout the library.
     */
    .
    .
    .

}

/*    card-catalog program*/

/*
 * 1. Read screen for author and title.
 * 2. Use semaphores to prevent reading index while it is being written.
 * 3. Use index to get position of book record in book file.
 * 4. Print book record on screen or indicate book was not found.
 * 5. Go to 1.
 */

#include        <stdio.h>
#include        <sys/types.h>
#include        <sys/ipc.h>
#include        <sys/sem.h>
#include     <fcntl.h>
#include     "liber.h"

void exit();
extern int errno;
struct sembuf sop[1];

main() {
    .
    .
    .
```

*continued*

```
while (1)
{
    /*
     * Read author/title/subject information from screen.
     */

    /*
     * Wait for write semaphore to reach 0 (index not being written).
     */
    sop[0].sem_op = 1;
    if (semop(wrtsem, sop, 1) == -1)
    {
            (void) fprintf(stderr, "semop failed: %d\n", errno);
            exit(1);
    }
    /*
     * Increment read semaphore so potential writer will wait
     * for us to finish reading the index.
     */
    sop[0].sem_op = 0;
    if (semop(rdsem, sop, 1) == -1)
    {
            (void) fprintf(stderr, "semop failed: %d\n", errno);
            exit(1);
    }

    /* Use index to find file pointer(s) for book(s) */

    /* Decrement read semaphore */
    sop[0].sem_op = -1;
    if (semop(rdsem, sop, 1) == -1)
    {
            (void) fprintf(stderr, "semop failed: %d\n", errno);
            exit(1);
    }

    /*
     * Now we use the file pointers found in the index to
     * read the book file.  Then we print the information
     * on the book(s) to the screen.
     */
} /* while */
}
/*    checkout program*/
```

*continued*

```
/*
 * 1. Read screen for Dewey Decimal number of book to be checked out.
 * 2. Use semaphores to prevent reading index while it is being written.
 * 3. Use index to get position of book record in book file.
 * 4. If book not found print message on screen, otherwise lock
 *    book record and read.
 * 5. If book already checked out print message on screen, otherwise
 *    mark record "checked out" and write back to book file.
 * 6. Unlock book record.
 * 7. Go to 1.
 */

#include         <stdio.h>
#include         <sys/types.h>
#include         <sys/ipc.h>
#include         <sys/sem.h>
#include     <fcntl.h>
#include     "liber.h"

void exit();
long lseek();
extern int errno;
struct flock flk;
struct sembuf sop[1];
long bookpos;

main()
{
        .
        .
        .
    while (1)
    {
        /*
         * Read Dewey Decimal number from screen.
         */
```

*continued*

```
/*
 * Wait for write semaphore to reach 0 (index not being written).
 */
sop[0].sem_flg = 0;
sop[0].sem_op = 0;
if (semop(wrtsem, sop, 1) == -1)
{
        (void) fprintf(stderr, "semop failed: %d\n", errno);
        exit(1);
}
/*
 * Increment read semaphore so potential writer will wait
 * for us to finish reading the index.
 */
sop[0].sem_op = 1;
if (semop(rdsem, sop, 1) == -1)
{
        (void) fprintf(stderr, "semop failed: %d\n", errno);
        exit(1);
}


/*
 * Now we can use the index to find the book's record position.
 * Assign this value to "bookpos".
 */

/* Decrement read semaphore */
sop[0].sem_op = -1;
if (semop(rdsem, sop, 1) == -1)
{
        (void) fprintf(stderr, "semop failed: %d\n", errno);
        exit(1);
}

/* Lock the book's record in book file, read the record. */
flk.l_type = F_WRLCK;
flk.l_whence = 0;
flk.l_start = bookpos;
flk.l_len = sizeof(BOOK);
if (fcntl(book_file, F_SETLKW, &flk) == -1)
```

*continued*

```
        {
                (void) fprintf(stderr, "trouble locking: %d\n", errno);
                exit(1);
        }
        if (lseek(book_file, bookpos, 0) == -1)
        {
                Error processing for lseek;
        }
        if (read(book_file, &book_buf, sizeof(BOOK)) == -1)
        {
                Error processing for read;
        }

        /*
         * If the book is checked out inform the client, otherwise
         * mark the book's record as checked out and write it
         * back into the book file.
         */

        /* Unlock the book's record in book file. */
        flk.l_type = F_UNLCK;
        if (fcntl(book_file, F_SETLK, &flk) == -1)
        {
                (void) fprintf(stderr, "trouble unlocking: %d\n", errno);
                exit(1);
        }
    } /* while */
}

/*    add-books program*/

/*
 * 1. Read a new book entry from screen.
 * 2. Insert book in book file.
 * 3. Use semaphore "wrtsem" to block new readers.
 * 4. Wait for semaphore "rdsem" to reach 0.
 * 5. Insert book into index.
 * 6. Decrement wrtsem.
 * 7. Go to 1.
 */
```

*continued*

```
#include <stdio.h>
#include   <sys/types.h>
#include   <sys/ipc.h>
#include   <sys/sem.h>
#include   "liber.h"

void exit();
extern int errno;
struct sembuf sop[1];
BOOK bookbuf;

main()
{
     .
     .
     .
     for (;;)
     {

          /*
           * Read information on new book from screen.
           */

          addscr(&bookbuf);

          /* write new record at the end of the bookfile.
           * Code not shown, but
           * addscr() returns a 1 if title information has
           * been entered, 0 if not.
           */

          /*
           * Increment write semaphore, blocking new readers from
           * accessing the index.
           */
          sop[0].sem_flg = 0;
          sop[0].sem_op = 1;
          if (semop(wrtsem, sop, 1) == -1)
          {
                    (void) fprintf(stderr, "semop failed: %d\n", errno);
                    exit(1);
          }
```

*continued*

```
        /*
         * Wait for read semaphore to reach 0 (all readers to finish
         * using the index).
         */
        sop[0].sem_op = 0;
        if (semop(rdsem, sop, 1) == -1)
        {
                (void) fprintf(stderr, "semop failed: %d\n", errno);
                exit(1);
        }
        /*
         * Now that we have exclusive access to the index we
         * insert our new book with its file pointer.
         */

        /* Decrement write semaphore, permitting readers to read index. */
        sop[0].sem_op = -1;
        if (semop(wrtsem, sop, 1) == -1)
        {
                (void) fprintf(stderr, "semop failed: %d\n", errno);
                exit(1);
        }
    } /* for */
    .
    .
    .
}
```

The example following, **addscr()**, illustrates two significant points about **curses** screens:

1.  Information read in from a **curses** window can be stored in fields that are part of a structure defined in the header file for the application.

2.  The address of the structure can be passed from another function where the record is processed.

```
                        /*  addscr is called from add-books.
                         *  The user is prompted for title
                         *  information.
                         */
#include <curses.h>

WINDOW *cmdwin;

addscr(bb)
struct BOOK *bb;
{
     int c;

     initscr();
     nonl();
     noecho();
     cbreak();

     cmdwin = newwin(6, 40, 3, 20);
     mvprintw(0, 0, "This screen is for adding titles to the data base");
     mvprintw(1, 0, "Enter  a  to add;  q  to quit: ");
     refresh();
     for (;;)
     {
         refresh();
         c = getch();
         switch (c) {
           case 'a':
                     werase(cmdwin);
                     box(cmdwin, '|', '-');
                     mvwprintw(cmdwin, 1, 1, "Enter title: ");
                     wmove(cmdwin, 2, 1);
                     echo();
                     wrefresh(cmdwin);
                     wgetstr(cmdwin, bb->title);
                     noecho();
                     werase(cmdwin);
                     box(cmdwin, '|', '-');
                     mvwprintw(cmdwin, 1, 1, "Enter author: ");
                     wmove(cmdwin, 2, 1);
                     echo();
                     wrefresh(cmdwin);
                     wgetstr(cmdwin, bb->author);
                     noecho();
                     werase(cmdwin);
```

*continued*

```
                    wrefresh(cmdwin);
                    endwin();
                    return(1);
            case 'q':
                    erase();
                    endwin();
                    return(0);
            }
        }
}

#
# Makefile for liber library system
#

CC = cc
CFLAGS = -O
all: startup add-books checkout card-catalog

startup: liber.h startup.c
    $(CC) $(CFLAGS) -o startup startup.c

add-books: add-books.o addscr.o
    $(CC) $(CFLAGS) -o add-books add-books.o addscr.o

add-books.o: liber.h

checkout: liber.h checkout.c
    $(CC) $(CFLAGS) -o checkout checkout.c

card-catalog: liber.h card-catalog.c
    $(CC) $(CFLAGS) -o card-catalog card-catalog.c
```

# CHAPTER 4: awk

## Introduction

**awk** is a file-processing programming language designed to make many common information and retrieval text manipulation tasks easy to state and perform. **awk**:

- generates reports

- matches patterns

- validates data

- filters data for transmission

In the first part of this chapter, we give a general statement of the **awk** syntax. Then, under the heading "Using **awk**," we provide a number of examples that show the syntax rules in use.

## Program Structure

An **awk** program is a sequence of statements of the form

```
pattern {action}
pattern {action}
    . . .
```

**awk** runs on a set of input files. The basic operation of **awk** is to scan a set of input lines, in order, one at a time. In each line, **awk** searches for the pattern described in the **awk** program. If that pattern is found in the input line, a corresponding action is performed. In this way, each statement of the **awk** program is executed for a given input line. When all the patterns are tested, the next input line is fetched; and the **awk** program is once again executed from the beginning.

In the **awk** command, either the pattern or the action may be omitted, but not both. If there is no action for a pattern, the matching line is simply printed. If there is no pattern for an action, then the action is performed for every input line. The null **awk** program does nothing. Since patterns and actions are both optional, actions are enclosed in braces to distinguish them from patterns.

For example, this **awk** program

```
/x/     {print}
```

prints every input line that has an **x** in it.

An **awk** program has the following structure:

- a **BEGIN** section
- a **record** or main section
- an **END** section

The **BEGIN** section is run before any input lines are read, and the **END** section is run after all the data files are processed. The **record** section is run over and over for each separate line of input. The words **BEGIN** and **END** are actually special patterns recognized by **awk**.

Values are assigned to variables from the **awk** command line. The **BEGIN** section is run before these assignments are made.

## Lexical Units

All **awk** programs are made up of lexical units called tokens. In **awk** there are eight token types:

1. numeric constants

2. string constants

3. keywords

4. identifiers

5. operators

6. record and field tokens

7. comments

8. tokens used for grouping

## Numeric Constants

A numeric constant is either a decimal constant or a floating constant. A decimal constant is a nonnull sequence of digits containing at most one decimal point as in **12, 12., 1.2,** and **.12.** A floating constant is a decimal constant followed by **e** or **E** followed by an optional + or − sign followed by a nonnull sequence of digits as in **12e3, 1.2e3, 1.2e−3,** and **1.2E+3.** The maximum size and precision of a numeric constant are machine dependent.

## String Constants

A string constant is a sequence of zero or more characters surrounded by double quotes as in **",", "a", "ab",** and **"12".** A double quote is put in a string by preceding it with a backslash, \, as in "He said, \" Sit! \"". A newline is put in a string by using **\n** in its place. No other characters need to be escaped. Strings can be (almost) any length.

## Keywords

Strings used as keywords are shown in Figure 4-1.

### Keywords

| | | |
|---|---|---|
| **BEGIN** | break | log |
| **END** | close | next |
| **FILENAME** | continue | number |
| **FS** | exit | print |
| **NF** | exp | printf |
| **NR** | for | split |
| **OFS** | getline | sprintf |
| **ORS** | if | sqrt |
| **OFMT** | in | string |
| **RS** | index | substr |
| | int | while |
| | length | |

Figure 4-1: **awk** Keywords

## Identifiers

Identifiers in **awk** serve to denote variables and arrays. An identifier is a sequence of letters, digits, and underscores, beginning with a letter or an underscore. Uppercase and lowercase letters are different.

## Operators

**awk** has assignment, arithmetic, relational, and logical operators similar to those in the C programming language and regular expression pattern matching operators similar to those in **egrep**(1) and **lex**(1).

Assignment operators are shown in Figure 4-2.

| Symbol | Usage | Description |
|:------:|-------|-------------|
| = | assignment | |
| += | **plus-equals** | **X += Y is similar to X = X+Y** |
| −= | minus-equals | **X−=Y is similar to X = X−Y** |
| *= | times-equals | **X *= Y is similar to X = X*Y** |
| /= | divide-equals | **X /= Y is similar to X = X/Y** |
| %= | mod-equals | **X %= Y is similar to X = X%Y** |
| ++ | **prefix and postfix increments** | **++X and X++ are similar to X=X+1** |
| −− | **prefix and postfix decrements** | **−−X and X−− are similar to X = X −1** |

Figure 4-2: **awk** Assignment Operators

Arithmetic operators are shown in Figure 4-3.

| Symbol | Description |
|--------|-------------|
| + | unary and binary plus |
| − | unary and binary minus |
| * | multiplication |
| / | division |
| % | modulus |
| (...) | grouping |

Figure 4-3: **awk** Arithmetic Operators

Relational operators are shown in Figure 4-4.

| Symbol | Description |
|--------|-------------|
| < | less than |
| <= | less than or equal to |
| == | equal to |
| != | not equal to |
| >= | greater than or equal to |
| > | greater than |

Figure 4-4: **awk** Relational Operators

Logical operators are shown in Figure 4-5.

| Symbol | Description |
| :----: | ----------- |
| && | and |
| \| | or |
| ! | not |

Figure 4-5: **awk** Logical Operators

Regular expression matching operators are shown in the Figure 4-6.

| Symbol | Description |
| :----: | -------------- |
| ~ | matches |
| !~ | does not match |

Figure 4-6: Operators for Matching Regular Expressions in **awk**

## Record and Field Tokens

**$0** is a special variable whose value is that of the current input record. **$1**, **$2**, and so forth, are special variables whose values are those of the first field, the second field, and so forth, of the current input record. The keyword **NF** (Number of Fields) is a special variable whose value is the number of fields in the current input record. Thus **$NF** has, as its value, the value of the last field of the current input record. Notice that the first field of each record is numbered 1 and that the number of fields can vary from record to record. None of these variables is defined in the action associated with a **BEGIN** or **END** pattern, where there is no current input record.

The keyword **NR** (Number of Records) is a variable whose value is the number of input records read so far. The first input record read is 1.

### Record Separators

The keyword **RS** (Record Separator) is a variable whose value is the current record separator. The value of **RS** is initially set to newline, indicating that adjacent input records are separated by a newline. Keyword **RS** may be changed to any character, $c$, by executing the assignment statement **RS** = "$c$" in an action.

### Field Separator

The keyword **FS** (Field Separator) is a variable indicating the current field separator. Initially, the value of **FS** is a blank, indicating that fields are separated by white space, i.e., any nonnull sequence of blanks and tabs. Keyword **FS** is changed to any single character, $c$, by executing the assignment statement **F** = "$c$" in an action or by using the optional command line argument −F$c$. Two values of $c$ have special meaning, **space** and \t. The assignment statement **FS** =" " makes white space (a tab or blank) the field separator; and on the command line, −F\t makes a tab the field separator.

If the field separator is not a blank, then there is a field in the record on each side of the separator. For instance, if the field separator is **1**, the record **1XXX1** has three fields. The first and last are null. If the field separator is blank, then fields are separated by white space, and none of the **NF** fields are null.

### Multiline Records

The assignment **RS** =" " makes an empty line the record separator and makes a nonnull sequence (consisting of blanks, tabs, and possibly a newline) the field separator. With this setting, none of the first **NF** fields of any record are null.

### Output Record and Field Separators

The value of **OFS** (Output Field Separator) is the output field separator. It is put between fields by **print**. The value of **ORS** (Output Record Separators) is put after each record by **print**. Initially, **ORS** is set to a newline and **OFS** to a space. These values may change to any string by assignments such as **ORS** = "abc" and **OFS** = "xyz".

## Comments

A comment is introduced by a **#** and terminated by a newline. For example:

```
#    this line is a comment
```

A comment can be appended to the end of any line of an **awk** program.

## Tokens Used for Grouping

Tokens in **awk** are usually separated by nonnull sequences of blanks, tabs, and newlines, or by other punctuation symbols such as commas and semicolons. Braces, {...}, surround actions, slashes, /.../, surround regular expression patterns, and double quotes, "...", surround string constants.

# Primary Expressions

In **awk**, patterns and actions are made up of expressions. The basic building blocks of expressions are the primary expressions:

- numeric constants
  string constants
  variables
  functions

Each expression has both a numeric and a string value, one of which is usually preferred. The rules for determining the preferred value of an expression are explained below.

## Numeric Constants

The format of a numeric constant was defined previously in "Lexical Units." Numeric values are stored as floating point numbers. The string value of a numeric constant is computed from the numeric value. The preferred value is the numeric value. Numeric values for string constants are in Figure 4-7.

| Numeric Constant | Numeric Value | String Value |
|:---:|:---:|:---:|
| 0 | 0 | 0 |
| 1 | 1 | 1 |
| .5 | 0.5 | .5 |
| .5e2 | 50 | 50 |

Figure 4-7: Numeric Values for String Constants

## String Constants

The format of a string constant was defined previously in "Lexical Units." The numeric value of a string constant is 0 unless the string is a numeric constant enclosed in double quotes. In this case, the numeric value is the number represented. The preferred value of a string constant is its string value. The string value of a string constant is always the string itself. String values for string constants are in Figure 4-8.

| String Constant | Numeric Value | String Value |
|:---:|:---:|:---|
| "" | 0 | empty space |
| "a" | 0 | a |
| "XYZ" | 0 | XYZ |
| "o" | 0 | 0 |
| "1" | 1 | 1 |
| ".5" | 0.5 | .5 |
| ".5e2" | 0.5 | .5e2 |

Figure 4-8: String Values for String Constants

## Variables

A variable is one of the following:

> *identifier*
> *identifier* [*expression*]
> $*term*

The numeric value of any uninitialized variable is 0, and the string value is the empty string.

An identifier by itself is a simple variable. A variable of the form *identifier* [*expression*] represents an element of an associative array named by *identifier*. The string value of *expression* is used as the index into the array. The preferred value of *identifier* or *identifier* [*expression*] is determined by context.

The variable **$0** refers to the current input record. Its string and numeric values are those of the current input record. If the current input record represents a number, then the numeric value of **$0** is the number and the string value is the literal string. The preferred value of **$0** is string unless the current input record is a number. **$0** cannot be changed by assignment.

The variables **$1**, **$2**, ... refer to fields 1, 2, and so forth, of the current input record. The string and numeric value of **$i** for $1<=i<=NF$ are those of the **i**th field of the current input record. As with **$0**, if the **i**th field represents a number, then the numeric value of **$i** is the number and the string value is the literal string. The preferred value of **$i** is string unless the **i**th field is a number. **$i** may be changed by assignment; the value of **$0** is changed accordingly.

In general, $*term* refers to the input record if *term* has the numeric value 0 and to field **i** if the greatest integer in the numeric value of *term* is **i**. If $i<0$ or if $i>=100$, then accessing **$i** causes **awk** to produce an error diagnostic. If $NF<i<=100$, then **$i** behaves like an uninitialized variable. Accessing **$i** for $i > NF$ does not change the value of **NF**.

## Functions

awk has a number of built-in functions that perform common arithmetic and string operations. The arithmetic functions are in Figure 4-9.

### Functions

exp (*expression*)
int (*expression*)
log (*expression*)
sqrt (*expression*)

Figure 4-9: Built-in Functions for Arithmetic and String Operations

These functions (**exp**, **int**, **log**, and **sqrt**) compute the exponential, integer part, natural logarithm, and square root, respectively, of the numeric value of *expression*. The (*expression*) may be omitted; then the function is applied to **$0**. The preferred value of an arithmetic function is numeric. String functions are shown in Figure 4-10.

## String Functions

---

**getline**
**index**(*expression1, expression2*)
**length**(*expression*)
**split**(*expression, identifier, expression2*)
**split**(*expression, identifier*)
**sprintf**(*format, expression1, expression2...*)
**substr**(*expression1, expression2*)
**substr**(*expression1, expression2, expression3*)

Figure 4-10: **awk** String Functions

---

The function **getline** causes the next input record to replace the current record. It returns 1 if there is a next input record or a 0 if there is no next input record. The value of **NR** is updated.

The function **index**(*e1,e2*) takes the string value of expressions *e1* and *e2* and returns the first position of where *e2* occurs as a substring in *e1*. If *e2* does not occur in *e1*, index returns 0. For example:

```
index ("abc", "bc")=2
index ("abc", "ac")=0.
```

The function **length** without an argument returns the number of characters in the current input record. With an expression argument, **length**(*e*) returns the number of characters in the string value of *e*. For example:

```
length ("abc")=3
length (17)=2.
```

The function **split** splits the string value of expression *e* into fields that are then stored in *array*[1], *array*[2], ..., *array*[*n*] using the string value of *sep* as the field separator. Split returns the number of fields found in The function **split** uses the current value of **FS** to indicate the field separator. For example, after invoking

```
n = split ($0, a), a[1],
```

a[2], ..., a[*n*] is the same sequence of values as **$1**, **$2** ..., **$NF**.

The function **sprintf**(*f, e1, e2, ...*) produces the value of expressions *e1, e2, ...* in the format specified by the string value of the expression *f*. The format control conventions are those of the **printf**(3S) statement in the C programming language (except that the use of the asterisk, *, for field width or precision is not allowed).

The function **substr** returns the suffix of *string* starting at position The function **substr** returns the substring of *string* that begins at position *pos* and is *length* characters long. If *pos* + *length* is greater than the length of *string* then **substr** is equivalent to **substr** For example:

```
substr("abc", 2, 1) = "b"
substr("abc", 2, 2) = "bc"
substr("abc", 2, 3) = "bc"
```

Positions less than 1 are taken as 1. A negative or zero length produces a null result. The preferred value of **sprintf** and **substr** is string. The preferred value of the remaining string functions is numeric.

## Terms

Various arithmetic operators are applied to primary expressions to produce larger syntactic units called terms. All arithmetic is done in floating point. A term has one of the following forms:

*primary expression*
*term binop term*
*unop term*
*incremented variable*
*(term)*

## Binary Terms

In a term of the form

term1 binop term2

*binop* can be one of the five binary arithmetic operators +, −, * (multiplication), /(division), % (modulus). The binary operator is applied to the numeric value of the operands *term1* and *term2*, and the result is the usual numeric value. This numeric value is the preferred value, but it can be interpreted as a string value (see **Numeric Constants**). The operators *, /, and % have higher precedence than + and −. All operators are left associative.

## Unary Term

In a term of the form

unop term

*unop* can be unary + or −. The unary operator is applied to the numeric value of *term*, and the result is the usual numeric value which is preferred. However, it can be interpreted as a string value. Unary + and − have higher precedence than *, /, and %.

## Incremented Vars

An incremented variable has one of the forms

++ var
− − var
var ++
var − −

The + + *var* has the value *var* + 1 and has the effect of *var* = *var* + 1. Similarly, − − *var* has the value *var* − 1 and has the effect of *var* = *var* − 1. Therefore, *var* + + has the same value as *var* and has the effect of *var* = *var* + 1. Similarly, *var* − − has the same value as *var* and has the effect of *var* = *var* − 1. The preferred value of an incremented variable is numeric.

## Parenthesized Terms

Parentheses are used to group terms in the usual manner.

# Expressions

An **awk** expression is one of the following:

> *term*
> *term term* ...
> *var asgnop expression*

## Concatenation of Terms

In an expression of the form *term1 term2* ..., the string value of the terms are concatenated. The preferred value of the resulting expression is a string value. Concatenation of terms has lower precedence than binary + and −. For example,

> 1+2  3+4

has the string (and numeric) value 37.

## Assignment Expressions

An assignment expression is one of the forms

> *var asgnop expression*

where *asgnop* is one of the six assignment operators:

> =
> +=
> −=
> *=
> /=
> %=

The preferred value of *var* is the same as that of *expression*.

In an expression of the form

> *var* = *expression*

the numeric and string values of *var* become those of *expression*.

> *var op* = *expression*

is equivalent to

*var = var op expression*

where *op* is one of: +, −, *, /, %. The *asgnops* are right associative and have the lowest precedence of any operator. Thus, a += b *= c−2 is equivalent to the sequence of assignments

```
b = b * (c-2)
a = a + b
```

# Using awk

The remainder of this chapter undertakes to show the syntax rules of **awk** in action. The material is organized under the following topics:

- input and output

- patterns

- actions

- special features

# Input and Output

## Presenting Your Program for Processing

There are two ways to present your program of pattern/action statements to **awk** for processing:

1. If the program is short (a line or two), it is often easiest to make the program the first argument on the command line:

    **awk** ' *program* ' [*filename...*]

    where *program* is your **awk** program, and *filename...* is an optional input file(s). Note that there are single quotes around the program name in order for the shell to accept the entire string (program) as the first argument to **awk**. For example, write to the shell

    **awk** ' /x/ {print} ' **file1**

    to run the **awk** program /x/ {print} on the input file **file1**. If no input file is specified, **awk** expects input from the standard input, **stdin**. You can also specify that input comes from **stdin** by using the hyphen, −, as one of the files. The pattern-action statement

    **awk** ' *program* ' **file1** −

    looks for input from **file1** and from **stdin**. It processes first from **file1** and then from **stdin**.

2. Alternately, if your **awk** program is long or is one you want to preserve for re-use in the future, it is convenient to put the program in a separate file, **awkprog**, for example, and tell **awk** to fetch it from there. This is done by using the −**f** option on the command line, as follows:

    **awk** −**f awkprog** *filename...* where *filename...* is an optional list of input

    files that may include **stdin** as is shown above.

These alternative ways of presenting your **awk** program for processing are illustrated by the following:

> **awk ' BEGIN {print "hello, world" exit} '**

prints

```
hello, world
```

on the standard output when given to the shell.

This **awk** program could be run by putting

```
BEGIN {print "hello, world" exit}
```

in a file named **awkprog**, and then the command

> **awk −f awkprog**

given to the shell would have the same effect as the first procedure.

## Input: Records and Fields

**awk** reads its input one record at a time. Unless changed by you, a record is a sequence of characters from the input ending with a newline character or with an end of file. **awk** reads in characters until it encounters a newline or end of file. The string of characters, thus read, is assigned to the variable **$0**.

Once **awk** has read in a record, it then views the record as being made up of fields. Unless changed by you, a field is a string of characters separated by blanks or tabs.

## Sample Input File, countries

For use as an example, we have created the file, **countries**. **countries** contains the area in thousands of square miles, the population in millions, and the continent for the ten largest countries in the world. (Figures are from 1978; Russia is placed in Asia.)

| Russia | 8650 | 262 | Asia |
|--------|------|-----|------|
| Canada | 3852 | 24 | North America |
| China | 3692 | 866 | Asia |
| USA | 3615 | 219 | North America |
| Brazil | 3286 | 116 | South America |
| Australia | 2968 | 14 | Australia |
| India | 1269 | 637 | Asia |
| Argentina | 1072 | 26 | South America |
| Sudan | 968 | 19 | Africa |
| Algeria | 920 | 18 | Africa |

Figure 4-11: Sample Input File, **countries**

The wide spaces are tabs in the original input and a single blank separates North and South from America. We use this data as the input for many of the **awk** programs in this chapter since it is typical of the type of material that **awk** is best at processing (a mixture of words and numbers arranged in fields or columns separated by blanks and tabs).

Each of these lines has either four or five fields if blanks and/or tabs separate the fields. This is what **awk** assumes unless told otherwise. In the above example, the first record is

    Russia  8650    262    Asia

When this record is read by **awk**, it is assigned to the variable **$0**. If you want to refer to this entire record, it is done through the variable, **$0**. For example, the following action:

    {print $0}

prints the entire record.

Fields within a record are assigned to the variables **$1**, **$2**, **$3**, and so forth; that is, the first field of the present record is referred to as **$1** by the **awk** program. The second field of the present record is referred to as **$2** by the **awk** program. The **i**th field of the present record is referred to as **$i** by the **awk** program. Thus, in the above example of the file **countries**, in the first record:

$1 is equal to the string "Russia"
$2 is equal to the integer 8650
$3 is equal to the integer 262
$4 is equal to the string "Asia"
$5 is equal to the null string

... and so forth.

To print the continent, followed by the name of the country, followed by its population, use the following command:

**awk '{print $4, $1, $3}' countries**

You'll notice that this does not produce exactly the output you may have wanted because the field separator defaults to white space (tabs or blanks). **North America** and **South America** inconveniently contain a blank. Try it again with the following command line:

**awk -F\t '{print $4, $1, $3}' countries**

# Input: From the Command Line

We have seen above, under "Presenting Your Program for Processing," that you can give your program to **awk** for processing by either including it on the command line enclosed by single quotes, or by putting it in a file and naming the file on the command line (preceded by the −**f** flag). It is also possible to set variables from the command line.

In **awk**, values may be assigned to variables from within an **awk** program. Because you do not declare types of variables, a variable is created simply by referring to it. An example of assigning a value to a variable is:

**x=5**

This statement in an **awk** program assigns the value **5** to the variable **x**. This type of assignment can be done from the command line. This provides another way to supply input values to **awk** programs. For example:

**awk ' {print x }' x=5 −**

will print the value **5** on the standard output. The minus sign at the end of this command is necessary to indicate that input is coming from **stdin** instead of a file called **x=5**. After entering the command, the user must proceed to enter input. The input is terminated with a CTRL-d.

If the input comes from a file, named **file1** in the example, the command is

> **awk '{print x}' file1**

It is not possible to assign values to variables used in the **BEGIN** section in this way.

If it is necessary to change the record separator and the field separator, it is useful to do so from the command line as in the following example:

> awk −f awkprog RS=":" file1

Here, the record separator is changed to the character :. This causes your program in the file **awkprog** to run with records separated by the colon instead of the newline character and with input coming from **file1**. It is similarly useful to change the field separator from the command line.

There is a separate option, **−F**$x$, that is placed directly after the command **awk**. This changes the field separator from white space to the character $x$. For example:

> **awk −F: −f awkprog file1**

changes the field separator, **FS**, to the character :. Note that if the field separator is specifically set to a tab (that is, with the −**F** option or by making a direct assignment to **FS**), then blanks are not recognized by **awk** as separating fields. However, the reverse is not true. Even if the field separator is specifically set to a blank, tabs are still recognized by **awk** as separating fields.

## Output: Printing

An action may have no pattern; in this case, the action is executed for all lines as in the simple printing program

> {print}

This is one of the simplest actions performed by **awk**. It prints each line of the input to the output. More useful is to print one or more fields from each line. For instance, using the file **countries** that was used earlier,

> **awk '{ print $1, $3 }' countries**

prints the name of the country and the population:

```
Russia 262
Canada 24
China 866
USA 219
Brazil 116
Australia 14
India 637
Argentina 14
Sudan 19
Algeria 18
```

A semicolon at the end of statements is optional. **awk** accepts

```
{print $1}
```

      and

```
{print $1;}
```

equally and takes them to mean the same thing. If you want to put two **awk** statements on the same line of an **awk** script, the semicolon is necessary, for example, if you want the number **5** printed:

```
{x=5; print x}
```

Parentheses are also optional with the print statement.

```
{print $3, $2}
```

is the same as

```
{print ($3, $2)}
```

Items separated by a comma in a **print** statement are separated by the current output field separator (normally spaces, even though the input is separated by tabs) when printed. The **OFS** is another special variable that can be changed by you. (These special variables are summarized below.) **print** also prints strings directly from your programs, as with the **awk** script

```
{print "hello, world"}
```

As we have already seen, **awk** makes available a number of special variables with useful values, for example, **FS** and **RS**. We introduce two other special variables in the next example. **NR** and **NF** are both integers that contain the number of the present record and the number of fields in the present record, respectively. Thus,

```
{print NR, NF, $0}
```

prints each record number and the number of fields in each record followed by the record itself. Using this program on the file **countries** yields:

```
 1 4 Russia      8650  262   Asia
 2 5 Canada      3852   24   North America
 3 4 China       3692  866   Asia
 4 5 USA         3615  219   North America
 5 5 Brazil      3286  116   South America
 6 4 Australia   2968   14   Australia
 7 4 India       1269  637   Asia
 8 5 Argentina   1072   26   South America
 9 4 Sudan        968   19   Africa
10 4 Algeria      920   18   Africa
```

and the program

```
{print NR, $1}
```

prints

```
 1 Russia
 2 Canada
 3 China
 4 USA
 5 Brazil
 6 Australia
 7 India
 8 Argentina
 9 Sudan
10 Algeria
```

This is an easy way to supply sequence numbers to a list. **print**, by itself, prints the input record. Use

```
{print ""}
```

to print an empty line.

**awk** also provides the statement **printf** so that you can format output as desired. **print** uses the default format **%.6g** for each numeric variable printed.

**printf** *"format"*, *expr, expr, ...*

formats the expressions in the list according to the specification in the string *format*, and prints them. The *format* statement is almost identical to that of **printf**(3S) in the C library. For example:

```
{ printf "%10s %6d %6d\n", $1, $2, $3 }
```

prints **$1** as a string of 10 characters (right justified). The second and third fields (6-digit numbers) make a neatly columned table.

```
   Russia  8650  262
   Canada  3852  244
    China  3692  866
      USA  3615  219
   Brazil  3286  116
Australia  2968   14
    India  1269  637
Argentina  1072   26
    Sudan   968   19
  Algeria   920   18
```

With **printf**, no output separators or newlines are produced automatically. You must add them as in this example. The escape characters **\n**, **\t**, **\b** (backspace), and **\r** (carriage return) may be specified.

There is a third way that printing can occur on standard output when a pattern without an action is specified. In this case, the entire record, **$0**, is printed. For example, the program

```
/x/
```

prints any record that contains the character **x**.

There are two special variables that go with printing, **OFS** and **ORS**. By default, these are set to blank and the newline character, respectively. The variable **OFS** is printed on the standard output when a comma occurs in a **print** statement such as

```
{ x="hello"; y="world"
print x,y
}
```

which prints

```
hello world
```

However, without the comma in the print statement as

```
{ x="hello"; y="world"
print x y
}
```

you get

```
helloworld
```

To get a comma on the output, you can either insert it in the print statement as in this case

```
{ x="hello"; y="world"
print x"," y
}
```

or you can change **OFS** in a **BEGIN** section as in

```
BEGIN {OFS=", "}
{ x="hello"; y="world"
print x, y
}
```

Both of these last two scripts yield

```
hello, world
```

Note that the output field separator is not used when **$0** is printed.

## Output: to Different Files

The UNIX operating system shell allows you to redirect standard output to a file. **awk** also lets you direct output to many different files from within your **awk** program. For example, with our input file **countries**, we want to print all the data from countries of Asia in a file called **ASIA**, all the data from countries in Africa in a file called **AFRICA**, and so forth. This is done with the following **awk** program:

```
{ if ($4 == "Asia") print > "ASIA"
  if ($4 == "Europe") print > "EUROPE"
  if ($4 == "North") print > "NORTH_AMERICA"
  if ($4 == "South") print > "SOUTH_AMERICA"
  if ($4 == "Australia") print > "AUSTRALIA"
  if ($4 == "Africa") print > "AFRICA"
}
```

Flow of control statements is discussed later.

In general, you may direct output into a file after a **print** or a **printf** statement by using a statement of the form

**print** > *"filename"*

where *filename* is the name of the file receiving the data. The **print** statement may have any legal arguments to it.

Notice that the filename is quoted. Without quotes, filenames are treated as uninitialized variables and all output then goes to **stdout**, unless redirected on the command line.

If > is replaced by >>, output is appended to the file rather than overwriting it. Notice that there is an upper limit to the number of files that are written in this way. At present it is ten.

## Output: to Pipes

It is also possible to direct printing into a pipe instead of a file. For example:

```
{
if ($2 == "XX") print | "mailx mary"
}
```

where **mary** is a person's login name. Any record with the second field equal
to **XX** is sent to the user, **mary**, as mail. **awk** waits until the entire program is
run before it executes the command that was piped to; in this case, the
**mailx**(1) command. For example:

```
{
print $1 | "sort"
}
```

takes the first field of each input record, sorts these fields, and then prints
them.

Another example of using a pipe for output is the following idiom, which
guarantees that its output always goes to your terminal:

```
{
print ... | "cat -v > /dev/tty"
}
```

Only one output statement to a pipe is permitted in an **awk** program. In
all output statements involving redirection of output, the files or pipes are
identified by their names, but they are created and opened only once in the
entire run.

# Patterns

A pattern in front of an action acts as a selector that determines if the action is to be executed.  A variety of expressions are used as patterns:

- certain keywords

- arithmetic relational expressions

- regular expressions

- combinations of these

## BEGIN and END

The keyword, **BEGIN**, is a special pattern that matches the beginning of the input before the first record is read.  The keyword, **END**, is a special pattern that matches the end of the input after the last line is processed.  **BEGIN** and **END** thus provide a way to gain control before and after processing for initialization and wrapping up.

As you have seen, you can use **BEGIN** to put column headings on the output

```
BEGIN {print "Country", "Area", "Population", "Continent"}
      {print}
```

which produces

```
Country Area Population Continent

Russia    8650   262   Asia
Canada    3852   24    North America
China     3692   866   Asia
USA       3615   219   North America
Brazil    3286   116   South America
Australia        2968  14Australia
India     1269   637   Asia
Argentina        1072  26South America
Sudan     968    19    Africa
Algeria   920    18    Africa
```

Formatting is not very good here; **printf** would do a better job and is generally used when appearance is important.

Recall also, that the **BEGIN** section is a good place to change special variables such as **FS** or **RS**. For example:

```
BEGIN { FS= "\t"
        printf "Country\t\t  Area\tPopulation\tContinent\n\n"}
        {printf "%-10s\t%6d\t%6d\t\t% -14s\n", $1, $2, $3, $4}
END     {print "The number of records is", NR}
```

In this program, **FS** is set to a tab in the **BEGIN** section and as a result all records in the file **countries** have exactly four fields. Note that if **BEGIN** is present it is the first pattern; **END** is the last if it is used.

## Relational Expressions

An **awk** pattern is any expression involving comparisons between strings of characters or numbers. For example, if you want to print only countries with more than 100 million population, use

```
$3 > 100
```

This tiny **awk** program is a pattern without an action so it prints each line whose third field is greater than 100 as follows:

```
Russia    8650    262    Asia
China     3692    866    Asia
USA       3615    219    North America
Brazil    3286    116    South America
India     1269    637    Asia
```

To print the names of the countries that are in Asia, type

```
$4 == "Asia" {print $1}
```

which produces

```
Russia
China
India
```

The conditions tested are $<$, $<=$, $==$, $!=$, $>=$, and $>$. In such relational tests if both operands are numeric, a numerical comparison is made. Otherwise, the operands are compared as strings. Thus,

```
$1 >= "S"
```

selects lines that begin with **S**, **T**, **U**, and greater, which in this case are

```
USA      3615    219     North America
Sudan    968     19      Africa
```

In the absence of other information, fields are treated as strings, so the program

```
$1 == $4
```

compares the first and fourth fields as strings of characters and prints the single line

```
Australia       2968        14 Australia
```


# Regular Expressions

**awk** provides more powerful capabilities for searching for strings of characters than were illustrated in the previous section. These are regular expressions. The simplest regular expression is a literal string of characters enclosed in slashes.

```
/Asia/
```

This is a complete **awk** program that prints all lines that contain any occurrence of the name **Asia**. If a line contains **Asia** as part of a larger word like **Asiatic**, it is also printed (but there are no such words in the **countries** file.)

**awk** regular expressions include regular expression forms found in the text editor, **ed**(1), and the pattern finder, **grep**(1), in which certain characters have special meanings.

For example, we could print all lines that begin with **A** with

```
/^A/
```

or all lines that begin with **A**, **B**, or **C** with

```
/^[ABC]/
```

or all lines that end with **ia** with

```
/ia$/
```

In general, the circumflex, ^, indicates the beginning of a line. The dollar sign, **$**, indicates the end of the line and characters enclosed in brackets, **[ ]**, match any one of the characters enclosed. In addition, **awk** allows parentheses for grouping, the pipe, |, for alternatives, + for one or more occurrences, and **?** for zero or one occurrences. For example:

    /x|y/ {print}

prints all records that contain either an **x** or a **y**.

    /ax+b/      {print}

prints all records that contain an **a** followed by one or more **x**'s followed by a **b**. For example, axb, Paxxxxxxb, QaxxbR.

    /ax?b/      {print}

prints all records that contain an **a** followed by zero or one **x** followed by a **b**. For example: ab, axb, yaxbPPP, CabD.

The two characters, **.** and **\***, have the same meaning as they have in **ed**(1) namely, **.** can stand for any character and **\*** means zero or more occurrences of the character preceding it. For example:

    **/a.b/**

matches any record that contains an **a** followed by any character followed by a **b**. That is, the record must contain an **a** and a **b** separated by exactly one character. For example, **/a.b/** matches axb, aPb and xxxxaXbxx, but not ab, axxb.

    /ax*c/

matches a record that contains an **a** followed by zero or more **x**'s followed by a **c**. For example, it matches

    ac
    axc
    pqraxxxxxxxxxxxc901

Just as in **ed**(1), it is possible to turn off the special meaning of metacharacters such as ^ and **\*** by preceding these characters with a backslash. An example of this is the pattern

    /\/*\//

which matches any string of characters enclosed in slashes.

One can also specify that any field or variable matches a regular expression (or does not match it) by using the operators ~ or !~. For example, with the input file **countries** as before, the program

```
$1 ~ /ia$/        {print $1}
```

prints all countries whose name ends in **ia**:

```
Russia
Australia
India
Algeria
```

which is indeed different from lines that end in **ia**.

## Combinations of Patterns

A pattern can be made up of similar patterns combined with the operators ¦¦ (OR), && (AND), ! (NOT), and parentheses. For example:

```
$2 >= 3000 && $3 >= 100
```

selects lines where both area and population are large. For example:

```
Russia   8650   262   Asia
China    3692   866   Asia
USA      3615   219   North America
Brazil   3286   116   South America
```

while

```
$4 == "Asia" ¦¦ $4 == "Africa"
```

selects lines with **Asia** or **Africa** as the fourth field. An alternate way to write this last expression is with a regular expression:

```
$4 ~ /^Asia¦Africa)$/
```

which says to select records where the 4th field matches **Africa** or begins with **Asia**.

&& and ¦¦ guarantee that their operands are evaluated from left to right; evaluation stops as soon as truth or falsehood is determined.

# Pattern Ranges

The pattern that selects an action may also consist of two patterns separated by a comma as in

*pattern1, pattern2*   { *action* }

In this case, the *action* is performed for each line between an occurrence of *pattern1* and the next occurrence of *pattern2* (inclusive). As an example with no action

/Canada/,/Brazil/

prints all lines between the one containing **Canada** and the line containing **Brazil**. For example:

```
Canada    3852    24     North America
China     3692    866    Asia
USA       3615    219    North America
Brazil    3286    116    South America
```

while

NR == 2, NR == 5 { ... }

does the action for lines 2 through 5 of the input. Different types of patterns may be mixed as in

/Canada/, $4 == "Africa"

which prints all lines from the first line containing **Canada** up to and including the next record whose fourth field is **Africa**.

The foregoing discussion of pattern matching pertains to the pattern portion of the pattern/action **awk** statement. Pattern matching can also take place inside an **if** or **while** statement in the action portion. See the section "Flow of Control."

# Actions

An **awk** action is a sequence of action statements separated by newlines or semicolons. These action statements do a variety of bookkeeping and string manipulating tasks.

## Variables, Expressions, and Assignments

**awk** provides the ability to do arithmetic and to store the results in variables for later use in the program. As an example, consider printing the population density for each country in the file **countries**.

```
{print $1, (1000000 * $3) / ($2 * 1000) }
```

(Recall that in this file the population is in millions and the area in thousands.) The result is population density in people per square mile.

```
Russia 30.289
Canada 6.23053
China 234.561
USA 60.5809
Brazil 35.3013
Australia 4.71698
India 501.97
Argentina 24.2537
Sudan 19.6281
Algeria 19.5652
```

The formatting is not good; using **printf** instead gives the program

```
{printf "%10s %6.1f\n", $1, (1000000 * $3) / ($2 * 1000)}
```

and the output

| | |
|---|---|
| Russia | 30.3 |
| Canada | 6.2 |
| China | 234.6 |
| USA | 60.6 |
| Brazil | 35.3 |
| Australia | 4.7 |
| India | 502.0 |
| Argentina | 24.3 |
| Sudan | 19.6 |
| Algeria | 19.6 |

Arithmetic is done internally in floating point. The arithmetic operators are +, −, *, /, and % (modulus).

To compute the total population and number of countries from Asia, we could write

```
/Asia/    { pop += $3; ++n }
END       {print "total population of ", n, "Asian countries is", pop }
```

which produces

```
    total population of 3 Asian countries is 1765.
```

The operators, ++, −−, −=, /=, * =, +=, and %= are available in **awk** as they are in C. The same is true of the ++ operator; it adds one to the value of a variable. The increment operators ++ and −− (as in C) are used as prefix or as postfix operators. These operators are also used in expressions.

## Initialization of Variables

In the previous example, we did not initialize **pop** nor **n**; yet everything worked properly. This is because (by default) variables are initialized to the null string, which has a numerical value of 0. This eliminates the need for most initialization of variables in **BEGIN** sections. We can use default initialization to advantage in this program, which finds the country with the largest population.

```
maxpop < $3 {
        maxpop = $3
        country = $1
        }
END     {print country, maxpop}
```

which produces

```
China 866
```

## Field Variables

Fields in **awk** share essentially all of the properties of variables. They are used in arithmetic and string operations, may be initialized to the null string, or have other values assigned to them. Thus, divide the second field by 1000 to convert the area to millions of square miles by

```
{ $2 /= 1000; print }
```

or process two fields into a third with

```
BEGIN   { FS = "\t" }
        { $4 = 1000 * $3 / $2; print }
```

or assign strings to a field as in

```
/USA/   { $1 = "United States" ; print }
```

which replaces **USA** by **United States** and prints the affected line:

```
United States 3615 219 North America
```

Fields are accessed by expressions; thus, **$NF** is the last field and **$(NF − 1)** is the second to the last. Note that the parentheses are needed since **$NF − 1** is 1 less than the value in the last field.

## String Concatenation

Strings are concatenated by writing them one after the other as in the following example:

```
{ x = "hello"
  x = x ", world"
  print x
}
```

which prints the usual

```
hello, world
```

With input from the file **countries**, the following program:

```
/A/        { s = s " " $1 }
END        { print s }
```

prints

```
Australia Argentina Algeria
```

Variables, string expressions, and numeric expressions may appear in concatenations; the numeric expressions are treated as strings in this case.


## Special Variables

Some variables in **awk** have special meanings. These are detailed here and the complete list given.

| | |
|---|---|
| **NR** | Number of the current record. |
| **NF** | Number of fields in the current record. |
| **FS** | Input field separator, by default it is set to a blank or tab. |
| **RS** | Input record separator, by default it is set to the newline character. |
| **$i** | The **i**th input field of the current record. |
| **$0** | The entire current input record. |
| **OFS** | Output field separator, by default it is set to a blank. |
| **ORS** | Output record separator, by default it is set to the newline character. |
| **OFMT** | The format for printing numbers, with the print statement, by default is %**.6g** |

      FILENAME      The name of the input file currently being read. This is useful because **awk** commands are typically of the form

                awk —f *program* **file1 file2 file3 ...**

# Type

Variables (and fields) take on numeric or string values according to context. For example, in

    pop += $3

**pop** is presumably a number, while in

    country = $1

**country** is a string. In

    maxpop < $3

the type of **maxpop** depends on the data found in **$3**. It is determined when the program is run.

In general, each variable and field is potentially a string or a number, or both at any time. When a variable is set by the assignment

    v = expr

its type is set to that of *expr*. (Assignment also includes +=, ++, —=, and so forth.) An arithmetic expression is of the type **number**; a concatenation of strings is of type **string**. If the assignment is a simple copy as in

    v1 = v2

then the type of **v1** becomes that of **v2**.

In comparisons, if both operands are numeric, the comparison is made numerically. Otherwise, operands are coerced to strings if necessary and the comparison is made on strings.

The type of any expression may be coerced to numeric by a subterfuge such as

```
expr + 0
```

and to string by

```
expr ""
```

This last expression is **string** concatenated with the null string.

## Arrays

As well as ordinary variables, **awk** provides 1-dimensional arrays. Array elements are not declared; they spring into existence by being mentioned. Subscripts may have any non-null value including non-numeric strings. As an example of a conventional numeric subscript, the statement

```
x[NR] = $0
```

assigns the current input line to the **NR**th element of the array **x**. In fact, it is possible in principle (though perhaps slow) to process the entire input in a random order with the following **awk** program:

```
        { x[NR] = $0 }
END     { ... program ... }
```

The first line of this program records each input line into the array **x**. In particular, the following program

```
{ x[NR] = $1}
```

(when run on the file **countries**) produces an array of elements with

```
x[1] = "Russia"
x[2] = "Canada"
x[3] = "China"
      ... and so forth.
```

Arrays are also indexed by non-numeric values that give **awk** a capability rather like the associative memory of Snobol tables. For example, we can write

```
/Asia/{pop["Asia"] += $3}
/Africa/{pop[Africa] += $3}
END     {print "Asia=" pop["Asia"], "Africa="pop["Africa"] }
```

which produces

```
Asia=1765 Africa=37
```

Notice the concatenation. Also, any expression can be used as a subscript in an array reference. Thus,

```
area[$1] = $2
```

uses the first field of a line (as a string) to index the array **area**.

# Special Features

In this final section we describe the use of some special **awk** features.

## Built-In Functions

The function **length** is provided by **awk** to compute the length of a string of characters. The following program prints each record preceded by its length:

```
{print length, $0 }
```

In this case the variable **length** means **length($0)**, the length of the present record. In general, **length**($x$) will return the length of $x$ as a string.

With input from the file **countries**, the following **awk** program will print the longest country name:

```
length($1) > max   {max = length($1); name = $1 }
END                {print name}
```

The function **split**

```
split(s, array)
```

assigns the fields of the string **s** to successive elements of the array, **array**.

For example;

```
split("Now is the time", w)
```

assigns the value **Now** to **w**[1], **is** to **w**[2], **the** to **w**[3], and **time** to **w**[4]. All other elements of the array **w**[ ], if any, are set to the null string. It is possible to have a character other than a blank as the separator for the elements of **w**. For this, use **split** with three elements.

```
n = split(s, array, sep)
```

This splits the string **s** into **array**[1], ..., **array**[n]. The number of elements found is returned as the value of **split**. If the *sep* argument is present, its first character is used as the field separator; otherwise, **FS** is used. This is useful if in the middle of an **awk** script, it is necessary to change the record separator for one record. Also provided by **awk** are the math functions

> **sqrt**
> **log**
> **exp**
> **int**

They provide the square root function, the base **e** logarithm function, exponential and integral part functions. This last function returns the greatest integer less than or equal to its argument. These functions are the same as those of the C math library (**int** corresponds to the **libm floor** function) and so they have the same return on error as those in **libm**. (See the *Programmer's Reference Manual*.)

The function **substr**

```
substr(s,m,n)
```

produces the substring of **s** that begins at position **m** and is at most *n* characters long. If the third argument (**n** in this case) is omitted, the substring goes to the end of **s**. For example, we could abbreviate the country names in the file **countries** by

```
{ $1 = substr($1, 1, 3); print }
```

which produces

```
Rus    8650    262    Asia
Can    3852     24    North America
Chi    3692    866    Asia
USA    3615    219    North America
Bra    3286    116    South America
Aus    2968     14    Australia
Ind    1269    637    Asia
Arg    1072     26    South America
Sud     968     19    Africa
Alg     920     18    Africa
```

If **s** is a number, **substr** uses its printed image:

```
substr(123456789,3,4)=3456.
```

The function **index**

```
index (s1,s2)
```

returns the leftmost position where the string **s2** occurs in **s1** or zero if **s2** does not occur in **s1**.

The function **sprintf** formats expressions as the **printf** statement does but assigns the resulting expression to a variable instead of sending the results to **stdout**. For example:

```
x = sprintf("%10s %6d", $1, $2)
```

sets **x** to the string produced by formatting the values of **$1** and **$2**. The **x** may then be used in subsequent computations.

The function **getline** immediately reads the next input record. Fields **NR** and **$0** are set but control is left at exactly the same spot in the **awk** program. **getline** returns 0 for the end of file and a 1 for a normal record.

# Flow of Control

**awk** provides the basic flow of control statements within actions

- **if-else**
- **while**
- **for**

with statement grouping as in C language.

The **if** statement is used as follows:

**if** ( *condition* ) *statement1* **else** *statement2*

The *condition* is evaluated; and if it is true, *statement1* is executed; otherwise, *statement2* is executed. The **else** part is optional. Several statements enclosed in braces, { }, are treated as a single statement. Rewriting the maximum population computation from the pattern section with an **if** statement results in

```
{       if (maxpop < $3) {
                maxpop = $3
                country = $1
        }
}
END     { print country, maxpop }
```

There is also a **while** statement in **awk**.

> **while** ( *condition* ) *statement*

The *condition* is evaluated; if it is true, the *statement* is executed. The *condition* is evaluated again, and if true, the *statement* is executed. The cycle repeats as long as the condition is true. For example, the following prints all input fields, one per line:

```
{       i = 1
        while (i <= NF) {
                print $i
                ++i
        }
}
```

Another example is the Euclidean algorithm for finding the greatest common divisor of **$1** and **$2**:

```
{printf "the greatest common divisor of " $1 "and ", $2, "is"
while ($1 != $2) {
   if ($1 > $2) $1 -= $2
   else      $2 -= $1
}
printf $1 "\n"
}
```

The **for** statement is like that of C, which is:

> **for** ( *expression1* ; *condition* ; *expression2* ) *statement*

So

```
{        for (i = 1 ; i <= NF; i++)
                print $i
}
```

is another **awk** program that prints all input fields, one per line.

There is an alternate form of the **for** statement that is useful for accessing the elements of an associative array in **awk**.

**for** (*i in array*) *statement*

executes *statement* with the variable **i** set in turn to each subscript of *array*. The subscripts are each accessed once but in undefined order. Chaos will ensue if the variable **i** is altered or if any new elements are created within the loop. For example, you could use the **for** statement to print the record number followed by the record of all input records after the main program is executed.

```
        { x[NR] = $0 }
END     { for(i in x) print i, x[i] }
```

A more practical example is the following use of strings to index arrays to add the populations of countries by continents:

```
BEGIN   {FS="\t"}
        {population[$4] += $3}
END     {for(i in population)
                print i, population[i]
        }
```

In this program, the body of the **for** loop is executed for **i** equal to the string **Asia**, then for **i** equal to the string **North America**, and so forth until all the possible values of **i** are exhausted; that is, until all the strings of names of countries are used. Note, however, the order the loops are executed is not specified. If the loop associated with **Canada** is executed before the loop associated with the string **Russia**, such a program produces

```
South America 26
Africa 16
Asia 637
Australia 14
North America 219
```

Note that the expression in the condition part of an **if, while**, or, **for** statement can include

- relational operators like $<$, $<=$, $>$, $>=$, $==$, and $!=$
- regular expressions that are used with the matching operators $\sim$ and $!\sim$
- the logical operators ¦¦, &&, and !
- parentheses for grouping

The **break** statement (when it occurs within a **while** or **for** loop) causes an immediate exit from the **while** or **for** loop.

The **continue** statement (when it occurs within a **while** or **for** loop) causes the next iteration of the loop to begin.

The **next** statement in an **awk** program causes **awk** to skip immediately to the next record and begin scanning patterns from the top of the program. (Note the difference between **getline** and **next**. **getline** does not skip to the top of the **awk** program.)

If an **exit** statement occurs in the **BEGIN** section of an **awk** program, the program stops executing and the **END** section is not executed (if there is one).

An **exit** that occurs in the main body of the **awk** program causes execution of the main body of the **awk** program to stop. No more records are read, and the **END** section is executed.

An **exit** in the **END** section causes execution to terminate at that point.

## Report Generation

The flow of control statements in the last section are especially useful when **awk** is used as a report generator. **awk** is useful for tabulating, summarizing, and formatting information. We have seen an example of **awk** tabulating populations in the last section. Here is another example of this. Suppose you have a file **prog.usage** that contains lines of three fields: **name**, **program**, and **usage:**

```
Smith     draw    3
Brown     eqn     1
Jones     nroff   4
Smith     nroff   1
Jones     spell   5
Brown     spell   9
Smith     draw    6
```

The first line indicates that Smith used the **draw** program three times. If you want to create a program that has the total usage of each program along with the names in alphabetical order and the total usage, use the following program, called **list1**:

```
        {use[$1 "" $2] += $3}
END     {for (np in use)
            print np "         " use[np] | "sort +0 +2nr"
        }
```

This program produces the following output when used on the input file, **prog.usage**.

```
Brown     eqn     1
Brown     spell   9
Jones     nroff   4
Jones     spell   5
Smith     draw    9
Smith     nroff   1
```

If you would like to format the previous output so that each name is printed only once, pipe the output of the previous **awk** program into the following program, called **format1**:

```
{       if ($1 != prev) {
            print $1 ":"
            prev = $1
        }
        print " " $2 " " $3
}
```

The variable **prev** is used to ensure each unique value of **$1** prints only once. The command

> **awk −f list1 prog.usage | awk −f format1**

gives the output

```
Brown:
         eqn     1
         spell   9
Jones:
         nroff   4
         spell   5
Smith:
         draw    9
         nroff   1
```

It is often useful to combine different **awk** scripts and other shell commands such as **sort**(1), as was done in the **list1** script.

## Cooperation with the Shell

Normally, an **awk** program is either contained in a file or enclosed within single quotes as in

> **awk '{print $1}' ...**

Since **awk** uses many of the same characters the shell does (such as **$** and the double quote) surrounding the program by single quotes ensures that the shell passes the program to **awk** intact.

Consider writing an **awk** program to print the $n$th field, where $n$ is a parameter determined when the program is run. That is, we want a program called **field** such that

> **field n**

runs the **awk** program

> **awk '{print $n}'**

How does the value of $n$ get into the **awk** program?

There are several ways to do this. One is to define **field** as follows:

**awk '{print $'$1'}'**

Spaces are critical here: as written there is only one argument, even though there are two sets of quotes. The **$1** is outside the quotes, visible to the shell, and therefore substituted properly when **field** is invoked.

Another way to do this job relies on the fact that the shell substitutes for **$** parameters within double quotes.

awk "{print \$ $1}"

Here the trick is to protect the first **$** with a \; the **$1** is again replaced by the number when **field** is invoked.

## Multidimensional Arrays

You can simulate the effect of multidimensional arrays by creating your own subscripts. For example:

```
for (i = 1; i <= 10; i++)
        for (j = 1; j <= 10; j++)
                mult[i "," j] = . . .
```

creates an array whose subscripts have the form **i,j**; that is, 1,1; 1,2 and so forth; and thus simulate a 2-dimensional array.

# CHAPTER 5: lex

## An Overview of lex Programming

**lex** is a software tool that lets you solve a wide class of problems drawn from text processing, code enciphering, compiler writing, and other areas. In text processing, you may check the spelling of words for errors; in code enciphering, you may translate certain patterns of characters into others; and in compiler writing, you may determine what the tokens (smallest meaningful sequences of characters) are in the program to be compiled. The problem common to all of these tasks is recognizing different strings of characters that satisfy certain characteristics. In the compiler writing case, creating the ability to solve the problem requires implementing the compiler's lexical analyzer. Hence the name **lex**.

It is not essential to use **lex** to handle problems of this kind. You could write programs in a standard language like C to handle them, too. In fact, what **lex** does is produce such C programs. (**lex** is therefore called a program generator.) What **lex** offers you, once you acquire a facility with it, is typically a faster, easier way to create programs that perform these tasks. Its weakness is that it often produces C programs that are longer than necessary for the task at hand and that execute more slowly than they otherwise might. In many applications this is a minor consideration, and the advantages of using **lex** considerably outweigh it.

To understand what **lex** does, see the diagram in Figure 5-1. We begin with the **lex** source (often called the **lex** specification) that you, the programmer, write to solve the problem at hand. This **lex** source consists of a list of rules specifying sequences of characters (expressions) to be searched for in an input text, and the actions to take when an expression is found. The source is read by the **lex** program generator. The output of the program generator is a C program that, in turn, must be compiled by a host language C compiler to generate the executable object program that does the lexical analysis. Note that this procedure is not typically automatic—user intervention is required. Finally, the lexical analyzer program produced by this process takes as input any source file and produces the desired output, such as altered text or a list of tokens.

**lex** can also be used to collect statistical data on features of the input, such as character count, word length, number of occurrences of a word, and so forth. In later sections of this chapter, we will see

- how to write **lex** source to do some of these tasks

- how to translate **lex** source

- how to compile, link, and execute the lexical analyzer in C

- how to run the lexical analyzer program

We will then be on our way to appreciating the power that **lex** provides.

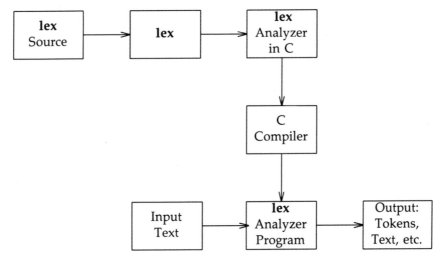

Figure 5-1: Creation and Use of a Lexical Analyzer with **lex**

# Writing lex Programs

A **lex** specification consists of at most three sections: definitions, rules, and user subroutines. The rules section is mandatory. Sections for definitions and user subroutines are optional, but if present, must appear in the indicated order.

## The Fundamentals of lex Rules

The mandatory rules section opens with the delimiter %%. If a subroutines section follows, another %% delimiter ends the rules section. If there is no second delimiter, the rules section is presumed to continue to the end of the program.

Each rule consists of a specification of the pattern sought and the action(s) to take on finding it. (Note the dual meaning of the term specification—it may mean either the entire **lex** source itself or, within it, a representation of a particular pattern to be recognized.) Whenever the input consists of patterns not sought, **lex** writes out the input exactly as it finds it. So, the simplest **lex** program is just the beginning rules delimiter, %%. It writes out the entire input to the output with no changes at all. Typically, the rules are more elaborate than that.

### Specifications

You specify the patterns you are interested in with a notation called regular expressions. A regular expression is formed by stringing together characters with or without operators. The simplest regular expressions are strings of text characters with no operators at all. For example,

> **apple**
> **orange**
> **pluto**

These three regular expressions match any occurrences of those character strings in an input text. If you want to have your lexical analyzer **a.out** remove every occurrence of **orange**, from the input text, you could specify the rule

> orange;

Because you did not specify an action on the right (before the semi-colon), **lex** does nothing but print out the original input text with every occurrence of this regular expression removed, that is, without any occurrence of the string **orange** at all.

Unlike **orange** above, most of the expressions that we want to search for cannot be specified so easily. The expression itself might simply be too long. More commonly, the class of desired expressions is too large; it may, in fact, be infinite. Thanks to the use of operators, we can form regular expressions signifying any expression of a certain class. The + operator, for instance, means one or more occurrences of the preceding expression, the **?** means 0 or 1 occurrence(s) of the preceding expression (this is equivalent, of course, to saying that the preceding expression is optional), and * means 0 or more occurrences of the preceding expression. (It may at first seem odd to speak of 0 occurrences of an expression and to need an operator to capture the idea, but it is often quite helpful. We will see an example in a moment.) So **m+** is a regular expression matching any string of **m**s such as each of the following:

```
mmm
m
mmmmmm
mm
```

and **7\*** is a regular expression matching any string of zero or more 7s:

```
77
77777

777
```

The string of blanks on the third line matches simply because it has no 7s in it at all.

Brackets, [ ], indicate any one character from the string of characters specified between the brackets. Thus, **[dgka]** matches a single **d**, **g**, **k**, or **a**. Note that commas are not included within the brackets. Any comma here would be taken as a character to be recognized in the input text. Ranges within a standard alphabetic or numeric order are indicated with a hyphen, −. The sequence **[a-z]**, for instance, indicates any lowercase letter. Somewhat more interestingly,

```
[A-Za-z0-9*&#]
```

is a regular expression that matches any letter (whether upper- or lowercase), any digit, an asterisk, an ampersand, or a sharp character. Given the input text

    $$$$?? ????!!!*$$ $$$$$$&+====r~~# ((

the lexical analyzer with the previous specification in one of its rules will recognize the *, &, r, and #, perform on each recognition whatever action the rule specifies (we have not indicated an action here), and print out the rest of the text as it stands.

The operators become especially powerful in combination. For example, the regular expression to recognize an identifier in many programming languages is

    [a-zA-Z][0-9a-zA-Z]*

An identifier in these languages is defined to be a letter followed by zero or more letters or digits, and that is just what the regular expression says. The first pair of brackets matches any letter. The second, if it were not followed by a *, would match any digit or letter. The two pairs of brackets with their enclosed characters would then match any letter followed by a digit or a letter. But with the asterisk, *, the example matches any letter followed by any number of letters or digits. In particular, it would recognize the following as identifiers:

    e
    pay
    distance
    pH
    EngineNo99
    R2D2

Note that it would not recognize the following as identifiers:

    not_idenTIFER
    5times
    $hello

because **not_idenTIFER** has an embedded underscore; **5times** starts with a digit, not a letter; and **$hello** starts with a special character. Of course, you may want to write the specifications for these three examples as an exercise.

A potential problem with operator characters is how we can refer to them as characters to look for in our search pattern. The last example, for instance, will not recognize text with an * in it. **lex** solves the problem in one of two ways: a character enclosed in quotation marks or a character preceded by a \ is taken literally, that is, as part of the text to be searched for. To use the backslash method to recognize, say, an * followed by any number of digits, we can use the pattern

    \*[1-9]*

To recognize a \ itself, we need two backslashes: \\.

## Actions

Once **lex** recognizes a string matching the regular expression at the start of a rule, it looks to the right of the rule for the action to be performed. Kinds of actions include recording the token type found and its value, if any; replacing one token with another; and counting the number of instances of a token or token type. What you want to do is write these actions as program fragments in the host language C. An action may consist of as many statements as are needed for the job at hand. You may want to print out a message noting that the text has been found or a message transforming the text in some way. Thus, to recognize the expression Amelia Earhart and to note such recognition, the rule

    "Amelia Earhart"   printf("found Amelia");

would do. And to replace in a text lengthy medical terms with their equivalent acronyms, a rule such as

    Electroencephalogram   printf("EEG");

would be called for. To count the lines in a text, we need to recognize end-of-lines and increment a linecounter. **lex** uses the standard escape sequences from C like \n for end-of-line. To count lines we might have

    \n   lineno++;

where **lineno**, like other C variables, is declared in the definitions section that we discuss later.

**lex** stores every character string that it recognizes in a character array called **yytext[]**. You can print or manipulate the contents of this array as you want. Sometimes your action may consist of two or more C statements and you must (or for style and clarity, you choose to) write it on several lines. To inform **lex** that the action is for one rule only, simply enclose the C code in braces. For example, to count the total number of all digit strings in an input text, print the running total of the number of digit strings (not their sum, here) and print out each one as soon as it is found, your **lex** code might be

```
+?[1-9]+              { digstrngcount++;
                        printf("%d",digstrngcount);
                        printf("%s", yytext);    }
```

This specification matches digit strings whether they are preceded by a plus sign or not, because the **?** indicates that the preceding plus sign is optional. In addition, it will catch negative digit strings because that portion following the minus sign, −, will match the specification. The next section explains how to distinguish negative from positive integers.

## Advanced lex Usage

**lex** provides a suite of features that lets you process input text riddled with quite complicated patterns. These include rules that decide what specification is relevant, when more than one seems so at first; functions that transform one matching pattern into another; and the use of definitions and subroutines. Before considering these features, you may want to affirm your understanding thus far by examining an example drawing together several of the points already covered.

```
%%
−[0-9]+         printf("negative integer");
+?[0-9]+        printf("positive integer");
−0.[0-9]+       printf("negative fraction, no whole number part");
rail[ ]+road    printf("railroad is one word");
crook           printf("Here's a crook");
function        subprogcount++;
G[a-zA-Z]*      { printf("may have a G word here: ", yytext);
                  Gstringcount++; }
```

The first three rules recognize negative integers, positive integers, and negative fractions between 0 and −1. The use of the terminating + in each specification ensures that one or more digits compose the number in question. Each of the next three rules recognizes a specific pattern. The specification for **railroad** matches cases where one or more blanks intervene between the two syllables of the word. In the cases of **railroad** and **crook**, you may have simply printed a synonym rather than the messages stated. The rule recognizing a **function** simply increments a counter. The last rule illustrates several points:

- The braces specify an action sequence extending over several lines.

- Its action uses the **lex** array **yytext[]**, which stores the recognized character string.

- Its specification uses the * to indicate that zero or more letters may follow the **G**.

## Some Special Features

Besides storing the recognized character string in **yytext[]**, **lex** automatically counts the number of characters in a match and stores it in the variable **yyleng**. You may use this variable to refer to any specific character just placed in the array **yytext[]**. Remember that C numbers locations in an array starting with 0, so to print out the third digit (if there is one) in a just recognized integer, you might write

```
[1–9]+      {if  (yyleng > 2)
             printf("%c", yytext[2]); }
```

**lex** follows a number of high-level rules to resolve ambiguities that may arise from the set of rules that you write. *Prima facie*, any reserved word, for instance, could match two rules. In the lexical analyzer example developed later in the section on **lex** and **yacc**, the reserved word **end** could match the second rule as well as the seventh, the one for identifiers.

 **lex** follows the rule that where there is a match with two or more rules in a specification, the first rule is the one whose action will be executed.

By placing the rule for **end** and the other reserved words before the rule for identifiers, we ensure that our reserved words will be duly recognized.

Another potential problem arises from cases where one pattern you are searching for is the prefix of another. For instance, the last two rules in the lexical analyzer example above are designed to recognize > and >= . If the text has the string >= at one point, you might worry that the lexical analyzer would stop as soon as it recognized the > character to execute the rule for > rather than read the next character and execute the rule for >=.

NOTE **lex** follows the rule that it matches the longest character string possible and executes the rule for that.

Here it would recognize the $>=$ and act accordingly. As a further example, the rule would enable you to distinguish $+$ from $++$ in a program in C.

Still another potential problem exists when the analyzer must read characters beyond the string you are seeking because you cannot be sure you've in fact found it until you've read the additional characters. These cases reveal the importance of trailing context. The classic example here is the DO statement in FORTRAN. In the statement

```
DO 50 k = 1 , 20, 1
```

we cannot be sure that the first 1 is the initial value of the index **k** until we read the first comma. Until then, we might have the assignment statement

```
DO50k = 1
```

(Remember that FORTRAN ignores all blanks.) The way to handle this is to use the forward-looking slash, / (not the backslash, \), which signifies that what follows is trailing context, something not to be stored in **yytext[]**, because it is not part of the token itself. So the rule to recognize the FORTRAN DO statement could be

```
30/[ ]*[0-9][ ]*[a-z A-Z0-9]+=[a-z A-Z0-9]+,    printf("found DO");
```

Different versions of FORTRAN have limits on the size of identifiers, here the index name. To simplify the example, the rule accepts an index name of any length.

**lex** uses the $ as an operator to mark a special trailing context—the end of line. (It is therefore equivalent to \n.) An example would be a rule to ignore all blanks and tabs at the end of a line:

```
[ \t]+$    ;
```

On the other hand, if you want to match a pattern only when it starts a line, **lex** offers you the circumflex, ^, as the operator. The formatter **nroff**, for example, demands that you never start a line with a blank, so you might want to check input to **nroff** with some such rule as:

```
^[ ]      printf("error: remove leading blank");
```

Finally, some of your action statements themselves may require your reading another character, putting one back to be read again a moment later, or writing a character on an output device. **lex** supplies three functions to handle these tasks—**input()**, **unput(c)**, and **output(c)**, respectively. One way to ignore all characters between two special characters, say between a pair of double quotation marks, would be to use **input()**, thus:

```
\"        while (input() != '"');
```

Upon finding the first double quotation mark, the generated **a.out** will simply continue reading all subsequent characters so long as none is a quotation mark, and not again look for a match until it finds a second double quotation mark.

To handle special I/O needs, such as writing to several files, you may use standard I/O routines in C to rewrite the functions **input()**, **unput(c)**, and **output**. These and other programmer-defined functions should be placed in your subroutine section. Your new routines will then replace the standard ones. The standard **input()**, in fact, is equivalent to **getchar()**, and the standard **output(c)** is equivalent to **putchar(c)**.

There are a number of **lex** routines that let you handle sequences of characters to be processed in more than one way. These include **yymore()**, **yyless(n)**, and **REJECT**. Recall that the text matching a given specification is stored in the array **yytext[]**. In general, once the action is performed for the specification, the characters in **yytext[]** are overwritten with succeeding characters in the input stream to form the next match. The function **yymore()**, by contrast, ensures that the succeeding characters recognized are appended to those already in **yytext[]**. This lets you do one thing and then another, when one string of characters is significant and a longer one including the first is significant as well. Consider a character string bound by **B**s and interspersed with one at an arbitrary location.

```
B...B...B
```

In a simple code deciphering situation, you may want to count the number of characters between the first and second **B**'s and add it to the number of characters between the second and third **B**. (Only the last **B** is not to be counted.) The code to do this is

```
B[^B]*      { if (flag = 0)
              save = yyleng;
              flag = 1;
              yymore();
          else    {
              importantno = save + yyleng;
              flag = 0; }
          }
```

where **flag, save**, and **importantno** are declared (and at least **flag** initialized to 0) in the definitions section. The **flag** distinguishes the character sequence terminating just before the second **B** from that terminating just before the third.

The function **yyless**(*n*) lets you reset the end point of the string to be considered to the *n*th character in the original **yytext[]**. Suppose you are again in the code deciphering business and the gimmick here is to work with only half the characters in a sequence ending with a certain one, say upper- or lowercase **Z**. The code you want might be

```
[a-yA-Y]+[Zz]     { yyless(yyleng/2);
                  ... process first half of string... }
```

Finally, the function REJECT lets you more easily process strings of characters even when they overlap or contain one another as parts. REJECT does this by immediately jumping to the next rule and its specification without changing the contents of **yytext[]**. If you want to count the number of occurrences both of the regular expression **snapdragon** and of its subexpression **dragon** in an input text, the following will do:

```
snapdragon       {countflowers++; REJECT;}
dragon           countmonsters++;
```

As an example of one pattern overlapping another, the following counts the number of occurrences of the expressions **comedian** and **diana**, even where the input text has sequences such as **comediana..**:

```
comedian        {comiccount++; REJECT;}
diana           princesscount++;
```

Note that the actions here may be considerably more complicated than simply incrementing a counter. In all cases, the counters and other necessary variables are declared in the definitions section commencing the **lex** specification.

## Definitions

The **lex** definitions section may contain any of several classes of items. The most critical are external definitions, **#include** statements, and abbreviations. Recall that for legal **lex** source this section is optional, but in most cases some of these items are necessary. External definitions have the form and function that they do in C. They declare that variables globally defined elsewhere (perhaps in another source file) will be accessed in your **lex**-generated **a.out**. Consider a declaration from an example to be developed later.

```
extern int tokval;
```

When you store an integer value in a variable declared in this way, it will be accessible in the routine, say a parser, that calls it. If, on the other hand, you want to define a local variable for use within the action sequence of one rule (as you might for the index variable for a loop), you can declare the variable at the start of the action itself right after the left brace, { .

The purpose of the **#include** statement is the same as in C: to include files of importance for your program. Some variable declarations and **lex** definitions might be needed in more than one **lex** source file. It is then advantageous to place them all in one file to be included in every file that needs them. One example occurs in using **lex** with **yacc**, which generates parsers that call a lexical analyzer. In this context, you should include the file **y.tab.h**, which may contain **#define**s for token names. Like the declarations, **#include** statements should come between %{ and }%, thus:

```
%{
#include "y.tab.h"
extern int tokval;
int lineno;
%}
```

In the definitions section, after the %} that ends your **#include**'s and declarations, you place your abbreviations for regular expressions to be used in the rules section. The abbreviation appears on the left of the line and, separated by one or more spaces, its definition or translation appears on the right. When you later use abbreviations in your rules, be sure to enclose them within braces.

NOTE    The purpose of abbreviations is to avoid needless repetition in writing your specifications and to provide clarity in reading them.

As an example, reconsider the **lex** source reviewed at the beginning of this section on advanced **lex** usage. The use of definitions simplifies our later reference to digits, letters, and blanks. This is especially true if the specifications appear several times:

```
D               [0-9]
L               [a-zA-Z]
B               [ ]
%%
-{D}+           printf("negative integer");
+?{D}+          printf("positive integer");
-0.{D}+         printf("negative fraction");
G{L}*           printf("may have a G word here");
rail{B}+road    printf("railroad is one word");
crook           printf("criminal");
 \"\./{B}+      printf(".\"");
   .                   .
   .                   .
```

The last rule, newly added to the example and somewhat more complex than the others, is used in the WRITER'S WORKBENCH Software, an AT&T software product for promoting good writing. (See the *UNIX System WRITER'S WORKBENCH Software Release 3.0 User's Guide* for information on this product.) The rule ensures that a period always precedes a quotation mark at the end of a sentence. It would change example". to example."

## Subroutines

You may want to use subroutines in **lex** for much the same reason that you do so in other programming languages. Action code that is to be used for several rules can be written once and called when needed. As with definitions, this can simplify the writing and reading of programs. The function **put_in_tabl**(), to be discussed in the next section on **lex** and **yacc**, is a good candidate for a subroutine.

Another reason to place a routine in this section is to highlight some code of interest or to simplify the rules section, even if the code is to be used for one rule only. As an example, consider the following routine to ignore comments in a language like C where comments occur between /* and */ :

```
"/*"                    skipcmnts();
.
.                       /* rest of rules */
%%
skipcmnts()
{
        for(;;)
        {
            while (input() != '*');
            if (input() != '/') {
                    unput(yytext[yyleng-1]);
            else return;
        }
}
```

There are three points of interest in this example. First, the **unput(c)** function (putting back the last character read) is necessary to avoid missing the final / if the comment ends unusually with a **\*/** . In this case, eventually having read an **\***, the analyzer finds that the next character is not the terminal / and must read some more. Second, the expression **yytext[yyleng−1]** picks out that last character read. Third, this routine assumes that the comments are not nested. (This is indeed the case with the C language.) If, unlike C, they are nested in the source text, after **input**()ing the first \*/ ending the inner group of comments, the **a.out** will read the rest of the comments as if they were part of the input to be searched for patterns.

Other examples of subroutines would be programmer-defined versions of the I/O routines **input()**, **unput(c)**, and **output()**, discussed above. Subroutines such as these that may be exploited by many different programs would probably do best to be stored in their own individual file or library to be called as needed. The appropriate **#include** statements would then be necessary in the definitions section.

# Using lex with yacc

If you work on a compiler project or develop a program to check the validity of an input language, you may want to use the UNIX system program tool **yacc**. **yacc** generates parsers, programs that analyze input to ensure that it is syntactically correct. (**yacc** is discussed in detail in Chapter 6 of this guide.) **lex** often forms a fruitful union with **yacc** in the compiler development context. Whether or not you plan to use **lex** with **yacc**, be sure to read this section because it covers information of interest to all **lex** programmers.

The lexical analyzer that **lex** generates (not the file that stores it) takes the name **yylex()**. This name is convenient because **yacc** calls its lexical analyzer by this very name. To use **lex** to create the lexical analyzer for the parser of a compiler, you want to end each **lex** action with the statement **return** *token*, where *token* is a defined term whose value is an integer. The integer value of the token returned indicates to the parser what the lexical analyzer has found. The parser, whose file is called **y.tab.c** by **yacc**, then resumes control and makes another call to the lexical analyzer when it needs another token.

In a compiler, the different values of the token indicate what, if any, reserved word of the language has been found or whether an identifier, constant, arithmetic operand, or relational operator has been found. In the latter cases, the analyzer must also specify the exact value of the token: what the identifier is, whether the constant, say, is 9 or 888, whether the operand is + or * (multiply), and whether the relational operator is = or >. Consider the following portion of **lex** source for a lexical analyzer for some programming language perhaps slightly reminiscent of Ada:

```
begin                    return(BEGIN);
end                        return(END);
while                      return(WHILE);
if                         return(IF);
package                    return(PACKAGE);
reverse                    return(REVERSE);
loop                       return(LOOP);
[a-zA-Z][a-zA-Z0-9]*     { tokval = put_in_tabl();
                             return(IDENTIFIER); }
[0-9]+                   { tokval = put_in_tabl();
                             return(INTEGER); }
\+                      { tokval = PLUS;
                             return(ARITHOP); }
\-                      { tokval = MINUS;
                             return(ARITHOP); }
>                       { tokval = GREATER;
                             return(RELOP); }
>=                      { tokval = GREATEREQL;
                             return(RELOP); }
```

Despite appearances, the tokens returned, and the values assigned to **tokval**, are indeed integers. Good programming style dictates that we use informative terms such as **BEGIN, END, WHILE,** and so forth to signify the integers the parser understands, rather than use the integers themselves. You establish the association by using **#define** statements in your parser calling routine in C. For example,

```
#define BEGIN  1
#define END   2
   .
#define PLUS 7
   .
```

If the need arises to change the integer for some token type, you then change the **#define** statement in the parser rather than hunt through the entire program, changing every occurrence of the particular integer. In using **yacc** to generate your parser, it is helpful to insert the statement

```
#include y.tab.h
```

into the definitions section of your **lex** source. The file **y.tab.h** provides **#define** statements that associate token names such as **BEGIN**, **END**, and so on with the integers of significance to the generated parser.

To indicate the reserved words in the example, the returned integer values suffice. For the other token types, the integer value of the token type is stored in the programmer-defined variable **tokval**. This variable, whose definition was an example in the definitions section, is globally defined so that the parser as well as the lexical analyzer can access it. **yacc** provides the variable **yylval** for the same purpose.

Note that the example shows two ways to assign a value to **tokval**. First, a function **put_in_tabl()** places the name and type of the identifier or constant in a symbol table so that the compiler can refer to it in this or a later stage of the compilation process. More to the present point, **put_in_tabl()** assigns a type value to **tokval** so that the parser can use the information immediately to determine the syntactic correctness of the input text. The function **put_in_tabl()** would be a routine that the compiler writer might place in the subroutines section discussed later. Second, in the last few actions of the example, **tokval** is assigned a specific integer indicating which operand or relational operator the analyzer recognized. If the variable PLUS, for instance, is associated with the integer 7 by means of the **#define** statement above, then when a + sign is recognized, the action assigns to **tokval** the value 7, which indicates the +. The analyzer indicates the general class of operator by the value it returns to the parser (in the example, the integer signified by ARITHOP or RELOP).

# Running lex under the UNIX System

As you review the following few steps, you might recall Figure 5-1 at the start of the chapter. To produce the lexical analyzer in C, run

**lex lex.l**

where **lex.l** is the file containing your **lex** specification. The name **lex.l** is conventionally the favorite, but you may use whatever name you want. The output file that **lex** produces is automatically called **lex.yy.c**; this is the lexical analyzer program that you created with lex. You then compile and link this as you would any C program, making sure that you invoke the **lex** library with the −ll option:

**cc lex.yy.c −ll**

The **lex** library provides a default **main()** program that calls the lexical analyzer under the name **yylex()**, so you need not supply your own **main()**.

If you have the **lex** specification spread across several files, you can run **lex** with each of them individually, but be sure to rename or move each **lex.yy.c** file (with **mv**) before you run **lex** on the next one. Otherwise, each will overwrite the previous one. Once you have all the generated **.c** files, you can compile all of them, of course, in one command line.

With the executable **a.out** produced, you are ready to analyze any desired input text. Suppose that the text is stored under the filename **textin** (this name is also arbitrary). The lexical analyzer **a.out** by default takes input from your terminal. To have it take the file **textin** as input, simply use redirection, thus:

**a.out < textin**

By default, output will appear on your terminal, but you can redirect this as well:

**a.out < textin > textout**

In running **lex** with **yacc**, either may be run first.

**yacc −d grammar.y**
**lex lex.l**

spawns a parser in the file **y.tab.c**. (The −d option creates the file **y.tab.h**, which contains the **#define** statements that associate the **yacc** assigned integer token values with the user-defined token names.) To compile and link the output files produced, run

**cc lex.yy.c y.tab.c −ly −ll**

Note that the **yacc** library is loaded (with the **−ly** option) before the **lex** library (with the **−ll** option) to ensure that the **main**() program supplied will call the **yacc** parser.

There are several options available with the **lex** command. If you use one or more of them, place them between the command name **lex** and the filename argument. If you care to see the C program, **lex.yy.c**, that **lex** generates on your terminal (the default output device), use the **−t** option.

**lex −t lex.l**

The **−v** option prints out for you a small set of statistics describing the so-called finite automata that **lex** produces with the C program **lex.yy.c**. (For a detailed account of finite automata and their importance for **lex**, see the Aho, Sethi, and Ullman text, *Compilers: Principles, Techniques, and Tools*, Addison-Wesley, 1986.)

**lex** uses a table (a two-dimensional array in C) to represent its finite automaton. The maximum number of states that the finite automaton requires is set by default to 500. If your **lex** source has a large number of rules or the rules are very complex, this default value may be too small. You can enlarge the value by placing another entry in the definitions section of your **lex** source, as follows:

%n 700

This entry tells **lex** to make the table large enough to handle as many as 700 states. (The **−v** option will indicate how large a number you should choose.) If you have need to increase the maximum number of state transitions beyond 2000, the designated parameter is **a**, thus:

%a 2800

Finally, check the *Programmer's Reference Manual* page on **lex** for a list of all the options available with the **lex** command. In addition, review the paper by Lesk (the originator of **lex**) and Schmidt, "Lex—A Lexical Analyzer Generator," in volume 5 of the *UNIX Programmer's Manual*, Holt, Rinehart, and Winston, 1986. It is somewhat dated, but offers several interesting examples.

This tutorial has introduced you to **lex** programming. As with any programming language, the way to master it is to write programs and then write some more.

# CHAPTER 6: yacc

## Introduction

**yacc** provides a general tool for imposing structure on the input to a computer program. The **yacc** user prepares a specification that includes:

- a set of rules to describe the elements of the input

- code to be invoked when a rule is recognized

- either a definition or declaration of a low-level routine to examine the input

**yacc** then turns the specification into a C language function that examines the input stream. This function, called a parser, works by calling the low-level input scanner. The low-level input scanner, called a lexical analyzer, picks up items from the input stream. The selected items are known as tokens. Tokens are compared to the input construct rules, called grammar rules. When one of the rules is recognized, the user code supplied for this rule, (an action) is invoked. Actions are fragments of C language code. They can return values and make use of values returned by other actions.

The heart of the **yacc** specification is the collection of grammar rules. Each rule describes a construct and gives it a name. For example, one grammar rule might be

```
date  :  month_name  day  ','  year   ;
```

where **date**, **month_name**, **day**, and **year** represent constructs of interest; presumably, **month_name**, **day**, and **year** are defined in greater detail elsewhere. In the example, the comma is enclosed in single quotes. This means that the comma is to appear literally in the input. The colon and semicolon merely serve as punctuation in the rule and have no significance in evaluating the input. With proper definitions, the input

```
July  4,  1776
```

might be matched by the rule.

The lexical analyzer is an important part of the parsing function. This user-supplied routine reads the input stream, recognizes the lower-level constructs, and communicates these as tokens to the parser. The lexical analyzer recognizes constructs of the input stream as terminal symbols; the parser recognizes constructs as nonterminal symbols. To avoid confusion, we will refer to terminal symbols as tokens.

There is considerable leeway in deciding whether to recognize constructs using the lexical analyzer or grammar rules. For example, the rules

```
month_name : 'J' 'a' 'n'  ;
month_name : 'F' 'e' 'b'  ;

        . . .

month_name : 'D' 'e' 'c'  ;
```

might be used in the above example. While the lexical analyzer only needs to recognize individual letters, such low-level rules tend to waste time and space, and may complicate the specification beyond the ability of **yacc** to deal with it. Usually, the lexical analyzer recognizes the month names and returns an indication that a **month_name** is seen. In this case, **month_name** is a token and the detailed rules are not needed.

Literal characters such as a comma must also be passed through the lexical analyzer and are also considered tokens.

Specification files are very flexible. It is relatively easy to add to the above example the rule

```
date  :  month '/' day '/' year   ;
```

allowing

```
7/4/1776
```

as a synonym for

```
July 4, 1776
```

on input. In most cases, this new rule could be slipped into a working system with minimal effort and little danger of disrupting existing input.

The input being read may not conform to the specifications. With a left-to-right scan input errors are detected as early as is theoretically possible. Thus, not only is the chance of reading and computing with bad input data substantially reduced, but the bad data usually can be found quickly. Error handling, provided as part of the input specifications, permits the reentry of bad data or the continuation of the input process after skipping over the bad data.

In some cases, **yacc** fails to produce a parser when given a set of specifications. For example, the specifications may be self-contradictory, or they may require a more powerful recognition mechanism than that available to **yacc**. The former cases represent design errors; the latter cases often can be corrected by making the lexical analyzer more powerful or by rewriting some of the grammar rules. While **yacc** cannot handle all possible specifications, its power compares favorably with similar systems. Moreover, the constructs that are difficult for **yacc** to handle are also frequently difficult for human beings to handle. Some users have reported that the discipline of formulating valid **yacc** specifications for their input revealed errors of conception or design early in the program development.

The remainder of this chapter describes the following subjects:

- basic process of preparing a **yacc** specification
- parser operation
- handling ambiguities
- handling operator precedences in arithmetic expressions
- error detection and recovery
- the operating environment and special features of the parsers **yacc** produces
- suggestions to improve the style and efficiency of the specifications
- advanced topics

In addition, there are two examples and a summary of the **yacc** input syntax.

# Basic Specifications

Names refer to either tokens or nonterminal symbols. **yacc** requires token names to be declared as such. While the lexical analyzer may be included as part of the specification file, it is perhaps more in keeping with modular design to keep it as a separate file. Like the lexical analyzer, other subroutines may be included as well. Thus, every specification file theoretically consists of three sections: the declarations, (grammar) rules, and subroutines. The sections are separated by double percent signs, %% (the percent sign is generally used in **yacc** specifications as an escape character).

A full specification file looks like:

*declarations*
%%
*rules*
%%
*subroutines*

when all sections are used. The *declarations* and *subroutines* sections are optional. The smallest legal **yacc** specification is

%%
**rules**

Blanks, tabs, and newlines are ignored, but they may not appear in names or multicharacter reserved symbols. Comments may appear wherever a name is legal. They are enclosed in /* ... */, as in the C language.

The rules section is made up of one or more grammar rules. A grammar rule has the form

A  :  BODY  ;

where **A** represents a nonterminal symbol, and BODY represents a sequence of zero or more names and literals. The colon and the semicolon are **yacc** punctuation.

Names may be of any length and may be made up of letters, dots, under-scores, and digits although a digit may not be the first character of a name. Uppercase and lowercase letters are distinct. The names used in the body of a grammar rule may represent tokens or nonterminal symbols.

A literal consists of a character enclosed in single quotes, '. As in the C language, the backslash, \, is an escape character within literals, and all the C language escapes are recognized. Thus:

| | |
|---|---|
| '\n' | newline |
| '\r' | return |
| '\'' | single quote ( ' ) |
| '\\' | backslash ( \ ) |
| '\t' | tab |
| '\b' | backspace |
| '\f' | form feed |
| '\xxx' | xxx in octal notation |

are understood by **yacc**. For a number of technical reasons, the NULL character (\0 or 0) should never be used in grammar rules.

If there are several grammar rules with the same left-hand side, the vertical bar, | can be used to avoid rewriting the left-hand side. In addition, the semicolon at the end of a rule is dropped before a vertical bar. Thus the grammar rules

```
A   :   B   C   D   ;
A   :   E   F   ;
A   :   G   ;
```

can be given to **yacc** as

```
A   :   B   C   D
    |   E   F
    |   G
    ;
```

by using the vertical bar. It is not necessary that all grammar rules with the same left side appear together in the grammar rules section although it makes the input more readable and easier to change.

If a nonterminal symbol matches the empty string, this can be indicated by

```
epsilon :   ;
```

The blank space following the colon is understood by **yacc** to be a nonterminal symbol named **epsilon**.

Names representing tokens must be declared. This is most simply done by writing

```
%token   name1  name2 ...
```

in the declarations section. Every name not defined in the declarations section is assumed to represent a nonterminal symbol. Every nonterminal symbol must appear on the left side of at least one rule.

Of all the nonterminal symbols, the start symbol has particular importance. By default, the start symbol is taken to be the left-hand side of the first grammar rule in the rules section. It is possible and desirable to declare the start symbol explicitly in the declarations section using the **%start** keyword.

```
%start   symbol
```

The end of the input to the parser is signaled by a special token, called the end-marker. The end-marker is represented by either a zero or a negative number. If the tokens up to but not including the end-marker form a construct that matches the start symbol, the parser function returns to its caller after the end-marker is seen and accepts the input. If the end-marker is seen in any other context, it is an error.

It is the job of the user-supplied lexical analyzer to return the end-marker when appropriate. Usually the end-marker represents some reasonably obvious I/O status, such as end of file or end of record.

## Actions

With each grammar rule, the user may associate actions to be performed when the rule is recognized. Actions may return values and may obtain the values returned by previous actions. Moreover, the lexical analyzer can return values for tokens if desired.

An action is an arbitrary C language statement and as such can do input and output, call subroutines, and alter arrays and variables. An action is specified by one or more statements enclosed in curly braces, {, and }. For example:

```
A   :  '('  B  ')'
       {
           hello( 1, "abc" );
       }
```

and

```
XXX    :   YYY  ZZZ
           {
               (void) printf("a message\n");
               flag = 25;
           }
```

are grammar rules with actions.

The dollar sign symbol, **$**, is used to facilitate communication between the actions and the parser, The pseudo-variable **$$** represents the value returned by the complete action. For example, the action

```
{   $$ = 1;   }
```

returns the value of one; in fact, that's all it does.

To obtain the values returned by previous actions and the lexical analyzer, the action may use the pseudo-variables **$1, $2, ... $n**. These refer to the values returned by components 1 through $n$ of the right side of a rule, with the components being numbered from left to right. If the rule is

```
A    :   B   C   D    ;
```

then **$2** has the value returned by **C**, and **$3** the value returned by **D**.

The rule

```
expr   :    '(' expr ')'   ;
```

provides a common example. One would expect the value returned by this rule to be the value of the *expr* within the parentheses. Since the first component of the action is the literal left parenthesis, the desired logical result can be indicated by

```
expr   :    '(' expr ')'
           {
               $$ = $2 ;
           }
```

By default, the value of a rule is the value of the first element in it (**$1**). Thus, grammar rules of the form

```
A    :   B    ;
```

frequently need not have an explicit action. In previous examples, all the actions came at the end of rules. Sometimes, it is desirable to get control before a rule is fully parsed. **yacc** permits an action to be written in the middle of a rule as well as at the end. This action is assumed to return a value accessible through the usual **$** mechanism by the actions to the right of it. In turn, it may access the values returned by the symbols to its left. Thus, in the rule below the effect is to set **x** to 1 and **y** to the value returned by **C**.

```
A   :   B
            {
                $$ = 1;
            }
            C
    {
            x = $2;
            y = $3;
    }
    ;
```

Actions that do not terminate a rule are handled by **yacc** by manufacturing a new nonterminal symbol name and a new rule matching this name to the empty string. The interior action is the action triggered by recognizing this added rule. **yacc** treats the above example as if it had been written

```
$ACT    :    /* empty */
        {
            $$ = 1;
        }
        ;


A       :    B  $ACT  C
        {
            x = $2;
            y = $3;
        }
        ;
```

where **$ACT** is an empty action.

In many applications, output is not done directly by the actions. A data structure, such as a parse tree, is constructed in memory and transformations are applied to it before output is generated. Parse trees are particularly easy to construct given routines to build and maintain the tree structure desired. For example, suppose there is a C function node written so that the call

```
node( L, n1, n2 )
```

creates a node with label **L** and descendants **n1** and **n2** and returns the index of the newly created node. Then a parse tree can be built by supplying actions such as

```
expr    :    expr  '+'  expr
        {
            $$ = node( '+', $1, $3 );
        }
```

in the specification.

The user may define other variables to be used by the actions. Declarations and definitions can appear in the declarations section enclosed in the marks %{ and %}. These declarations and definitions have global scope, so they are known to the action statements and can be made known to the lexical analyzer. For example:

```
%{    int variable = 0;    %}
```

could be placed in the declarations section making **variable** accessible to all of the actions. Users should avoid names beginning with **yy** because the **yacc** parser uses only such names. In the examples shown thus far all the values are integers. A discussion of values of other types is found in the section "Advanced Topics."

## Lexical Analysis

The user must supply a lexical analyzer to read the input stream and communicate tokens (with values, if desired) to the parser. The lexical analyzer is an integer-valued function called **yylex**. The function returns an integer, the *token number*, representing the kind of token read. If there is a value associated with that token, it should be assigned to the external variable **yylval**.

The parser and the lexical analyzer must agree on these token numbers in order for communication between them to take place. The numbers may be chosen by **yacc** or the user. In either case, the **#define** mechanism of C language is used to allow the lexical analyzer to return these numbers symbolically. For example, suppose that the token name DIGIT has been defined in the declarations section of the **yacc** specification file. The relevant portion of the lexical analyzer might look like

```
int yylex()
{
        extern int yylval;
        int c;
        ...
        c = getchar();
        ...
        switch (c)
        {
          ...
          case '0':
          case '1':
          ...
          case '9':
          yylval = c - '0';
          return (DIGIT);
          ...
        }
        ...
}
```

to return the appropriate token.

The intent is to return a token number of DIGIT and a value equal to the numerical value of the digit. Provided that the lexical analyzer code is placed in the subroutines section of the specification file, the identifier DIGIT is defined as the token number associated with the token DIGIT.

This mechanism leads to clear, easily modified lexical analyzers. The only pitfall to avoid is using any token names in the grammar that are reserved or significant in C language or the parser. For example, the use of token names **if** or **while** will almost certainly cause severe difficulties when the lexical analyzer is compiled. The token name **error** is reserved for error handling and should not be used naively.

In the default situation, token numbers are chosen by **yacc**. The default token number for a literal character is the numerical value of the character in the local character set. Other names are assigned token numbers starting at 257. If the **yacc** command is invoked with the −**d** option a file called **y.tab.h** is generated. **y.tab.h** contains **#define** statements for the tokens.

If the user prefers to assign the token numbers, the first appearance of the token name or literal in the declarations section must be followed immediately by a nonnegative integer. This integer is taken to be the token number of the name or literal. Names and literals not defined this way are assigned default definitions by **yacc**. The potential for duplication exists here. Care must be taken to make sure that all token numbers are distinct.

For historical reasons, the end-marker must have token number 0 or negative. This token number cannot be redefined by the user. Thus, all lexical analyzers should be prepared to return 0 or a negative number as a token upon reaching the end of their input.

A very useful tool for constructing lexical analyzers is the **lex** utility. Lexical analyzers produced by **lex** are designed to work in close harmony with **yacc** parsers. The specifications for these lexical analyzers use regular expressions instead of grammar rules. **lex** can be easily used to produce quite complicated lexical analyzers, but there remain some languages (such as FORTRAN), which do not fit any theoretical framework and whose lexical analyzers must be crafted by hand.

# Parser Operation

**yacc** turns the specification file into a C language procedure, which parses the input according to the specification given. The algorithm used to go from the specification to the parser is complex and will not be discussed here. The parser itself, though, is relatively simple and understanding its usage will make treatment of error recovery and ambiguities easier.

The parser produced by **yacc** consists of a finite state machine with a stack. The parser is also capable of reading and remembering the next input token (called the look-ahead token). The current state is always the one on the top of the stack. The states of the finite state machine are given small integer labels. Initially, the machine is in state 0 (the stack contains only state 0) and no look-ahead token has been read.

The machine has only four actions available—**shift**, **reduce**, **accept**, and **error**. A step of the parser is done as follows:

1. Based on its current state, the parser decides if it needs a look-ahead token to choose the action to be taken. If it needs one and does not have one, it calls **yylex** to obtain the next token.

2. Using the current state and the look-ahead token if needed, the parser decides on its next action and carries it out. This may result in states being pushed onto the stack or popped off of the stack and in the look-ahead token being processed or left alone.

The shift action is the most common action the parser takes. Whenever a shift action is taken, there is always a look-ahead token. For example, in state 56 there may be an action

```
IF   shift 34
```

which says, in state 56, if the look-ahead token is IF, the current state (56) is pushed down on the stack, and state 34 becomes the current state (on the top of the stack). The look-ahead token is cleared.

The **reduce** action keeps the stack from growing without bounds. **reduce** actions are appropriate when the parser has seen the right-hand side of a grammar rule and is prepared to announce that it has seen an instance of the rule replacing the right-hand side by the left-hand side. It may be necessary to consult the look-ahead token to decide whether or not to **reduce** (usually it is not necessary). In fact, the default action (represented by a dot) is often a **reduce** action.

**reduce** actions are associated with individual grammar rules. Grammar rules are also given small integer numbers, and this leads to some confusion. The action

. reduce 18

refers to grammar rule 18, while the action

IF   shift 34

refers to state 34.

Suppose the rule

A   :   x   y   z    ;

is being reduced. The **reduce** action depends on the left-hand symbol (A in this case) and the number of symbols on the right-hand side (three in this case). To reduce, first pop off the top three states from the stack. (In general, the number of states popped equals the number of symbols on the right side of the rule.) In effect, these states were the ones put on the stack while recognizing x, y, and z and no longer serve any useful purpose. After popping these states, a state is uncovered, which was the state the parser was in before beginning to process the rule. Using this uncovered state and the symbol on the left side of the rule, perform what is in effect a shift of **A**. A new state is obtained, pushed onto the stack, and parsing continues. There are significant differences between the processing of the left-hand symbol and an ordinary shift of a token, however, so this action is called a **goto** action. In particular, the look-ahead token is cleared by a shift but is not affected by a **goto**. In any case, the uncovered state contains an entry such as

A   goto 20

causing state 20 to be pushed onto the stack and become the current state.

In effect, the **reduce** action turns back the clock in the parse popping the states off the stack to go back to the state where the right-hand side of the rule was first seen. The parser then behaves as if it had seen the left side at that time. If the right-hand side of the rule is empty, no states are popped off of the stacks. The uncovered state is in fact the current state.

The **reduce** action is also important in the treatment of user-supplied actions and values. When a rule is reduced, the code supplied with the rule is executed before the stack is adjusted. In addition to the stack holding the states, another stack running in parallel with it holds the values returned from the lexical analyzer and the actions. When a **shift** takes place, the external variable **yylval** is copied onto the value stack. After the return from the user code, the reduction is carried out. When the **goto** action is done, the external variable **yyval** is copied onto the value stack. The pseudo-variables **$1**, **$2**, etc., refer to the value stack.

The other two parser actions are conceptually much simpler. The **accept** action indicates that the entire input has been seen and that it matches the specification. This action appears only when the look-ahead token is the end-marker and indicates that the parser has successfully done its job. The **error** action, on the other hand, represents a place where the parser can no longer continue parsing according to the specification. The input tokens it has seen (together with the look-ahead token) cannot be followed by anything that would result in a legal input. The parser reports an error and attempts to recover the situation and resume parsing. The error recovery (as opposed to the detection of error) will be discussed later.

Consider:

```
%token   DING   DONG   DELL
%%
rhyme    :    sound   place
         ;
sound    :    DING   DONG
         ;
place    :    DELL
         ;
```

as a **yacc** specification.

When **yacc** is invoked with the **−v** option, a file called **y.output** is produced with a human-readable description of the parser. The **y.output** file corresponding to the above grammar (with some statistics stripped off the end) follows.

```
state 0
      $accept  :  _rhyme  $end

      DING  shift 3
      .  error

      rhyme  goto 1
      sound  goto 2

state 1
      $accept  :  rhyme_$end

      $end  accept
      .  error

state 2
      rhyme  :  sound_place

      DELL  shift 5
      .  error

      place  goto 4

state 3
      sound  :  DING_DONG

      DONG  shift 6
      .  error

state 4
      rhyme  :  sound place_     (1)

      .  reduce  1

state 5
      place  :  DELL_     (3)

      .  reduce  3

state 6
      sound  :  DING DONG_     (2)

      .  reduce  2
```

The actions for each state are specified and there is a description of the parsing rules being processed in each state. The _ character is used to indicate what has been seen and what is yet to come in each rule. The following input

        DING   DONG   DELL

can be used to track the operations of the parser. Initially, the current state is state 0. The parser needs to refer to the input in order to decide between the actions available in state 0, so the first token, DING, is read and becomes the look-ahead token. The action in state 0 on DING is **shift 3**, state 3 is pushed onto the stack, and the look-ahead token is cleared. State 3 becomes the current state. The next token, DONG, is read and becomes the look-ahead token. The action in state 3 on the token DONG is **shift 6**, state 6 is pushed onto the stack, and the look-ahead is cleared. The stack now contains 0, 3, and 6. In state 6, without even consulting the look-ahead, the parser reduces by

        sound   :   DING   DONG

which is rule 2. Two states, 6 and 3, are popped off of the stack uncovering state 0. Consulting the description of state 0 (looking for a **goto** on **sound**),

        sound    goto 2

is obtained. State 2 is pushed onto the stack and becomes the current state.

   In state 2, the next token, DELL, must be read. The action is **shift 5**, so state 5 is pushed onto the stack, which now has 0, 2, and 5 on it, and the look-ahead token is cleared. In state 5, the only action is to reduce by rule 3. This has one symbol on the right-hand side, so one state, 5, is popped off, and state 2 is uncovered. The **goto** in state 2 on **place** (the left side of rule 3) is state 4. Now, the stack contains 0, 2, and 4. In state 4, the only action is to reduce by rule 1. There are two symbols on the right, so the top two states are popped off, uncovering state 0 again. In state 0, there is a **goto** on **rhyme** causing the parser to enter state 1. In state 1, the input is read and the end-marker is obtained indicated by **$end** in the **y.output** file. The action in state 1 (when the end-marker is seen) successfully ends the parse.

   The reader is urged to consider how the parser works when confronted with such incorrect strings as DING DONG DONG, DING DONG, DING DONG DELL DELL, etc. A few minutes spent with this and other simple examples is repaid when problems arise in more complicated contexts.

# Ambiguity and Conflicts

A set of grammar rules is ambiguous if there is some input string that can be structured in two or more different ways. For example, the grammar rule

> expr  :  expr  '−'  expr

is a natural way of expressing the fact that one way of forming an arithmetic expression is to put two other expressions together with a minus sign between them. Unfortunately, this grammar rule does not completely specify the way that all complex inputs should be structured. For example, if the input is

> expr  −  expr  −  expr

the rule allows this input to be structured as either

> (  expr  −  expr  )  −  expr

or as

> expr  −  (  expr  −  expr  )

(The first is called left association, the second right association.)

**yacc** detects such ambiguities when it is attempting to build the parser. Given the input

> expr  −  expr  −  expr

consider the problem that confronts the parser. When the parser has read the second *expr*, the input seen

> expr  −  expr

matches the right side of the grammar rule above. The parser could reduce the input by applying this rule. After applying the rule, the input is reduced to **expr** (the left side of the rule). The parser would then read the final part of the input

> −  expr

and again reduce. The effect of this is to take the left associative interpretation.

Alternatively, if the parser sees

> expr  −  expr

it could defer the immediate application of the rule and continue reading the input until

$$expr \; - \; expr \; - \; expr$$

is seen. It could then apply the rule to the rightmost three symbols reducing them to *expr*, which results in

$$expr \; - \; expr$$

being left. Now the rule can be reduced once more. The effect is to take the right associative interpretation. Thus, having read

$$expr \; - \; expr$$

the parser can do one of two legal things, a shift or a reduction. It has no way of deciding between them. This is called a **shift-reduce** conflict. It may also happen that the parser has a choice of two legal reductions. This is called a **reduce-reduce** conflict. Note that there are never any **shift-shift** conflicts.

When there are **shift-reduce** or **reduce-reduce** conflicts, **yacc** still produces a parser. It does this by selecting one of the valid steps wherever it has a choice. A rule describing the choice to make in a given situation is called a disambiguating rule.

**yacc** invokes two default disambiguating rules:

1. In a **shift-reduce** conflict, the default is to do the shift.

2. In a **reduce-reduce** conflict, the default is to reduce by the earlier grammar rule (in the **yacc** specification).

Rule 1 implies that reductions are deferred in favor of shifts when there is a choice. Rule 2 gives the user rather crude control over the behavior of the parser in this situation, but **reduce-reduce** conflicts should be avoided when possible.

Conflicts may arise because of mistakes in input or logic or because the grammar rules (while consistent) require a more complex parser than **yacc** can construct. The use of actions within rules can also cause conflicts if the action must be done before the parser can be sure which rule is being recognized. In these cases, the application of disambiguating rules is inappropriate and leads to an incorrect parser. For this reason, **yacc** always reports the number of **shift-reduce** and **reduce-reduce** conflicts resolved by Rule 1 and Rule 2.

In general, whenever it is possible to apply disambiguating rules to produce a correct parser, it is also possible to rewrite the grammar rules so that the same inputs are read but there are no conflicts. For this reason, most previous parser generators have considered conflicts to be fatal errors. Our experience has suggested that this rewriting is somewhat unnatural and produces slower parsers. Thus, **yacc** will produce parsers even in the presence of conflicts.

As an example of the power of disambiguating rules, consider

```
stat    :   IF  '('  cond  ')'  stat
        |   IF  '('  cond  ')'  stat  ELSE  stat
        ;
```

which is a fragment from a programming language involving an **if-then-else** statement. In these rules, IF and ELSE are tokens, *cond* is a nonterminal symbol describing conditional (logical) expressions, and *stat* is a nonterminal symbol describing statements. The first rule will be called the simple **if** rule and the second the **if-else** rule.

These two rules form an ambiguous construction because input of the form

```
IF  ( C1 )  IF  ( C2 )  S1  ELSE  S2
```

can be structured according to these rules in two ways

```
IF   ( C1 )
{
        IF   ( C2 )
            S1
}
ELSE
        S2
```

or

```
IF   ( C1 )
{
        IF   ( C2 )
            S1
        ELSE
            S2
}
```

where the second interpretation is the one given in most programming languages having this construct; each ELSE is associated with the last preceding un-ELSE'd IF. In this example, consider the situation where the parser has seen

        IF  (  C1  )  IF  (  C2  )  S1

and is looking at the ELSE. It can immediately reduce by the simple **if** rule to get

        IF  (  C1  )  stat

and then read the remaining input

        ELSE  S2

and reduce

        IF  (  C1  )  stat  ELSE  S2

by the **if-else** rule. This leads to the first of the above groupings of the input.

On the other hand, the ELSE may be shifted, S2 read, and then the right-hand portion of

        IF  (  C1  )  IF  (  C2  )  S1  ELSE  S2

can be reduced by the if-else rule to get

        IF  (  C1  )  stat

which can be reduced by the simple **if** rule. This leads to the second of the above groupings of the input which is usually desired.

Once again, the parser can do two valid things—there is a **shift-reduce** conflict. The application of disambiguating rule 1 tells the parser to shift in this case, which leads to the desired grouping.

This **shift-reduce** conflict arises only when there is a particular current input symbol, ELSE, and particular inputs, such as

        IF  (  C1  )  IF  (  C2  )  S1

have already been seen. In general, there may be many conflicts, and each one will be associated with an input symbol and a set of previously read inputs. The previously read inputs are characterized by the state of the parser.

The conflict messages of **yacc** are best understood by examining the verbose (−**v**) option output file. For example, the output corresponding to the above conflict state might be

```
23: shift-reduce conflict (shift 45, reduce 18) on ELSE

state 23

    stat  :  IF  (  cond  )  stat_           (18)
    stat  :  IF  (  cond  )  stat_ELSE  stat

    ELSE      shift 45
    .         reduce 18
```

where the first line describes the conflict—giving the state and the input symbol. The ordinary state description gives the grammar rules active in the state and the parser actions. Recall that the underline marks the portion of the grammar rules, which has been seen. Thus in the example, in state 23 the parser has seen input corresponding to

```
    IF  (  cond  )  stat
```

and the two grammar rules shown are active at this time. The parser can do two possible things. If the input symbol is ELSE, it is possible to shift into state 45. State 45 will have, as part of its description, the line

```
    stat  :  IF  (  cond  )  stat  ELSE_stat
```

because the ELSE will have been shifted in this state. In state 23, the alternative action (describing a dot, .), is to be done if the input symbol is not mentioned explicitly in the actions. In this case, if the input symbol is not ELSE, the parser reduces to

```
    stat  :  IF  '('  cond  ')'  stat
```

by grammar rule 18.

Once again, notice that the numbers following shift commands refer to other states, while the numbers following reduce commands refer to grammar rule numbers. In the **y.output** file, the rule numbers are printed in parentheses after those rules, which can be reduced. In most states, there is a reduce action possible in the state and this is the default command. The user who encounters unexpected **shift-reduce** conflicts will probably want to look at the verbose output to decide whether the default actions are appropriate.

# Precedence

There is one common situation where the rules given above for resolving conflicts are not sufficient. This is in the parsing of arithmetic expressions. Most of the commonly used constructions for arithmetic expressions can be naturally described by the notion of precedence levels for operators, together with information about left or right associativity. It turns out that ambiguous grammars with appropriate disambiguating rules can be used to create parsers that are faster and easier to write than parsers constructed from unambiguous grammars. The basic notion is to write grammar rules of the form

        expr  :  expr  OP  expr

and

        expr  :  UNARY  expr

for all binary and unary operators desired. This creates a very ambiguous grammar with many parsing conflicts. As disambiguating rules, the user specifies the precedence or binding strength of all the operators and the associativity of the binary operators. This information is sufficient to allow **yacc** to resolve the parsing conflicts in accordance with these rules and construct a parser that realizes the desired precedences and associativities.

The precedences and associativities are attached to tokens in the declarations section. This is done by a series of lines beginning with a **yacc** keyword: **%left**, **%right**, or **%nonassoc**, followed by a list of tokens. All of the tokens on the same line are assumed to have the same precedence level and associativity; the lines are listed in order of increasing precedence or binding strength. Thus:

        %left  '+'  '−'
        %left  '*'  '/'

describes the precedence and associativity of the four arithmetic operators. Plus and minus are left associative and have lower precedence than star and slash, which are also left associative. The keyword **%right** is used to describe right associative operators, and the keyword **%nonassoc** is used to describe operators, like the operator **.LT.** in FORTRAN, that may not associate with themselves. Thus:

        A  . LT.  B  . LT.  C

is illegal in FORTRAN and such an operator would be described with the keyword **%nonassoc** in **yacc**. As an example of the behavior of these declarations, the description

```
%right   '='
%left    '+'  '-'
%left    '*'  '/'

%%

expr   :   expr  '='  expr
       |   expr  '+'  expr
       |   expr  '-'  expr
       |   expr  '*'  expr
       |   expr  '/'  expr
       |   NAME
       ;
```

might be used to structure the input

$$a = b = c*d - e - f*g$$

as follows

$$a = ( b = ( ((c*d)-e) - (f*g) ) )$$

in order to perform the correct precedence of operators. When this mechanism is used, unary operators must, in general, be given a precedence. Sometimes a unary operator and a binary operator have the same symbolic representation but different precedences. An example is unary and binary minus, −.

Unary minus may be given the same strength as multiplication, or even higher, while binary minus has a lower strength than multiplication. The keyword, **%prec**, changes the precedence level associated with a particular grammar rule. The keyword **%prec** appears immediately after the body of the grammar rule, before the action or closing semicolon, and is followed by a token name or literal. It causes the precedence of the grammar rule to become that of the following token name or literal. For example, the rules

```
%left  '+'  '-'
%left  '*'  '/'

%%

expr   :   expr  '+'  expr
       |   expr  '-'  expr
       |   expr  '*'  expr
       |   expr  '/'  expr
       |   '-'  expr       %prec  '*'
       |   NAME
       ;
```

might be used to give unary minus the same precedence as multiplication.

A token declared by **%left**, **%right**, and **%nonassoc** need not be, but may be, declared by **%token** as well.

Precedences and associativities are used by **yacc** to resolve parsing conflicts. They give rise to the following disambiguating rules:

1. Precedences and associativities are recorded for those tokens and literals that have them.

2. A precedence and associativity is associated with each grammar rule. It is the precedence and associativity of the last token or literal in the body of the rule. If the **%prec** construction is used, it overrides this default. Some grammar rules may have no precedence and associativity associated with them.

3. When there is a **reduce-reduce** conflict or there is a **shift-reduce** conflict and either the input symbol or the grammar rule has no precedence and associativity, then the two default disambiguating rules given at the beginning of the section are used, and the conflicts are reported.

4.  If there is a **shift-reduce** conflict and both the grammar rule and the input character have precedence and associativity associated with them, then the conflict is resolved in favor of the action—**shift** or **reduce**—associated with the higher precedence. If precedences are equal, then associativity is used. Left associative implies **reduce**; right associative implies **shift**; nonassociating implies **error**.

Conflicts resolved by precedence are not counted in the number of **shift-reduce** and **reduce-reduce** conflicts reported by **yacc**. This means that mistakes in the specification of precedences may disguise errors in the input grammar. It is a good idea to be sparing with precedences and use them in a cookbook fashion until some experience has been gained. The **y.output** file is very useful in deciding whether the parser is actually doing what was intended.

# Error Handling

Error handling is an extremely difficult area, and many of the problems are semantic ones. When an error is found, for example, it may be necessary to reclaim parse tree storage, delete or alter symbol table entries, and/or, typically, set switches to avoid generating any further output.

It is seldom acceptable to stop all processing when an error is found. It is more useful to continue scanning the input to find further syntax errors. This leads to the problem of getting the parser restarted after an error. A general class of algorithms to do this involves discarding a number of tokens from the input string and attempting to adjust the parser so that input can continue.

To allow the user some control over this process, **yacc** provides the token name **error**. This name can be used in grammar rules. In effect, it suggests places where errors are expected and recovery might take place. The parser pops its stack until it enters a state where the token **error** is legal. It then behaves as if the token **error** were the current look-ahead token and performs the action encountered. The look-ahead token is then reset to the token that caused the error. If no special error rules have been specified, the processing halts when an error is detected.

In order to prevent a cascade of error messages, the parser, after detecting an error, remains in error state until three tokens have been successfully read and shifted. If an error is detected when the parser is already in error state, no message is given, and the input token is quietly deleted.

As an example, a rule of the form

    stat   :   error

means that on a syntax error the parser attempts to skip over the statement in which the error is seen. More precisely, the parser scans ahead, looking for three tokens that might legally follow a statement, and start processing at the first of these. If the beginnings of statements are not sufficiently distinctive, it may make a false start in the middle of a statement and end up reporting a second error where there is in fact no error.

Actions may be used with these special error rules. These actions might attempt to reinitialize tables, reclaim symbol table space, etc.

Error rules such as the above are very general but difficult to control. Rules such as

```
stat   :   error  ';'
```

are somewhat easier.  Here, when there is an error, the parser attempts to skip over the statement but does so by skipping to the next semicolon.  All tokens after the error and before the next semicolon cannot be shifted and are discarded.  When the semicolon is seen, this rule will be reduced and any cleanup action associated with it performed.

Another form of **error** rule arises in interactive applications where it may be desirable to permit a line to be reentered after an error.  The following example

```
input   :   error  '\n'
                {
                        (void) printf( "Reenter last line: " );
                }
                input
            {
                $$ = $4;
            }
            ;
```

is one way to do this.  There is one potential difficulty with this approach. The parser must correctly process three input tokens before it admits that it has correctly resynchronized after the error.  If the reentered line contains an error in the first two tokens, the parser deletes the offending tokens and gives no message.  This is clearly unacceptable.  For this reason, there is a mechanism that can force the parser to believe that error recovery has been accomplished.  The statement

```
yyerrok ;
```

in an action resets the parser to its normal mode.  The last example can be rewritten as

```
input    :   error  '\n'
                 {
                     yyerrok;
                     (void) printf( "Reenter last line: " );
                 }
                 input
         {
             $$ = $4;
         }
         ;
```

which is somewhat better.

As previously mentioned, the token seen immediately after the **error** symbol is the input token at which the error was discovered. Sometimes, this is inappropriate; for example, an error recovery action might take upon itself the job of finding the correct place to resume input. In this case, the previous look-ahead token must be cleared. The statement

    yyclearin ;

in an action will have this effect. For example, suppose the action after **error** were to call some sophisticated resynchronization routine (supplied by the user) that attempted to advance the input to the beginning of the next valid statement. After this routine is called, the next token returned by **yylex** is presumably the first token in a legal statement. The old illegal token must be discarded and the **error** state reset. A rule similar to

```
stat    :    error
        {
            resynch();
            yyerrok  ;
            yyclearin;
        }
        ;
```

could perform this.

These mechanisms are admittedly crude but do allow for a simple, fairly effective recovery of the parser from many errors. Moreover, the user can get control to deal with the error actions required by other portions of the program.

# The yacc **Environment**

When the user inputs a specification to **yacc**, the output is a file of C language subroutines, called **y.tab.c**. The function produced by **yacc** is called **yyparse**(); it is an integer valued function. When it is called, it in turn repeatedly calls **yylex**(), the lexical analyzer supplied by the user (see "Lexical Analysis"), to obtain input tokens. Eventually, an error is detected, **yyparse**() returns the value 1, and no error recovery is possible, or the lexical analyzer returns the end-marker token and the parser accepts. In this case, **yyparse**() returns the value 0.

The user must provide a certain amount of environment for this parser in order to obtain a working program. For example, as with every C language program, a routine called **main**() must be defined that eventually calls **yparse**(). In addition, a routine called **yyerror**() is needed to print a message when a syntax error is detected.

These two routines must be supplied in one form or another by the user. To ease the initial effort of using **yacc**, a library has been provided with default versions of **main**() and **yerror**(). The library is accessed by a −**ly** argument to the **cc**(1) command or to the loader. The source codes

```
main( )
{
    return (yyparse( ));
}
```

and

```
# include <stdio.h>

yyerror(s)
        char *s;
{
        (void) fprintf(stderr, "%s\n", s);
}
```

show the triviality of these default programs. The argument to **yerror**() is a string containing an error message, usually the string **syntax error**. The average application wants to do better than this. Ordinarily, the program should keep track of the input line number and print it along with the message when a syntax error is detected. The external integer variable *yychar* contains the look-ahead token number at the time the error was detected. This may be of some interest in giving better diagnostics. Since the **main**()

routine is probably supplied by the user (to read arguments, etc.), the **yacc** library is useful only in small projects or in the earliest stages of larger ones.

The external integer variable **yydebug** is normally set to 0. If it is set to a nonzero value, the parser will output a verbose description of its actions including a discussion of the input symbols read and what the parser actions are. It is possible to set this variable by using **sdb**.

# Hints for Preparing Specifications

This part contains miscellaneous hints on preparing efficient, easy to change, and clear specifications. The individual subsections are more or less independent.

## Input Style

It is difficult to provide rules with substantial actions and still have a readable specification file. The following are a few style hints.

1. Use all uppercase letters for token names and all lowercase letters for nonterminal names. This is useful in debugging.

2. Put grammar rules and actions on separate lines. It makes editing easier.

3. Put all rules with the same left-hand side together. Put the left-hand side in only once and let all following rules begin with a vertical bar.

4. Put a semicolon only after the last rule with a given left-hand side and put the semicolon on a separate line. This allows new rules to be easily added.

5. Indent rule bodies by one tab stop and action bodies by two tab stops.

6. Put complicated actions into subroutines defined in separate files.

Example 1 is written following this style, as are the examples in this section (where space permits). The user must decide about these stylistic questions. The central problem, however, is to make the rules visible through the morass of action code.

## Left Recursion

The algorithm used by the **yacc** parser encourages so called left recursive grammar rules. Rules of the form

```
name  :  name rest_of_rule ;
```

match this algorithm. These rules such as

```
list   :   item
       |   list  ','  item
       ;
```

and

```
seq    :   item
       |   seq  item
       ;
```

frequently arise when writing specifications of sequences and lists. In each of these cases, the first rule will be reduced for the first item only; and the second rule will be reduced for the second and all succeeding items.

With right recursive rules, such as

```
seq    :   item
       |   item  seq
       ;
```

the parser is a bit bigger; and the items are seen and reduced from right to left. More seriously, an internal stack in the parser is in danger of overflowing if a very long sequence is read. Thus, the user should use left recursion wherever reasonable.

It is worth considering if a sequence with zero elements has any meaning, and if so, consider writing the sequence specification as

```
seq    :   /* empty */
       |   seq  item
       ;
```

using an empty rule. Once again, the first rule would always be reduced exactly once before the first item was read, and then the second rule would be reduced once for each item read. Permitting empty sequences often leads to increased generality. However, conflicts might arise if **yacc** is asked to decide which empty sequence it has seen when it hasn't seen enough to know!

## Lexical Tie-Ins

Some lexical decisions depend on context. For example, the lexical analyzer might want to delete blanks normally, but not within quoted strings, or names might be entered into a symbol table in declarations but not in expressions. One way of handling these situations is to create a global flag that is examined by the lexical analyzer and set by actions. For example,

```
%{
    int dflag;
%}
    ... other declarations ...

%%

prog    :   decls  stats
        ;

decls   :   /* empty */
        {
                dflag = 1;
        }
        |   decls  declaration
        ;

stats   :   /* empty */
        {
                dflag = 0;
        }
        |   stats  statement
        ;

    ... other rules ...
```

specifies a program that consists of zero or more declarations followed by zero or more statements. The flag **dflag** is now 0 when reading statements and 1 when reading declarations, except for the first token in the first statement.

This token must be seen by the parser before it can tell that the declaration section has ended and the statements have begun. In many cases, this single token exception does not affect the lexical scan.

This kind of back-door approach can be elaborated to a noxious degree. Nevertheless, it represents a way of doing some things that are difficult, if not impossible, to do otherwise.

# Reserved Words

Some programming languages permit you to use words like **if**, which are normally reserved as label or variable names, provided that such use does not conflict with the legal use of these names in the programming language. This is extremely hard to do in the framework of **yacc**. It is difficult to pass information to the lexical analyzer telling it this instance of **if** is a keyword and that instance is a variable. The user can make a stab at it using the mechanism described in the last subsection, but it is difficult.

A number of ways of making this easier are under advisement. Until then, it is better that the keywords be reserved, i.e., forbidden for use as variable names. There are powerful stylistic reasons for preferring this.

# Advanced Topics

This part discusses a number of advanced features of **yacc**.

## Simulating error and accept in Actions

The parsing actions of **error** and **accept** can be simulated in an action by use of macros YYACCEPT and YYERROR. The YYACCEPT macro causes **yyparse()** to return the value 0; YYERROR causes the parser to behave as if the current input symbol had been a syntax error; **yyerror()** is called, and error recovery takes place. These mechanisms can be used to simulate parsers with multiple end-markers or context sensitive syntax checking.

## Accessing Values in Enclosing Rules

An action may refer to values returned by actions to the left of the current rule. The mechanism is simply the same as with ordinary actions, a dollar sign followed by a digit.

```
sent    :   adj  noun  verb  adj  noun
        {
            look at the sentence ...
        }
        ;
adj     :   THE
        {
                $$ = THE;
        }
        |   YOUNG
        {
                $$ = YOUNG;
        }
        ...
        ;
noun    :   DOG
        {
            $$ = DOG;
        }
        |   CRONE
        {
            if( $0 == YOUNG )
            {
                (void) printf( "what?\n" );
            }
            $$ = CRONE;
        }
        ;
        ...
```

In this case, the digit may be 0 or negative. In the action following the word CRONE, a check is made that the preceding token shifted was not YOUNG. Obviously, this is only possible when a great deal is known about what might precede the symbol **noun** in the input. There is also a distinctly unstructured flavor about this. Nevertheless, at times this mechanism prevents a great deal of trouble especially when a few combinations are to be excluded from an otherwise regular structure.

# Support for Arbitrary Value Types

By default, the values returned by actions and the lexical analyzer are integers. **yacc** can also support values of other types including structures. In addition, **yacc** keeps track of the types and inserts appropriate union member names so that the resulting parser is strictly type checked. **yacc** value stack is declared to be a **union** of the various types of values desired. The user declares the union and associates union member names with each token and nonterminal symbol having a value. When the value is referenced through a **$$** or **$n** construction, **yacc** will automatically insert the appropriate union name so that no unwanted conversions take place. In addition, type checking commands such as **lint** are far more silent.

There are three mechanisms used to provide for this typing. First, there is a way of defining the union. This must be done by the user since other subroutines, notably the lexical analyzer, must know about the union member names. Second, there is a way of associating a union member name with tokens and nonterminals. Finally, there is a mechanism for describing the type of those few values where **yacc** cannot easily determine the type.

To declare the union, the user includes

```
%union
{
    body of union ...
}
```

in the declaration section. This declares the **yacc** value stack and the external variables **yylval** and **yyval** to have type equal to this union. If **yacc** was invoked with the −**d** option, the union declaration is copied onto the **y.tab.h** file as YYSTYPE.

Once YYSTYPE is defined, the union member names must be associated with the various terminal and nonterminal names. The construction

```
<name>
```

is used to indicate a union member name. If this follows one of the keywords **%token**, **%left**, **%right**, and **%nonassoc**, the union member name is associated with the tokens listed. Thus, saying

```
%left  <optype>  '+'  '−'
```

causes any reference to values returned by these two tokens to be tagged with the union member name **optype**. Another keyword, **%type**, is used to associate union member names with nonterminals. Thus, one might say

```
%type  <nodetype>  expr  stat
```

to associate the union member **nodetype** with the nonterminal symbols **expr** and **stat**.

There remain a couple of cases where these mechanisms are insufficient. If there is an action within a rule, the value returned by this action has no *a priori* type. Similarly, reference to left context values (such as **$0**) leaves **yacc** with no easy way of knowing the type. In this case, a type can be imposed on the reference by inserting a union member name between < and > immediately after the first $. The example

```
rule    :    aaa
                        {
                            $<intval>$ = 3;
                        }
                        bbb
            {
                fun( $<intval>2, $<other>0 );
            }
            ;
```

shows this usage. This syntax has little to recommend it, but the situation arises rarely.

A sample specification is given in Example 2. The facilities in this subsection are not triggered until they are used. In particular, the use of **%type** will turn on these mechanisms. When they are used, there is a fairly strict level of checking. For example, use of **$n** or **$$** to refer to something with no defined type is diagnosed. If these facilities are not triggered, the **yacc** value stack is used to hold **int**s.

## yacc **Input Syntax**

This section has a description of the **yacc** input syntax as a **yacc** specification. Context dependencies, etc. are not considered. Ironically, although **yacc** accepts an LALR(1) grammar, the **yacc** input specification language is most naturally specified as an LR(2) grammar; the sticky part comes when an identifier is seen in a rule immediately following an action. If this identifier is followed by a colon, it is the start of the next rule; otherwise, it is a continuation of the current rule, which just happens to have an action embedded in it. As implemented, the lexical analyzer looks ahead after seeing an identifier and decides whether the next token (skipping blanks, newlines, and comments, etc.) is a colon. If so, it returns the token C_IDENTIFIER. Otherwise, it returns IDENTIFIER. Literals (quoted strings) are also returned as IDENTIFIERs but never as part of C_IDENTIFIERs.

```
    /* grammar for the input to yacc */

    /* basic entries */
%token    IDENTIFIER    /* includes identifiers and literals */
%token    C_IDENTIFIER  /* identifier (but not literal) followed by a : */
%token    NUMBER        /* [0-9]+ */

    /*    reserved words: %type=>TYPE %left=>LEFT,etc. */

%token    LEFT RIGHT NONASSOC TOKEN PREC TYPE START UNION

%token    MARK    /* the %% mark */
%token    LCURL   /* the %{ mark */
%token    RCURL   /* the %} mark */

    /* ASCII character literals stand for themselves */

%token    spec

%%

spec    :    defs MARK rules tail
        ;
```

*continued*

```
tail    :    MARK
        {

                In this action, eat up the rest of the file

        }
        |    /* empty: the second MARK is optional */
        ;


defs    :    /* empty */
        |    defs def
        ;
def     :    START IDENTIFIER
        |    UNION
        {

              Copy union definition to output

        }
        |    LCURL
        {

                Copy C code to output file

        }
             RCURL
        |    rword tag nlist
        ;


rword   :    TOKEN
        |    LEFT
        |    RIGHT
        |    NONASSOC
        |    TYPE
        ;


tag     :    /* empty: union tag is optional */
        |    '<' IDENTIFIER '>'
        ;


nlist   :    nmno
        |    nlist nmno
        |    nlist ',' nmno
        ;
```

*continued*

```
nmno    :   IDENTIFIER          /* Note: literal illegal with % type */
        |   IDENTIFIER NUMBER    /* Note: illegal with % type */
        ;

    /* rule section */

rules   :   C_IDENTIFIER rbody prec
        |   rules rule
        ;
rule    :   C_IDENTIFIER rbody prec
        |   '|' rbody prec
        ;


rbody   :   /* empty */
        |   rbody IDENTIFIER
        |   rbody act
        ;

act     :   '{'
            {
                Copy action translate $$ etc.
            }
            '}'
        ;

prec    :   /* empty */
        |   PREC IDENTIFIER
        |   PREC IDENTIFIER act
        |   prec ';'
        ;
```

# Examples

## 1. A Simple Example

This example gives the complete **yacc** applications for a small desk calculator; the calculator has 26 registers labeled **a** through **z** and accepts arithmetic expressions made up of the operators

> +, −, *, /, % (mod operator), & (bitwise and), ¦ (bitwise or), and assignments.

If an expression at the top level is an assignment, only the assignment is done; otherwise, the expression is printed. As in the C language, an integer that begins with 0 (zero) is assumed to be octal; otherwise, it is assumed to be decimal.

As an example of a **yacc** specification, the desk calculator does a reasonable job of showing how precedence and ambiguities are used and demonstrates simple recovery. The major oversimplifications are that the lexical analyzer is much simpler than for most applications, and the output is produced immediately line by line. Note the way that decimal and octal integers are read in by grammar rules. This job is probably better done by the lexical analyzer.

```
%{
# include <stdio.h>
# include <ctype.h>

int regs[26];
int base;

%}

%start list

%token DIGIT LETTER

%left '¦'
%left '&'
%left '+' '−'
%left '*' '/' '%'
```

*continued*

```
%left UMINUS  /* supplies precedence for unary minus */

%%         /* beginning of rules section */

list      :  /* empty */
          |  list stat '\n'
          |  list error '\n'
          {
             yyerrok;
          }
          ;

stat      :  expr
          {
             (void) printf( "%d\n", $1 );
          }
          |  LETTER '=' expr
          {
             regs[$1] = $3;
          }
          ;

expr      :  '(' expr ')'
          {
                $$ = $2;
          }
          |  expr '+' expr
          {
                $$ = $1 + $3;
          }
          |  expr '-' expr
          {
          {
          |  expr '*' expr
          {
                $$ = $1 * $3;
          }
          |  expr '/' expr
          {
                $$ = $1 / $3;
          }
          |   exp '%' expr
          {
                $$ = $1 % $3;
```

*continued*

```
        }
        |   expr '&' expr
        {
            $$ = $1 & $3;
        }
        |   expr '|' expr
        {
            $$ = $1 | $3;
        }
        |   '-' expr  %prec UMINUS
        {
            $$ = -$2;
        }
        |   LETTER
        {
            $$ = reg[$1];
        }
        |   number
        ;

number  :   DIGIT
        {
            $$ = $1; base = ($1==0) ? 8 ; 10;
        }
        |   number DIGIT
        {
            $$ = base * $1 + $2;
        }
        ;

%%              /* beginning of subroutines section */

int yylex( )    /* lexical analysis routine */
{               /* return LETTER for lowercase letter, */
                /* yylval = 0 through 25 */
                /* returns DIGIT for digit, yylval = 0 through 9 */
                /* all other characters are returned immediately */
```

*continued*

```
int c;
            /*skip blanks*/
while ((c = getchar()) == ' ')
        ;

        /* c is now nonblank */

if (islower(c))
{
        yylval = c - 'a';
        return (LETTER);
}
if (isdigit(c))
}
        yylval = c - '0';
        return (DIGIT);

}
return (c);
}
```

## 2. An Advanced Example

This section gives an example of a grammar using some of the advanced features. The desk calculator example in Example 1 is modified to provide a desk calculator that does floating point interval arithmetic. The calculator understands floating point constants; the arithmetic operations +, − *, /, unary − **a** through **z**. Moreover, it also understands intervals written

    (X,Y)

where **X** is less than or equal to **Y**. There are 26 interval valued variables **A** through **Z** that may also be used. The usage is similar to that in Example 1; assignments return no value and print nothing while expressions print the (floating or interval) value.

This example explores a number of interesting features of **yacc** and C. Intervals are represented by a structure consisting of the left and right endpoint values stored as doubles. This structure is given a type name, INTERVAL, by using **typedef**. **yacc** value stack can also contain floating point scalars and integers (used to index into the arrays holding the variable values). Notice that the entire strategy depends strongly on being able to assign structures and unions in C language. In fact, many of the actions call functions that return structures as well.

It is also worth noting the use of YYERROR to handle error conditions—division by an interval containing 0 and an interval presented in the wrong order. The error recovery mechanism of **yacc** is used to throw away the rest of the offending line.

In addition to the mixing of types on the value stack, this grammar also demonstrates an interesting use of syntax to keep track of the type (for example, scalar or interval) of intermediate expressions. Note that scalar can be automatically promoted to an interval if the context demands an interval value. This causes a large number of conflicts when the grammar is run through **yacc**: 18 **shift**-**reduce** and 26 **reduce**-**reduce**. The problem can be seen by looking at the two input lines.

```
2.5 + (3.5 – 4.)
```

and

```
2.5 + (3.5, 4)
```

Notice that the 2.5 is to be used in an interval value expression in the second example, but this fact is not known until the comma is read. By this time, 2.5 is finished, and the parser cannot go back and change its mind. More generally, it might be necessary to look ahead an arbitrary number of tokens to decide whether to convert a scalar to an interval. This problem is evaded by having two rules for each binary interval valued operator—one when the left operand is a scalar and one when the left operand is an interval. In the second case, the right operand must be an interval, so the conversion will be applied automatically. Despite this evasion, there are still many cases where the conversion may be applied or not, leading to the above conflicts. They are resolved by listing the rules that yield scalars first in the specification file; in this way, the conflict will be resolved in the direction of keeping scalar valued expressions scalar valued until they are forced to become intervals.

This way of handling multiple types is very instructive. If there were many kinds of expression types instead of just two, the number of rules needed would increase dramatically and the conflicts even more dramatically. Thus, while this example is instructive, it is better practice in a more normal programming language environment to keep the type information as part of the value and not as part of the grammar.

Finally, a word about the lexical analysis. The only unusual feature is the treatment of floating point constants. The C language library routine **atof()** is used to do the actual conversion from a character string to a double-precision value. If the lexical analyzer detects an error, it responds by returning a token that is illegal in the grammar provoking a syntax error in the parser and thence error recovery.

```
%{

#include <stdio.h>
#include <ctype.h>

typedef struct interval
{
     double lo, hi;
}  INTERVAL;

INTERVAL vmul(), vdiv();

double atof();

double dreg[26];
INTERVAL vreg[26];

%}

%start line

%union
{
  int ival;
  double dval;
  INTERVAL vval;
}
```

**Examples** ─────────────────────────────────────────────

*continued*

```
%token <ival> DREG VREG   /* indices into dreg, vreg arrays */


%token <dval> CONST       /* floating point constant */

%type <dval> dexp         /* expression */

%type <vval> vexp         /* interval expression */

  /* precedence information about the operators */

%left   '+' '-'
%left   '*' '/'
%left   UMINUS   /* precedence for unary minus */

%%               /* beginning of rules section */

lines   : /* empty */
        | lines line
        ;
line    : dexp '\n'
        {
                (void) printf("%15.8f\n",$1);
        }
        | vexp '\n'
        {
                (void) printf("(%15.8f, %15.8f)\n", $1.lo, $1.hi);

        }
        | DREG '=' dexp '\n'
        {
                dreg[$1] = $3;
        }
        | VREG '=' vexp '\n'
        {
                vreg[$1] = $3;
        }
        | error '\n'
        {
                yyerrok;
        }
        ;

dexp    : CONST
        | DREG
```

*continued*

```
             {
                     $$ = dreg[$1];
             }
           | dexp '+' dexp
             {
                     $$ = $1 + $3;
             }
           | dexp '−' dexp
             {
                     $$ = $1 − $3;
             }
           | dexp '*' dexp
             {
                     $$ = $1 * $3;
             }
           | dexp '/' dexp
             {
                     $$ = $1 / $3;
             }
           | '−' dexp    %prec UMINUS
             {
                     $$ = −$2;
             }
           | '(' dexp ')'
             {
                     $$ = $2;
             }
           ;

vexp      : dexp
             {
                     $$.hi = $$.lo = $1;
             }
           | '(' dexp ',' dexp ')'
             {
                     $$.lo = $2;
                     $$.hi = $4;
                     if( $$.lo > $$.hi )
```

*continued*

```
        {
                (void) printf("interval out of order \n");
                YYERROR;
        }
}
|  VREG
{
        $$ = vreg[$1];
}
|  vexp '+' vexp
{
      $$.hi = $1.hi + $3.hi;
      $$.lo = $1.lo + $3.lo;
}
|  dexp '+' vexp
{
      $$.hi = $1 + $3.hi;
      $$.lo = $1 + $3.lo;
}
|  vexp '−' vexp
{
      $$.hi = $1.hi − $3.lo;
      $$.lo = $1.lo − $3.hi;
}
|  dvep '−' vdep
{
      $$.hi = $1 − $3.lo;
      $$.lo = $1 − $3.hi
}
|  vexp '*' vexp
{
      $$ = vmul( $1.lo,$.hi,$3 )
}
|  dexp '*' vexp
{
      $$ = vmul( $1, $1, $3 )
}
|  vexp '/' vexp
```

*continued*

```
        {
                if( dcheck( $3 ) ) YYERROR;
                $$ = vdiv( $1.lo, $1.hi, $3 )
        }
     |  dexp '/' vexp
        {
                 if( dcheck( $3 ) ) YYERROR;
                 $$ = vdiv( $1.lo, $1.hi, $3 )
        }
     |  '-' vexp      %prec UMINUS
        {
                $$.hi = -$2.lo;$$.lo = -$2.hi
        }
     |  '(' vexp ')'
        }
                $$ = $2
        }
        ;

%%                              /* beginning of subroutines section */

# define BSZ 50    /* buffer size for floating point number */

        /* lexical analysis */

int yylex( )
{
        register int c;

                        /* skip over blanks */
        while ((c = getchar()) == ' ')
                ;
        if (isupper(c))
        {
            yylval.ival = c - 'A'
            return (VREG);
        }
        if (islower(c))
```

*continued*

```
{
    yylval.ival = c - 'a',
    return( DREG );
}

    /* gobble up digits. points, exponents */

if (isdigit(c) || c == '.')
{
    char buf[BSZ+1], *cp = buf;
    int dot = 0, exp = 0;

    for(; (cp - buf) < BSZ ; ++cp, c = getchar())
        {
            *cp = c;
            if (isdigit(c))
              continue;
            if (c == '.')
            {
             if (dot++ || exp)
               return ('.');   /* will cause syntax error */
             continue;
            }
            if( c == 'e' )
            {
             if (exp++)
               return ('e');   /* will cause syntax error */
             continue;
            }
                /* end of number */
            break;
        }

    *cp = ' ';
    if (cp - buf >= BSZ)
        (void) printf("constant too long - truncated\n");
    else
        ungetc(c, stdin);   /* push back last char read */
    yylval.dval = atof(buf);
    return (CONST);
}
```

*continued*

```
        return (c);
}
INTERVAL
hilo(a, b, c, d)
        double a, b, c, d;
{
        /* returns the smallest interval containing a, b, c, and d */

        /* used by *,/ routine */
        INTERVAL v;

        if (a > b)
        {
            v.hi = a;
            v.lo = b;
        }
        else
        {
            v.hi = b;
            v.lo = a;
        }
        if (c > d)
        {
            if (c > v.hi)
                v.hi = c;
            if (d < v.lo)
                v.lo = d;
        }
        else
        }
            if (d > v.hi)
                v.hi = d;
            if (c < v.lo)
                v.lo = c;
        }
        return (v);
}
```

*continued*

```
INTERVAL
vmul(a, b, v)
        double a, b;
        INTERVAL v;
{
        return (hilo(a * v.hi, a * v,lo, b * v.hi, b * v.lo));
}
dcheck(v)
        INTERVAL v;
{
        if (v.hi >= 0. && v.lo <= 0.)
        {
            (void) printf("divisor interval contains 0.\n");
            return (1);
        }
        return (0);
{

INTERVAL
vdiv(a, b, v)
        double a, b;
        INTERVAL v;
{
   return (hilo(a / v.hi, a / v,lo, b / v.hi, b / v.lo));
}
```

# CHAPTER 7: FILE AND RECORD LOCKING

## Introduction

Mandatory and advisory file and record locking both are available on current releases of the UNIX system. The intent of this capability to is provide a synchronization mechanism for programs accessing the same stores of data simultaneously. Such processing is characteristic of many multi-user applications, and the need for a standard method of dealing with the problem has been recognized by standards advocates like */usr/group*, an organization of UNIX system users from businesses and campuses across the country.

Advisory file and record locking can be used to coordinate self-synchronizing processes. In mandatory locking, the standard I/O subroutines and I/O system calls enforce the locking protocol. In this way, at the cost of a little efficiency, mandatory locking double checks the programs against accessing the data out of sequence.

The remainder of this chapter describes how file and record locking capabilities can be used. Examples are given for the correct use of record locking. Misconceptions about the amount of protection that record locking affords are dispelled. Record locking should be viewed as a synchronization mechanism, not a security mechanism.

The manual pages for the **fcntl**(2) system call, the **lockf**(3) library function, and **fcntl**(5) data structures and commands are referred to throughout this section. You should read them before continuing.

# Terminology

Before discussing how record locking should be used, let us first define a few terms.

Record

A contiguous set of bytes in a file. The UNIX operating system does not impose any record structure on files. This may be done by the programs that use the files.

Cooperating Processes

Processes that work together in some well defined fashion to accomplish the tasks at hand. Processes that share files must request permission to access the files before using them. File access permissions must be carefully set to restrict non-cooperating processes from accessing those files. The term process will be used interchangeably with cooperating process to refer to a task obeying such protocols.

Read (Share) Locks

These are used to gain limited access to sections of files. When a read lock is in place on a record, other processes may also read lock that record, in whole or in part. No other process, however, may have or obtain a write lock on an overlapping section of the file. If a process holds a read lock it may assume that no other process will be writing or updating that record at the same time. This access method also permits many processes to read the given record. This might be necessary when searching a file, without the contention involved if a write or exclusive lock were to be used.

Write (Exclusive) Locks

These are used to gain complete control over sections of files. When a write lock is in place on a record, no other process may read or write lock that record, in whole or in part. If a process holds a write lock it may assume that no other process will be reading or writing that record at the same time.

Advisory Locking

A form of record locking that does not interact with the I/O subsystem (i.e. **creat**(2), **open**(2), **read**(2), and **write**(2)). The control over records is accomplished by requiring an appropriate record lock request before I/O operations. If appropriate requests are always made by all processes accessing the file, then the accessibility of the file will be controlled by the interaction of these requests. Advisory locking depends on the individual processes to enforce the record locking protocol; it does not require an accessibility check at the time of each I/O request.

Mandatory Locking

A form of record locking that does interact with the I/O subsystem. Access to locked records is enforced by the **creat**(2), **open**(2), **read**(2), and **write**(2) system calls. If a record is locked, then access of that record by any other process is restricted according to the type of lock on the record. The control over records should still be performed explicitly by requesting an appropriate record lock before I/O operations, but an additional check is made by the system before each I/O operation to ensure the record locking protocol is being honored. Mandatory locking offers an extra synchronization check, but at the cost of some additional system overhead.

# File Protection

There are access permissions for UNIX system files to control who may read, write, or execute such a file. These access permissions may only be set by the owner of the file or by the superuser. The permissions of the directory in which the file resides can also affect the ultimate disposition of a file. Note that if the directory permissions allow anyone to write in it, then files within the directory may be removed, even if those files do not have read, write or execute permission for that user. Any information that is worth protecting, is worth protecting properly. If your application warrants the use of record locking, make sure that the permissions on your files and directories are set properly. A record lock, even a mandatory record lock, will only protect the portions of the files that are locked. Other parts of these files might be corrupted if proper precautions are not taken.

Only a known set of programs and/or administrators should be able to read or write a data base. This can be done easily by setting the set-group-ID bit (see **chmod**(1)) of the data base accessing programs. The files can then be accessed by a known set of programs that obey the record locking protocol. An example of such file protection, although record locking is not used, is the **mail**(1) command. In that command only the particular user and the **mail** command can read and write in the unread mail files.

## Opening a File for Record Locking

The first requirement for locking a file or segment of a file is having a valid open file descriptor. If read locks are to be done, then the file must be opened with at least read accessibility and likewise for write locks and write accessibility. For our example we will open our file for both read and write access:

```
#include <stdio.h>
#include <errno.h>
#include <fcntl.h>


int fd;  /* file descriptor */
char *filename;

main(argc, argv)
int argc;
char *argv[];
{
        extern void exit(), perror();

        /* get data base file name from command line and open the
         * file for read and write access.
         */
        if (argc < 2) {
        (void) fprintf(stderr, "usage: %s filename\n", argv[0]);
        exit(2);
        }
        filename = argv[1];
        fd = open(filename, O_RDWR);
        if (fd < 0) {
        perror(filename);
        exit(2);
        }
        .
        .
        .
```

The file is now open for us to perform both locking and I/O functions. We then proceed with the task of setting a lock.

## Setting a File Lock

There are several ways for us to set a lock on a file. In part, these methods depend upon how the lock interacts with the rest of the program. There are also questions of performance as well as portability. Two methods will be given here, one using the **fcntl**(2) system call, the other using the */usr/group* standards compatible **lockf**(3) library function call.

Locking an entire file is just a special case of record locking. For both these methods the concept and the effect of the lock are the same. The file is locked starting at a byte offset of zero (0) until the end of the maximum file size. This point extends beyond any real end of the file so that no lock can be placed on this file beyond this point. To do this the value of the size of the lock is set to zero. The code using the **fcntl**(2) system call is as follows:

```
#include <fcntl.h>
#define MAX_TRY 10
int try;
struct flock lck;

try = 0;

/* set up the record locking structure, the address of which
 * is passed to the fcntl system call.
 */
lck.l_type = F_WRLCK;/* setting a write lock */
lck.l_whence = 0;/* offset l_start from beginning of file */
lck.l_start = 0L;
lck.l_len = 0L;/* until the end of the file address space */

/* Attempt locking MAX_TRY times before giving up.
 */
while (fcntl(fd, F_SETLK, &lck) < 0) {
if (errno == EAGAIN || errno == EACCES) {
/* there might be other errors cases in which
 * you might try again.
 */
if (++try < MAX_TRY) {
(void) sleep(2);
continue;
}
(void) fprintf(stderr,"File busy try again later!\n");
return;
}
perror("fcntl");
exit(2);
}
.
.
.
```

This portion of code tries to lock a file. This is attempted several times until one of the following things happens:

- the file is locked

- an error occurs

- it gives up trying because MAX_TRY has been exceeded

To perform the same task using the **lockf**(3) function, the code is as follows:

```
#include <unistd.h>
#define MAX_TRY 10
int try;
try = 0;

/* make sure the file pointer
 * is at the beginning of the file.
 */
lseek(fd, 0L, 0);

/* Attempt locking MAX_TRY times before giving up.
 */
while (lockf(fd, F_TLOCK, 0L) < 0) {
if (errno == EAGAIN || errno == EACCES) {
/* there might be other errors cases in which
 * you might try again.
 */
if (++try < MAX_TRY) {
sleep(2);
continue;
}
(void) fprintf(stderr,"File busy try again later!\n");
return;
}
perror("lockf");
exit(2);
}
    .
    .
    .
```

It should be noted that the **lockf**(3) example appears to be simpler, but the **fcntl**(2) example exhibits additional flexibility. Using the **fcntl**(2) method, it is possible to set the type and start of the lock request simply by setting a few structure variables. **lockf**(3) merely sets write (exclusive) locks; an additional system call (**lseek**(2)) is required to specify the start of the lock.

## Setting and Removing Record Locks

Locking a record is done the same way as locking a file except for the differing starting point and length of the lock. We will now try to solve an interesting and real problem. There are two records (these records may be in the same or different file) that must be updated simultaneously so that other processes get a consistent view of this information. (This type of problem comes up, for example, when updating the interrecord pointers in a doubly linked list.) To do this you must decide the following questions:

- What do you want to lock?

- For multiple locks, what order do you want to lock and unlock the records?

- What do you do if you succeed in getting all the required locks?

- What do you do if you fail to get all the locks?

In managing record locks, you must plan a failure strategy if one cannot obtain all the required locks. It is because of contention for these records that we have decided to use record locking in the first place. Different programs might:

- wait a certain amount of time, and try again

- abort the procedure and warn the user

- let the process sleep until signaled that the lock has been freed

- some combination of the above

Let us now look at our example of inserting an entry into a doubly linked list. For the example, we will assume that the record after which the new record is to be inserted has a read lock on it already. The lock on this record must be changed or promoted to a write lock so that the record may be edited.

Promoting a lock (generally from read lock to write lock) is permitted if no other process is holding a read lock in the same section of the file. If there are processes with pending write locks that are sleeping on the same section of the file, the lock promotion succeeds and the other (sleeping) locks wait. Promoting (or demoting) a write lock to a read lock carries no restrictions. In either case, the lock is merely reset with the new lock type. Because the */usr/group* **lockf** function does not have read locks, lock promotion is not applicable to that call. An example of record locking with lock promotion follows:

```
struct record {
        .
        ./* data portion of record */
        .
        long prev;/* index to previous record in the list */
        long next;/* index to next record in the list */
};

/* Lock promotion using fcntl(2)
 * When this routine is entered it is assumed that there are read
 * locks on "here" and "next".
 * If write locks on "here" and "next" are obtained:
 *     Set a write lock on "this".
 *     Return index to "this" record.
 * If any write lock is not obtained:
 *     Restore read locks on "here" and "next".
 *     Remove all other locks.
 *     Return a -1.
 */
long
set3lock (this, here, next)
long this, here, next;
{
        struct flock lck;

        lck.l_type = F_WRLCK;/* setting a write lock */
        lck.l_whence = 0;/* offset l_start from beginning of file */
        lck.l_start = here;
        lck.l_len = sizeof(struct record);

        /* promote lock on "here" to write lock */
        if (fcntl(fd, F_SETLKW, &lck) < 0) {
        return (-1);
        }
```

*continued*

```
            /* lock "this" with write lock */
            lck.l_start = this;
            if (fcntl(fd, F_SETLKW, &lck) < 0) {
            /* Lock on "this" failed;
             * demote lock on "here" to read lock.
             */
            lck.l_type = F_RDLCK;
            lck.l_start = here;
            (void) fcntl(fd, F_SETLKW, &lck);
            return (-1);
            }
            /* promote lock on "next" to write lock */
            lck.l_start = next;
            if (fcntl(fd, F_SETLKW, &lck) < 0) {
            /* Lock on "next" failed;
             * demote lock on "here" to read lock,
             */
            lck.l_type = F_RDLCK;
            lck.l_start = here;
            (void) fcntl(fd, F_SETLK, &lck);
            /* and remove lock on "this".
             */
            lck.l_type = F_UNLCK;
            lck.l_start = this;
            (void) fcntl(fd, F_SETLK, &lck);
            return (-1);/* cannot set lock, try again or quit */
            }

            return (this);
        }
```

The locks on these three records were all set to wait (sleep) if another process was blocking them from being set. This was done with the F_SETLKW command. If the F_SETLK command was used instead, the **fcntl** system calls would fail if blocked. The program would then have to be changed to handle the blocked condition in each of the error return sections.

Let us now look at a similar example using the **lockf** function. Since there are no read locks, all (write) locks will be referenced generically as locks.

```
/* Lock promotion using lockf(3)
 * When this routine is entered it is assumed that there are
 * no locks on "here" and "next".
 * If locks are obtained:
 *     Set a lock on "this".
 *     Return index to "this" record.
 * If any lock is not obtained:
 *     Remove all other locks.
 *     Return a -1.
 */

#include <unistd.h>

long
set3lock (this, here, next)
long this, here, next;

{

        /* lock "here" */
        (void) lseek(fd, here, 0);
        if (lockf(fd, F_LOCK, sizeof(struct record)) < 0) {
        return (-1);
        }
        /* lock "this" */
        (void) lseek(fd, this, 0);
        if (lockf(fd, F_LOCK, sizeof(struct record)) < 0) {
        /* Lock on "this" failed.
         * Clear lock on "here".
         */
        (void) lseek(fd, here, 0);
        (void) lockf(fd, F_ULOCK, sizeof(struct record));
        return (-1);

        }

        /* lock "next" */
        (void) lseek(fd, next, 0);
        if (lockf(fd, F_LOCK, sizeof(struct record)) < 0) {

        /* Lock on "next" failed.
```

*continued*

```
     * Clear lock on "here",
     */
    (void) lseek(fd, here, 0);
    (void) lockf(fd, F_ULOCK, sizeof(struct record));

    /* and remove lock on "this".
     */
    (void) lseek(fd, this, 0);
    (void) lockf(fd, F_ULOCK, sizeof(struct record));
    return (-1);/* cannot set lock, try again or quit */

    }

    return (this);
}
```

Locks are removed in the same manner as they are set, only the lock type is different (F_UNLCK or F_ULOCK). An unlock cannot be blocked by another process and will only affect locks that were placed by this process. The unlock only affects the section of the file defined in the previous example by **lck**. It is possible to unlock or change the type of lock on a subsection of a previously set lock. This may cause an additional lock (two locks for one system call) to be used by the operating system. This occurs if the subsection is from the middle of the previously set lock.

## Getting Lock Information

One can determine which processes, if any, are blocking a lock from being set. This can be used as a simple test or as a means to find locks on a file. A lock is set up as in the previous examples and the F_GETLK command is used in the **fcntl** call. If the lock passed to **fcntl** would be blocked, the first blocking lock is returned to the process through the structure passed to **fcntl**. That is, the lock data passed to **fcntl** is overwritten by blocking lock information. This information includes two pieces of data that have not been discussed yet, **l_pid** and **l_sysid**, that are only used by F_GETLK. (For systems that do not support a distributed architecture the value in **l_sysid** should be ignored.) These fields uniquely identify the process holding the lock.

If a lock passed to **fcntl** using the F_GETLK command would not be blocked by another process' lock, then the **l_type** field is changed to F_UNLCK and the remaining fields in the structure are unaffected. Let us use this capability to print all the segments locked by other processes. Note that if there are several read locks over the same segment only one of these will be found.

```
struct flock lck;

/* Find and print "write lock" blocked segments of this file. */
        (void) printf("sysid    pid type     start    length\n");
        lck.l_whence = 0;
        lck.l_start = 0L;
        lck.l_len = 0L;
        do {
        lck.l_type = F_WRLCK;
        (void) fcntl(fd, F_GETLK, &lck);
        if (lck.l_type != F_UNLCK) {
        (void) printf("%5d %5d    %c   %8d %8d\n",
        lck.l_sysid,
        lck.l_pid,
        (lck.l_type == F_WRLCK) ? 'W' : 'R',
        lck.l_start,
        lck.l_len);
        /* if this lock goes to the end of the address
         * space, no need to look further, so break out.
         */
        if (lck.l_len == 0)
        break;
        /* otherwise, look for new lock after the one
         * just found.
         */
        lck.l_start += lck.l_len;
        }
        } while (lck.l_type != F_UNLCK);
```

**fcntl** with the F_GETLK command will always return correctly (that is, it will not sleep or fail) if the values passed to it as arguments are valid.

The **lockf** function with the F_TEST command can also be used to test if there is a process blocking a lock. This function does not, however, return the information about where the lock actually is and which process owns the lock. A routine using **lockf** to test for a lock on a file follows:

```
/* find a blocked record. */

/* seek to beginning of file */
(void) lseek(fd, 0, 0L);
/* set the size of the test region to zero (0)
 * to test until the end of the file address space.
 */
if (lockf(fd, F_TEST, 0L) < 0) {
switch (errno) {
case EACCES:
case EAGAIN:
(void) printf("file is locked by another process\n");
break;
case EBADF:
/* bad argument passed to lockf */
perror("lockf");
break;
default:
(void) printf("lockf: unknown error <%d>\n", errno);
break;
}
}
```

When a process forks, the child receives a copy of the file descriptors that the parent has opened. The parent and child also share a common file pointer for each file. If the parent were to seek to a point in the file, the child's file pointer would also be at that location. This feature has important implications when using record locking. The current value of the file pointer is used as the reference for the offset of the beginning of the lock, as described by **l_start**, when using a **l_whence** value of 1. If both the parent and child process set locks on the same file, there is a possibility that a lock will be set using a file pointer that was reset by the other process. This problem appears in the **lockf**(3) function call as well and is a result of the */usr/group* requirements for record locking. If forking is used in a record locking program, the child process should close and reopen the file if either locking method is used. This will result in the creation of a new and separate file pointer that can be manipulated without this problem occurring. Another solution is to use the **fcntl** system call with a **l_whence** value of 0 or 2. This makes the locking function atomic, so that even processes sharing file pointers can be locked without difficulty.

## Deadlock Handling

There is a certain level of deadlock detection/avoidance built into the record locking facility. This deadlock handling provides the same level of protection granted by the */usr/group* standard **lockf** call. This deadlock detection is only valid for processes that are locking files or records on a single system. Deadlocks can only potentially occur when the system is about to put a record locking system call to sleep. A search is made for constraint loops of processes that would cause the system call to sleep indefinitely. If such a situation is found, the locking system call will fail and set **errno** to the deadlock error number. If a process wishes to avoid the use of the systems deadlock detection it should set its locks using F_GETLK instead of F_GETLKW.

# Selecting Advisory or Mandatory Locking

The use of mandatory locking is not recommended for reasons that will be made clear in a subsequent section. Whether or not locks are enforced by the I/O system calls is determined at the time the calls are made and the state of the permissions on the file (see **chmod**(2)). For locks to be under mandatory enforcement, the file must be a regular file with the set-group-ID bit on and the group execute permission off. If either condition fails, all record locks are advisory. Mandatory enforcement can be assured by the following code:

```
#include <sys/types.h>
#include <sys/stat.h>

int mode;
struct stat buf;
        .
        .
        .
        if (stat(filename, &buf) < 0) {
        perror("program");
        exit (2);
        }
        /* get currently set mode */
        mode = buf.st_mode;
        /* remove group execute permission from mode */
        mode &= ~(S_IEXEC>>3);
        /* set 'set group id bit' in mode */
        mode |= S_ISGID;
        if (chmod(filename, mode) < 0) {
        perror("program");
        exit(2);
        }
        .
        .
        .
```

Files that are to be record locked should never have any type of execute permission set on them. This is because the operating system does not obey the record locking protocol when executing a file.

The **chmod**(1) command can also be easily used to set a file to have mandatory locking. This can be done with the command:

   **chmod +l** *filename*

The **ls**(1) command was also changed to show this setting when you ask for the long listing format:

   **ls -l** *filename*

causes the following to be printed:

```
-rw---l---   1 abc      other     1048576 Dec  3 11:44 filename
```


# Caveat Emptor—Mandatory Locking

- Mandatory locking only protects those portions of a file that are locked. Other portions of the file that are not locked may be accessed according to normal UNIX system file permissions.

- If multiple reads or writes are necessary for an atomic transaction, the process should explicitly lock all such pieces before any I/O begins. Thus advisory enforcement is sufficient for all programs that perform in this way.

- As stated earlier, arbitrary programs should not have unrestricted access permission to files that are important enough to record lock.

- Advisory locking is more efficient because a record lock check does not have to be performed for every I/O request.

# Record Locking and Future Releases of the UNIX System

Provisions have been made for file and record locking in a UNIX system environment. In such an environment the system on which the locking process resides may be remote from the system on which the file and record locks reside. In this way multiple processes on different systems may put locks upon a single file that resides on one of these or yet another system. The record locks for a file reside on the system that maintains the file. It is also important to note that deadlock detection/avoidance is only determined by the record locks being held by and for a single system. Therefore, it is necessary that a process only hold record locks on a single system at any given time for the deadlock mechanism to be effective. If a process needs to maintain locks over several systems, it is suggested that the process avoid the **sleep-when-blocked** features of **fcntl** or **lockf** and that the process maintain its own deadlock detection. If the process uses the **sleep-when-blocked** feature, then a timeout mechanism should be provided by the process so that it does not hang waiting for a lock to be cleared.

# CHAPTER 8: SHARED LIBRARIES

## Introduction

With the UNIX system running on smaller machines, such as the AT&T 3B2 Computer, efficient use of disk storage space, memory, and computer power is becoming increasingly important. A shared library can offer savings in all three areas. For example, if constructed properly, a shared library can make **a.out** files (executable object files) smaller on disk storage and processes (**a.out** files that are executing) smaller in memory.

The first part of this chapter, "Using a Shared Library," is designed to help you use UNIX System V shared libraries. It describes what a shared library is and how to use one to build **a.out** files. It also offers advice about when and when not to use a shared library and how to determine whether an **a.out** uses a shared library.

The second part in this chapter, "Building a Shared Library," describes how to build a shared library. You do not need to read this part to use shared libraries. It addresses library developers, advanced programmers who are expected to build their own shared libraries. Specifically, this part describes how to use the UNIX system tool **mkshlib**(1) (documented in the *Programmer's Reference Manual*) and how to write C code for shared libraries on a UNIX system. An example is included. Read this part of the chapter only if you have to build a shared library.

 NOTE    Shared libraries are a new feature of UNIX System V Release 3.0. An executable object file that needs shared libraries will not run on previous releases of UNIX System V.

# Using a Shared Library

If you are accustomed to using libraries to build your applications programs, shared libraries should blend into your work easily. This part of the
chapter explains what shared libraries are and how and when to use them on
the UNIX system.

## What is a Shared Library?

A shared library is a file containing object code that several **a.out** files may
use simultaneously while executing. A shared library, like a library that is not
shared, is an archive file. For simplicity, however, we refer to an archive file
with shared library members as a shared library and one without as an
archive library.

When a program is compiled or link edited with a shared library, the
library code that defines the program's external references is not copied into
the program's object file. Instead, a special section called **.lib** that identifies
the library code is created in the object file. When the UNIX system executes
the resulting **a.out** file, it uses the information in this section to bring the
required shared library code into the address space of the process.

A shared library offers several benefits by not copying code into **a.out**
files. It can

- save disk storage space

  Because shared library code is not copied into all the **a.out** files that use
  the code, these files are smaller and use less disk space.

- save memory

  By sharing library code at run time, the dynamic memory needs of
  processes are reduced.

- make executable files using library code easier to maintain

  As mentioned above, shared library code is brought into a process'
  address space at run time. Updating a shared library effectively
  updates all executable files that use the library, because the operating
  system brings the updated version into new processes. If an error in
  shared library code is fixed, all processes automatically use the
  corrected code.

Archive libraries cannot, of course, offer this benefit: changes to archive libraries do not affect executable files, because code from the libraries is copied to the files during link editing, not during execution.

"Deciding Whether to Use a Shared Library" in this chapter describes shared libraries in more detail.

## The UNIX System Shared Libraries

AT&T provides the C shared library with UNIX System V Release 3.0, and later releases; the networking library included with the Networking Support Utilities is also a shared library. Other shared libraries may be available now from software vendors and in the future from AT&T.

These libraries, like all shared libraries, are made up of two files called the host library and the target library. The host library is the file that the link editor searches when linking programs to create the **.lib** sections in **a.out** files; the target library is the file that the UNIX system uses when running those files. Naturally, the target library must be present for the **a.out** file to run.

| Shared Library | Host Library Command Line Option | Target Library Path Name |
|---|---|---|
| C Library | −lc_s | /shlib/libc_s |
| Networking Library | −lnsl_s | /shlib/libnsl_s |

Notice the _s suffix on the library names; we use it to identify both host and target shared libraries. For example, it distinguishes the standard relocatable C library **libc** from the shared C library **libc_s**. The _s also indicates that the libraries are statically linked.

The relocatable C library is still available on the UNIX system; this library is searched by default during the compilation or link editing of C programs. All other archive libraries from previous releases of the system are also available. Just as you use the archive libraries' names, you must use a shared library's name when you want to use it to build your **a.out** files. You tell the link editor its name with the −l option, as shown below.

## Building an a.out File

You direct the link editor to search a shared library the same way you direct a search of an archive library on the UNIX system:

> **cc**  *file*.**c**  **−o** *file*  ...  **−l***library_file*  ...

To direct a search of the networking library, for example, you use the following command line.

> **cc**  *file*.**c**  **−o** *file*  ...  **−lnsl_s**  ...

And to link all the files in your current directory together with the shared C library you'd use the following command line:

> **cc**  **\*.c**  **−lc_s**

Normally, you should include the **−lc_s** argument after all other **−l** arguments on a command line. The shared C library will then be treated like the relocatable C library, which is searched by default after all other libraries specified on a command line are searched.


## Coding an Application

Application source code in C or assembly language is compatible with both archive libraries and shared libraries. As a result, you should not have to change the code in any applications you already have when you use a shared library with them. When coding a new application for use with a shared library, you should just observe your standard coding conventions.

However, do keep the following two points in mind, which apply when using either an archive or a shared library:

- Don't define symbols in your application with the same names as those in a library.

  Although there are exceptions, you should avoid redefining standard library routines, such as **printf**(3S) and **strcmp**(3C). Replacements that are incompatibly defined can cause any library, shared or unshared, to behave incorrectly.

- Don't use undocumented archive routines.

  Use only the functions and data mentioned on the manual pages describing the routines in Section 3 of the *Programmer's Reference Manual*. For example, don't try to outsmart the **ctype** design by manipulating the underlying implementation.

## Deciding Whether to Use a Shared Library

You should base your decision to use a shared library on whether it saves space in disk storage and memory for your program. A well-designed shared library almost always saves space. So, as a general rule, use a shared library when it is available.

To determine what savings are gained from using a shared library, you might build the same application with both an archive and a shared library, assuming both kinds of library are available. Remember, that you may do this because source code is compatible between shared libraries and archive libraries. (See the above section "Coding an Application.") Then compare the two versions of the application for size and performance. For example,

```
$ cat hello.c
main( )
{
    printf("Hello\n");
}
$ cc -o unshared hello.c
$ cc -o shared hello.c -lc_s
$ size unshared shared
unshared: 8680 + 1388 + 2248 = 12316
shared: 300 + 680 + 2248 = 3228
```

If the application calls only a few library members, it is possible that using a shared library could take more disk storage or memory. The following section gives a more detailed discussion about when a shared library does and does not save space.

When making your decision about using shared libraries, also remember that they are not available on UNIX System V releases prior to Release 3.0. If your program must run on previous releases, you will need to use archive libraries.

# More About Saving Space

This section is designed to help you better understand why your programs will usually benefit from using a shared library. It explains

- how shared libraries save space that archive libraries cannot

- how shared libraries are implemented on the UNIX system

- how shared libraries might increase space usage

## How Shared Libraries Save Space

To better understand how a shared library saves space, we need to compare it to an archive library.

A host shared library resembles an archive library in three ways. First, as noted earlier, both are archive files. Second, the object code in the library typically defines commonly used text symbols and data symbols. The symbols defined inside and made available outside the library are called exported symbols. Note that the library may also have imported symbols, symbols that it uses but usually does not define. Third, the link editor searches the library for these symbols when linking a program to resolve its external references. By resolving the references, the link editor produces an executable version of the program, the **a.out** file.

 NOTE Note that the link editor on the UNIX system is a static linking tool; static linking requires that all symbolic references in a program be resolved before the program may be executed. The link editor uses static linking with both an archive library and a shared library.

Although these similarities exist, a shared library differs significantly from an archive library. The major differences relate to how the libraries are handled to resolve symbolic references, a topic already discussed briefly.

Consider how the UNIX system handles both types of libraries during link editing. To produce an **a.out** file using an archive library, the link editor copies the library code that defines a program's unresolved external reference from the library into appropriate **.text** and **.data** sections in the program's object file. In contrast, to produce an **a.out** file using a shared library, the link editor does not copy any code from the library into the program's object file. Instead, it creates a special section called **.lib** in the file that identifies the library code needed at run time and resolves the external references to shared library symbols with their correct values. When the UNIX system executes the resulting **a.out** file, it uses the information in the **.lib** section to bring the required shared library code into the address space of the process.

Figure 8-1 depicts the **a.out** files produced using a regular archive version and a shared version of the standard C library to compile the following program:

```
main()
{
    ...
    printf( "How do you like this manual?\n" );
    ...
    result = strcmp( "I do.", answer );
    ...
}
```

Notice that the shared version is smaller. Figure 8-2 depicts the process images in memory of these two files when they are executed.

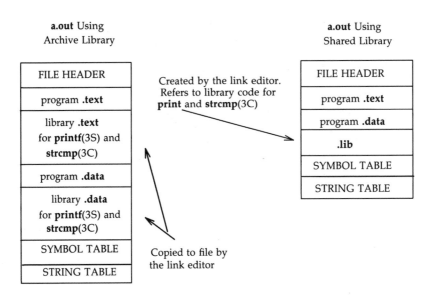

Figure 8-1: **a.out** Files Created Using an Archive Library and a Shared Library

Now consider what happens when several **a.out** files need the same code from a library. When using an archive library, each file gets its own copy of the code. This results in duplication of the same code on the disk and in memory when the **a.out** files are run as processes. In contrast, when a shared library is used, the library code remains separate from the code in the **a.out** files, as indicated in Figure 8-2. This separation enables all processes using the same shared library to reference a single copy of the code.

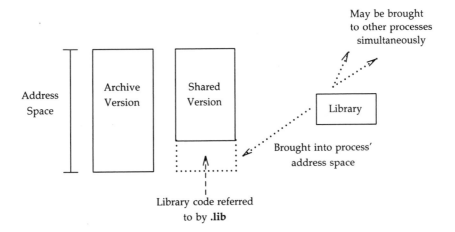

Figure 8-2: Processes Using an Archive and a Shared Library

## How Shared Libraries Are Implemented

Now that you have a better understanding of how shared libraries save space, you need to consider their implementation on the UNIX system to understand how they might increase space usage (this happens seldomly).

### The Host Library and Target Library

As previously mentioned, every shared library has two parts: the host library used for linking that resides on the host machine and the target library used for execution that resides on the target machine. The host machine is the machine on which you build an **a.out** file; the target machine is the machine on which you run the file. Of course, the host and target may be the same machine, but they don't have to be.

The host library is just like an archive library. Each of its members (typically a complete object file) defines some text and data symbols in its symbol table. The link editor searches this file when a shared library is used during the compilation or link editing of a program.

The search is for definitions of symbols referenced in the program but not defined there. However, as mentioned earlier, the link editor does not copy the library code defining the symbols into the program's object file. Instead, it uses the library members to locate the definitions and then places symbols in the file that tell where the library code is. The result is the special section in the **a.out** file mentioned earlier (see the section "What is a Shared Library?") and shown in Figure 8-1 as **.lib**.

The target library used for execution resembles an **a.out** file. The UNIX operating system reads this file during execution if a process needs a shared library. The special **.lib** section in the **a.out** file tells which shared libraries are needed. When the UNIX system executes the **a.out** file, it uses this section to bring the appropriate library code into the address space of the process. In this way, before the process starts to run, all required library code has been made available.

Shared libraries enable the sharing of **.text** sections in the target library, which is where text symbols are defined. Although processes that use the shared library have their own virtual address spaces, they share a single physical copy of the library's text among them. That is, the UNIX system uses the same physical code for each process that attaches a shared library's text.

The target library cannot share its **.data** sections. Each process using data from the library has its own private data region (contiguous area of virtual address space that mirrors the **.data** section of the target library). Processes that share text do not share data and stack area so that they do not interfere with one another.

As suggested above, the target library is a lot like an **a.out** file, which can also share its text, but not its data. Also, a process must have execute permission for a target library to execute an **a.out** file that uses the library.

### The Branch Table

When the link editor resolves an external reference in a program, it gets the address of the referenced symbol from the host library. This is because a static linking loader like **ld** binds symbols to addresses during link editing. In this way, the **a.out** file for the program has an address for each referenced symbol.

What happens if library code is updated and the address of a symbol changes? Nothing happens to an **a.out** file built with an archive library, because that file already has a copy of the code defining the symbol. (Even though it isn't the updated copy, the **a.out** file will still run.) However, the change can adversely affect an **a.out** file built with a shared library. This file has only a symbol telling where the required library code is. If the library code were updated, the location of that code might change. Therefore, if the **a.out** file ran after the change took place, the operating system could bring in the wrong code. To keep the **a.out** file current, you might have to recompile a program that uses a shared library after each library update.

To prevent the need to recompile, a shared library is implemented with a branch table on the UNIX system. A branch table associates text symbols with an absolute address that does not change even when library code is changed. Each address labels a jump instruction to the address of the code that defines a symbol. Instead of being directly associated with the addresses of code, text symbols have addresses in the branch table.

Figure 8-3 shows two **a.out** files executing that make a call to **printf**(3S). The process on the left was built using an archive library. It already has a copy of the library code defining the **printf**(3S) symbol. The process on the right was built using a shared library. This file references an absolute address (10) in the branch table of the shared library at run time; at this address, a jump instruction references the needed code.

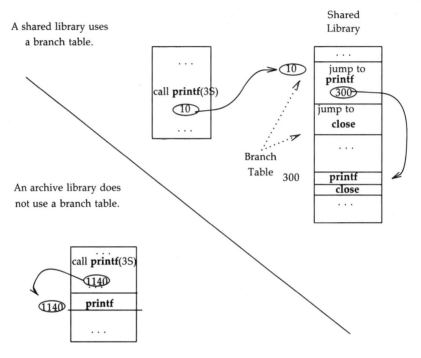

Figure 8-3: A Branch Table in a Shared Library

## How Shared Libraries Might Increase Space Usage

A host library might add space to an **a.out** file. Recall that UNIX System V Release 3.0 uses static linking, which requires that all external references in a program be resolved before it is executed. Also recall that a shared library may have imported symbols, which are used but not defined by the library. These symbols might introduce unresolved references during the linking process. To resolve these references, the link editor has to add the **.text** and **.data** sections defining the referenced imported symbols to the **a.out** file. These sections increase the size of the **a.out** file.

A target library might also add space to a process. Again recall from "How Shared Libraries are Implemented" in this chapter that a shared library's target file may have both text and data regions connected to a process. While the text region is shared by all processes that use the library, the data region is not. Every process that uses the library gets its own private copy of the entire library data region. Naturally, this region adds to the process's memory requirements. As a result, if an application uses only a small part of a shared library's text and data, executing the application might require more memory with a shared library than without one. For example, it would be unwise to use the shared C library to access only **strcmp**(3C). Although sharing **strcmp**(3C) saves disk storage and memory, the memory cost for sharing all the shared C library's private data region outweighs the savings. The archive version of the library would be more appropriate.

## Identifying a.out Files that Use Shared Libraries

Suppose you have an executable file and you want to know whether it uses a shared library. You can use the **dump**(1) command (documented in the *Programmer's Reference Manual*) to look at the section headers for the file:

    **dump**  −**hv**  **a.out**

If the file has a **.lib** section, a shared library is needed. If the **a.out** does not have a **.lib** section, it does not use shared libraries.

With a little more work, you can even tell what libraries a file uses by looking at the **.lib** section contents.

    **dump**  −**L**  **a.out**

## Debugging a.out Files that Use Shared Libraries

Debugging support for shared libraries is currently limited. Shared library data are not dumped to core files, and **sdb**(1) (documented in the *Programmer's Reference Manual*) does not read shared libraries' symbol tables. If you encounter an error that appears not to be in your application code, you may find debugging easier if you rebuild the application with the archive version of the library used.

# Building a Shared Library

This part of the chapter explains how to build a shared library. It covers the major steps to the building process, the use of the UNIX system tool **mkshlib**(1) which builds the host and target libraries, and some guidelines for writing shared library code.

This part assumes that you are an advanced C programmer faced with the task of building a shared library. It also assumes you are familiar with the archive library building process. You do not need to read this part of the chapter if you only plan to use the UNIX system shared libraries or other shared libraries that have already been built.

## The Building Process

To build a shared library on the UNIX system, you have to complete six major tasks:

- Choose region addresses.
- Choose the path name for the shared library target file.
- Select the library contents.
- Rewrite existing library code to be included in the shared library.
- Write the library specification file.
- Use the **mkshlib** tool to build the host and target libraries.

Here each of these tasks is discussed.

### Step 1: Choosing Region Addresses

The first thing you need to do is choose region addresses for your shared library.

Shared library regions on the AT&T 3B2 Computer correspond to memory management unit (MMU) segment size, each of which is 128 KB. The following table gives a list of the segment assignments on the 3B2 Computer (as of the copyright date for this guide) and shows what virtual addresses are available for libraries you might build.

| Start Address | Contents | Target Path Name |
|---|---|---|
| 0x80000000 | Reserved for AT&T | |
| ... | UNIX Shared C Library | /shlib/libc_s |
| | AT&T Networking Library | /shlib/libnsl_s |
| 0x803E0000 | | |
| 0x80400000 | Generic Database Library | Unassigned |
| 0x80420000 | | |
| 0x80440000 | Generic Statistical Library | Unassigned |
| 0x80460000 | | |
| 0x80480000 | Generic User Interface Library | Unassigned |
| 0x804A0000 | | |
| 0x804C0000 | Generic Screen Handling Library | Unassigned |
| 0x804E0000 | | |
| 0x80500000 | Generic Graphics Library | Unassigned |
| 0x80520000 | | |
| 0x80540000 | Generic Networking Library | Unassigned |
| 0x80560000 | | |
| 0x80580000 | Generic − to be defined | Unassigned |
| ... | | |
| 0x80660000 | | |
| 0x80680000 | For private use | Unassigned |
| ... | | |
| 0x807E0000 | | |

What does this table tell you? First, the AT&T shared C library and the networking library reside at the path names given above and use addresses in the range reserved for AT&T. If you build a shared library that uses reserved addresses you run the risk of conflicting with future AT&T products.

Second, a number of segments are allocated for shared libraries that provide various services such as graphics, database access, and so on. These categories are intended to reduce the chance of address conflicts among commercially available libraries. Although two libraries of the same type may conflict, that doesn't matter. A single process should not usually need to use two shared libraries of the same type. If the need arises, a program can use one shared library and one archive library.

Any number of libraries can use the same virtual addresses, even on the same machine. Conflicts occur only within a single process, not among separate processes. Thus two shared libraries can have the same region addresses without causing problems, as long as a single **a.out** file doesn't need to use both libraries.

Third, several segments are reserved for private use. If you are building a large system with many **a.out** files and processes, shared libraries might improve its performance. As long as you don't intend to release the shared libraries as separate products, you should use the private region addresses. You can put your shared libraries into these segments and avoid conflicting with commercial shared libraries. You should also use the private areas when you will own all the **a.out** files that access your shared library. Don't risk address conflicts.

If you plan to build a commercial shared library, you are strongly encouraged to provide a compatible, relocatable archive as well. Some of your customers might not find the shared library appropriate for their applications. Others might want their applications to run on versions of the UNIX system without shared library support.

## Step 2: Choosing the Target Library Path Name

After you choose the region addresses for your shared library, you should choose the path name for the target library. We chose **/shlib/libc_s** for the shared C library and **/shlib/libnsl_s** for the networking library. (As mentioned earlier, we use the _s suffix in the path names of all statically linked shared libraries.) To choose a path name for your shared library, consult the established list of names for your computer or see your system administrator. Also keep in mind that shared libraries needed to boot a UNIX system should normally be located in **/shlib**; other application libraries normally reside in **/usr/lib** or in private application directories. Of course, if your shared library is for personal use, you can choose any convenient path name for the target library.

## Step 3: Selecting Library Contents

Selecting the contents for your shared library is the most important task in the building process. Some routines are prime candidates for sharing; others are not. For example, it's a good idea to include large, frequently used routines in a shared library but to exclude smaller routines that aren't used as much. What you include will depend on the individual needs of the programmers and other users for whom you are building the library. There are some general guidelines you should follow, however. They are discussed in the section "Choosing Library Members" in this chapter. Also see the guidelines in the following sections "Importing Symbols" and "Tuning the Shared Library Code."

## Step 4: Rewriting Existing Library Code

If you choose to include some existing code from an archive library in a shared library, changing some of the code will make the shared code easier to maintain. See the section "Changing Existing Code for the Shared Library" in this chapter.

## Step 5: Writing the Library Specification File

After you select and edit all the code for your shared library, you have to build the shared library specification file. The library specification file contains all the information that **mkshlib** needs to build both the host and target libraries. An example specification file is shown in the next section, "An Example." The contents and format of the specification file are given by the following directives (see also the **mkshlib**(1) manual page):

**#address** *sectname address*

Specifies the start address, *address*, of section *sectname* for the target file. This directive is typically used to specify the start addresses of the **.text** and **.data** sections.

**#target** *pathname*

Specifies the path name, *pathname*, of the target shared library on the target machine. This is the location where the operating system looks for the shared library during execution. Normally, *pathname* will be an absolute path name, but it does not have to be.

This directive can be specified only once per shared library specification file.

**#branch**

Starts the branch table specifications. The lines following this directive are taken to be branch table specification lines.

Branch table specification lines have the following format:

*funcname* <white space> *position*

*funcname* is the name of the symbol given a branch table entry and *position* specifies the position of *funcname's* branch table entry. *position* may be a single integer or a range of integers of the form *position1-position2*. Each *position* must be greater than or equal to one. The same position cannot be specified more than once, and every position from one to the highest given position must be accounted for.

If a symbol is given more than one branch table entry by associating a range of positions with the symbol or by specifying the same symbol on more than one branch table specification line, then the symbol is defined to have the address of the highest associated branch table entry. All other branch table entries for the symbol can be thought of as empty slots and can be replaced by new entries in future versions of the shared library.

Finally, only functions should be given branch table entries, and those functions must be external.

This directive can be specified only once per shared library specification file.

**#objects**

Specifies the names of the object files constituting the target shared library. The lines following this directive are taken to be the list of input object files in the order they are to be loaded into the target. The list simply consists of each filename followed by white space. This list of objects will be used to build the shared library.

This directive can be specified only once per shared library specification file.

**#init** *object*      Specifies that the object file, *object*, requires initialization code. The lines following this directive are taken to be initialization specification lines.

Initialization specification lines have the following format:

*pimport* <white space> *import*

*pimport* is a pointer to the associated imported symbol, *import*, and must be defined in the current specified object file, *object*. The initialization code generated for each line resembles the C assignment statement:

*pimport* = &*import*;

The assignments set the pointers to default values. All initializations for a particular object file must be given at once and multiple specifications of the same object file are not allowed.

**#ident** *"string"*  *Specifies a string, string, to be included in the* **.comment** *section of the target shared library and the* **.comment** *sections of every member of the host shared library. Only one* **#ident** *directive is permitted per shared library specification file.*

**##**          Specifies a comment. The rest of the line is ignored.

All directives that are followed by multi-line specifications are valid until the next directive or the end of file.

## Step 6: Using mkshlib to Build the Host and Target

The UNIX system command **mkshlib**(1) builds both the host and target libraries. **mkshlib** invokes other tools such as the assembler, **as**(1), and link editor, **ld**(1). Tools are invoked through the use of **execvp** (see **exec**(2)) which searches directories in a user's $PATH environment variable. Also, prefixes to **mkshlib** are parsed in much the same manner as prefixes to the **cc**(1) command and invoked tools are given the prefix, where appropriate. For example, **3b2mkshlib** invokes **3b2ld**. These commands all are documented in the *Programmer's Reference Manual*.

The user input to **mkshlib** consists of the library specification file and command line options. We just discussed the specification file; let's take a look at the options now. The shared library build tool has the following syntax:

**mkshlib** −**s** *specfil* −**t** *target* [−**h** *host*] [−**n**] [−**q**]

−**s** *specfil*    Specifies the shared library specification file, *specfil*. This file contains all the information necessary to build a shared library, as described in Step 5. Its contents include the branch table specifications for the target, the path name in which the target should be installed, the start addresses of text and data for the target, the initialization specifications for the host, and the list of object files to be included in the shared library.

−**t** *target*    Specifies the name, *target*, of the target shared library produced on the host machine. When *target* is moved to the target machine, it should be installed at the location given in the specification file (see the **#target** directive in the section "Writing the Library Specification File"). If the −**n** option is given, then a new target shared library will not be generated.

−**h** *host*    Specifies the name of the host shared library, *host*. If this option is not given, then the host shared library will not be produced.

−**n**    Prevents a new target shared library from being generated. This option is useful when producing only a new host shared library. The −**t** option must still be supplied since a version of the target shared library is needed to build the host shared library.

−**q**    Suppresses the printing of certain warning messages.

## An Example

Follow each of the steps in the library building process to build a small example shared library. While building this library, appropriate guidelines will be displayed amidst text. Note that the example code is contrived to show samples of problem areas, not to do anything useful.

The name of our library will be **libexam**. Assume the original code was a single source file, as shown below.

```
/* Original exam.c */

#include <stdio.h>

extern int      strlen();
extern char     *malloc(), *strcpy();

int     count   = 0;
char    *Error;

char *
excopy(e)
        char    *e;
{
        char    *new;

        ++count;
        if ( (new = malloc(strlen(e)+1)) == 0 )
        {
                Error = "no memory";
                return 0;
        }
        return strcpy(new, e);
}

excount()
{
        fprintf(stderr, "excount %d\n", count);
        return count;
}
```

To begin, let's choose the region address spaces for the library's **.text** and **.data** sections from the segments reserved for private use on the 3B2 Computer; note that the region addresses must be on a segment boundary (128K):

```
.text   0x80680000
.data   0x806a0000
```

Also choose the path name for our target library:

/my/directory/libexam_s

Now you need to identify the imported symbols in the library code. (See the guidelines in the section about "Importing Symbols": **malloc, strcpy, strlen, fprintf**, and **_iob**.) A header file defines C preprocessor macros for these symbols; note that you don't use **_iob** directly except through the macro **stderr** from <**stdio.h**>. Also notice the **_libexam_** prefixes for the symbols. The pointers for imported symbols are exported and, therefore, might conflict with other symbols. Using the library name as a prefix reduces the chance of a conflict occurring.

```
/* New file import.h */

#define malloc      (*_libexam_malloc)
#define strcpy      (*_libexam_strcpy)
#define strlen      (*_libexam_strlen)
#define fprintf     (*_libexam_fprintf)
#define _iob        (*_libexam__iob)

extern char    *malloc();
extern char    *strcpy();
extern int     strlen();
extern int     fprintf();
```

NOTE    The file **import.h** does not declare **_iob** as **extern**; it relies on the header file <**stdio.h**> for this information.

You will also need a new source file to hold definitions of the imported symbol pointers. Remember that all global data need to be initialized:

```
/* New file import.c */

#include <stdio.h>

char    *(*_libexam_malloc)()    = 0;
char    *(*_libexam_strcpy)()    = 0;
int     (*_libexam_strlen)()     = 0;
int     (*_libexam_fprintf)()    = 0;
FILE    (*_libexam__iob)[]       = 0;
```

Next, look at the library's global data to see what needs to be visible externally. (See the guideline "Minimize Global Data.") The variable **count** does not need to be external, because it is accessed through **excount()**. Make it static. (This should have been done for the relocatable version.)

Now the library's global data need to be moved into separate source files. (See the guideline "Define Text and Global Data in Separate Source Files.") The only global datum left is **Error**, and it needs to be initialized. (See the guideline "Initialize Global Data.") **Error** must remain global, because it passes information back to the calling routine:

```
/* New file global.c */

char    *Error   = 0;
```

Integrating these changes into the original source file, we get the following (notice that the symbol names must be declared as **extern**s):

```
/* Modified exam.c */

#include "import.h"

#include <stdio.h>

extern int      strlen();
extern char     *malloc(), *strcpy();

static int      count = 0;
extern char     *Error;

char *
excopy(e)
        char    *e;
{
        char    *new;

        ++count;
        if ( (new = malloc(strlen(e)+1)) == 0 )
        {
                Error = "no memory";
                return 0;
        }
        return strcpy(new, e);
}

excount()
{
        fprintf(stderr, "excount %d\n", count);
        return count;
}
```

NOTE

The new header file **import.h** must be included before **<stdio.h>**.

Next, we must write the shared library specification file for **mkshlib**:

```
        /* New file libexam.sl */
1       #target /my/directory/libexam_s
2       #address .text 0x80680000
3       #address .data 0x806a0000

4       #branch
5               excopy          1
6               excount         2

7       #objects
8               import.o
9               global.o
10              exam.o

11      #init import.o
12              _libexam_malloc  malloc
13              _libexam_strcpy  strcpy
14              _libexam_strlen  strlen
15              _libexam_fprintf fprintf
16              _libexam__iob    _iob
```

Briefly, here is what the specification file does. Line 1 gives the path name of the shared library on the target machine. The target shared library must be installed there for **a.out** files that use it to work correctly. Lines 2 and 3 give the virtual addresses for the shared library text and data regions, respectively. Line 4 through 6 specify the branch table. Lines 5 and 6 assign the functions **excopy()** and **excount()** to branch table entries 1 and 2. Only external text symbols, such as C functions, should be placed in the branch table.

Lines 7 through 10 give the list of object files that will be used to construct the host and target shared libraries. When building the host shared library archive, each file listed here will reside in its own archive member. When building the target library, the order of object files will be preserved. The data files must be first. Otherwise, a change in the size of static data in **exam.o** would move external data symbols and break compatibility.

Lines 11 through 16 give imported symbol information for the object file **import.o**. You can imagine assignments of the symbol values on the right to the symbols on the left. Thus **_libexam_malloc** will hold a pointer to **malloc**, and so on.

Now, we have to compile the **.o** files as we would for any other library:

    **cc −c import.c global.c exam.c**

Finally, we need to invoke **mkshlib** to build our host and target libraries:

    **mkshlib −s libexam.sl −t libexam_s −h libexam_s.a**

Presuming all of the source files have been compiled appropriately, the **mkshlib** command line shown above will create both the host library, **libexam_s.a**, and the target library, **libexam_s**.

## Guidelines for Writing Shared Library Code

Because the main advantage of a shared library over an archive library is sharing and the space it saves, these guidelines stress ways to increase sharing while avoiding the disadvantages of a shared library. The guidelines also stress upward compatibility. When appropriate, we describe our experience with building the shared C library to illustrate how following a particular guideline helped us.

We recommend that you read these guidelines once from beginning to end to get a perspective of the things you need to consider when building a shared library. Then use it as a checklist to guide your planning and decision-making.

Before we consider these guidelines, let's consider the restrictions to building a shared library common to all the guidelines. These restrictions involve static linking. Here's a summary of them, some of which are discussed in more detail later. Keep them in mind when reading the guidelines in this section:

- Exported symbols have fixed addresses.

     If an exported symbol moves, you have to re-link all **a.out** files that use the library. This restriction applies both to text and data symbols.

- If the library's text changes for one process at run time, it changes for all processes.

  Therefore, any library changes that apply only to a single process must occur in data, not in text, because only the data region is private. (Besides, the text region is read-only.)

- If the library uses a symbol directly, that symbol's run time value (address) must be known when the library is built.

- Imported symbols cannot be referenced directly.

  Their addresses are not known when you build the library, and they can be different for different processes. You can use imported symbols by adding an indirection through a pointer in the library's data.

## Choosing Library Members

### Include Large, Frequently Used Routines

These routines are prime candidates for sharing. Placing them in a shared library saves code space for individual **a.out** files and saves memory, too, when several concurrent processes need the same code. **printf**(3S) and related C library routines (which are documented in the *Programmer's Reference Manual*) are good examples.

> ### When we built the shared C library...
>
> The **printf**(3S) family of routines is used frequently. Consequently, we included **printf**(3S) and related routines in the shared C library.

### Exclude Infrequently Used Routines

Putting these routines in a shared library can degrade performance, particularly on paging systems. Traditional **a.out** files contain all code they need at run time. By definition, the code in an **a.out** file is (at least distantly) related to the process. Therefore, if a process calls a function, it may already be in memory because of its proximity to other text in the process.

If the function is in the shared library, a page fault may be more likely to occur, because the surrounding library code may be unrelated to the calling process. Only rarely will any single **a.out** file use everything in the shared C library. If a shared library has unrelated functions, and unrelated processes make random calls to those functions, the locality of reference may be decreased. The decreased locality may cause more paging activity and, thereby, decrease performance. See also "Organize to Improve Locality."

---

### When we built the shared C library...

Our original shared C library had about 44 KB of text. After profiling the code in the library, we removed small routines that were not often used. The current library has under 29 KB of text. The point is that functions used only by a few **a.out** files do not save much disk space by being in a shared library, and their inclusion can cause more paging and decrease performance.

---

### Exclude Routines that Use Much Static Data

These modules increase the size of processes. As "How Shared Libraries are Implemented" and "Deciding Whether to Use a Shared Library" explain, every process that uses a shared library gets its own private copy of the library's data, regardless of how much of the data is needed. Library data is static: it is not shared and cannot be loaded selectively with the provision that unreferenced pages may be removed from the working set.

For example, **getgrent**(3C), which is documented in the *Programmer's Reference Manual*, is not used by many standard UNIX commands. Some versions of the module define over 1400 bytes of unshared, static data. It probably should not be included in a shared library. You can import global data, if necessary, but not local, static data.

### Exclude Routines that Complicate Maintenance

All exported symbols must remain at constant addresses. The branch table makes this easy for text symbols, but data symbols don't have an equivalent mechanism. The more data a library has, the more likely some of them will have to change size. Any change in the size of exported data may affect symbol addresses and break compatibility.

### Include Routines the Library Itself Needs

It usually pays to make the library self-contained. For example, **printf**(3S) requires much of the standard I/O library. A shared library containing **printf**(3S) should contain the rest of the standard I/O routines, too.

 NOTE This guideline should not take priority over the others in this section. If you exclude some routine that the library itself needs based on a previous guideline, consider leaving the symbol out of the library and importing it.

## Changing Existing Code for the Shared Library

All C code that works in a shared library will also work in an archive library. However, the reverse is not true because a shared library must explicitly handle imported symbols. The following guidelines are meant to help you produce shared library code that is still valid for archive libraries (although it may be slightly bigger and slower). The guidelines mostly explain how to structure data for ease of maintenance, since most compatibility problems involve restructuring data from a shared library to an archive library.

### Minimize Global Data

In the current shared library implementation, all external data symbols are global; they are visible to applications. This can make maintenance difficult. You should try to reduce global data, as described below.

First, try to use automatic (stack) variables. Don't use permanent storage if automatic variables work. Using automatic variables saves static data space and reduces the number of symbols visible to application processes.

Second, see whether variables really must be external. Static symbols are not visible outside the library, so they may change addresses between library versions. Only external variables must remain constant.

Third, allocate buffers at run time instead of defining them at compile time. This does two important things. It reduces the size of the library's data region for all processes and, therefore, saves memory; only the processes that actually need the buffers get them. It also allows the size of the buffer to change from one release to the next without affecting compatibility. Statically allocated buffers cannot change size without affecting the addresses of other symbols and, perhaps, breaking compatibility.

### Define Text and Global Data in Separate Source Files

Separating text from global data makes it easier to prevent data symbols from moving. If new exported variables are needed, they can be added at the end of the old definitions to preserve the old symbols' addresses.

Archive libraries let the link editor extract individual members. This sometimes encourages programmers to define related variables and text in the same source file. This works fine for relocatable files, but shared libraries have a different set of restrictions. Suppose exported variables were scattered throughout the library modules. Then visible and hidden data would be inter-mixed. Changing hidden data, such as a string, like **hello** in the following example, moves subsequent data symbols, even the exported symbols:

| Before | Broken Successor |
|--------|------------------|
| `int head = 0;` | `int head = 0;` |
| `func()` | `func()` |
| `{` | `{` |
| `    ...` | `    ...` |
| `    p = "hello";` | `    p = "hello, world";` |
| `    ...` | `    ...` |
| `}` | `}` |
| `int tail = 0;` | `int tail = 0;` |

Assume the relative virtual address of **head** is 0 for both examples. The string literals will have the same address too, but they have different lengths. The old and new addresses of **tail** thus will be 12 and 20, respectively. If **tail** is supposed to be visible outside the library, the two versions will not be compatible.

Adding new exported variables to a shared library may change the addresses of static symbols, but this doesn't affect compatibility. An **a.out** file has no way to reference static library symbols directly, so it cannot depend on their values. Thus it pays to group all exported data symbols and place them at lower addresses than the static (hidden) data. You can write the specification file to control this. In the list of object files, make the global data files first.

```
#objects
    data1.o
    ...
    lastdata.o
    text1.o
    text2.o
    ...
```

If the data modules are not first, a seemingly harmless change (such as a new string literal) can break existing **a.out** files.

Shared library users get all library data at run time, regardless of the source file organization. Consequently, you can put all exported variables' definitions in a single source file without a penalty. You can also use several source files for data definitions.

### Initialize Global Data

Initialize exported variables, including the pointers for imported symbols. Although this uses more disk space in the target shared library, the expansion is limited to a single file. Using initialized variables is another way to prevent address changes.

The C compilation system on UNIX System V puts uninitialized variables in a common area, and the link editor assigns addresses to them in an unpredictable way. In other words, the order of uninitialized symbols may change from one link editor run to the next. However, the link editor will not change the order of initialized variables, thus allowing a library developer to preserve compatibility.

### Preserve Branch Table Order

You should add new functions only at the end of the branch table. After you have a specification file for the library, try to maintain compatibility with previous versions. You may add new functions without breaking old **a.out** files as long as previous assignments are not changed. This lets you distribute a new library without having to re-link all of the **a.out** files that used a previous version of the library.

## Importing Symbols

Shared library code cannot directly use symbols defined outside a library, but an escape hatch exists. You can define pointers in the data area and arrange for those pointers to be initialized to the addresses of imported symbols. Library code then accesses imported symbols indirectly, delaying symbol binding until run time. Libraries can import both text and data symbols. Moreover, imported symbols can come from the user's code, another library, or even the library itself. In Figure 8-4, the symbols **_libc.ptr1** and **_libc.ptr2** are imported from user's code and the symbol **_libc_malloc** from the library itself.

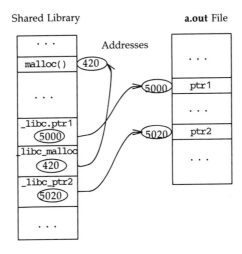

Figure 8-4: Imported Symbols in a Shared Library

The following guidelines describe when and how to use imported symbols.

### Imported Symbols that the Library Does Not Define

Archive libraries typically contain relocatable files, which allow undefined references. Although the host shared library is an archive, too, that archive is constructed to mirror the target library, which more closely resembles an **a.out** file. Neither target shared libraries nor **a.out** files can have unresolved symbols.

Consequently, shared libraries must import any symbols they use but do not define. Some shared libraries will derive from existing archive libraries. For the reasons stated above, it may not be appropriate to include all the archive's modules in the target shared library. If you leave something out that the library calls, you have to make an imported symbol pointer for it.

### Imported Symbols that Users Must Be Able to Redefine

Optionally, shared libraries can import their own symbols. At first this might appear to be an unnecessary complication, but consider the following. Two standard libraries, **libc** and **libmalloc**, provide a **malloc** family. Even though most UNIX commands use the **malloc** from the C library, they can choose either library or define their own.

---

> ## When we built the shared C library...
>
> Three possible strategies existed for the shared C library. First, we could have excluded **malloc**(3X). Other library members would have needed it, and so it would have been an imported symbol. This would have worked, but it would have meant less savings.
>
> Second, we could have included the **malloc**(3X) family and not imported it. This would have given us more savings for typical commands, but it had a price. Other library routines call **malloc**(3X) directly, and those calls could not have been overridden. If an application tried to redefine **malloc**(3X), the library calls would not have used the alternate version. Furthermore, the link editor would have found multiple definitions of **malloc**(3X) while building the application. To resolve this the library developer would have to change source code to remove the custom **malloc**(3X), or the developer would have to refrain from using the shared library.
>
> Finally, we could have included **malloc**(3X) in the shared library, treating it as an imported symbol. This is what we did. Even though **malloc**(3X) is in the library, nothing else there refers to it directly. If the application does not redefine **malloc**(3X), both application and library calls are routed to the library version. All calls are mapped to the alternate, if present.

You might want to permit redefinition of all library symbols in some libraries. You can do this by importing all symbols the library defines, in addition to those it uses but does not define. Although this adds a little space and time overhead to the library, the technique allows a shared library to be one hundred percent compatible with an existing archive at link time and run time.

### Mechanics of Importing Symbols

Let's assume a shared library wants to import the symbol **malloc**. The original archive code and the shared library code appear below.

Archive Code

Shared Library Code

```
                              /* See pointers.c on next page */

extern char *malloc();        extern char *(*_libc_malloc)();

export()                      export()
{                             {
    ...                           ...
    p = malloc(n);                p = (*_libc_malloc)(n);
    ...                           ...
}                             }
```

Making this transformation is straightforward, but two sets of source code would be necessary to support both an archive and a shared library. Some simple macro definitions can hide the transformations and allow source code compatibility. A header file defines the macros, and a different version of this header file would exist for each type of library. The −I flag to **cpp**(1) would direct the C preprocessor to look in the appropriate directory to find the desired file.

Archive **import.h**

Shared **import.h**

```
/* empty */          /*
                      *  Macros for importing
                      *  symbols.  One #define
                      *  per symbol.
                      */

                      ...
                      #define malloc   (*_libc_malloc)
                      ...
                      extern char *malloc();
                      ...
```

These header files allow one source both to serve the original archive source and to serve a shared library, too, because they supply the indirections for imported symbols. The declaration of **malloc** in **import.h** actually declares the pointer **_libc_malloc**.

Common Source

```
#include "import.h"

extern char *malloc();

export()
{
    ...
    p = malloc(n);
    ...
}
```

Alternatively, one can hide the #include with #ifdef:

Common Source

```
#ifdef SHLIB
#       include "import.h"
#endif

extern char *malloc();

export()
{
    ...
    p = malloc(n);
    ...
}
```

Of course the transformation is not complete. You must define the pointer **_libc_malloc**.

File **pointers.c**

```
char *(*_libc_malloc)() = 0;
```

Note that **_libc_malloc** is initialized to zero, because it is an exported data symbol.

Special initialization code sets the pointers. Shared library code should not use the pointer before it contains the correct value. In the example the address of **malloc** must be assigned to **_libc_malloc**. Tools that build the shared library generate the initialization code according to the library specification file.

### Pointer Initialization Fragments

A host shared library archive member can define one or many imported symbol pointers. Regardless of the number, every imported symbol pointer should have initialization code.

This code goes into the **a.out** file and does two things. First, it creates an unresolved reference to make sure the symbol being imported gets resolved. Second, initialization fragments set the imported symbol pointers to their values before the process reaches **main**. If the imported symbol pointer can be used at run time, the imported symbol will be present, and the imported symbol pointer will be set properly.

 NOTE | Initialization fragments reside in the host, not the target, shared library. The link editor copies initialization code into **a.out** files to set imported pointers to their correct values.

Library specification files describe how to initialize the imported symbol pointers. For example, the following specification line would set **_libc_malloc** to the address of **malloc**:

```
#init pmalloc.o
_libc_malloc    malloc
```

When **mkshlib** builds the host library, it modifies the file **pmalloc.o**, adding relocatable code to perform the following assignment statement:

**_libc_malloc = &malloc;**

When the link editor extracts **pmalloc.o** from the host library, the relocatable code goes into the **a.out** file. As the link editor builds the final **a.out** file, it resolves the unresolved references and collects all initialization fragments. When the **a.out** file is executed, the run time startup (**crt1**) executes the initialization fragments to set the library pointers.

### Selectively Loading Imported Symbols

Defining fewer pointers in each archive member increases the granularity of symbol selection and can prevent unnecessary objects from being linked into the **a.out** file. For example, if an archive member defines three pointers to imported symbols, the link editor will resolve all three, even though only one might be needed.

You can reduce unnecessary loading by writing C source files that define imported symbol pointers singly or in related groups. If an imported symbol must be individually selectable, put its pointer in its own source file (and archive member). This will give the link editor a finer granularity to use when it resolves the symbols.

Let's look at some examples. In the coarse method, a single source file might define all pointers to imported symbols:

Old **pointers.c**

```
...
int (*_libc_ptr1)() = 0;
char *(*_libc_malloc)() = 0;
int (*_libc_ptr2)() = 0;
...
```

Being able to use them individually requires multiple source files and archive members. Each of the new files defines a single pointer or a small group of related pointers:

| File | Contents |
|------|----------|
| **ptr1.c** | `int (*_libc_ptr1)() = 0;` |
| **pmalloc.c** | `char *(*_libc_malloc)() = 0;` |
| **ptr2.c** | `int (*_libc_ptr2)() = 0;` |

Originally, a single object file, **pointers.o**, defines all pointers. Extracting it requires definitions for **ptr1, malloc,** and **ptr2.** The modified example lets one extract each pointer individually, thus avoiding the unresolved reference for unnecessary symbols.

## Providing Archive Library Compatibility

Having compatible libraries makes it easy to substitute one for the other. In almost all cases, this can be done without makefile or source file changes. Perhaps the best way to explain this guideline is by example:

---

### When we built the shared C library...

We had an existing archive library to use as the base. This obviously gave us code for individual routines, and the archive library also gave us a model to use for the shared library itself.

We wanted the host library archive file to be compatible with the relocatable archive C library. However, we did not want the shared library target file to include all routines from the archive: including them all would have hurt performance.

Reaching these goals was, perhaps, easier than you might think. We did it by building the host library in two steps. First, we used the available shared library tools to create the host library to match exactly the target. The resulting archive file was not compatible with the archive C library at this point. Second, we added to the host library the set of relocatable objects residing in the archive C library that were missing from the host library. Although this set is not in the shared library target, its inclusion in the host library makes the relocatable and shared C libraries compatible.

---

## Tuning the Shared Library Code

Some suggestions for how to organize shared library code to improve performance are presented here. They apply to paging systems, such as UNIX System V Release 3.0. The suggestions come from the experience of building the shared C library.

The archive C library contains several diverse groups of functions. Many processes use different combinations of these groups, making the paging behavior of any shared C library difficult to predict. A shared library should offer greater benefits for more homogeneous collections of code. For example, a data base library probably could be organized to reduce system paging substantially, if its static and dynamic calling dependencies were more predictable.

### Profile the Code

To begin, profile the code that might go into the shared library.

### Choose Library Contents

Based on profiling information, make some decisions about what to include in the shared library. **a.out** file size is a static property, and paging is a dynamic property. These static and dynamic characteristics may conflict, so you have to decide whether the performance lost is worth the disk space gained. See "Choosing Library Members" in this chapter for more information.

### Organize to Improve Locality

When a function is in **a.out** files, it probably resides in a page with other code that is used more often (see "Exclude Infrequently Used Routines"). Try to improve locality of reference by grouping dynamically related functions. If every call of **funcA** generates calls to **funcB** and **funcC**, try to put them in the same page. cflow(1) (documented in the *Programmer's Reference Manual*) generates this static dependency information. Combine it with profiling to see what things actually are called, as opposed to what things might be called.

### Align for Paging

The key is to arrange the shared library target's object files so that frequently used functions do not unnecessarily cross page boundaries. When arranging object files within the target library, be sure to keep the text and data files separate. You can reorder text object files without breaking compatibility; the same is not true for object files that define global data. Once again, an example might best explain this guideline:

### When we built the shared C library...

We used a 3B2 Computer to build the library; the architecture of the 3B2 Computer uses 2 KB pages. Using name lists and disassemblies of the shared library target file, we determined where the page boundaries fell.

After grouping related functions, we broke them into page-sized chunks. Although some object files and functions are larger than a single page, most of them are smaller. Then we used the infrequently called functions as glue between the chunks. Because the glue between pages is referenced less frequently than the page contents, the probability of a page fault decreased.

After determining the branch table, we rearranged the library's object files without breaking compatibility. We put frequently used, unrelated functions together, because we figured they would be called randomly enough to keep the pages in memory. System calls went into another page as a group, and so on. The following example shows how to change the order of the library's object files:

```
    Before              After

    #objects            #objects
      ...                 ...
      printf.o            strcmp.o
      fopen.o             malloc.o
      malloc.o            printf.o
      strcmp.o            fopen.o
      ...                 ...
```

### Avoid Hardware Thrashing

Finally, you may have to consider the hardware you're using to obtain better performance. Using the 3B2 Computer, for example, you need to consider its memory management. Part of the memory management hardware is an 8-entry cache for translating virtual to physical addresses. Each segment (128 KB) is mapped to one of the eight entries. Consequently, segments 0, 8, 16, ... use entry 0; segments 1, 9, 17, ... use entry 1; and so on.

You get better performance by arranging the typical process to avoid cache entry conflicts. If a heavily used library had both its text and its data segment mapped to the same cache entry, the performance penalty would be particularly severe. Every library instruction would bring the text segment information into the cache. Instructions that referenced data would flush the entry to load the data segment. Of course, the next instruction would reference text and flush the cache entry, again.

---

### When we built the shared C library...

We avoided the cache entry conflicts. At least with the 3B2 Computer architecture, a library's text and data segment numbers should differ by something other than eight.

---

## Making A Shared Library Upward Compatible

The following guidelines explain how to build upward-compatible shared libraries. Note, however, that upward compatibility may not always be an issue. Consider the case in which a shared library is one piece of a larger system and is not delivered as a separate product. In this restricted case, you can identify all **a.out** files that use a particular library. As long as you rebuild all the **a.out** files every time the library changes, versions of the library may be incompatible with each other. This may complicate development, but it is possible.

### Comparing Previous Versions of the Library

Shared library developers normally want newer versions of a library to be compatible with previous ones. As mentioned before, **a.out** files will not execute properly otherwise.

The following procedures let you check libraries for compatibility. In these tests, two libraries are said to be compatible if their exported symbols have the same addresses. Although this criterion usually works, it is not foolproof. For example, if a library developer changes the number of arguments a function requires, the new function may not be compatible with the old. This kind of change may not alter symbol addresses, but it will break old **a.out** files.

Let's assume we want to compare two target shared libraries: **new.libx_s** and **old.libx_s**. We use the **nm**(1) command to look at their symbols and **sed**(1) to delete everything except external symbols. A small **sed** program simplifies the job.

New file **cmplib.sed**

```
sed     '/|extern|.*/!d
        s///
        /^.bt/d
        /^etext /d
        /^edata /d
        /^end /d'
```

The first line of the **sed** script deletes all lines except those for external symbols. The second line leaves only symbol names and values in the output. The last four lines delete special symbols that have no bearing on library compatibility; they are not visible to application programs. You will have to create your own file to hold the **sed** script.

Now we are ready to create lists of symbol names and values for the new and old libraries:

```
nm old.libx_s | sed -f cmplib.sed >old.nm
nm new.libx_s | sed -f cmplib.sed >new.nm
```

Next, we compare the symbol values to identify differences:

```
diff old.nm new.nm
```

If all symbols in the two libraries have the same values, the **diff**(1) command will produce no output, and the libraries are compatible. Otherwise, some symbols are different and the two libraries may be incompatible. **diff**(1), **nm**(1), and **sed**(1) are documented in the *User's Reference Manual*.

### Dealing with Incompatible Libraries

When you determine that two libraries are incompatible, you have to deal with the incompatibility. You can deal with it in one of two ways. First, you can rebuild all the **a.out** files that use your library. If feasible, this is probably the best choice. Unfortunately, you might not be able to find those **a.out** files, let alone force their owners to rebuild them with your new library.

So your second choice is to give a different target path name to the new version of the library. The host and target path names are independent; so you don't have to change the host library path name. New **a.out** files will use your new target library, but old **a.out** files will continue to access the old library.

As the library developer, it is your responsibility to check for compatibility and, probably, to provide a new target library path name for a new version of a library that is incompatible with older versions. If you fail to resolve compatibility problems, **a.out** files that use your library will not work properly.

NOTE

You should try to avoid multiple library versions. If too many copies of the same shared library exist, they might actually use more disk space and more memory than the equivalent relocatable version would have.

# Summary

This chapter described the UNIX system shared libraries and explained how to use them. It also explained how to build your own shared libraries. Using any shared library almost always saves disk storage space, memory, and computer power; and running the UNIX system on smaller machines makes the efficient use of these resources increasingly important. Therefore, you should normally use a shared library whenever it's available.

# CHAPTER 9: INTERPROCESS COMMUNICATION

## Introduction

The UNIX system supports three types of Inter-Process Communication (IPC):

- messages
- semaphores
- shared memory

This chapter describes the system calls for each type of IPC.

Included in the chapter are several example programs that show the use of the IPC system calls. All of the example programs have been compiled and run on an AT&T 3B2 Computer.

Since there are many ways in the C Programming Language to accomplish the same task or requirement, keep in mind that the example programs were written for clarity and not for program efficiency. Usually, system calls are embedded within a larger user-written program that makes use of a particular function that the calls provide.

# Messages

The message type of IPC allows processes (executing programs) to communicate through the exchange of data stored in buffers. This data is transmitted between processes in discrete portions called messages. Processes using this type of IPC can perform two operations:

- sending

- receiving

Before a message can be sent or received by a process, a process must have the UNIX operating system generate the necessary software mechanisms to handle these operations. A process does this by using the **msgget**(2) system call. While doing this, the process becomes the owner/creator of the message facility and specifies the initial operation permissions for all other processes, including itself. Subsequently, the owner/creator can relinquish ownership or change the operation permissions using the **msgctl**(2) system call. However, the creator remains the creator as long as the facility exists. Other processes with permission can use **msgctl**() to perform various other control functions.

Processes which have permission and are attempting to send or receive a message can suspend execution if they are unsuccessful at performing their operation. That is, a process which is attempting to send a message can wait until the process which is to receive the message is ready and vice versa. A process which specifies that execution is to be suspended is performing a "blocking message operation." A process which does not allow its execution to be suspended is performing a "nonblocking message operation."

A process performing a blocking message operation can be suspended until one of three conditions occurs:

- It is successful.

- It receives a signal.

- The facility is removed.

System calls make these message capabilities available to processes. The calling process passes arguments to a system call, and the system call either successfully or unsuccessfully performs its function. If the system call is successful, it performs its function and returns applicable information.

Otherwise, a known error code ($-1$) is returned to the process, and an external error number variable **errno** is set accordingly.

Before a message can be sent or received, a uniquely identified message queue and data structure must be created. The unique identifier created is called the message queue identifier (**msqid**); it is used to identify or reference the associated message queue and data structure.

The message queue is used to store (header) information about each message that is being sent or received. This information includes the following for each message:

- pointer to the next message on queue

- message type

- message text size

- message text address

There is one associated data structure for the uniquely identified message queue. This data structure contains the following information related to the message queue:

- operation permissions data (operation permission structure)

- pointer to first message on the queue

- pointer to last message on the queue

- current number of bytes on the queue

- number of messages on the queue

- maximum number of bytes on the queue

- process identification (PID) of last message sender

- PID of last message receiver

- last message send time

- last message receive time

- last change time

NOTE

All include files discussed in this chapter are located in the **/usr/include** or **/usr/include/sys** directories.

The C Programming Language data structure definition for the message information contained in the message queue is as follows:

```
struct msg
{
        struct msg      *msg_next;  /* ptr to next message on q */
        long            msg_type;   /* message type */
        short           msg_ts;     /* message text size */
        short           msg_spot;   /* message text map address */
};
```

It is located in the **/usr/include/sys/msg.h** header file.

Likewise, the structure definition for the associated data structure is as follows:

```
struct msqid_ds
{
        struct ipc_perm  msg_perm;    /* operation permission struct */
        struct msg       *msg_first;  /* ptr to first message on q */
        struct msg       *msg_last;   /* ptr to last message on q */
        ushort           msg_cbytes;  /* current # bytes on q */
        ushort           msg_qnum;    /* # of messages on q */
        ushort           msg_qbytes;  /* max # of bytes on q */
        ushort           msg_lspid;   /* pid of last msgsnd */
        ushort           msg_lrpid;   /* pid of last msgrcv */
        time_t           msg_stime;   /* last msgsnd time */
        time_t           msg_rtime;   /* last msgrcv time */
        time_t           msg_ctime;   /* last change time */
};
```

It is located in the **#include <sys/msg.h>** header file also. Note that the **msg_perm** member of this structure uses **ipc_perm** as a template. The breakout for the operation permissions data structure is shown in Figure 9-1.

The definition of the **ipc_perm** data structure is as follows:

```
struct ipc_perm
{
        ushort    uid;      /* owner's user id */
        ushort    gid;      /* owner's group id */
        ushort    cuid;     /* creator's user id */
        ushort    cgid;     /* creator's group id */
        ushort    mode;     /* access modes */
        ushort    seq;      /* slot usage sequence number */
        key_t     key;      /* key */
};
```

Figure 9-1: **ipc_perm** Data Structure

---

It is located in the **#include <sys/ipc.h>** header file; it is common for all IPC facilities.

The **msgget(2)** system call is used to perform two tasks when only the IPC_CREAT flag is set in the **msgflg** argument that it receives:

- to get a new **msqid** and create an associated message queue and data structure for it

- to return an existing **msqid** that already has an associated message queue and data structure

The task performed is determined by the value of the **key** argument passed to the **msgget()** system call.  For the first task, if the **key** is not already in use for an existing **msqid**, a new **msqid** is returned with an associated message queue and data structure created for the **key**.  This occurs provided no system tunable parameters would be exceeded.

There is also a provision for specifying a **key** of value zero which is known as the private **key** (IPC_PRIVATE = 0); when specified, a new **msqid** is always returned with an associated message queue and data structure created for it unless a system tunable parameter would be exceeded.  When the **ipcs** command is performed, for security reasons the KEY field for the **msqid** is all zeros.

For the second task, if a **msqid** exists for the **key** specified, the value of the existing **msqid** is returned. If you do not desire to have an existing **msqid** returned, a control command (IPC_EXCL) can be specified (set) in the **msgflg** argument passed to the system call. The details of using this system call are discussed in the "Using **msgget**" section of this chapter.

When performing the first task, the process which calls **msgget** becomes the owner/creator, and the associated data structure is initialized accordingly. Remember, ownership can be changed but the creating process always remains the creator; see the "Controlling Message Queues" section in this chapter. The creator of the message queue also determines the initial operation permissions for it.

Once a uniquely identified message queue and data structure are created, message operations [**msgop()**] and message control [**msgctl()**] can be used.

Message operations, as mentioned previously, consist of sending and receiving messages. System calls are provided for each of these operations; they are **msgsnd()** and **msgrcv()**. Refer to the "Operations for Messages" section in this chapter for details of these system calls.

Message control is done by using the **msgctl(2)** system call. It permits you to control the message facility in the following ways:

- to determine the associated data structure status for a message queue identifier (**msqid**)

- to change operation permissions for a message queue

- to change the **size (msg_qbytes)** of the message queue for a particular **msqid**

- to remove a particular **msqid** from the UNIX operating system along with its associated message queue and data structure

Refer to the "Controlling Message Queues" section in this chapter for details of the **msgctl()** system call.

## Getting Message Queues

This section gives a detailed description of using the **msgget**(2) system call along with an example program illustrating its use.

### Using msgget

The synopsis found in the **msgget**(2) entry in the *Programmer's Reference Manual* is as follows:

```
#include   <sys/types.h>
#include   <sys/ipc.h>
#include   <sys/msg.h>

int  msgget (key, msgflg)
key_t  key;
int msgflg;
```

All of these include files are located in the **/usr/include/sys** directory of the UNIX operating system.

The following line in the synopsis:

```
int msgget (key, msgflg)
```

informs you that **msgget**() is a function with two formal arguments that returns an integer type value, upon successful completion (**msqid**). The next two lines:

```
key_t  key;
int msgflg;
```

declare the types of the formal arguments. **key_t** is declared by a **typedef** in the **types.h** header file to be an integer.

The integer returned from this function upon successful completion is the message queue identifier (**msqid**) that was discussed earlier.

As declared, the process calling the **msgget**() system call must supply two arguments to be passed to the formal **key** and **msgflg** arguments.

A new **msqid** with an associated message queue and data structure is provided if either

- **key** is equal to IPC_PRIVATE,

or

- **key** is passed a unique hexadecimal integer, and **msgflg** ANDed with IPC_CREAT is TRUE.

The value passed to the **msgflg** argument must be an integer type octal value and it will specify the following:

- access permissions
- execution modes
- control fields (commands)

Access permissions determine the read/write attributes and execution modes determine the user/group/other attributes of the **msgflg** argument.

They are collectively referred to as "operation permissions." Figure 9-2 reflects the numeric values (expressed in octal notation) for the valid operation permissions codes.

| Operation Permissions | Octal Value |
|---|---|
| Read by User | 00400 |
| Write by User | 00200 |
| Read by Group | 00040 |
| Write by Group | 00020 |
| Read by Others | 00004 |
| Write by Others | 00002 |

Figure 9-2: Operation Permissions Codes

―――――――――――――――――――――――――――――――

A specific octal value is derived by adding the octal values for the operation permissions desired. That is, if read by user and read/write by others is desired, the code value would be 00406 (00400 plus 00006). There are constants located in the **msg.h** header file which can be used for the user (OWNER).

Control commands are predefined constants (represented by all uppercase letters). Figure 9-3 contains the names of the constants which apply to the **msgget**() system call along with their values. They are also referred to as flags and are defined in the **ipc.h** header file.

| Control Command | Value |
|---|---|
| IPC_CREAT | 0001000 |
| IPC_EXCL | 0002000 |

Figure 9-3: Control Commands (Flags)

―――――――――――――――――――――――――――――――

The value for **msgflg** is therefore a combination of operation permissions and control commands. After determining the value for the operation permissions as previously described, the desired flag(s) can be specified. This is accomplished by bitwise ORing (|) them with the operation permissions; the bit positions and values for the control commands in relation to those of the operation permissions make this possible. It is illustrated as follows:

|  |  | Octal Value | Binary Value |
|---|---|---|---|
| IPC_CREAT | = | 0 1 0 0 0 | 0 000 001 000 000 000 |
| ¦ ORed by User | = | 0 0 4 0 0 | 0 000 000 100 000 000 |
| **msgflg** | = | 0 1 4 0 0 | 0 000 001 100 000 000 |

The **msgflg** value can be easily set by using the names of the flags in conjunction with the octal operation permissions value:

```
msqid = msgget (key, (IPC_CREAT ¦ 0400));

msqid = msgget (key, (IPC_CREAT ¦ IPC_EXCL ¦ 0400));
```

As specified by the **msgget(2)** page in the *Programmer's Reference Manual*, success or failure of this system call depends upon the argument values for **key** and **msgflg** or system tunable parameters. The system call will attempt to return a new **msqid** if one of the following conditions is true:

- Key is equal to IPC_PRIVATE (0)

- Key does not already have a **msqid** associated with it, and (**msgflg** & IPC_CREAT) is "true" (not zero).

The **key** argument can be set to IPC_PRIVATE in the following ways:

```
msqid = msgget (IPC_PRIVATE, msgflg);

        or

msqid = msgget ( 0 , msgflg);
```

This alone will cause the system call to be attempted because it satisfies the first condition specified. Exceeding the MSGMNI system tunable parameter always causes a failure. The MSGMNI system tunable parameter determines the maximum number of unique message queues (**msqid**'s) in the UNIX operating system.

The second condition is satisfied if the value for **key** is not already associated with a **msqid** and the bitwise ANDing of **msgflg** and IPC_CREAT is "true" (not zero). This means that the **key** is unique (not in use) within the UNIX operating system for this facility type and that the IPC_CREAT flag is set (**msgflg** | IPC_CREAT). The bitwise ANDing (&), which is the logical way of testing if a flag is set, is illustrated as follows:

$$
\begin{array}{lll}
\textbf{msgflg} & = \text{x 1 x x x} & (x = \text{immaterial}) \\
\& \text{ IPC\_CREAT} & = \text{0 1 0 0 0} & \\
 & & \\
\text{result} & = \text{0 1 0 0 0} & (\text{not zero})
\end{array}
$$

Since the result is not zero, the flag is set or "true."

IPC_EXCL is another control command used in conjunction with IPC_CREAT to exclusively have the system call fail if, and only if, a **msqid** exists for the specified **key** provided. This is necessary to prevent the process from thinking that it has received a new (unique) **msqid** when it has not. In other words, when both IPC_CREAT and IPC_EXCL are specified, a new **msqid** is returned if the system call is successful.

Refer to the **msgget**(2) page in the *Programmer's Reference Manual* for specific associated data structure initialization for successful completion. The specific failure conditions with error names are contained there also.

## Example Program

The example program in this section (Figure 9-4) is a menu driven program which allows all possible combinations of using the **msgget**(2) system call to be exercised.

From studying this program, you can observe the method of passing arguments and receiving return values. The user-written program requirements are pointed out.

This program begins (lines 4-8) by including the required header files as specified by the **msgget**(2) entry in the *Programmer's Reference Manual*. Note that the **errno.h** header file is included as opposed to declaring **errno** as an external variable; either method will work.

Variable names have been chosen to be as close as possible to those in the synopsis for the system call. Their declarations are self-explanatory. These names make the program more readable, and it is perfectly legal since they are local to the program. The variables declared for this program and their purposes are as follows:

- **key**—used to pass the value for the desired **key**

- **opperm**—used to store the desired operation permissions

- **flags**—used to store the desired control commands (flags)

- **opperm_flags**—used to store the combination from the logical ORing of the **opperm** and **flags** variables; it is then used in the system call to pass the **msgflg** argument

- **msqid**—used for returning the message queue identification number for a successful system call or the error code (−1) for an unsuccessful one.

The program begins by prompting for a hexadecimal **key**, an octal operation permissions code, and finally for the control command combinations (flags) which are selected from a menu (lines 15-32). All possible combinations are allowed even though they might not be viable. This allows observing the errors for illegal combinations.

Next, the menu selection for the flags is combined with the operation permissions, and the result is stored at the address of the **opperm_flags** variable (lines 36-51).

The system call is made next, and the result is stored at the address of the **msqid** variable (line 53).

Since the **msqid** variable now contains a valid message queue identifier or the error code (−1), it is tested to see if an error occurred (line 55). If **msqid** equals −1, a message indicates that an error resulted, and the external **errno** variable is displayed (lines 57, 58).

If no error occurred, the returned message queue identifier is displayed (line 62).

The example program for the **msgget**(2) system call follows. It is suggested that the source program file be named **msgget.c** and that the executable file be named **msgget**. When compiling C programs that use floating point operations, the −**f** option should be used on the **cc** command line. If this option is not used, the program will compile successfully, but when the program is executed it will fail.

```
 1    /*This is a program to illustrate
 2    **the message get, msgget(),
 3    **system call capabilities.*/

 4    #include    <stdio.h>
 5    #include    <sys/types.h>
 6    #include    <sys/ipc.h>
 7    #include    <sys/msg.h>
 8    #include    <errno.h>

 9    /*Start of main C language program*/
10    main()
11    {
12        key_t key;              /*declare as long integer*/
13        int opperm, flags;
14        int msqid, opperm_flags;
15        /*Enter the desired key*/
16        printf("Enter the desired key in hex = ");
17        scanf("%x", &key);


18        /*Enter the desired octal operation
19          permissions.*/
20        printf("\nEnter the operation\n");
21        printf("permissions in octal = ");
22        scanf("%o", &opperm);
```

Figure 9-4: **msgget**() System Call Example (Sheet 1 of 3)

```
23          /*Set the desired flags.*/
24          printf("\nEnter corresponding number to\n");
25          printf("set the desired flags:\n");
26          printf("No flags                  = 0\n");
27          printf("IPC_CREAT                 = 1\n");
28          printf("IPC_EXCL                  = 2\n");
29          printf("IPC_CREAT and IPC_EXCL    = 3\n");
30          printf("          Flags           = ");

31          /*Get the flag(s) to be set.*/
32          scanf("%d", &flags);

33          /*Check the values.*/
34          printf ("\nkey =0x%x, opperm = 0%o, flags = 0%o\n",
35              key, opperm, flags);

36          /*Incorporate the control fields (flags) with
37            the operation permissions*/
38          switch (flags)
39          {
40          case 0:   /*No flags are to be set.*/
41              opperm_flags = (opperm | 0);
42              break;
43          case 1:   /*Set the IPC_CREAT flag.*/
44              opperm_flags = (opperm | IPC_CREAT);
45              break;
46          case 2:   /*Set the IPC_EXCL flag.*/
47              opperm_flags = (opperm | IPC_EXCL);
48              break;
49          case 3:     /*Set the IPC_CREAT and IPC_EXCL flags.*/
50              opperm_flags = (opperm | IPC_CREAT | IPC_EXCL);
51          }
```

Figure 9-4: **msgget**() System Call Example (Sheet 2 of 3)

```
52        /*Call the msgget system call.*/
53        msqid = msgget (key, opperm_flags);

54        /*Perform the following if the call is unsuccessful.*/
55        if(msqid == -1)
56        {
57            printf ("\nThe msgget system call failed!\n");
58            printf ("The error number = %d\n", errno);
59        }

60        /*Return the msqid upon successful completion.*/
61        else
62            printf ("\nThe msqid = %d\n", msqid);
63        exit(0);
64    }
```

Figure 9-4: **msgget**() System Call Example (Sheet 3 of 3)

# Controlling Message Queues

This section gives a detailed description of using the **msgctl** system call along with an example program which allows all of its capabilities to be exercised.

## Using msgctl

The synopsis found in the **msgctl**(2) entry in the *Programmer's Reference Manual* is as follows:

```
#include <sys/types.h>
#include <sys/ipc.h>
#include <sys/msg.h>

int msgctl (msqid, cmd, buf)
int msqid, cmd;
struct msqid_ds *buf;
```

The **msgctl()** system call requires three arguments to be passed to it, and it returns an integer value.

Upon successful completion, a zero value is returned; and when unsuccessful, it returns a −1.

The **msqid** variable must be a valid, non-negative, integer value. In other words, it must have already been created by using the **msgget()** system call.

The **cmd** argument can be replaced by one of the following control commands (flags):

IPC_STAT    return the status information contained in the associated data structure for the specified **msqid**, and place it in the data structure pointed to by the **\*buf** pointer in the user memory area.

IPC_SET    for the specified **msqid**, set the effective user and group identification, operation permissions, and the number of bytes for the message queue.

IPC_RMID    remove the specified **msqid** along with its associated message queue and data structure.

A process must have an effective user identification of OWNER/CREATOR or super-user to perform an IPC_SET or IPC_RMID control command. Read permission is required to perform the IPC_STAT control command.

The details of this system call are discussed in the example program for it. If you have problems understanding the logic manipulations in this program, read the "Using **msgget**" section of this chapter; it goes into more detail than what would be practical to do for every system call.

## Example Program

The example program in this section (Figure 9-5) is a menu driven program which allows all possible combinations of using the **msgctl**(2) system call to be exercised.

From studying this program, you can observe the method of passing arguments and receiving return values. The user-written program requirements are pointed out.

This program begins (lines 5-9) by including the required header files as specified by the **msgctl**(2) entry in the *Programmer's Reference Manual*. Note in this program that **errno** is declared as an external variable, and therefore, the **errno.h** header file does not have to be included.

Variable and structure names have been chosen to be as close as possible to those in the synopsis for the system call. Their declarations are self-explanatory. These names make the program more readable, and it is perfectly legal since they are local to the program. The variables declared for this program and their purpose are as follows:

| | |
|---|---|
| **uid** | used to store the IPC_SET value for the effective user identification |
| **gid** | used to store the IPC_SET value for the effective group identification |
| **mode** | used to store the IPC_SET value for the operation permissions |
| **bytes** | used to store the IPC_SET value for the number of bytes in the message queue (**msg_qbytes**) |
| **rtrn** | used to store the return integer value from the system call |
| **msqid** | used to store and pass the message queue identifier to the system call |
| **command** | used to store the code for the desired control command so that subsequent processing can be performed on it |

| | |
|---|---|
| **choice** | used to determine which member is to be changed for the IPC_SET control command |
| **msqid_ds** | used to receive the specified message queue indentifier's data structure when an IPC_STAT control command is performed |
| **∗buf** | a pointer passed to the system call which locates the data structure in the user memory area where the IPC_STAT control command is to place its return values or where the IPC_SET command gets the values to set |

Note that the **msqid_ds** data structure in this program (line 16) uses the data structure located in the **msg.h** header file of the same name as a template for its declaration. This is a perfect example of the advantage of local variables.

The next important thing to observe is that although the **∗buf** pointer is declared to be a pointer to a data structure of the **msqid_ds** type, it must also be initialized to contain the address of the user memory area data structure (line 17). Now that all of the required declarations have been explained for this program, this is how it works.

First, the program prompts for a valid message queue identifier which is stored at the address of the **msqid** variable (lines 19, 20). This is required for every **msgctl** system call.

Then the code for the desired control command must be entered (lines 21-27), and it is stored at the address of the command variable. The code is tested to determine the control command for subsequent processing.

If the IPC_STAT control command is selected (code 1), the system call is performed (lines 37, 38) and the status information returned is printed out (lines 39-46); only the members that can be set are printed out in this program. Note that if the system call is unsuccessful (line 106), the status information of the last successful call is printed out. In addition, an error message is displayed and the **errno** variable is printed out (lines 108, 109). If the system call is successful, a message indicates this along with the message queue identifier used (lines 111-114).

If the IPC_SET control command is selected (code 2), the first thing done is to get the current status information for the message queue identifier specified (lines 50-52). This is necessary because this example program provides for changing only one member at a time, and the system call changes all of them. Also, if an invalid value happened to be stored in the user memory area for one of these members, it would cause repetitive failures for this control command until corrected. The next thing the program does is to prompt for a code corresponding to the member to be changed (lines 53-59). This code is stored at the address of the choice variable (line 60). Now, depending upon the member picked, the program prompts for the new value (lines 66-95). The value is placed at the address of the appropriate member in the user memory area data structure, and the system call is made (lines 96-98). Depending upon success or failure, the program returns the same messages as for IPC_STAT above.

If the IPC_RMID control command (code 3) is selected, the system call is performed (lines 100-103), and the **msqid** along with its associated message queue and data structure are removed from the UNIX operating system. Note that the *****buf** pointer is not required as an argument to perform this control command, and its value can be zero or NULL. Depending upon the success or failure, the program returns the same messages as for the other control commands.

The example program for the **msgctl()** system call follows. It is suggested that the source program file be named **msgctl.c** and that the executable file be named **msgctl**. When compiling C programs that use floating point operations, the −**f** option should be used on the **cc** command line. If this option is not used, the program will compile successfully, but when the program is executed it will fail.

```
1     /*This is a program to illustrate
2     **the message control, msgctl(),
3     **system call capabilities.
4     */

5     /*Include necessary header files.*/
6     #include    <stdio.h>
7     #include    <sys/types.h>
8     #include    <sys/ipc.h>
9     #include    <sys/msg.h>

10    /*Start of main C language program*/
11    main()
12    {
13        extern int errno;
14        int uid, gid, mode, bytes;
15        int rtrn, msqid, command, choice;
16        struct msqid_ds msqid_ds, *buf;
17        buf = &msqid_ds;

18        /*Get the msqid, and command.*/
19        printf("Enter the msqid = ");
20        scanf("%d", &msqid);
21        printf("\nEnter the number for\n");
22        printf("the desired command:\n");
23        printf("IPC_STAT    = 1\n");
24        printf("IPC_SET     = 2\n");
25        printf("IPC_RMID    = 3\n");
26        printf("Entry       = ");
27        scanf("%d", &command);
```

Figure 9-5: **msgctl**() System Call Example (Sheet 1 of 4)

```
28          /*Check the values.*/
29          printf ("\nmsqid =%d, command = %d\n",
30              msqid, command);

31          switch (command)
32          {
33          case 1:     /*Use msgctl() to duplicate
34                  the data structure for
35                          msqid in the msqid_ds area pointed
36                          to by buf and then print it out.*/
37              rtrn = msgctl(msqid, IPC_STAT,
38                  buf);
39              printf ("\nThe USER ID = %d\n",
40                  buf->msg_perm.uid);
41              printf ("The GROUP ID = %d\n",
42                  buf->msg_perm.gid);
43              printf ("The operation permissions = 0%o\n",
44                  buf->msg_perm.mode);
45              printf ("The msg_qbytes = %d\n",
46                  buf->msg_qbytes);
47              break;
48          case 2:     /*Select and change the desired
49                          member(s) of the data structure.*/
50              /*Get the original data for this msqid
51                  data structure first.*/
52              rtrn = msgctl(msqid, IPC_STAT, buf);
53              printf("\nEnter the number for the\n");
54              printf("member to be changed:\n");
55              printf("msg_perm.uid    = 1\n");
56              printf("msg_perm.gid    = 2\n");
57              printf("msg_perm.mode   = 3\n");
58              printf("msg_qbytes      = 4\n");
59              printf("Entry           = ");
```

Figure 9-5: **msgctl**() System Call Example (Sheet 2 of 4)

```
60          scanf("%d", &choice);
61          /*Only one choice is allowed per
62            pass as an illegal entry will
63                cause repetitive failures until
64            msqid_ds is updated with
65                IPC_STAT.*/

66          switch(choice){
67          case 1:
68              printf("\nEnter USER ID = ");
69              scanf ("%d", &uid);
70              buf->msg_perm.uid = uid;
71              printf("\nUSER ID = %d\n",
72                  buf->msg_perm.uid);
73              break;
74          case 2:
75              printf("\nEnter GROUP ID = ");
76              scanf("%d", &gid);
77              buf->msg_perm.gid = gid;
78              printf("\nGROUP ID = %d\n",
79                  buf->msg_perm.gid);
80              break;
81          case 3:
82              printf("\nEnter MODE = ");
83              scanf("%o", &mode);
84              buf->msg_perm.mode = mode;
85              printf("\nMODE = 0%o\n",
86                  buf->msg_perm.mode);
87              break;
```

Figure 9-5: **msgctl**() System Call Example (Sheet 3 of 4)

```
88          case 4:
89              printf("\nEnter msq_bytes = ");
90              scanf("%d", &bytes);
91              buf->msg_qbytes = bytes;
92              printf("\nmsg_qbytes = %d\n",
93                  buf->msg_qbytes);
94              break;
95          }

96          /*Do the change.*/
97          rtrn = msgctl(msqid, IPC_SET,
98              buf);
99          break;

100     case 3:     /*Remove the msqid along with its
101                     associated message queue
102                     and data structure.*/
103         rtrn = msgctl(msqid, IPC_RMID, NULL);
104     }
105     /*Perform the following if the call is unsuccessful.*/
106     if(rtrn == -1)
107     {
108         printf ("\nThe msgctl system call failed!\n");
109         printf ("The error number = %d\n", errno);
110     }
111     /*Return the msqid upon successful completion.*/
112     else
113         printf ("\nMsgctl was successful for msqid = %d\n",
114             msqid);
115     exit (0);
116 }
```

Figure 9-5: **msgctl**() System Call Example (Sheet 4 of 4)

# Operations for Messages

This section gives a detailed description of using the **msgsnd**(2) and **msgrcv**(2) system calls, along with an example program which allows all of their capabilities to be exercised.

## Using msgop

The synopsis found in the **msgop**(2) entry in the *Programmer's Reference Manual* is as follows:

```
#include <sys/types.h>
#include <sys/ipc.h>
#include <sys/msg.h>

int msgsnd (msqid, msgp, msgsz, msgflg)
int msqid;
struct msgbuf *msgp;
int msgsz, msgflg;

int msgrcv (msqid, msgp, msgsz, msgtyp, msgflg)
int msqid;
struct msgbuf *msgp;
int msgsz;
long msgtyp;
int msgflg;
```

### Sending a Message

The **msgsnd** system call requires four arguments to be passed to it. It returns an integer value.

Upon successful completion, a zero value is returned; and when unsuccessful, **msgsnd**() returns a −1.

The **msqid** argument must be a valid, non-negative, integer value. In other words, it must have already been created by using the **msgget**() system call.

The **msgp** argument is a pointer to a structure in the user memory area that contains the type of the message and the message to be sent.

The **msgsz** argument specifies the length of the character array in the data structure pointed to by the **msgp** argument. This is the length of the message. The maximum **size** of this array is determined by the MSGMAX system tunable parameter.

The **msg_qbytes** data structure member can be lowered from MSGMNB by using the **msgctl**() IPC_SET control command, but only the super-user can raise it afterwards.

The **msgflg** argument allows the "blocking message operation" to be performed if the IPC_NOWAIT flag is not set (**msgflg** & IPC_NOWAIT = 0); this would occur if the total number of bytes allowed on the specified message queue are in use (**msg_qbytes** or MSGMNB), or the total system-wide number of messages on all queues is equal to the system imposed limit (MSGTQL). If the IPC_NOWAIT flag is set, the system call will fail and return a −1.

Further details of this system call are discussed in the example program for it. If you have problems understanding the logic manipulations in this program, read the "Using **msgget**" section of this chapter; it goes into more detail than what would be practical to do for every system call.

### Receiving Messages

The **msgrcv**() system call requires five arguments to be passed to it, and it returns an integer value.

Upon successful completion, a value equal to the number of bytes received is returned and when unsuccessful it returns a −1.

The **msqid** argument must be a valid, non-negative, integer value. In other words, it must have already been created by using the **msgget**() system call.

The **msgp** argument is a pointer to a structure in the user memory area that will receive the message type and the message text.

The **msgsz** argument specifies the length of the message to be received. If its value is less than the message in the array, an error can be returned if desired; see the **msgflg** argument.

The **msgtyp** argument is used to pick the first message on the message queue of the particular type specified. If it is equal to zero, the first message on the queue is received; if it is greater than zero, the first message of the same type is received; if it is less than zero, the lowest type that is less than or equal to its absolute value is received.

The **msgflg** argument allows the "blocking message operation" to be performed if the IPC_NOWAIT flag is not set (**msgflg** & IPC_NOWAIT = 0); this would occur if there is not a message on the message queue of the desired type (**msgtyp**) to be received. If the IPC_NOWAIT flag is set, the system call will fail immediately when there is not a message of the desired type on the queue. Msgflg can also specify that the system call fail if the message is longer than the **size** to be received; this is done by not setting the MSG_NOERROR flag in the **msgflg** argument (**msgflg** & MSG_NOERROR = 0). If the MSG_NOERROR flag is set, the message is truncated to the length specified by the **msgsz** argument of **msgrcv**().

Further details of this system call are discussed in the example program for it. If you have problems understanding the logic manipulations in this program, read the "Using **msgget**" section of this chapter; it goes into more detail than what would be practical to do for every system call.

## Example Program

The example program in this section (Figure 9-6) is a menu driven program which allows all possible combinations of using the **msgsnd**() and **msgrcv**(2) system calls to be exercised.

From studying this program, you can observe the method of passing arguments and receiving return values. The user-written program requirements are pointed out.

This program begins (lines 5-9) by including the required header files as specified by the **msgop**(2) entry in the *Programmer's Reference Manual*. Note that in this program **errno** is declared as an external variable, and therefore, the **errno.h** header file does not have to be included.

Variable and structure names have been chosen to be as close as possible to those in the synopsis. Their declarations are self-explanatory. These names make the program more readable, and this is perfectly legal since they are local to the program. The variables declared for this program and their purposes are as follows:

**sndbuf**  used as a buffer to contain a message to be sent (line 13); it uses the **msgbuf1** data structure as a template (lines 10-13) The **msgbuf1** structure (lines 10-13) is almost an exact duplicate of the **msgbuf** structure contained in the **msg.h** header file. The only difference is that the character array for **msgbuf1** contains the maximum message **size** (MSGMAX) for the 3B2 Computer where in **msgbuf** it is set to one (1) to satisfy the compiler. For this reason **msgbuf** cannot be used directly as a template for the user-written program. It is there so you can determine its members.

**rcvbuf**  used as a buffer to receive a message (line 13); it uses the **msgbuf1** data structure as a template (lines 10-13)

**\*msgp**  used as a pointer (line 13) to both the **sndbuf** and **rcvbuf** buffers

**i**  used as a counter for inputting characters from the keyboard, storing them in the array, and keeping track of the message length for the **msgsnd**() system call; it is also used as a counter to output the received message for the **msgrcv**() system call

**c**  used to receive the input character from the **getchar**() function (line 50)

**flag**  used to store the code of IPC_NOWAIT for the **msgsnd**() system call (line 61)

**flags**  used to store the code of the IPC_NOWAIT or MSG_NOERROR flags for the **msgrcv**() system call (line 117)

**choice**  used to store the code for sending or receiving (line 30)

**rtrn**  used to store the return values from all system calls

**msqid**  used to store and pass the desired message queue identifier for both system calls

| | |
|---|---|
| **msgsz** | used to store and pass the **size** of the message to be sent or received |
| **msgflg** | used to pass the value of flag for sending or the value of flags for receiving |
| **msgtyp** | used for specifying the message type for sending, or used to pick a message type for receiving. |

Note that a **msqid_ds** data structure is set up in the program (line 21) with a pointer which is initialized to point to it (line 22); this will allow the data structure members that are affected by message operations to be observed. They are observed by using the **msgctl()** (IPC_STAT) system call to get them for the program to print them out (lines 80-92 and lines 161-168).

The first thing the program prompts for is whether to send or receive a message. A corresponding code must be entered for the desired operation, and it is stored at the address of the choice variable (lines 23-30). Depending upon the code, the program proceeds as in the following **msgsnd** or **msgrcv** sections.

### msgsnd

When the code is to send a message, the **msgp** pointer is initialized (line 33) to the address of the send data structure, **sndbuf**. Next, a message type must be entered for the message; it is stored at the address of the variable **msgtyp** (line 42), and then (line 43) it is put into the mtype member of the data structure pointed to by **msgp**.

The program now prompts for a message to be entered from the keyboard and enters a loop of getting and storing into the mtext array of the data structure (lines 48-51). This will continue until an end of file is recognized which for the **getchar()** function is a control-d (CTRL-D) immediately following a carriage return (<CR>). When this happens, the **size** of the message is determined by adding one to the **i** counter (lines 52, 53) as it stored the message beginning in the zero array element of mtext. Keep in mind that the message also contains the terminating characters, and the message will therefore appear to be three characters short of **msgsz**.

The message is immediately echoed from the mtext array of the **sndbuf** data structure to provide feedback (lines 54-56).

The next and final thing that must be decided is whether to set the IPC_NOWAIT flag. The program does this by requesting that a code of a 1 be entered for yes or anything else for no (lines 57-65). It is stored at the address of the flag variable. If a 1 is entered, IPC_NOWAIT is logically ORed with **msgflg**; otherwise, **msgflg** is set to zero.

The **msgsnd**() system call is performed (line 69). If it is unsuccessful, a failure message is displayed along with the error number (lines 70-72). If it is successful, the returned value is printed which should be zero (lines 73-76).

Every time a message is successfully sent, there are three members of the associated data structure which are updated. They are described as follows:

**msg_qnum**  represents the total number of messages on the message queue; it is incremented by one.

**msg_lspid**  contains the Process Identification (PID) number of the last process sending a message; it is set accordingly.

**msg_stime**  contains the time in seconds since January 1, 1970, Greenwich Mean Time (GMT) of the last message sent; it is set accordingly.

These members are displayed after every successful message send operation (lines 79-92).

**msgrcv**

If the code specifies that a message is to be received, the program continues execution as in the following paragraphs.

The **msgp** pointer is initialized to the **rcvbuf** data structure (line 99).

Next, the message queue identifier of the message queue from which to receive the message is requested, and it is stored at the address of **msqid** (lines 100-103).

The message type is requested, and it is stored at the address of **msgtyp** (lines 104-107).

The code for the desired combination of control flags is requested next, and it is stored at the address of flags (lines 108-117). Depending upon the selected combination, **msgflg** is set accordingly (lines 118-133).

Finally, the number of bytes to be received is requested, and it is stored at the address of **msgsz** (lines 134-137).

The **msgrcv**() system call is performed (line 144). If it is unsuccessful, a message and error number is displayed (lines 145-148). If successful, a message indicates so, and the number of bytes returned is displayed followed by the received message (lines 153-159).

When a message is successfully received, there are three members of the associated data structure which are updated; they are described as follows:

**msg_qnum**   contains the number of messages on the message queue; it is decremented by one.

**msg_lrpid**   contains the process identification (PID) of the last process receiving a message; it is set accordingly.

**msg_rtime**   contains the time in seconds since January 1, 1970, Greenwich Mean Time (GMT) that the last process received a message; it is set accordingly.

The example program for the **msgop**() system calls follows. It is suggested that the program be put into a source file called **msgop.c** and then into an executable file called **msgop**.

When compiling C programs that use floating point operations, the −**f** option should be used on the **cc** command line. If this option is not used, the program will compile successfully, but when the program is executed it will fail.

```
1    /*This is a program to illustrate
2    **the message operations, msgop(),
3    **system call capabilities.
4    */

5    /*Include necessary header files.*/
6    #include    <stdio.h>
7    #include    <sys/types.h>
8    #include    <sys/ipc.h>
9    #include    <sys/msg.h>

10   struct msgbuf1 {
11       long    mtype;
12       char    mtext[8192];
13   } sndbuf, rcvbuf, *msgp;

14   /*Start of main C language program*/
15   main()
16   {
17       extern int errno;
18       int i, c, flag, flags, choice;
19       int rtrn, msqid, msgsz, msgflg;
20       long mtype, msgtyp;
21       struct msqid_ds msqid_ds, *buf;
22       buf = &msqid_ds;
```

Figure 9-6: **msgop**() System Call Example (Sheet 1 of 7)

```
23        /*Select the desired operation.*/
24        printf("Enter the corresponding\n");
25        printf("code to send or\n");
26        printf("receive a message:\n");
27        printf("Send            =  1\n");
28        printf("Receive         =  2\n");
29        printf("Entry           =  ");
30        scanf("%d", &choice);

31        if(choice == 1) /*Send a message.*/
32        {
33            msgp = &sndbuf; /*Point to user send structure.*/

34            printf("\nEnter the msqid of\n");
35            printf("the message queue to\n");
36            printf("handle the message = ");
37            scanf("%d", &msqid);

38            /*Set the message type.*/
39            printf("\nEnter a positive integer\n");
40            printf("message type (long) for the\n");
41            printf("message = ");
42            scanf("%d", &msgtyp);
43            msgp->mtype = msgtyp;

44            /*Enter the message to send.*/
45            printf("\nEnter a message: \n");

46            /*A control-d (^d) terminates as
47               EOF.*/
```

Figure 9-6: **msgop**() System Call Example (Sheet 2 of 7)

```
48          /*Get each character of the message
49            and put it in the mtext array.*/
50          for(i = 0; ((c = getchar()) != EOF); i++)
51              sndbuf.mtext[i] = c;

52          /*Determine the message size.*/
53          msgsz = i + 1;

54          /*Echo the message to send.*/
55          for(i = 0; i < msgsz; i++)
56              putchar(sndbuf.mtext[i]);

57          /*Set the IPC_NOWAIT flag if
58            desired.*/
59          printf("\nEnter a 1 if you want the\n");
60          printf("the IPC_NOWAIT flag set:  ");
61          scanf("%d", &flag);
62          if(flag == 1)
63              msgflg |= IPC_NOWAIT;
64          else
65              msgflg = 0;

66          /*Check the msgflg.*/
67          printf("\nmsgflg = 0%o\n", msgflg);

68          /*Send the message.*/
69          rtrn = msgsnd(msqid, msgp, msgsz, msgflg);
70          if(rtrn == -1)
71          printf("\nMsgsnd failed.  Error = %d\n",
72                  errno);
73          else {
74              /*Print the value of test which
75                  should be zero for successful.*/
76              printf("\nValue returned = %d\n", rtrn);
```

Figure 9-6: **msgop**() System Call Example (Sheet 3 of 7)

```
77              /*Print the size of the message
78                sent.*/
79              printf("\nMsgsz = %d\n", msgsz);

80              /*Check the data structure update.*/
81              msgctl(msqid, IPC_STAT, buf);

82              /*Print out the affected members.*/

83              /*Print the incremented number of
84                messages on the queue.*/
85              printf("\nThe msg_qnum = %d\n",
86                  buf->msg_qnum);
87              /*Print the process id of the last sender.*/
88              printf("The msg_lspid = %d\n",
89                  buf->msg_lspid);
90              /*Print the last send time.*/
91              printf("The msg_stime = %d\n",
92                  buf->msg_stime);
93          }
94      }

95      if(choice == 2)   /*Receive a message.*/
96      {
97          /*Initialize the message pointer
98            to the receive buffer.*/
99          msgp = &rcvbuf;

100         /*Specify the message queue which contains
101             the desired message.*/
102         printf("\nEnter the msqid = ");
103         scanf("%d", &msqid);
```

Figure 9-6: **msgop**() System Call Example (Sheet 4 of 7)

```
104         /*Specify the specific message on the queue
105              by using its type.*/
106         printf("\nEnter the msgtyp = ");
107         scanf("%d", &msgtyp);

108         /*Configure the control flags for the
109              desired actions.*/
110         printf("\nEnter the corresponding code\n");
111         printf("to select the desired flags: \n");
112         printf("No flags                   =  0\n");
113         printf("MSG_NOERROR                =  1\n");
114         printf("IPC_NOWAIT                 =  2\n");
115         printf("MSG_NOERROR and IPC_NOWAIT =  3\n");
116         printf("                   Flags   =  ");
117         scanf("%d", &flags);

118         switch(flags) {
119            /*Set msgflg by ORing it with the appropriate
120                     flags (constants).*/
121         case 0:
122            msgflg = 0;
123            break;
124         case 1:
125            msgflg |= MSG_NOERROR;
126            break;
127         case 2:
128            msgflg |= IPC_NOWAIT;
129            break;
130         case 3:
131            msgflg |= MSG_NOERROR | IPC_NOWAIT;
132            break;
133         }
```

Figure 9-6: **msgop**() System Call Example (Sheet 5 of 7)

```
134          /*Specify the number of bytes to receive.*/
135          printf("\nEnter the number of bytes\n");
136          printf("to receive (msgsz) = ");
137          scanf("%d", &msgsz);

138          /*Check the values for the arguments.*/
139          printf("\nmsqid =%d\n", msqid);
140          printf("\nmsgtyp = %d\n", msgtyp);
141          printf("\nmsgsz = %d\n", msgsz);
142          printf("\nmsgflg = 0%o\n", msgflg);

143          /*Call msgrcv to receive the message.*/
144          rtrn = msgrcv(msqid, msgp, msgsz, msgtyp, msgflg);

145          if(rtrn == -1)  {
146              printf("\nMsgrcv failed.  ");
147              printf("Error = %d\n", errno);
148          }
149          else {
150              printf ("\nMsgctl was successful\n");
151              printf("for msqid = %d\n",
152                  msqid);

153              /*Print the number of bytes received,
154                it is equal to the return
155                value.*/
156              printf("Bytes received = %d\n", rtrn);
```

Figure 9-6: **msgop**() System Call Example (Sheet 6 of 7)

```
157              /*Print the received message.*/
158              for(i = 0; i<=rtrn; i++)
159                  putchar(rcvbuf.mtext[i]);
160          }
161          /*Check the associated data structure.*/
162          msgctl(msqid, IPC_STAT, buf);
163          /*Print the decremented number of messages.*/
164          printf("\nThe msg_qnum = %d\n", buf->msg_qnum);
165          /*Print the process id of the last receiver.*/
166          printf("The msg_lrpid = %d\n", buf->msg_lrpid);
167          /*Print the last message receive time*/
168          printf("The msg_rtime = %d\n", buf->msg_rtime);
169      }
170  }
```

Figure 9-6: **msgop**() System Call Example (Sheet 7 of 7)

# Semaphores

The semaphore type of IPC allows processes to communicate through the exchange of semaphore values. A semaphore is a positive integer (0 through 32,767). Since many applications require the use of more than one semaphore, the UNIX operating system has the ability to create sets or arrays of semaphores. A semaphore set can contain one or more semaphores up to a limit set by the system administrator. The tunable parameter, SEMMSL has a default value of 25. Semaphore sets are created by using the **semget**(2) system call.

The process performing the **semget**(2) system call becomes the owner/creator, determines how many semaphores are in the set, and sets the operation permissions for the set, including itself. This process can subsequently relinquish ownership of the set or change the operation permissions using the **semctl**(), semaphore control, system call. The creating process always remains the creator as long as the facility exists. Other processes with permission can use **semctl**() to perform other control functions.

Provided a process has alter permission, it can manipulate the semaphore(s). Each semaphore within a set can be manipulated in two ways with the **semop**(2) system call (which is documented in the *Programmer's Reference Manual*):

- incremented
- decremented

To increment a semaphore, an integer value of the desired magnitude is passed to the **semop**(2) system call. To decrement a semaphore, a minus (−) value of the desired magnitude is passed.

The UNIX operating system ensures that only one process can manipulate a semaphore set at any given time. Simultaneous requests are performed sequentially in an arbitrary manner.

A process can test for a semaphore value to be greater than a certain value by attempting to decrement the semaphore by one more than that value. If the process is successful, then the semaphore value is greater than that certain value. Otherwise, the semaphore value is not. While doing this, the process can have its execution suspended (IPC_NOWAIT flag not set) until the semaphore value would permit the operation (other processes increment the semaphore), or the semaphore facility is removed.

The ability to suspend execution is called a "blocking semaphore operation." This ability is also available for a process which is testing for a semaphore to become zero or equal to zero; only read permission is required for this test, and it is accomplished by passing a value of zero to the **semop**(2) system call.

On the other hand, if the process is not successful and the process does not request to have its execution suspended, it is called a "nonblocking semaphore operation." In this case, the process is returned a known error code (−1), and the external **errno** variable is set accordingly.

The blocking semaphore operation allows processes to communicate based on the values of semaphores at different points in time. Remember also that IPC facilities remain in the UNIX operating system until removed by a permitted process or until the system is reinitialized.

Operating on a semaphore set is done by using the **semop**(2), semaphore operation, system call.

When a set of semaphores is created, the first semaphore in the set is semaphore number zero. The last semaphore number in the set is one less than the total in the set.

An array of these "blocking/nonblocking operations" can be performed on a set containing more than one semaphore. When performing an array of operations, the "blocking/nonblocking operations" can be applied to any or all of the semaphores in the set. Also, the operations can be applied in any order of semaphore number. However, no operations are done until they can all be done successfully. This requirement means that preceding changes made to semaphore values in the set must be undone when a "blocking semaphore operation" on a semaphore in the set cannot be completed successfully; no changes are made until they can all be made. For example, if a process has successfully completed three of six operations on a set of ten semaphores but is "blocked" from performing the fourth operation, no changes are made to the set until the fourth and remaining operations are successfully performed. Additionally, any operation preceding or succeeding the "blocked" operation, including the blocked operation, can specify that at such time that all operations can be performed successfully, that the operation be undone. Otherwise, the operations are performed and the semaphores are changed or one "nonblocking operation" is unsuccessful and none are changed. All of this is commonly referred to as being "atomically performed."

The ability to undo operations requires the UNIX operating system to maintain an array of "undo structures" corresponding to the array of semaphore operations to be performed. Each semaphore operation which is to be undone has an associated adjust variable used for undoing the operation, if necessary.

Remember, any unsuccessful "nonblocking operation" for a single semaphore or a set of semaphores causes immediate return with no operations performed at all. When this occurs, a known error code (−1) is returned to the process, and the external variable **errno** is set accordingly.

System calls make these semaphore capabilities available to processes.The calling process passes arguments to a system call, and the system call either successfully or unsuccessfully performs its function. If the system call is successful, it performs its function and returns the appropriate information. Otherwise, a known error code (-1) is returned to the process, and the external variable **errno** is set accordingly.

# Using Semaphores

Before semaphores can be used (operated on or controlled) a uniquely identified **data structure** and **semaphore set** (array) must be created. The unique identifier is called the semaphore identifier (**semid**); it is used to identify or reference a particular data structure and semaphore set.

The semaphore set contains a predefined number of structures in an array, one structure for each semaphore in the set. The number of semaphores (**nsems**) in a semaphore set is user selectable. The following members are in each structure within a semaphore set:

- semaphore text map address

- process identification (PID) performing last operation

- number of processes awaiting the semaphore value to become greater than its current value

- number of processes awaiting the semaphore value to equal zero

There is one associated data structure for the uniquely identified semaphore set. This data structure contains information related to the semaphore set as follows:

- operation permissions data (operation permissions structure)
- pointer to first semaphore in the set (array)
- number of semaphores in the set
- last semaphore operation time
- last semaphore change time

The C Programming Language data structure definition for the semaphore set (array member) is as follows:

```
struct sem
{
        ushort  semval;     /* semaphore text map address */
        short   sempid;     /* pid of last operation */
        ushort  semncnt;    /* # awaiting semval > cval */
        ushort  semzcnt;    /* # awaiting semval = 0 */
};
```

It is located in the **#include <sys/sem.h>** header file.

Likewise, the structure definition for the associated semaphore data structure is as follows:

```
struct semid_ds
{
        struct ipc_perm sem_perm;    /* operation permission struct */
        struct sem      *sem_base;   /* ptr to first semaphore in set */
        ushort          sem_nsems;   /* # of semaphores in set */
        time_t          sem_otime;   /* last semop time */
        time_t          sem_ctime;   /* last change time */
};
```

It is also located in the **#include <sys/sem.h>** header file. Note that the **sem_perm** member of this structure uses **ipc_perm** as a template. The breakout for the operation permissions data structure is shown in Figure 9-1.

The **ipc_perm** data structure is the same for all IPC facilities, and it is located in the **#include <sys/ipc.h>** header file. It is shown in the "Messages" section.

The **semget**(2) system call is used to perform two tasks when only the IPC_CREAT flag is set in the **semflg** argument that it receives:

- to get a new **semid** and create an associated data structure and semaphore set for it

- to return an existing **semid** that already has an associated data structure and semaphore set

The task performed is determined by the value of the **key** argument passed to the **semget**(2) system call. For the first task, if the **key** is not already in use for an existing **semid**, a new **semid** is returned with an associated data structure and semaphore set created for it provided no system tunable parameter would be exceeded.

There is also a provision for specifying a **key** of value zero (0) which is known as the private **key** (IPC_PRIVATE = 0); when specified, a new **semid** is always returned with an associated data structure and semaphore set created for it unless a system tunable parameter would be exceeded. When the **ipcs** command is performed, the KEY field for the **semid** is all zeros.

When performing the first task, the process which calls **semget()** becomes the owner/creator, and the associated data structure is initialized accordingly. Remember, ownership can be changed, but the creating process always remains the creator; see the "Controlling Semaphores" section in this chapter. The creator of the semaphore set also determines the initial operation permissions for the facility.

For the second task, if a **semid** exists for the **key** specified, the value of the existing **semid** is returned. If it is not desired to have an existing **semid** returned, a control command (IPC_EXCL) can be specified (set) in the **semflg** argument passed to the system call. The system call will fail if it is passed a value for the number of semaphores (**nsems**) that is greater than the number actually in the set; if you do not know how many semaphores are in the set, use 0 for **nsems**. The details of using this system call are discussed in the "Using **semget**" section of this chapter.

Once a uniquely identified semaphore set and data structure are created, semaphore operations [**semop**(2)] and semaphore control [**semctl**()] can be used.

Semaphore operations consist of incrementing, decrementing, and testing for zero. A single system call is used to perform these operations. It is called **semop**(). Refer to the "Operations on Semaphores" section in this chapter for details of this system call.

Semaphore control is done by using the **semctl**(2) system call. These control operations permit you to control the semaphore facility in the following ways:

- to return the value of a semaphore
- to set the value of a semaphore
- to return the process identification (PID) of the last process performing an operation on a semaphore set
- to return the number of processes waiting for a semaphore value to become greater than its current value
- to return the number of processes waiting for a semaphore value to equal zero
- to get all semaphore values in a set and place them in an array in user memory

- to set all semaphore values in a semaphore set from an array of values in user memory

- to place all data structure member values, status, of a semaphore set into user memory area

- to change operation permissions for a semaphore set

- to remove a particular **semid** from the UNIX operating system along with its associated data structure and semaphore set

Refer to the "Controlling Semaphores" section in this chapter for details of the **semctl**(2) system call.

# Getting Semaphores

This section contains a detailed description of using the **semget**(2) system call along with an example program illustrating its use.

### Using semget

The synopsis found in the **semget**(2) entry in the *Programmer's Reference Manual* is as follows:

```
#include  <sys/types.h>
#include  <sys/ipc.h>
#include  <sys/sem.h>

int  semget (key, nsems, semg)
key_t  key;
int nsems, semg;
```

The following line in the synopsis:

```
int semget (key, nsems, semflg)
```

informs you that **semget()** is a function with three formal arguments that returns an integer type value, upon successful completion (**semid**). The next two lines:

```
key_t  key;
int nsems, semflg;
```

declare the types of the formal arguments. **key_t** is declared by a **typedef** in the **types.h** header file to be an integer.

The integer returned from this system call upon successful completion is the semaphore set identifier (**semid**) that was discussed above.

As declared, the process calling the **semget()** system call must supply three actual arguments to be passed to the formal **key**, **nsems**, and **semflg** arguments.

A new **semid** with an associated semaphore set and data structure is provided if either

- **key** is equal to IPC_PRIVATE,

    **or**

- **key** is passed a unique hexadecimal integer, and **semflg** ANDed with IPC_CREAT is TRUE.

The value passed to the **semflg** argument must be an integer type octal value and will specify the following:

- access permissions
- execution modes
- control fields (commands)

Access permissions determine the read/alter attributes and execution modes determine the user/group/other attributes of the **semflg** argument. They are collectively referred to as "operation permissions." Figure 9-7 reflects the numeric values (expressed in octal notation) for the valid operation permissions codes.

| Operation Permissions | Octal Value |
|---|---|
| Read by User | 00400 |
| Alter by User | 00200 |
| Read by Group | 00040 |
| Alter by Group | 00020 |
| Read by Others | 00004 |
| Alter by Others | 00002 |

Figure 9-7: Operation Permissions Codes

A specific octal value is derived by adding the octal values for the operation permissions desired. That is, if read by user and read/alter by others is desired, the code value would be 00406 (00400 plus 00006). There are constants **#define**'d in the **sem.h** header file which can be used for the user (OWNER). They are as follows:

```
SEM_A    0200    /* alter permission by owner */
SEM_R    0400    /* read permission by owner */
```

Control commands are predefined constants (represented by all uppercase letters). Figure 9-8 contains the names of the constants which apply to the **semget**(2) system call along with their values. They are also referred to as flags and are defined in the **ipc.h** header file.

| Control Command | Value |
|---|---|
| IPC_CREAT | 0001000 |
| IPC_EXCL | 0002000 |

Figure 9-8: Control Commands (Flags)

The value for **semflg** is, therefore, a combination of operation permissions and control commands. After determining the value for the operation permissions as previously described, the desired flag(s) can be specified. This specification is accomplished by bitwise ORing (|) them with the operation permissions; the bit positions and values for the control commands in relation to those of the operation permissions make this possible.  It is illustrated as follows:

|  |  | Octal Value | Binary Value |
|---|---|---|---|
| IPC_CREAT | = | 0 1 0 0 0 | 0 000 001 000 000 000 |
| CW\| ORed by User | = | 0 0 4 0 0 | 0 000 000 100 000 000 |
| **semflg** | = | 0 1 4 0 0 | 0 000 001 100 000 000 |

The **semflg** value can be easily set by using the names of the flags in conjunction with the octal operation permissions value:

```
semid = semget (key, nsems, (IPC_CREAT | 0400));
```

```
semid = semget (key, nsems, (IPC_CREAT | IPC_EXCL | 0400));
```

As specified by the **semget**(2) entry in the *Programmer's Reference Manual,* success or failure of this system call depends upon the actual argument values for **key, nsems, semflg** or system tunable parameters.  The system call will attempt to return a new **semid** if one of the following conditions is true:

- Key is equal to IPC_PRIVATE (0)

- Key does not already have a **semid** associated with it, and (**semflg** & IPC_CREAT) is "true" (not zero).

The **key** argument can be set to IPC_PRIVATE in the following ways:

```
semid = semget (IPC_PRIVATE, nsems, semflg);
```

**or**

```
semid = semget ( 0, nsems, semflg);
```

This alone will cause the system call to be attempted because it satisfies the first condition specified.

Exceeding the SEMMNI, SEMMNS, or SEMMSL system tunable parameters will always cause a failure. The SEMMNI system tunable parameter determines the maximum number of unique semaphore sets (**semid**'s) in the UNIX operating system. The SEMMNS system tunable parameter determines the maximum number of semaphores in all semaphore sets system wide. The SEMMSL system tunable parameter determines the maximum number of semaphores in each semaphore set.

The second condition is satisfied if the value for **key** is not already associated with a **semid**, and the bitwise ANDing of **semflg** and IPC_CREAT is "true" (not zero). This means that the **key** is unique (not in use) within the UNIX operating system for this facility type and that the IPC_CREAT flag is set (**semflg**|IPC_CREAT). The bitwise ANDing (&), which is the logical way of testing if a flag is set, is illustrated as follows:

```
    semflg = x 1 x x x   (x = immaterial)
 &  IPC_CREAT = 0 1 0 0 0

    result = 0 1 0 0 0   (not zero)
```

Since the result is not zero, the flag is set or "true." SEMMNI, SEMMNS, and SEMMSL apply here also, just as for condition one.

IPC_EXCL is another control command used in conjunction with IPC_CREAT to exclusively have the system call fail if, and only if, a **semid** exists for the specified key provided. This is necessary to prevent the process from thinking that it has received a new (unique) **semid** when it has not. In other words, when both IPC_CREAT and IPC_EXCL are specified, a new **semid** is returned if the system call is successful. Any value for **semflg** returns a new **semid** if the key equals zero (IPC_PRIVATE) and no system tunable parameters are exceeded.

Refer to the **semget**(2) manual page for specific associated data structure initialization for successful completion.

## Example Program

The example program in this section (Figure 9-9) is a menu driven program which allows all possible combinations of using the **semget**(2) system call to be exercised.

From studying this program, you can observe the method of passing arguments and receiving return values. The user-written program requirements are pointed out.

This program begins (lines 4-8) by including the required header files as specified by the **semget(2)** entry in the *Programmer's Reference Manual*. Note that the **errno.h** header file is included as opposed to declaring **errno** as an external variable; either method will work.

Variable names have been chosen to be as close as possible to those in the synopsis. Their declarations are self-explanatory. These names make the program more readable, and this is perfectly legal since they are local to the program. The variables declared for this program and their purpose are as follows:

- **key**—used to pass the value for the desired key

- **opperm**—used to store the desired operation permissions

- **flags**—used to store the desired control commands (flags)

- **opperm_flags**—used to store the combination from the logical ORing of the **opperm** and **flags** variables; it is then used in the system call to pass the **semflg** argument

- **semid**—used for returning the semaphore set identification number for a successful system call or the error code (−1) for an unsuccessful one.

The program begins by prompting for a hexadecimal **key**, an octal operation permissions code, and the control command combinations (flags) which are selected from a menu (lines 15-32). All possible combinations are allowed even though they might not be viable. This allows observing the errors for illegal combinations.

Next, the menu selection for the flags is combined with the operation permissions, and the result is stored at the address of the **opperm_flags** variable (lines 36-52).

Then, the number of semaphores for the set is requested (lines 53-57), and its value is stored at the address of **nsems**.

The system call is made next, and the result is stored at the address of the **semid** variable (lines 60, 61).

Since the **semid** variable now contains a valid semaphore set identifier or the error code (−1), it is tested to see if an error occurred (line 63). If **semid** equals −1, a message indicates that an error resulted and the external **errno** variable is displayed (lines 65, 66). Remember that the external **errno** variable is only set when a system call fails; it should only be tested immediately following system calls.

If no error occurred, the returned semaphore set identifier is displayed (line 70).

The example program for the **semget**(2) system call follows. It is suggested that the source program file be named **semget.c** and that the executable file be named **semget**.

```
1    /*This is a program to illustrate
2    **the semaphore get, semget(),
3    **system call capabilities.*/

4    #include    <stdio.h>
5    #include    <sys/types.h>
6    #include    <sys/ipc.h>
7    #include    <sys/sem.h>
8    #include    <errno.h>

9    /*Start of main C language program*/
10   main()
11   {
12       key_t key;      /*declare as long integer*/
13       int opperm, flags, nsems;
14       int semid, opperm_flags;

15       /*Enter the desired key*/
16       printf("\nEnter the desired key in hex = ");
17       scanf("%x", &key);

18       /*Enter the desired octal operation
19            permissions.*/
20       printf("\nEnter the operation\n");
21       printf("permissions in octal = ");
22       scanf("%o", &opperm);
```

Figure 9-9: **semget()** System Call Example (Sheet 1 of 3)

```
23      /*Set the desired flags.*/
24      printf("\nEnter corresponding number to\n");
25      printf("set the desired flags:\n");
26      printf("No flags              = 0\n");
27      printf("IPC_CREAT             = 1\n");
28      printf("IPC_EXCL              = 2\n");
29      printf("IPC_CREAT and IPC_EXCL  = 3\n");
30      printf("          Flags       = ");
31      /*Get the flags to be set.*/
32      scanf("%d", &flags);

33      /*Error checking (debugging)*/
34      printf ("\nkey =0x%x, opperm = 0%o, flags = 0%o\n",
35          key, opperm, flags);
36      /*Incorporate the control fields (flags) with
37          the operation permissions.*/
38      switch (flags)
39      {
40      case 0:    /*No flags are to be set.*/
41          opperm_flags = (opperm | 0);
42          break;
43      case 1:    /*Set the IPC_CREAT flag.*/
44          opperm_flags = (opperm | IPC_CREAT);
45          break;
46      case 2:    /*Set the IPC_EXCL flag.*/
47          opperm_flags = (opperm | IPC_EXCL);
48          break;
49      case 3: /*Set the IPC_CREAT and IPC_EXCL
50                  flags.*/
51          opperm_flags = (opperm | IPC_CREAT | IPC_EXCL);
52      }
```

Figure 9-9: **semget**() System Call Example (Sheet 2 of 3)

```
53      /*Get the number of semaphores for this set.*/
54      printf("\nEnter the number of\n");
55      printf("desired semaphores for\n");
56      printf("this set (25 max) = ");
57      scanf("%d", &nsems);

58      /*Check the entry.*/
59      printf("\nNsems = %d\n", nsems);

60      /*Call the semget system call.*/
61      semid = semget(key, nsems, opperm_flags);

62      /*Perform the following if the call is unsuccessful.*/
63      if(semid == -1)
64      {
65          printf("The semget system call failed!\n");
66          printf("The error number = %d\n", errno);
67      }
68      /*Return the semid upon successful completion.*/
69      else
70          printf("\nThe semid = %d\n", semid);
71      exit(0);
72  }
```

Figure 9-9: **semget**() System Call Example (Sheet 3 of 3)

# Controlling Semaphores

This section contains a detailed description of using the **semctl**(2) system call along with an example program which allows all of its capabilities to be exercised.

## Using semctl

The synopsis found in the **semctl**(2) entry in the *Programmer's Reference Manual* is as follows:

```
#include <sys/types.h>
#include <sys/ipc.h>
#include <sys/sem.h>

int semctl (semid, semnum, cmd, arg)
int semid, cmd;
int semnum;
union semun
{
        int val;
        struct semid_ds *bu;
        ushort array[];
} arg;
```

The **semctl**(2) system call requires four arguments to be passed to it, and it returns an integer value.

The **semid** argument must be a valid, non-negative, integer value that has already been created by using the **semget**(2) system call.

The **semnum** argument is used to select a semaphore by its number. This relates to array (atomically performed) operations on the set. When a set of semaphores is created, the first semaphore is number 0, and the last semaphore has the number of one less than the total in the set.

The **cmd** argument can be replaced by one of the following control commands (flags):

- GETVAL—return the value of a single semaphore within a semaphore set

- SETVAL—set the value of a single semaphore within a semaphore set

- GETPID—return the Process Identifier (PID) of the process that performed the last operation on the semaphore within a semaphore set

- GETNCNT—return the number of processes waiting for the value of a particular semaphore to become greater than its current value

- GETZCNT—return the number of processes waiting for the value of a particular semaphore to be equal to zero

- GETALL—return the values for all semaphores in a semaphore set

- SETALL—set all semaphore values in a semaphore set

- IPC_STAT—return the status information contained in the associated data structure for the specified **semid**, and place it in the data structure pointed to by the *****buf** pointer in the user memory area; **arg.buf** is the union member that contains the value of **buf**

- IPC_SET—for the specified semaphore set (**semid**), set the effective user/group identification and operation permissions

- IPC_RMID—remove the specified (**semid**) semaphore set along with its associated data structure.

A process must have an effective user identification of OWNER/CREATOR or super-user to perform an IPC_SET or IPC_RMID control command. Read/alter permission is required as applicable for the other control commands.

The **arg** argument is used to pass the system call the appropriate union member for the control command to be performed:

- **arg.val**

- **arg.buf**

- **arg.array**

The details of this system call are discussed in the example program for it. If you have problems understanding the logic manipulations in this program, read the "Using **semget**" section of this chapter; it goes into more detail than what would be practical to do for every system call.

## Example Program

The example program in this section (Figure 9-10) is a menu driven program which allows all possible combinations of using the **semctl**(2) system call to be exercised.

From studying this program, you can observe the method of passing arguments and receiving return values. The user-written program requirements are pointed out.

This program begins (lines 5-9) by including the required header files as specified by the **semctl**(2) entry in the *Programmer's Reference Manual* Note that in this program **errno** is declared as an external variable, and therefore the **errno.h** header file does not have to be included.

Variable, structure, and union names have been chosen to be as close as possible to those in the synopsis. Their declarations are self-explanatory. These names make the program more readable, and this is perfectly legal since they are local to the program. Those declared for this program and their purpose are as follows:

- **semid_ds**—used to receive the specified semaphore set identifier's data structure when an IPC_STAT control command is performed

- **c**—used to receive the input values from the **scanf**(3S) function, (line 117) when performing a SETALL control command

- **i**—used as a counter to increment through the union **arg.array** when displaying the semaphore values for a GETALL (lines 97-99) control command, and when initializing the **arg.array** when performing a SETALL (lines 115-119) control command

- **length**—used as a variable to test for the number of semaphores in a set against the **i** counter variable (lines 97, 115)

- **uid**—used to store the IPC_SET value for the effective user identification

- **gid**—used to store the IPC_SET value for the effective group identification

- **mode**—used to store the IPC_SET value for the operation permissions

- **rtrn**—used to store the return integer from the system call which depends upon the control command or a −1 when unsuccessful

- **semid**—used to store and pass the semaphore set identifier to the system call

- **semnum**—used to store and pass the semaphore number to the system call

- **cmd**—used to store the code for the desired control command so that subsequent processing can be performed on it

- **choice**—used to determine which member (**uid, gid, mode**) for the IPC_SET control command that is to be changed

- **arg.val**—used to pass the system call a value to set (SETVAL) or to store (GETVAL) a value returned from the system call for a single semaphore (union member)

- **arg.buf**—a pointer passed to the system call which locates the data structure in the user memory area where the IPC_STAT control command is to place its return values, or where the IPC_SET command gets the values to set (union member)

- **arg.array**—used to store the set of semaphore values when getting (GETALL) or initializing (SETALL) (union member).

Note that the **semid_ds** data structure in this program (line 14) uses the data structure located in the **sem.h** header file of the same name as a template for its declaration. This is a perfect example of the advantage of local variables.

The **arg** union (lines 18-22) serves three purposes in one. The compiler allocates enough storage to hold its largest member. The program can then use the union as any member by referencing union members as if they were regular structure members. Note that the array is declared to have 25 elements (0 through 24).This number corresponds to the maximum number of semaphores allowed per set (SEMMSL), a system tunable parameter.

The next important program aspect to observe is that although the *****buf** pointer member (**arg.buf**) of the union is declared to be a pointer to a data structure of the **semid_ds** type, it must also be initialized to contain the address of the user memory area data structure (line 24). Because of the way this program is written, the pointer does not need to be reinitialized later. If it was used to increment through the array, it would need to be reinitialized just before calling the system call.

Now that all of the required declarations have been presented for this program, this is how it works.

First, the program prompts for a valid semaphore set identifier, which is stored at the address of the **semid** variable (lines 25-27). This is required for all **semctl**(2) system calls.

Then, the code for the desired control command must be entered (lines 28-42), and the code is stored at the address of the **cmd** variable. The code is tested to determine the control command for subsequent processing.

If the GETVAL control command is selected (code 1), a message prompting for a semaphore number is displayed (lines 49, 50). When it is entered, it is stored at the address of the **semnum** variable (line 51). Then, the system call is performed, and the semaphore value is displayed (lines 52-55). If the system call is successful, a message indicates this along with the semaphore set identifier used (lines 195, 196); if the system call is unsuccessful, an error message is displayed along with the value of the external **errno** variable (lines 191-193).

If the SETVAL control command is selected (code 2), a message prompting for a semaphore number is displayed (lines 56, 57). When it is entered, it is stored at the address of the **semnum** variable (line 58). Next, a message prompts for the value to which the semaphore is to be set, and it is stored as the **arg.val** member of the union (lines 59, 60). Then, the system call is performed (lines 61, 63). Depending upon success or failure, the program returns the same messages as for GETVAL above.

If the GETPID control command is selected (code 3), the system call is made immediately since all required arguments are known (lines 64-67), and the PID of the process performing the last operation is displayed. Depending upon success or failure, the program returns the same messages as for GETVAL above.

If the GETNCNT control command is selected (code 4), a message prompting for a semaphore number is displayed (lines 68-72). When entered, it is stored at the address of the **semnum** variable (line 73). Then, the system call is performed, and the number of processes waiting for the semaphore to become greater than its current value is displayed (lines 74-77). Depending upon success or failure, the program returns the same messages as for GETVAL above.

If the GETZCNT control command is selected (code 5), a message prompting for a semaphore number is displayed (lines 78-81). When it is entered, it is stored at the address of the **semnum** variable (line 82). Then the system call is performed, and the number of processes waiting for the semaphore value to become equal to zero is displayed (lines 83, 86). Depending upon success or failure, the program returns the same messages as for GETVAL above.

If the GETALL control command is selected (code 6), the program first performs an IPC_STAT control command to determine the number of semaphores in the set (lines 88-93). The length variable is set to the number of semaphores in the set (line 91). Next, the system call is made and, upon success, the **arg.array** union member contains the values of the semaphore set (line 96). Now, a loop is entered which displays each element of the **arg.array** from zero to one less than the value of length (lines 97-103). The semaphores in the set are displayed on a single line, separated by a space. Depending upon success or failure, the program returns the same messages as for GETVAL above.

If the SETALL control command is selected (code 7), the program first performs an IPC_STAT control command to determine the number of semaphores in the set (lines 106-108). The length variable is set to the number of semaphores in the set (line 109). Next, the program prompts for the values to be set and enters a loop which takes values from the keyboard and initializes the **arg.array** union member to contain the desired values of the semaphore set (lines 113-119). The loop puts the first entry into the array position for semaphore number zero and ends when the semaphore number that is filled in the array equals one less than the value of length. The system call is then made (lines 120-122). Depending upon success or failure, the program returns the same messages as for GETVAL above.

If the IPC_STAT control command is selected (code 8), the system call is performed (line 127), and the status information returned is printed out (lines 128-139); only the members that can be set are printed out in this program. Note that if the system call is unsuccessful, the status information of the last successful one is printed out. In addition, an error message is displayed, and the **errno** variable is printed out (lines 191, 192).

If the IPC_SET control command is selected (code 9), the program gets the current status information for the semaphore set identifier specified (lines 143-146). This is necessary because this example program provides for changing only one member at a time, and the **semctl(2)** system call changes all of them. Also, if an invalid value happened to be stored in the user memory area for one of these members, it would cause repetitive failures for this control command until corrected. The next thing the program does is to prompt for a code corresponding to the member to be changed (lines 147-153). This code is stored at the address of the choice variable (line 154). Now, depending upon the member picked, the program prompts for the new value (lines 155-178). The value is placed at the address of the appropriate member in the user memory area data structure, and the system call is made (line 181). Depending upon success or failure, the program returns the same messages as for GETVAL above.

If the IPC_RMID control command (code 10) is selected, the system call is performed (lines 183-185). The **semid** along with its associated data structure and semaphore set is removed from the UNIX operating system. Depending upon success or failure, the program returns the same messages as for the other control commands.

The example program for the **semctl**(2) system call follows. It is suggested that the source program file be named **semctl.c** and that the executable file be named **semctl**.

```
1     /*This is a program to illustrate
2     **the semaphore control, semctl(),
3     **system call capabilities.
4     */

5     /*Include necessary header files.*/
6     #include    <stdio.h>
7     #include    <sys/types.h>
8     #include    <sys/ipc.h>
9     #include    <sys/sem.h>

10    /*Start of main C language program*/
11    main()
12    {
13        extern int errno;
14        struct semid_ds semid_ds;
15        int c, i, length;
16        int uid, gid, mode;
17        int retrn, semid, semnum, cmd, choice;
18        union semun  {
19            int val;
20            struct semid_ds *buf;
21            ushort array[25];
22        } arg;

23        /*Initialize the data structure pointer.*/
24        arg.buf = &semid_ds;
```

Figure 9-10: **semctl()** System Call Example (Sheet 1 of 7)

```
25        /*Enter the semaphore ID.*/
26        printf("Enter the semid = ");
27        scanf("%d", &semid);

28        /*Choose the desired command.*/
29        printf("\nEnter the number for\n");
30        printf("the desired cmd:\n");
31        printf("GETVAL       =   1\n");
32        printf("SETVAL       =   2\n");
33        printf("GETPID       =   3\n");
34        printf("GETNCNT      =   4\n");
35        printf("GETZCNT      =   5\n");
36        printf("GETALL       =   6\n");
37        printf("SETALL       =   7\n");
38        printf("IPC_STAT     =   8\n");
39        printf("IPC_SET      =   9\n");
40        printf("IPC_RMID     =   10\n");
41        printf("Entry        =   ");
42        scanf("%d", &cmd);

43        /*Check entries.*/
44        printf ("\nsemid =%d, cmd = %d\n\n",
45            semid, cmd);

46        /*Set the command and do the call.*/
47        switch (cmd)
48        {
```

Figure 9-10: **semctl**() System Call Example (Sheet 2 of 7)

```
49          case 1: /*Get a specified value.*/
50                  printf("\nEnter the semnum = ");
51                  scanf("%d", &semnum);
52                  /*Do the system call.*/
53                  retrn = semctl(semid, semnum, GETVAL, 0);
54                  printf("\nThe semval = %d\n", retrn);
55                  break;
56          case 2: /*Set a specified value.*/
57                  printf("\nEnter the semnum = ");
58                  scanf("%d", &semnum);
59                  printf("\nEnter the value = ");
60                  scanf("%d", &arg.val);
61                  /*Do the system call.*/
62                  retrn = semctl(semid, semnum, SETVAL, arg.val);
63                  break;
64          case 3: /*Get the process ID.*/
65                  retrn = semctl(semid, 0, GETPID, 0);
66                  printf("\nThe sempid = %d\n", retrn);
67                  break;
68          case 4: /*Get the number of processes
69                     waiting for the semaphore to
70                     become greater than its current
71                         value.*/
72                  printf("\nEnter the semnum = ");
73                  scanf("%d", &semnum);
74                  /*Do the system call.*/
75                  retrn = semctl(semid, semnum, GETNCNT, 0);
76                  printf("\nThe semncnt = %d", retrn);
77                  break;
```

Figure 9-10: **semctl**() System Call Example (Sheet 3 of 7)

```
78          case 5: /*Get the number of processes
79              waiting for the semaphore
80                      value to become zero.*/
81              printf("\nEnter the semnum = ");
82              scanf("%d", &semnum);
83              /*Do the system call.*/
84              retrn = semctl(semid, semnum, GETZCNT, 0);
85              printf("\nThe semzcnt = %d", retrn);
86              break;

87          case 6: /*Get all of the semaphores.*/
88              /*Get the number of semaphores in
89                the semaphore set.*/
90              retrn = semctl(semid, 0, IPC_STAT, arg.buf);
91              length = arg.buf->sem_nsems;
92              if(retrn == -1)
93                  goto ERROR;
94              /*Get and print all semaphores in the
95                specified set.*/
96              retrn = semctl(semid, 0, GETALL, arg.array);
97              for (i = 0; i < length; i++)
98              {
99                  printf("%d", arg.array[i]);
100                 /*Seperate each
101                   semaphore.*/
102                 printf("%c", ' ');
103             }
104             break;
```

Figure 9-10: **semctl**() System Call Example (Sheet 4 of 7)

```
105      case 7: /*Set all semaphores in the set.*/
106          /*Get the number of semaphores in
107            the set.*/
108          retrn = semctl(semid, 0, IPC_STAT, arg.buf);
109          length = arg.buf->sem_nsems;
110          printf("Length = %d\n", length);
111          if(retrn == -1)
112              goto ERROR;
113          /*Set the semaphore set values.*/
114          printf("\nEnter each value:\n");
115          for(i = 0; i < length ; i++)
116          {
117              scanf("%d", &c);
118              arg.array[i] = c;
119          }
120          /*Do the system call.*/
121          retrn = semctl(semid, 0, SETALL, arg.array);
122          break;

123      case 8: /*Get the status for the semaphore set.*/
125          /*Get and print the current status values.*/
127          retrn = semctl(semid, 0, IPC_STAT, arg.buf);
128          printf ("\nThe USER ID = %d\n",
129              arg.buf->sem_perm.uid);
130          printf ("The GROUP ID = %d\n",
131              arg.buf->sem_perm.gid);
132          printf ("The operation permissions = 0%o\n",
133              arg.buf->sem_perm.mode);
134          printf ("The number of semaphores in set = %d\n",
135              arg.buf->sem_nsems);
136          printf ("The last semop time = %d\n",
137              arg.buf->sem_otime);
```

Figure 9-10: **semctl**() System Call Example (Sheet 5 of 7)

```
138              printf ("The last change time  = %d\n",
139                  arg.buf->sem_ctime);
140              break;

141      case 9:     /*Select and change the desired
142                      member of the data structure.*/
143              /*Get the current status values.*/
144              retrn = semctl(semid, 0, IPC_STAT, arg.buf);
145              if(retrn == -1)
146                  goto ERROR;
147              /*Select the member to change.*/
148              printf("\nEnter the number for the\n");
149              printf("member to be changed:\n");
150              printf("sem_perm.uid  = 1\n");
151              printf("sem_perm.gid  = 2\n");
152              printf("sem_perm.mode = 3\n");
153              printf("Entry         = ");
154              scanf("%d", &choice);
155              switch(choice){

156              case 1: /*Change the user ID.*/
157                  printf("\nEnter USER ID = ");
158                  scanf ("%d", &uid);
159                  arg.buf->sem_perm.uid = uid;
160                  printf("\nUSER ID = %d\n",
161                      arg.buf->sem_perm.uid);
162                  break;

163              case 2: /*Change the group ID.*/
164                  printf("\nEnter GROUP ID = ");
165                  scanf("%d", &gid);
166                  arg.buf->sem_perm.gid = gid;
167                  printf("\nGROUP ID = %d\n",
168                      arg.buf->sem_perm.gid);
169                  break;
```

Figure 9-10: **semctl**() System Call Example (Sheet 6 of 7)

```
170              case 3: /*Change the mode portion of
171                  the operation
172                          permissions.*/
173              printf("\nEnter MODE = ");
174              scanf("%o", &mode);
175              arg.buf->sem_perm.mode = mode;
176              printf("\nMODE = 0%o\n",
177                  arg.buf->sem_perm.mode);
178              break;
179          }
180          /*Do the change.*/
181          retrn = semctl(semid, 0, IPC_SET, arg.buf);
182          break;
183      case 10:    /*Remove the semid along with its
184                  data structure.*/
185          retrn = semctl(semid, 0, IPC_RMID, 0);
186      }
187      /*Perform the following if the call is unsuccessful.*/
188      if(retrn == -1)
189      {
190  ERROR:
191          printf ("\n\nThe semctl system call failed!\n");
192          printf ("The error number = %d\n", errno);
193          exit(0);
194      }
195      printf ("\n\nThe semctl system call was successful\n");
196      printf ("for semid = %d\n", semid);
197      exit (0);
198  }
```

Figure 9-10: **semctl**() System Call Example (Sheet 7 of 7)

# Operations on Semaphores

This section contains a detailed description of using the **semop**(2) system call along with an example program which allows all of its capabilities to be exercised.

## Using semop

The synopsis found in the **semop**(2) entry in the *Programmer's Reference Manual* is as follows:

```
#include <sys/types.h>
#include <sys/ipc.h>
#include <sys/sem.h>

int semop (semid, sops, nsops)
int semid;
struct sembuf **sops;
unsigned nsops;
```

The **semop**(2) system call requires three arguments to be passed to it, and it returns an integer value.

Upon successful completion, a zero value is returned and when unsuccessful it returns a −1.

The **semid** argument must be a valid, non-negative, integer value. In other words, it must have already been created by using the **semget**(2) system call.

The **sops** argument is a pointer to an array of structures in the user memory area that contains the following for each semaphore to be changed:

- the semaphore number

- the operation to be performed

- the control command (flags)

The **sops** declaration means that a pointer can be initialized to the address of the array, or the array name can be used since it is the address of the first element of the array. Sem**buf** is the *tag* name of the data structure used as the template for the structure members in the array; it is located in the **#include <sys/sem.h>** header file.

The **nsops** argument specifies the length of the array (the number of structures in the array). The maximum **size** of this array is determined by the SEMOPM system tunable parameter. Therefore, a maximum of SEMOPM operations can be performed for each **semop**(2) system call.

The semaphore number determines the particular semaphore within the set on which the operation is to be performed.

The operation to be performed is determined by the following:

- a positive integer value means to increment the semaphore value by its value

- a negative integer value means to decrement the semaphore value by its value

- a value of zero means to test if the semaphore is equal to zero

The following operation commands (flags) can be used:

- IPC_NOWAIT—this operation command can be set for any operations in the array. The system call will return unsuccessfully without changing any semaphore values at all if any operation for which IPC_NOWAIT is set cannot be performed successfully. The system call will be unsuccessful when trying to decrement a semaphore more than its current value, or when testing for a semaphore to be equal to zero when it is not.

- SEM_UNDO—this operation command allows any operations in the array to be undone when any operation in the array is unsuccessful and does not have the IPC_NOWAIT flag set. That is, the blocked operation waits until it can perform its operation; and when it and all succeeding operations are successful, all operations with the SEM_UNDO flag set are undone. Remember, no operations are performed on any semaphores in a set until all operations are successful. Undoing is accomplished by using an array of adjust values for the operations that are to be undone when the blocked operation and all subsequent operations are successful.

## Example Program

The example program in this section (Figure 9-11) is a menu driven program which allows all possible combinations of using the **semop**(2) system call to be exercised.

From studying this program, you can observe the method of passing arguments and receiving return values. The user-written program requirements are pointed out.

This program begins (lines 5-9) by including the required header files as specified by the **shmop**(2) entry in the *Programmer's Reference Manual* Note that in this program **errno** is declared as an external variable, and therefore, the **errno.h** header file does not have to be included.

Variable and structure names have been chosen to be as close as possible to those in the synopsis. Their declarations are self-explanatory. These names make the program more readable, and this is perfectly legal since the declarations are local to the program. The variables declared for this program and their purpose are as follows:

- **sembuf[10]**—used as an array buffer (line 14) to contain a maximum of ten **sembuf** type structures; ten equals SEMOPM, the maximum number of operations on a semaphore set for each **semop**(2) system call

- ***sops**—used as a pointer (line 14) to **sembuf[10]** for the system call and for accessing the structure members within the array

- **rtrn**—used to store the return values from the system call

- **flags**—used to store the code of the IPC_NOWAIT or SEM_UNDO flags for the **semop**(2) system call (line 60)

- **i**—used as a counter (line 32) for initializing the structure members in the array, and used to print out each structure in the array (line 79)

- **nsops**—used to specify the number of semaphore operations for the system call—must be less than or equal to SEMOPM

- **semid**—used to store the desired semaphore set identifier for the system call

First, the program prompts for a semaphore set identifier that the system call is to perform operations on (lines 19-22). Semid is stored at the address of the **semid** variable (line 23).

A message is displayed requesting the number of operations to be performed on this set (lines 25-27). The number of operations is stored at the address of the **nsops** variable (line 28).

Next, a loop is entered to initialize the array of structures (lines 30-77). The semaphore number, operation, and operation command (flags) are entered for each structure in the array. The number of structures equals the number of semaphore operations (**nsops**) to be performed for the system call, so **nsops** is tested against the **i** counter for loop control. Note that **sops** is used as a pointer to each element (structure) in the array, and **sops** is incremented just like **i**. **sops** is then used to point to each member in the structure for setting them.

After the array is initialized, all of its elements are printed out for feedback (lines 78-85).

The **sops** pointer is set to the address of the array (lines 86, 87). Sem**buf** could be used directly, if desired, instead of **sops** in the system call.

The system call is made (line 89), and depending upon success or failure, a corresponding message is displayed. The results of the operation(s) can be viewed by using the **semctl**() GETALL control command.

The example program for the **semop**(2) system call follows. It is suggested that the source program file be named **semop.c** and that the executable file be named **semop**.

```
 1    /*This is a program to illustrate
 2    **the semaphore operations, semop(),
 3    **system call capabilities.
 4    */

 5    /*Include necessary header files.*/
 6    #include    <stdio.h>
 7    #include    <sys/types.h>
 8    #include    <sys/ipc.h>
 9    #include    <sys/sem.h>
10    /*Start of main C language program*/
11    main()
12    {
13        extern int errno;
14        struct sembuf sembuf[10], *sops;
15        char string[];
16        int retrn, flags, sem_num, i, semid;
17        unsigned nsops;
18        sops = sembuf; /*Pointer to array sembuf.*/

19        /*Enter the semaphore ID.*/
20        printf("\nEnter the semid of\n");
21        printf("the semaphore set to\n");
22        printf("be operated on = ");
23        scanf("%d", &semid);
24        printf("\nsemid = %d", semid);
```

Figure 9-11: **semop**(2) System Call Example (Sheet 1 of 4)

```
25        /*Enter the number of operations.*/
26        printf("\nEnter the number of semaphore\n");
27        printf("operations for this set = ");
28        scanf("%d", &nsops);
29        printf("\nnosops = %d", nsops);

30        /*Initialize the array for the
31          number of operations to be performed.*/
32        for(i = 0; i < nsops; i++, sops++)
33        {

34            /*This determines the semaphore in
35               the semaphore set.*/
36            printf("\nEnter the semaphore\n");
37            printf("number (sem_num) = ");
38            scanf("%d", &sem_num);
39            sops->sem_num = sem_num;
40            printf("\nThe sem_num = %d", sops->sem_num);

41            /*Enter a (-)number to decrement,
42               an unsigned number (no +) to increment,
43               or zero to test for zero.  These values
44               are entered into a string and converted
45               to integer values.*/
46            printf("\nEnter the operation for\n");
47            printf("the semaphore (sem_op) = ");
48            scanf("%s", string);
49            sops->sem_op = atoi(string);
50            printf("\nsem_op = %d\n", sops->sem_op);
```

Figure 9-11: **semop**(2) System Call Example (Sheet 2 of 4)

```
51          /*Specify the desired flags.*/
52          printf("\nEnter the corresponding\n");
53          printf("number for the desired\n");
54          printf("flags:\n");
55          printf("No flags              = 0\n");
56          printf("IPC_NOWAIT            = 1\n");
57          printf("SEM_UNDO              = 2\n");
58          printf("IPC_NOWAIT and SEM_UNDO = 3\n");
59          printf("            Flags     = ");
60          scanf("%d", &flags);

61          switch(flags)
62          {
63          case 0:
64              sops->sem_flg = 0;
65              break;
66          case 1:
67              sops->sem_flg = IPC_NOWAIT;
68              break;
69          case 2:
70              sops->sem_flg = SEM_UNDO;
71              break;
72          case 3:
73              sops->sem_flg = IPC_NOWAIT | SEM_UNDO;
74              break;
75          }
76          printf("\nFlags = 0%o\n", sops->sem_flg);
77      }
```

Figure 9-11: **semop**(2) System Call Example (Sheet 3 of 4)

```
78          /*Print out each structure in the array.*/
79          for(i = 0; i < nsops; i++)
80          {
81              printf("\nsem_num = %d\n", sembuf[i].sem_num);
82              printf("sem_op = %d\n", sembuf[i].sem_op);
83              printf("sem_flg = %o\n", sembuf[i].sem_flg);
84              printf("%c", ' ');
85          }

86          sops = sembuf; /*Reset the pointer to
87                          sembuf[0].*/

88          /*Do the semop system call.*/
89          retrn = semop(semid, sops, nsops);
90          if(retrn == -1)  {
91              printf("\nSemop failed.  ");
92              printf("Error = %d\n", errno);
93          }
94          else {
95              printf ("\nSemop was successful\n");
96              printf("for semid = %d\n", semid);

97              printf("Value returned = %d\n", retrn);
98          }
99      }
```

Figure 9-11: **semop**(2) System Call Example (Sheet 4 of 4)

# Shared Memory

The shared memory type of IPC allows two or more processes (executing programs) to share memory and consequently the data contained there. This is done by allowing processes to set up access to a common virtual memory address space. This sharing occurs on a segment basis, which is memory management hardware dependent.

This sharing of memory provides the fastest means of exchanging data between processes.

A process initially creates a shared memory segment facility using the **shmget**(2) system call. Upon creation, this process sets the overall operation permissions for the shared memory segment facility, sets its size in bytes, and can specify that the shared memory segment is for reference only (read-only) upon attachment. If the memory segment is not specified to be for reference only, all other processes with appropriate operation permissions can read from or write to the memory segment.

There are two operations that can be performed on a shared memory segment:

- **shmat**(2) — shared memory attach
- **shmdt**(2) — shared memory detach

Shared memory attach allows processes to associate themselves with the shared memory segment if they have permission. They can then read or write as allowed.

Shared memory detach allows processes to disassociate themselves from a shared memory segment. Therefore, they lose the ability to read from or write to the shared memory segment.

The original owner/creator of a shared memory segment can relinquish ownership to another process using the **shmctl**(2) system call. However, the creating process remains the creator until the facility is removed or the system is reinitialized. Other processes with permission can perform other functions on the shared memory segment using the **shmctl**(2) system call.

System calls, which are documented in the *Programmer's Reference Manual*, make these shared memory capabilities available to processes. The calling process passes arguments to a system call, and the system call either successfully or unsuccessfully performs its function. If the system call is successful, it performs its function and returns the appropriate information. Otherwise, a known error code (−1) is returned to the process, and the external variable **errno** is set accordingly.

## Using Shared Memory

The sharing of memory between processes occurs on a virtual segment basis. There is one and only one instance of an individual shared memory segment existing in the UNIX operating system at any point in time.

Before sharing of memory can be realized, a uniquely identified shared memory segment and data structure must be created. The unique identifier created is called the shared memory identifier (**shmid**); it is used to identify or reference the associated data structure. The data structure includes the following for each shared memory segment:

- operation permissions
- segment size
- segment descriptor
- process identification performing last operation
- process identification of creator
- current number of processes attached
- in memory number of processes attached
- last attach time
- last detach time
- last change time

The C Programming Language data structure definition for the shared memory segment data structure is located in the **/usr/include/sys/shm.h** header file. It is as follows:

```
/*
**      There is a shared mem id data structure for
**      each segment in the system.
*/

struct shmid_ds {
    struct ipc_perm     shm_perm;       /* operation permission struct */
    int                 shm_segsz;      /* segment size */
    struct region       *shm_reg;       /* ptr to region structure */
    char                pad[4];         /* for swap compatibility */
    ushort              shm_lpid;       /* pid of last shmop */
    ushort              shm_cpid;       /* pid of creator */
    ushort              shm_nattch;     /* used only for shminfo */
    ushort              shm_cnattch;    /* used only for shminfo */
    time_t              shm_atime;      /* last shmat time */
    time_t              shm_dtime;      /* last shmdt time */
    time_t              shm_ctime;      /* last change time */
};
```

Note that the **shm_perm** member of this structure uses **ipc_perm** as a template. The breakout for the operation permissions data structure is shown in Figure 9-1.

The **ipc_perm** data structure is the same for all IPC facilities, and it is located in the **#include <sys/ipc.h>** header file. It is shown in the introduction section of "Messages."

Figure 9-12 is a table that shows the shared memory state information.

Shared Memory States

| Lock Bit | Swap Bit | Allocated Bit | Implied State |
|---|---|---|---|
| 0 | 0 | 0 | Unallocated Segment |
| 0 | 0 | 1 | Incore |
| 0 | 1 | 0 | Unused |
| 0 | 1 | 1 | On Disk |
| 1 | 0 | 1 | Locked Incore |
| 1 | 1 | 0 | Unused |
| 1 | 0 | 0 | Unused |
| 1 | 1 | 1 | Unused |

Figure 9-12: Shared Memory State Information

The implied states of Figure 9-12 are as follows:

- **Unallocated Segment**—the segment associated with this segment descriptor has not been allocated for use.

- **Incore**—the shared segment associated with this descriptor has been allocated for use. Therefore, the segment does exist and is currently resident in memory.

- **On Disk**—the shared segment associated with this segment descriptor is currently resident on the swap device.

- **Locked Incore**—the shared segment associated with this segment descriptor is currently locked in memory and will not be a candidate for swapping until the segment is unlocked. Only the super-user may lock and unlock a shared segment.

- **Unused**—this state is currently unused and should never be encountered by the normal user in shared memory handling.

The **shmget**(2) system call is used to perform two tasks when only the IPC_CREAT flag is set in the **shmflg** argument that it receives:

- to get a new **shmid** and create an associated shared memory segment data structure for it

- to return an existing **shmid** that already has an associated shared memory segment data structure

The task performed is determined by the value of the **key** argument passed to the **shmget**(2) system call. For the first task, if the **key** is not already in use for an existing **shmid**, a new **shmid** is returned with an associated shared memory segment data structure created for it provided no system tunable parameters would be exceeded.

There is also a provision for specifying a **key** of value zero which is known as the private **key** (IPC_PRIVATE = 0); when specified, a new **shmid** is always returned with an associated shared memory segment data structure created for it unless a system tunable parameter would be exceeded. When the **ipcs** command is performed, the KEY field for the **shmid** is all zeros.

For the second task, if a **shmid** exists for the **key** specified, the value of the existing **shmid** is returned. If it is not desired to have an existing **shmid** returned, a control command (IPC_EXCL) can be specified (set) in the **shmflg** argument passed to the system call. The details of using this system call are discussed in the "Using **shmget**" section of this chapter.

When performing the first task, the process that calls **shmget** becomes the owner/creator, and the associated data structure is initialized accordingly. Remember, ownership can be changed, but the creating process always remains the creator; see the "Controlling Shared Memory" section in this chapter. The creator of the shared memory segment also determines the initial operation permissions for it.

Once a uniquely identified shared memory segment data structure is created, shared memory segment operations [**shmop**()] and control [**shmctl**(2)] can be used.

Shared memory segment operations consist of attaching and detaching shared memory segments. System calls are provided for each of these operations; they are **shmat**(2) and **shmdt**(2). Refer to the "Operations for Shared Memory" section in this chapter for details of these system calls.

Shared memory segment control is done by using the **shmctl**(2) system call. It permits you to control the shared memory facility in the following ways:

- to determine the associated data structure status for a shared memory segment (**shmid**)

- to change operation permissions for a shared memory segment

- to remove a particular **shmid** from the UNIX operating system along with its associated shared memory segment data structure

- to lock a shared memory segment in memory

- to unlock a shared memory segment

Refer to the "Controlling Shared Memory" section in this chapter for details of the **shmctl**(2) system call.

## Getting Shared Memory Segments

This section gives a detailed description of using the **shmget**(2) system call along with an example program illustrating its use.

### Using shmget

The synopsis found in the **shmget**(2) entry in the *Programmer's Reference Manual* is as follows:

```
#include  <sys/types.h>
#include  <sys/ipc.h>
#include  <sys/shm.h>

int  shmget (key, size, shmflg)
key_t  key;
int size, shmflg;
```

All of these include files are located in the **/usr/include/sys** directory of the UNIX operating system. The following line in the synopsis:

```
int shmget (key, size, shmflg)
```

informs you that **shmget**(2) is a function with three formal arguments that returns an integer type value, upon successful completion (**shmid**). The next two lines:

```
key_t  key;
int size, shmflg;
```

declare the types of the formal arguments. The variable **key_t** is declared by a **typedef** in the **types.h** header file to be an integer.

The integer returned from this function upon successful completion is the shared memory identifier (**shmid**) that was discussed earlier.

As declared, the process calling the **shmget**(2) system call must supply three arguments to be passed to the formal **key**, **size**, and **shmflg** arguments.

A new **shmid** with an associated shared memory data structure is provided if either

- **key** is equal to IPC_PRIVATE,

or

- **key** is passed a unique hexadecimal integer, and **shmflg** ANDed with IPC_CREAT is TRUE.

The value passed to the **shmflg** argument must be an integer type octal value and will specify the following:

- access permissions
- execution modes
- control fields (commands)

Access permissions determine the read/write attributes and execution modes determine the user/group/other attributes of the **shmflg** argument. They are collectively referred to as "operation permissions." Figure 9-13 reflects the numeric values (expressed in octal notation) for the valid operation permissions codes.

| Operation Permissions | Octal Value |
|---|---|
| Read by User | 00400 |
| Write by User | 00200 |
| Read by Group | 00040 |
| Write by Group | 00020 |
| Read by Others | 00004 |
| Write by Others | 00002 |

Figure 9-13: Operation Permissions Codes

A specific octal value is derived by adding the octal values for the operation permissions desired. That is, if read by user and read/write by others is desired, the code value would be 00406 (00400 plus 00006). There are constants located in the **shm.h** header file which can be used for the user (OWNER). They are as follows:

```
SHM_R              0400
SHM_W              0200
```

Control commands are predefined constants (represented by all uppercase letters). Figure 9-14 contains the names of the constants that apply to the **shmget()** system call along with their values. They are also referred to as flags and are defined in the **ipc.h** header file.

| Control Command | Value |
|---|---|
| IPC_CREAT | 0001000 |
| IPC_EXCL | 0002000 |

Figure 9-14: Control Commands (Flags)

The value for **shmflg** is, therefore, a combination of operation permissions and control commands. After determining the value for the operation permissions as previously described, the desired flag(s) can be specified. This is accomplished by bitwise ORing (|) them with the operation permissions; the bit positions and values for the control commands in relation to those of the operation permissions make this possible. It is illustrated as follows:

|  |  | Octal Value | Binary Value |
|---|---|---|---|
| IPC_CREAT | = | 0 1 0 0 0 | 0 000 001 000 000 000 |
| ¦ ORed by User | = | 0 0 4 0 0 | 0 000 000 100 000 000 |
| shmflg | = | 0 1 4 0 0 | 0 000 001 100 000 000 |

The **shmflg** value can be easily set by using the names of the flags in conjunction with the octal operation permissions value:

```
shmid = shmget (key, size, (IPC_CREAT ¦ 0400));
```

```
shmid = shmget (key, size, (IPC_CREAT ¦ IPC_EXCL ¦ 0400));
```

As specified by the **shmget**(2) entry in the *Programmer's Reference Manual*, success or failure of this system call depends upon the argument values for **key**, **size**, and **shmflg** or system tunable parameters. The system call will attempt to return a new **shmid** if one of the following conditions is true:

- Key is equal to IPC_PRIVATE (0).

- Key does not already have a **shmid** associated with it, and (**shmflg** & IPC_CREAT) is "true" (not zero).

The **key** argument can be set to IPC_PRIVATE in the following ways:

```
shmid = shmget (IPC_PRIVATE, size, shmflg);
```

**or**

```
shmid = shmget ( 0 , size, shmflg);
```

This alone will cause the system call to be attempted because it satisfies the first condition specified. Exceeding the SHMMNI system tunable parameter always causes a failure. The SHMMNI system tunable parameter determines the maximum number of unique shared memory segments (**shmid**s) in the UNIX operating system.

The second condition is satisfied if the value for **key** is not already associated with a **shmid** and the bitwise ANDing of **shmflg** and IPC_CREAT is "true" (not zero). This means that the **key** is unique (not in use) within the UNIX operating system for this facility type and that the IPC_CREAT flag is set (**shmflg** | IPC_CREAT). The bitwise ANDing (&), which is the logical way of testing if a flag is set, is illustrated as follows:

```
    shmflg = x 1 x x x   (x = immaterial)
& IPC_CREAT = 0 1 0 0 0

    result = 0 1 0 0 0   (not zero)
```

Because the result is not zero, the flag is set or "true." SHMMNI applies here also, just as for condition one.

IPC_EXCL is another control command used in conjunction with IPC_CREAT to exclusively have the system call fail if, and only if, a **shmid** exists for the specified **key** provided. This is necessary to prevent the process from thinking that it has received a new (unique) **shmid** when it has not. In other words, when both IPC_CREAT and IPC_EXCL are specified, a unique **shmid** is returned if the system call is successful. Any value for **shmflg** returns a new **shmid** if the **key** equals zero (IPC_PRIVATE).

The system call will fail if the value for the **size** argument is less than SHMMIN or greater than SHMMAX. These tunable parameters specify the minimum and maximum shared memory segment **size**s.

Refer to the **shmget**(2) manual page for specific associated data structure initialization for successful completion. The specific failure conditions with error names are contained there also.

## Example Program

The example program in this section (Figure 9-15) is a menu driven program which allows all possible combinations of using the **shmget**(2) system call to be exercised.

From studying this program, you can observe the method of passing arguments and receiving return values. The user-written program requirements are pointed out.

This program begins (lines 4-7) by including the required header files as specified by the **shmget**(2) entry in the *Programmer's Reference Manual*. Note that the **errno.h** header file is included as opposed to declaring **errno** as an external variable; either method will work.

Variable names have been chosen to be as close as possible to those in the synopsis for the system call. Their declarations are self-explanatory. These names make the program more readable, and this is perfectly legal since they are local to the program. The variables declared for this program and their purposes are as follows:

- **key**—used to pass the value for the desired **key**
- **opperm**—used to store the desired operation permissions
- **flags**—used to store the desired control commands (flags)
- **opperm_flags**—used to store the combination from the logical ORing of the **opperm** and **flags** variables; it is then used in the system call to pass the **shmflg** argument
- **shmid**—used for returning the message queue identification number for a successful system call or the error code (−1) for an unsuccessful one
- **size**—used to specify the shared memory segment size.

The program begins by prompting for a hexadecimal **key**, an octal operation permissions code, and finally for the control command combinations (flags) which are selected from a menu (lines 14-31). All possible combinations are allowed even though they might not be viable. This allows observing the errors for illegal combinations.

Next, the menu selection for the flags is combined with the operation permissions, and the result is stored at the address of the **opperm_flags** variable (lines 35-50).

A display then prompts for the **size** of the shared memory segment, and it is stored at the address of the **size** variable (lines 51-54).

The system call is made next, and the result is stored at the address of the **shmid** variable (line 56).

Since the **shmid** variable now contains a valid message queue identifier or the error code (−1), it is tested to see if an error occurred (line 58). If **shmid** equals −1, a message indicates that an error resulted and the external **errno** variable is displayed (lines 60, 61).

If no error occurred, the returned shared memory segment identifier is displayed (line 65).

The example program for the **shmget**(2) system call follows. It is suggested that the source program file be named **shmget.c** and that the executable file be named **shmget**.

When compiling C programs that use floating point operations, the −**f** option should be used on the **cc** command line. If this option is not used, the program will compile successfully, but when the program is executed it will fail.

```
1      /*This is a program to illustrate
2      **the shared memory get, shmget(),
3      **system call capabilities.*/

4      #include     <sys/types.h>
5      #include     <sys/ipc.h>
6      #include     <sys/shm.h>
7      #include     <errno.h>

8      /*Start of main C language program*/
9      main()
10     {
11         key_t key;                /*declare as long integer*/
12         int opperm, flags;
13         int shmid, size, opperm_flags;
14         /*Enter the desired key*/
15         printf("Enter the desired key in hex = ");
16         scanf("%x", &key);

17         /*Enter the desired octal operation
18           permissions.*/
19         printf("\nEnter the operation\n");
20         printf("permissions in octal = ");
21         scanf("%o", &opperm);
```

Figure 9-15: **shmget**(2) System Call Example (Sheet 1 of 3)

```
22      /*Set the desired flags.*/
23      printf("\nEnter corresponding number to\n");
24      printf("set the desired flags:\n");
25      printf("No flags                   = 0\n");
26      printf("IPC_CREAT                  = 1\n");
27      printf("IPC_EXCL                   = 2\n");
28      printf("IPC_CREAT and IPC_EXCL     = 3\n");
29      printf("            Flags          = ");
30      /*Get the flag(s) to be set.*/
31      scanf("%d", &flags);

32      /*Check the values.*/
33      printf ("\nkey =0x%x, opperm = 0%o, flags = 0%o\n",
34          key, opperm, flags);

35      /*Incorporate the control fields (flags) with
36        the operation permissions*/
37      switch (flags)
38      {
39      case 0:    /*No flags are to be set.*/
40          opperm_flags = (opperm | 0);
41          break;
42      case 1:    /*Set the IPC_CREAT flag.*/
43          opperm_flags = (opperm | IPC_CREAT);
44          break;
45      case 2:    /*Set the IPC_EXCL flag.*/
46          opperm_flags = (opperm | IPC_EXCL);
47          break;
48      case 3:    /*Set the IPC_CREAT and IPC_EXCL flags.*/
49          opperm_flags = (opperm | IPC_CREAT | IPC_EXCL);
50      }
```

Figure 9-15: **shmget**(2) System Call Example (Sheet 2 of 3)

```
51        /*Get the size of the segment in bytes.*/
52        printf ("\nEnter the segment");
53        printf ("\nsize in bytes = ");
54        scanf ("%d", &size);

55        /*Call the shmget system call.*/
56        shmid = shmget (key, size, opperm_flags);

57        /*Perform the following if the call is unsuccessful.*/
58        if(shmid == -1)
59        {
60            printf ("\nThe shmget system call failed!\n");
61            printf ("The error number = %d\n", errno);
62        }
63        /*Return the shmid upon successful completion.*/
64        else
65            printf ("\nThe shmid = %d\n", shmid);
66        exit(0);
67    }
```

Figure 9-15: **shmget**(2) System Call Example (Sheet 3 of 3)

# Controlling Shared Memory

This section gives a detailed description of using the **shmctl**(2) system call along with an example program which allows all of its capabilities to be exercised.

## Using shmctl

The synopsis found in the **shmctl**(2) entry in the *Programmer's Reference Manual* is as follows:

```
#include <sys/types.h>
#include <sys/ipc.h>
#include <sys/shm.h>

int shmctl (shmid, cmd, buf)
int shmid, cmd;
struct shmid_ds *buf;
```

The **shmctl**(2) system call requires three arguments to be passed to it, and **shmctl**(2) returns an integer value.

Upon successful completion, a zero value is returned; and when unsuccessful, **shmctl**() returns a −1.

The **shmid** variable must be a valid, non-negative, integer value. In other words, it must have already been created by using the **shmget**(2) system call.

The **cmd** argument can be replaced by one of following control commands (flags):

- IPC_STAT—return the status information contained in the associated data structure for the specified **shmid** and place it in the data structure pointed to by the ∗**buf** pointer in the user memory area

- IPC_SET—for the specified **shmid**, set the effective user and group identification, and operation permissions

- IPC_RMID—remove the specified **shmid** along with its associated shared memory segment data structure

- SHM_LOCK—lock the specified shared memory segment in memory, must be super-user

■ SHM_UNLOCK—unlock the shared memory segment from memory, must be super-user.

A process must have an effective user identification of OWNER/CREATOR or super-user to perform an IPC_SET or IPC_RMID control command. Only the super-user can perform a SHM_LOCK or SHM_UNLOCK control command. A process must have read permission to perform the IPC_STAT control command.

The details of this system call are discussed in the example program for it. If you have problems understanding the logic manipulations in this program, read the "Using **shmget**" section of this chapter; it goes into more detail than what would be practical to do for every system call.

## Example Program

The example program in this section (Figure 9-16) is a menu driven program which allows all possible combinations of using the **shmctl**(2) system call to be exercised.

From studying this program, you can observe the method of passing arguments and receiving return values. The user-written program requirements are pointed out.

This program begins (lines 5-9) by including the required header files as specified by the **shmctl**(2) entry in the *Programmer's Reference Manual*. Note in this program that **errno** is declared as an external variable, and therefore, the **errno.h** header file does not have to be included.

Variable and structure names have been chosen to be as close as possible to those in the synopsis for the system call. Their declarations are self-explanatory. These names make the program more readable, and it is perfectly legal since they are local to the program. The variables declared for this program and their purposes are as follows:

■ **uid**—used to store the IPC_SET value for the effective user identification

■ **gid**—used to store the IPC_SET value for the effective group identification

■ **mode**—used to store the IPC_SET value for the operation permissions

- **rtrn**—used to store the return integer value from the system call

- **shmid**—used to store and pass the shared memory segment identifier to the system call

- **command**—used to store the code for the desired control command so that subsequent processing can be performed on it

- **choice**—used to determine which member for the IPC_SET control command that is to be changed

- **shmid_ds**—used to receive the specified shared memory segment identifier's data structure when an IPC_STAT control command is performed

- **\*buf**—a pointer passed to the system call which locates the data structure in the user memory area where the IPC_STAT control command is to place its return values or where the IPC_SET command gets the values to set.

Note that the **shmid_ds** data structure in this program (line 16) uses the data structure located in the **shm.h** header file of the same name as a template for its declaration. This is a perfect example of the advantage of local variables.

The next important thing to observe is that although the **\*buf** pointer is declared to be a pointer to a data structure of the **shmid_ds** type, it must also be initialized to contain the address of the user memory area data structure (line 17).

Now that all of the required declarations have been explained for this program, this is how it works.

First, the program prompts for a valid shared memory segment identifier which is stored at the address of the **shmid** variable (lines 18-20). This is required for every **shmctl(2)** system call.

Then, the code for the desired control command must be entered (lines 21-29), and it is stored at the address of the command variable. The code is tested to determine the control command for subsequent processing.

If the IPC_STAT control command is selected (code 1), the system call is performed (lines 39, 40) and the status information returned is printed out (lines 41-71). Note that if the system call is unsuccessful (line 146), the status information of the last successful call is printed out. In addition, an error message is displayed and the **errno** variable is printed out (lines 148, 149). If the system call is successful, a message indicates this along with the shared memory segment identifier used (lines 151-154).

If the IPC_SET control command is selected (code 2), the first thing done is to get the current status information for the message queue identifier specified (lines 90-92). This is necessary because this example program provides for changing only one member at a time, and the system call changes all of them. Also, if an invalid value happened to be stored in the user memory area for one of these members, it would cause repetitive failures for this control command until corrected. The next thing the program does is to prompt for a code corresponding to the member to be changed (lines 93-98). This code is stored at the address of the choice variable (line 99). Now, depending upon the member picked, the program prompts for the new value (lines 105-127). The value is placed at the address of the appropriate member in the user memory area data structure, and the system call is made (lines 128-130). Depending upon success or failure, the program returns the same messages as for IPC_STAT above.

If the IPC_RMID control command (code 3) is selected, the system call is performed (lines 132-135), and the **shmid** along with its associated message queue and data structure are removed from the UNIX operating system. Note that the **∗buf** pointer is not required as an argument to perform this control command and its value can be zero or NULL. Depending upon the success or failure, the program returns the same messages as for the other control commands.

If the SHM_LOCK control command (code 4) is selected, the system call is performed (lines 137,138). Depending upon the success or failure, the program returns the same messages as for the other control commands.

If the SHM_UNLOCK control command (code 5) is selected, the system call is performed (lines 140-142). Depending upon the success or failure, the program returns the same messages as for the other control commands.

The example program for the **shmctl**(2) system call follows. It is suggested that the source program file be named **shmctl.c** and that the executable file be named **shmctl**.

When compiling C programs that use floating point operations, the −**f** option should be used on the **cc** command line. If this option is not used, the program will compile successfully, but when the program is executed it will fail.

```
1    /*This is a program to illustrate
2    **the shared memory control, shmctl(),
3    **system call capabilities.
4    */

5    /*Include necessary header files.*/
6    #include    <stdio.h>
7    #include    <sys/types.h>
8    #include    <sys/ipc.h>
9    #include    <sys/shm.h>

10   /*Start of main C language program*/
11   main()
12   {
13       extern int errno;
14       int uid, gid, mode;
15       int rtrn, shmid, command, choice;
16       struct shmid_ds shmid_ds, *buf;
17       buf = &shmid_ds;

18       /*Get the shmid, and command.*/
19       printf("Enter the shmid = ");
20       scanf("%d", &shmid);
21       printf("\nEnter the number for\n");
22       printf("the desired command:\n");
```

Figure 9-16: **shmctl**(2) System Call Example (Sheet 1 of 6)

```
23          printf("IPC_STAT    =  1\n");
24          printf("IPC_SET     =  2\n");
25          printf("IPC_RMID    =  3\n");
26          printf("SHM_LOCK    =  4\n");
27          printf("SHM_UNLOCK  =  5\n");
28          printf("Entry       =  ");
29          scanf("%d", &command);

30          /*Check the values.*/
31          printf ("\nshmid =%d, command = %d\n",
32              shmid, command);

33          switch (command)
34          {
35          case 1:    /*Use shmctl() to duplicate
36              the data structure for
37                      shmid in the shmid_ds area pointed
38                      to by buf and then print it out.*/
39              rtrn = shmctl(shmid, IPC_STAT,
40                  buf);
41              printf ("\nThe USER ID = %d\n",
42                  buf->shm_perm.uid);
43              printf ("The GROUP ID = %d\n",
44                  buf->shm_perm.gid);
45              printf ("The creator's ID = %d\n",
46                  buf->shm_perm.cuid);
47              printf ("The creator's group ID = %d\n",
48                  buf->shm_perm.cgid);
49              printf ("The operation permissions = 0%o\n",
50                  buf->shm_perm.mode);
51              printf ("The slot usage sequence\n");
```

Figure 9-16: **shmctl**(2) System Call Example (Sheet 2 of 6)

```
52              printf ("number = 0%x\n",
53                  buf->shm_perm.seq);
54              printf ("The key= 0%x\n",
55                  buf->shm_perm.key);
56              printf ("The segment size = %d\n",
57                  buf->shm_segsz);
58              printf ("The pid of last shmop = %d\n",
59                  buf->shm_lpid);
60              printf ("The pid of creator = %d\n",
61                  buf->shm_cpid);
62              printf ("The current # attached = %d\n",
63                  buf->shm_nattch);
64              printf("The in memory # attached = %d\n",
65                  buf->shm_cnattach);
66              printf("The last shmat time = %d\n",
67                  buf->shm_atime);
68              printf("The last shmdt time = %d\n",
69                  buf->shm_dtime);
70              printf("The last change time = %d\n",
71                  buf->shm_ctime);
72              break;

                /* Lines 73 - 87 deleted */
```

Figure 9-16: **shmctl**(2) System Call Example (Sheet 3 of 6)

```
 88        case 2:     /*Select and change the desired
 89                        member(s) of the data structure.*/

 90            /*Get the original data for this shmid
 91                data structure first.*/
 92            rtrn = shmctl(shmid, IPC_STAT, buf);

 93            printf("\nEnter the number for the\n");
 94            printf("member to be changed:\n");
 95            printf("shm_perm.uid   = 1\n");
 96            printf("shm_perm.gid   = 2\n");
 97            printf("shm_perm.mode  = 3\n");
 98            printf("Entry          = ");
 99            scanf("%d", &choice);
100            /*Only one choice is allowed per
101              pass as an illegal entry will
102                 cause repetitive failures until
103              shmid_ds is updated with
104                 IPC_STAT.*/
```

Figure 9-16: **shmctl**(2) System Call Example (Sheet 4 of 6)

```
105         switch(choice){
106         case 1:
107             printf("\nEnter USER ID = ");
108             scanf ("%d", &uid);
109             buf->shm_perm.uid = uid;
110             printf("\nUSER ID = %d\n",
111                 buf->shm_perm.uid);
112             break;

113         case 2:
114             printf("\nEnter GROUP ID = ");
115             scanf("%d", &gid);
116             buf->shm_perm.gid = gid;
117             printf("\nGROUP ID = %d\n",
118                 buf->shm_perm.gid);
119             break;

120         case 3:
121             printf("\nEnter MODE = ");
122             scanf("%o", &mode);
123             buf->shm_perm.mode = mode;
124             printf("\nMODE = 0%o\n",
125                 buf->shm_perm.mode);
126             break;
127         }
128         /*Do the change.*/
129         rtrn = shmctl(shmid, IPC_SET,
130             buf);
131         break;
```

Figure 9-16: **shmctl**() System Call Example (Sheet 5 of 6)

```
132        case 3:    /*Remove the shmid along with its
133                       associated
134                       data structure.*/
135            rtrn = shmctl(shmid, IPC_RMID, NULL);
136            break;

137        case 4: /*Lock the shared memory segment*/
138            rtrn = shmctl(shmid, SHM_LOCK, NULL);
139            break;
140        case 5: /*Unlock the shared memory
141                      segment.*/
142            rtrn = shmctl(shmid, SHM_UNLOCK, NULL);
143            break;
144        }
145        /*Perform the following if the call is unsuccessful.*/
146        if(rtrn == −1)
147        {
148            printf ("\nThe shmctl system call failed!\n");
149            printf ("The error number = %d\n", errno);
150        }
151        /*Return the shmid upon successful completion.*/
152        else
153            printf ("\nShmctl was successful for shmid = %d\n",
154                shmid);
155        exit (0);
156    }
```

Figure 9-16: **shmctl**(2) System Call Example (Sheet 6 of 6)

# Operations for Shared Memory

This section gives a detailed description of using the **shmat**(2) and **shmdt**(2) system calls, along with an example program which allows all of their capabilities to be exercised.

## Using shmop

The synopsis found in the **shmop**(2) entry in the *Programmer's Reference Manual* is as follows:

```
#include <sys/types.h>
#include <sys/ipc.h>
#include <sys/shm.h>

char *shmat (shmid, shmaddr, shmflg)
int shmid;
char *shmaddr;
int shmflg;

int shmdt (shmaddr)
char *shmaddr;
```

### Attaching a Shared Memory Segment

The **shmat**(2) system call requires three arguments to be passed to it, and it returns a character pointer value.

The system call can be cast to return an integer value. Upon successful completion, this value will be the address in core memory where the process is attached to the shared memory segment and when unsuccessful it will be a −1.

The **shmid** argument must be a valid, non-negative, integer value. In other words, it must have already been created by using the **shmget**(2) system call.

The shm**addr** argument can be zero or user supplied when passed to the **shmat**(2) system call. If it is zero, the UNIX operating system picks the address of where the shared memory segment will be attached. If it is user supplied, the address must be a valid address that the UNIX operating system would pick. The following illustrates some typical address ranges; these are for the 3B2 Computer:

> 0xc00c0000
> 0xc00e0000
> 0xc0100000
> 0xc0120000

Note that these addresses are in chunks of 20,000 hexadecimal. It would be wise to let the operating system pick addresses so as to improve portability.

The **shmflg** argument is used to pass the SHM_RND and SHM_RDONLY flags to the **shmat**() system call.

Further details are discussed in the example program for **shmop**(). If you have problems understanding the logic manipulations in this program, read the "Using **shmget**" section of this chapter; it goes into more detail than what would be practical to do for every system call.

### Detaching Shared Memory Segments

The **shmdt**(2) system call requires one argument to be passed to it, and **shmdt**(2) returns an integer value.

Upon successful completion, zero is returned; and when unsuccessful, **shmdt**(2) returns a −1.

Further details of this system call are discussed in the example program. If you have problems understanding the logic manipulations in this program, read the "Using **shmget**" section of this chapter; it goes into more detail than what would be practical to do for every system call.

## Example Program

The example program in this section (Figure 9-17) is a menu driven program which allows all possible combinations of using the **shmat**(2) and **shmdt**(2) system calls to be exercised.

From studying this program, you can observe the method of passing arguments and receiving return values. The user-written program requirements are pointed out.

This program begins (lines 5-9) by including the required header files as specified by the **shmop**(2) entry in the *Programmer's Reference Manual*. Note that in this program that **errno** is declared as an external variable, and therefore, the **errno.h** header file does not have to be included.

Variable and structure names have been chosen to be as close as possible to those in the synopsis. Their declarations are self-explanatory. These names make the program more readable, and this is perfectly legal since they are local to the program. The variables declared for this program and their purposes are as follows:

- **flags**—used to store the codes of SHM_RND or SHM_RDONLY for the **shmat**(2) system call

- **addr**—used to store the address of the shared memory segment for the **shmat**(2) and **shmdt**(2) system calls

- **i**—used as a loop counter for attaching and detaching

- **attach**—used to store the desired number of attach operations

- **shmid**—used to store and pass the desired shared memory segment identifier

- **shmflg**—used to pass the value of flags to the **shmat**(2) system call

- **retrn**—used to store the return values from both system calls

- **detach**—used to store the desired number of detach operations

This example program combines both the **shmat**(2) and **shmdt**(2) system calls. The program prompts for the number of attachments and enters a loop until they are done for the specified shared memory identifiers. Then, the program prompts for the number of detachments to be performed and enters a loop until they are done for the specified shared memory segment addresses.

### shmat

The program prompts for the number of attachments to be performed, and the value is stored at the address of the attach variable (lines 17-21).

A loop is entered using the attach variable and the i counter (lines 23-70) to perform the specified number of attachments.

In this loop, the program prompts for a shared memory segment identifier (lines 24-27) and it is stored at the address of the **shmid** variable (line 28). Next, the program prompts for the address where the segment is to be attached (lines 30-34), and it is stored at the address of the **addr** variable (line 35). Then, the program prompts for the desired flags to be used for the attachment (lines 37-44), and the code representing the flags is stored at the address of the flags variable (line 45). The flags variable is tested to determine the code to be stored for the **shmflg** variable used to pass them to the **shmat**(2) system call (lines 46-57). The system call is made (line 60). If successful, a message stating so is displayed along with the attach address (lines 66-68). If unsuccessful, a message stating so is displayed and the error code is displayed (lines 62, 63). The loop then continues until it finishes.

### shmdt

After the attach loop completes, the program prompts for the number of detach operations to be performed (lines 71-75), and the value is stored at the address of the detach variable (line 76).

A loop is entered using the detach variable and the i counter (lines 78-95) to perform the specified number of detachments.

In this loop, the program prompts for the address of the shared memory segment to be detached (lines 79-83), and it is stored at the address of the **addr** variable (line 84). Then, the **shmdt**(2) system call is performed (line 87). If successful, a message stating so is displayed along with the address that the segment was detached from (lines 92,93). If unsuccessful, the error number is displayed (line 89). The loop continues until it finishes.

The example program for the **shmop**(2) system calls follows. It is suggested that the program be put into a source file called **shmop.c** and then into an executable file called **shmop**.

When compiling C programs that use floating point operations, the −**f** option should be used on the **cc** command line. If this option is not used, the program will compile successfully, but when the program is executed it will fail.

```
1    /*This is a program to illustrate
2    **the shared memory operations, shmop(),
3    **system call capabilities.
4    */

5    /*Include necessary header files.*/
6    #include     <stdio.h>
7    #include     <sys/types.h>
8    #include     <sys/ipc.h>
9    #include     <sys/shm.h>
10   /*Start of main C language program*/
11   main()
12   {
13       extern int errno;
14       int flags, addr, i, attach;
15       int shmid, shmflg, retrn, detach;



16       /*Loop for attachments by this process.*/
17       printf("Enter the number of\n");
18       printf("attachments for this\n");
19       printf("process (1-4).\n");
20       printf("     Attachments = ");

21       scanf("%d", &attach);
22       printf("Number of attaches = %d\n", attach);
```

Figure 9-17: **shmop**() System Call Example (Sheet 1 of 4)

```
23          for(i = 1; i <= attach; i++) {
24              /*Enter the shared memory ID.*/
25              printf("\nEnter the shmid of\n");
26              printf("the shared memory segment to\n");
27              printf("be operated on = ");
28              scanf("%d", &shmid);
29              printf("\nshmid = %d\n", shmid);


30              /*Enter the value for shmaddr.*/
31              printf("\nEnter the value for\n");
32              printf("the shared memory address\n");
33              printf("in hexadecimal:\n");
34              printf("          Shmaddr = ");
35              scanf("%x", &addr);
36              printf("The desired address = 0x%x\n", addr);

37              /*Specify the desired flags.*/
38              printf("\nEnter the corresponding\n");
39              printf("number for the desired\n");
40              printf("flags:\n");
41              printf("SHM_RND               = 1\n");
42              printf("SHM_RDONLY            = 2\n");
43              printf("SHM_RND and SHM_RDONLY = 3\n");
44              printf("              Flags    = ");
45              scanf("%d", &flags);
```

Figure 9-17: **shmop**() System Call Example (Sheet 2 of 4)

```
46          switch(flags)
47          {
48          case 1:
49              shmflg = SHM_RND;
50              break;
51          case 2:
52              shmflg = SHM_RDONLY;
53              break;
54          case 3:
55              shmflg = SHM_RND | SHM_RDONLY;
56              break;
57          }
58          printf("\nFlags = 0%o\n", shmflg);

59          /*Do the shmat system call.*/
60          retrn = (int)shmat(shmid, addr, shmflg);
61          if(retrn == -1)  {
62              printf("\nShmat failed.  ");
63              printf("Error = %d\n", errno);
64          }
65          else {
66              printf ("\nShmat was successful\n");
67              printf("for shmid = %d\n", shmid);
68              printf("The address = 0x%x\n", retrn);
69          }
70      }

71      /*Loop for detachments by this process.*/
72      printf("Enter the number of\n");
73      printf("detachments for this\n");
74      printf("process (1-4).\n");
75      printf("        Detachments = ");
```

Figure 9-17: **shmop**() System Call Example (Sheet 3 of 4)

```
76          scanf("%d", &detach);
77          printf("Number of attaches = %d\n", detach);
78          for(i = 1; i <= detach; i++) {

79              /*Enter the value for shmaddr.*/
80              printf("\nEnter the value for\n");
81              printf("the shared memory address\n");
82              printf("in hexadecimal:\n");
83              printf("          Shmaddr = ");
84              scanf("%x", &addr);
85              printf("The desired address = 0x%x\n", addr);

86              /*Do the shmdt system call.*/
87              retrn = (int)shmdt(addr);
88              if(retrn == -1)   {
89                  printf("Error = %d\n", errno);
90              }
91              else {
92                  printf ("\nShmdt was successful\n");
93                  printf("for address  = 0%x\n", addr);

94              }
95          }
96      }
```

Figure 9-17: **shmop**() System Call Example (Sheet 4 of 4)

# CHAPTER 10: curses/terminfo

## Introduction

Screen management programs are a common component of many commercial computer applications. These programs handle input and output at a video display terminal. A screen program might move a cursor, print a menu, divide a terminal screen into windows, or draw a display on the screen to help users enter and retrieve information from a database.

This tutorial explains how to use the Terminal Information Utilities package, commonly called **curses/terminfo**, to write screen management programs on a UNIX system. This package includes a library of C routines, a database, and a set of UNIX system support tools. To start you writing screen management programs as soon as possible, the tutorial does not attempt to cover every part of the package. For instance, it covers only the most frequently used routines and then points you to **curses**(3X) and **terminfo**(4) in the *Programmer's Reference Manual* for more information. Keep the manual close at hand; you'll find it invaluable when you want to know more about one of these routines or about other routines not discussed here.

Because the routines are compiled C functions, you should be familiar with the C programming language before using **curses/terminfo**. You should also be familiar with the UNIX system/C language standard I/O package (see "System Calls and Subroutines" and "Input/Output" in Chapter 2 and **stdio**(3S)). With that knowledge and an appreciation for the UNIX philosophy of building on the work of others, you can design screen management programs for many purposes.

This chapter has five sections:

- Overview

  This section briefly describes **curses**, **terminfo**, and the other components of the Terminal Information Utilities package.

- Working with **curses** Routines

  This section describes the basic routines making up the **curses**(3X) library. It covers the routines for writing to a screen, reading from a screen, and building windows. It also covers routines for more advanced screen management programs that draw line graphics, use a terminal's soft labels, and work with more than one terminal at the same time. Many examples are included to show the effect of using these routines.

■ Working with **terminfo** Routines

This section describes the routines in the **curses** library that deal directly with the **terminfo** database to handle certain terminal capabilities, such as programming function keys.

■ Working with the **terminfo** Database

This section describes the **terminfo** database, related support tools, and their relationship to the **curses** library.

■ **curses** Program Examples

This section includes six programs that illustrate uses of **curses** routines.

# Overview

## What is curses?

**curses**(3X) is the library of routines that you use to write screen management programs on the UNIX system. The routines are C functions and macros; many of them resemble routines in the standard C library. For example, there's a routine **printw**() that behaves much like **printf**(3S) and another routine **getch**() that behaves like **getc**(3S). The automatic teller program at your bank might use **printw**() to print its menus and **getch**() to accept your requests for withdrawals (or, better yet, deposits). A visual screen editor like the UNIX system screen editor **vi**(1) might also use these and other **curses** routines.

The **curses** routines are usually located in **/usr/lib/libcurses.a**. To compile a program using these routines, you must use the **cc**(1) command and include **−lcurses** on the command line so that the link editor can locate and load them:

      **cc**  *file*.**c**   **−lcurses**   **−o**   *file*

The name **curses** comes from the cursor optimization that this library of routines provides. Cursor optimization minimizes the amount a cursor has to move around a screen to update it. For example, if you designed a screen editor program with **curses** routines and edited the sentence

      curses/terminfo is a great package for creating screens.

to read

      curses/terminfo is the best package for creating screens.

the program would output only the best in place of a great. The other characters would be preserved. Because the amount of data transmitted—the output—is minimized, cursor optimization is also referred to as output optimization.

Cursor optimization takes care of updating the screen in a manner appropriate for the terminal on which a **curses** program is run. This means that the **curses** library can do whatever is required to update many different terminal types. It searches the **terminfo** database (described below) to find the correct description for a terminal.

How does cursor optimization help you and those who use your programs? First, it saves you time in describing in a program how you want to update screens. Second, it saves a user's time when the screen is updated. Third, it reduces the load on your UNIX system's communication lines when the updating takes place. Fourth, you don't have to worry about the myriad of terminals on which your program might be run.

Here's a simple **curses** program. It uses some of the basic **curses** routines to move a cursor to the middle of a terminal screen and print the character string BullsEye. Each of these routines is described in the following section "Working with **curses** Routines" in this chapter. For now, just look at their names and you will get an idea of what each of them does:

```
#include <curses.h>

main()
{
    initscr();

    move( LINES/2 - 1, COLS/2 - 4 );
    addstr("Bulls");
    refresh();
    addstr("Eye");
    refresh();
    endwin();
}
```

Figure 10-1: A Simple **curses** Program

# What Is terminfo?

**terminfo** refers to both of the following:

- It is a group of routines within the **curses** library that handles certain terminal capabilities. You can use these routines to program function keys, if your terminal has programmable keys, or write filters, for example. Shell programmers, as well as C programmers, can use the **terminfo** routines in their programs.

- It is a database containing the descriptions of many terminals that can be used with **curses** programs. These descriptions specify the capabilities of a terminal and the way it performs various operations—for example, how many lines and columns it has and how its control characters are interpreted.

Each terminal description in the database is a separate, compiled file. You use the source code that **terminfo**(4) describes to create these files and the command **tic**(1M) to compile them.

The compiled files are normally located in the directories **/usr/lib/terminfo/?**. These directories have single character names, each of which is the first character in the name of a terminal. For example, an entry for the AT&T Teletype 5425 is normally located in the file **/usr/lib/terminfo/a/att5425**.

Here's a simple shell script that uses the **terminfo** database.

```
#    Clear the screen and show the 0,0 position.
#
tput clear
tput cup 0 0          # or tput home
echo "<- this is 0 0"

#
#    Show the 5,10 position.
#
tput cup 5 10
echo "<- this is 5 10"
```

Figure 10-2: A Shell Script Using **terminfo** Routines

# How curses **and terminfo Work Together**

A screen management program with **curses** routines refers to the **terminfo** database at run time to obtain the information it needs about the terminal being used—what we'll call the current terminal from here on.

For example, suppose you are using an AT&T Teletype 5425 terminal to run the simple **curses** program shown in Figure 10-1. To execute properly, the program needs to know how many lines and columns the terminal screen has to print the BullsEye in the middle of it. The description of the AT&T Teletype 5425 in the **terminfo** database has this information. All the **curses** program needs to know before it goes looking for the information is the name of your terminal. You tell the program the name by putting it in the environment variable **$TERM** when you log in or by setting and exporting **$TERM** in your **.profile** file (see **profile**(4)). Knowing **$TERM**, a **curses** program run on the current terminal can search the **terminfo** database to find the correct terminal description.

For example, assume that the following example lines are in a **.profile**:

```
TERM=5425
export TERM
tput init
```

The first line names the terminal type, and the second line exports it. (See **profile**(4) in the *Programmer's Reference Manual*.) The third line of the example tells the UNIX system to initialize the current terminal. That is, it makes sure that the terminal is set up according to its description in the **terminfo** database. (The order of these lines is important. **$TERM** must be defined and exported first, so that when **tput** is called the proper initialization for the current terminal takes place.) If you had these lines in your **.profile** and you ran a **curses** program, the program would get the information that it needs about your terminal from the file **/usr/lib/terminfo/a/att5425**, which provides a match for **$TERM**.

## Other Components of the Terminal Information Utilities

We said earlier that the Terminal Information Utilities is commonly referred to as **curses/terminfo**. The package, however, has other components. We've mentioned some of them, for instance **tic**(1M). Here's a complete list of the components discussed in this tutorial:

| | |
|---|---|
| **captoinfo**(1M) | a tool for converting terminal descriptions developed on earlier releases of the UNIX system to **terminfo** descriptions |
| **curses**(3X) | |
| **infocmp**(1M) | a tool for printing and comparing compiled terminal descriptions |
| **tabs**(1) | a tool for setting non-standard tab stops |
| **terminfo**(4) | |
| **tic**(1M) | a tool for compiling terminal descriptions for the **terminfo** database |

**tput**(1)  a tool for initializing the tab stops on a terminal and for outputting the value of a terminal capability

We also refer to **profile**(4), **scr_dump**(4), **term**(4), and **term**(5). For more information about any of these components, see the *Programmer's Reference Manual* and the *User's Reference Manual*.

# Working with curses Routines

This section describes the basic **curses** routines for creating interactive screen management programs. It begins by describing the routines and other program components that every **curses** program needs to work properly. Then it tells you how to compile and run a **curses** program. Finally, it describes the most frequently used **curses** routines that

- write output to and read input from a terminal screen

- control the data output and input — for example, to print output in bold type or prevent it from echoing (printing back on a screen)

- manipulate multiple screen images (windows)

- draw simple graphics

- manipulate soft labels on a terminal screen

- send output to and accept input from more than one terminal.

To illustrate the effect of using these routines, we include simple example programs as the routines are introduced. We also refer to a group of larger examples located in the section "**curses** Program Examples" in this chapter. These larger examples are more challenging; they sometimes make use of routines not discussed here. Keep the **curses**(3X) manual page handy.

## What Every curses Program Needs

All **curses** programs need to include the header file <**curses.h**> and call the routines **initscr()**, **refresh()** or similar related routines, and **endwin()**.

### The Header File <curses.h>

The header file <**curses.h**> defines several global variables and data structures and defines several **curses** routines as macros.

To begin, let's consider the variables and data structures defined. <**curses.h**> defines all the parameters used by **curses** routines. It also defines the integer variables **LINES** and **COLS**; when a **curses** program is run on a particular terminal, these variables are assigned the vertical and horizontal dimensions of the terminal screen, respectively, by the routine **initscr()**

described below. The header file defines the constants **OK** and **ERR**, too. Most **curses** routines have return values; the **OK** value is returned if a routine is properly completed, and the **ERR** value if some error occurs.

LINES and COLS are external (global) variables that represent the size of a terminal screen. Two similar variables, **$LINES** and **$COLUMNS**, may be set in a user's shell environment; a **curses** program uses the environment variables to determine the size of a screen. Whenever we refer to the environment variables in this chapter, we will use the **$** to distinguish them from the C declarations in the <**curses.h**> header file.

For more information about these variables, see the following sections "The Routines **initscr()**, **refresh()**, and **endwin()**" and "More about **initscr()** and Lines and Columns."

Now let's consider the macro definitions. <**curses.h**> defines many **curses** routines as macros that call other macros or **curses** routines. For instance, the simple routine **refresh()** is a macro. The line

```
#define refresh( ) wrefresh(stdscr)
```

shows when **refresh** is called, it is expanded to call the **curses** routine **wrefresh()**. The latter routine in turn calls the two **curses** routines **wnoutrefresh()** and **doupdate()**. Many other routines also group two or three routines together to achieve a particular result.

Macro expansion in **curses** programs may cause problems with certain sophisticated C features, such as the use of automatic incrementing variables.

One final point about <**curses.h**>: it automatically includes <**stdio.h**> and the <**termio.h**> tty driver interface file. Including either file again in a program is harmless but wasteful.

### The Routines initscr(), refresh(), endwin()

The routines **initscr()**, **refresh()**, and **endwin()** initialize a terminal screen to an "in **curses** state," update the contents of the screen, and restore the terminal to an "out of **curses** state," respectively. Use the simple program that we introduced earlier to learn about each of these routines:

```
#include <curses.h>

main()
{
    initscr();      /* initialize terminal settings and <curses.h>
                       data structures and variables */

    move( LINES/2 - 1, COLS/2 - 4 );
    addstr("Bulls");
    refresh();      /* send output to (update) terminal screen */
    addstr("Eye");
    refresh();      /* send more output to terminal screen */
    endwin();       /* restore all terminal settings */
}
```

Figure 10-3: The Purposes of **initscr()**, **refresh()**, and **endwin()** in a Program

A **curses** program usually starts by calling **initscr()**; the program should call **initscr()** only once. Using the environment variable **$TERM** as the section "How **curses** and **terminfo** Work Together" describes, this routine determines what terminal is being used. It then initializes all the declared data structures and other variables from **<curses.h>**. For example, **initscr()** would initialize **LINES** and **COLS** for the sample program on whatever terminal it was run. If the Teletype 5425 were used, this routine would initialize **LINES** to 24 and **COLS** to 80. Finally, this routine writes error messages to **stderr** and exits if errors occur.

During the execution of the program, output and input is handled by routines like **move**() and **addstr**() in the sample program. For example,

```
move( LINES/2 - 1, COLS/2 - 4 );
```

says to move the cursor to the left of the middle of the screen. Then the line

```
addstr("Bulls");
```

says to write the character string Bulls. For example, if the Teletype 5425 were used, these routines would position the cursor and write the character string at (11,36).

NOTE    All **curses** routines that move the cursor move it from its home position in the upper left corner of a screen. The **(LINES,COLS)** coordinate at this position is (0,0) not (1,1). Notice that the vertical coordinate is given first and the horizontal second, which is the opposite of the more common 'x,y' order of screen (or graph) coordinates. The −1 in the sample program takes the (0,0) position into account to place the cursor on the center line of the terminal screen.

Routines like **move**() and **addstr**() do not actually change a physical terminal screen when they are called. The screen is updated only when **refresh**() is called. Before this, an internal representation of the screen called a window is updated. This is a very important concept, which we discuss below under "More about **refresh**() and Windows."

Finally, a **curses** program ends by calling **endwin**(). This routine restores all terminal settings and positions the cursor at the lower left corner of the screen.

## Compiling a curses Program

You compile programs that include **curses** routines as C language programs using the **cc**(1) command (documented in the *Programmer's Reference Manual*), which invokes the C compiler (see Chapter 2 in this guide for details).

The routines are usually stored in the library **/usr/lib/libcurses.a**. To direct the link editor to search this library, you must use the −**l** option with the **cc** command.

The general command line for compiling a **curses** program follows:

**cc** *file*.**c** −**lcurses** −**o** *file*

*file*.**c** is the name of the source program; and *file* is the executable object module.

## Running a curses Program

**curses** programs count on certain information being in a user's environment to run properly. Specifically, users of a **curses** program should usually include the following three lines in their **.profile** files:

```
TERM=current terminal type
export TERM
tput init
```

For an explanation of these lines, see the section "How **curses** and **terminfo** Work Together" in this chapter. Users of a **curses** program could also define the environment variables **$LINES**, **$COLUMNS**, and **$TERMINFO** in their **.profile** files. However, unlike **$TERM**, these variables do not have to be defined.

If a **curses** program does not run as expected, you might want to debug it with **sdb**(1), which is documented in the *Programmer's Reference Manual*). When using **sdb**, you have to keep a few points in mind. First, a **curses** program is interactive and always has knowledge of where the cursor is located. An interactive debugger like **sdb**, however, may cause changes to the contents of the screen of which the **curses** program is not aware.

Second, a **curses** program outputs to a window until **refresh()** or a similar routine is called. Because output from the program may be delayed, debugging the output for consistency may be difficult.

Third, setting break points on **curses** routines that are macros, such as **refresh()**, does not work. You have to use the routines defined for these macros, instead; for example, you have to use **wrefresh()** instead of **refresh()**. See the above section, "The Header File **<curses.h>**," for more information about macros.

# More about initscr() and Lines and Columns

After determining a terminal's screen dimensions, **initscr**() sets the variables **LINES** and **COLS**. These variables are set from the **terminfo** variables **lines** and **columns**. These, in turn, are set from the values in the **terminfo** database, unless these values are overridden by the values of the environment **$LINES** and **$COLUMNS**.

# More about refresh() and Windows

As mentioned above, **curses** routines do not update a terminal until **refresh**() is called. Instead, they write to an internal representation of the screen called a window. When **refresh**() is called, all the accumulated output is sent from the window to the current terminal screen.

A window acts a lot like a buffer does when you use a UNIX system editor. When you invoke **vi**(1), for instance, to edit a file, the changes you make to the contents of the file are reflected in the buffer. The changes become part of the permanent file only when you use the **w** or **ZZ** command. Similarly, when you invoke a screen program made up of **curses** routines, they change the contents of a window. The changes become part of the current terminal screen only when **refresh**() is called.

<**curses.h**> supplies a default window named **stdscr** (standard screen), which is the size of the current terminal's screen, for all programs using **curses** routines. The header file defines **stdscr** to be of the type **WINDOW\***, a pointer to a C structure which you might think of as a two-dimensional array of characters representing a terminal screen. The program always keeps track of what is on the physical screen, as well as what is in **stdscr**. When **refresh**() is called, it compares the two screen images and sends a stream of characters to the terminal that make the current screen look like **stdscr**. A **curses** program considers many different ways to do this, taking into account the various capabilities of the terminal and similarities between what is on the screen and what is on the window. It optimizes output by printing as few characters as is possible. Figure 10-4 illustrates what happens when you execute the sample curses program that prints BullsEye at the center of a terminal screen (see Figure 10-1). Notice in the figure that the terminal screen retains whatever garbage is on it until the first **refresh**() is called. This **refresh**() clears the screen and updates it with the current contents of **stdscr**.

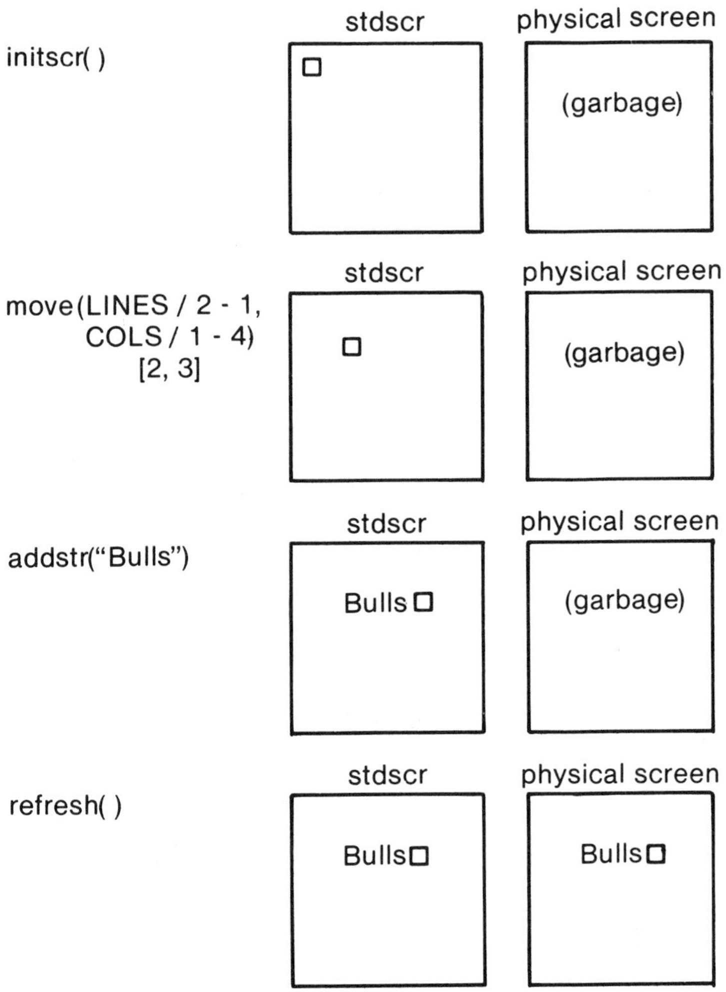

Figure 10-4: The Relationship between **stdscr** and a Terminal Screen (Sheet 1 of 2)

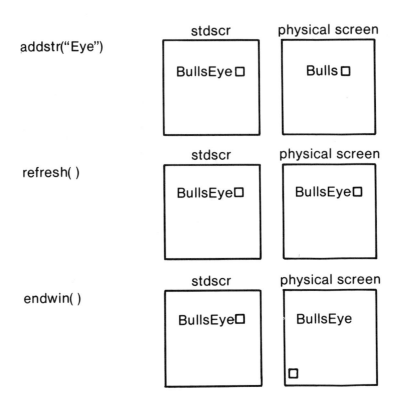

Figure 10-4: The Relationship Between **stdscr** and a Terminal Screen  (Sheet 2 of 2)

You can create other windows and use them instead of **stdscr**. Windows are useful for maintaining several different screen images. For example, many data entry and retrieval applications use two windows: one to control input and output and one to print error messages that don't mess up the other window.

It's possible to subdivide a screen into many windows, refreshing each one of them as desired. When windows overlap, the contents of the current screen show the most recently refreshed window. It's also possible to create a window within a window; the smaller window is called a subwindow. Assume that you are designing an application that uses forms, for example, an expense voucher, as a user interface. You could use subwindows to control access to certain fields on the form.

Some **curses** routines are designed to work with a special type of window called a pad. A pad is a window whose size is not restricted by the size of a screen or associated with a particular part of a screen. You can use a pad when you have a particularly large window or only need part of the window on the screen at any one time. For example, you might use a pad for an application with a spread sheet.

Figure 10-5 represents what a pad, a subwindow, and some other windows could look like in comparison to a terminal screen.

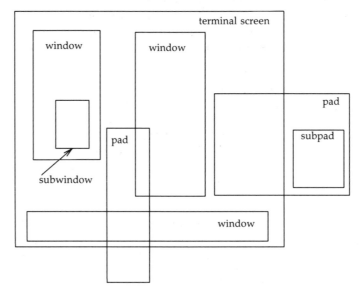

Figure 10-5: Multiple Windows and Pads Mapped to a Terminal Screen

The section "Building Windows and Pads" in this chapter describes the routines you use to create and use them. If you'd like to see a **curses** program with windows now, you can turn to the **window** program under the section "**curses** Program Examples" in this chapter.

# Getting Simple Output and Input

### Output

The routines that **curses** provides for writing to **stdscr** are similar to those provided by the **stdio**(3S) library for writing to a file. They let you

- write a character at a time — **addch**()

- write a string — **addstr**()

- format a string from a variety of input arguments — **printw**()

- move a cursor or move a cursor and print character(s) — **move**(), **mvaddch**(), **mvaddstr**(), **mvprintw**()

- clear a screen or a part of it — **clear**(), **erase**(), **clrtoeol**(), **clrtobot**()

Following are descriptions and examples of these routines.

 The **curses** library provides its own set of output and input functions. You should not use other I/O routines or system calls, like **read**(2) and **write**(2), in a **curses** program. They may cause undesirable results when you run the program.

**addch()**

SYNOPSIS

**#include <curses.h>**

**int addch(ch)**
**chtype ch;**

NOTES

- **addch()** writes a single character to **stdscr**.

- The character is of the type **chtype**, which is defined in **<curses.h>**. **chtype** contains data and attributes (see "Output Attributes" in this chapter for information about attributes).

- When working with variables of this type, make sure you declare them as **chtype** and not as the basic type (for example, **short**) that **chtype** is declared to be in **<curses.h>**. This will ensure future compatibility.

- **addch()** does some translations. For example, it converts

  □ the **<NL>** character to a clear to end of line and a move to the next line

  □ the tab character to an appropriate number of blanks

  □ other control characters to their ^X notation

- **addch()** normally returns **OK**. The only time **addch()** returns **ERR** is after adding a character to the lower right-hand corner of a window that does not scroll.

- **addch()** is a macro.

EXAMPLE

```
#include <curses.h>

main()
{
    initscr();
    addch('a');
    refresh();
    endwin();
}
```

The output from this program will appear as follows:

```
a



$□
```

Also see the **show** program under **"curses** Example Programs" in this chapter.

**addstr()**

SYNOPSIS

**#include <curses.h>**

**int addstr(str)**
**char *str;**

NOTES

- **addstr()** writes a string of characters to **stdscr**.

- **addstr()** calls **addch()** to write each character.

- **addstr()** follows the same translation rules as **addch()**.

- **addstr()** returns **OK** on success and **ERR** on error.

- **addstr()** is a macro.

EXAMPLE

Recall the sample program that prints the character string BullsEye. See Figures 10-1, 10-2, and 10-4.

**printw()**

SYNOPSIS

**#include <curses.h>**

**int printw(fmt [,arg...])**
**char *fmt**

NOTES

- **printw**() handles formatted printing on **stdscr**.

- Like **printf**, **printw**() takes a format string and a variable number of arguments.

- Like **addstr**(), **printw**() calls **addch**() to write the string.

- **printw**() returns **OK** on success and **ERR** on error.

EXAMPLE

```
#include <curses.h>

main()
{
    char* title = "Not specified";
    int no = 0;

        /* Missing code. */

    initscr();

        /* Missing code. */

    printw("%s is not in stock.\n", title);
    printw("Please ask the cashier to order %d for you.\n", no);

    refresh();
    endwin();
}
```

The output from this program will appear as follows:

```
Not specified is not in stock.
Please ask the cashier to order 0 for you.



$□
```

**move()**

SYNOPSIS

**#include <curses.h>**

**int move(y, x);**
**int y, x;**

NOTES

- **move()** positions the cursor for **stdscr** at the given row **y** and the given column **x**.

- Notice that **move()** takes the **y** coordinate before the **x** coordinate. The upper left-hand coordinates for **stdscr** are (0,0), the lower right-hand (**LINES** - 1, **COLS** - 1). See the section "The Routines **initscr()**, **refresh()**, and **endwin()**" for more information.

- **move()** may be combined with the write functions to form

  - **mvaddch( y, x, ch )**, which moves to a given position and prints a character

  - **mvaddstr( y, x, str )**, which moves to a given position and prints a string of characters

  - **mvprintw( y, x, fmt** [,*arg*...]**)**, which moves to a given position and prints a formatted string.

- **move()** returns **OK** on success and **ERR** on error. Trying to move to a screen position of less than (0,0) or more than (**LINES** - 1, **COLS** - 1) causes an error.

- **move()** is a macro.

EXAMPLE

```
#include <curses.h>

main()
{
    initscr();
    addstr("Cursor should be here --> if move() works.");
    printw("\n\n\nPress <CR> to end test.");
    move(0,25);
    refresh();
    getch();      /* Gets <CR>; discussed below. */
    endwin();
}
```

Here's the output generated by running this program:

```
Cursor should be here -->□if move() works.


Press <CR> to end test.
```

After you press **<CR>**, the screen looks like this:

```
Cursor should be here -->


Press <CR> to end test.
$□
```

See the **scatter** program under **"curses** Program Examples" in this chapter for another example of using **move()**.

**clear() and** erase()

SYNOPSIS

**#include <curses.h>**

**int clear()**
**int erase()**

NOTES

- Both routines change **stdscr** to all blanks.

- **clear**() also assumes that the screen may have garbage that it doesn't know about; this routine first calls **erase**() and then **clearok**() which clears the physical screen completely on the next call to **refresh**() for **stdscr**. See the **curses**(3X) manual page for more information about **clearok**().

- **initscr**() automatically calls **clear**().

- **clear**() always returns **OK**; **erase**() returns no useful value.

- Both routines are macros.

**clrtoeol() and clrtobot()**

SYNOPSIS

**#include <curses.h>**

**int clrtoeol()**
**int clrtobot()**

NOTES

- **clrtoeol()** changes the remainder of a line to all blanks.

- **clrtobot()** changes the remainder of a screen to all blanks.

- Both begin at the current cursor position inclusive.

- Neither returns any useful value.

EXAMPLE

The following sample program uses **clrtobot()**.

```
#include <curses.h>

main()
{
    initscr();
    addstr("Press <CR> to delete from here to the end of the line and on.");
    addstr("\nDelete this too.\nAnd this.");
    move(0,30);
    refresh();
    getch();
    clrtobot();
    refresh();
    endwin();
}
```

Here's the output generated by running this program:

```
Press <CR> to delete from here□to the end of the line and on.
Delete this too.
And this.
```

Notice the two calls to **refresh()**: one to send the full screen of text to a terminal, the other to clear from the position indicated to the bottom of a screen.

Here's what the screen looks like when you press **<CR>**:

```
Press <CR> to delete from here

$□
```

See the **show** and **two** programs under "**curses** Example Programs" for examples of uses for **clrtoeol**().

## Input

**curses** routines for reading from the current terminal are similar to those provided by the **stdio**(3S) library for reading from a file. They let you

- read a character at a time — **getch()**

- read a <NL>-terminated string — **getstr()**

- parse input, converting and assigning selected data to an argument list — **scanw()**

The primary routine is **getch()**, which processes a single input character and then returns that character. This routine is like the C library routine **getchar()**(3S) except that it makes several terminal- or system-dependent options available that are not possible with **getchar()**. For example, you can use **getch()** with the **curses** routine **keypad()**, which allows a **curses** program to interpret extra keys on a user's terminal, such as arrow keys, function keys, and other special keys that transmit escape sequences, and treat them as just another key. See the descriptions of **getch()** and **keypad()** on the **curses**(3X) manual page for more information about **keypad()**.

The following pages describe and give examples of the basic routines for getting input in a screen program.

**getch()**
  SYNOPSIS

**#include <curses.h>**

**int getch()**

NOTES

- **getch()** reads a single character from the current terminal.

- **getch()** returns the value of the character or **ERR** on 'end of file,' receipt of signals, or non-blocking read with no input.

- **getch()** is a macro.

- See the discussions about **echo(), noecho(), cbreak(), nocbreak(), raw(), noraw(), halfdelay(), nodelay(),** and **keypad()** below and in **curses**(3X).

EXAMPLE

```
#include <curses.h>

main()
{
    int ch;

    initscr();
    cbreak();                /* Explained later in the section "Input Options" */
    addstr("Press any character:  ");
    refresh();
    ch = getch();
    printw("\n\n\nThe character entered was a '%c'.\n", ch);
    refresh();
    endwin();
}
```

The output from this program follows.  The first **refresh**() sends the **addstr**() character string from **stdscr** to the terminal:

```
Press any character:  □
```

Then assume that a **w** is typed at the keyboard.  **getch**() accepts the character and assigns it to **ch**.  Finally, the second **refresh**() is called and the screen appears as follows:

```
Press any character:  w


The character entered was a 'w'.


$□
```

For another example of **getch**(), see the **show** program under "**curses** Example Programs" in this chapter.

**getstr()**

SYNOPSIS

**#include <curses.h>**

**int getstr(str)**
**char *str;**

NOTES

- **getstr()** reads characters and stores them in a buffer until a **<CR>**, **<NL>**, or **<ENTER>** is received from **stdscr**. **getstr()** does not check for buffer overflow.

- The characters read and stored are in a character string.

- **getstr()** is a macro; it calls **getch()** to read each character.

- **getstr()** returns **ERR** if **getch()** returns **ERR** to it. Otherwise it returns **OK**.

- See the discussions about **echo()**, **noecho()**, **cbreak()**, **nocbreak()**, **raw()**, **noraw()**, **halfdelay()**, **nodelay()**, and **keypad()** below and in **curses**(3X).

EXAMPLE

```
#include <curses.h>

main()
{
char str[256];

    initscr();
    cbreak();        /* Explained later in the section "Input Options" */
    addstr("Enter a character string terminated by <CR>:\n\n");
    refresh()
    getstr(str);
    printw("\n\n\nThe string entered was \n'%s'\n", str);
    refresh();
    endwin();
}
```

Assume you entered the string 'I enjoy learning about the UNIX system.' The final screen (after entering **<CR>**) would appear as follows:

```
Enter a character string terminated by <CR>:

I enjoy learning about the UNIX system.


The string entered was
'I enjoy learning about the UNIX system.'

$□
```

**scanw()**

SYNOPSIS

**#include <curses.h>**

**int scanw(fmt [, arg...])**
**char *fmt;**

NOTES

- **scanw()** calls **getstr()** and parses an input line.

- Like **scanf**(3S), **scanw()** uses a format string to convert and assign to a variable number of arguments.

- **scanw()** returns the same values as **scanf()**.

- See **scanf**(3S) for more information.

EXAMPLE

```
#include <curses.h>

main()
{
    char string[100];
    float number;

    initscr();
    cbreak();                /* Explained later in the   */
    echo();                  /* section "Input Options" */
    addstr("Enter a number and a string separated by a comma: ");
    refresh();
    scanw("%f,%s",&number,string);
    clear();
    printw("The string was \"%s\" and the number was %f.",string,number);
    refresh();
    endwin();
}
```

Notice the two calls to **refresh()**. The first call updates the screen with the character string passed to **addstr()**, the second with the string returned from **scanw()**. Also notice the call to **clear()**. Assume you entered the following when prompted: **2,twin**. After running this program, your terminal screen would appear, as follows:

```
The string was "twin" and the number was 2.000000.


$□
```

# Controlling Output and Input

## Output Attributes

When we talked about **addch**(), we said that it writes a single character of the type **chtype** to **stdscr**. **chtype** has two parts: a part with information about the character itself and another part with information about a set of attributes associated with the character. The attributes allow a character to be printed in reverse video, bold, underlined, and so on.

**stdscr** always has a set of current attributes that it associates with each character as it is written. However, using the routine **attrset**() and related **curses** routines described below, you can change the current attributes. Below is a list of the attributes and what they mean:

- A_BLINK — blinking

- A_BOLD — extra bright or bold

- A_DIM — half bright

- A_REVERSE — reverse video

- A_STANDOUT — a terminal's best highlighting mode

- A_UNDERLINE — underlining

- A_ALTCHARSET — alternate character set (see the section "Drawing Lines and Other Graphics" in this chapter)

To use these attributes, you must pass them as arguments to **attrset**() and related routines; they can also be ORed with the bitwise OR (|) to **addch**().

NOTE   Not all terminals are capable of displaying all attributes. If a particular terminal cannot display a requested attribute, a **curses** program attempts to find a substitute attribute. If none is possible, the attribute is ignored.

Let's consider a use of one of these attributes. To display a word in bold, you would use the following code:

```
    ...
   printw("A word in ");
   attrset(A_BOLD);
   printw("boldface");
   attrset(0);
   printw(" really stands out.\n");
    ...
   refresh();
```

Attributes can be turned on singly, such as **attrset**(A_BOLD) in the example, or in combination. To turn on blinking bold text, for example, you would use **attrset**(A_BLINK|A_BOLD). Individual attributes can be turned on and off with the **curses** routines **attron**() and **attroff**() without affecting other attributes. **attrset(0)** turns all attributes off.

Notice the attribute called A_STANDOUT. You might use it to make text attract the attention of a user. The particular hardware attribute used for standout is the most visually pleasing attribute a terminal has. Standout is typically implemented as reverse video or bold. Many programs don't really need a specific attribute, such as bold or reverse video, but instead just need to highlight some text. For such applications, the A_STANDOUT attribute is recommended. Two convenient functions, **standout**() and **standend**() can be used to turn on and off this attribute. **standend**(), in fact, turns of all attributes.

In addition to the attributes listed above, there are two bit masks called A_CHARTEXT and A_ATTRIBUTES. You can use these bit masks with the **curses** function **inch**() and the C logical AND ( **&** ) operator to extract the character or attributes of a position on a terminal screen. See the discussion of **inch**() on the **curses**(3X) manual page.

Following are descriptions of **attrset**() and the other **curses** routines that you can use to manipulate attributes.

**attron(), attrset(), and attroff()**

SYNOPSIS

**#include <curses.h>**

**int attron( attrs )**
**chtype attrs;**

**int attrset( attrs )**
**chtype attrs;**

**int attroff( attrs )**
**chtype attrs;**

NOTES

- **attron**() turns on the requested attribute **attrs** in addition to any that are currently on. **attrs** is of the type **chtype** and is defined in **<curses.h>**.

- **attrset**() turns on the requested attributes **attrs** instead of any that are currently turned on.

- **attroff**() turns off the requested attributes **attrs** if they are on.

- The attributes may be combined using the bitwise OR ( | ).

- All return **OK**.

EXAMPLE

See the **highlight** program under "**curses** Example Programs" in this chapter.

**standout() and** standend()

SYNOPSIS

**#include** <curses.h>

**int standout()**
**int standend()**

NOTES

- **standout()** turns on the preferred highlighting attribute, A_STANDOUT, for the current terminal. This routine is equivalent to **attron(A_STANDOUT)**.

- **standend()** turns off all attributes. This routine is equivalent to **attrset(0)**.

- Both always return **OK**.

EXAMPLE

See the **highlight** program under **"curses** Example Programs" in this chapter.

## Bells, Whistles, and Flashing Lights

Occasionally, you may want to get a user's attention. Two **curses** routines were designed to help you do this. They let you ring the terminal's chimes and flash its screen.

**flash**() flashes the screen if possible, and otherwise rings the bell. Flashing the screen is intended as a bell replacement, and is particularly useful if the bell bothers someone within ear shot of the user. The routine **beep**() can be called when a real beep is desired. (If for some reason the terminal is unable to beep, but able to flash, a call to **beep**() will flash the screen.)

**beep() and flash()**

SYNOPSIS

**#include <curses.h>**

**int flash()**
**int beep()**

NOTES

- **flash**() tries to flash the terminals screen, if possible, and, if not, tries to ring the terminal bell.

- **beep**() tries to ring the terminal bell, if possible, and, if not, tries to flash the terminal screen.

- Neither returns any useful value.

## Input Options

The UNIX system does a considerable amount of processing on input before an application ever sees a character. For example, it does the following:

- echoes (prints back) characters to a terminal as they are typed

- interprets an erase character (typically **#**) and a line kill character (typically **@**)

- interprets a CTRL-D (control d) as end of file (EOF)

- interprets interrupt and quit characters

- strips the character's parity bit

- translates **<CR>** to **<NL>**

Because a **curses** program maintains total control over the screen, **curses** turns off echoing on the UNIX system and does echoing itself. At times, you may not want the UNIX system to process other characters in the standard way in an interactive screen management program. Some **curses** routines, **noecho()** and **cbreak()**, for example, have been designed so that you can change the standard character processing. Using these routines in an application controls how input is interpreted. Figure 10-6 shows some of the major routines for controlling input.

Every **curses** program accepting input should set some input options. This is because when the program starts running, the terminal on which it runs may be in **cbreak()**, **raw()**, **nocbreak()**, or **noraw()** mode. Although the **curses** program starts up in **echo()** mode, as Figure 10-6 shows, none of the other modes are guaranteed.

The combination of **noecho()** and **cbreak()** is most common in interactive screen management programs. Suppose, for instance, that you don't want the characters sent to your application program to be echoed wherever the cursor currently happens to be; instead, you want them echoed at the bottom of the screen. The **curses** routine **noecho()** is designed for this purpose. However, when **noecho()** turns off echoing, normal erase and kill processing is still on. Using the routine **cbreak()** causes these characters to be uninterpreted.

| Input Options | Characters | |
|---|---|---|
| | **Interpreted** | **Uninterpreted** |
| Normal 'out of **curses** state' | interrupt, quit stripping \<CR\> to \<NL\> echoing erase, kill EOF | |
| Normal **curses** 'start up state' | echoing (simulated) | All else undefined. |
| **cbreak()** and **echo()** | interrupt, quit stripping echoing | erase, kill EOF |
| **cbreak()** and **noecho()** | interrupt, quit stripping | echoing erase, kill EOF |
| **nocbreak()** and **noecho()** | break, quit stripping erase, kill EOF | echoing |
| **nocbreak()** and **echo()** | See caution below. | |
| **nl()** | \<CR\> to \<NL\> | |
| **nonl()** | | \<CR\> to \<NL\> |
| **raw()** (instead of **cbreak()**) | | break, quit stripping |

Figure 10-6: Input Option Settings for **curses** Programs

Do not use the combination **nocbreak()** and **noecho()**. If you use it in a program and also use **getch()**, the program will go in and out of **cbreak()** mode to get each character. Depending on the state of the tty driver when each character is typed, the program may produce undesirable output.

In addition to the routines noted in Figure 10-6, you can use the **curses** routines **noraw(), halfdelay()**, and **nodelay()** to control input. See the **curses**(3X) manual page for discussions of these routines.

The next few pages describe **noecho()**, **cbreak()** and the related routines **echo()** and **nocbreak()** in more detail.

**echo() and noecho()**

SYNOPSIS

**#include** **<curses.h>**

**int echo()**
**int noecho()**

NOTES

- **echo**() turns on echoing of characters by **curses** as they are read in. This is the initial setting.

- **noecho**() turns off the echoing.

- Neither returns any useful value.

- **curses** programs may not run properly if you turn on echoing with **nocbreak**(). See Figure 10-6 and accompanying caution. After you turn echoing off, you can still echo characters with **addch**().

EXAMPLE

See the **editor** and **show** programs under "**curses** Program Examples" in this chapter.

cbreak() **and** nocbreak()

SYNOPSIS

**#include < curses.h >**
**int cbreak()**
**int nocbreak()**

NOTES

- **cbreak()** turns on 'break for each character' processing. A program gets each character as soon as it is typed, but the erase, line kill, and CTRL-D characters are not interpreted.

- **nocbreak()** returns to normal 'line at a time' processing. This is typically the initial setting.

- Neither returns any useful value.

- A **curses** program may not run properly if **cbreak()** is turned on and off within the same program or if the combination **nocbreak()** and **echo()** is used.

- See Figure 10-6 and accompanying caution.

EXAMPLE

See the **editor** and **show** programs under "**curses** Program Examples" in this chapter.

# Building Windows and Pads

An earlier section in this chapter, "More about **refresh**() and Windows" explained what windows and pads are and why you might want to use them. This section describes the **curses** routines you use to manipulate and create windows and pads.

## Output and Input

The routines that you use to send output to and get input from windows and pads are similar to those you use with **stdscr**. The only difference is that you have to give the name of the window to receive the action. Generally, these functions have names formed by putting the letter **w** at the beginning of the name of a **stdscr** routine and adding the window name as the first parameter. For example, **addch**('c') would become **waddch**(**mywin**, 'c') if you wanted to write the character **c** to the window **mywin**. Here's a list of the window (or **w**) versions of the output routines discussed in "Getting Simple Output and Input."

- **waddch**(*win, ch*)

- **mvwaddch**(*win, y, x, ch*)

- **waddstr**(*win, str*)

- **mvwaddstr**(*win, y, x, str*)

- **wprintw**(*win, fmt [, arg...]*)

- **mvwprintw**(*win, y, x, fmt [, arg...]*)

- **wmove**(*win, y, x*)

- **wclear**(*win*) and **werase**(*win*)

- **wclrtoeol**(*win*) and **wclrtobot**(*win*)

- **wrefresh**()

You can see from their declarations that these routines differ from the versions that manipulate **stdscr** only in their names and the addition of a *win* argument. Notice that the routines whose names begin with **mvw** take the *win* argument before the *y, x* coordinates, which is contrary to what the names imply. See **curses**(3X) for more information about these routines or the versions of the input routines **getch, getstr**(), and so on that you should use with windows.

All **w** routines can be used with pads except for **wrefresh**() and **wnoutrefresh**() (see below). In place of these two routines, you have to use **prefresh**() and **pnoutrefresh**() with pads.

## The Routines wnoutrefresh() and doupdate()

If you recall from the earlier discussion about **refresh**(), we said that it sends the output from **stdscr** to the terminal screen. We also said that it was a macro that expands to **wrefresh(stdscr)** (see "What Every **curses** Program Needs" and "More about **refresh**() and Windows").

The **wrefresh**() routine is used to send the contents of a window (**stdscr** or one that you create) to a screen; it calls the routines **wnoutrefresh**() and **doupdate**(). Similarly, **prefresh**() sends the contents of a pad to a screen by calling **pnoutrefresh**() and **doupdate**().

Using **wnoutrefresh**()—or **pnoutrefresh**() (this discussion will be limited to the former routine for simplicity)—and **doupdate**(), you can update terminal screens with more efficiency than using **wrefresh**() by itself. **wrefresh**() works by first calling **wnoutrefresh**(), which copies the named window to a data structure referred to as the virtual screen. The virtual screen contains what a program intends to display at a terminal. After calling **wnoutrefresh**(), **wrefresh**() then calls **doupdate**(), which compares the virtual screen to the physical screen and does the actual update. If you want to output several windows at once, calling **wrefresh**() will result in alternating calls to **wnoutrefresh**() and **doupdate**(), causing several bursts of output to a screen. However, by calling **wnoutrefresh**() for each window and then **doupdate**() only once, you can minimize the total number of characters transmitted and the processor time used. The following sample program uses only one **doupdate**():

```
#include <curses.h>

main()
{
    WINDOW *w1, *w2;

    initscr();
    w1 = newwin(2,6,0,3);
    w2 = newwin(1,4,5,4);
    waddstr(w1, "Bulls");
    wnoutrefresh(w1);
    waddstr(w2, "Eye");
    wnoutrefresh(w2);
    doupdate();
    endwin();
}
```

Notice from the sample that you declare a new window at the beginning of a **curses** program. The lines

```
    w1 = newwin(2,6,0,3);
    w2 = newwin(1,4,5,4);
```

declare two windows named w1 and w2 with the routine **newwin()** according to certain specifications. **newwin()** is discussed in more detail below.

Figure 10-7 illustrates the effect of **wnoutrefresh()** and **doupdate()** on these two windows, the virtual screen, and the physical screen:

initscr ( )

stdscr@ (0,0)    virtual screen    physical screen

(garbage)

w1 = newwin
(2,6,0,3,)

stdscr@ (0,0)    virtual screen    physical screen

(garbage)

w1 @ (0,3)

w2 = newwin
(1,4,5,4)

stdscr@ (0,0)    virtual screen    physical screen

(garbage)

w1 @ (0,3)    w2 @ (5,4)

Figure 10-7: The Relationship Between a Window and a Terminal Screen
(Sheet 1 of 3)

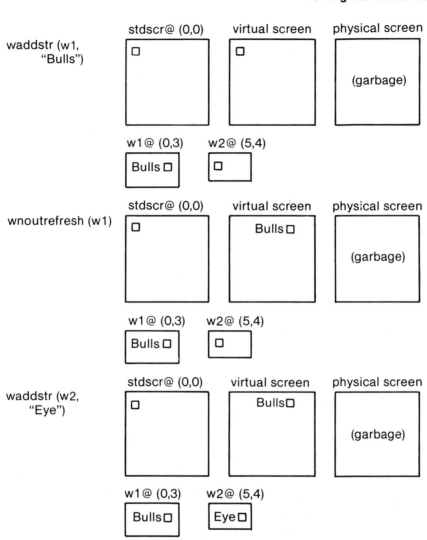

Figure 10-7: The Relationship Between a Window and a Terminal Screen
(Sheet 2 of 3)

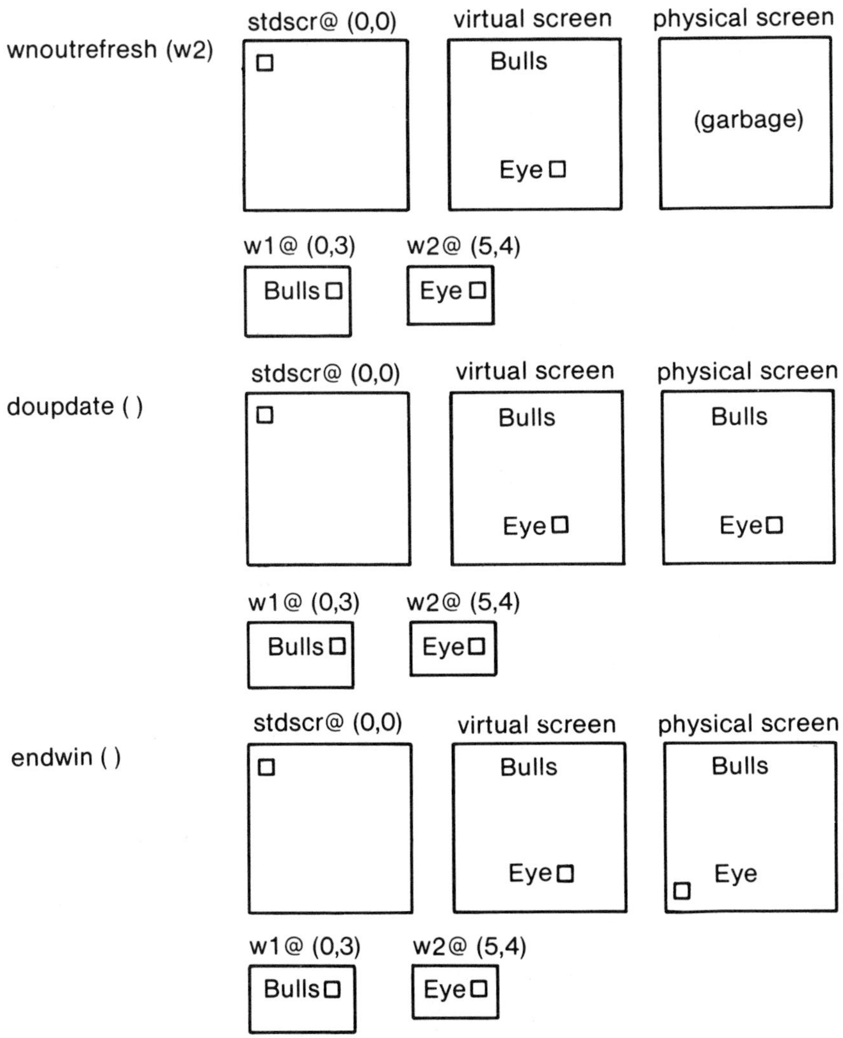

Figure 10-7: The Relationship Between a Window and a Terminal Screen (Sheet 3 of 3)

## New Windows

Following are descriptions of the routines **newwin**() and **subwin**(), which you use to create new windows. For information about creating new pads with **newpad**() and **subpad**(), see the **curses**(3X) manual page.

**newwin()**

SYNOPSIS

**#include** <**curses.h**>

**WINDOW** *newwin(nlines, ncols, begin_y, begin_x)
**int nlines, ncols, begin_y, begin_x;**

NOTES

■ **newwin**() returns a pointer to a new window with a new data area.

■ The variables **nlines** and **ncols** give the size of the new window.

■ **begin_y** and **begin_x** give the screen coordinates from (0,0) of the upper left corner of the window as it is refreshed to the current screen.

EXAMPLE

Recall the sample program using two windows; see Figure 10-7. Also see the **window** program under "**curses** Program Examples" in this chapter.

**subwin()**

SYNOPSIS

**#include <curses.h>**

**WINDOW \*subwin(orig, nlines, ncols, begin_y, begin_x)**
**WINDOW \*orig;**
**int nlines, ncols, begin_y, begin_x;**

NOTES

- **subwin**() returns a new window that points to a section of another window, **orig**.

- **nlines** and **ncols** give the size of the new window.

- **begin_y** and **begin_x** give the screen coordinates of the upper left corner of the window as it is refreshed to the current screen.

- Subwindows and original windows can accidentally overwrite one another.

 Subwindows of subwindows do not work (as of the copyright date of this *Programmer's Guide*).

EXAMPLE

```
#include <curses.h>

main()
{
 WINDOW *sub;

  initscr();
  box(stdscr,'w','w');      /* See the curses(3X) manual page for box() */
  mvwaddstr(stdscr,7,10,"------- this is 10,10");
  mvwaddch(stdscr,8,10,'!');
  mvwaddch(stdscr,9,10,'v');
  sub = subwin(stdscr,10,20,10,10);
  box(sub,'s','s');
  wnoutrefresh(stdscr);
  wrefresh(sub);
  endwin();
}
```

This program prints a border of **w**s around the stdscr (the sides of your terminal screen) and a border of s's around the subwindow **sub** when it is run. For another example, see the **window** program under "**curses** Program Examples" in this chapter.

# Using Advanced curses Features

Knowing how to use the basic **curses** routines to get output and input and to work with windows, you can design screen management programs that meet the needs of many users. The **curses** library, however, has routines that let you do more in a program than handle I/O and multiple windows. The following few pages briefly describe some of these routines and what they can help you do—namely, draw simple graphics, use a terminal's soft labels, and work with more than one terminal in a single **curses** program.

You should be comfortable using the routines previously discussed in this chapter and the other routines for I/O and window manipulation discussed on the **curses**(3X) manual page before you try to use the advanced **curses** features.

 The routines described under "Routines for Drawing Lines and Other Graphics" and "Routines for Using Soft Labels" are features that are new for UNIX System V Release 3.0. If a program uses any of these routines, it may not run on earlier releases of the UNIX system. You must use the Release 3.0 version of the **curses** library on UNIX System V Release 3.0 to work with these routines.

## Routines for Drawing Lines and Other Graphics

Many terminals have an alternate character set for drawing simple graphics (or glyphs or graphic symbols). You can use this character set in **curses** programs. **curses** use the same names for glyphs as the VT100 line drawing character set.

To use the alternate character set in a **curses** program, you pass a set of variables whose names begin with ACS_ to the **curses** routine **waddch**() or a related routine. For example, ACS_ULCORNER is the variable for the upper left corner glyph. If a terminal has a line drawing character for this glyph, ACS_ULCORNER's value is the terminal's character for that glyph OR'd ( | ) with the bit-mask A_ALTCHARSET. If no line drawing character is available for that glyph, a standard ASCII character that approximates the glyph is stored in its place. For example, the default character for ACS_HLINE, a horizontal line, is a − (minus sign). When a close approximation is not available, a + (plus sign) is used. All the standard ACS_ names and their defaults are listed on the **curses**(3X) manual page.

Part of an example program that uses line drawing characters follows. The example uses the **curses** routine **box**() to draw a box around a menu on a screen. **box**() uses the line drawing characters by default or when | (the pipe) and − are chosen. (See **curses**(3X).) Up and down more indicators are drawn on the box border (using **ACS_UARROW** and **ACS_DARROW**) if the menu contained within the box continues above or below the screen:

```
box(menuwin, ACS_VLINE, ACS_HLINE);
 ...

/* output the up/down arrows */
wmove(menuwin, maxy, maxx - 5);

/* output up arrow or horizontal line */
if (moreabove)
    waddch(menuwin, ACS_UARROW);
else
    addch(menuwin, ACS_HLINE);

/*output down arrow or horizontal line */
if (morebelow)
    waddch(menuwin, ACS_DARROW);
else
    waddch(menuwin, ACS_HLINE);
```

Here's another example. Because a default down arrow (like the lowercase letter v) isn't very discernible on a screen with many lowercase characters on it, you can change it to an uppercase V.

```
if ( ! (ACS_DARROW & A_ALTCHARSET))
    ACS_DARROW = 'v';
```

For more information, see **curses**(3X) in the *Programmer's Reference Manual*.

## Routines for Using Soft Labels

Another feature available on most terminals is a set of soft labels across the bottom of their screens. A terminal's soft labels are usually matched with a set of hard function keys on the keyboard. There are usually eight of these labels, each of which is usually eight characters wide and one or two lines high.

The **curses** library has routines that provide a uniform model of eight soft labels on the screen. If a terminal does not have soft labels, the bottom line of its screen is converted into a soft label area. It is not necessary for the keyboard to have hard function keys to match the soft labels for a **curses** program to make use of them.

Let's briefly discuss most of the **curses** routines needed to use soft labels: **slk_init**(), **slk_set**(), **slk_refresh**() and **slk_noutrefresh**(), **slk_clear**, and **slk_restore**.

When you use soft labels in a **curses** program, you have to call the routine **slk_int**() before **initscr**(). This sets an internal flag for **initscr**() to look at that says to use the soft labels. If **initscr**() discovers that there are fewer than eight soft labels on the screen, that they are smaller than eight characters in size, or that there is no way to program them, then it will remove a line from the bottom of **stdscr** to use for the soft labels. The size of **stdscr** and the **LINES** variable will be reduced by 1 to reflect this change. A properly written program, one that is written to use the **LINES** and **COLS** variables, will continue to run as if the line had never existed on the screen.

**slk_init()** takes a single argument. It determines how the labels are grouped on the screen should a line get removed from **stdscr**. The choices are between a 3-2-3 arrangement as appears on AT&T terminals, or a 4-4 arrangement as appears on Hewlett-Packard terminals. The **curses** routines adjust the width and placement of the labels to maintain the pattern. The widest label generated is eight characters.

The routine **slk_set()** takes three arguments, the label number (1-8), the string to go on the label (up to eight characters), and the justification within the label (0 = left justified, 1 = centered, and 2 = right justified).

The routine **slk_noutrefresh()** is comparable to **wnoutrefresh()** in that it copies the label information onto the internal screen image, but it does not cause the screen to be updated. Since a **wrefresh()** commonly follows, **slk_noutrefresh()** is the function that is most commonly used to output the labels.

Just as **wrefresh()** is equivalent to a **wnoutrefresh()** followed by a **doupdate()**, so too the function **slk_refresh()** is equivalent to a **slk_noutrefresh()** followed by a **doupdate()**.

To prevent the soft labels from getting in the way of a shell escape, **slk_clear()** may be called before doing the **endwin()**. This clears the soft labels off the screen and does a **doupdate()**. The function **slk_restore()** may be used to restore them to the screen. See the **curses**(3X) manual page for more information about the routines for using soft labels.

## Working with More than One Terminal

A **curses** program can produce output on more than one terminal at the same time. This is useful for single process programs that access a common database, such as multi-player games.

Writing programs that output to multiple terminals is a difficult business, and the **curses** library does not solve all the problems you might encounter. For instance, the programs—not the library routines—must determine the file name of each terminal line, and what kind of terminal is on each of those lines. The standard method, checking **$TERM** in the environment, does not work, because each process can only examine its own environment.

Another problem you might face is that of multiple programs reading from one line. This situation produces a race condition and should be avoided. However, a program trying to take over another terminal cannot just shut off whatever program is currently running on that line. (Usually, security reasons would also make this inappropriate. But, for some applications, such as an inter-terminal communication program, or a program that takes over unused terminal lines, it would be appropriate.) A typical solution to this problem requires each user logged in on a line to run a program that notifies a master program that the user is interested in joining the master program and tells it the notification program's process ID, the name of the tty line, and the type of terminal being used. Then the program goes to sleep until the master program finishes. When done, the master program wakes up the notification program and all programs exit.

A **curses** program handles multiple terminals by always having a current terminal. All function calls always affect the current terminal. The master program should set up each terminal, saving a reference to the terminals in its own variables. When it wishes to affect a terminal, it should set the current terminal as desired, and then call ordinary **curses** routines.

References to terminals in a **curses** program have the type **SCREEN***. A new terminal is initialized by calling **newterm(***type, outfd, infd***)**. **newterm** returns a screen reference to the terminal being set up. *type* is a character string, naming the kind of terminal being used. *outfd* is a **stdio**(3S) file pointer (**FILE***) used for output to the terminal and *infd* a file pointer for input from the terminal. This call replaces the normal call to **initscr**(), which calls **newterm(getenv("TERM"), stdout, stdin)**.

To change the current terminal, call **set_term(***sp***)** where *sp* is the screen reference to be made current. **set_term**() returns a reference to the previous terminal.

It is important to realize that each terminal has its own set of windows and options. Each terminal must be initialized separately with **newterm**(). Options such as **cbreak**() and **noecho**() must be set separately for each terminal. The functions **endwin**() and **refresh**() must be called separately for each terminal. Figure 10-8 shows a typical scenario to output a message to several terminals.

```
for (i=0; i<nterm; i++)
{
    set_term(terms[i]);
    mvaddstr(0, 0, "Important message");
    refresh();
}
```

Figure 10-8: Sending a Message to Several Terminals

See the **two** program under "**curses** Program Examples" in this chapter for a more complete example.

# Working with terminfo Routines

Some programs need to use lower level routines (i.e., primitives) than those offered by the **curses** routines. For such programs, the **terminfo** routines are offered. They do not manage your terminal screen, but rather give you access to strings and capabilities which you can use yourself to manipulate the terminal.

There are three circumstances when it is proper to use **terminfo** routines. The first is when you need only some screen management capabilities, for example, making text standout on a screen. The second is when writing a filter. A typical filter does one transformation on an input stream without clearing the screen or addressing the cursor. If this transformation is terminal dependent and clearing the screen is inappropriate, use of the **terminfo** routines is worthwhile. The third is when you are writing a special purpose tool that sends a special purpose string to the terminal, such as programming a function key, setting tab stops, sending output to a printer port, or dealing with the status line. Otherwise, you are discouraged from using these routines: the higher level **curses** routines make your program more portable to other UNIX systems and to a wider class of terminals.

 You are discouraged from using **terminfo** routines except for the purposes noted, because **curses** routines take care of all the glitches present in physical terminals. When you use the **terminfo** routines, you must deal with the glitches yourself. Also, these routines may change and be incompatible with previous releases.

# What Every terminfo Program Needs

A **terminfo** program typically includes the header files and routines shown in Figure 10-9.

```
#include <curses.h>
#include <term.h>
...
    setupterm( (char*)0, 1, (int*)0 );
    ...
    putp(clear_screen);
    ...
    reset_shell_mode();
    exit(0);
```

Figure 10-9: Typical Framework of a **terminfo** Program

The header files **<curses.h>** and **<term.h>** are required because they contain the definitions of the strings, numbers, and flags used by the **terminfo** routines. **setupterm**() takes care of initialization. Passing this routine the values **(char*)0, 1,** and **(int*)0** invokes reasonable defaults. If **setupterm**() can't figure out what kind of terminal you are on, it prints an error message and exits. **reset_shell_mode**() performs functions similar to **endwin**() and should be called before a **terminfo** program exits.

A global variable like **clear_screen** is defined by the call to **setupterm**(). It can be output using the **terminfo** routines **putp**() or **tputs**(), which gives a user more control. This string should not be directly output to the terminal using the C library routine **printf**(3S), because it contains padding information. A program that directly outputs strings will fail on terminals that require padding or that use the **xon/xoff** flow control protocol.

At the **terminfo** level, the higher level routines like **addch**() and **getch**() are not available. It is up to you to output whatever is needed. For a list of capabilities and a description of what they do, see **terminfo**(4); see **curses**(3X) for a list of all the **terminfo** routines.

# Compiling and Running a terminfo Program

The general command line for compiling and the guidelines for running a program with **terminfo** routines are the same as those for compiling any other **curses** program. See the sections "Compiling a **curses** Program" and "Running a **curses** Program" in this chapter for more information.

# An Example terminfo Program

The example program **termhl** shows a simple use of **terminfo** routines. It is a version of the **highlight** program (see "**curses** Program Examples") that does not use the higher level **curses** routines. **termhl** can be used as a filter. It includes the strings to enter bold and underline mode and to turn off all attributes.

```
/*
 * A terminfo level version of the highlight program.
 */


#include <curses.h>
#include <term.h>

int ulmode = 0;                    /* Currently underlining */

main(argc, argv)
  int argc;
  char **argv;
{
   FILE *fd;
   int c, c2;
   int outch();

   if (argc > 2)
   {
      fprintf(stderr, "Usage: termhl [file]\n");
      exit(1);
   }

   if (argc == 2)
```

*continued*

```
{
    fd = fopen(argv[1], "r");
    if (fd == NULL)
    {
        perror(argv[1]);
        exit(2);
    }
}
else
{
    fd = stdin;
}
setupterm((char*)0, 1, (int*)0);

for (;;)
{
    c = getc(fd);
    if (c == EOF)
    break;
    if (c == '\')
    {
        c2 = getc(fd);
        switch (c2)
        {
            case 'B':
            tputs(enter_bold_mode, 1, outch);
            continue;
            case 'U':
            tputs(enter_underline_mode, 1, outch);
            ulmode = 1;
            continue;
            case 'N':
            tputs(exit_attribute_mode, 1, outch);
            ulmode = 0;
            continue;
        }
        putch(c);
        putch(c2);
    }
    else
        putch(c);
```

continued

```
      }
      fclose(fd);
      fflush(stdout);
      resetterm();
      exit(0);
}

/*
 * This function is like putchar, but it checks for underlining.
 */
putch(c)
    int c;
{
    outch(c);
    if (ulmode && underline_char)
    {
        outch('\b');
        tputs(underline_char, 1, outch);
    }
}

/*
 * Outchar is a function version of putchar that can be passed to
 * tputs as a routine to call.
 */
outch(c)
    int c;
{
    putchar(c);
}
```

Let's discuss the use of the function **tputs(***cap, affcnt, outc***)** in this program to gain some insight into the **terminfo** routines. **tputs()** applies padding information. Some terminals have the capability to delay output. Their terminal descriptions in the **terminfo** database probably contain strings like **$<20>**, which means to pad for 20 milliseconds (see the following section "Specify Capabilities" in this chapter). **tputs** generates enough pad characters to delay for the appropriate time.

**tput**() has three parameters. The first parameter is the string capability to be output. The second is the number of lines affected by the capability. (Some capabilities may require padding that depends on the number of lines affected. For example, **insert_line** may have to copy all lines below the current line, and may require time proportional to the number of lines copied. By convention *affcnt* is 1 if no lines are affected. The value 1 is used, rather than 0, for safety, since *affcnt* is multiplied by the amount of time per item, and anything multiplied by 0 is 0.) The third parameter is a routine to be called with each character.

For many simple programs, *affcnt* is always 1 and *outc* always calls **putchar**. For these programs, the routine **putp(***cap***)** is a convenient abbreviation. **termhl** could be simplified by using **putp**().

Now to understand why you should use the **curses** level routines instead of **terminfo** level routines whenever possible, note the special check for the **underline_char** capability in this sample program. Some terminals, rather than having a code to start underlining and a code to stop underlining, have a code to underline the current character. **termhl** keeps track of the current mode, and if the current character is supposed to be underlined, outputs **underline_char**, if necessary. Low level details such as this are precisely why the **curses** level is recommended over the terminfo level. **curses** takes care of terminals with different methods of underlining and other terminal functions. Programs at the **terminfo** level must handle such details themselves.

**termhl** was written to illustrate a typical use of the **terminfo** routines. It is more complex than it need be in order to illustrate some properties of **terminfo** programs. The routine **vidattr** (see **curses**(3X)) could have been used instead of directly outputting **enter_bold_mode**, **enter_underline_mode**, and **exit_attribute_mode**. In fact, the program would be more robust if it did, since there are several ways to change video attribute modes.

# Working with the terminfo Database

The **terminfo** database describes the many terminals with which **curses** programs, as well as some UNIX system tools, like **vi**(1), can be used. Each terminal description is a compiled file containing the names that the terminal is known by and a group of comma-separated fields describing the actions and capabilities of the terminal. This section describes the **terminfo** database, related support tools, and their relationship to the **curses** library.

## Writing Terminal Descriptions

Descriptions of many popular terminals are already described in the **terminfo** database. However, it is possible that you'll want to run a **curses** program on a terminal for which there is not currently a description. In that case, you'll have to build the description.

The general procedure for building a terminal description is as follows:

1.  Give the known names of the terminal.

2.  Learn about, list, and define the known capabilities.

3.  Compile the newly-created description entry.

4.  Test the entry for correct operation.

5.  Go back to step 2, add more capabilities, and repeat, as necessary.

Building a terminal description is sometimes easier when you build small parts of the description and test them as you go along. These tests can expose deficiencies in the ability to describe the terminal. Also, modifying an existing description of a similar terminal can make the building task easier. (Lest we forget the UNIX motto: Build on the work of others.)

In the next few pages, we follow each step required to build a terminal description for the fictitious terminal named "myterm."

## Name the Terminal

The name of a terminal is the first information given in a **terminfo** terminal description. This string of names, assuming there is more than one name, is separated by pipe symbols ( | ). The first name given should be the most common abbreviation for the terminal. The last name given should be a long name that fully identifies the terminal. The long name is usually the manufacturer's formal name for the terminal. All names between the first and last entries should be known synonyms for the terminal name. All names but the formal name should be typed in lowercase letters and contain no blanks. Naturally, the formal name is entered as closely as possible to the manufacturer's name.

Here is the name string from the description of the AT&T Teletype 5420 Buffered Display Terminal:

```
5420|att5420|AT&T Teletype 5420,
```

Notice that the first name is the most commonly used abbreviation and the last is the long name. Also notice the comma at the end of the name string.

Here's the name string for our fictitious terminal, myterm:

```
myterm|mytm|mine|fancy|terminal|My FANCY Terminal,
```

Terminal names should follow common naming conventions. These conventions start with a root name, like 5425 or myterm, for example. The root name should not contain odd characters, like hyphens, that may not be recognized as a synonym for the terminal name. Possible hardware modes or user preferences should be shown by adding a hyphen and a 'mode indicator' at the end of the name. For example, the 'wide mode' (which is shown by a —w) version of our fictitious terminal would be described as **myterm—w**. **term**(5) describes mode indicators in greater detail.

## Learn About the Capabilities

After you complete the string of terminal names for your description, you have to learn about the terminal's capabilities so that you can properly describe them. To learn about the capabilities your terminal has, you should do the following:

- See the owner's manual for your terminal. It should have information about the capabilities available and the character strings that make up the sequence transmitted from the keyboard for each capability.

- Test the keys on your terminal to see what they transmit, if this information is not available in the manual. You can test the keys in one of the following ways — type:

  **stty —echo; cat —vu**
  *Type in the keys you want to test;*
  *for example, see what right arrow (→) transmits.*
  **<CR>**
  **<CTRL-D>**
  **stty echo**

  or

  **cat >dev/null**
  *Type in the escape sequences you want to test;*
  *for example, see what \E[H transmits.*
  **<CTRL-D>**

- The first line in each of these testing methods sets up the terminal to carry out the tests. The **<CTRL-D>** helps return the terminal to its normal settings.

- See the **terminfo**(4) manual page. It lists all the capability names you have to use in a terminal description. The following section, "Specify Capabilities," gives details.

## Specify Capabilities

Once you know the capabilities of your terminal, you have to describe them in your terminal description. You describe them with a string of comma-separated fields that contain the abbreviated **terminfo** name and, in some cases, the terminal's value for each capability. For example, **bel** is the abbreviated name for the beeping or ringing capability. On most terminals, a CTRL-G is the instruction that produces a beeping sound. Therefore, the beeping capability would be shown in the terminal description as **bel=^G,**.

The list of capabilities may continue onto multiple lines as long as white space (that is, tabs and spaces) begins every line but the first of the description. Comments can be included in the description by putting a **#** at the beginning of the line.

The **terminfo**(4) manual page has a complete list of the capabilities you can use in a terminal description. This list contains the name of the capability, the abbreviated name used in the database, the two-letter code that corresponds to the old **termcap** database name, and a short description of the capability. The abbreviated name that you will use in your database descriptions is shown in the column titled "Capname."

NOTE

For a **curses** program to run on any given terminal, its description in the **terminfo** database must include, at least, the capabilities to move a cursor in all four directions and to clear the screen.

A terminal's character sequence (value) for a capability can be a keyed operation (like CTRL-G), a numeric value, or a parameter string containing the sequence of operations required to achieve the particular capability. In a terminal description, certain characters are used after the capability name to show what type of character sequence is required. Explanations of these characters follow:

\#      This shows a numeric value is to follow. This character follows a capability that needs a number as a value. For example, the number of columns is defined as **cols#80,**.

\=      This shows that the capability value is the character string that follows. This string instructs the terminal how to act and may actually be a sequence of commands. There are certain characters used in the instruction strings that have special meanings. These special characters follow:

     ^      This shows a control character is to be used. For example, the beeping sound is produced by a CTRL-G. This would be shown as ^**G**.

\E or \e These characters followed by another character show an escape instruction. An entry of \EC would transmit to the terminal as ESCAPE-C.

\n      These characters provide a <**NL**> character sequence.

\l      These characters provide a linefeed character sequence.

\r    These characters provide a return character sequence.

\t    These characters provide a tab character sequence.

\b    These characters provide a backspace character sequence.

\f    These characters provide a formfeed character sequence.

\s    These characters provide a space character sequence.

\nnn  This is a character whose three-digit octal is *nnn*, where *nnn* can be one to three digits.

$< >  These symbols are used to show a delay in milliseconds. The desired length of delay is enclosed inside the "less than/greater than" symbols (< >). The amount of delay may be a whole number, a numeric value to one decimal place (tenths), or either form followed by an asterisk (*). The * shows that the delay will be proportional to the number of lines affected by the operation. For example, a 20-millisecond delay per line would appear as **$<20*>**. See the **terminfo**(4) manual page for more information about delays and padding.

Sometimes, it may be necessary to comment out a capability so that the terminal ignores this particular field. This is done by placing a period ( . ) in front of the abbreviated name for the capability. For example, if you would like to comment out the beeping capability, the description entry would appear as

    .bel=ˆG,

With this background information about specifying capabilities, let's add the capability string to our description of myterm. We'll consider basic, screen-oriented, keyboard-entered, and parameter string capabilities.

### Basic Capabilities

Some capabilities common to most terminals are bells, columns, lines on the screen, and overstriking of characters, if necessary. Suppose our fictitious terminal has these and a few other capabilities, as listed below. Note that the list gives the abbreviated **terminfo** name for each capability in the parentheses following the capability description:

- An automatic wrap around to the beginning of the next line whenever the cursor reaches the right-hand margin (**am**).

- The ability to produce a beeping sound. The instruction required to produce the beeping sound is ^G (**bel**).

- An 80-column wide screen (**cols**).

- A 30-line long screen (**lines**).

- Use of xon/xoff protocol (**xon**).

By combining the name string (see the section "Name the Terminal") and the capability descriptions that we now have, we get the following general **terminfo** database entry:

```
myterm|mytm|mine|fancy|terminal|My FANCY terminal,
          am, bel=^G, cols#80, lines#30, xon,
```

### Screen-Oriented Capabilities

Screen-oriented capabilities manipulate the contents of a screen. Our example terminal myterm has the following screen-oriented capabilities. Again, the abbreviated command associated with the given capability is shown in parentheses.

- A <CR> is a CTRL-M (**cr**).

- A cursor up one line motion is a CTRL-K (**cuu1**).

- A cursor down one line motion is a CTRL-J (**cud1**).

- Moving the cursor to the left one space is a CTRL-H (**cub1**).

- Moving the cursor to the right one space is a CTRL-L (**cuf1**).

- Entering reverse video mode is an ESCAPE-D (**smso**).

- Exiting reverse video mode is an ESCAPE-Z (**rmso**).

- A clear to the end of a line sequence is an ESCAPE-K and should have a 3-millisecond delay (**el**).

- A terminal scrolls when receiving a <NL> at the bottom of a page (**ind**).

The revised terminal description for myterm including these screen-oriented capabilities follows:

```
myterm|mytm|mine|fancy|terminal|My FANCY Terminal,
        am, bel=^G, cols#80, lines#30, xon,
        cr=^M, cuu1=^K, cud1=^J, cub1=^H, cuf1=^L,
        smso=\ED, rmso=\EZ, el=\EK$<3>, ind=\n,
```

### Keyboard-Entered Capabilities

Keyboard-entered capabilities are sequences generated when a key is typed on a terminal keyboard. Most terminals have, at least, a few special keys on their keyboard, such as arrow keys and the backspace key. Our example terminal has several of these keys whose sequences are, as follows:

- The backspace key generates a CTRL-H (**kbs**).

- The up arrow key generates an ESCAPE-[ A (**kcuu1**).

- The down arrow key generates an ESCAPE-[ B (**kcud1**).

- The right arrow key generates an ESCAPE-[ C (**kcuf1**).

- The left arrow key generates an ESCAPE-[ D (**kcub1**).

- The home key generates an ESCAPE-[ H (**khome**).

Adding this new information to our database entry for myterm produces:

```
myterm|mytm|mine|fancy|terminal|My FANCY Terminal,
        am, bel=^G, cols#80, lines#30, xon,
        cr=^M, cuu1=^K, cud1=^J, cub1=^H, cuf1=^L,
        smso=\ED, rmso=\EZ, el=\EK$<3>, ind=0
        kbs=^H, kcuu1=\E[A, kcud1=\E[B, kcuf1=\E[C,
        kcub1=\E[D, khome=\E[H,
```

### Parameter String Capabilities

Parameter string capabilities are capabilities that can take parameters — for example, those used to position a cursor on a screen or turn on a combination of video modes. To address a cursor, the **cup** capability is used and is passed two parameters: the row and column to address. String capabilities, such as **cup** and set attributes (**sgr**) capabilities, are passed arguments in a **terminfo** program by the **tparm()** routine.

The arguments to string capabilities are manipulated with special '%' sequences similar to those found in a **printf**(3S) statement. In addition, many of the features found on a simple stack-based RPN calculator are available. **cup**, as noted above, takes two arguments: the row and column. **sgr**, takes nine arguments, one for each of the nine video attributes. See **terminfo**(4) for the list and order of the attributes and further examples of **sgr**.

Our fancy terminal's cursor position sequence requires a row and column to be output as numbers separated by a semicolon, preceded by ESCAPE-[ and followed with H. The coordinate numbers are 1-based rather than 0-based. Thus, to move to row 5, column 18, from (0,0), the sequence

Integer arguments are pushed onto the stack with a '%p' sequence followed by the argument number, such as '%p2' to push the second argument. A shorthand sequence to increment the first two arguments is '%i'. To output the top number on the stack as a decimal, a '%d' sequence is used, exactly as in **printf**. Our terminal's **cup** sequence is built up as follows:

| cup= | Meaning |
|------|---------|
| \E[ | output ESCAPE-[ |
| %i | increment the two arguments |
| %p1 | push the 1st argument (the row) onto the stack |
| %d | output the row as a decimal |
| ; | output a semi-colon |
| %p2 | push the 2nd argument (the column) onto the stack |
| %d | output the column as a decimal |
| H | output the trailing letter |

or

cup=\E[%i%p1%d;%p2%dH,

Adding this new information to our database entry for myterm produces:

```
myterm|mytm|mine|fancy|terminal|My FANCY Terminal,
            am, bel=^G, cols#80, lines#30, xon,
            cr=^M, cuu1=^K, cud1=^J, cub1=^H, cuf1=^L,
            smso=\ED, rmso=\EZ, el=\EK$<3>, ind=0
            kbs=^H, kcuu1=\E[A, kcud1=\E[B, kcuf1=\E[C,
            kcub1=\E[D, khome=\E[H,
            cup=\E[%i%p1%d;%p2%dH,
```

See **terminfo**(4) for more information about parameter string capabilities.

## Compile the Description

The **terminfo** database entries are compiled using the **tic** compiler. This compiler translates **terminfo** database entries from the source format into the compiled format.

The source file for the description is usually in a file suffixed with **.ti**. For example, the description of myterm would be in a source file named **myterm.ti**. The compiled description of myterm would usually be placed in **/usr/lib/terminfo/m/myterm**, since the first letter in the description entry is **m**. Links would also be made to synonyms of **myterm**, for example, to **/f/fancy**. If the environment variable **$TERMINFO** were set to a directory and exported before the entry was compiled, the compiled entry would be placed in the **$TERMINFO** directory. All programs using the entry would then look in the new directory for the description file if **$TERMINFO** were set, before looking in the default **/usr/lib/terminfo**. The general format for the **tic** compiler is as follows:

> **tic** [−v] [−c] *file*

The **−v** option causes the compiler to trace its actions and output information about its progress. The **−c** option causes a check for errors; it may be combined with the **−v** option. *file* shows what file is to be compiled. If you want to compile more than one file at the same time, you have to first use **cat**(1) to join them together. The following command line shows how to compile the **terminfo** source file for our fictitious terminal:

> **tic −v myterm.ti <CR>**
> (The trace information appears as the compilation
>   proceeds.)

Refer to the **tic**(1M) manual page in the *System Administrator's Reference Manual* for more information about the compiler.

## Test the Description

Let's consider three ways to test a terminal description. First, you can test it by setting the environment variable **$TERMINFO** to the path name of the directory containing the description. If programs run the same on the new terminal as they did on the older known terminals, then the new description is functional.

Second, you can test for correct insert line padding by commenting out **xon** in the description and then editing (using **vi**(1)) a large file (over 100 lines) at 9600 baud (if possible), and deleting about 15 lines from the middle of the screen. Type **u** (undo) several times quickly. If the terminal messes up, then more padding is usually required. A similar test can be used for inserting a character.

Third, you can use the **tput**(1) command. This command outputs a string or an integer according to the type of capability being described. If the capability is a Boolean expression, then **tput** sets the exit code (0 for TRUE, 1 for FALSE) and produces no output. The general format for the **tput** command is as follows:

> **tput** [−T*type*] *capname*

The type of terminal you are requesting information about is identified with the −T*type* option. Usually, this option is not necessary because the default terminal name is taken from the environment variable **$TERM**. The *capname* field is used to show what capability to output from the **terminfo** database.

The following command line shows how to output the "clear screen" character sequence for the terminal being used:

> **tput clear**
> (The screen is cleared.)

The following command line shows how to output the number of columns for the terminal being used:

> **tput cols**
> (The number of columns used by the terminal appears here.)

The **tput**(1) manual page found in the *User's Reference Manual* contains more information on the usage and possible messages associated with this command.

# Comparing or Printing terminfo Descriptions

Sometime you may want to compare two terminal descriptions or quickly look at a description without going to the **terminfo** source directory. The **infocmp**(1M) command was designed to help you with both of these tasks. Compare two descriptions of the same terminal; for example,

```
mkdir /tmp/old /tmp/new
TERMINFO=/tmp/old tic old5420.ti
TERMINFO=/tmp/new tic new5420.ti
infocmp -A /tmp/old -B /tmp/new -d 5420 5420
```

compares the old and new 5420 entries.

To print out the **terminfo** source for the 5420, type

```
infocmp -I 5420
```

# Converting a terminfo Description to a terminfo Description

 The **terminfo** database is designed to take the place of the **termcap** database. Because of the many programs and processes that have been written with and for the **termcap** database, it is not feasible to do a complete cutover at one time. Any conversion from **termcap** to **terminfo** requires some experience with both databases. All entries into the databases should be handled with extreme caution. These files are important to the operation of your terminal.

The **captoinfo**(1M) command converts **termcap**(4) descriptions to **terminfo**(4) descriptions. When a file is passed to **captoinfo**, it looks for **termcap** descriptions and writes the equivalent **terminfo** descriptions on the standard output. For example,

**captoinfo /etc/termcap**

converts the file **/etc/termcap** to **terminfo** source, preserving comments and other extraneous information within the file. The command line

**captoinfo**

looks up the current terminal in the **termcap** database, as specified by the **$TERM** and **$TERMCAP** environment variables and converts it to **terminfo**.

If you must have both **termcap** and **terminfo** terminal descriptions, keep the **terminfo** description only and use **infocmp -C** to get the **termcap** descriptions.

If you have been using cursor optimization programs with the −**ltermcap** or −**ltermlib** option in the **cc** command line, those programs will still be functional. However, these options should be replaced with the −**lcurses** option.

# curses Program Examples

The following examples demonstrate uses of **curses** routines.

## The editor Program

This program illustrates how to use **curses** routines to write a screen editor. For simplicity, **editor** keeps the buffer in **stdscr**; obviously, a real screen editor would have a separate data structure for the buffer. This program has many other simplifications: no provision is made for files of any length other than the size of the screen, for lines longer than the width of the screen, or for control characters in the file.

Several points about this program are worth making. First, it uses the **move()**, **mvaddstr()**, **flash()**, **wnoutrefresh()** and **clrtoeol()** routines. These routines are all discussed in this chapter under "Working with **curses** Routines."

Second, it also uses some **curses** routines that we have not discussed. For example, the function to write out a file uses the **mvinch()** routine, which returns a character in a window at a given position. The data structure used to write out a file does not keep track of the number of characters in a line or the number of lines in the file, so trailing blanks are eliminated when the file is written. The program also uses the **insch()**, **delch()**, **insertln()**, and **deleteln()** routines. These functions insert and delete a character or line. See **curses**(3X) for more information about these routines.

Third, the editor command interpreter accepts special keys, as well as ASCII characters. On one hand, new users find an editor that handles special keys easier to learn about. For example, it's easier for new users to use the arrow keys to move a cursor than it is to memorize that the letter h means left, j means down, k means up, and l means right. On the other hand, experienced users usually like having the ASCII characters to avoid moving their hands from the home row position to use special keys.

 NOTE Because not all terminals have arrow keys, your **curses** programs will work on more terminals if there is an ASCII character associated with each special key.

Fourth, the CTRL-L command illustrates a feature most programs using **curses** routines should have. Often some program beyond the control of the routines writes something to the screen (for instance, a broadcast message) or some line noise affects the screen so much that the routines cannot keep track of it. A user invoking **editor** can type CTRL-L, causing the screen to be cleared and redrawn with a call to **wrefresh(curscr)**.

Finally, another important point is that the input command is terminated by CTRL-D, not the escape key. It is very tempting to use escape as a command, since escape is one of the few special keys available on every keyboard. (Return and break are the only others.) However, using escape as a separate key introduces an ambiguity. Most terminals use sequences of characters beginning with escape (i.e., escape sequences) to control the terminal and have special keys that send escape sequences to the computer. If a computer receives an escape from a terminal, it cannot tell whether the user depressed the escape key or whether a special key was pressed.

**editor** and other **curses** programs handle the ambiguity by setting a timer. If another character is received during this time, and if that character might be the beginning of a special key, the program reads more input until either a full special key is read, the time out is reached, or a character is received that could not have been generated by a special key. While this strategy works most of the time, it is not foolproof. It is possible for the user to press escape, then to type another key quickly, which causes the **curses** program to think a special key has been pressed. Also, a pause occurs until the escape can be passed to the user program, resulting in a slower response to the escape key.

Many existing programs use escape as a fundamental command, which cannot be changed without infuriating a large class of users. These programs cannot make use of special keys without dealing with this ambiguity, and at best must resort to a time-out solution. The moral is clear: when designing your **curses** programs, avoid the escape key.

```
/* editor: A screen-oriented editor.  The user
 * interface is similar to a subset of vi.
 * The buffer is kept in stdscr to simplify
 * the program.
 */

#include <stdio.h>
#include <curses.h>
```

*continued*

```
#define CTRL(c) ((c) & 037)

main(argc, argv)
int argc;
char **argv;
{
        extern void perror(), exit();
        int i, n, l;
        int c;
        int line = 0;
        FILE *fd;

        if (argc != 2)
        {
                fprintf(stderr, "Usage: %s file\n", argv[0]);
                exit(1);
        }

        fd = fopen(argv[1], "r");
        if (fd == NULL)
        {
                perror(argv[1]);
                exit(2);
        }

        initscr();
        cbreak();
        nonl();
        noecho();
        idlok(stdscr, TRUE);
        keypad(stdscr, TRUE);

        /* Read in the file */
        while ((c = getc(fd)) != EOF)
        {
                if (c == '\n')
                        line++;
                if (line > LINES - 2)
                        break;
                addch(c);
        }
```

*continued*

```
        fclose(fd);

        move(0,0);
        refresh();
        edit();

        /* Write out the file */
        fd = fopen(argv[1], "w");
        for (1 = 0; 1 < LINES - 1; 1++)
        {
                n = len(1);
                for (i = 0; i < n; i++)
                        putc(mvinch(1, i) & A_CHARTEXT, fd);
                putc('\n', fd);
        }
        fclose(fd);

        endwin();
        exit(0);
}

len(lineno)
int lineno;
{
        int linelen = COLS - 1;

        while (linelen >= 0 && mvinch(lineno, linelen) == ' ')
                linelen--;
        return linelen + 1;
}

/* Global value of current cursor position */
int row, col;

edit()
{
        int c;

        for (;;)
```

*continued*

```
{
        move(row, col);
        refresh();
        c = getch();

        /* Editor commands */
        switch (c)
        {

        /* hjkl and arrow keys: move cursor
         * in direction indicated */
        case 'h':
        case KEY_LEFT:
                if (col > 0)
                        col--;
                else
                        flash();
                break;

        case 'j':
        case KEY_DOWN:
                if (row < LINES - 1)
                        row++;
                else
                        flash();
                break;

        case 'k':
        case KEY_UP:
                if (row > 0)
                        row--;
                else
                        flash();
                break;

        case 'l':
        case KEY_RIGHT:
                if (col < COLS - 1)
                        col++;
                else
                        flash();
                break;
```

*continued*

```
/* i: enter input mode */
case KEY_IC:
case 'i':
        input();
        break;

/* x: delete current character */
case KEY_DC:
case 'x':
        delch();
        break;

/* o: open up a new line and enter input mode */
case KEY_IL:
case 'o':
        move(++row, col = 0);
        insertln();
        input();
        break;

/* d: delete current line */
case KEY_DL:
case 'd':
        deleteln();
        break;

/* ^L: redraw screen */
case KEY_CLEAR:
case CTRL('L'):
        wrefresh(curscr);
        break;

/* w: write and quit */
case 'w':
        return;
```

*continued*

```
                        /* q: quit without writing */
                        case 'q':
                                endwin();
                                exit(2);
                        default:
                                flash();
                                break;
                        }
                }
        }

/*
 * Insert mode: accept characters and insert them.
 *  End with ^D or EIC
 */
input()
{
        int c;

        standout();
        mvaddstr(LINES - 1, COLS - 20, "INPUT MODE");
        standend();
        move(row, col);
        refresh();
        for (;;)
        {
                c = getch();
                if (c == CTRL('D') || c == KEY_EIC)
                        break;
                insch(c);
                move(row, ++col);
                refresh();
        }
        move(LINES - 1, COLS - 20);
        clrtoeol();
        move(row, col);
        refresh();
}
```

# The highlight Program

This program illustrates a use of the routine **attrset()**. **highlight** reads a text file and uses embedded escape sequences to control attributes. **\U** turns on underlining, **\B** turns on bold, and **\N** restores the default output attributes.

Note the first call to **scrollok()**, a routine that we have not previously discussed (see **curses**(3X)). This routine allows the terminal to scroll if the file is longer than one screen. When an attempt is made to draw past the bottom of the screen, **scrollok()** automatically scrolls the terminal up a line and calls **refresh()**.

```
/*
 * highlight: a program to turn \U, \B, and
 * \N sequences into highlighted
 * output, allowing words to be
 * displayed underlined or in bold.
 */

#include <stdio.h>
#include <curses.h>

main(argc, argv)
int argc;
char **argv;
{
        FILE *fd;
        int c, c2;
        void exit(), perror();

        if (argc != 2)
        {
                fprintf(stderr, "Usage: highlight file\n");
                exit(1);
        }

        fd = fopen(argv[1], "r");

        if (fd == NULL)
```

*continued*

```
        {
                perror(argv[1]);
                exit(2);
        }

        initscr();
        scrollok(stdscr, TRUE);
        nonl();
        while ((c = getc(fd)) != EOF)
        {
                if (c == '\\')
                {
                        c2 = getc(fd);
                        switch (c2)
                        {
                        case 'B':
                                attrset(A_BOLD);
                                continue;
                        case 'U':
                                attrset(A_UNDERLINE);
                                continue;
                        case 'N':
                                attrset(0);
                                continue;
                        }
                        addch(c);
                        addch(c2);
                }
                else
                        addch(c);
        }
        fclose(fd);
        refresh();
        endwin();
        exit(0);
}
```

## The scatter **Program**

This program takes the first **LINES** − 1 lines of characters from the standard input and displays the characters on a terminal screen in a random order. For this program to work properly, the input file should not contain tabs or non-printing characters.

```
/*
 *        The scatter program.
 */

#include <curses.h>
#include <sys/types.h>

extern time_t time();

#define MAXLINES 120
#define MAXCOLS   160
char s[MAXLINES][MAXCOLS];          /* Screen Array */
int  T[MAXLINES][MAXCOLS];          /* Tag Array - Keeps track of   *
                                     * the number of characters     *
                                     * printed and their positions. */

main()
{
        register int row = 0,col = 0;
        register int c;
        int char_count = 0;
        time_t t;
        void exit(), srand();

        initscr();
        for(row = 0;row < MAXLINES;row++)
                for(col = 0;col < MAXCOLS;col++)
                        s[row][col]=' ';

        col = row = 0;
        /* Read screen in */
        while ((c=getchar()) != EOF && row < LINES ) {

                if(c != '\n')
```

*continued*

```
        {
                /* Place char in screen array */
                s[row][col++] = c;
                if(c != ' ')
                        char_count++;
        }
        else
        {
                col = 0;
                row++;
        }
}

time(&t);/* Seed the random number generator */
srand((unsigned)t);

while (char_count)
{
        row = rand() % LINES;
        col = (rand() >> 2) % COLS;
        if (T[row][col] != 1 && s[row][col] != ' ')
        {
                move(row, col);
                addch(s[row][col]);
                T[row][col] = 1;
                char_count--;
                refresh();
        }
}
endwin();
exit(0);
}
```

## The show **Program**

**show** pages through a file, showing one screen of its contents each time
you depress the space bar. The program calls **cbreak**() so that you can
depress the space bar without having to hit return; it calls **noecho**() to prevent
the space from echoing on the screen. The **nonl**() routine, which we have not
previously discussed, is called to enable more cursor optimization. The
**idlok**() routine, which we also have not discussed, is called to allow insert and
delete line. (See **curses**(3X) for more information about these routines). Also
notice that **clrtoeol**() and **clrtobot**() are called.

By creating an input file for **show** made up of screen-sized (about 24
lines) pages, each varying slightly from the previous page, nearly any exercise
for a **curses**() program can be created. This type of input file is called a show
script.

```
#include <curses.h>
#include <signal.h>

main(argc, argv)
int argc;
char *argv[];
{
        FILE *fd;
        char linebuf[BUFSIZ];
        int line;
        void done(), perror(), exit();

        if (argc != 2)
        {
                fprintf(stderr, "usage: %s file\n", argv[0]);
                exit(1);
        }

        if ((fd=fopen(argv[1], "r")) == NULL)
        {

                perror(argv[1]);
                exit(2);
        }
```

*continued*

```
        signal(SIGINT, done);

        initscr();
        noecho();
        cbreak();
        nonl();
        idlok(stdscr, TRUE);

        while(1)
        {
                move(0,0);
                for (line = 0; line < LINES; line++)
                {
                        if (!fgets(linebuf, sizeof linebuf, fd))
                        {
                                clrtobot();
                                done();
                        }
                        move(line, 0);
                        printw("%s", linebuf);
                }
                refresh();
                if (getch() == 'q')
                        done();
        }
}

void done()
{
        move(LINES - 1, 0);
        clrtoeol();
        refresh();
        endwin();
        exit(0);
}
```

# The two Program

This program pages through a file, writing one page to the terminal from which the program is invoked and the next page to the terminal named on the command line. It then waits for a space to be typed on either terminal and writes the next page to the terminal at which the space is typed.

**two** is just a simple example of a two-terminal **curses** program. It does not handle notification; instead, it requires the name and type of the second terminal on the command line. As written, the command **"sleep 100000"** must be typed at the second terminal to put it to sleep while the program runs, and the user of the first terminal must have both read and write permission on the second terminal.

```
#include <curses.h>
#include <signal.h>

SCREEN *me, *you;
SCREEN *set_term();

FILE *fd, *fdyou;
char linebuf[512];

main(argc, argv)
int argc;
char **argv;
{
        void done(), exit();
        unsigned sleep();
        char *getenv();
        int c;

        if (argc != 4)
        {
            fprintf(stderr, "Usage: two othertty otherttytype inputfile\n");
            exit(1);
        }
```

*continued*

```
fd = fopen(argv[3], "r");
fdyou = fopen(argv[1], "w+");
signal(SIGINT, done);       /* die gracefully */

me = newterm(getenv("TERM"), stdout, stdin);  /* initialize my tty */
you = newterm(argv[2], fdyou, fdyou);/* Initialize the other terminal */

set_term(me);      /* Set modes for my terminal */
noecho();/* turn off tty echo */
cbreak();/* enter cbreak mode */
nonl();            /* Allow linefeed */
nodelay(stdscr, TRUE);      /* No hang on input */

set_term(you);     /* Set modes for other terminal */
noecho();
cbreak();
nonl();
nodelay(stdscr,TRUE);

/* Dump first screen full on my terminal */
dump_page(me);

/* Dump second screen full on the other terminal */
dump_page(you);

for (;;) /* for each screen full */
{
    set_term(me);
    c = getch();
    if (c == 'q')/* wait for user to read it */
    done();
    if (c == ' ')
    dump_page(me);

    set_term(you);
    c = getch();
    if (c == 'q')/* wait for user to read it */
    done();
    if (c == ' ')
    dump_page(you);
    sleep(1);
}
}
```

*continued*

```
dump_page(term)
  SCREEN *term;
{
        int line;

        set_term(term);
        move(0, 0);
        for (line = 0; line < LINES - 1; line++) {
            if (fgets(linebuf, sizeof linebuf, fd) == NULL) {
            clrtobot();
            done();
            }
            mvaddstr(line, 0, linebuf);
        }
        standout();
        mvprintw(LINES - 1, 0, "--More--");
        standend();
        refresh();          /* sync screen */
}
/*
 * Clean up and exit.
 */
void done()
{
        /* Clean up first terminal */
        set_term(you);
        move(LINES - 1,0);/* to lower left corner */

        clrtoeol();          /* clear bottom line */
        refresh();           /* flush out everything */
        endwin();/* curses cleanup */

        /* Clean up second terminal */
        set_term(me);
        move(LINES - 1,0);/* to lower left corner */
        clrtoeol();          /* clear bottom line */
        refresh();           /* flush out everything */
        endwin();/* curses cleanup */
        exit(0);
}
```

## The window Program

This example program demonstrates the use of multiple windows. The main display is kept in **stdscr**. When you want to put something other than what is in **stdscr** on the physical terminal screen temporarily, a new window is created covering part of the screen. A call to **wrefresh**() for that window causes it to be written over the **stdscr** image on the terminal screen. Calling **refresh**() on **stdscr** results in the original window being redrawn on the screen. Note the calls to the **touchwin**() routine (which we have not discussed — see **curses**(3X)) that occur before writing out a window over an existing window on the terminal screen. This routine prevents screen optimization in a **curses** program. If you have trouble refreshing a new window that overlaps an old window, it may be necessary to call **touchwin**() for the new window to get it completely written out.

```
#include <curses.h>

WINDOW *cmdwin;

main()

{
        int i, c;
        char buf[120];
        void exit();

        initscr();
        nonl();
        noecho();
        cbreak();

        cmdwin = newwin(3, COLS, 0, 0);/* top 3 lines */
        for (i = 0; i < LINES; i++)
                mvprintw(i, 0, "This is line %d of stdscr", i);
```

*continued*

```
for (;;)

{
        refresh();
        c = getch();
        switch (c)

        {

        case 'c':/* Enter command from keyboard */
                werase(cmdwin);
                wprintw(cmdwin, "Enter command:");
                wmove(cmdwin, 2, 0);
                for (i = 0; i < COLS; i++)
                        waddch(cmdwin, '-');
                wmove(cmdwin, 1, 0);
                touchwin(cmdwin);
                wrefresh(cmdwin);
                wgetstr(cmdwin, buf);
                touchwin(stdscr);

                /*
                 * The command is now in buf.
                 * It should be processed here.
                 */

        case 'q':
                endwin();
                exit(0);
        }

}

}
```

# CHAPTER 11: THE COMMON OBJECT FILE FORMAT (COFF)

## The Common Object File Format (COFF)

This section describes the Common Object File Format (COFF) used on AT&T computers with the UNIX operating system. COFF is the format of the output file produced by the assembler, **as**, and the link editor, **ld**.

Some key features of COFF are

- applications can add system-dependent information to the object file without causing access utilities to become obsolete

- space is provided for symbolic information used by debuggers and other applications

- programmers can modify the way the object file is constructed by providing directives at compile time

The object file supports user-defined sections and contains extensive information for symbolic software testing. An object file contains

- a file header
- optional header information
- a table of section headers
- data corresponding to the section headers
- relocation information
- line numbers
- a symbol table
- a string table

Figure 11-1 shows the overall structure.

| FILE HEADER |
| Optional Information |
| Section 1 Header |
| ... |
| Section *n* Header |
| Raw Data for Section 1 |
| ... |
| Raw Data for Section *n* |
| Relocation Info for Sect. 1 |
| ... |
| Relocation Info for Sect. *n* |
| Line Numbers for Sect. 1 |
| ... |
| Line Numbers for Sect. *n* |
| SYMBOL TABLE |
| STRING TABLE |

Figure 11-1: Object File Format

The last four sections (relocation, line numbers, symbol table, and the string table) may be missing if the program is linked with the −s option of the **ld** command, or if the line number information, symbol table, and string table are removed by the **strip** command. The line number information does not appear unless the program is compiled with the −g option of the **cc** command. Also, if there are no unresolved external references after linking, the relocation information is no longer needed and is absent. The string table is also absent if the source file does not contain any symbols with names longer than eight characters.

An object file that contains no errors or unresolved references is considered executable.

# Definitions and Conventions

Before proceeding further, you should become familiar with the following terms and conventions.

## Sections

A section is the smallest portion of an object file that is relocated and treated as one separate and distinct entity. In the most common case, there are three sections named **.text**, **.data**, and **.bss**. Additional sections accommodate comments, multiple text or data segments, shared data segments, or user-specified sections. However, the UNIX operating system loads only **.text**, **.data**, and **.bss** into memory when the file is executed.

 NOTE

It a mistake to assume that every COFF file will have a certain number of sections, or to assume characteristics of sections such as their order, their location in the object file, or the address at which they are to be loaded. This information is available only after the object file has been created. Programs manipulating COFF files should obtain it from file and section headers in the file.

## Physical and Virtual Addresses

The physical address of a section or symbol is the offset of that section or symbol from address zero of the address space. The term physical address as used in COFF does not correspond to general usage. The physical address of an object is not necessarily the address at which the object is placed when the process is executed. For example, on a system with paging, the address is located with respect to address zero of virtual memory and the system performs another address translation. The section header contains two address fields, a physical address, and a virtual address; but in all versions of COFF on UNIX systems, the physical address is equivalent to the virtual address.

## Target Machine

Compilers and link editors produce executable object files that are intended to be run on a particular computer. In the case of cross-compilers, the compilation and link editing are done on one computer with the intent of creating an object file that can be executed on another computer. The term target machine refers to the computer on which the object file is destined to run. In the majority of cases, the target machine is the exact same computer on which the object file is being created.

## File Header

The file header contains the 20 bytes of information shown in Figure 11-2. The last 2 bytes are flags that are used by **ld** and object file utilities.

| Bytes | Declaration | Name | Description |
|-------|-------------|------|-------------|
| 0-1 | **unsigned short** | **f_magic** | Magic number |
| 2-3 | **unsigned short** | **f_nscns** | Number of sections |
| 4-7 | **long int** | **f_timdat** | Time and date stamp indicating when the file was created, expressed as the number of elapsed seconds since 00:00:00 GMT, January 1, 1970 |
| 8-11 | **long int** | **f_symptr** | File pointer containing the starting address of the symbol table |
| 12-15 | **long int** | **f_nsyms** | Number of entries in the symbol table |
| 16-17 | **unsigned short** | **f_opthdr** | Number of bytes in the optional header |
| 18-19 | **unsigned short** | **f_flags** | Flags (see Figure 11-3) |

Figure 11-2: File Header Contents

### Magic Numbers

The magic number specifies the target machine on which the object file is executable.

## Flags

The last 2 bytes of the file header are flags that describe the type of the object file. Currently defined flags are found in the header file **filehdr.h**, and are shown in Figure 11-3.

| Mnemonic | Flag | Meaning |
|----------|------|---------|
| F_RELFLG | 00001 | Relocation information stripped from the file |
| F_EXEC | 00002 | File is executable (i.e., no unresolved external references) |
| F_LNNO | 00004 | Line numbers stripped from the file |
| F_LSYMS | 00010 | Local symbols stripped from the file |
| F_AR32W | 0001000 | 32 bit word |
| F_BM32B | 0020000 | 32100 required |
| F_BM32MAU | 0040000 | MAU required |

Figure 11-3: File Header Flags (3B2 Computer)

## File Header Declaration

The C structure declaration for the file header is given in Figure 11-4. This declaration may be found in the header file **filehdr.h**.

```
struct filehdr
{
    unsigned short   f_magic;    /* magic number */
    unsigned short   f_nscns;    /* number of section */

    long             f_timdat;   /* time and date stamp */

    long             f_symptr;   /* file ptr to symbol table */

    long             f_nsyms;    /* number entries in the symbol table */

    unsigned short   f_opthdr;   /* size of optional header */

    unsigned short   f_flags;    /* flags */
};

#define FILHDR struct filehdr
#define FILHSZ sizeof(FILHDR)
```

Figure 11-4: File Header Declaration

## Optional Header Information

The template for optional information varies among different systems that use COFF. Applications place all system-dependent information into this record. This allows different operating systems access to information that only that operating system uses without forcing all COFF files to save space for that information. General utility programs (for example, the symbol table access library functions, the disassembler, etc.) are made to work properly on any common object file. This is done by seeking past this record using the size of optional header information in the file header field **f_opthdr**.

## Standard UNIX System a.out Header

By default, files produced by the link editor for a UNIX system always have a standard UNIX system **a.out** header in the optional header field. The UNIX system **a.out** header is 28 bytes. The fields of the optional header are described in Figure 11-5.

| Bytes | Declaration | Name | Description |
|-------|-------------|------|-------------|
| 0-1 | short | magic | Magic number |
| 2-3 | short | vstamp | Version stamp |
| 4-7 | long int | tsize | Size of text in bytes |
| 8-11 | long int | dsize | Size of initialized data in bytes |
| 12-15 | long int | bsize | Size of uninitialized data in bytes |
| 16-19 | long int | entry | Entry point |
| 20-23 | long int | text_start | Base address of text |
| 24-27 | long int | data_start | Base address of data |

Figure 11-5: Optional Header Contents (3B2, 3B5, 3B15 Computers)

Whereas, the magic number in the file header specifies the machine on which the object file runs, the magic number in the optional header supplies information telling the operating system on that machine how that file should be executed. The magic numbers recognized by the 3B2/3B5/3B15 UNIX operating system are given in Figure 11-6.

| Value | Meaning |
|-------|---------|
| 0407 | The text segment is not write-protected or sharable; the data segment is contiguous with the text segment. |
| 0410 | The data segment starts at the next segment following the text segment and the text segment is write protected. |
| 0413 | Text and data segments are aligned within **a.out** so it can be directly paged. |

Figure 11-6: UNIX System Magic Numbers (3B2, 3B5, 3B15 Computers)

### Optional Header Declaration

The C language structure declaration currently used for the UNIX system **a.out** file header is given in Figure 11-7. This declaration may be found in the header file **aouthdr.h**.

```
typedef struct aouthdr
{
        short    magic;      /* magic number */
        short    vstamp;     /* version stamp */
        long     tsize;      /* text size in bytes, padded */

                             /* to full word boundary */

        long     dsize;      /* initialized data size */

        long     bsize;      /* uninitialized data size */

        long     entry;      /* entry point */

        long     text_start; /* base of text for this file */

        long     data_start  /* base of data for this file */

} AOUTHDR;
```

Figure 11-7: **aouthdr** Declaration

# Section Headers

Every object file has a table of section headers to specify the layout of data within the file. The section header table consists of one entry for every section in the file. The information in the section header is described in Figure 11-8.

| Bytes | Declaration | Name | Description |
|-------|-------------|------|-------------|
| 0-7 | char | s_name | 8-character null padded section name |
| 8-11 | long int | s_paddr | Physical address of section |
| 12-15 | long int | s_vaddr | Virtual address of section |
| 16-19 | long int | s_size | Section size in bytes |
| 20-23 | long int | s_scnptr | File pointer to raw data |
| 24-27 | long int | s_relptr | File pointer to relocation entries |
| 28-31 | long int | s_lnnoptr | File pointer to line number entries |
| 32-33 | unsigned short | s_nreloc | Number of relocation entries |
| 34-35 | unsigned short | s_nlnno | Number of line number entries |
| 36-39 | long int | s_flags | Flags (see Figure 11-9) |

Figure 11-8: Section Header Contents

The size of a section is padded to a multiple of 4 bytes. File pointers are byte offsets that can be used to locate the start of data, relocation, or line number entries for the section. They can be readily used with the UNIX system function **fseek**(3S).

## Flags

The lower 2 bytes of the flag field indicate a section type. The flags are described in Figure 11-9.

| Mnemonic | Flag | Meaning |
|----------|------|---------|
| STYP_REG | 0x00 | Regular section (allocated, relocated, loaded) |
| STYP_DSECT | 0x01 | Dummy section (not allocated, relocated, not loaded) |
| STYP_NOLOAD | 0x02 | Noload section (allocated, relocated, not loaded) |
| STYP_GROUP | 0x04 | Grouped section (formed from input sections) |
| STYP_PAD | 0x08 | Padding section (not allocated, not relocated, loaded) |
| STYP_COPY | 0x10 | Copy section (for a decision function used in updating fields; not allocated, not relocated, loaded, relocation and line number entries processed normally) |
| STYP_TEXT | 0x20 | Section contains executable text |
| STYP_DATA | 0x40 | Section contains initialized data |
| STYP_BSS | 0x80 | Section contains only uninitialized data |
| STYP_INFO | 0x200 | Comment section (not allocated, not relocated, not loaded) |
| STYP_OVER | 0x400 | Overlay section (relocated, not allocated, not loaded) |
| STYP_LIB | 0x800 | For **.lib** section (treated like STYP_INFO) |

Figure 11-9: Section Header Flags

## Section Header Declaration

The C structure declaration for the section headers is described in Figure 11-10. This declaration may be found in the header file **scnhdr.h**.

```
struct scnhdr
{
        char      s_name[8];        /* section name */
        long      s_paddr;          /* physical address */
        long      s_vaddr;          /* virtual address */
        long      s_size;           /* section size */
        long      s_scnptr;         /* file ptr to section raw data */

        long      s_relptr;         /* file ptr to relocation */

        long      s_lnnoptr;        /* file ptr to line number */

        unsigned short  s_nreloc;   /* number of relocation entries */

        unsigned short  s_nlnno;    /* number of line number entries */

        long      s_flags;          /* flags */

};

#define   SCNHDR   struct scnhdr
#define   SCNHSZ   sizeof(SCNHDR)
```

Figure 11-10: Section Header Declaration

## .bss Section Header

The one deviation from the normal rule in the section header table is the entry for uninitialized data in a **.bss** section. A **.bss** section has a size and symbols that refer to it, and symbols that are defined in it. At the same time, a **.bss** section has no relocation entries, no line number entries, and no data. Therefore, a **.bss** section has an entry in the section header table but occupies no space elsewhere in the file. In this case, the number of relocation and line number entries, as well as all file pointers in a **.bss** section header, are 0. The same is true of the STYP_NOLOAD and STYP_DSECT sections.

## Sections

Figure 11-1 shows that section headers are followed by the appropriate number of bytes of text or data. The raw data for each section begins on a 4-byte boundary in the file.

Link editor SECTIONS directives (see Chapter 12) allow users to, among other things:

- describe how input sections are to be combined
- direct the placement of output sections
- rename output sections

If no SECTIONS directives are given, each input section appears in an output section of the same name. For example, if a number of object files, each with a **.text** section, are linked together the output object file contains a single **.text** section made up of the combined input **.text** sections.

## Relocation Information

Object files have one relocation entry for each relocatable reference in the text or data. The relocation information consists of entries with the format described in Figure 11-11.

| Bytes | Declaration | Name | Description |
|-------|-------------|------|-------------|
| 0-3 | **long int** | **r_vaddr** | (Virtual) address of reference |
| 4-7 | **long int** | **r_symndx** | Symbol table index |
| 8-9 | **unsigned short** | **r_type** | Relocation type |

Figure 11-11: Relocation Section Contents

The first 4 bytes of the entry are the virtual address of the text or data to which this entry applies. The next field is the index, counted from 0, of the symbol table entry that is being referenced. The type field indicates the type of relocation to be applied.

As the link editor reads each input section and performs relocation, the relocation entries are read. They direct how references found within the input section are treated. The currently recognized relocation types are given in Figure 11-12.

| Mnemonic | Flag | Meaning |
|----------|------|---------|
| R_ABS | 0 | Reference is absolute; no relocation is necessary. The entry will be ignored. |
| R_DIR32 | 06 | Direct 32-bit reference to the symbol's virtual address. |
| R_DIR32S | 012 | Direct 32-bit reference to the symbol's virtual address, with the 32-bit value stored in the reverse order in the object file. |

Figure 11-12: Relocation Types (3B2, 3B5, 3B15 Computers)

## Relocation Entry Declaration

The structure declaration for relocation entries is given in Figure 11-13. This declaration may be found in the header file **reloc.h**.

```
struct reloc
{
    long            r_vaddr;    /* virtual address of reference */

    long            r_symndx;   /* index into symbol table */

    unsigned short  r_type;     /* relocation type */
};

#define RELOC    struct reloc

#define RELSZ    10
```

Figure 11-13: Relocation Entry Declaration

## Line Numbers

When invoked with the −g option, the **cc**, and **f77** commands cause an entry in the object file for every source line where a breakpoint can be inserted. You can then reference line numbers when using a software debugger like **sdb**. All line numbers in a section are grouped by function as shown in Figure 11-14.

| symbol index | 0 |
|---|---|
| physical address | line number |
| physical address | line number |
| . | . |
| . | . |
| . | . |
| symbol index | 0 |
| physical address | line number |
| physical address | line number |

Figure 11-14: Line Number Grouping

The first entry in a function grouping has line number 0 and has, in place of the physical address, an index into the symbol table for the entry containing the function name. Subsequent entries have actual line numbers and addresses of the text corresponding to the line numbers. The line number entries are relative to the beginning of the function, and appear in increasing order of address.

## Line Number Declaration

The structure declaration currently used for line number entries is given in Figure 11-15.

```
struct lineno
{
        union
        {
                long    l_symndx;   /* symtbl index of func name */

                long    l_paddr;    /* paddr of line number */
        } l_addr;
        unsigned short  l_lnno;     /* line number */

};

#define LINENO      struct lineno
#define LINESZ      6
```

Figure 11-15: Line Number Entry Declaration

# Symbol Table

Because of symbolic debugging requirements, the order of symbols in the symbol table is very important. Symbols appear in the sequence shown in Figure 11-16.

| |
|---|
| filename 1 |
| function 1 |
| local symbols for function 1 |
| function 2 |
| local symbols for function 2 |
| . . . |
| statics |
| . . . |
| filename 2 |
| function 1 |
| local symbols for function 1 |
| . . . |
| statics |
| . . . |
| defined global symbols |
| undefined global symbols |

Figure 11-16: COFF Symbol Table

The word statics in Figure 11-16 means symbols defined with the C language storage class static outside any function. The symbol table consists of at least one fixed-length entry per symbol with some symbols followed by auxiliary entries of the same size. The entry for each symbol is a structure that holds the value, the type, and other information.

## Special Symbols

The symbol table contains some special symbols that are generated by **as**, and other tools. These symbols are given in Figure 11-17.

| Symbol | Meaning |
|--------|---------|
| .file | filename |
| .text | address of .text section |
| .data | address of .data section |
| .bss | address of .bss section |
| .bb | address of start of inner block |
| .eb | address of end of inner block |
| .bf | address of start of function |
| .ef | address of end of function |
| .target | pointer to the structure or union returned by a function |
| .xfake | dummy tag name for structure, union, or enumeration |
| .eos | end of members of structure, union, or enumeration |
| etext | next available address after the end of the output section .text |
| edata | next available address after the end of the output section .data |
| end | next available address after the end of the output section .bss |

Figure 11-17: Special Symbols in the Symbol Table

Six of these special symbols occur in pairs. The **.bb** and **.eb** symbols indicate the boundaries of inner blocks; a **.bf** and **.ef** pair brackets each function. An **.xfake** and **.eos** pair names and defines the limit of structures, unions, and enumerations that were not named. The **.eos** symbol also appears after named structures, unions, and enumerations.

When a structure, union, or enumeration has no tag name, the compiler invents a name to be used in the symbol table. The name chosen for the symbol table is *.xfake*, where *x* is an integer. If there are three unnamed structures, unions, or enumerations in the source, their tag names are **.0fake**, **.1fake**, and **.2fake**. Each of the special symbols has different information stored in the symbol table entry as well as the auxiliary entries.

## Inner Blocks

The C language defines a block as a compound statement that begins and ends with braces, {, and }. An inner block is a block that occurs within a function (which is also a block).

For each inner block that has local symbols defined, a special symbol, **.bb**, is put in the symbol table immediately before the first local symbol of that block. Also a special symbol, **.eb**, is put in the symbol table immediately after the last local symbol of that block. The sequence is shown in Figure 11-18.

| **.bb** |
| --- |
| local symbols for that block |
| **.eb** |

Figure 11-18: Special Symbols (**.bb** and **.eb**)

───────────────────────────────────────────────

Because inner blocks can be nested by several levels, the **.bb**-**.eb** pairs and associated symbols may also be nested. See Figure 11-19.

```
{                          /* block 1 */
    int i;
    char c;
    ...
    {                      /* block 2 */
        long a;
        ...
        {                  /* block 3 */
            int x;
            ....
        }                  /* block 3 */

    }                      /* block 2 */

    {                      /* block 4 */
        long i;
        ...
    }                      /* block 4 */
}                          /* block 1 */
```

Figure 11-19: Nested blocks

The symbol table would look like Figure 11-20.

| |
|---|
| **.bb** for block 1 |
| i |
| c |
| **.bb** for block 2 |
| a |
| **.bb** for block 3 |
| x |
| **.eb** for block 3 |
| **.eb** for block 2 |
| **.bb** for block 4 |
| i |
| **.eb** for block 4 |
| **.eb** for block 1 |

Figure 11-20: Example of the Symbol Table

## Symbols and Functions

For each function, a special symbol **.bf** is put between the function name and the first local symbol of the function in the symbol table. Also, a special symbol **.ef** is put immediately after the last local symbol of the function in the symbol table. The sequence is shown in Figure 11-21.

| |
|---|
| function name |
| **.bf** |
| local symbol |
| **.ef** |

Figure 11-21: Symbols for Functions

## Symbol Table Entries

All symbols, regardless of storage class and type, have the same format for their entries in the symbol table. The symbol table entries each contain 18 bytes of information. The meaning of each of the fields in the symbol table entry is described in Figure 11-22. It should be noted that indices for symbol table entries begin at 0 and count upward. Each auxiliary entry also counts as one symbol.

| Bytes | Declaration | Name | Description |
|-------|-------------|------|-------------|
| 0-7 | (see text below) | _n | These 8 bytes contain either a symbol name or an index to a symbol |
| 8-11 | long int | n_value | Symbol value; storage class dependent |
| 12-13 | short | n_scnum | Section number of symbol |
| 14-15 | unsigned short | n_type | Basic and derived type specification |
| 16 | char | n_sclass | Storage class of symbol |
| 17 | char | n_numaux | Number of auxiliary entries |

Figure 11-22: Symbol Table Entry Format

### Symbol Names

The first 8 bytes in the symbol table entry are a union of a character array and two longs. If the symbol name is eight characters or less, the (null-padded) symbol name is stored there. If the symbol name is longer than eight characters, then the entire symbol name is stored in the string table. In this case, the 8 bytes contain two long integers, the first is zero, and the second is the offset (relative to the beginning of the string table) of the name in the string table. Since there can be no symbols with a null name, the zeroes on the first 4 bytes serve to distinguish a symbol table entry with an offset from one with a name in the first 8 bytes as shown in Figure 11-23.

| Bytes | Declaration | Name | Description |
|-------|-------------|------|-------------|
| 0-7 | char | n_name | 8-character null-padded symbol name |
| 0-3 | long | n_zeroes | Zero in this field indicates the name is in the string table |
| 4-7 | long | n_offset | Offset of the name in the string table |

Figure 11-23: Name Field

Special symbols generated by the C Compilation System are discussed above in "Special Symbols."

**Storage Classes**

The storage class field has one of the values described in Figure 11-24. These **#define**'s may be found in the header file **storclass.h**.

| Mnemonic | Value | Storage Class |
|----------|-------|---------------|
| C_EFCN | −1 | physical end of a function |
| C_NULL | 0 | − |
| C_AUTO | 1 | automatic variable |
| C_EXT | 2 | external symbol |
| C_STAT | 3 | static |
| C_REG | 4 | register variable |
| C_EXTDEF | 5 | external definition |
| C_LABEL | 6 | label |
| C_ULABEL | 7 | undefined label |
| C_MOS | 8 | member of structure |
| C_ARG | 9 | function argument |
| C_STRTAG | 10 | structure tag |
| C_MOU | 11 | member of union |
| C_UNTAG | 12 | union tag |
| C_TPDEF | 13 | type definition |
| C_USTATIC | 14 | uninitialized static |
| C_ENTAG | 15 | enumeration tag |
| C_MOE | 16 | member of enumeration |
| C_REGPARM | 17 | register parameter |
| C_FIELD | 18 | bit field |

Figure 11-24: Storage Classes (Sheet 1 of 2)

| Mnemonic | Value | Storage Class |
|----------|-------|---------------|
| C_BLOCK | 100 | beginning and end of block |
| C_FCN | 101 | beginning and end of function |
| C_EOS | 102 | end of structure |
| C_FILE | 103 | filename |
| C_LINE | 104 | used only by utility programs |
| C_ALIAS | 105 | duplicated tag |
| C_HIDDEN | 106 | like static, used to avoid name conflicts |

Figure 11-24: Storage Classes (Sheet 2 of 2)

All of these storage classes except for C_ALIAS and C_HIDDEN are generated by the **cc** or **as** commands. The compress utility, **cprs**, generates the C_ALIAS mnemonic. This utility (described in the *User's Reference Manual*) removes duplicated structure, union, and enumeration definitions and puts alias entries in their places. The storage class C_HIDDEN is not used by any UNIX system tools.

Some of these storage classes are used only internally by the C Compilation Systems. These storage classes are C_EFCN, C_EXTDEF, C_ULABEL, C_USTATIC, and C_LINE.

### Storage Classes for Special Symbols

Some special symbols are restricted to certain storage classes. They are given in Figure 11-25.

| Special Symbol | Storage Class |
|---|---|
| .file | C_FILE |
| .bb | C_BLOCK |
| .eb | C_BLOCK |
| .bf | C_FCN |
| .ef | C_FCN |
| .target | C_AUTO |
| .xfake | C_STRTAG, C_UNTAG, C_ENTAG |
| .eos | C_EOS |
| .text | C_STAT |
| .data | C_STAT |
| .bss | C_STAT |

Figure 11-25: Storage Class by Special Symbols

Also some storage classes are used only for certain special symbols. They are summarized in Figure 11-26.

| Storage Class | Special Symbol |
|---|---|
| C_BLOCK | .bb, .eb |
| C_FCN | .bf, .ef |
| C_EOS | .eos |
| C_FILE | .file |

Figure 11-26: Restricted Storage Classes

**Symbol Value Field**

The meaning of the value of a symbol depends on its storage class. This relationship is summarized in Figure 11-27.

| Storage Class | Meaning of Value |
|---|---|
| C_AUTO | stack offset in bytes |
| C_EXT | relocatable address |
| C_STAT | relocatable address |
| C_REG | register number |
| C_LABEL | relocatable address |
| C_MOS | offset in bytes |
| C_ARG | stack offset in bytes |
| C_STRTAG | 0 |
| C_MOU | 0 |
| C_UNTAG | 0 |
| C_TPDEF | 0 |
| C_ENTAG | 0 |
| C_MOE | enumeration value |
| C_REGPARM | register number |
| C_FIELD | bit displacement |
| C_BLOCK | relocatable address |
| C_FCN | relocatable address |
| C_EOS | size |
| C_FILE | (see text below) |
| C_ALIAS | tag index |
| C_HIDDEN | relocatable address |

Figure 11-27: Storage Class and Value

If a symbol has storage class C_FILE, the value of that symbol equals the symbol table entry index of the next **.file** symbol. That is, the **.file** entries form a one-way linked list in the symbol table. If there are no more **.file** entries in the symbol table, the value of the symbol is the index of the first global symbol.

Relocatable symbols have a value equal to the virtual address of that symbol. When the section is relocated by the link editor, the value of these symbols changes.

### Section Number Field

Section numbers are listed in Figure 11-28.

| Mnemonic | Section Number | Meaning |
|----------|:--------------:|---------|
| N_DEBUG | −2 | Special symbolic debugging symbol |
| N_ABS | −1 | Absolute symbol |
| N_UNDEF | 0 | Undefined external symbol |
| N_SCNUM | 1-077777 | Section number where symbol is defined |

Figure 11-28: Section Number

A special section number (−2) marks symbolic debugging symbols, including structure/union/enumeration tag names, typedefs, and the name of the file. A section number of −1 indicates that the symbol has a value but is not relocatable. Examples of absolute-valued symbols include automatic and register variables, function arguments, and **.eos** symbols.

With one exception, a section number of 0 indicates a relocatable external symbol that is not defined in the current file. The one exception is a multiply defined external symbol (i.e., FORTRAN common or an uninitialized variable defined external to a function in C). In the symbol table of each file where the symbol is defined, the section number of the symbol is 0 and the value of the symbol is a positive number giving the size of the symbol. When the files are combined to form an executable object file, the link editor combines all the input symbols of the same name into one symbol with the section number of the **.bss** section. The maximum size of all the input symbols with the same name is used to allocate space for the symbol and the value becomes the address of the symbol. This is the only case where a symbol has a section number of 0 and a non-zero value.

### Section Numbers and Storage Classes

Symbols having certain storage classes are also restricted to certain section numbers.  They are summarized in Figure 11-29.

| Storage Class | Section Number |
|---|---|
| C_AUTO | N_ABS |
| C_EXT | N_ABS, N_UNDEF, N_SCNUM |
| C_STAT | N_SCNUM |
| C_REG | N_ABS |
| C_LABEL | N_UNDEF, N_SCNUM |
| C_MOS | N_ABS |
| C_ARG | N_ABS |
| C_STRTAG | N_DEBUG |
| C_MOU | N_ABS |
| C_UNTAG | N_DEBUG |
| C_TPDEF | N_DEBUG |
| C_ENTAG | N_DEBUG |
| C_MOE | N_ABS |
| C_REGPARM | N_ABS |
| C_FIELD | N_ABS |
| C_BLOCK | N_SCNUM |
| C_FCN | N_SCNUM |
| C_EOS | N_ABS |
| C_FILE | N_DEBUG |
| C_ALIAS | N_DEBUG |

Figure 11-29: Section Number and Storage Class

**Type Entry**

The type field in the symbol table entry contains information about the basic and derived type for the symbol. This information is generated by the C Compilation System only if the **−g** option is used. Each symbol has exactly one basic or fundamental type but can have more than one derived type. The format of the 16-bit type entry is

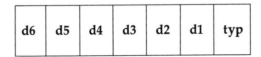

Bits 0 through 3, called **typ**, indicate one of the fundamental types given in Figure 11-30.

| Mnemonic | Value | Type |
|----------|-------|------|
| T_NULL | 0 | type not assigned |
| T_VOID | 1 | void |
| T_CHAR | 2 | character |
| T_SHORT | 3 | short integer |
| T_INT | 4 | integer |
| T_LONG | 5 | long integer |
| T_FLOAT | 6 | floating point |
| T_DOUBLE | 7 | double word |
| T_STRUCT | 8 | structure |
| T_UNION | 9 | union |
| T_ENUM | 10 | enumeration |
| T_MOE | 11 | member of enumeration |
| T_UCHAR | 12 | unsigned character |
| T_USHORT | 13 | unsigned short |
| T_UINT | 14 | unsigned integer |
| T_ULONG | 15 | unsigned long |

Figure 11-30: Fundamental Types

Bits 4 through 15 are arranged as six 2-bit fields marked **d1** through **d6**. These **d** fields represent levels of the derived types given in Figure 11-31.

| Mnemonic | Value | Type |
|----------|-------|------|
| DT_NON | 0 | no derived type |
| DT_PTR | 1 | pointer |
| DT_FCN | 2 | function |
| DT_ARY | 3 | array |

Figure 11-31: Derived Types

The following examples demonstrate the interpretation of the symbol table entry representing type.

```
char *func();
```

Here **func** is the name of a function that returns a pointer to a character. The fundamental type of **func** is 2 (character), the **d1** field is 2 (function), and the **d2** field is 1 (pointer). Therefore, the type word in the symbol table for **func** contains the hexadecimal number 0x62, which is interpreted to mean a function that returns a pointer to a character.

```
short *tabptr[10][25][3];
```

Here **tabptr** is a three-dimensional array of pointers to short integers. The fundamental type of **tabptr** is 3 (short integer); the **d1**, **d2**, and **d3** fields each contains a 3 (array), and the **d4** field is 1 (pointer). Therefore, the type entry in the symbol table contains the hexadecimal number 0x7f3 indicating a three-dimensional array of pointers to short integers.

### Type Entries and Storage Classes

Figure 11-32 shows the type entries that are legal for each storage class.

| Storage Class | d Entry | | | typ Entry Basic Type |
|---|---|---|---|---|
| | Function? | Array? | Pointer? | |
| C_AUTO | no | yes | yes | Any except T_MOE |
| C_EXT | yes | yes | yes | Any except T_MOE |
| C_STAT | yes | yes | yes | Any except T_MOE |
| C_REG | no | no | yes | Any except T_MOE |
| C_LABEL | no | no | no | T_NULL |
| C_MOS | no | yes | yes | Any except T_MOE |
| C_ARG | yes | no | yes | Any except T_MOE |
| C_STRTAG | no | no | no | T_STRUCT |
| C_MOU | no | yes | yes | Any except T_MOE |
| C_UNTAG | no | no | no | T_UNION |

Figure 11-32: Type Entries by Storage Class (Sheet 1 of 2)

| Storage Class | d Entry | | | typ Entry Basic Type |
|---|---|---|---|---|
| | Function? | Array? | Pointer? | |
| C_TPDEF | no | yes | yes | Any except T_MOE |
| C_ENTAG | no | no | no | T_ENUM |
| C_MOE | no | no | no | T_MOE |
| C_REGPARM | no | no | yes | Any except T_MOE |
| C_FIELD | no | no | no | T_ENUM, T_UCHAR, T_USHORT, T_UNIT, T_ULONG |
| C_BLOCK | no | no | no | T_NULL |
| C_FCN | no | no | no | T_NULL |
| C_EOS | no | no | no | T_NULL |
| C_FILE | no | no | no | T_NULL |
| C_ALIAS | no | no | no | T_STRUCT, T_UNION, T_ENUM |

Figure 11-32: Type Entries by Storage Class (Sheet 2 of 2)

Conditions for the **d** entries apply to **d1** through **d6**, except that it is impossible to have two consecutive derived types of function.

Although function arguments can be declared as arrays, they are changed to pointers by default. Therefore, no function argument can have array as its first derived type.

### Structure for Symbol Table Entries

The C language structure declaration for the symbol table entry is given in Figure 11-33. This declaration may be found in the header file **syms.h**.

```
struct syment
{
   union
   {
        char            _n_name[SYMNMLEN];    /* symbol name*/
        struct
        {
            long    _n_zeroes;    /* symbol name */

            long    _n_offset;    /* location in string table */
        } _n_n;
        char            *_n_nptr[2]; /* allows overlaying */
   } _n;
   unsigned long    n_value;               /* value of symbol */

   short            n_scnum;               /* section number */

   unsigned short   n_type;                /* type and derived */

   char             n_sclass;              /* storage class */

   char             n_numaux;              /* number of aux entries */
};

#define  n_name         _n._n_name
#define  n_zeroes       _n._n_n._n_zeroes
#define  n_offset       _n._n_n._n_offset
#define  n_nptr         _n._n_nptr[1]

#define  SYMNMLEN   8
#define  SYMESZ     18    /* size of a symbol table entry */
```

Figure 11-33: Symbol Table Entry Declaration

## Auxiliary Table Entries

An auxiliary table entry of a symbol contains the same number of bytes as the symbol table entry. However, unlike symbol table entries, the format of an auxiliary table entry of a symbol depends on its type and storage class. They are summarized in Figure 11-34.

| Name | Storage Class | Type Entry | | Auxiliary Entry Format |
|------|---------------|------|------|------------------|
| | | d1 | typ | |
| **.file** | C_FILE | DT_NON | T_NULL | filename |
| **.text,.data, .bss** | C_STAT | DT_NON | T_NULL | section |
| *tagname* | C_STRTAG C_UNTAG C_ENTAG | DT_NON | T_NULL | tag name |
| **.eos** | C_EOS | DT_NON | T_NULL | end of structure |
| *fcname* | C_EXT C_STAT | DT_FCN | (Note 1) | function |
| *arrname* | (Note 2) | DT_ARY | (Note 1) | array |
| **.bb,.eb** | C_BLOCK | DT_NON | T_NULL | beginning and end of block |
| **.bf,.ef** | C_FCN | DT_NON | T_NULL | beginning and end of function |
| name related to structure, union, enumeration | (Note 2) | DT_PTR, DT_ARR, DT_NON | T_STRUCT, T_UNION, T_ENUM | name related to structure, union, enumeration |

Figure 11-34: Auxiliary Symbol Table Entries

Notes to Figure 11-34:
1. Any except T_MOE.
2. C_AUTO, C_STAT, C_MOS, C_MOU, C_TPDEF.

In Figure 11-34, *tagname* means any symbol name including the special symbol .*xfake*, and *fcname* and *arrname* represent any symbol name for a function or an array respectively. Any symbol that satisfies more than one condition in Figure 11-34 should have a union format in its auxiliary entry.

It is a mistake to assume how many auxiliary entries are associated with any given symbol table entry. This information is available, and should be obtained from the **n_numaux** field in the symbol table.

### Filenames

Each of the auxiliary table entries for a filename contains a 14-character filename in bytes 0 through 13. The remaining bytes are 0.

### Sections

The auxiliary table entries for sections have the format as shown in Figure 11-35.

| Bytes | Declaration | Name | Description |
|-------|-------------|------|-------------|
| 0-3 | **long int** | **x_scnlen** | section length |
| 4-5 | **unsigned short** | **x_nreloc** | number of relocation entries |
| 6-7 | **unsigned short** | **x_nlinno** | number of line numbers |
| 8-17 | − | − | unused (filled with zeroes) |

Figure 11-35: Format for Auxiliary Table Entries for Sections

### Tag Names

The auxiliary table entries for tag names have the format shown in Figure 11-36.

| Bytes | Declaration | Name | Description |
|-------|-------------|------|-------------|
| 0-5 | — | — | unused (filled with zeroes) |
| 6-7 | **unsigned short** | **x_size** | size of structure, union, and enumeration |
| 8-11 | — | — | unused (filled with zeroes) |
| 12-15 | **long int** | **x_endndx** | index of next entry beyond this structure, union, or enumeration |
| 16-17 | — | — | unused (filled with zeroes) |

Figure 11-36: Tag Names Table Entries

### End of Structures

The auxiliary table entries for the end of structures have the format shown in Figure 11-37:

| Bytes | Declaration | Name | Description |
|-------|-------------|------|-------------|
| 0-3 | **long int** | **x_tagndx** | tag index |
| 4-5 | — | — | unused (filled with zeroes) |
| 6-7 | **unsigned short** | **x_size** | size of structure, union, or enumeration |
| 8-17 | — | — | unused (filled with zeroes) |

Figure 11-37: Table Entries for End of Structures

### Functions

The auxiliary table entries for functions have the format shown in Figure 11-38:

| Bytes | Declaration | Name | Description |
|-------|-------------|------|-------------|
| 0-3 | long int | x_tagndx | tag index |
| 4-7 | long int | x_fsize | size of function (in bytes) |
| 8-11 | long int | x_lnnoptr | file pointer to line number |
| 12-15 | long int | x_endndx | index of next entry beyond this point |
| 16-17 | unsigned short | x_tvndx | index of the function's address in the transfer vector table (not used in UNIX system) |

Figure 11-38: Table Entries for Functions

### Arrays

The auxiliary table entries for arrays have the format shown in Figure 11-39. Defining arrays having more than four dimensions produces a warning message.

| Bytes | Declaration | Name | Description |
|-------|-------------|------|-------------|
| 0-3 | long int | x_tagndx | tag index |
| 4-5 | unsigned short | x_lnno | line number of declaration |
| 6-7 | unsigned short | x_size | size of array |
| 8-9 | unsigned short | x_dimen[0] | first dimension |
| 10-11 | unsigned short | x_dimen[1] | second dimension |
| 12-13 | unsigned short | x_dimen[2] | third dimension |
| 14-15 | unsigned short | x_dimen[3] | fourth dimension |
| 16-17 | — | — | unused (filled with zeroes) |

Figure 11-39: Table Entries for Arrays

### End of Blocks and Functions

The auxiliary table entries for the end of blocks and functions have the format shown in Figure 11-40:

| Bytes | Declaration | Name | Description |
|-------|-------------|------|-------------|
| 0-3 | — | — | unused (filled with zeroes) |
| 4-5 | unsigned short | x_lnno | C-source line number |
| 6-17 | — | — | unused (filled with zeroes) |

Figure 11-40: End of Block and Function Entries

### Beginning of Blocks and Functions

The auxiliary table entries for the beginning of blocks and functions have the format shown in Figure 11-41:

| Bytes | Declaration | Name | Description |
|---|---|---|---|
| 0-3 | – | – | unused (filled with zeroes) |
| 4-5 | unsigned short | x_lnno | C-source line number |
| 6-11 | – | – | unused (filled with zeroes) |
| 12-15 | long int | x_endndx | index of next entry past this block |
| 16-17 | – | – | unused (filled with zeroes) |

Figure 11-41: Format for Beginning of Block and Function

---

### Names Related to Structures, Unions, and Enumerations

The auxiliary table entries for structure, union, and enumeration symbols have the format shown in Figure 11-42:

| Bytes | Declaration | Name | Description |
|---|---|---|---|
| 0-3 | long int | x_tagndx | tag index |
| 4-5 | – | – | unused (filled with zeroes) |
| 6-7 | unsigned short | x_size | size of the structure, union, or enumeration |
| 8-17 | – | – | unused (filled with zeroes) |

Figure 11-42: Entries for Structures, Unions, and Enumerations

---

Aggregates defined by **typedef** may or may not have auxiliary table entries. For example,

```
typedef struct people STUDENT;

struct people
{
        char name[20];
        long id;
};

typedef struct people EMPLOYEE;
```

The symbol EMPLOYEE has an auxiliary table entry in the symbol table but symbol STUDENT will not because it is a forward reference to a structure.

### Auxiliary Entry Declaration

The C language structure declaration for an auxiliary symbol table entry is given in Figure 11-43. This declaration may be found in the header file **syms.h**.

```
union auxent
{
    struct
    {
        long    x_tagndx;
        union
        {
            struct
            {
                unsigned short    x_lnno;
                unsigned short    x_size;
            } x_lnsz;
            long    x_fsize;
        } x_misc;
        union
        {
            struct
                .
                .
                .
```

Figure 11-43: Auxiliary Symbol Table Entry (Sheet 1 of 2)

```
            .
            .
            .
                {
                        long    x_lnnoptr;
                        long    x_endndx;
                } x_fcn;
                struct
                {
                        unsigned short   x_dimen[DIMNUM];
                } x_ary;
            } x_fcnary;
            unsigned short   x_tvndx;
        } x_sym;
        struct
        {
            char   x_fname[FILNMLEN];
        } x_file;
        struct
        {
            long   x_scnlen;
            unsigned short   x_nreloc;
            unsigned short   x_nlinno;
        } x_scn;
        struct
        {
            long   x_tvfill;
            unsigned short   x_tvlen;
            unsigned short   x_tvran[2];
        } x_tv;
}
#define FILNMLEN   14
#define DIMNUM     4
#define AUXENT     union auxent
#define AUXESZ     18
```

Figure 11-43: Auxiliary Symbol Table Entry (Sheet 2 of 2)

## String Table

Symbol table names longer than eight characters are stored contiguously in the string table with each symbol name delimited by a null byte. The first four bytes of the string table are the size of the string table in bytes; offsets into the string table, therefore, are greater than or equal to 4. For example, given a file containing two symbols (with names longer then eight characters, **long_name_1** and **another_one**) the string table has the format as shown in Figure 11-44:

| | | | |
|---|---|---|---|
| 'l' | 'o' | 'n' | 'g' |
| '_' | 'n' | 'a' | 'm' |
| 'e' | '_' | 'l' | '\0' |
| 'a' | 'n' | 'o' | 't' |
| 'h' | 'e' | 'r' | '_' |
| 'o' | 'n' | 'e' | '\0' |

Figure 11-44: String Table

The index of **long_name_1** in the string table is 4 and the index of **another_one** is 16.

# Access Routines

UNIX system releases contain a set of access routines that are used for reading the various parts of a common object file. Although the calling program must know the detailed structure of the parts of the object file it processes, the routines effectively insulate the calling program from the knowledge of the overall structure of the object file.

The access routines can be divided into four categories:

1. functions that open or close an object file

2. functions that read header or symbol table information

3. functions that position an object file at the start of a particular section of the object file

4. a function that returns the symbol table index for a particular symbol

These routines can be found in the library **libld.a** and are listed in Section 3 of the *Programmer's Reference Manual*. A summary of what is available can be found in the *Programmer's Reference Manual* under **ldfcn**(4).

# CHAPTER 12: THE LINK EDITOR

## The Link Editor

In Chapter 2 there was a discussion of link editor command line options (some of which may also be provided on the cc(1) command line). This chapter contains information on the Link Editor Command Language.

The command language enables you to

- specify the memory configuration of the target machine

- combine the sections of an object file in arrangements other than the default

- bind sections to specific addresses or within specific portions of memory

- define or redefine global symbols

Under most normal circumstances there is no compelling need to have such tight control over object files and where they are located in memory. When you do need to be very precise in controlling the link editor output, you do it by means of the command language.

Link editor command language directives are passed in a file named on the ld(1) command line. Any file named on the command line that is not identifiable as an object module or an archive library is assumed to contain directives. The following paragraphs define terms and describe conditions with which you need to be familiar before you begin to use the command language.

## Memory Configuration

The virtual memory of the target machine is, for purposes of allocation, partitioned into configured and unconfigured memory. The default condition is to treat all memory as configured. It is common with microprocessor applications, however, to have different types of memory at different addresses. For example, an application might have 3K of PROM (Programmable Read-Only Memory) beginning at address 0, and 8K of ROM (Read-Only Memory) starting at 20K. Addresses in the range 3K to 20K−1 are then not configured. Unconfigured memory is treated as reserved or unusable by ld(1). Nothing can ever be linked into unconfigured memory. Thus, specifying a certain memory range to be unconfigured is one way of marking the addresses (in that range) illegal or nonexistent with respect to the linking process. Memory configurations other than the default must be explicitly specified by you (the user).

Unless otherwise specified, all discussion in this document of memory, addresses, etc. are with respect to the configured sections of the address space.

## Sections

A section of an object file is the smallest unit of relocation and must be a contiguous block of memory. A section is identified by a starting address and a size. Information describing all the sections in a file is stored in section headers at the start of the file. Sections from input files are combined to form output sections that contain executable text, data, or a mixture of both. Although there may be holes or gaps between input sections and between output sections, storage is allocated contiguously within each output section and may not overlap a hole in memory.

## Addresses

The physical address of a section or symbol is the relative offset from address zero of the address space. The physical address of an object is not necessarily the location at which it is placed when the process is executed. For example, on a system with paging, the address is with respect to address zero of the virtual space, and the system performs another address translation.

## Binding

It is often necessary to have a section begin at a specific, predefined address in the address space. The process of specifying this starting address is called binding, and the section in question is said to be bound to or bound at the required address. While binding is most commonly relevant to output sections, it is also possible to bind special absolute global symbols with an assignment statement in the **ld**(1) command language.

## Object File

Object files are produced both by the assembler (typically as a result of calling the compiler) and by **ld**(1). **ld**(1) accepts relocatable object files as input and produces an output object file that may or may not be relocatable. Under certain special circumstances, the input object files given to **ld**(1) can also be absolute files.

Files produced from the compilation system may contain, among others, sections called **.text** and **.data**. The **.text** section contains the instruction text (executable instructions), **.data** contains initialized data variables. For example, if a C program contained the global (i.e., not inside a function) declaration

        int i = 100;

and the assignment

        i = 0;

then compiled code from the C assignment is stored in **.text**, and the variable **i** is located in **.data**.

# Link Editor Command Language

## Expressions

Expressions may contain global symbols, constants, and most of the basic C language operators. (See Figure 12-2, "Syntax Diagram for Input Directives.") Constants are as in C with a number recognized as decimal unless preceded with 0 for octal or 0x for hexadecimal. All numbers are treated as long integers's. Symbol names may contain uppercase or lowercase letters, digits, and the underscore, _. Symbols within an expression have the value of the address of the symbol only. **ld**(1) does not do symbol table lookup to find the contents of a symbol, the dimensionality of an array, structure elements declared in a C program, etc.

**ld**(1) uses a **lex**-generated input scanner to identify symbols, numbers, operators, etc. The current scanner design makes the following names reserved and unavailable as symbol names or section names:

| ADDR | BLOCK | GROUP | NEXT | RANGE | SPARE |
|------|-------|-------|------|-------|-------|
| ALIGN | COMMON | INFO | NOLOAD | REGIONS | PHY |
| ASSIGN | COPY | LENGTH | ORIGIN | SECTIONS | TV |
| BIND | DSECT | MEMORY | OVERLAY | SIZEOF | |

| addr | block | length | origin | sizeof |
|------|-------|--------|--------|--------|
| align | group | next | phy | spare |
| assign | l | o | range | |
| bind | len | org | s | |

The operators that are supported, in order of precedence from high to low, are shown in Figure 12-1:

| symbol |
|---|
| ! ~ − (UNARY Minus) |
| * / % |
| + − (BINARY Minus) |
| >> << |
| == != > < <= >= |
| & |
| \| |
| && |
| \| |
| = += −= *= /= |

Figure 12-1: Operator Symbols

The above operators have the same meaning as in the C language. Operators on the same line have the same precedence.

## Assignment Statements

External symbols may be defined and assigned addresses via the assignment statement. The syntax of the assignment statement is

    symbol = expression;

or

    symbol op= expression;

where *op* is one of the operators +, −, *, or / . Assignment statements must be terminated by a semicolon.

All assignment statements (with the exception of the one case described in the following paragraph) are evaluated after allocation has been performed. This occurs after all input-file-defined symbols are appropriately relocated but before the actual relocation of the text and data itself. Therefore, if an assignment statement expression contains any symbol name, the address used for that symbol in the evaluation of the expression reflects the symbol address in the output object file. References within text and data (to symbols given a value through an assignment statement) access this latest assigned value.

Assignment statements are processed in the same order in which they are input to **ld**(1).

Assignment statements are normally placed outside the scope of section-definition directives (see "Section Definition Directives" under "Link Editor Command Language"). However, there exists a special symbol, called **dot**, ., that can occur only within a section-definition directive. This symbol refers to the current address of **ld**(1)'s location counter. Thus, assignment expressions involving . are evaluated during the allocation phase of **ld**(1). Assigning a value to the . symbol within a section-definition directive can increment (but not decrement) **ld**(1)'s location counter and can create holes within the section, as described in "Section Definition Directives." Assigning the value of the . symbol to a conventional symbol permits the final allocated address (of a particular point within the link edit run) to be saved.

**align** is provided as a shorthand notation to allow alignment of a symbol to an $n$-byte boundary within an output section, where $n$ is a power of 2. For example, the expression

    align(n)

is equivalent to

$$(. + n - 1) \mathbin{\&} {\sim} (n - 1)$$

SIZEOF and ADDR are pseudo-functions that, given the name of a section, return the size or address of the section respectively. They may be used in symbol definitions outside of section directives.

Link editor expressions may have either an absolute or a relocatable value. When **ld**(1) creates a symbol through an assignment statement, the symbol's value takes on that type of expression. That type depends on the following rules:

- An expression with a single relocatable symbol (and zero or more constants or absolute symbols) is relocatable.

- The difference of two relocatable symbols from the same section is absolute.

- All other expressions are combinations of the above.

# Specifying a Memory Configuration

MEMORY directives are used to specify

1.   The total size of the virtual space of the target machine.

2.   The configured and unconfigured areas of the virtual space.

If no directives are supplied, **ld**(1) assumes that all memory is configured. The size of the default memory is dependent upon the target machine.

By means of MEMORY directives, an arbitrary name of up to eight characters is assigned to a virtual address range. Output sections can then be forced to be bound to virtual addresses within specifically named memory areas. Memory names may contain uppercase or lowercase letters, digits, and the special characters **$**, **.**, or **_**. Names of memory ranges are used by **ld**(1) only and are not carried in the output file symbol table or headers.

When MEMORY directives are used, all virtual memory not described in a MEMORY directive is considered to be unconfigured. Unconfigured memory is not used in **ld**(1)'s allocation process; hence nothing except DSECT sections can be link edited or bound to an address within unconfigured memory.

As an option on the MEMORY directive, attributes may be associated with a named memory area. In future releases this may be used to provide error checking. Currently, error checking of this type is not implemented.

The attributes currently accepted are

1.   R : readable memory

2.   W : writable memory

3.   X : executable, i.e., instructions may reside in this memory

4.   I : initializable, i.e., stack areas are typically not initialized

Other attributes may be added in the future if necessary. If no attributes are specified on a MEMORY directive or if no MEMORY directives are supplied, memory areas assume the attributes of R, W, X, and I.

The syntax of the MEMORY directive is

```
MEMORY
{
        name1 (attr) : origin = n1, length = n2
        name2 (attr) : origin = n3, length = n4
        etc.
}
```

The keyword **origin** (or **org** or **o**) must precede the origin of a memory range, and **length** (or **len** or **l**) must precede the length as shown in the above prototype. The **origin** operand refers to the virtual address of the memory range. **origin** and **length** are entered as long integer constants in either decimal, octal, or hexadecimal (standard C syntax). **origin** and **length** specifications, as well as individual MEMORY directives, may be separated by white space or a comma.

By specifying MEMORY directives, **ld**(1) can be told that memory is configured in some manner other than the default. For example, if it is necessary to prevent anything from being linked to the first 0x10000 words of memory, a MEMORY directive can accomplish this.

```
MEMORY
{
        valid : org = 0x10000, len = 0xFE0000
}
```

# Section Definition Directives

The purpose of the SECTIONS directive is to describe how input sections are to be combined, to direct where to place output sections (both in relation to each other and to the entire virtual memory space), and to permit the renaming of output sections.

In the default case where no SECTIONS directives are given, all input sections of the same name appear in an output section of that name. If two object files are linked, one containing sections s1 and s2 and the other containing sections s3 and s4, the output object file contains the four sections s1, s2, s3, and s4. The order of these sections would depend on the order in which the link editor sees the input files.

The basic syntax of the SECTIONS directive is

```
SECTIONS
{
        secname1 :
        {
                file_specifications,
                assignment_statements
        }
        secname2 :
        {
                file_specifications,
                assignment_statements
        }
etc.
}
```

The various types of section definition directives are discussed in the remainder of this section.

## File Specifications

Within a section definition, the files and sections of files to be included in the output section are listed in the order in which they are to appear in the output section. Sections from an input file are specified by

```
filename ( secname )
```

or

```
filename ( secnam1 secnam2 . . . )
```

Sections of an input file are separated either by white space or commas as are the file specifications themselves.

```
filename [COMMON]
```

may be used in the same way to refer to all the uninitialized, unallocated global symbols in a file.

If a file name appears with no sections listed, then all sections from the file (but not the uninitialized, unallocated globals) are linked into the current output section. For example,

```
SECTIONS
{
        outsec1:
        {
                file1.o (sec1)
                file2.o
                file3.o (sec1, sec2)
        }
}
```

According to this directive, the order in which the input sections appear in the output section **outsec1** would be

1.  section **sec1** from file **file1.o**

2.  all sections from **file2.o**, in the order they appear in the file

3.  section **sec1** from file **file3.o**, and then section **sec2** from file **file3.o**

If there are any additional input files that contain input sections also named **outsec1**, these sections are linked following the last section named in the definition of **outsec1**. If there are any other input sections in **file1.o** or **file3.o**, they will be placed in output sections with the same names as the input sections unless they are included in other file specifications.

The code

```
*(secname)
```

may be used to indicate all previously unallocated input sections of the given name, regardless of what input file they are contained in.

## Load a Section at a Specified Address

Bonding of an output section to a specific virtual address is accomplished by an **ld**(1) option as shown in the following SECTIONS directive example:

```
SECTIONS
{
        outsec addr:
        {
                . . .
        }
        etc.
}
```

The *addr* is the bonding address expressed as a C constant. If **outsec** does not fit at *addr* (perhaps because of holes in the memory configuration or because **outsec** is too large to fit without overlapping some other output section), **ld**(1) issues an appropriate error message. *addr* may also be the word BIND, followed by a parenthesized expression. The expression may use the pseudo-functions SIZEOF, ADDR or NEXT. NEXT accepts a constant and returns the first multiple of that value that falls into configured unallocated memory; SIZEOF and ADDR accept previously defined sections.

As long as output sections do not overlap and there is enough space, they can be bound anywhere in configured memory. The SECTIONS directives defining output sections need not be given to **ld**(1) in any particular order, unless SIZEOF or ADDR is used.

**ld**(1) does not ensure that each section's size consists of an even number of bytes or that each section starts on an even byte boundary. The assembler ensures that the size (in bytes) of a section is evenly divisible by 4. **ld**(1) directives can be used to force a section to start on an odd byte boundary although this is not recommended. If a section starts on an odd byte boundary, the section's contents are either accessed incorrectly or are not executed properly. When a user specifies an odd byte boundary, **ld**(1) issues a warning message.

## Aligning an Output Section

It is possible to request that an output section be bound to a virtual address that falls on an $n$-byte boundary, where $n$ is a power of 2. The ALIGN option of the SECTIONS directive performs this function, so that the option

    ALIGN(n)

is equivalent to specifying a bonding address of

$$( \; . \; + n - 1) \; \&^{\sim} (n - 1)$$

For example

```
SECTIONS
{
        outsec  ALIGN(0x20000) :
        {
                . . .
        }
        etc.
}
```

The output section **outsec** is not bound to any given address but is placed at some virtual address that is a multiple of 0x20000 (e.g., at address 0x0, 0x20000, 0x40000, 0x60000, etc.).

## Grouping Sections Together

The default allocation algorithm for **ld**(1)

1.  Links all input **.init** sections together, followed by **.text** sections, into one output section. This output section is called **.text** and is bound to an address of 0x0 plus the size of all headers in the output file.

2.  Links all input **.data** sections together into one output section. This output section is called **.data** and, in paging systems, is bound to an address aligned to a machine dependent constant plus a number dependent on the size of headers and text.

3. Links all input **.bss** sections together with all uninitialized, unallocated global symbols, into one output section. This output section is called **.bss** and is allocated so as to immediately follow the output section **.data**. Note that the output section **.bss** is not given any particular address alignment.

Specifying any SECTIONS directives results in this default allocation not being performed. Rather than relying on the **ld**(1) default algorithm, if you are manipulating COFF files, the one certain way of determining address and order information is to take it from the file and section headers. The default allocation of **ld**(1) is equivalent to supplying the following directive:

```
SECTIONS
{
        .text sizeof_headers : { *(.init) *(.text) }
        GROUP BIND( NEXT(align_value) +
                    ((SIZEOF(.text) + ADDR(.text)) % 0x2000)) :
        {
                .data    : { }
                .bss     : { }
        }
}
```

where *align_value* is a machine dependent constant. The GROUP command ensures that the two output sections, **.data** and **.bss**, are allocated (e.g., grouped) together. Bonding or alignment information is supplied only for the group and not for the output sections contained within the group. The sections making up the group are allocated in the order listed in the directive.

If **.text**, **.data**, and **.bss** are to be placed in the same segment, the following SECTIONS directive is used:

```
SECTIONS
{
        GROUP                   :
        {
                .text           : { }
                .data           : { }
                .bss            : { }
        }
}
```

Note that there are still three output sections (**.text**, **.data**, and **.bss**), but now they are allocated into consecutive virtual memory.

This entire group of output sections could be bound to a starting address or aligned simply by adding a field to the GROUP directive. To bind to 0xC0000, use

```
GROUP 0xC0000 : {
```

To align to 0x10000, use

```
GROUP ALIGN(0x10000) : {
```

With this addition, first the output section **.text** is bound at 0xC0000 (or is aligned to 0x10000); then the remaining members of the group are allocated in order of their appearance into the next available memory locations.

When the GROUP directive is not used, each output section is treated as an independent entity:

```
SECTIONS
{
        .text    : { }
        .data ALIGN(0x20000)  : { }
        .bss     : { }
}
```

The **.text** section starts at virtual address 0x0 (if it is in configured memory) and the **.data** section at a virtual address aligned to 0x20000. The **.bss** section follows immediately after the **.text** section if there is enough space. If there is not, it follows the **.data** section. The order in which output sections are defined to **ld**(1) cannot be used to force a certain allocation order in the output file.

## Creating Holes Within Output Sections

The special symbol dot, ., appears only within section definitions and assignment statements. When it appears on the left side of an assignment statement, . causes **ld**(1)'s location counter to be incremented or reset and a hole left in the output section. Holes built into output sections in this manner take up physical space in the output file and are initialized using a fill character (either the default fill character (0x00) or a supplied fill character). See the definition of the −**f** option in "Using the Link Editor" and the discussion of filling holes in "Initialized Section Holes" or **.bss** Sections." in this chapter.

Consider the following section definition:

```
outsec:
{
        . += 0x1000;
        f1.o (.text)
        . += 0x100;
        f2.o (.text)
        . = align (4);
        f3.o (.text)
}
```

The effect of this command is as follows:

1.  A 0x1000 byte hole, filled with the default fill character, is left at the beginning of the section. Input section **f1.o (.text)** is linked after this hole.

2.  The **.text** section of input file **f2.o** begins at 0x100 bytes following the end of **f1.o (.text)**.

3.  The **.text** section of **f3.o** is linked to start at the next full word boundary following the **.text** section of **f2.o** with respect to the beginning of **outsec**.

For the purposes of allocating and aligning addresses within an output section, **ld**(1) treats the output section as if it began at address zero. As a result, if, in the above example, **outsec** ultimately is linked to start at an odd address, then the part of **outsec** built from **f3.o (.text)** also starts at an odd address—even though **f3.o (.text)** is aligned to a full word boundary. This is prevented by specifying an alignment factor for the entire output section.

```
outsec ALIGN(4) : {
```

It should be noted that the assembler, **as**, always pads the sections it generates to a full word length making explicit alignment specifications unnecessary. This also holds true for the compiler.

Expressions that decrement **.** are illegal. For example, subtracting a value from the location counter is not allowed since overwrites are not allowed. The most common operators in expressions that assign a value to **.** are **+=** and **align**.

## Creating and Defining Symbols at Link-Edit Time

The assignment instruction of **ld**(1) can be used to give symbols a value that is link-edit dependent. Typically, there are three types of assignments:

1.   Use of **.** to adjust **ld**(1)'s location counter during allocation.

2.   Use of **.** to assign an allocation-dependent value to a symbol.

3.   Assigning an allocation-independent value to a symbol.

Case 1) has already been discussed in the previous section.

Case 2) provides a means to assign addresses (known only after allocation) to symbols. For example,

```
SECTIONS
{
        outsc1: {...}
        outsc2:
        {
                file1.o (s1)
                s2_start = . ;
                file2.o (s2)
                s2_end = . − 1;
        }
}
```

The symbol **s2_start** is defined to be the address of **file2.o(s2)**, and **s2_end** is the address of the last byte of **file2.o(s2)**.

Consider the following example:

```
SECTIONS
{
        outsc1:
        {
                file1.o ( .data)
                mark = .;
                . += 4;
                file2.o ( .data)
        }
}
```

In this example, the symbol **mark** is created and is equal to the address of the first byte beyond the end of **file1.o**'s **.data** section. Four bytes are reserved for a future run-time initialization of the symbol **mark**. The type of the symbol is a long integer (32 bits).

Assignment instructions involving . must appear within SECTIONS definitions since they are evaluated during allocation. Assignment instructions that do not involve . can appear within SECTIONS definitions but typically do not. Such instructions are evaluated after allocation is complete. Reassignment of a defined symbol to a different address is dangerous. For example, if a symbol within **.data** is defined, initialized, and referenced within a set of object files being link-edited, the symbol table entry for that symbol is changed to reflect the new, reassigned physical address. However, the associated initialized data is not moved to the new address, and there may be references to the old address. The **ld**(1) issues warning messages for each defined symbol that is being redefined within an ifile. However, assignments of absolute values to new symbols are safe because there are no references or initialized data associated with the symbol.

## Allocating a Section Into Named Memory

It is possible to specify that a section be linked (somewhere) within a specific named memory (as previously specified on a MEMORY directive). (The > notation is borrowed from the UNIX system concept of redirected output.) For example,

```
MEMORY
{
        mem1:           o=0x000000     1=0x10000
        mem2 (RW):      o=0x020000     1=0x40000
        mem3 (RW):      o=0x070000     1=0x40000
        mem1:           o=0x120000     1=0x04000
}

SECTIONS
{
        outsec1: { f1.o( .data) } > mem1
        outsec2: { f2.o( .data) } > mem3
}
```

This directs **ld**(1) to place **outsec1** anywhere within the memory area named **mem1** (i.e., somewhere within the address range 0x0-0xFFFF or 0x120000-0x123FFF). The **outsec2** is to be placed somewhere in the address range 0x70000-0xAFFFF.

## Initialized Section Holes or .bss Sections

When holes are created within a section (as in the example in "Creating Holes within Output Sections"), **ld**(1) normally puts out bytes of zero as fill. By default, **.bss** sections are not initialized at all; that is, no initialized data is generated for any **.bss** section by the assembler nor supplied by the link editor, not even zeros.

Initialization options can be used in a SECTIONS directive to set such holes or output **.bss** sections to an arbitrary 2-byte pattern. Such initialization options apply only to **.bss** sections or holes. As an example, an application might want an uninitialized data table to be initialized to a constant value without recompiling the **.o** file or a hole in the text area to be filled with a transfer to an error routine.

Either specific areas within an output section or the entire output section may be specified as being initialized. However, since no text is generated for an uninitialized **.bss** section, if part of such a section is initialized, then the entire section is initialized. In other words, if a **.bss** section is to be combined with a **.text** or **.data** section (both of which are initialized) or if part of an output **.bss** section is to be initialized, then one of the following will hold:

1. Explicit initialization options must be used to initialize all **.bss** sections in the output section.

2. **ld**(1) will use the default fill value to initialize all **.bss** sections in the output section.

Consider the following **ld**(1) ifile:

```
SECTIONS
{
        sec1:
        {
                f1.o
                . =+ 0x200;
                f2.o (.text)
        } = 0xDFFF
        sec2:
        {
                f1.o (.bss)
                f2.o (.bss) = 0x1234
        }
        sec3:
        {
                f3.o (.bss)
                . . .
        } = 0xFFFF
        sec4: { f4.o (.bss) }
}
```

In the example above, the 0x200 byte hole in section **sec1** is filled with the value 0xDFFF. In section **sec2, f1.o(.bss)** is initialized to the default fill value of 0x00, and **f2.o(.bss)** is initialized to 0x1234. All **.bss** sections within sec3 as well as all holes are initialized to 0xFFFF. Section **sec4** is not initialized; that is, no data is written to the object file for this section.

# Notes and Special Considerations

## Changing the Entry Point

The UNIX system **a.out** optional header contains a field for the (primary) entry point of the file. This field is set using one of the following rules (listed in the order they are applied):

1.  The value of the symbol specified with the −**e** option, if present, is used.

2.  The value of the symbol _**start**, if present, is used.

3.  The value of the symbol **main**, if present, is used.

4.  The value zero is used.

Thus, an explicit entry point can be assigned to this **a.out** header field through the −**e** option or by using an assignment instruction in an ifile of the form

        _start   =   expression;

If **ld**(1) is called through **cc**(1), a startup routine is automatically linked in. Then, when the program is executed, the routine **exit**(1) is called after the main routine finishes to close file descriptors and do other cleanup. The user must therefore be careful when calling **ld**(1) directly or when changing the entry point. The user must supply the startup routine or make sure that the program always calls exit rather than falling through the end. Otherwise, the program will dump core.

## Use of Archive Libraries

Each member of an archive library (e.g., **libc.a**) is a complete object file. Archive libraries are created with the **ar**(1) command from object files generated by **cc** or **as**. An archive library is always processed using selective inclusion: only those members that resolve existing undefined-symbol references are taken from the library for link editing. Libraries can be placed both inside and outside section definitions. In both cases, a member of a library is included for linking whenever

1. There exists a reference to a symbol defined in that member.

2. The reference is found by **ld**(1) prior to the actual scanning of the library.

When a library member is included by searching the library inside a SECTIONS directive, all input sections from the library member are included in the output section being defined. When a library member is included by searching the library outside of a SECTIONS directive, all input sections from the library member are included into the output section with the same name. If necessary, new output sections are defined to provide a place to put the input sections. Note, however, that

1. Specific members of a library cannot be referenced explicitly in an ifile.

2. The default rules for the placement of members and sections cannot be overridden when they apply to archive library members.

The −1 option is a shorthand notation for specifying an input file coming from a predefined set of directories and having a predefined name. By convention, such files are archive libraries. However, they need not be so. Furthermore, archive libraries can be specified without using the −1 option by simply giving the (full or relative) UNIX system file path.

The ordering of archive libraries is important since for a member to be extracted from the library it must satisfy a reference that is known to be unresolved at the time the library is searched. Archive libraries can be specified more than once. They are searched every time they are encountered. Archive files have a symbol table at the beginning of the archive. **ld**(1) will cycle through this symbol table until it has determined that it cannot resolve any more references from that library.

Consider the following example:

1. The input files **file1.o** and **file2.o** each contain a reference to the external function FCN.

2. Input **file1.o** contains a reference to symbol ABC.

3. Input **file2.o** contains a reference to symbol XYZ.

4. Library **liba.a**, member 0, contains a definition of XYZ.

5. Library **libc.a**, member 0, contains a definition of ABC.

6. Both libraries have a member 1 that defines FCN.

If the **ld**(1) command were entered as

      **ld file1.o −la file2.o −lc**

then the FCN references are satisfied by **liba.a**, member 1, ABC is obtained from **libc.a**, member 0, and XYZ remains undefined (because the library **liba.a** is searched before **file2.o** is specified). If the **ld**(1) command were entered as

      **ld file1.o file2.o −la −lc**

then the FCN references is satisfied by **liba.a**, member 1, ABC is obtained from **libc.a**, member 0, and XYZ is obtained from **liba.a**, member 0. If the **ld**(1) command were entered as

      **ld file1.o file2.o −lc −la**

then the FCN references is satisfied by **libc.a**, member 1, ABC is obtained from **libc.a**, member 0, and XYZ is obtained from **liba.a**, member 0.

The **−u** option is used to force the linking of library members when the link edit run does not contain an actual external reference to the members. For example,

      **ld −u rout1 −la**

creates an undefined symbol called **rout1** in **ld**(1)'s global symbol table. If any member of library **liba.a** defines this symbol, it (and perhaps other members as well) is extracted. Without the **−u** option, there would have been no unresolved references or undefined symbols to cause **ld**(1) to search the archive library.

# Dealing With Holes in Physical Memory

When memory configurations are defined such that unconfigured areas exist in the virtual memory, each application or user must assume the responsibility of forming output sections that will fit into memory. For example, assume that memory is configured as follows:

```
MEMORY
{
        mem1:        o = 0x00000        1 = 0x02000
        mem2:        o = 0x40000        1 = 0x05000
        mem3:        o = 0x20000        1 = 0x10000
}
```

Let the files **f1.o**, **f2.o**, . . . **fn.o** each contain three sections **.text**, **.data**, and **.bss**, and suppose the combined **.text** section is 0x12000 bytes. There is no configured area of memory in which this section can be placed. Appropriate directives must be supplied to break up the **.text** output section so **ld**(1) may do allocation. For example,

```
SECTIONS
{
        txt1:
        {
                f1.o ( .text)
                f2.o ( .text)
                f3.o ( .text)
        }
        txt2:
        {
                f4.o ( .text)
                f5.o ( .text)
                f6.o ( .text)
        }
        etc.
}
```

## Allocation Algorithm

An output section is formed either as a result of a SECTIONS directive, by combining input sections of the same name, or by combining **.text** and **.init** into **.text**. An output section can have zero or more input sections comprising it. After the composition of an output section is determined, it must then be allocated into configured virtual memory. **ld**(1) uses an algorithm that attempts to minimize fragmentation of memory, and hence increases the possibility that a link edit run will be able to allocate all output sections within the specified virtual memory configuration. The algorithm proceeds as follows:

1.  Any output sections for which explicit bonding addresses were specified are allocated.

2.  Any output sections to be included in a specific named memory are allocated. In both this and the succeeding step, each output section is placed into the first available space within the (named) memory with any alignment taken into consideration.

3.  Output sections not handled by one of the above steps are allocated.

If all memory is contiguous and configured (the default case), and no SECTIONS directives are given, then output sections are allocated in the order they appear to **ld**(1). Otherwise, output sections are allocated in the order they were defined or made known to **ld**(1) into the first available space they fit.

## Incremental Link Editing

As previously mentioned, the output of **ld**(1) can be used as an input file to subsequent **ld**(1) runs providing that the relocation information is retained (**−r** option). Large applications may find it desirable to partition their C programs into subsystems, link each subsystem independently, and then link edit the entire application. For example,

Step 1:

    **ld −r −o outfile1  ifile1 infile1.o**

```
/* ifile1  */
SECTIONS
{
        ss1:
        {
                f1.o
                f2.o
                . . .
                fn.o
        }
}
```

Step 2:

    **ld −r −o outfile2  ifile2  infile2.o**

```
/* ifile2  */
SECTIONS
{
        ss2:
        {
                g1.o
                g2.o
                . . .
                gn.o
        }
}
```

Step 3:

    **ld  −a −o final.out outfile1 outfile2**

By judiciously forming subsystems, applications may achieve a form of incremental link editing whereby it is necessary to relink only a portion of the total link edit when a few files are recompiled.

    To apply this technique, there are two simple rules

1.    Intermediate link edits should contain only SECTIONS declarations and be concerned only with the formation of output sections from input files and input sections. No binding of output sections should be done in these runs.

2.    All allocation and memory directives, as well as any assignment statements, are included only in the final **ld**(1) call.

## DSECT, COPY, NOLOAD, INFO, and OVERLAY Sections

    Sections may be given a type in a section definition as shown in the following example:

```
SECTIONS
{
        name1 0x200000 (DSECT)        : { file1.o }
        name2 0x400000 (COPY)         : { file2.o }
        name3 0x600000 (NOLOAD)       : { file3.o }
        name4          (INFO)         : { file4.o }
        name5 0x900000 (OVERLAY)      : { file5.o }

}
```

The DSECT option creates what is called a dummy section. A dummy section has the following properties:

1.  It does not participate in the memory allocation for output sections. As a result, it takes up no memory and does not show up in the memory map generated by **ld**(1).

2.  It may overlay other output sections and even unconfigured memory. DSECTs may overlay other DSECTs.

3.  The global symbols defined within the dummy section are relocated normally. That is, they appear in the output file's symbol table with the same value they would have had if the DSECT were actually loaded at its virtual address. DSECT-defined symbols may be referenced by other input sections. Undefined external symbols found within a DSECT cause specified archive libraries to be searched and any members which define such symbols are link edited normally (i.e., not as a DSECT).

4.  None of the section contents, relocation information, or line number information associated with the section is written to the output file.

In the above example, none of the sections from **file1.o** are allocated, but all symbols are relocated as though the sections were link edited at the specified address. Other sections could refer to any of the global symbols and they are resolved correctly.

A copy section created by the COPY option is similar to a dummy section. The only difference between a copy section and a dummy section is that the contents of a copy section and all associated information is written to the output file.

An INFO section is the same as a COPY section but its purpose is to carry information about the object file whereas the COPY section may contain valid text and data. INFO sections are usually used to contain file version identification information.

A section with the type of NOLOAD differs in only one respect from a normal output section: its text and/or data is not written to the output file. A NOLOAD section is allocated virtual space, appears in the memory map, etc.

An OVERLAY section is relocated and written to the output file. It is different from a normal section in that it is not allocated and may overlay other sections or unconfigured memory.

## Output File Blocking

The BLOCK option (applied to any output section or GROUP directive) is used to direct **ld**(1) to align a section at a specified byte offset in the output file. It has no effect on the address at which the section is allocated nor on any part of the link edit process. It is used purely to adjust the physical position of the section in the output file.

```
SECTIONS
{
        .text BLOCK(0x200) : { }
        .data ALIGN(0x20000) BLOCK(0x200) : { }
}
```

With this SECTIONS directive, **ld**(1) assures that each section, **.text** and **.data**, is physically written at a file offset, which is a multiple of 0x200 (e.g., at an offset of 0, 0x200, 0x400, and so forth, in the file).

## Nonrelocatable Input Files

If a file produced by **ld**(1) is intended to be used in a subsequent **ld**(1) run, the first **ld**(1) run should have the −**r** option set. This preserves relocation information and permits the sections of the file to be relocated by the subsequent run.

If an input file to **ld**(1) does not have relocation or symbol table information (perhaps from the action of a **strip**(1) command, or from being link edited without a −**r** option or with a −**s** option), the link edit run continues using the nonrelocatable input file.

For such a link edit to be successful (i.e., to actually and correctly link edit all input files, relocate all symbols, resolve unresolved references, etc.), two conditions on the nonrelocatable input files must be met.

1.  Each input file must have no unresolved external references.

2.  Each input file must be bound to the exact same virtual address as it was bound to in the **ld**(1) run that created it.

If these two conditions are not met for all nonrelocatable input files, no error messages are issued. Because of this fact, extreme care must be taken when supplying such input files to **ld**(1).

# Syntax Diagram for Input Directives

| Directives | Expanded Directives |
|---|---|
| \<ifile\> | \{\<cmd\>\} |
| \<cmd\> | \<memory\> |
| | \<sections\> |
| | \<assignment\> |
| | \<filename\> |
| | \<flags\> |
| \<memory\> | MEMORY \{ \<memory_spec\> |
| \<memory_spec\> | \<name\> **[** \<attributes\> **]** : |
| \<attributes\> | ( \{ R \| W \| X \| I \} ) |
| \<origin_spec\> | \<origin\> = \<long\> |
| \<lenth_spec\> | \<length\> = \<long\> |
| \<origin\> | ORIGIN \| o \| org \| origin |
| \<length\> | LENGTH \| l \| len \| length |

Figure 12-2: Syntax Diagram for Input Directives (Sheet 1 of 4)

---

NOTE

Two punctuation symbols, square brackets and curly braces, do double duty in this diagram.

Where the actual symbols, [] and {} are used, they are part of the syntax and must be present when the directive is specified.

Where you see the symbols **[** and **]** (larger and in bold), it means the material enclosed is optional.

Where you see the symbols **{** and **}** (larger and in bold), it means multiple occurrences of the material enclosed are permitted.

| Directives | Expanded Directives |
|---|---|
| <sections> | SECTIONS { {<sec_or_group>} } |
| <sec_or_group> | <section> \| <group> \| <library> |
| <group> | GROUP <group_options> : { |
| <section_list> | <section> { [,] <section> } |
| <section> | <name> <sec_options> : |
| <group_options> | [<addr>] \| [<align_option>] [<block_option>] |
| <sec_options> | [<addr>] \| [<align_option>] |
| <addr> | <long> \| <bind>( <expr> ) |
| <alignoption> | <align> ( <expr> ) |
| <align> | ALIGN \| align |
| <block_option> | <block> ( <long> ) |
| <block> | BLOCK \| block |
| <type_option> | (DSECT) \| (NOLOAD) \| (COPY) |
| <fill> | = <long> |
| <mem_spec> | > <name> |
| | > <attributes> |
| <statement> | <filename> |
| | <filename>  ( <name_list> ) \| [COMMON] |
| | * ( <name_list> ) \| [COMMON] |
| | <assignment> |
| | <library> |
| | *null* |

Figure 12-2: Syntax Diagram for Input Directives (Sheet 2 of 4)

| Directives | Expanded Directives |
|---|---|
| <name_list> | <section_name> **[,]** { <section_name> } |
| <library> | −l<name> |
| <bind> | BIND \| bind |
| <assignment> | <lside>  <assign_op>  <expr>  <end> |
| <lside> | <name> \| . |
| <assign_op> | = \| += \| −= \| *= \|/ = |
| <end> | ; \| , |
| <expr> | <expr>  <binary_op>  <expr> |
|  | <term> |
| <binary_op> | * \| / \| % |
|  | + \| − |
|  | >> \| << |
|  | == \| != \| > \| < \| <= \| >= |
|  | & |
|  | \| |
|  | && |
|  | \| |
| <term> | <long> |
|  | <name> |
|  | <align> ( <term> ) |
|  | ( <expr> ) |
|  | <unary_op>  <term> |
|  | <phy> (<lside>) |
|  | <sizeof>(<sectionname>) |
|  | <next>(<long>) |
|  | <addr>(<sectionname>) |
| <unary_op> | ! \| − |
| <phy> | PHY \| phy |
| <sizeof> | SIZEOF \| sizeof |

Figure 12-2: Syntax Diagram for Input Directives (Sheet 3 of 4)

| Directives | Expanded Directives |
|---|---|
| <next> | NEXT | next |
| <addr> | ADDR | addr |
| <flags> | −e <wht_space> <name> |
|  | −f <wht_space> <long> |
|  | −h <wht_space> <long> |
|  | −l <name> |
|  | −m |
|  | −o <wht_space> <filename> |
|  | −r |
|  | −s |
|  | −t |
|  | −u <wht_space> <name> |
|  | −z |
|  | −H |
|  | −L <path_name> |
|  | −M |
|  | −N |
|  | −S |
|  | −V |
|  | −VS <wht_space> <long> |
|  | −a |
|  | −x |
| <name> | Any valid symbol name |
| <long> | Any valid long integer constant |
| <wht_space> | Blanks, tabs, and newlines |
| <filename> | Any valid UNIX operating system |
| <sectionname> | Any valid section name, |
| <path_name> | Any valid UNIX operating system |

Figure 12-2: Syntax Diagram for Input Directives (Sheet 4 of 4)

# CHAPTER 13: make

## Introduction

The trend toward increased modularity of programs means that a project may have to cope with a large assortment of individual files. There may also be a wide range of generation procedures needed to turn the assortment of individual files into the final executable product.

**make**(1) provides a method for maintaining up-to-date versions of programs that consist of a number of files that may be generated in a variety of ways.

An individual programmer can easily forget

- file-to-file dependencies

- files that were modified and the impact that has on other files

- the exact sequence of operations needed to generate a new version of the program

In a description file, **make** keeps track of the commands that create files and the relationship between files. Whenever a change is made in any of the files that make up a program, the **make** command creates the finished program by recompiling only those portions directly or indirectly affected by the change.

The basic operation of **make** is to

- find the target in the description file

- ensure that all the files on which the target depends, the files needed to generate the target, exist and are up to date

- create the target file if any of the generators have been modified more recently than the target

The description file that holds the information on interfile dependencies and command sequences is conventionally called **makefile**, **Makefile**, or **s.[mM]akefile**. If this naming convention is followed, the simple command **make** is usually sufficient to regenerate the target regardless of the number files edited since the last **make**. In most cases, the description file is not difficult to write and changes infrequently. Even if only a single file has been edited, rather than typing all the commands to regenerate the target, typing the **make** command ensures the regeneration is done in the prescribed way.

# Basic Features

The basic operation of **make** is to update a target file by ensuring that all of the files on which the target file depends exist and are up to date. The target file is regenerated if it has not been modified since the dependents were modified. The **make** program searches the graph of dependencies. The operation of **make** depends on its ability to find the date and time that a file was last modified.

The **make** program operates using three sources of information:

- a user-supplied description file
- filenames and last-modified times from the file system
- built-in rules to bridge some of the gaps

To illustrate, consider a simple example in which a program named **prog** is made by compiling and loading three C language files **x.c**, **y.c**, and **z.c** with the **math** library. By convention, the output of the C language compilations will be found in files named **x.o**, **y.o**, and **z.o**. Assume that the files **x.c** and **y.c** share some declarations in a file named **defs.h**, but that **z.c** does not. That is, **x.c** and **y.c** have the line

```
#include "defs.h"
```

The following specification describes the relationships and operations:

```
prog :  x.o  y.o  z.o
        cc  x.o  y.o  z.o   -lm  -o  prog

x.o  y.o :   defs.h
```

If this information were stored in a file named **makefile**, the command

```
make
```

would perform the operations needed to regenerate **prog** after any changes had been made to any of the four source files **x.c**, **y.c**, **z.c**, or **defs.h**. In the example above, the first line states that **prog** depends on three .o files. Once these object files are current, the second line describes how to load them to create **prog**. The third line states that **x.o** and **y.o** depend on the file **defs.h**. From the file system, **make** discovers that there are three .c files corresponding to the needed .o files and uses built-in rules on how to generate an object from a C source file (i.e., issue a **cc** −**c** command).

If **make** did not have the ability to determine automatically what needs to be done, the following longer description file would be necessary:

```
prog :  x.o  y.o  z.o
        cc  x.o  y.o  z.o  -lm  -o  prog
x.o :  x.c  defs.h
       cc  -c  x.c
y.o :  y.c  defs.h
       cc  -c  y.c
z.o :  z.c
       cc  -c  z.c
```

If none of the source or object files have changed since the last time **prog** was made, and all of the files are current, the command **make** announces this fact and stops. If, however, the **defs.h** file has been edited, **x.c** and **y.c** (but not **z.c**) are recompiled; and then **prog** is created from the new **x.o** and **y.o** files, and the existing **z.o** file. If only the file **y.c** had changed, only it is recompiled; but it is still necessary to reload **prog**. If no target name is given on the **make** command line, the first target mentioned in the description is created; otherwise, the specified targets are made. The command

   **make x.o**

would regenerate **x.o** if **x.c** or **defs.h** had changed.

A method often useful to programmers is to include rules with mnemonic names and commands that do not actually produce a file with that name. These entries can take advantage of **make**'s ability to generate files and substitute macros (for information about macros, see "Description Files and Substitutions" below.) Thus, an entry "save" might be included to copy a certain set of files, or an entry "clean" might be used to throw away unneeded intermediate files.

If a file exists after such commands are executed, the file's time of last modification is used in further decisions. If the file does not exist after the commands are executed, the current time is used in making further decisions.

You can maintain a zero-length file purely to keep track of the time at which certain actions were performed. This technique is useful for maintaining remote archives and listings.

A simple macro mechanism for substitution in dependency lines and command strings is used by **make**. Macros can either be defined by command-line arguments or included in the description file. In either case, a macro consists of a name followed by an equals sign followed by what the macro stands for. A macro is invoked by preceding the name by a dollar sign. Macro names longer than one character must be parenthesized. The following are valid macro invocations:

```
$(CFLAGS)
$2
$(xy)
$Z
$(Z)
```

The last two are equivalent.

**$***, **$@**, **$?**, and **$<** are four special macros that change values during the execution of the command. (These four macros are described later in this chapter under "Description Files and Substitutions.") The following fragment shows assignment and use of some macros:

```
OBJECTS = x.o y.o z.o
LIBES = -lm
prog: $(OBJECTS)
        cc $(OBJECTS)  $(LIBES)  -o prog
    . . .
```

The command

**make  LIBES="-ll -lm"**

loads the three objects with both the **lex** (**-ll**) and the **math** (**-lm**) libraries, because macro definitions on the command line override definitions in the description file. (In UNIX system commands, arguments with embedded blanks must be quoted.)

As an example of the use of **make**, a description file that might be used to maintain the **make** command itself is given. The code for **make** is spread over a number of C language source files and has a **yacc** grammar. The description file contains the following:

```
# Description file for the make command

FILES = Makefile defs.h main.c doname.c misc.c
        files.c dosys.c gram.y
OBJECTS = main.o doname.o misc.o files.o
          dosys.o gram.o
LIBES= -lld
LINT = lint -p
CFLAGS = -O
LP = /usr/bin/lp

make:   $(OBJECTS)
        $(CC) $(CFLAGS) $(OBJECTS) $(LIBES) -o make
        @size make

$(OBJECTS):  defs.h

cleanup:
        -rm *.o gram.c
        -du

install:
        @size make /usr/bin/make
        cp make /usr/bin/make && rm make

lint :  dosys.c doname.c files.c main.c misc.c gram.c
        $(LINT) dosys.c doname.c files.c main.c misc.c \
        gram.c

                # print files that are out-of-date
                # with respect to "print" file.

print:  $(FILES)
        pr $? | $(LP)
        touch print
```

The **make** program prints out each command before issuing it.

The following output results from typing the command **make** in a directory containing only the source and description files:

```
cc  -o -c main.c
cc  -o -c doname.c
cc  -o -c misc.c
cc  -o -c files.c
cc  -o -c dosys.c
yacc  gram.y
mv y.tab.c gram.c
cc  -o -c gram.c
cc  main.o doname.o misc.o files.o dosys.o
    gram.o  -lld -o make
13188 + 3348 + 3044 = 19580
```

The string of digits results from the **size make** command. The printing of the command line itself was suppressed by an at sign, **@**, in the description file.

# Description Files and Substitutions

The following section will explain the customary elements of the description file.

## Comments

The comment convention is that a sharp, #, and all characters on the same line after a sharp are ignored. Blank lines and lines beginning with a sharp are totally ignored.

## Continuation Lines

If a noncomment line is too long, the line can be continued by using a backslash. If the last character of a line is a backslash, then the backslash, the new line, and all following blanks and tabs are replaced by a single blank.

## Macro Definitions

A macro definition is an identifier followed by an equal sign. The identifier must not be preceded by a colon or a tab. The name (string of letters and digits) to the left of the equal sign (trailing blanks and tabs are stripped) is assigned the string of characters following the equal sign (leading blanks and tabs are stripped). The following are valid macro definitions:

```
2 = xyz
abc = -11 -ly -lm
LIBES =
```

The last definition assigns LIBES the null string. A macro that is never explicitly defined has the null string as its value. Remember, however, that some macros are explicitly defined in **make**'s own rules. (See Figure 13-2 at the end of the chapter.)

# General Form

The general form of an entry in a description file is

```
target1 [target2 ...] :[:] [dependent1 ...] [; commands] [# ...]
[ \t commands] [# ...]
  . . .
```

Items inside brackets may be omitted and targets and dependents are strings of letters, digits, periods, and slashes. Shell metacharacters such as * and **?** are expanded when the line is evaluated. Commands may appear either after a semicolon on a dependency line or on lines beginning with a tab immediately following a dependency line. A command is any string of characters not including a sharp, #, except when the sharp is in quotes.

# Dependency Information

A dependency line may have either a single or a double colon. A target name may appear on more than one dependency line, but all of those lines must be of the same (single or double colon) type. For the more common single-colon case, a command sequence may be associated with at most one dependency line. If the target is out of date with any of the dependents on any of the lines and a command sequence is specified (even a null one following a semicolon or tab), it is executed; otherwise, a default rule may be invoked. In the double-colon case, a command sequence may be associated with more than one dependency line. If the target is out of date with any of the files on a particular line, the associated commands are executed. A built-in rule may also be executed. The double colon form is particularly useful in updating archive-type files, where the target is the archive library itself. (An example is included in the "Archive Libraries" section later in this chapter.)

# Executable Commands

If a target must be created, the sequence of commands is executed. Normally, each command line is printed and then passed to a separate invocation of the shell after substituting for macros. The printing is suppressed in the silent mode (−s option of the **make** command) or if the command line in the description file begins with an **@** sign. **make** normally stops if any command signals an error by returning a nonzero error code. Errors are ignored if the −i flag has been specified on the **make** command line, if the fake target name .IGNORE appears in the description file, or if the command string in the description file begins with a hyphen. If a program is known to return a meaningless status, a hyphen in front of the command that invokes it is appropriate. Because each command line is passed to a separate invocation of the shell, care must be taken with certain commands (e.g., **cd** and shell control commands) that have meaning only within a single shell process. These results are forgotten before the next line is executed.

Before issuing any command, certain internally maintained macros are set. The **$@** macro is set to the full target name of the current target. The **$@** macro is evaluated only for explicitly named dependencies. The **$?** macro is set to the string of names that were found to be younger than the target. The **$?** macro is evaluated when explicit rules from the **makefile** are evaluated. If the command was generated by an implicit rule, the **$<** macro is the name of the related file that caused the action; and the **$\*** macro is the prefix shared by the current and the dependent filenames. If a file must be made but there are no explicit commands or relevant built-in rules, the commands associated with the name DEFAULT are used. If there is no such name, **make** prints a message and stops.

In addition, a description file may also use the following related macros: **$(@D)**, **$(@F)**, **$(\*D)**, **$(\*F)**, **$(<D)**, and **$(<F)** (see below).

# Extensions of $*, $@, and $<

The internally generated macros $*, $@, and $< are useful generic terms for current targets and out-of-date relatives. To this list has been added the following related macros: **$(@D)**, **$(@F)**, **$(*D)**, **$(*F)**, **$(<D)**, and **$(<F)**. The **D** refers to the directory part of the single character macro. The **F** refers to the filename part of the single character macro. These additions are useful when building hierarchical **makefiles**. They allow access to directory names for purposes of using the **cd** command of the shell. Thus, a command can be

**cd $(<D); $(MAKE) $(<F)**

# Output Translations

Macros in shell commands are translated when evaluated. The form is as follows:

    $(macro:string1=string2)

The meaning of **$(macro)** is evaluated. For each appearance of **string1** in the evaluated macro, **string2** is substituted. The meaning of finding **string1** in **$(macro)** is that the evaluated **$(macro)** is considered as a series of strings each delimited by white space (blanks or tabs). Thus, the occurrence of **string1** in **$(macro)** means that a regular expression of the following form has been found:

    .*<string1>[TAB│BLANK]

This particular form was chosen because **make** usually concerns itself with suffixes. The usefulness of this type of translation occurs when maintaining archive libraries. Now, all that is necessary is to accumulate the out-of-date members and write a shell script, which can handle all the C language programs (i.e., those files ending in **.c**). Thus, the following fragment optimizes the executions of **make** for maintaining an archive library:

```
$(LIB):  $(LIB)(a.o) $(LIB)(b.o) $(LIB)(c.o)
         $(CC) -c $(CFLAGS) $(?:.o=.c)
         $(AR) $(ARFLAGS) $(LIB) $?
         rm $?
```

A dependency of the preceding form is necessary for each of the different types of source files (suffixes) that define the archive library. These translations are added in an effort to make more general use of the wealth of information that **make** generates.

# Recursive Makefiles

Another feature of **make** concerns the environment and recursive invocations. If the sequence $(MAKE) appears anywhere in a shell command line, the line is executed even if the **−n** flag is set. Since the **−n** flag is exported across invocations of **make** (through the MAKEFLAGS variable), the only thing that is executed is the **make** command itself. This feature is useful when a hierarchy of **makefile**(s) describes a set of software subsystems. For testing purposes, **make −n ...** can be executed and everything that would have been done will be printed including output from lower level invocations of **make**.

# Suffixes and Transformation Rules

**make** uses an internal table of rules to learn how to transform a file with one suffix into a file with another suffix. If the **−r** flag is used on the **make** command line, the internal table is not used.

The list of suffixes is actually the dependency list for the name .SUFFIXES. **make** searches for a file with any of the suffixes on the list. If it finds one, **make** transforms it into a file with another suffix. The transformation rule names are the concatenation of the before and after suffixes. The name of the rule to transform a **.r** file to a **.o** file is thus **.r.o**. If the rule is present and no explicit command sequence has been given in the user's description files, the command sequence for the rule **.r.o** is used. If a command is generated by using one of these suffixing rules, the macro **$∗** is given the value of the stem (everything but the suffix) of the name of the file to be made; and the macro **$<** is the full name of the dependent that caused the action.

The order of the suffix list is significant since the list is scanned from left to right. The first name formed that has both a file and a rule associated with it is used. If new names are to be appended, the user can add an entry for .SUFFIXES in the description file. The dependents are added to the usual list. A .SUFFIXES line without any dependents deletes the current list. It is necessary to clear the current list if the order of names is to be changed.

## Implicit Rules

**make** uses a table of suffixes and a set of transformation rules to supply default dependency information and implied commands.  The default suffix list is as follows:

.o   Object file

.c   C source file

.c~   SCCS C source file

.f   FORTRAN source file

.f~   SCCS FORTRAN source file

.s   Assembler source file

.s~   SCCS Assembler source file

.y   **yacc** source grammar

.y~   SCCS **yacc** source grammar

.l   **lex** source grammar

.l~   SCCS **ex** source grammar

.h   Header file

.h~   SCCS header file

.sh   Shell file

.sh~   SCCS shell file

Figure 13-1 summarizes the default transformation paths.  If there are two paths connecting a pair of suffixes, the longer one is used only if the intermediate file exists or is named in the description.

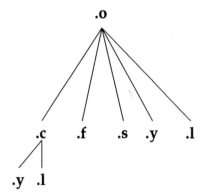

Figure 13-1: Summary of Default Transformation Path

If the file **x.o** is needed and an **x.c** is found in the description or directory, the **x.o** file would be compiled. If there is also an **x.l**, that source file would be run through **lex** before compiling the result. However, if there is no **x.c** but there is an **x.l**, **make** would discard the intermediate C language file and use the direct link as shown in Figure 13-1.

It is possible to change the names of some of the compilers used in the default or the flag arguments with which they are invoked by knowing the macro names used. The compiler names are the macros AS, CC, F77, YACC, and LEX. The command

    **make CC=newcc**

will cause the **newcc** command to be used instead of the usual C language compiler. The macros ASFLAGS, CFLAGS, F77FLAGS, YFLAGS, and LFLAGS may be set to cause these commands to be issued with optional flags. Thus

    **make "CFLAGS=−g"**

causes the **cc** command to include debugging information.

## Archive Libraries

The **make** program has an interface to archive libraries. A user may name a member of a library in the following manner:

```
projlib(object.o)
    or
projlib((entrypt))
```

where the second method actually refers to an entry point of an object file within the library. (**make** looks through the library, locates the entry point, and translates it to the correct object filename.)

To use this procedure to maintain an archive library, the following type of **makefile** is required:

```
projlib::    projlib(pfile1.o)
        $(CC) -c -O pfile1.c
        $(AR) $(ARFLAGS) projlib pfile1.o
        rm pfile1.o
projlib::    projlib(pfile2.o)
        $(CC) -c -O pfile2.c
        $(AR) $(ARFLAGS) projlib pfile2.o
        rm pfile2.o
```

... and so on for each object ...

This is tedious and error prone. Obviously, the command sequences for adding a C language file to a library are the same for each invocation; the filename being the only difference each time. (This is true in most cases.)

The **make** command also gives the user access to a rule for building libraries. The handle for the rule is the **.a** suffix. Thus, a **.c.a** rule is the rule for compiling a C language source file, adding it to the library, and removing the **.o** cadaver. Similarly, the **.y.a**, the **.s.a**, and the **.l.a** rules rebuild **yacc**, assembler, and **lex** files, respectively. The archive rules defined internally are **.c.a**, **.c~.a**, **.f.a**, **.f~.a**, and **.s~.a**. (The tilde, ~, syntax will be described shortly.) The user may define other needed rules in the description file.

The above two-member library is then maintained with the following shorter **makefile**:

```
projlib:        projlib(pfile1.o) projlib(pfile2.o)
                @echo projlib up-to-date.
```

The internal rules are already defined to complete the preceding library maintenance. The actual **.c.a** rule is as follows:

```
.c.a:
        $(CC) -c $(CFLAGS) $<
        $(AR) $(ARFLAGS) $@ $*.o
        rm -f $*.o
```

Thus, the **$@** macro is the **.a** target (**projlib**); the **$<** and **$\*** macros are set to the out-of-date C language file; and the filename minus the suffix, respectively (**pfile1.c** and **pfile1**). The **$<** macro (in the preceding rule) could have been changed to **$\*.c**.

It might be useful to go into some detail about exactly what **make** does when it sees the construction

```
projlib:    projlib(pfile1.o)
            @echo projlib up-to-date
```

Assume the object in the library is out of date with respect to **pfile1.c**. Also, there is no **pfile1.o** file.

1. **make projlib**.

2. Before **make**ing **projlib**, check each dependent of **projlib**.

3. **projlib(pfile1.o)** is a dependent of **projlib** and needs to be generated.

4. Before generating **projlib(pfile1.o)**, check each dependent of **projlib(pfile1.o)**. (There are none.)

5. Use internal rules to try to create **projlib(pfile1.o)**. (There is no explicit rule.) Note that **projlib(pfile1.o)** has a parenthesis in the name to identify the target suffix as **.a**. This is the key. There is no explicit **.a** at the end of the **projlib** library name. The parenthesis implies the **.a** suffix. In this sense, the **.a** is hard-wired into **make**.

6. Break the name **projlib(pfile1.o)** up into **projlib** and **pfile1.o**. Define two macros, **$@** (=**projlib**) and **$\*** (=**pfile1**).

7. Look for a rule .*X*.**a** and a file **$**∗.*X*. The first .*X* (in the .SUFFIXES list) which fulfills these conditions is .**c** so the rule is .**c.a**, and the file is **pfile1.c**. Set **$**< to be **pfile1.c** and execute the rule. In fact, **make** must then compile **pfile1.c**.

8. The library has been updated. Execute the command associated with the **projlib:** dependency; namely

   ```
   @echo projlib up-to-date
   ```

It should be noted that to let **pfile1.o** have dependencies, the following syntax is required:

```
projlib(pfile1.o):        $(INCDIR)/stdio.h  pfile1.c
```

There is also a macro for referencing the archive member name when this form is used. The **$%** macro is evaluated each time **$@** is evaluated. If there is no current archive member, **$%** is null. If an archive member exists, then **$%** evaluates to the expression between the parenthesis.

# Source Code Control System Filenames: The Tilde

The syntax of **make** does not directly permit referencing of prefixes. For most types of files on UNIX operating system machines, this is acceptable since nearly everyone uses a suffix to distinguish different types of files. The SCCS files are the exception. Here, **s.** precedes the filename part of the complete path name.

To allow **make** easy access to the prefix **s.** the tilde, ~, is used as an identifier of SCCS files. Hence, **.c~.o** refers to the rule which transforms an SCCS C language source file into an object file. Specifically, the internal rule is

```
.c~.o:
        $(GET) $(GFLAGS) $<
        $(CC) $(CFLAGS) —c $*.c
        —rm —f $*.c
```

Thus, the tilde appended to any suffix transforms the file search into an SCCS filename search with the actual suffix named by the dot and all characters up to (but not including) the tilde.

The following SCCS suffixes are internally defined:

```
.c~
.f~
.y~
.l~
.s~
.sh~
.h~
```

The following rules involving SCCS transformations are internally defined:

```
.c~:
.f~:
.sh~:
.c~.a:
.c~.c:
.c~.o:
.f~.a:
.f~.f:
.f~.o:
.s~.a:
.s~.s:
.s~.o:
.y~.c:
.y~.o:
.l~.l:
.l~.o:
.h~.h:
```

Obviously, the user can define other rules and suffixes, which may prove useful. The tilde provides a handle on the SCCS filename format so that this is possible.

## The Null Suffix

There are many programs that consist of a single source file. **make** handles this case by the null suffix rule. Thus, to maintain the UNIX system program **cat**, a rule in the **makefile** of the following form is needed:

```
.c:
        $(CC) $(CFLAGS) $< -o $@
```

In fact, this **.c:** rule is internally defined so no **makefile** is necessary at all. The user only needs to type

**make cat dd echo date**

(these are all UNIX system single-file programs) and all four C language source files are passed through the above shell command line associated with the **.c:** rule. The internally defined single suffix rules are

```
.c:
.c~:
.f:
.f~:
.sh:
.sh~:
```

Others may be added in the **makefile** by the user.

## include Files

The **make** program has a capability similar to the **#include** directive of the C preprocessor. If the string **include** appears as the first seven letters of a line in a **makefile** and is followed by a blank or a tab, the rest of the line is assumed to be a filename, which the current invocation of **make** will read. Macros may be used in filenames. The file descriptors are stacked for reading **include** files so that no more than 16 levels of nested **include**s are supported.

## SCCS Makefiles

Makefiles under SCCS control are accessible to **make**. That is, if **make** is typed and only a file named **s.makefile** or **s.Makefile** exists, **make** will do a **get** on the file, then read and remove the file.

## Dynamic Dependency Parameters

The parameter has meaning only on the dependency line in a makefile. The **$$@** refers to the current "thing" to the left of the colon (which is **$@**). Also the form **$$(@F)** exists, which allows access to the file part of **$@**. Thus, in the following:

```
cat:      $$@.c
```

the dependency is translated at execution time to the string **cat.c**. This is useful for building a large number of executable files, each of which has only one source file. For instance, the UNIX software command directory could have a **makefile** like:

```
CMDS = cat dd echo date cmp comm chown

$(CMDS):        $$@.c
        $(CC) -o $? -o $@
```

Obviously, this is a subset of all the single file programs. For multiple file programs, a directory is usually allocated and a separate **makefile** is made. For any particular file that has a peculiar compilation procedure, a specific entry must be made in the **makefile**.

The second useful form of the dependency parameter is **$$(@F)**. It represents the filename part of **$$@**. Again, it is evaluated at execution time. Its usefulness becomes evident when trying to maintain the **/usr/include** directory from a makefile in the **/usr/src/head** directory. Thus, the **/usr/src/head/makefile** would look like

```
INCDIR = /usr/include

INCLUDES = \
        $(INCDIR)/stdio.h \
        $(INCDIR)/pwd.h \
        $(INCDIR)/dir.h \
        $(INCDIR)/a.out.h

$(INCLUDES): $$(@F)
        cp $? $@
        chmod 0444 $@
```

This would completely maintain the **/usr/include** directory whenever one of the above files in **/usr/src/head** was updated.

# Command Usage

The **make** command description is found under **make**(1) in the *Programmer's Reference Manual*.

## The make Command

The **make** command takes macro definitions, options, description filenames, and target filenames as arguments in the form:

**make** [ *options* ] [ *macro definitions* ] [ *targets* ]

The following summary of command operations explains how these arguments are interpreted.

First, all macro definition arguments (arguments with embedded equal signs) are analyzed and the assignments made. Command-line macros override corresponding definitions found in the description files. Next, the option arguments are examined. The permissible options are as follows:

−**i**  Ignore error codes returned by invoked commands. This mode is entered if the fake target name .IGNORE appears in the description file.

−**s**  Silent mode. Do not print command lines before executing. This mode is also entered if the fake target name .SILENT appears in the description file.

−**r**  Do not use the built-in rules.

−**n**  No execute mode. Print commands, but do not execute them. Even lines beginning with an **@** sign are printed.

−**t**  Touch the target files (causing them to be up to date) rather than issue the usual commands.

−**q**  Question. The **make** command returns a zero or nonzero status code depending on whether the target file is or is not up to date.

−**p**  Print out the complete set of macro definitions and target descriptions.

−**k**  Abandon work on the current entry if something goes wrong, but continue on other branches that do not depend on the current entry.

−**e**  Environment variables override assignments within **makefile**s.

−**f**  Description filename.  The next argument is assumed to be the name of a description file.  A filename of − denotes the standard input.  If there are no −**f** arguments, the file named **makefile** or **Makefile** or **s.[mM]akefile** in the current directory is read.  The contents of the description files override the built-in rules if they are present.

The following two arguments are evaluated in the same manner as flags:

.DEFAULT    If a file must be made but there are no explicit commands or relevant built-in rules, the commands associated with the name .DEFAULT are used if it exists.

.PRECIOUS   Dependents on this target are not removed when quit or interrupt is pressed.

Finally, the remaining arguments are assumed to be the names of targets to be made and the arguments are done in left-to-right order.  If there are no such arguments, the first name in the description file that does not begin with a period is made.

## Environment Variables

Environment variables are read and added to the macro definitions each time **make** executes.  Precedence is a prime consideration in doing this properly.  The following describes **make**'s interaction with the environment.  A macro, MAKEFLAGS, is maintained by **make**.  The macro is defined as the collection of all input flag arguments into a string (without minus signs).  The macro is exported and thus accessible to further invocations of **make**.  Command line flags and assignments in the **makefile** update MAKEFLAGS.  Thus, to describe how the environment interacts with **make**, the MAKEFLAGS macro (environment variable) must be considered.

When executed, **make** assigns macro definitions in the following order:

1.  Read the MAKEFLAGS environment variable.  If it is not present or null, the internal **make** variable MAKEFLAGS is set to the null string.  Otherwise, each letter in MAKEFLAGS is assumed to be an input flag argument and is processed as such.  (The only exceptions are the −**f**, −**p**, and −**r** flags.)

2. Read the internal list of macro definitions.

3. Read the environment. The environment variables are treated as macro definitions and marked as **exported** (in the shell sense).

4. Read the **makefile**(s). The assignments in the **makefile**(s) overrides the environment. This order is chosen so that when a **makefile** is read and executed, you know what to expect. That is, you get what is seen unless the −**e** flag is used. The −**e** is the line flag, which tells **make** to have the environment override the **makefile** assignments. Thus, if **make** −**e** ... is typed, the variables in the environment override the definitions in the **makefile**. Also MAKEFLAGS override the environment if assigned. This is useful for further invocations of **make** from the current **makefile**.

It may be clearer to list the precedence of assignments. Thus, in order from least binding to most binding, the precedence of assignments is as follows:

1. internal definitions

2. environment

3. **makefile**(s)

4. command line

The −**e** flag has the effect of rearranging the order to:

1. internal definitions

2. **makefile**(s)

3. environment

4. command line

This order is general enough to allow a programmer to define a **makefile** or set of **makefile**s whose parameters are dynamically definable.

# Suggestions and Warnings

The most common difficulties arise from **make**'s specific meaning of dependency. If file **x.c** has a

```
#include "defs.h"
```

line, then the object file **x.o** depends on **defs.h**; the source file **x.c** does not. If **defs.h** is changed, nothing is done to the file **x.c** while file **x.o** must be recreated.

To discover what **make** would do, the −**n** option is very useful. The command

```
make −n
```

orders **make** to print out the commands that **make** would issue without actually taking the time to execute them. If a change to a file is absolutely certain to be mild in character (e.g., adding a comment to an **include** file), the −**t** (touch) option can save a lot of time. Instead of issuing a large number of superfluous recompilations, **make** updates the modification times on the affected file. Thus, the command

```
make −ts
```

(touch silently) causes the relevant files to appear up to date. Obvious care is necessary because this mode of operation subverts the intention of **make** and destroys all memory of the previous relationships.

# Internal Rules

The standard set of internal rules used by **make** are reproduced below.

```
#
#          SUFFIXES RECOGNIZED BY MAKE
#
.SUFFIXES: .o .c .c~ .y .y~ .l .l~ .s .s~ .h .h~ .sh .sh~ .f .f~

#
#          PREDEFINED MACROS
#
MAKE=make
AR=ar
ARFLAGS=-rv
AS=as
ASFLAGS=
CC=cc
CFLAGS=-O
F77=f77
F77FLAGS=
GET=get
GFLAGS=
LEX=lex
LFLAGS=
LD=ld
LDFLAGS=
YACC=yacc
YFLAGS=
```

Figure 13-2: **make** Internal Rules (Sheet 1 of 5)

```
#
#          SINGLE SUFFIX RULES
#
.c:
          $(CC) $(CFLAGS) $(LDFLAGS) $< -o $@
.c~ :

          $(GET) $(GFLAGS) $<
          $(CC) $(CFLAGS) $(LDFLAGS) $*.c -o $*
          -rm -f $*.c

.f:
          $(F77) $(F77FLAGS) $(LDFLAGS) $< -o $@
.f~ :

          $(GET) $(GFLAGS) $<
          $(F77) $(F77FLAGS) $(LDFLAGS) $< -o $*
          -rm -f $*.f

.sh:
          cp $< $@; chmod 0777 $@
.sh~ :

          $(GET) $(GFLAGS) $<
          cp $*.sh $*; chmod 0777 $@
          -rm -f $*.sh
```

Figure 13-2: **make** Internal Rules (Sheet 2 of 5)

```
#
#        DOUBLE SUFFIX RULES
#
.c~.c  .f~.f  .s~.s  .sh~.sh  .y~.y  .l~.l  .h~.h:
        $(GET) $(GFLAGS) $<

.c.a:
        $(CC) -c $(CFLAGS) $<
        $(AR) $(ARFLAGS) $@ $*.o
        rm -f $*.o

.c~.a:
        $(GET) $(GFLAGS) $<
        $(CC) -c $(CFLAGS) $*.c
        $(AR) $(ARFLAGS) $@ $*.o
        rm -f $*.[co]

.c.o:
        $(CC) $(CFLAGS) -c $<

.c~.o:
        $(GET) $(GFLAGS) $<
        $(CC) $(CFLAGS) -c $*.c
        -rm -f $*.c

.f.a:
        $(F77) $(F77FLAGS) $(LDFLAGS) -c $*.f
        $(AR) $(ARFLAGS) $@ $*.o
        -rm -f $*.o

.f~.a:
        $(GET) $(GFLAGS) $<
        $(F77) $(F77FLAGS) $(LDFLAGS) -c $*.f
        $(AR) $(ARFLAGS) $@ $*.o
        -rm -f $*.[fo]
```

Figure 13-2: **make** Internal Rules (Sheet 3 of 5)

```
.f.o:
        $(F77) $(F77FLAGS) $(LDFLAGS) -c $*.f
.f~.o:
        $(GET) $(GFLAGS) $<
        $(F77) $(F77FLAGS) $(LDFLAGS) -c $*.f
        -rm -f $*.f
.s~.a:
        $(GET) $(GFLAGS) $<
        $(AS) $(ASFLAGS) -o $*.o $*.s
        $(AR) $(ARFLAGS) $@ $*.o
        -rm -f $*.[so]
.s.o:
        $(AS) $(ASFLAGS) -o $@ $<
.s~.o:
        $(GET) $(GFLAGS) $<
        $(AS) $(ASFLAGS) -o $*.o $*.s
        -rm -f $*.s
.l.c :
        $(LEX) $(LFLAGS) $<
        mv lex.yy.c $@
.l~.c:
        $(GET) $(GFLAGS) $<
        $(LEX) $(LFLAGS) $*.l
        mv lex.yy.c $@
```

Figure 13-2: **make** Internal Rules (Sheet 4 of 5)

```
.l.o:
        $(LEX) $(LFLAGS) $<
        $(CC) $(CFLAGS) -c lex.yy.c
        rm lex.yy.c
        mv lex.yy.o $@
        -rm -f $*.l
.l~.o:
        $(GET) $(GFLAGS) $<
        $(LEX) $(LFLAGS) $*.l
        $(CC) $(CFLAGS) -c lex.yy.c
        rm -f lex.yy.c $*.l
        mv lex.yy.o $*.o

.y.c :
        $(YACC) $(YFLAGS) $<
        mv y.tab.c $@
.y~.c :
        $(GET) $(GFLAGS) $<
        $(YACC) $(YFLAGS) $*.y
        mv y.tab.c $*.c
        -rm -f $*.y

.y.o:
        $(YACC) $(YFLAGS) $<
        $(CC) $(CFLAGS) -c y.tab.c
        rm y.tab.c
        mv y.tab.o $@

.y~.o:
        $(GET) $(GFLAGS) $<
        $(YACC) $(YFLAGS) $*.y
        $(CC) $(CFLAGS) -c y.tab.c
        rm -f y.tab.c $*.y
        mv y.tab.o $*.o
```

Figure 13-2: **make** Internal Rules (Sheet 5 of 5)

# CHAPTER 14: SOURCE CODE CONTROL
## SYSTEM (SCCS)

## Introduction

The Source Code Control System (SCCS) is a maintenance and enhancement tracking tool that runs under the UNIX system. SCCS takes custody of a file and, when changes are made, identifies and stores them in the file with the original source code and/or documentation. As other changes are made, they too are identified and retained in the file.

Retrieval of the original or any set of changes is possible. Any version of the file as it develops can be reconstructed for inspection or additional modification. History data can be stored with each version: why the changes were made, who made them, when they were made.

This guide covers the following:

- SCCS for Beginners: how to make, retrieve, and update an SCCS file

- Delta Numbering: how versions of an SCCS file are named

- SCCS Command Conventions: what rules apply to SCCS commands

- SCCS Commands: the fourteen SCCS commands and their more useful arguments

- SCCS Files: protection, format, and auditing of SCCS files

Neither the implementation of SCCS nor the installation procedure for SCCS is described in this guide.

# SCCS For Beginners

Several terminal session fragments are presented in this section. Try them all. The best way to learn SCCS is to use it.

## Terminology

A delta is a set of changes made to a file under SCCS custody. To identify and keep track of a delta, it is assigned an SID (SCCS IDentification) number. The SID for any original file turned over to SCCS is composed of release number 1 and level number 1, stated as 1.1. The SID for the first set of changes made to that file, that is, its first delta is release 1 version 2, or 1.2. The next delta would be 1.3, the next 1.4, and so on. More on delta numbering later. At this point, it is enough to know that by default SCCS assigns SIDs automatically.

## Creating an SCCS File via admin

Suppose, for example, you have a file called **lang** that is simply a list of five programming language names. Use a text editor to create file **lang** containing the following list.

```
C
PL/1
FORTRAN
COBOL
ALGOL
```

Custody of your **lang** file can be given to SCCS using the **admin** command (i.e., administer SCCS file). The following creates an SCCS file from the **lang** file:

> admin −ilang s.lang

All SCCS files must have names that begin with **s.**, hence **s.lang**. The −**i** keyletter, together with its value **lang**, means **admin** is to create an SCCS file and initialize it with the contents of the file **lang**.

The **admin** command replies

```
No id keywords (cm7)
```

This is a warning message that may also be issued by other SCCS commands. Ignore it for now. Its significance is described later with the **get** command under "SCCS Commands." In the following examples, this warning message is not shown although it may be issued.

Remove the **lang** file. It is no longer needed because it exists now under SCCS as **s.lang**.

    **rm lang**

# Retrieving a File via get

Use the **get** command as follows:

    **get s.lang**

This retrieves **s.lang** and prints

```
1.1
5 lines
```

This tells you that **get** retrieved version 1.1 of the file, which is made up of five lines of text.

The retrieved text has been placed in a new file known as a "g.file." SCCS forms the g.file name by deleting the prefix **s.** from the name of the SCCS file. Thus, the original **lang** file has been recreated.

If you list, **ls**(1), the contents of your directory, you will see both **lang** and **s.lang**. SCCS retains **s.lang** for use by other users.

The **get s.lang** command creates **lang** as read-only and keeps no information regarding its creation. Because you are going to make changes to it, **get** must be informed of your intention to do so. This is done as follows:

    **get −e s.lang**

**get −e** causes SCCS to create **lang** for both reading and writing (editing). It also places certain information about **lang** in another new file, called the "p.file" (**p.lang** in this case), which is needed later by the **delta** command.

**get** −**e** prints the same messages as **get**, except that now the SID for the first delta you will create is issued:

```
1.1
new delta   1.2
5 lines
```

Change **lang** by adding two more programming languages:

```
SNOBOL
ADA
```

# Recording Changes via delta

Next, use the **delta** command as follows:

**delta  s.lang**

**delta** then prompts with

```
comments?
```

Your response should be an explanation of why the changes were made. For example,

**added more languages**

**delta** now reads the p.file, **p.lang**, and determines what changes you made to **lang**. It does this by doing its own **get** to retrieve the original version and applying the **diff**(1) command to the original version and the edited version. Next, **delta** stores the changes in **s.lang** and destroys the no longer needed **p.lang** and **lang** files.

When this process is complete, **delta** outputs

```
1.2
2 inserted
0 deleted
5 unchanged
```

The number 1.2 is the SID of the delta you just created, and the next three lines summarize what was done to **s.lang**.

## Additional Information about get

The command,

**get s.lang**

retrieves the latest version of the file **s.lang**, now 1.2. SCCS does this by starting, with the original version of the file and applying the delta you made. If you use the **get** command now, any of the following will retrieve version 1.2.

**get s.lang**
**get −r1 s.lang**
**get −r1.2 s.lang**

The numbers following −**r** are SIDs. When you omit the level number of the SID (as in **get** −r1 **s.lang**), the default is the highest level number that exists within the specified release. Thus, the second command requests the retrieval of the latest version in release 1, namely 1.2. The third command specifically requests the retrieval of a particular version, in this case also 1.2.

Whenever a major change is made to a file, you may want to signify it by changing the release number, the first number of the SID. This, too, is done with the **get** command.

**get −e −r2 s.lang**

Because release 2 does not exist, **get** retrieves the latest version before release 2. **get** also interprets this as a request to change the release number of the new delta to 2, thereby naming it 2.1 rather than 1.3. The output is

```
1.2
new delta 2.1
7 lines
```

which means version 1.2 has been retrieved, and 2.1 is the version **delta** will create. If the file is now edited, for example, by deleting COBOL from the list of languages, and **delta** is executed

> **delta  s.lang**
> comments? **deleted cobol from list of languages**

you will see by **delta**'s output that version 2.1 is indeed created.

```
2.1
0 inserted
1 deleted
6 unchanged
```

Deltas can now be created in release 2 (deltas 2.2, 2.3, etc.), or another new release can be created in a similar manner.

# The help Command

If the command

> **get  lang**

is now executed, the following message will be output:

```
ERROR [lang]: not an SCCS file (co1)
```

The code **co1** can be used with **help** to print a fuller explanation of the message.

> **help  co1**

This gives the following explanation of why **get lang** produced an error message:

```
co1:
"not an SCCS file"
A file that you think is an SCCS file
does not begin with the characters "s.".
```

**help** is useful whenever there is doubt about the meaning of almost any SCCS message.

# Delta Numbering

Think of deltas as the nodes of a tree in which the root node is the original version of the file. The root is normally named 1.1 and deltas (nodes) are named 1.2, 1.3, etc. The components of these SIDs are called release and level numbers, respectively. Thus, normal naming of new deltas proceeds by incrementing the level number. This is done automatically by SCCS whenever a delta is made.

Because the user may change the release number to indicate a major change, the release number then applies to all new deltas unless specifically changed again. Thus, the evolution of a particular file could be represented by Figure 14-1.

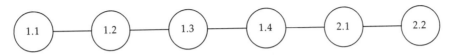

Figure 14-1: Evolution of an SCCS File

---

This is the normal sequential development of an SCCS file, with each delta dependent on the preceding deltas. Such a structure is called the trunk of an SCCS tree.

There are situations that require branching an SCCS tree. That is, changes are planned to a given delta that will not be dependent on all previous deltas. For example, consider a program in production use at version 1.3 and for which development work on release 2 is already in progress. Release 2 may already have a delta in progress as shown in Figure 14-1. Assume that a production user reports a problem in version 1.3 that cannot wait to be repaired in release 2. The changes necessary to repair the trouble will be applied as a delta to version 1.3 (the version in production use). This creates a new version that will then be released to the user but will not affect the changes being applied for release 2 (i.e., deltas 1.4, 2.1, 2.2, etc.). This new delta is the first node of a new branch of the tree.

Branch delta names always have four SID components: the same release number and level number as the trunk delta, plus a branch number and sequence number. The format is as follows:

*release.level.branch.sequence*

The branch number of the first delta branching off any trunk delta is always 1, and its sequence number is also 1. For example, the full SID for a delta branching off trunk delta 1.3 will be 1.3.1.1. As other deltas on that same branch are created, only the sequence number changes: 1.3.1.2, 1.3.1.3, etc. This is shown in Figure 14-2.

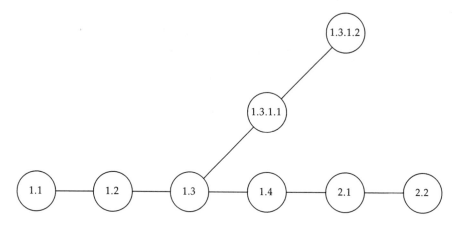

Figure 14-2: Tree Structure with Branch Deltas

The branch number is incremented only when a delta is created that starts a new branch off an existing branch, as shown in Figure 14-3. As this secondary branch develops, the sequence numbers of its deltas are incremented (1.3.2.1, 1.3.2.2, etc.), but the secondary branch number remains the same.

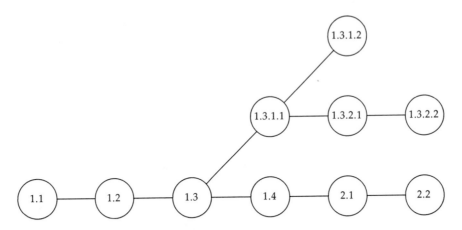

Figure 14-3: Extended Branching Concept

The concept of branching may be extended to any delta in the tree, and the numbering of the resulting deltas proceeds as shown above. SCCS allows the generation of complex tree structures. Although this capability has been provided for certain specialized uses, the SCCS tree should be kept as simple as possible. Comprehension of its structure becomes difficult as the tree becomes complex.

# SCCS Command Conventions

SCCS commands accept two types of arguments:

- keyletters
- filenames

Keyletters are options that begin with a minus sign, −, followed by a lowercase letter and, in some cases, a value.

File and/or directory names specify the file(s) the command is to process. Naming a directory is equivalent to naming all the SCCS files within the directory. Non-SCCS files and unreadable files (because of permission modes via **chmod**(1)) in the named directories are silently ignored.

In general, filename arguments may not begin with a minus sign. If a filename of − (a lone minus sign) is specified, the command will read the standard input (usually your terminal) for lines and take each line as the name of an SCCS file to be processed. The standard input is read until end-of-file. This feature is often used in pipelines with, for example, the commands **find**(1) or **ls**(1).

Keyletters are processed before filenames. Therefore, the placement of keyletters is arbitrary—that is, they may be interspersed with filenames. Filenames, however, are processed left to right. Somewhat different conventions apply to **help**(1), **what**(1), **sccsdiff**(1), and **val**(1), detailed later under "SCCS Commands."

Certain actions of various SCCS commands are controlled by flags appearing in SCCS files. Some of these flags will be discussed, but for a complete description see **admin**(1) in the *Programmer's Reference Manual*.

The distinction between real user (see **passwd**(1)) and effective user will be of concern in discussing various actions of SCCS commands. For now, assume that the real and effective users are the same—the person logged into the UNIX system.

# x.files and z.files

All SCCS commands that modify an SCCS file do so by writing a copy called the "x.file." This is done to ensure that the SCCS file is not damaged if processing terminates abnormally. SCCS names the x.file by replacing the **s.** of the SCCS filename with **x.**. The x.file is created in the same directory as the SCCS file, given the same mode (see **chmod**(1)), and is owned by the effective user. When processing is complete, the old SCCS file is destroyed and the modified x.file is renamed (**x.** is relaced by **s.**) and becomes the new SCCS file.

To prevent simultaneous updates to an SCCS file, the same modifying commands also create a lock-file called the "z.file." SCCS forms its name by replacing the **s.** of the SCCS filename with a **z.** prefix. The z.file contains the process number of the command that creates it, and its existence prevents other commands from processing the SCCS file. The z.file is created with access permission mode 444 (read only) in the same directory as the SCCS file and is owned by the effective user. It exists only for the duration of the execution of the command that creates it.

In general, users can ignore x.files and z.files. They are useful only in the event of system crashes or similar situations.

# Error Messages

SCCS commands produce error messages on the diagnostic output in this format:

      ERROR [name-of-file-being-processed]: message text (code)

The code in parentheses can be used as an argument to the **help** command to obtain a further explanation of the message. Detection of a fatal error during the processing of a file causes the SCCS command to stop processing that file and proceed with the next file specified.

# SCCS Commands

This section describes the major features of the fourteen SCCS commands and their most common arguments. Full descriptions with details of all arguments are in the *Programmer's Reference Manual*.

Here is a quick-reference overview of the commands:

**get**    retrieves versions of SCCS files

**unget**    undoes the effect of a **get** −**e** prior to the file being **delta**ed

**delta**    applies deltas (changes) to SCCS files and creates new versions

**admin**    initializes SCCS files, manipulates their descriptive text, and controls delta creation rights

**prs**    prints portions of an SCCS file in user specified format

**sact**    prints information about files that are currently out for edit

**help**    gives explanations of error messages

**rmdel**    removes a delta from an SCCS file allows removal of deltas created by mistake

**cdc**    changes the commentary associated with a delta

**what**    searches any UNIX system file(s) for all occurrences of a special pattern and prints out what follows it useful in finding identifying information inserted by the **get** command

**sccsdiff**    shows differences between any two versions of an SCCS file

**comb**    combines consecutive deltas into one to reduce the size of an SCCS file

**val**    validates an SCCS file

**vc**    a filter that may be used for version control

# The get **Command**

The **get**(1) command creates a file that contains a specified version of an SCCS file. The version is retrieved by beginning with the initial version and then applying deltas, in order, until the desired version is obtained. The resulting file is called the "g.file." It is created in the current directory and is owned by the real user. The mode assigned to the g.file depends on how the **get** command is used.

The most common use of **get** is

> **get  s.abc**

which normally retrieves the latest version of file **abc** from the SCCS file tree trunk and produces (for example) on the standard output

```
1.3
67 lines
No id keywords (cm7)
```

meaning version 1.3 of file **s.abc** was retrieved (assuming 1.3 is the latest trunk delta), it has 67 lines of text, and no ID keywords were substituted in the file.

The generated g.file (file **abc**) is given access permission mode 444 (read only). This particular way of using **get** is intended to produce g.files only for inspection, compilation, etc. It is not intended for editing (making deltas).

When several files are specified, the same information is output for each one. For example,

> **get  s.abc  s.xyz**

produces

```
s.abc:
1.3
67 lines
No id keywords (cm7)

s.xyz:
1.7
85 lines
No id keywords (cm7)
```

## ID Keywords

In generating a g.file for compilation, it is useful to record the date and time of creation, the version retrieved, the module's name, etc. within the g.file. This information appears in a load module when one is eventually created. SCCS provides a convenient mechanism for doing this automatically. Identification (ID) keywords appearing anywhere in the generated file are replaced by appropriate values according to the definitions of those ID keywords. The format of an ID keyword is an uppercase letter enclosed by percent signs, %. For example,

%I%

is the ID keyword replaced by the SID of the retrieved version of a file. Similarly, %H% and %M% are the names of the g.file. Thus, executing **get** on an SCCS file that contains the PL/I declaration,

DCL ID CHAR(100) VAR INIT('%M% %I% %H%');

gives (for example) the following:

DCL ID CHAR(100) VAR INIT('MODNAME 2.3 07/18/85');

When no ID keywords are substituted by **get**, the following message is issued:

No id keywords (cm7)

This message is normally treated as a warning by **get** although the presence of the **i** flag in the SCCS file causes it to be treated as an error. For a complete list of the approximately twenty ID keywords provided, see **get**(1) in the *Programmer's Reference Manual*.

## Retrieval of Different Versions

The version of an SCCS file **get** retrieves is the most recently created delta of the highest numbered trunk release. However, any other version can be retrieved with **get** −r by specifying the version's SID. Thus,

get −r1.3 s.abc

retrieves version 1.3 of file **s.abc** and produces (for example) on the standard output

1.3
64 lines

A branch delta may be retrieved similarly,

> **get** −r1.5.2.3  **s.abc**

which produces (for example) on the standard output

```
1.5.2.3
234 lines
```

When a SID is specified and the particular version does not exist in the SCCS file, an error message results.

Omitting the level number, as in

> **get** −r3  **s.abc**

causes retrieval of the trunk delta with the highest level number within the given release. Thus, the above command might output,

```
3.7
213 lines
```

If the given release does not exist, **get** retrieves the trunk delta with the highest level number within the highest-numbered existing release that is lower than the given release. For example, assume release 9 does not exist in file **s.abc** and release 7 is the highest-numbered release below 9. Executing

> **get** −r9  **s.abc**

might produce

```
7.6
420 lines
```

which indicates that trunk delta 7.6 is the latest version of file **s.abc** below release 9. Similarly, omitting the sequence number, as in

> **get** −r4.3.2  **s.abc**

results in the retrieval of the branch delta with the highest sequence number on the given branch. (If the given branch does not exist, an error message results.) This might result in the following output:

```
4.3.2.8
89 lines
```

get −t will retrieve the latest (top) version of a particular release when no −r is used or when its value is simply a release number. The latest version is the delta produced most recently, independent of its location on the SCCS file tree. Thus, if the most recent delta in release 3 is 3.5,

> get −r3 −t s.abc

might produce

> 3.5
> 59 lines

However, if branch delta 3.2.1.5 were the latest delta (created after delta 3.5), the same command might produce

> 3.2.1.5
> 46 lines

## Retrieval With Intent to Make a Delta

get −e indicates an intent to make a delta. First, get checks the following.

1.  The user list to determine if the login name or group ID of the person executing get is present. The login name or group ID must be present for the user to be allowed to make deltas. (See "The admin Command" for a discussion of making user lists.)

2.  The release number (R) of the version being retrieved satisfies the relation

    > floor is less than or equal to R, which is
    > less than or equal to ceiling

    to determine if the release being accessed is a protected release. The floor and ceiling are flags in the SCCS file representing start and end of range.

3.  The R is not locked against editing. The lock is a flag in the SCCS file.

4.  Whether multiple concurrent edits are allowed for the SCCS file by the j flag in the SCCS file.

A failure of any of the first three conditions causes the processing of the corresponding SCCS file to terminate.

If the above checks succeed, **get** −**e** causes the creation of a g.file in the current directory with mode 644 (readable by everyone, writable only by the owner) owned by the real user. If a writable g.file already exists, **get** terminates with an error. This is to prevent inadvertent destruction of a g.file being edited for the purpose of making a delta.

Any ID keywords appearing in the g.file are not substituted by **get** −**e** because the generated g.file is subsequently used to create another delta. Replacement of ID keywords causes them to be permanently changed in the SCCS file. Because of this, **get** does not need to check for their presence in the g.file. Thus, the message

```
No id keywords (cm7)
```

is never output when **get** −**e** is used.

In addition, **get** −**e** causes the creation (or updating) of a p.file that is used to pass information to the **delta** command.

The following

**get** −**e** **s.abc**

produces (for example) on the standard output

```
1.3
new delta 1.4
67 lines
```

## Undoing a get −e

There may be times when a file is retrieved for editing in error; there is really no editing that needs to be done at this time. In such cases, the **unget** command can be used to cancel the delta reservation that was set up.

## Additional get Options

If **get** −**r** and/or −**t** are used together with −**e**, the version retrieved for editing is the one specified with −**r** and/or −**t**.

get −i and −x are used to specify a list (see **get**(1) in the *Programmer's Reference Manual* for the syntax of such a list) of deltas to be included and excluded, respectively. Including a delta means forcing its changes to be included in the retrieved version. This is useful in applying the same changes to more than one version of the SCCS file. Excluding a delta means forcing it not to be applied. This may be used to undo the effects of a previous delta in the version to be created.

Whenever deltas are included or excluded, **get** checks for possible interference with other deltas. Two deltas can interfere, for example, when each one changes the same line of the retrieved g.file. A warning shows the range of lines within the retrieved g.file where the problem may exist. The user should examine the g.file to determine what the problem is and take appropriate corrective steps (e.g., edit the file).

 **get** −i and **get** −x should be used with extreme care.

**get** −k is used either to regenerate a g.file that may have been accidentally removed or ruined after **get** −e, or simply to generate a g.file in which the replacement of ID keywords has been suppressed. A g.file generated by **get** −k is identical to one produced by **get** −e, but no processing related to the p.file takes place.

## Concurrent Edits of Different SID

The ability to retrieve different versions of an SCCS file allows several deltas to be in progress at any given time. This means that several **get** −e commands may be executed on the same file as long as no two executions retrieve the same version (unless multiple concurrent edits are allowed).

The p.file created by **get** −e is named by automatic replacement of the SCCS filename's prefix **s.** with **p.**. It is created in the same directory as the SCCS file, given mode 644 (readable by everyone, writable only by the owner), and owned by the effective user. The p.file contains the following information for each delta that is still in progress:

- the SID of the retrieved version

- the SID given to the new delta when it is created

■ the login name of the real user executing **get**

The first execution of **get** −**e** causes the creation of a p.file for the corresponding SCCS file. Subsequent executions only update the p.file with a line containing the above information. Before updating, however, **get** checks to assure that no entry already in the p.file specifies that the SID of the version to be retrieved is already retrieved (unless multiple concurrent edits are allowed). If the check succeeds, the user is informed that other deltas are in progress and processing continues. If the check fails, an error message results.

It should be noted that concurrent executions of **get** must be carried out from different directories. Subsequent executions from the same directory will attempt to overwrite the g.file, which is an SCCS error condition. In practice, this problem does not arise since each user normally has a different working directory. See "Protection" under "SCCS Files" for a discussion of how different users are permitted to use SCCS commands on the same files.

Figure 14-4 shows the possible SID components a user can specify with **get** (left-most column), the version that will then be retrieved by **get**, and the resulting SID for the delta, which **delta** will create (right-most column).

| SID Specified in get* | −b Key-Letter Used† | Other Conditions | SID Retrieved by get | SID of Delta To be Created by delta |
|---|---|---|---|---|
| none‡ | no | R defaults to mR | mR.mL | mR.(mL+1) |
| none‡ | yes | R defaults to mR | mR.mL | mR.mL.(mB+1) |
| R | no | R > mR | mR.mL | R.1§ |
| R | no | R = mR | mR.mL | mR.(mL+1) |
| R | yes | R > mR | mR.mL | mR.mL.(mB+1).1 |
| R | yes | R = mR | mR.mL | mR.mL.(mB+1).1 |
| R | — | R < mR and R does not exist | hR.mL** | hR.mL.(mB+1).1 |
| R | — | Trunk successor number in release > R and R exists | R.mL | R.mL.(mB+1).1 |
| R.L. | no | No trunk successor | R.L | R.(L+1) |
| R.L. | yes | No trunk successor | R.L | R.L.(mB+1).1 |

Figure 14-4: Determination of New SID (sheet 1 of 2)

| SID Specified in get* | −b Key-Letter used† | Other Condition | SID Retrieved by get | SID of Delta to be Created by delta |
|---|---|---|---|---|
| R.L | − | Trunk successor in release ≥ R | R.L | R.L.(mS+1).1 |
| R.L.B | no | No branch successor | R.L.B.mS | R.L.B.(mS+1) |
| R.L.B | yes | No branch successor | R.L.B.mS | R.L.(mB+1).1 |
| R.L.B.S | no | No branch successor | R.L.B.S | R.L.B.(S+1) |
| R.L.B.S | yes | No branch successor | R.L.B.S | R.L.(mB+1).1 |
| R.L.B.S | − | Branch successor | R.L.B.S | R.L.(mB+1).1 |

Figure 14-4: Determination of New SID (sheet 2 of 2)

**Footnotes to Figure 14-4:**

\*     R, L, B, and S mean release, level, branch, and sequence numbers in the SID, and m means maximum. Thus, for example, R.mL means the maximum level number within release R. R.L.(mB+1).1 means the first sequence number on the new branch (i.e., maximum branch number plus 1) of level L within release R. Note that if the SID specified is R.L, R.L.B, or R.L.B.S, each of these specified SID numbers must exist.

†     The −b keyletter is effective only if the b flag (see **admin(1)**) is present in the file. An entry of − means irrelevant.

‡   This case applies if the **d** (default SID) flag is not present.  If the **d** flag is present in the file, the SID is interpreted as if specified on the command line.  Thus, one of the other cases in this figure applies.

§   This is used to force the creation of the first delta in a new release.

**   hR is the highest existing release that is lower than the specified, nonexistent release R.

## Concurrent Edits of Same SID

Under normal conditions, more than one **get** −**e** for the same SID is not permitted.  That is, **delta** must be executed before a subsequent **get** −**e** is executed on the same SID.

Multiple concurrent edits are allowed if the **j** flag is set in the SCCS file.  Thus:

```
get  −e  s.abc
1.1
new delta 1.2
5 lines
```

may be immediately followed by

```
get  −e  s.abc
1.1
new delta 1.1.1.1
5 lines
```

without an intervening **delta**.  In this case, a **delta** after the first **get** will produce delta 1.2 (assuming 1.1 is the most recent trunk delta), and a **delta** after the second **get** will produce delta 1.1.1.1.

## Keyletters That Affect Output

**get** −**p** causes the retrieved text to be written to the standard output rather than to a g.file.  In addition, all output normally directed to the standard output (such as the SID of the version retrieved and the number of lines retrieved) is directed instead to the diagnostic output.  **get** −**p** is used, for example, to create a g.file with an arbitrary name, as in

```
get  −p  s.abc  >  arbitrary-file-name
```

**get** −s suppresses output normally directed to the standard output, such as the SID of the retrieved version and the number of lines retrieved, but it does not affect messages normally directed to the diagnostic output. **get** −s is used to prevent nondiagnostic messages from appearing on the user's terminal and is often used with −**p** to pipe the output, as in

get −p −s s.abc | pg

**get** −**g** suppresses the retrieval of the text of an SCCS file. This is useful in several ways. For example, to verify a particular SID in an SCCS file

get −g −r4.3 s.abc

outputs the SID 4.3 if it exists in the SCCS file **s.abc** or an error message if it does not. Another use of **get** −**g** is in regenerating a p.file that may have been accidentally destroyed, as in

get −e −g s.abc

**get** −l causes SCCS to create an "l.file." It is named by replacing the **s.** of the SCCS filename with **l.**, created in the current directory with mode 444 (read only) and owned by the real user. The l.file contains a table (whose format is described under **get**(1) in the *Programmer's Reference Manual*) showing the deltas used in constructing a particular version of the SCCS file. For example

get −r2.3 −l s.abc

generates an l.file showing the deltas applied to retrieve version 2.3 of file **s.abc**. Specifying **p** with −**l**, as in

get −lp −r2.3 s.abc

causes the output to be written to the standard output rather than to the l.file. **get** −**g** can be used with −**l** to suppress the retrieval of the text.

**get** −**m** identifies the changes applied to an SCCS file. Each line of the g.file is preceded by the SID of the delta that caused the line to be inserted. The SID is separated from the text of the line by a tab character.

**get** −**n** causes each line of a g.file to be preceded by the value of the ID keyword and a tab character. This is most often used in a pipeline with **grep**(1). For example, to find all lines that match a given pattern in the latest version of each SCCS file in a directory, the following may be executed:

get −p −n −s *directory* | **grep** *pattern*

If both −**m** and −**n** are specified, each line of the generated g.file is preceded by the value of the **chap3.13** ID keyword and a tab (this is the effect of −**n**) and is followed by the line in the format produced by −**m**. Because use of −**m** and/or −**n** causes the contents of the g.file to be modified, such a g.file must not be used for creating a delta. Therefore, neither −**m** nor −**n** may be specified together with **get** −**e**.

 See **get**(1) in the *Programmer's Reference Manual* for a full description of additional keyletters.

## The delta **Command**

The **delta**(1) command is used to incorporate changes made to a g.file into the corresponding SCCS file—that is, to create a delta and, therefore, a new version of the file.

The **delta** command requires the existence of a p.file (created via **get** −**e**). It examines the p.file to verify the presence of an entry containing the user's login name. If none is found, an error message results.

**get** −**e** performs. If all checks are successful, **delta** determines what has been changed in the g.file by comparing it via **diff**(1) with its own temporary copy of the g.file as it was before editing. This temporary copy of the g.file is called the d.file and is obtained by performing an internal **get** on the SID specified in the p.file entry.

The required p.file entry is the one containing the login name of the user executing **delta**, because the user who retrieved the g.file must be the one who creates the delta. However, if the login name of the user appears in more than one entry, the same user has executed **get** −**e** more than once on the same SCCS file. Then, **delta** −**r** must be used to specify the SID that uniquely identifies the p.file entry. This entry is then the one used to obtain the SID of the delta to be created.

In practice, the most common use of **delta** is

**delta  s.abc**

which prompts

comments?

to which the user replies with a description of why the delta is being made, ending the reply with a newline character. The user's response may be up to 512 characters long with newlines (not intended to terminate the response) escaped by backslashes, \.

If the SCCS file has a **v** flag, **delta** first prompts with

MRs?

(Modification Requests), on the standard output. The standard input is then read for MR numbers, separated by blanks and/or tabs, ended with a newline character. A Modification Request is a formal way of asking for a correction or enhancement to the file. In some controlled environments where changes to source files are tracked, deltas are permitted only when initiated by a trouble report, change request, trouble ticket, etc., collectively called MRs. Recording MR numbers within deltas is a way of enforcing the rules of the change management process.

**delta** −**y** and/or −**m** can be used to enter comments and MR numbers on the command line rather than through the standard input, as in

**delta**  −**y**"*descriptive comment*"  −**m**"*mrnum1 mrnum2*"  **s.abc**

In this case, the prompts for comments and MRs are not printed, and the standard input is not read. These two keyletters are useful when **delta** is executed from within a shell procedure (see **sh**(1) in the *Programmer's Reference Manual*).

NOTE **delta** −**m** is allowed only if the SCCS file has a **v** flag.

No matter how comments and MR numbers are entered with **delta**, they are recorded as part of the entry for the delta being created. Also, they apply to all SCCS files specified with the **delta**.

If **delta** is used with more than one file argument and the first file named has a **v** flag, all files named must have this flag. Similarly, if the first file named does not have the flag, none of the files named may have it.

When **delta** processing is complete, the standard output displays the SID of the new delta (from the p.file) and the number of lines inserted, deleted, and left unchanged. For example:

```
1.4
14 inserted
7 deleted
345 unchanged
```

If line counts do not agree with the user's perception of the changes made to a g.file, it may be because there are various ways to describe a set of changes, especially if lines are moved around in the g.file. However, the total number of lines of the new delta (the number inserted plus the number left unchanged) should always agree with the number of lines in the edited g.file.

If you are in the process of making a delta, the **delta** command finds no ID keywords in the edited g.file, the message

```
No id keywords (cm7)
```

is issued after the prompts for commentary but before any other output. This means that any ID keywords that may have existed in the SCCS file have been replaced by their values or deleted during the editing process. This could be caused by making a delta from a g.file that was created by a **get** without −**e** (ID keywords are replaced by **get** in such a case). It could also be caused by accidentally deleting or changing ID keywords while editing the g.file. Or, it is possible that the file had no ID keywords. In any case, the delta will be created unless there is an **i** flag in the SCCS file (meaning the error should be treated as fatal), in which case the delta will not be created.

After the processing of an SCCS file is complete, the corresponding p.file entry is removed from the p.file. All updates to the p.file are made to a temporary copy, the "q.file," whose use is similar to the use of the x.file described earlier under "SCCS Command Conventions." If there is only one entry in the p.file, then the p.file itself is removed.

In addition, **delta** removes the edited g.file unless −**n** is specified. For example

**delta** −**n** **s.abc**

will keep the g.file after processing.

**delta** −s suppresses all output normally directed to the standard output, other than comments? and MRs?. Thus, use of −s with −y (and/or −m) causes **delta** to neither read the standard input nor write the standard output.

The differences between the g.file and the d.file constitute the delta and may be printed on the standard output by using **delta** −p. The format of this output is similar to that produced by **diff**(1).

## The admin Command

The **admin**(1) command is used to administer SCCS files—that is, to create new SCCS files and change the parameters of existing ones. When an SCCS file is created, its parameters are initialized by use of keyletters with **admin** or are assigned default values if no keyletters are supplied. The same keyletters are used to change the parameters of existing SCCS files.

Two keyletters are used in detecting and correcting corrupted SCCS files (see "Auditing" under "SCCS Files").

Newly created SCCS files are given access permission mode 444 (read only) and are owned by the effective user. Only a user with write permission in the directory containing the SCCS file may use the **admin** command on that file.

## Creation of SCCS Files

An SCCS file can be created by executing the command

**admin** −i**first** s.abc

in which the value **first** with −**i** is the name of a file from which the text of the initial delta of the SCCS file **s.abc** is to be taken. Omission of a value with −**i** means **admin** is to read the standard input for the text of the initial delta.

The command

**admin** −i s.abc < **first**

is equivalent to the previous example.

If the text of the initial delta does not contain ID keywords, the message

```
No id keywords (cm7)
```

is issued by **admin** as a warning. However, if the command also sets the **i** flag (not to be confused with the −**i** keyletter), the message is treated as an error and the SCCS file is not created. Only one SCCS file may be created at a time using **admin** −**i**.

**admin** −**r** is used to specify a release number for the first delta. Thus:

**admin** −**ifirst** −**r3 s.abc**

means the first delta should be named 3.1 rather than the normal 1.1. Because −**r** has meaning only when creating the first delta, its use is permitted only with −**i**.

## Inserting Commentary for the Initial Delta

When an SCCS file is created, the user may want to record why this was done. Comments (**admin** −**y**) and/or MR numbers (−**m**) can be entered in exactly the same way as a **delta**.

If −**y** is omitted, a comment line of the form

date and time created YY/MM/DD HH:MM:SS by logname

is automatically generated.

If it is desired to supply MR numbers (**admin** −**m**), the **v** flag must be set via −**f**. The **v** flag simply determines whether MR numbers must be supplied when using any SCCS command that modifies a delta commentary (see **sccsfile**(4) in the *Programmer's Reference Manual*) in the SCCS file. Thus:

**admin** −**ifirst** −**m***mrnum1* −**fv s.abc**

Note that −**y** and −**m** are effective only if a new SCCS file is being created.

## Initialization and Modification of SCCS File Parameters

Part of an SCCS file is reserved for descriptive text, usually a summary of the file's contents and purpose. It can be initialized or changed by using **admin** −**t**.

When an SCCS file is first being created and −**t** is used, it must be followed by the name of a file from which the descriptive text is to be taken. For example, the command admin −ifirst −tdesc s.abc

specifies that the descriptive text is to be taken from file **desc**.

When processing an existing SCCS file, −t specifies that the descriptive text (if any) currently in the file is to be replaced with the text in the named file. Thus:

admin −tdesc s.abc

specifies that the descriptive text of the SCCS file is to be replaced by the contents of **desc**. Omission of the filename after the −t keyletter as in

admin −t s.abc

causes the removal of the descriptive text from the SCCS file.

The flags of an SCCS file may be initialized or changed by **admin −f**, or deleted via −**d**.

SCCS file flags are used to direct certain actions of the various commands. (See **admin**(1) in the *Programmer's Reference Manual* for a description of all the flags.) For example, the **i** flag specifies that a warning message (stating that there are no ID keywords contained in the SCCS file) should be treated as an error. The **d** (default SID) flag specifies the default version of the SCCS file to be retrieved by the **get** command.

**admin −f** is used to set flags and, if desired, their values. For example

admin −ifirst −fi −fm*modname* s.abc

sets the **i** and **m** (module name) flags. The value *modname* specified for the **m** flag is the value that the **get** command will use to replace the %M% ID keyword. (In the absence of the **m** flag, the name of the g.file is used as the replacement for the %M% ID keyword.) Several −**f** keyletters may be supplied on a single **admin**, and they may be used whether the command is creating a new SCCS file or processing an existing one.

**admin −d** is used to delete a flag from an existing SCCS file. As an example, the command

admin −dm s.abc

removes the **m** flag from the SCCS file. Several −**d** keyletters may be used with one **admin** and may be intermixed with −**f**.

SCCS files contain a list of login names and/or group IDs of users who are allowed to create deltas. This list is empty by default, allowing anyone to create deltas. To create a user list (or add to an existing one), **admin −a** is used. For example,

> **admin −axyz −awql −a1234 s.abc**

adds the login names **xyz** and **wql** and the group ID **1234** to the list. **admin −a** may be used whether creating a new SCCS file or processing an existing one.

> **admin −e** (erase) is used to remove login names or group IDs from the list.

# The prs Command

The **prs**(1) command is used to print all or part of an SCCS file on the standard output. If **prs −d** is used, the output will be in a format called data specification. Data specification is a string of SCCS file data keywords (not to be confused with **get** ID keywords) interspersed with optional user text.

Data keywords are replaced by appropriate values according to their definitions. For example,

> :I:

is defined as the data keyword replaced by the SID of a specified delta. Similarly, **:F:** is the data keyword for the SCCS filename currently being processed, and **:C:** is the comment line associated with a specified delta. All parts of an SCCS file have an associated data keyword. For a complete list, see **prs**(1) in the *Programmer's Reference Manual*.

There is no limit to the number of times a data keyword may appear in a data specification. Thus, for example,

> **prs −d":I: this is the top delta for :F: :I:" s.abc**

may produce on the standard output

> 2.1 this is the top delta for s.abc 2.1

Information may be obtained from a single delta by specifying its SID using **prs** −r. For example,

**prs** −d":F:: :I: comment line is: :C:" −r1.4 s.abc

may produce the following output:

s.abc: **1.4 comment line is:** THIS IS A COMMENT

If −r is not specified, the value of the SID defaults to the most recently created delta.

In addition, information from a range of deltas may be obtained with −l or −e. The use of **prs** −e substitutes data keywords for the SID designated via −r and all deltas created earlier, while **prs** −l substitutes data keywords for the SID designated via −r and all deltas created later. Thus, the command

**prs** −d:I: −r1.4 −e s.abc

may output

```
1.4
1.3
1.2.1.1
1.2
1.1
```

and the command

**prs** −d:I: −r1.4 −l s.abc

may produce

```
3.3
3.2
3.1
2.2.1.1
2.2
2.1
1.4
```

Substitution of data keywords for all deltas of the SCCS file may be obtained by specifying both −e and −l.

# The sact **Command**

**sact**(1) is like a special form of the **prs** command that produces a report about files that are out for edit. The command takes only one type of argument: a list of file or directory names. The report shows the SID of any file in the list that is out for edit, the SID of the impending delta, the login of the user who executed the **get** −e command, and the date and time the **get** −e was executed. It is a useful command for an administrator.

# The help **Command**

The **help**(1) command prints the syntax of SCCS commands and of messages that may appear on the user's terminal. Arguments to **help** are simply SCCS commands or the code numbers that appear in parentheses after SCCS messages. (If no argument is given, **help** prompts for one.) Explanatory information is printed on the standard output. If no information is found, an error message is printed. When more than one argument is used, each is processed independently, and an error resulting from one will not stop the processing of the others.

NOTE    There is no conflict between the **help**(1) command of SCCS and the UNIX system **help**(1) utilities. The installation procedure for each package checks for the prior existence of the other.

Explanatory information related to a command is a synopsis of the command. For example,

**help ge5 rmdel**

produces

```
ge5:
"nonexistent sid"
The specified sid does not exist in the
given file.
Check for typos.

rmdel:
  rmdel  -rSID  name  ...
```

# The rmdel Command

The **rmdel**(1) command allows removal of a delta from an SCCS file. Its use should be reserved for deltas in which incorrect global changes were made. The delta to be removed must be a leaf delta. That is, it must be the most recently created delta on its branch or on the trunk of the SCCS file tree. In Figure 14-3, only deltas 1.3.1.2, 1.3.2.2, and 2.2 can be removed. Only after they are removed can deltas 1.3.2.1 and 2.1 be removed.

To be allowed to remove a delta, the effective user must have write permission in the directory containing the SCCS file. In addition, the real user must be either the one who created the delta being removed or the owner of the SCCS file and its directory.

The −r keyletter is mandatory with **rmdel**. It is used to specify the complete SID of the delta to be removed. Thus,

>    **rmdel  −r2.3  s.abc**

specifies the removal of trunk delta 2.3.

Before removing the delta, **rmdel** checks that the release number (R) of the given SID satisfies the relation:

>    floor less than or equal to R less than or equal to ceiling

The **rmdel** command also checks the SID to make sure it is not for a version on which a **get** for editing has been executed and whose associated **delta** has not yet been made. In addition, the login name or group ID of the user must appear in the file's user list (or the user list must be empty). Also, the release specified cannot be locked against editing. That is, if the **l** flag is set (see **admin**(1) in the *Programmer's Reference Manual*), the release must not be contained in the list. If these conditions are not satisfied, processing is terminated, and the delta is not removed.

Once a specified delta has been removed, its type indicator in the delta table of the SCCS file is changed from D (delta) to R (removed).

# The cdc Command

The **cdc**(1) command is used to change the commentary made when the delta was created. It is similar to the **rmdel** command (e.g., −**r** and full SID are necessary), although the delta need not be a leaf delta. For example,

> **cdc −r3.4 s.abc**

specifies that the commentary of delta 3.4 is to be changed. New commentary is then prompted for as with **delta**.

The old commentary is kept, but it is preceded by a comment line indicating that it has been superseded, and the new commentary is entered ahead of the comment line. The inserted comment line records the login name of the user executing **cdc** and the time of its execution.

The **cdc** command also allows for the insertion of new and deletion of old ("!" prefix) MR numbers. Thus,

> **cdc −r1.4 s.abc**
> MRs? **mrnum3 !mrnum1**　　　　　*(The MRs? prompt appears only*
> 　　　　　　　　　　　　　　　　*if the v flag has been set.)*
> comments? **deleted wrong MR number and inserted correct MR number**

inserts **mrnum3** and deletes **mrnum1** for delta 1.4.

An MR (Modification Request) is described above under the **delta** command.

# The what Command

The **what**(1) command is used to find identifying information within any UNIX file whose name is given as an argument. No keyletters are accepted. The **what** command searches the given file(s) for all occurrences of the string **@(#)**, which is the replacement for the %Z% ID keyword (see **get**(1)). It prints on the standard output whatever follows the string until the first double quote, ", greater than, >, backslash, \, newline, or nonprinting NUL character.

For example, if an SCCS file called **s.prog.c** (a C language program) contains the following line:

```
char  id[ ]= "%W%";
```

and the command

> **get  −r3.4  s.prog.c**

is used, the resulting g.file is compiled to produce **prog.o** and **a.out**. Then, the command

> **what  prog.c  prog.o  a.out**

produces

```
prog.c:
  prog.c:  3.4
prog.o:
  prog.c:  3.4
a.out:
  prog.c:  3.4
```

The string searched for by **what** need not be inserted via an ID keyword of **get**; it may be inserted in any convenient manner.

# The sccsdiff Command

The **sccsdiff**(1) command determines (and prints on the standard output) the differences between any two versions of an SCCS file. The versions to be compared are specified with **sccsdiff** −**r** in the same way as with **get** −**r**. SID numbers must be specified as the first two arguments. Any following keyletters are interpreted as arguments to the **pr**(1) command (which prints the differences) and must appear before any filenames. The SCCS file(s) to be processed are named last. Directory names and a name of − (a lone minus sign) are not acceptable to **sccsdiff**.

The following is an example of the format of **sccsdiff**:

    **sccsdiff** −**r3.4** −**r5.6** **s.abc**

The differences are printed the same way as by **diff**(1).

# The comb Command

The **comb**(1) command lets the user try to reduce the size of an SCCS file. It generates a shell procedure (see **sh**(1) in the *Programmer's Reference Manual*) on the standard output, which reconstructs the file by discarding unwanted deltas and combining other specified deltas. (It is not recommended that **comb** be used as a matter of routine.)

In the absence of any keyletters, **comb** preserves only leaf deltas and the minimum number of ancestor deltas necessary to preserve the shape of an SCCS tree. The effect of this is to eliminate middle deltas on the trunk and on all branches of the tree. Thus, in Figure 14-3, deltas 1.2, 1.3.2.1, 1.4, and 2.1 would be eliminated.

Some of the keyletters used with this command are:

**comb** −**s**   This option generates a shell procedure that produces a report of the percentage space (if any) the user will save. This is often useful as an advance step.

**comb** −**p**   This option is used to specify the oldest delta the user wants preserved.

comb −c   This option is used to specify a list (see **get**(1) in the *Programmer's Reference Manual* for its syntax) of deltas the user wants preserved. All other deltas will be discarded.

The shell procedure generated by **comb** is not guaranteed to save space. A reconstructed file may even be larger than the original. Note, too, that the shape of an SCCS file tree may be altered by the reconstruction process.

## The val Command

The **val**(1) command is used to determine whether a file is an SCCS file meeting the characteristics specified by certain keyletters. It checks for the existence of a particular delta when the SID for that delta is specified with −**r**.

The string following −**y** or −**m** is used to check the value set by the **t** or **m** flag, respectively. See **admin**(1) in the *Programmer's Reference Manual* for descriptions of these flags.

The **val** command treats the special argument − differently from other SCCS commands. It allows **val** to read the argument list from the standard input instead of from the command line, and the standard input is read until an end-of-file (CTRL-D) is entered. This permits one **val** command with different values for keyletters and file arguments. For example,

     val − −yc −mabc  s.abc −mxyz  −ypl1  s.xyz

first checks if file **s.abc** has a value **c** for its type flag and value **abc** for the module name flag. Once this is done, **val** processes the remaining file, in this case **s.xyz**.

The **val** command returns an 8-bit code. Each bit set shows a specific error (see **val**(1) for a description of errors and codes). In addition, an appropriate diagnostic is printed unless suppressed by −**s**. A return code of 0 means all files met the characteristics specified.

## The vc **Command**

The **vc**(1) command is an **awk**-like tool used for version control of sets of files. While it is distributed as part of the SCCS package, it does not require the files it operates on to be under SCCS control. A complete description of **vc** may be found in the *Programmer's Reference Manual*.

# SCCS Files

This section covers protection mechanisms used by SCCS, the format of SCCS files, and the recommended procedures for auditing SCCS files.

## Protection

SCCS relies on the capabilities of the UNIX system for most of the protection mechanisms required to prevent unauthorized changes to SCCS files—that is, changes by non-SCCS commands. Protection features provided directly by SCCS are the release lock flag, the release floor and ceiling flags, and the user list.

Files created by the **admin** command are given access permission mode 444 (read only). This mode should remain unchanged because it prevents modification of SCCS files by non-SCCS commands. Directories containing SCCS files should be given mode 755, which allows only the owner of the directory to modify it.

SCCS files should be kept in directories that contain only SCCS files and any temporary files created by SCCS commands. This simplifies their protection and auditing. The contents of directories should be logical groupings—subsystems of the same large project, for example.

SCCS files should have only one link (name) because commands that modify them do so by creating a copy of the file (the x.file; see "SCCS Command Conventions"). When processing is done, the old file is automatically removed and the x.file renamed (**s.** prefix). If the old file had additional links, this breaks them. Then, rather than process such files, SCCS commands will produce an error message.

When only one person uses SCCS, the real and effective user IDs are the same; and the user ID owns the directories containing SCCS files. Therefore, SCCS may be used directly without any preliminary preparation.

When several users with unique user IDs are assigned SCCS responsibilities (e.g., on large development projects), one user—that is, one user ID—must be chosen as the owner of the SCCS files. This person will administer the files (e.g. use the **admin** command) and will be SCCS administrator for the project. Because other users do not have the same privileges and permissions as the SCCS administrator, they are not able to execute directly those commands that require write permission in the directory containing the SCCS files. Therefore, a project-dependent program is required to provide an interface to the **get**, **delta**, and, if desired, **rmdel** and **cdc** commands.

The interface program must be owned by the SCCS administrator and must have the set user ID on execution bit on (see **chmod**(1) in the *User's Reference Manual*). This assures that the effective user ID is the user ID of the SCCS administrator. With the privileges of the interface program during command execution, the owner of an SCCS file can modify it at will. Other users whose login names or group IDs are in the user list for that file (but are not the owner) are given the necessary permissions only for the duration of the execution of the interface program. Thus, they may modify SCCS only with **delta** and, possibly, **rmdel** and **cdc**.

A project-dependent interface program, as its name implies, can be custom built for each project. Its creation is discussed later under "An SCCS Interface Program."

## Formatting

SCCS files are composed of lines of ASCII text arranged in six parts as follows:

Checksum           a line containing the logical sum of all the characters of the file (not including the checksum itself)

Delta Table        information about each delta, such as type, SID, date and time of creation, and commentary

User Names         list of login names and/or group IDs of users who are allowed to modify the file by adding or removing deltas

Flags              indicators that control certain actions of SCCS commands

Descriptive Text   usually a summary of the contents and purpose of the file

Body               the text administered by SCCS, intermixed with internal SCCS control lines

Details on these file sections may be found in **sccsfile**(4). The checksum is discussed below under "Auditing."

Since SCCS files are ASCII files they can be processed by non-SCCS commands like **ed**(1), **grep**(1), and **cat**(1). This is convenient when an SCCS file must be modified manually (e.g., a delta's time and date were recorded incorrectly because the system clock was set incorrectly), or when a user wants simply to look at the file.

 Extreme care should be exercised when modifying SCCS files with non-SCCS commands.

## Auditing

When a system or hardware malfunction destroys an SCCS file, any command will issue an error message. Commands also use the checksum stored in an SCCS file to determine whether the file has been corrupted since it was last accessed (possibly by having lost one or more blocks or by having been modified with **ed**(1)). No SCCS command will process a corrupted SCCS file except the **admin** command with −h or −z, as described below.

SCCS files should be audited for possible corruptions on a regular basis. The simplest and fastest way to do an audit is to use **admin** −h and specify all SCCS files:

> **admin** −h **s.***file1* **s.***file2* ...
>     or
> **admin** −h *directory1 directory2* ...

If the new checksum of any file is not equal to the checksum in the first line of that file, the message

```
corrupted file (co6)
```

is produced for that file. The process continues until all specified files have been examined. When examining directories (as in the second example above), the checksum process will not detect missing files. A simple way to learn whether files are missing from a directory is to execute the **ls**(1) command periodically, and compare the outputs. Any file whose name appeared in a previous output but not in the current one no longer exists.

When a file has been corrupted, the way to restore it depends on the extent of the corruption. If damage is extensive, the best solution is to contact the local UNIX system operations group and request that the file be restored from a backup copy. If the damage is minor, repair through editing may be possible. After such a repair, the **admin** command must be executed:

>   **admin** −**z** s.*file*

The purpose of this is to recompute the checksum and bring it into agreement with the contents of the file. After this command is executed, any corruption that existed in the file will no longer be detectable.

# CHAPTER 15: sdb—THE SYMBOLIC DEBUGGER

## Introduction

This chapter describes the symbolic debugger, **sdb**(1), as implemented for C language and Fortran 77 programs on the UNIX operating system. The **sdb** program is useful both for examining core images of aborted programs and for providing an environment in which execution of a program can be monitored and controlled.

The **sdb** program allows interaction with a debugged program at the source language level. When debugging a core image from an aborted program, **sdb** reports which line in the source program caused the error and allows all variables to be accessed symbolically and to be displayed in the correct format.

When executing, breakpoints may be placed at selected statements or the program may be single stepped on a line-by-line basis. To facilitate specification of lines in the program without a source listing, **sdb** provides a mechanism for examining the source text. Procedures may be called directly from the debugger. This feature is useful both for testing individual procedures and for calling user-provided routines, which provide formatted printouts of structured data.

# Using sdb

In order to use **sdb** to its full capabilities, it is necessary to compile the source program with the −**g** option. This causes the compiler to generate additional information about the variables and statements of the compiled program. When the −**g** option has been specified, **sdb** can be used to obtain a trace of the called functions at the time of the abort and interactively display the values of variables.

A typical sequence of shell commands for debugging a core image is

```
cc −g prgm.c −o prgm
prgm
Bus error - core dumped
sdb prgm
main:25:     x[i] = 0;
*
```

The program **prgm** was compiled with the −**g** option and then executed. An error occurred, which caused a core dump. The **sdb** program is then invoked to examine the core dump to determine the cause of the error. It reports that the bus error occurred in function **main** at line 25 (line numbers are always relative to the beginning of the file) and outputs the source text of the offending line. The **sdb** program then prompts the user with an *, which shows that it is waiting for a command.

It is useful to know that **sdb** has a notion of current function and current line. In this example, they are initially set to **main** and 25, respectively.

Here **sdb** was called with one argument, **prgm**. In general, it takes three arguments on the command line. The first is the name of the executable file that is to be debugged; it defaults to **a.out** when not specified. The second is the name of the core file, defaulting to **core**; and the third is the list of the directories (separated by colons) containing the source of the program being debugged. The default is the current working directory. In the example, the second and third arguments defaulted to the correct values, so only the first was specified.

If the error occurred in a function that was not compiled with the −**g** option, **sdb** prints the function name and the address at which the error occurred. The current line and function are set to the first executable line in **main**. If **main** was not compiled with the −**g** option, **sdb** will print an error message, but debugging can continue for those routines that were compiled with the −**g** option.

Figure 15-1 at the end of the chapter, shows a more extensive example of **sdb** use.

## Printing a Stack Trace

It is often useful to obtain a listing of the function calls that led to the error. This is obtained with the **t** command. For example:

```
*t
sub(x=2,y=3)        [prgm.c:25]
inter(i=16012)      [prgm.c:96]
main(argc=1,argv=0x7fffff54,envp=0x7fffff5c) [prgm.c:15]
```

This indicates that the program was stopped within the function **sub** at line 25 in file **prgm.c**. The **sub** function was called with the arguments **x**=2 and **y**=3 from **inter** at line 96. The **inter** function was called from **main** at line 15. The **main** function is always called by a startup routine with three arguments often referred to as **argc**, **argv**, and **envp**. Note that **argv** and **envp** are pointers, so their values are printed in hexadecimal.

## Examining Variables

The **sdb** program can be used to display variables in the stopped program. Variables are displayed by typing their name followed by a slash, so

```
*errflag/
```

causes **sdb** to display the value of variable **errflag**. Unless otherwise specified, variables are assumed to be either local to or accessible from the current function. To specify a different function, use the form

```
*sub:i/
```

to display variable **i** in function **sub**. FORTRAN 77 users can specify a common block variable in the same manner, provided it is on the call stack.

The **sdb** program supports a limited form of pattern matching for variable and function names. The symbol ∗ is used to match any sequence of characters of a variable name and **?** to match any single character. Consider the following commands

```
*x*/
*sub:y?/
**/
```

The first prints the values of all variables beginning with **x**, the second prints the values of all two letter variables in function **sub** beginning with **y**, and the last prints all variables. In the first and last examples, only variables accessible from the current function are printed. The command

```
**:*/
```

displays the variables for each function on the call stack.

The **sdb** program normally displays the variable in a format determined by its type as declared in the source program. To request a different format, a specifier is placed after the slash. The specifier consists of an optional length specification followed by the format. The length specifiers are:

**b**  one byte

**h**  two bytes (half word)

**l**  four bytes (long word)

The length specifiers are effective only with the formats **d**, **o**, **x**, and **u**. If no length is specified, the word length of the host machine is used. A number can be used with the **s** or **a** formats to control the number of characters printed. The **s** and **a** formats normally print characters until either a null is reached or 128 characters have been printed. The number specifies exactly how many characters should be printed.

There are a number of format specifiers available:

**c**  character

**d**  decimal

**u**  decimal unsigned

**o**  octal

**x**  hexadecimal

**f**  32-bit single-precision floating point

**g**  64-bit double-precision floating point

**s**  Assume variable is a string pointer and print characters starting at the address pointed to by the variable until a null is reached.

**a**  Print characters starting at the variable's address until a null is reached.

**p**  Pointer to function.

**i**  Interpret as a machine-language instruction.

For example, the variable **i** can be displayed with

```
*i/x
```

which prints out the value of **i** in hexadecimal.

**sdb** also knows about structures, arrays, and pointers so that all of the following commands work.

```
*array[2][3]/
*sym.id/
*psym->usage/
*xsym[20].p->usage/
```

The only restriction is that array subscripts must be numbers.  Note that as a special case:

```
*psym[0]
```

displays the structure pointed to by **psym** in decimal.

Core locations can also be displayed by specifying their absolute addresses.  The command

```
*1024/
```

displays location 1024 in decimal.  As in C language, numbers may also be specified in octal or hexadecimal so the above command is equivalent to both

```
*02000/
```

and

```
*0x400/
```

It is possible to mix numbers and variables so that

```
*1000.x/
```

refers to an element of a structure starting at address 1000, and

    *1000—>x/

refers to an element of a structure whose address is at 1000.  For commands
of the type *1000.x/ and *1000—>x/, the **sdb** program uses the structure
template of the last structured referenced.

    The address of a variable is printed with =, so

    *i=

displays the address of **i**.  Another feature whose usefulness will become
apparent later is the command

    *./

which redisplays the last variable typed.


# Source File Display and Manipulation

    The **sdb** program has been designed to make it easy to debug a program
without constant reference to a current source listing.  Facilities are provided
that perform context searches within the source files of the program being
debugged and that display selected portions of the source files.  The commands are similar to those of the UNIX system text editor **ed**(1).  Like the
editor, **sdb** has a notion of current file and line within the current file.  **sdb**
also knows how the lines of a file are partitioned into functions, so it also has
a notion of current function.  As noted in other parts of this document, the
current function is used by a number of **sdb** commands.

## Displaying the Source File

    Four commands exist for displaying lines in the source file.  They are
useful for perusing the source program and for determining the context of the
current line.  The commands are:

| | |
|---|---|
| **p** | Prints the current line. |
| **w** | Window; prints a window of ten lines around the current line. |
| **z** | Prints ten lines starting at the current line.  Advances the current line by ten. |
| **control-d** | Scrolls; prints the next ten lines and advances the current line by ten.  This command is used to cleanly display long seg-ments of the program. |

When a line from a file is printed, it is preceded by its line number. This not only gives an indication of its relative position in the file, but it is also used as input by some **sdb** commands.

## Changing the Current Source File or Function

The **e** command is used to change the current source file. Either of the forms

```
*e function
*e file.c
```

may be used. The first causes the file containing the named function to become the current file, and the current line becomes the first line of the function. The other form causes the named file to become current. In this case, the current line is set to the first line of the named file. Finally, an **e** command with no argument causes the current function and file named to be printed.

## Changing the Current Line in the Source File

The **z** and **control-d** commands have a side effect of changing the current line in the source file. The following paragraphs describe other commands that change the current line.

There are two commands for searching for instances of regular expressions in source files. They are

```
*/regular expression/
*?regular expression?
```

The first command searches forward through the file for a line containing a string that matches the regular expression and the second searches backwards. The trailing / and **?** may be omitted from these commands. Regular expression matching is identical to that of **ed**(1).

The + and − commands may be used to move the current line forward or backward by a specified number of lines. Typing a new-line advances the current line by one, and typing a number causes that line to become the current line in the file. These commands may be combined with the display commands so that

```
*+15z
```

advances the current line by 15 and then prints ten lines.

# A Controlled Environment for Program Testing

One very useful feature of **sdb** is breakpoint debugging. After entering **sdb**, breakpoints can be set at certain lines in the source program. The program is then started with an **sdb** command. Execution of the program proceeds as normal until it is about to execute one of the lines at which a breakpoint has been set. The program stops and **sdb** reports the breakpoint where the program stopped. Now, **sdb** commands may be used to display the trace of function calls and the values of variables. If the user is satisfied the program is working correctly to this point, some breakpoints can be deleted and others set; then program execution may be continued from the point where it stopped.

A useful alternative to setting breakpoints is single stepping. **sdb** can be requested to execute the next line of the program and then stop. This feature is especially useful for testing new programs, so they can be verified on a statement-by-statement basis. If an attempt is made to single step through a function that has not been compiled with the −**g** option, execution proceeds until a statement in a function compiled with the −**g** option is reached. It is also possible to have the program execute one machine level instruction at a time. This is particularly useful when the program has not been compiled with the −**g** option.

## Setting and Deleting Breakpoints

Breakpoints can be set at any line in a function compiled with the −**g** option. The command format is:

```
*12b
*proc:12b
*proc:b
*b
```

The first form sets a breakpoint at line 12 in the current file. The line numbers are relative to the beginning of the file as printed by the source file display commands. The second form sets a breakpoint at line 12 of function **proc**, and the third sets a breakpoint at the first line of **proc**. The last sets a breakpoint at the current line.

Breakpoints are deleted similarly with the **d** command:

```
*12d
*proc: 12d
*proc:d
```

In addition, if the command **d** is given alone, the breakpoints are deleted interactively. Each breakpoint location is printed, and a line is read from the user. If the line begins with a **y** or **d**, the breakpoint is deleted.

A list of the current breakpoints is printed in response to a **B** command, and the **D** command deletes all breakpoints. It is sometimes desirable to have **sdb** automatically perform a sequence of commands at a breakpoint and then have execution continue. This is achieved with another form of the **b** command.

```
*12b t;x/
```

causes both a trace back and the value of $x$ to be printed each time execution gets to line 12. The **a** command is a variation of the above command. There are two forms:

```
*proc:a
*proc: 12a
```

The first prints the function name and its arguments each time it is called, and the second prints the source line each time it is about to be executed. For both forms of the **a** command, execution continues after the function name or source line is printed.

## Running the Program

The **r** command is used to begin program execution. It restarts the program as if it were invoked from the shell. The command

```
*r args
```

runs the program with the given arguments as if they had been typed on the shell command line. If no arguments are specified, then the arguments from the last execution of the program within **sdb** are used. To run a program with no arguments, use the **R** command.

After the program is started, execution continues until a breakpoint is encountered, a signal such as INTERRUPT or QUIT occurs, or the program terminates. In all cases after an appropriate message is printed, control returns to the user.

The **c** command may be used to continue execution of a stopped program. A line number may be specified, as in:

    *proc: 12c

This places a temporary breakpoint at the named line. The breakpoint is deleted when the **c** command finishes. There is also a **C** command that continues but passes the signal that stopped the program back to the program. This is useful for testing user-written signal handlers. Execution may be continued at a specified line with the **g** command. For example:

    *17 g

continues at line 17 of the current function. A use for this command is to avoid executing a section of code that is known to be bad. The user should not attempt to continue execution in a function different than that of the breakpoint.

The **s** command is used to run the program for a single statement. It is useful for slowly executing the program to examine its behavior in detail. An important alternative is the **S** command. This command is like the **s** command but does not stop within called functions. It is often used when one is confident that the called function works correctly but is interested in testing the calling routine.

The **i** command is used to run the program one machine level instruction at a time while ignoring the signal that stopped the program. Its uses are similar to the **s** command. There is also an **I** command that causes the program to execute one machine level instruction at a time, but also passes the signal that stopped the program back to the program.

## Calling Functions

It is possible to call any of the functions of the program from **sdb**. This feature is useful both for testing individual functions with different arguments and for calling a user-supplied function to print structured data. There are two ways to call a function:

    *proc(arg1, arg2, . . .)
    *proc(arg1, arg2, . . .)/m

The first simply executes the function. The second is intended for calling functions (it executes the function and prints the value that it returns). The value is printed in decimal unless some other format is specified by *m*. Arguments to functions may be integer, character or string constants, or variables that are accessible from the current function.

An unfortunate bug in the current implementation is that if a function is called when the program is not stopped at a breakpoint (such as when a core image is being debugged) all variables are initialized before the function is started. This makes it impossible to use a function that formats data from a dump.

## Machine Language Debugging

The **sdb** program has facilities for examining programs at the machine language level. It is possible to print the machine language statements associated with a line in the source and to place breakpoints at arbitrary addresses. The **sdb** program can also be used to display or modify the contents of the machine registers.

### Displaying Machine Language Statements

To display the machine language statements associated with line 25 in function **main**, use the command

        *main:25?

The **?** command is identical to the **/** command except that it displays from text space. The default format for printing text space is the **i** format, which interprets the machine language instruction. The **control-d** command may be used to print the next ten instructions.

Absolute addresses may be specified instead of line numbers by appending a : to them so that

        *0x1024:?

displays the contents of address 0x1024 in text space. Note that the command

        *0x1024?

displays the instruction corresponding to line 0x1024 in the current function. It is also possible to set or delete a breakpoint by specifying its absolute address;

        *0x1024:b

sets a breakpoint at address 0x1024.

### Manipulating Registers

The **x** command prints the values of all the registers. Also, individual registers may be named by appending a % sign to their name so that

    *r3%

displays the value of register **r3**.

## Other Commands

To exit **sdb**, use the **q** command.

The **!** command (when used immediately after the * prompt) is identical to that in **ed**(1) and is used to have the shell execute a command. The **!** can also be used to change the values of variables or registers when the program is stopped at a breakpoint. This is done with the command

    *variable!value
    *r3!value

which sets the variable or the named register to the given value. The value may be a number, character constant, register, or the name of another variable. If the variable is of type **float** or **double**, the value can also be a floating-point constant (specified according to the standard C language format).

## An sdb Session

An example of a debugging session using **sdb** is shown in Figure 15-1. Comments (preceded by a pound sign, **#**) have been added to help you see what is happening.

```
sdb myoptim - .:../common    # enter sdb command
Source path: .:../common
No core image
*window:b                    # set a breakpoint at start of window
0x80802462 (window:1459+2) b
*r < m.s > out.m.s           # run the program
Breakpoint at
0x80802462 in window:1459: window(size, func) register int size;
boolean(*func)(); {
*t                           # print stack trace
window(size=2,func=w2opt)    [optim.c:1459]
peep()    [peep.c:34]
pseudo(s=.def^Imain;^I.val^I.;^I.scl^I-1;^I.endef)    [local.c:483]
yylex()    [local.c:229]
main(argc=0,argv=0xc00201bc,-1073610300)    [optim.c:227]
```

Figure 15-1: Example of **sdb** Usage (Sheet 1 of 3)

```
*z                          # print 10 lines of source
1459: window(size, func) register int size; boolean (*func)(); {
1460:
1461:    extern NODE *initw();
1462:    register NODE *pl;
1463:    register int i;
1464:
1465:    TRACE(window);
1466:
1467:    /* find first window */
1468:
*s                          # step
window:1459: window(size, func) register int size; boolean (*func)(); {
*s                          # step
window:1465:    TRACE(window);
*s                          # step
window:1469:    wsize = size;
*s                          # step
window:1470:    if ((pl = initw(n0.forw)) == NULL)
*S                          # step through procedure call
window:1475:    for (opf = pf->back; ; opf = pf->back) {
*pl                         # show variable pl
0x80886b38
*x                          # print the register contents
  r0/ 0x80886b38       r1/ 0              r2/ 0x8088796c
  r3/ 0x80885830       r4/ 0xc0020470     r5/ 0xc00203f0
  r6/ 0xc0020478       r7/ 0x80886b38     r8/ 2
  ap/ 0xc00202dc       fp/ 0xc0020308     sp/ 0xc0020308
 psw/ 0x201f73         pc/ 0x808024b0
0x808024b0 (window:1475):       MOVW     0x80880d8c,%r0  [-0x7f77f274,%r0]
```

Figure 15-1: Example of **sdb** Usage (Sheet 2 of 3)

```
*pl[0]                        # dereference the pointer
pl[0].forw/ 0x80886b6c
pl[0].back/ 0x80886ac8
pl[0].ops[0]/ pushw
pl[0].uniqid/ 0
pl[0].op/ 123
pl[0].nlive/ 3588
pl[0].ndead/ 4096
*pl->forw[0]                  # dereference the pointer
pl->forw[0].forw/ 0x80886ca0
pl->forw[0].back/ 0x80886b38
pl->forw[0].ops[0]/ call
pl->forw[0].uniqid/ 0
pl->forw[0].op/ 9
pl->forw[0].nlive/ 3584
pl->forw[0].ndead/ 4099
*pl!pl->forw                  # replace pl with pl->forw
*pl                           # show pl
0x80886b6c
*c                            # continue
Breakpoint at
0x80802462 in window:1459: window(size, func) register int size;
boolean (*func)(); {
*s                            # step
window:1459: window(size, func) register int size; boolean (*func)(); {
*s                            # step
window:1465:    TRACE(window);
*size                         # show function argument size
3
*D                            # delete all breakpoints
All breakpoints deleted
*c                            # continue
Process terminated
*q                            # quit sdb
$
```

Figure 15-1: Example of **sdb** Usage (Sheet 3 of 3)

# CHAPTER 16: lint

## Introduction

The **lint** program examines C language source programs detecting a number of bugs and obscurities. It enforces the type rules of C language more strictly than the C compiler. It may also be used to enforce a number of portability restrictions involved in moving programs between different machines and/or operating systems. Another option detects a number of wasteful or error prone constructions, which nevertheless are legal. **lint** accepts multiple input files and library specifications and checks them for consistency.

# Usage

The **lint** command has the form:

**lint** [*options*] *files ... library-descriptors ...*

where *options* are optional flags to control **lint** checking and messages; *files* are the files to be checked which end with **.c** or **.ln**; and *library-descriptors* are the names of libraries to be used in checking the program.

The options that are currently supported by the **lint** command are:

**−a**    Suppress messages about assignments of long values to variables that are not long.

**−b**    Suppress messages about break statements that cannot be reached.

**−c**    Only check for intra-file bugs; leave external information in files suffixed with **.ln**.

**−h**    Do not apply heuristics (which attempt to detect bugs, improve style, and reduce waste).

**−n**    Do not check for compatibility with either the standard or the portable **lint** library.

**−o** *name*    Create a lint library from input files named **llib−l***name***.ln**.

**−p**    Attempt to check portability.

**−u**    Suppress messages about function and external variables used and not defined or defined and not used.

**−v**    Suppress messages about unused arguments in functions.

**−x**    Do not report variables referred to by external declarations but never used.

When more than one option is used, they should be combined into a single argument, such as **−ab** or **−xha**.

The names of files that contain C language programs should end with the suffix **.c**, which is mandatory for **lint** and the C compiler.

**lint** accepts certain arguments, such as:

  **−lm**

These arguments specify libraries that contain functions used in the C language program. The source code is tested for compatibility with these libraries. This is done by accessing library description files whose names are constructed from the library arguments. These files all begin with the comment:

  `/* LINTLIBRARY */`

which is followed by a series of dummy function definitions. The critical parts of these definitions are the declaration of the function return type, whether the dummy function returns a value, and the number and types of arguments to the function. The VARARGS and ARGSUSED comments can be used to specify features of the library functions. The next section, "**lint** Message Types," describes how it is done.

  **lint** library files are processed almost exactly like ordinary source files. The only difference is that functions which are defined in a library file but are not used in a source file do not result in messages. **lint** does not simulate a full library search algorithm and will print messages if the source files contain a redefinition of a library routine.

  By default, **lint** checks the programs it is given against a standard library file that contains descriptions of the programs that are normally loaded when a C language program is run. When the **−p** option is used, another file is checked containing descriptions of the standard library routines which are expected to be portable across various machines. The **−n** option can be used to suppress all library checking.

# lint Message Types

The following paragraphs describe the major categories of messages printed by **lint**.

## Unused Variables and Functions

As sets of programs evolve and develop, previously used variables and arguments to functions may become unused. It is not uncommon for external variables or even entire functions to become unnecessary and yet not be removed from the source. These types of errors rarely cause working programs to fail, but are a source of inefficiency and make programs harder to understand and change. Also, information about such unused variables and functions can occasionally serve to discover bugs.

**lint** prints messages about variables and functions which are defined but not otherwise mentioned, unless the message is suppressed by means of the −**u** or −**x** option.

Certain styles of programming may permit a function to be written with an interface where some of the function's arguments are optional. Such a function can be designed to accomplish a variety of tasks depending on which arguments are used. Normally **lint** prints messages about unused arguments; however, the −**v** option is available to suppress the printing of these messages. When −**v** is in effect, no messages are produced about unused arguments except for those arguments which are unused and also declared as register arguments. This can be considered an active (and preventable) waste of the register resources of the machine.

Messages about unused arguments can be suppressed for one function by adding the comment:

        /* ARGSUSED */

to the source code before the function. This has the effect of the −**v** option for only one function. Also, the comment:

        /* VARARGS */

can be used to suppress messages about variable number of arguments in calls to a function. The comment should be added before the function definition. In some cases, it is desirable to check the first several arguments and leave the later arguments unchecked. This can be done with a digit giving the number of arguments which should be checked. For example:

```
/* VARARGS2 */
```

will cause only the first two arguments to be checked.

When **lint** is applied to some but not all files out of a collection that are to be loaded together, it issues complaints about unused or undefined variables. This information is, of course, more distracting than helpful. Functions and variables that are defined may not be used; conversely, functions and variables defined elsewhere may be used. The −**u** option suppresses the spurious messages.

## Set/Used Information

**lint** attempts to detect cases where a variable is used before it is set. **lint** detects local variables (automatic and register storage classes) whose first use appears physically earlier in the input file than the first assignment to the variable. It assumes that taking the address of a variable constitutes a "use" since the actual use may occur at any later time, in a data dependent fashion.

The restriction to the physical appearance of variables in the file makes the algorithm very simple and quick to implement since the true flow of control need not be discovered. It does mean that **lint** can print error messages about program fragments that are legal, but these programs would probably be considered bad on stylistic grounds. Because static and external variables are initialized to zero, no meaningful information can be discovered about their uses. The **lint** program does deal with initialized automatic variables.

The set/used information also permits recognition of those local variables that are set and never used. These form a frequent source of inefficiencies and may also be symptomatic of bugs.

## Flow of Control

**lint** attempts to detect unreachable portions of a program. It will print messages about unlabeled statements immediately following **goto**, **break**, **continue**, or **return** statements. It attempts to detect loops that cannot be left at the bottom and to recognize the special cases **while(1)** and **for(;;)** as infinite loops. **lint** also prints messages about loops that cannot be entered at the top. Valid programs may have such loops, but they are considered to be bad style. If you do not want messages about unreached portions of the program, use the −**b** option.

**lint** has no way of detecting functions that are called and never return. Thus, a call to **exit** may cause unreachable code which **lint** does not detect. The most serious effects of this are in the determination of returned function values (see "Function Values"). If a particular place in the program is thought to be unreachable in a way that is not apparent to **lint**, the comment

```
/* NOTREACHED */
```

can be added to the source code at the appropriate place. This comment will inform **lint** that a portion of the program cannot be reached, and **lint** will not print a message about the unreachable portion.

Programs generated by **yacc** and especially **lex** may have hundreds of unreachable **break** statements, but messages about them are of little importance. There is typically nothing the user can do about them, and the resulting messages would clutter up the **lint** output. The recommendation is to invoke **lint** with the −**b** option when dealing with such input.

## Function Values

Sometimes functions return values that are never used. Sometimes programs incorrectly use function values that have never been returned. **lint** addresses this problem in a number of ways.

Locally, within a function definition, the appearance of both

```
return( expr );
```

and

```
return ;
```

statements is cause for alarm; **lint** will give the message

```
function name has return(e) and return
```

The most serious difficulty with this is detecting when a function return is implied by flow of control reaching the end of the function. This can be seen with a simple example:

```
f ( a ) {
        if ( a ) return ( 3 );
        g ();
        }
```

Notice that, if **a** tests false, **f** will call **g** and then return with no defined return value; this will trigger a message from **lint**. If **g**, like **exit**, never returns, the message will still be produced when in fact nothing is wrong. A comment

```
/*NOTREACHED*/
```

in the source code will cause the message to be suppressed. In practice, some potentially serious bugs have been discovered by this feature.

On a global scale, **lint** detects cases where a function returns a value that is sometimes or never used. When the value is never used, it may constitute an inefficiency in the function definition that can be overcome by specifying the function as being of type (void). For example:

```
(void) fprintf(stderr,"File busy. Try again later!\n");
```

When the value is sometimes unused, it may represent bad style (e.g., not testing for error conditions).

The opposite problem, using a function value when the function does not return one, is also detected. This is a serious problem.

# Type Checking

**lint** enforces the type checking rules of C language more strictly than the compilers do. The additional checking is in four major areas:

- across certain binary operators and implied assignments
- at the structure selection operators
- between the definition and uses of functions
- in the use of enumerations

There are a number of operators which have an implied balancing between types of the operands. The assignment, conditional ( **?:** ), and relational operators have this property. The argument of a **return** statement and expressions used in initialization suffer similar conversions. In these operations, **char**, **short**, **int**, **long**, **unsigned**, **float**, and **double** types may be freely intermixed. The types of pointers must agree exactly except that arrays of *x*s can, of course, be intermixed with pointers to *x*s.

The type checking rules also require that, in structure references, the left operand of the $->$ be a pointer to structure, the left operand of the . be a structure, and the right operand of these operators be a member of the structure implied by the left operand. Similar checking is done for references to unions.

Strict rules apply to function argument and return value matching. The types **float** and **double** may be freely matched, as may the types **char**, **short**, **int**, and **unsigned**. Also, pointers can be matched with the associated arrays. Aside from this, all actual arguments must agree in type with their declared counterparts.

With enumerations, checks are made that enumeration variables or members are not mixed with other types or other enumerations and that the only operations applied are =, initialization, ==, !=, and function arguments and return values.

If it is desired to turn off strict type checking for an expression, the comment

```
/* NOSTRICT */
```

should be added to the source code immediately before the expression. This comment will prevent strict type checking for only the next line in the program.

## Type Casts

The type cast feature in C language was introduced largely as an aid to producing more portable programs. Consider the assignment

```
p = 1 ;
```

where **p** is a character pointer. **lint** will print a message as a result of detecting this. Consider the assignment

```
p = (char *)1 ;
```

in which a cast has been used to convert the integer to a character pointer. The programmer obviously had a strong motivation for doing this and has clearly signaled his intentions. Nevertheless, **lint** will continue to print messages about this.

# Nonportable Character Use

On some systems, characters are signed quantities with a range from −128 to 127. On other C language implementations, characters take on only positive values. Thus, **lint** will print messages about certain comparisons and assignments as being illegal or nonportable. For example, the fragment

```
char c;
    . . .
if( (c = getchar( )) < 0 ) . . .
```

will work on one machine but will fail on machines where characters always take on positive values. The real solution is to declare c as an integer since **getchar** is actually returning integer values. In any case, **lint** will print the message

```
nonportable character comparison
```

A similar issue arises with bit fields. When assignments of constant values are made to bit fields, the field may be too small to hold the value. This is especially true because on some machines bit fields are considered as signed quantities. While it may seem logical to consider that a two-bit field declared of type **int** cannot hold the value 3, the problem disappears if the bit field is declared to have type **unsigned**

# Assignments of longs to ints

Bugs may arise from the assignment of **long** to an **int**, which will truncate the contents. This may happen in programs which have been incompletely converted to use **typedefs**. When a **typedef** variable is changed from **int** to **long**, the program can stop working because some intermediate results may be assigned to **ints**, which are truncated. The −**a** option can be used to suppress messages about the assignment of **long**s to **int**s.

## Strange Constructions

Several perfectly legal, but somewhat strange, constructions are detected by **lint**. The messages hopefully encourage better code quality, clearer style, and may even point out bugs. The −**h** option is used to suppress these checks. For example, in the statement

        *p++ ;

the * does nothing. This provokes the message

        null effect

from **lint**. The following program fragment:

        unsigned x ;
        if( x < 0 ) . . .

results in a test that will never succeed. Similarly, the test

        if( x > 0 ) . . .

is equivalent to

        if( x != 0 )

which may not be the intended action. **lint** will print the message

        degenerate unsigned comparison

in these cases. If a program contains something similar to

        if( 1 != 0 ) . . .

**lint** will print the message

        constant in conditional context

since the comparison of 1 with 0 gives a constant result.

Another construction detected by **lint** involves operator precedence. Bugs which arise from misunderstandings about the precedence of operators can be accentuated by spacing and formatting, making such bugs extremely hard to find. For example, the statements

        if( x&077 == 0 ) . . .

and

```
x<<2 + 40
```

probably do not do what was intended. The best solution is to parenthesize such expressions, and **lint** encourages this by an appropriate message.

## Old Syntax

Several forms of older syntax are now illegal. These fall into two classes: assignment operators and initialization.

The older forms of assignment operators (e.g., =+, =−, ...) could cause ambiguous expressions, such as:

```
a =−1 ;
```

which could be taken as either

```
a =− 1 ;
```

or

```
a = −1 ;
```

The situation is especially perplexing if this kind of ambiguity arises as the result of a macro substitution. The newer and preferred operators (e.g., +=, −=, ...) have no such ambiguities. To encourage the abandonment of the older forms, **lint** prints messages about these old-fashioned operators.

A similar issue arises with initialization. The older language allowed

```
int x 1 ;
```

to initialize *x* to 1. This also caused syntactic difficulties. For example, the initialization

```
int x ( −1 ) ;
```

looks somewhat like the beginning of a function definition:

```
int x ( y ) { . . .
```

and the compiler must read past *x* in order to determine the correct meaning. Again, the problem is even more perplexing when the initializer involves a macro. The current syntax places an equals sign between the variable and the initializer:

```
int x = −1 ;
```

This is free of any possible syntactic ambiguity.

## Pointer Alignment

Certain pointer assignments may be reasonable on some machines and illegal on others due entirely to alignment restrictions. **lint** tries to detect cases where pointers are assigned to other pointers and such alignment problems might arise. The message

        possible pointer alignment problem

results from this situation.


## Multiple Uses and Side Effects

In complicated expressions, the best order in which to evaluate subexpressions may be highly machine dependent. For example, on machines in which the stack runs backwards, function arguments will probably be best evaluated from right to left. On machines with a stack running forward, left to right seems most attractive. Function calls embedded as arguments of other functions may or may not be treated similarly to ordinary arguments. Similar issues arise with other operators that have side effects, such as the assignment operators and the increment and decrement operators.

In order that the efficiency of C language on a particular machine not be unduly compromised, the C language leaves the order of evaluation of complicated expressions up to the local compiler. In fact, the various C compilers have considerable differences in the order in which they will evaluate complicated expressions. In particular, if any variable is changed by a side effect and also used elsewhere in the same expression, the result is explicitly undefined.

**lint** checks for the important special case where a simple scalar variable is affected. For example, the statement

        a[i] = b[i++];

will cause **lint** to print the message

        warning: i evaluation order undefined

in order to call attention to this condition.

# CHAPTER 17: C LANGUAGE

## Introduction

This chapter contains a summary of the grammar and syntax rules of the C Programming Language. The implementation described is that found on the AT&T line of 3B Computers. A consistent attempt is made to point out where other implementations may differ.

# Lexical Conventions

There are six classes of tokens: identifiers, keywords, constants, string literals, operators, and other separators. Blanks, tabs, new-lines, and comments (collectively, "white space") as described below are ignored except as they serve to separate tokens. Some white space is required to separate otherwise adjacent identifiers, keywords, and constants.

If the input stream has been parsed into tokens up to a given character, the next token is taken to include the longest string of characters that could possibly constitute a token.

## Comments

The characters /* introduce a comment that terminates with the characters */. Comments do not nest.

## Identifiers (Names)

An identifier is a sequence of letters and digits. The first character must be a letter. The underscore (_) counts as a letter. Uppercase and lowercase letters are different. There is no limit on the length of a name. Other implementations may collapse case distinctions for external names, and may reduce the number of significant characters for both external and non-external names.

## Keywords

The following identifiers are reserved for use as keywords and may not be used otherwise:

| | | | | |
|---|---|---|---|---|
| asm | default | float | register | switch |
| auto | do | for | return | typedef |
| break | double | goto | short | union |
| case | else | if | sizeof | unsigned |
| char | enum | int | static | void |
| continue | external | long | struct | while |

Some implementations also reserve the word **fortran.**

# Constants

There are several kinds of constants. Each has a type; an introduction to types is given in "Storage Class and Type."

## Integer Constants

An integer constant consisting of a sequence of digits is taken to be octal if it begins with **0** (digit zero). An octal constant consists of the digits **0** through **7** only. A sequence of digits preceded by **0x** or **0X** (digit zero) is taken to be a hexadecimal integer. The hexadecimal digits include **a** or **A** through **f** or **F** with values 10 through 15. Otherwise, the integer constant is taken to be decimal. A decimal constant whose value exceeds the largest signed machine integer is taken to be **long**; an octal or hex constant that exceeds the largest unsigned machine integer is likewise taken to be **long**. Otherwise, integer constants are **int**.

## Explicit Long Constants

A decimal, octal, or hexadecimal integer constant immediately followed by **l** (letter ell) or **L** is a long constant. As discussed below, on AT&T 3B Computers integer and long values may be considered identical.

## Character Constants

A character constant is a character enclosed in single quotes, as in **'x'**. The value of a character constant is the numerical value of the character in the machine's character set. Certain nongraphic characters, the single quote (') and the backslash (\), may be represented according to the table of escape sequences shown in Figure 17-1:

```
new-line           NL (LF)   \n
horizontal tab     HT        \t
vertical tab       VT        \v
backspace          BS        \b
carriage return    CR        \r
form feed          FF        \f
backslash          \         \\
single quote       '         \'
bit pattern        ddd       \ddd
```

Figure 17-1: Escape Sequences for Nongraphic Characters

The escape \ddd consists of the backslash followed by 1, 2, or 3 octal digits that are taken to specify the value of the desired character. A special case of this construction is \0 (not followed by a digit), which indicates the ASCII character **NUL**. If the character following a backslash is not one of those specified, the behavior is undefined. An explicit new-line character is illegal in a character constant. The type of a character constant is **int**.

## Floating Constants

A floating constant consists of an integer part, a decimal point, a fraction part, an **e** or **E**, and an optionally signed integer exponent. The integer and fraction parts both consist of a sequence of digits. Either the integer part or the fraction part (not both) may be missing. Either the decimal point or the **e** and the exponent (not both) may be missing. Every floating constant has type **double**.

## Enumeration Constants

Names declared as enumerators (see "Structure, Union, and Enumeration Declarations" under "Declarations") have type **int**.

# String Literals

A string literal is a sequence of characters surrounded by double quotes, as in "...". A string literal has type "array of **char**" and storage class **static** (see "Storage Class and Type") and is initialized with the given characters. The compiler places a null byte (\0) at the end of each string literal so that programs that scan the string literal can find its end. In a string literal, the double quote character (") must be preceded by a \; in addition, the same escapes as described for character constants may be used.

A \ and the immediately following new-line are ignored. All string literals, even when written identically, are distinct.

# Syntax Notation

Syntactic categories are indicated by *italic* type and literal words and characters by **bold** type. Alternative categories are listed on separate lines. An optional entry is indicated by the subscript "opt," so that

$$\{ \ expression_{opt} \ \}$$

indicates an optional expression enclosed in braces. The syntax is summarized in "Syntax Summary" at the end of the chapter.

# Storage Class and Type

The C language bases the interpretation of an identifier upon two attributes of the identifier: its storage class and its type. The storage class determines the location and lifetime of the storage associated with an identifier; the type determines the meaning of the values found in the identifier's storage.

## Storage Class

There are four declarable storage classes:

- automatic
- static
- external
- register

Automatic variables are local to each invocation of a block (see "Compound Statement or Block" in "Statements") and are discarded upon exit from the block. Static variables are local to a block but retain their values upon reentry to a block even after control has left the block. External variables exist and retain their values throughout the execution of the entire program and may be used for communication between functions, even separately compiled functions. Register variables are (if possible) stored in the fast registers of the machine; like automatic variables, they are local to each block and disappear on exit from the block.

## Type

The C language supports several fundamental types of objects. Objects declared as characters (**char**) are large enough to store any member of the implementation's character set. If a genuine character from that character set is stored in a **char** variable, its value is equivalent to the integer code for that character. Other quantities may be stored into character variables, but the implementation is machine dependent. In particular, **char** may be signed or unsigned by default. In this implementation the default is unsigned.

Up to three sizes of integer, declared **short int**, **int**, and **long int**, are available.  Longer integers provide no less storage than shorter ones, but the implementation may make either short integers or long integers, or both, equivalent to plain integers.  Plain integers have the natural size suggested by the host machine architecture.  The other sizes are provided to meet special needs.  The sizes for the AT&T 3B Computer are shown in Figure 17-2.

| AT&T 3B Computer (ASCII) | |
|---|---|
| char | 8 bits |
| int | 32 |
| short | 16 |
| long | 32 |
| float | 32 |
| double | 64 |
| float range | $\pm 10^{\pm 38}$ |
| double range | $\pm 10^{\pm 38}$ |

Figure 17-2: AT&T 3B Computer Hardware Characteristics

The properties of **enum** types (see "Structure, Union, and Enumeration Declarations" under "Declarations") are identical to those of some integer types.  The implementation may use the range of values to determine how to allot storage.

Unsigned integers, declared **unsigned,** obey the laws of arithmetic modulo $2^n$ where $n$ is the number of bits in the representation.

Single-precision floating point (**float**) and double precision floating point (**double**) may be synonymous in some implementations.

Because objects of the foregoing types can usefully be interpreted as numbers, they will be referred to as arithmetic types.  **Char**, **int** of all sizes whether **unsigned** or not, and **enum** will collectively be called integral types. The **float** and **double** types will collectively be called floating types.

The **void** type specifies an empty set of values. It is used as the type returned by functions that generate no value.

Besides the fundamental arithmetic types, there is a conceptually infinite class of derived types constructed from the fundamental types in the following ways:

- arrays of objects of most types
- functions that return objects of a given type
- pointers to objects of a given type
- structures containing a sequence of objects of various types
- unions capable of containing any one of several objects of various types

In general these methods of constructing objects can be applied recursively.

## Objects and lvalues

An object is a manipulatable region of storage. An lvalue is an expression referring to an object. An obvious example of an lvalue expression is an identifier. There are operators that yield lvalues: for example, if **E** is an expression of pointer type, then *E is an lv lue expression referring to the object to which **E** points. The name "lvalue" comes from the assignment expression **E1 = E2** in which the left operand **E1** must be an lvalue expression. The discussion of each operator below indicates whether it expects lvalue operands and whether it yields an lvalue.

# Operator Conversions

A number of operators may, depending on their operands, cause conversion of the value of an operand from one type to another. This part explains the result to be expected from such conversions. The conversions demanded by most ordinary operators are summarized under "Arithmetic Conversions." The summary will be supplemented as required by the discussion of each operator.

## Characters and Integers

A character or a short integer may be used wherever an integer may be used. In all cases the value is converted to an integer. Conversion of a shorter integer to a longer preserves sign. On the 3B Computers sign extension of **char** variables does not occur. It is guaranteed that a member of the standard character set is non-negative.

On machines that treat characters as signed, the characters of the ASCII set are all non-negative. However, a character constant specified with an octal escape suffers sign extension and may appear negative; for example, '\377' has the value −1.

When a longer integer is converted to a shorter integer or to a **char,** it is truncated on the left. Excess bits are simply discarded.

## Float and Double

All floating arithmetic in C is carried out in double precision. Whenever a **float** appears in an expression it is lengthened to **double** by zero padding its fraction. When a **double** must be converted to **float**, for example by an assignment, the **double** is rounded before truncation to **float** length. This result is undefined if it cannot be represented as a float.

# Floating and Integral

Conversions of floating values to integral type are rather machine dependent. In particular, the direction of truncation of negative numbers varies. The result is undefined if it will not fit in the space provided.

Conversions of integral values to floating type behave well. Some loss of accuracy occurs if the destination lacks sufficient bits.

# Pointers and Integers

An expression of integral type may be added to or subtracted from a pointer; in such a case, the first is converted as specified in the discussion of the addition operator. Two pointers to objects of the same type may be subtracted; in this case, the result is converted to an integer as specified in the discussion of the subtraction operator.

# Unsigned

Whenever an unsigned integer and a plain integer are combined, the plain integer is converted to unsigned and the result is unsigned. The value is the least unsigned integer congruent to the signed integer (modulo $2^{wordsize}$). In a 2's complement representation, this conversion is conceptual; and there is no actual change in the bit pattern.

When an unsigned **short** integer is converted to **long**, the value of the result is the same numerically as that of the unsigned integer. Thus, the conversion amounts to padding with zeros on the left.

# Arithmetic Conversions

A great many operators cause conversions and yield result types in a similar way. This pattern will be called the "usual arithmetic conversions."

1. First, any operands of type **char** or **short** are converted to **int**, and any operands of type **unsigned char** or **unsigned short** are converted to **unsigned int**.

2.  Then, if either operand is **double,** the other is converted to **double** and that is the type of the result.

3.  Otherwise, if either operand is **unsigned long**, the other is converted to **unsigned long** and that is the type of the result.

4.  Otherwise, if either operand is **long**, the other is converted to **long** and that is the type of the result.

5.  Otherwise, if one operand is **long**, and the other is **unsigned int**, they are both converted to **unsigned long** and that is the type of the result.

6.  Otherwise, if either operand is **unsigned,** the other is converted to **unsigned** and that is the type of the result.

7.  Otherwise, both operands must be **int**, and that is the type of the result.

# Void

The (nonexistent) value of a **void** object may not be used in any way, and neither explicit nor implicit conversion may be applied. Because a void expression denotes a nonexistent value, such an expression may be used only as an expression statement (see "Expression Statement" under "Statements") or as the left operand of a comma expression (see "Comma Operator" under "Expressions").

An expression may be converted to type **void** by use of a cast. For example, this makes explicit the discarding of the value of a function call used as an expression statement.

# Expressions and Operators

The precedence of expression operators is the same as the order of the major subsections of this section, highest precedence first. Thus, for example, the expressions referred to as the operands of + (see "Additive Operators") are those expressions defined under "Primary Expressions", "Unary Operators", and "Multiplicative Operators". Within each subpart, the operators have the same precedence. Left- or right-associativity is specified in each subsection for the operators discussed therein. The precedence and associativity of all the expression operators are summarized in the grammar of "Syntax Summary".

Otherwise, the order of evaluation of expressions is undefined. In particular, the compiler considers itself free to compute subexpressions in the order it believes most efficient even if the subexpressions involve side effects. Expressions involving a commutative and associative operator (*, +, &, |, ^) may be rearranged arbitrarily even in the presence of parentheses; to force a particular order of evaluation, an explicit temporary must be used.

The handling of overflow and divide check in expression evaluation is undefined. Most existing implementations of C ignore integer overflows; treatment of division by 0 and all floating-point exceptions varies between machines and is usually adjustable by a library function.

## Primary Expressions

Primary expressions involving ., ->, subscripting, and function calls group left to right.

> *primary-expression:*
>     *identifier*
>     *constant*
>     *string literal*
>     *( expression )*
>     *primary-expression [ expression ]*
>     *primary-expression ( expression-list$_{opt}$ )*
>     *primary-expression . identifier*
>     *primary-expression -> identifier*

> *expression-list:*
>     *expression*
>     *expression-list , expression*

An identifier is a primary expression provided it has been suitably declared as discussed below. Its type is specified by its declaration. If the type of the identifier is "array of ...", then the value of the identifier expression is a pointer to the first object in the array; and the type of the expression is "pointer to ...". Moreover, an array identifier is not an lvalue expression. Likewise, an identifier that is declared "function returning ...", when used except in the function-name position of a call, is converted to "pointer to function returning ...".

A constant is a primary expression. Its type may be **int**, **long**, or **double** depending on its form. Character constants have type **int** and floating constants have type **double**.

A string literal is a primary expression. Its type is originally "array of **char**", but following the same rule given above for identifiers, this is modified to "pointer to **char**" and the result is a pointer to the first character in the string literal. (There is an exception in certain initializers; see "Initialization" under "Declarations.")

A parenthesized expression is a primary expression whose type and value are identical to those of the unadorned expression. The presence of parentheses does not affect whether the expression is an lvalue.

A primary expression followed by an expression in square brackets is a primary expression. The intuitive meaning is that of a subscript. Usually, the primary expression has type "pointer to ...", the subscript expression is **int**, and the type of the result is "...". The expression **E1[E2]** is identical (by definition) to **\*((E1)+(E2))**. All the clues needed to understand this notation are contained in this subpart together with the discussions in "Unary Operators" and "Additive Operators" on identifiers, **\*** and **+**, respectively. The implications are summarized under "Arrays, Pointers, and Subscripting" under "Types Revisited."

A function call is a primary expression followed by parentheses containing a possibly empty, comma-separated list of expressions that constitute the actual arguments to the function. The primary expression must be of type "function returning ...", and the result of the function call is of type "...". As indicated below, a hitherto unseen identifier followed immediately by a left parenthesis is contextually declared to represent a function returning an integer.

Any actual arguments of type **float** are converted to **double** before the call. Any of type **char** or **short** are converted to **int**. Array names are converted to pointers. No other conversions are performed automatically; in particular, the compiler does not compare the types of actual arguments with those of formal arguments. If conversion is needed, use a cast; see "Unary Operators" and "Type Names" under "Declarations."

In preparing for the call to a function, a copy is made of each actual parameter. Thus, all argument passing in C is strictly by value. A function may change the values of its formal parameters, but these changes cannot affect the values of the actual parameters. It is possible to pass a pointer on the understanding that the function may change the value of the object to which the pointer points. An array name is a pointer expression. The order of evaluation of arguments is undefined by the language; take note that the various compilers differ. Recursive calls to any function are permitted.

A primary expression followed by a dot followed by an identifier is an expression. The first expression must be a structure or a union, and the identifier must name a member of the structure or union. The value is the named member of the structure or union, and it is an lvalue if the first expression is an lvalue.

A primary expression followed by an arrow (built from $-$ and $>$ ) followed by an identifier is an expression. The first expression must be a pointer to a structure or a union and the identifier must name a member of that structure or union. The result is an lvalue referring to the named member of the structure or union to which the pointer expression points. Thus the expression **E1−>MOS** is the same as **(∗E1).MOS**. Structures and unions are discussed in "Structure, Union, and Enumeration Declarations" under "Declarations."

# Unary Operators

Expressions with unary operators group right to left.

> *unary-expression:*
>     * *expression*
>     & *lvalue*
>     − *expression*
>     ! *expression*
>     ~ *expression*
>     ++ *lvalue*
>     −−*lvalue*
>     *lvalue* ++
>     *lvalue* −−
>     ( *type-name* ) *expression*
>     sizeof *expression*
>     sizeof ( *type-name* )

The unary * operator means "indirection"; the expression must be a pointer, and the result is an lvalue referring to the object to which the expression points. If the type of the expression is "pointer to ...," the type of the result is "...".

The result of the unary **&** operator is a pointer to the object referred to by the lvalue. If the type of the lvalue is "...", the type of the result is "pointer to ...".

The result of the unary − operator is the negative of its operand. The usual arithmetic conversions are performed. The negative of an unsigned quantity is computed by subtracting its value from $2^n$ where $n$ is the number of bits in the corresponding signed type.

There is no unary + operator.

The result of the logical negation operator **!** is one if the value of its operand is zero, zero if the value of its operand is nonzero. The type of the result is **int**. It is applicable to any arithmetic type or to pointers.

The ~ operator yields the one's complement of its operand. The usual arithmetic conversions are performed. The type of the operand must be integral.

The object referred to by the lvalue operand of prefix ++ is incremented. The value is the new value of the operand but is not an lvalue. The expression ++**x** is equivalent to **x** += **1**. See the discussions "Additive Operators" and "Assignment Operators" for information on conversions.

The lvalue operand of prefix −− is decremented analogously to the prefix ++ operator.

When postfix ++ is applied to an lvalue, the result is the value of the object referred to by the lvalue. After the result is noted, the object is incremented in the same manner as for the prefix ++ operator. The type of the result is the same as the type of the lvalue expression.

When postfix −− is applied to an lvalue, the result is the value of the object referred to by the lvalue. After the result is noted, the object is decremented in the manner as for the prefix −− operator. The type of the result is the same as the type of the lvalue expression.

An expression preceded by the parenthesized name of a data type causes conversion of the value of the expression to the named type. This construction is called a cast. Type names are described in "Type Names" under "Declarations."

The **sizeof** operator yields the size in bytes of its operand. (A byte is undefined by the language except in terms of the value of **sizeof**. However, in all existing implementations, a byte is the space required to hold a **char**.) When applied to an array, the result is the total number of bytes in the array. The size is determined from the declarations of the objects in the expression. This expression is semantically an **unsigned** constant and may be used anywhere a constant is required. Its major use is in communication with routines like storage allocators and I/O systems.

The **sizeof** operator may also be applied to a parenthesized type name. In that case it yields the size in bytes of an object of the indicated type.

The construction **sizeof**(*type*) is taken to be a unit, so the expression **sizeof**(*type*)−**2** is the same as (**sizeof**(*type*))−**2**.

## Multiplicative Operators

The multiplicative operators *, /, and % group left to right. The usual arithmetic conversions are performed.

> *multiplicative expression:*
>     *expression * expression*
>     *expression / expression*
>     *expression % expression*

The binary * operator indicates multiplication. The * operator is associative, and expressions with several multiplications at the same level may be rearranged by the compiler. The binary / operator indicates division.

The binary % operator yields the remainder from the division of the first expression by the second. The operands must be integral.

When positive integers are divided, truncation is toward 0; but the form of truncation is machine-dependent if either operand is negative. On all machines covered by this manual, the remainder has the same sign as the dividend. It is always true that **(a/b)*b + a%b** is equal to **a** (if **b** is not 0).

## Additive Operators

The additive operators + and − group left to right. The usual arithmetic conversions are performed. There are some additional type possibilities for each operator.

> *additive-expression:*
>     *expression + expression*
>     *expression − expression*

The result of the + operator is the sum of the operands. A pointer to an object in an array and a value of any integral type may be added. The latter is in all cases converted to an address offset by multiplying it by the length of the object to which the pointer points. The result is a pointer of the same type as the original pointer that points to another object in the same array, appropriately offset from the original object. Thus if **P** is a pointer to an object in an array, the expression **P+1** is a pointer to the next object in the array. No further type combinations are allowed for pointers.

The + operator is associative, and expressions with several additions at the same level may be rearranged by the compiler.

The result of the − operator is the difference of the operands. The usual arithmetic conversions are performed. Additionally, a value of any integral type may be subtracted from a pointer, and then the same conversions for addition apply.

If two pointers to objects of the same type are subtracted, the result is converted (by division by the length of the object) to an **int** representing the number of objects separating the pointed-to objects. This conversion will in general give unexpected results unless the pointers point to objects in the same array, since pointers, even to objects of the same type, do not necessarily differ by a multiple of the object length.

## Shift Operators

The shift operators $<<$ and $>>$ group left to right. Both perform the usual arithmetic conversions on their operands, each of which must be integral. Then the right operand is converted to **int**; the type of the result is that of the left operand. The result is undefined if the right operand is negative or greater than or equal to the length of the object in bits.

> *shift-expression:*
>     *expression* $<<$ *expression*
>     *expression* $>>$ *expression*

The value of **E1**$<<$**E2** is **E1** (interpreted as a bit pattern) left-shifted **E2** bits. Vacated bits are 0 filled. The value of **E1**$>>$**E2** is **E1** right-shifted **E2** bit positions. The right shift is guaranteed to be logical (0 fill) if **E1** is **unsigned**; otherwise, it may be arithmetic.

## Relational Operators

The relational operators group left to right.

> *relational-expression:*
>     *expression* $<$ *expression*
>     *expression* $>$ *expression*
>     *expression* $<=$ *expression*
>     *expression* $>=$ *expression*

The operators < (less than), > (greater than), <= (less than or equal to), and >= (greater than or equal to) all yield 0 if the specified relation is false and 1 if it is true. The type of the result is **int**. The usual arithmetic conversions are performed. Two pointers may be compared; the result depends on the relative locations in the address space of the pointed-to objects. Pointer comparison is portable only when the pointers point to objects in the same array.

# Equality Operators

> *equality-expression:*
>> *expression* == *expression*
>> *expression* != *expression*

The == (equal to) and the != (not equal to) operators are exactly analogous to the relational operators except for their lower precedence. (Thus **a<b == c<d** is 1 whenever **a<b** and **c<d** have the same truth value.)

A pointer may be compared to an integer only if the integer is the constant 0. A pointer to which 0 has been assigned is guaranteed not to point to any object and will appear to be equal to 0. In conventional usage, such a pointer is considered to be null.

# Bitwise AND Operator

> *and-expression:*
>> *expression* & *expression*

The **&** operator is associative, and expressions involving **&** may be rearranged. The usual arithmetic conversions are performed. The result is the bitwise AND function of the operands. The operator applies only to integral operands.

# Bitwise Exclusive OR Operator

*exclusive-or-expression:*
   *expression ^ expression*

The ^ operator is associative, and expressions involving ^ may be rearranged. The usual arithmetic conversions are performed; the result is the bitwise exclusive OR function of the operands. The operator applies only to integral operands.

# Bitwise Inclusive OR Operator

*inclusive-or-expression:*
   *expression | expression*

The | operator is associative, and expressions involving | may be rearranged. The usual arithmetic conversions are performed; the result is the bitwise inclusive OR function of its operands. The operator applies only to integral operands.

# Logical AND Operator

*logical-and-expression:*
   *expression && expression*

The **&&** operator groups left to right. It returns 1 if both its operands evaluate to nonzero, 0 otherwise. Unlike **&**, **&&** guarantees left to right evaluation; moreover, the second operand is not evaluated if the first operand evaluates to 0.

The operands need not have the same type, but each must have one of the fundamental types or be a pointer. The result is always **int**.

## Logical OR Operator

*logical-or-expression:*
   *expression | expression*

The | operator groups left to right. It returns 1 if either of its operands evaluates to nonzero, 0 otherwise. Unlike |, | guarantees left to right evaluation; moreover, the second operand is not evaluated if the value of the first operand evaluates to nonzero.

The operands need not have the same type, but each must have one of the fundamental types or be a pointer. The result is always **int**.

## Conditional Operator

*conditional-expression:*
   *expression ? expression : expression*

Conditional expressions group right to left. The first expression is evaluated; and if it is nonzero, the result is the value of the second expression, otherwise that of third expression. If possible, the usual arithmetic conversions are performed to bring the second and third expressions to a common type. If both are structures or unions of the same type, the result has the type of the structure or union. If both pointers are of the same type, the result has the common type. Otherwise, one must be a pointer and the other the constant 0, and the result has the type of the pointer. Only one of the second and third expressions is evaluated.

## Assignment Operators

There are a number of assignment operators, all of which group right to left. All require an lvalue as their left operand, and the type of an assignment expression is that of its left operand. The value is the value stored in the left operand after the assignment has taken place. The two parts of a compound assignment operator are separate tokens.

*assignment-expression:*
      *lvalue = expression*
      *lvalue += expression*
      *lvalue −= expression*
      *lvalue *= expression*
      *lvalue /= expression*
      *lvalue %= expression*
      *lvalue >>= expression*
      *lvalue <<= expression*
      *lvalue &= expression*
      *lvalue ^= expression*
      *lvalue |= expression*

In the simple assignment with =, the value of the expression replaces that of the object referred to by the lvalue. If both operands have arithmetic type, the right operand is converted to the type of the left preparatory to the assignment. Second, both operands may be structures or unions of the same type. Finally, if the left operand is a pointer, the right operand must in general be a pointer of the same type. However, the constant 0 may be assigned to a pointer; it is guaranteed that this value will produce a null pointer distinguishable from a pointer to any object.

The behavior of an expression of the form **E1** *op* = **E2** may be inferred by taking it as equivalent to **E1** = **E1** *op* (**E2**); however, **E1** is evaluated only once. In += and −=, the left operand may be a pointer, in which case the (integral) right operand is converted as explained in "Additive Operators." All right operands and all nonpointer left operands must have arithmetic type.

# Comma Operator

*comma-expression:*
  *expression , expression*

A pair of expressions separated by a comma is evaluated left to right, and the value of the left expression is discarded. The type and value of the result are the type and value of the right operand. This operator groups left to right. In contexts where comma is given a special meaning, e.g., in lists of actual arguments to functions (see "Primary Expressions") and lists of initializers (see "Initialization" under "Declarations"), the comma operator as described in this subpart can only appear in parentheses. For example,

**f(a, (t=3, t+2), c)**

has three arguments, the second of which has the value 5.

# Declarations

Declarations are used to specify the interpretation that C gives to each identifier; they do not necessarily reserve storage associated with the identifier. Declarations have the form

> *declaration:*
> *decl-specifiers declarator-list*$_{opt}$ ;

The declarators in the declarator-list contain the identifiers being declared. The decl-specifiers consist of a sequence of type and storage class specifiers.

> *decl-specifiers:*
> *type-specifier decl-specifiers*$_{opt}$
> *sc-specifier decl-specifiers*$_{opt}$

The list must be self-consistent in a way described below.


## Storage Class Specifiers

The sc-specifiers are:

> *sc-specifier:*
> **auto**
> **static**
> **extern**
> **register**
> **typedef**

The **typedef** specifier does not reserve storage and is called a "storage class specifier" only for syntactic convenience. See **"typedef"** for more information. The meanings of the various storage classes were discussed in "Names."

The **auto**, **static**, and **register** declarations also serve as definitions in that they cause an appropriate amount of storage to be reserved. In the **extern** case, there must be an external definition (see "External Definitions") for the given identifiers somewhere outside the function in which they are declared.

A **register** declaration is best thought of as an **auto** declaration, together with a hint to the compiler that the variables declared will be heavily used. Only the first few such declarations in each function are effective. Moreover, only variables of certain types will be stored in registers. One other restriction applies to variables declared using register storage class: the address-of operator, **&**, cannot be applied to them. Smaller, faster programs can be expected if register declarations are used appropriately.

At most, one sc-specifier may be given in a declaration. If the sc-specifier is missing from a declaration, it is taken to be **auto** inside a function, **extern** outside. Exception: functions are never automatic.

# Type Specifiers

The type-specifiers are

> *type-specifier:*
>> *struct-or-union-specifier*
>> *typedef-name*
>> *enum-specifier*
> *basic-type-specifier:*
>> *basic-type*
>> *basic-type basic-type-specifiers*
> *basic-type:*
>> **char**
>> **short**
>> **int**
>> **long**
>> **unsigned**
>> **float**
>> **double**
>> **void**

At most one of the words **long** or **short** may be specified in conjunction with **int**; the meaning is the same as if **int** were not mentioned. The word **long** may be specified in conjunction with **float**; the meaning is the same as **double**. The word **unsigned** may be specified alone, or in conjunction with **int** or any of its short or long varieties, or with **char**.

Otherwise, at most on type-specifier may be given in a declaration. In particular, adjectival use of **long**, **short**, or **unsigned** is not permitted with **typedef** names. If the type-specifier is missing from a declaration, it is taken to be **int**.

Specifiers for structures, unions, and enumerations are discussed in "Structure, Union, and Enumeration Declarations." Declarations with **typedef** names are discussed in "**typedef**."

# Declarators

The declarator-list appearing in a declaration is a comma-separated sequence of declarators, each of which may have an initializer:

> *declarator-list:*
> > *init-declarator*
> > *init-declarator , declarator-list*

> *init-declarator:*
> > *declarator initializer*$_{opt}$

Initializers are discussed in "Initialization." The specifiers in the declaration indicate the type and storage class of the objects to which the declarators refer. Declarators have the syntax:

> *declarator:*
> > *identifier*
> > *( declarator )*
> > *∗ declarator*
> > *declarator ()*
> > *declarator [ constant-expression*$_{opt}$ *]*

The grouping is the same as in expressions.

# Meaning of Declarators

Each declarator is taken to be an assertion that when a construction of the same form as the declarator appears in an expression, it yields an object of the indicated type and storage class.

Each declarator contains exactly one identifier; it is this identifier that is declared. If an unadorned identifier appears as a declarator, then it has the type indicated by the specifier heading the declaration.

A declarator in parentheses is identical to the unadorned declarator, but the binding of complex declarators may be altered by parentheses. See the examples below.

Now imagine a declaration

**T D1**

where **T** is a type-specifier (like **int**, etc.) and **D1** is a declarator. Suppose this declaration makes the identifier have type "... **T** ," where the "..." is empty if **D1** is just a plain identifier (so that the type of **x** in "**int x**" is just **int**). Then if **D1** has the form

**∗D**

the type of the contained identifier is "... pointer to **T** ."

If **D1** has the form

**D()**

then the contained identifier has the type "... function returning **T**."

If **D1** has the form

**D**[*constant-expression*]

or

**D[]**

then the contained identifier has type "... array of **T**." In the first case, the constant expression is an expression whose value is determinable at compile time, whose type is **int**, and whose value is positive. (Constant expressions are defined precisely in "Constant Expressions.") When several "array of" specifications are adjacent, a multi-dimensional array is created; the constant expressions that specify the bounds of the arrays may be missing only for the first member of the sequence. This elision is useful when the array is external and the actual definition, which allocates storage, is given elsewhere. The first constant expression may also be omitted when the declarator is followed by initialization. In this case the size is calculated from the number of initial elements supplied.

An array may be constructed from one of the basic types, from a pointer, from a structure or union, or from another array (to generate a multi-dimensional array).

Not all the possibilities allowed by the syntax above are actually permitted. The restrictions are as follows: functions may not return arrays or functions although they may return pointers; there are no arrays of functions although there may be arrays of pointers to functions. Likewise, a structure or union may not contain a function; but it may contain a pointer to a function.

As an example, the declaration

**int i, \*ip, f(), \*fip(), (\*pfi)();**

declares an integer **i**, a pointer **ip** to an integer, a function **f** returning an integer, a function **fip** returning a pointer to an integer, and a pointer **pfi** to a function, which returns an integer. It is especially useful to compare the last two. The binding of **\*fip()** is **\*(fip())**. The declaration suggests, and the same construction in an expression requires, the calling of a function **fip**, and then using indirection through the (pointer) result to yield an integer. In the declarator **(\*pfi)()**, the extra parentheses are necessary, as they are also in an expression, to indicate that indirection through a pointer to a function yields a function, which is then called; it returns an integer.

As another example,

**float fa[17], \*afp[17];**

declares an array of **float** numbers and an array of pointers to **float** numbers. Finally,

**static int x3d[3][5][7];**

declares a static 3-dimensional array of integers, with rank 3×5×7. In complete detail, **x3d** is an array of three items; each item is an array of five arrays; each of the latter arrays is an array of seven integers. Any of the expressions **x3d**, **x3d[i]**, **x3d[i][j]**, **x3d[i][j][k]** may reasonably appear in an expression. The first three have type "array" and the last has type **int**.

# Structure and Union Declarations

A structure is an object consisting of a sequence of named members. Each member may have any type. A union is an object that may, at a given time, contain any one of several members. Structure and union specifiers have the same form.

*struct-or-union-specifier:*
    *struct-or-union { struct-decl-list }*
    *struct-or-union identifier { struct-decl-list }*
    *struct-or-union identifier*


*struct-or-union:*
    **struct**
    **union**

The struct-decl-list is a sequence of declarations for the members of the structure or union:

*struct-decl-list:*
    *struct-declaration*
    *struct-declaration struct-decl-list*

*struct-declaration:*
    *type-specifier struct-declarator-list ;*

*struct-declarator-list:*
    *struct-declarator*
    *struct-declarator , struct-declarator-list*

In the usual case, a struct-declarator is just a declarator for a member of a structure or union. A structure member may also consist of a specified number of bits. Such a member is also called a field; its length, a non-negative constant expression, is set off from the field name by a colon.

*struct-declarator:*
    *declarator*
    *declarator : constant-expression*
    *: constant-expression*

Within a structure, the objects declared have addresses that increase as the declarations are read left to right. Each non-field member of a structure begins on an addressing boundary appropriate to its type; therefore, there may be unnamed holes in a structure. Field members are packed into machine integers; they do not straddle words. A field that does not fit into the space remaining in a word is put into the next word. No field may be wider than a word. (See Figure 17-2 for sizes of basic types on 3B Computers.)

A struct-declarator with no declarator, only a colon and a width, indicates an unnamed field useful for padding to conform to externally-imposed layouts. As a special case, a field with a width of 0 specifies alignment of the next field at an implementation dependent boundary.

The language does not restrict the types of things that are declared as fields. Moreover, even **int** fields may be considered to be unsigned. For these reasons, it is strongly recommended that fields be declared as **unsigned** where that is the intent. There are no arrays of fields, and the address-of operator, **&,** may not be applied to them, so that there are no pointers to fields.

A union may be thought of as a structure all of whose members begin at offset 0 and whose size is sufficient to contain any of its members. At most, one of the members can be stored in a union at any time.

A structure or union specifier of the second form, that is, one of

> **struct** *identifier* { *struct-decl-list* }
> **union** *identifier* { *struct-decl-list* }

declares the identifier to be the *structure tag* (or union tag) of the structure specified by the list. A subsequent declaration may then use the third form of specifier, one of

> **struct** *identifier*
> **union** *identifier*

Structure tags allow definition of self-referential structures. Structure tags also permit the long part of the declaration to be given once and used several times. It is illegal to declare a structure or union that contains an instance of itself, but a structure or union may contain a pointer to an instance of itself.

The third form of a structure or union specifier may be used prior to a declaration that gives the complete specification of the structure or union in situations in which the size of the structure or union is unnecessary. The size is unnecessary in two situations: when a pointer to a structure or union is being declared and when a **typedef** name is declared to be a synonym for a structure or union. This, for example, allows the declaration of a pair of structures that contain pointers to each other.

The names of members and tags do not conflict with each other or with ordinary variables. A particular name may not be used twice in the same structure, but the same name may be used in several different structures in the same scope.

**Declarations**

A simple but important example of a structure declaration is the following binary tree structure:

```
struct tnode
{
        char tword[20];
        int count;
        struct tnode *left;
        struct tnode *right;
};
```

which contains an array of 20 characters, an integer, and two pointers to similar structures. Once this declaration has been given, the declaration

**struct tnode s, \*sp;**

declares **s** to be a structure of the given sort and **sp** to be a pointer to a structure of the given sort. With these declarations, the expression

**sp->count**

refers to the **count** field of the structure to which **sp** points;

**s.left**

refers to the left subtree pointer of the structure **s**; and

**s.right->tword[0]**

refers to the first character of the **tword** member of the right subtree of **s**.

# Enumeration Declarations

Enumeration variables and constants have integral type.

*enum-specifier:*
> **enum** { *enum-list* }
> **enum** *identifier* { *enum-list* }
> **enum** *identifier*

*enum-list:*
> *enumerator*
> *enum-list , enumerator*

*enumerator:*
> *identifier*
> *identifier = constant-expression*

The identifiers in an enum-list are declared as constants and may appear wherever constants are required. If no enumerators with = appear, then the values of the corresponding constants begin at 0 and increase by 1 as the declaration is read from left to right. An enumerator with = gives the associated identifier the value indicated; subsequent identifiers continue the progression from the assigned value.

The names of enumerators in the same scope must all be distinct from each other and from those of ordinary variables.

The role of the identifier in the enum-specifier is entirely analogous to that of the structure tag in a struct-specifier; it names a particular enumeration. For example,

```
enum color { chartreuse, burgundy, claret=20, winedark };
...
enum color *cp, col;
...
col = claret;
cp = &col;
...
if (*cp == burgundy) ...
```

makes **color** the enumeration-tag of a type describing various colors, and then declares **cp** as a pointer to an object of that type and **col** as an object of that type. The possible values are drawn from the set $\{0,1,20,21\}$.

## Initialization

A declarator may specify an initial value for the identifier being declared. The initializer is preceded by = and consists of an expression or a list of values nested in braces.

> *initializer:*
> > = *expression*
> > = { *initializer-list* }
> > = { *initializer-list ,* }

> *initializer-list:*
> > *expression*
> > *initializer-list , initializer-list*
> > { *initializer-list* }
> > { *initializer-list ,* }

All the expressions in an initializer for a static or external variable must be constant expressions, which are described in "Constant Expressions," or expressions that reduce to the address of a previously declared variable, possibly offset by a constant expression. Automatic or register variables may be initialized by arbitrary expressions involving constants and previously declared variables and functions.

Static and external variables that are not initialized are guaranteed to start off as zero. Automatic and register variables that are not initialized are guaranteed to start off as garbage.

When an initializer applies to a scalar (a pointer or an object of arithmetic type), it consists of a single expression, perhaps in braces. The initial value of the object is taken from the expression; the same conversions as for assignment are performed.

When the declared variable is an aggregate (a structure or array), the initializer consists of a brace-enclosed, comma-separated list of initializers for the members of the aggregate written in increasing subscript or member order. If the aggregate contains subaggregates, this rule applies recursively to the members of the aggregate. If there are fewer initializers in the list than there are members of the aggregate, then the aggregate is padded with zeros. It is not permitted to initialize unions or automatic aggregates.

Braces may in some cases be omitted. If the initializer begins with a left brace, then the succeeding comma-separated list of initializers initializes the members of the aggregate; it is erroneous for there to be more initializers than members. If, however, the initializer does not begin with a left brace, then only enough elements from the list are taken to account for the members of the aggregate; any remaining members are left to initialize the next member of the aggregate of which the current aggregate is a part.

A final abbreviation allows a **char** array to be initialized by a string literal. In this case successive characters of the string literal initialize the members of the array.

For example,

> **int x[] = { 1, 3, 5 };**

declares and initializes **x** as a one-dimensional array that has three members, since no size was specified and there are three initializers.

> **float y[4][3] =**
> **{**
>     **{ 1, 3, 5 },**
>     **{ 2, 4, 6 },**
>     **{ 3, 5, 7 },**
> **};**

is a completely-bracketed initialization: 1, 3, and 5 initialize the first row of the array **y[0]**, namely **y[0][0]**, **y[0][1]**, and **y[0][2]**. Likewise, the next two lines initialize **y[1]** and **y[2]**. The initializer ends early and therefore **y[3]** is initialized with 0. Precisely, the same effect could have been achieved by

    **float y[4][3] =**
    **{**

        **1, 3, 5, 2, 4, 6, 3, 5, 7**

    **};**

The initializer for **y** begins with a left brace but that for **y[0]** does not; there-fore, three elements from the list are used. Likewise, the next three are taken successively for **y[1]** and **y[2]**. Also,

    **float y[4][3] =**
    **{**

        **{ 1 }, { 2 }, { 3 }, { 4 }**

    **};**

initializes the first column of **y** (regarded as a two-dimensional array) and leaves the rest 0.

    Finally,

    **char msg[] = "Syntax error on line %s\n";**

shows a character array whose members are initialized with a string literal. The length of the string (or size of the array) includes the terminating NUL character, \0.

## Type Names

In two contexts (to specify type conversions explicitly by means of a cast and as an argument of **sizeof**), it is desired to supply the name of a data type. This is accomplished using a "type name," which in essence is a declaration for an object of that type that omits the name of the object.

    *type-name:*
        *type-specifier abstract-declarator*

    *abstract-declarator:*
        *empty*
        *( abstract-declarator )*
        \* *abstract-declarator*
        *abstract-declarator ()*
        *abstract-declarator [ constant-expression$_{opt}$ ]*

To avoid ambiguity, in the construction

( *abstract-declarator* )

the abstract-declarator is required to be nonempty. Under this restriction, it is possible to identify uniquely the location in the abstract-declarator where the identifier would appear if the construction were a declarator in a declaration. The named type is then the same as the type of the hypothetical identifier. For example,

```
int
int *
int *[3]
int (*)[3]
int *()
int (*)()
int (*[3])()
```

name respectively the types "integer," "pointer to integer," "array of three pointers to integers," "pointer to an array of three integers," "function returning pointer to integer," "pointer to function returning an integer," and "array of three pointers to functions returning an integer."

## Implicit Declarations

It is not always necessary to specify both the storage class and the type of identifiers in a declaration. The storage class is supplied by the context in external definitions and in declarations of formal parameters and structure members. In a declaration inside a function, if a storage class but no type is given, the identifier is assumed to be **int**; if a type but no storage class is indicated, the identifier is assumed to be **auto**. An exception to the latter rule is made for functions because **auto** functions do not exist. If the type of an identifier is "function returning ...," it is implicitly declared to be **extern**.

In an expression, an identifier followed by **(** and not already declared is contextually declared to be "function returning **int**."

# typedef

Declarations whose "storage class" is **typedef** do not define storage but instead define identifiers that can be used later as if they were type keywords naming fundamental or derived types.

>*typedef-name:*
>>*identifier*

Within the scope of a declaration involving **typedef**, each identifier appearing as part of any declarator therein becomes syntactically equivalent to the type keyword naming the type associated with the identifier in the way described in "Meaning of Declarators." For example, after

>**typedef int MILES, \*KLICKSP;**
>**typedef struct { double re, im; } complex;**

the constructions

>**MILES distance;**
>**extern KLICKSP metricp;**
>**complex z, \*zp;**

are all legal declarations; the type of **distance** is **int**, that of **metricp** is "pointer to **int**," and that of **z** is the specified structure. The **zp** is a pointer to such a structure.

The **typedef** does not introduce brand-new types, only synonyms for types that could be specified in another way. Thus in the example above **distance** is considered to have exactly the same type as any other **int** object.

# Statements

Except as indicated, statements are executed in sequence.

## Expression Statement

Most statements are expression statements, which have the form

*expression ;*

Usually expression statements are assignments or function calls.

## Compound Statement or Block

So that several statements can be used where one is expected, the compound statement (also, and equivalently, called "block") is provided:

*compound-statement:*
    { *declaration-list*$_{opt}$ *statement-list*$_{opt}$ }

*declaration-list:*
    *declaration*
    *declaration declaration-list*

*statement-list:*
    *statement*
    *statement statement-list*

If any of the identifiers in the declaration-list were previously declared, the outer declaration is pushed down for the duration of the block, after which it resumes its force.

Any initializations of **auto** or **register** variables are performed each time the block is entered at the top. It is currently possible (but a bad practice) to transfer into a block; in that case the initializations are not performed. Initializations of **static** variables are performed only once when the program begins execution. Inside a block, **extern** declarations do not reserve storage so initialization is not permitted.

## Conditional Statement

The two forms of the conditional statement are

> **if** ( *expression* ) *statement*
> **if** ( *expression* ) *statement* **else** *statement*

In both cases, the expression is evaluated; if it is nonzero, the first substatement is executed. In the second case, the second substatement is executed if the expression is 0. The **else** ambiguity is resolved by connecting an **else** with the last encountered **else**-less **if**.

## while Statement

The **while** statement has the form

> **while** ( *expression* ) *statement*

The substatement is executed repeatedly so long as the value of the expression remains nonzero. The test takes place before each execution of the statement.

## do Statement

The **do** statement has the form

> **do** *statement* **while** ( *expression* ) ;

The substatement is executed repeatedly until the value of the expression becomes 0. The test takes place after each execution of the statement.

## for Statement

The **for** statement has the form:

> **for** ( $exp-1_{opt}$ ; $exp-2_{opt}$ ; $exp-3_{opt}$ ) *statement*

Except for the behavior of **continue**, this statement is equivalent to

```
exp-1 ;
while ( exp-2 )
{
        statement
        exp-3 ;
}
```

Thus the first expression specifies initialization for the loop; the second specifies a test, made before each iteration, such that the loop is exited when the expression becomes 0. The third expression often specifies an incrementing that is performed after each iteration.

Any or all of the expressions may be dropped. A missing *exp-2* makes the implied **while** clause equivalent to **while(1)**; other missing expressions are simply dropped from the expansion above.

## switch **Statement**

The **switch** statement causes control to be transferred to one of several statements depending on the value of an expression. It has the form

> **switch** ( *expression* ) *statement*

The usual arithmetic conversion is performed on the expression, but the result must be **int**. The statement is typically compound. Any statement within the statement may be labeled with one or more case prefixes as follows:

> **case** *constant-expression* :

where the constant expression must be **int**. No two of the case constants in the same switch may have the same value. Constant expressions are precisely defined in "Constant Expressions."

There may also be at most one statement prefix of the form

> **default :**

which properly goes at the end of the case constants.

When the **switch** statement is executed, its expression is evaluated and compared in turn with each case constant. If one of the case constants is equal to the value of the expression, control is passed to the statement following the matched case prefix. If no case constant matches the expression and if there is a **default** prefix, control passes to the statement prefixed by

**default**. If no case matches and if there is no **default**, then none of the statements in the switch is executed.

The prefixes **case** and **default** do not alter the flow of control, which continues unimpeded across such prefixes. That is, once a case constant is matched, all **case** statements (and the **default**) from there to the end of the **switch** are executed. To exit from a switch, see "**break** Statement."

Usually, the statement that is the subject of a switch is compound. Declarations may appear at the head of this statement, but initializations of automatic or register variables are ineffective. A simple example of a complete **switch** statement is:

```
switch (c) {
        case 'o':
                oflag = TRUE;
                break;
        case 'p':
                pflag = TRUE;
                break;
        case 'r':
                rflag = TRUE;
                break;
        default :
                (void) fprintf(stderr, "Unknown option\n");
                exit(2);
        }
```

# break **Statement**

The statement **break ;** causes termination of the smallest enclosing **while**, **do**, **for**, or **switch** statement; control passes to the statement following the terminated statement.

## continue **Statement**

The statement **continue ;** causes control to pass to the loop-continuation portion of the smallest enclosing **while, do,** or **for** statement; that is to the end of the loop. More precisely, in each of the statements

```
while (...)        do                for (...)
{                  {                  {
    ...                ...                ...
contin: ;          contin: ;          contin: ;
}                  } while (...);     }
```

a **continue** is equivalent to **goto contin.** (Following the **contin:** is a null statement; see "Null Statement.")

## return **Statement**

A function returns to its caller by means of the **return** statement, which has one of the forms

> **return ;**
> **return** *expression* ;

In the first case, the returned value is undefined. In the second case, the value of the expression is returned to the caller of the function. If required, the expression is converted, as if by assignment, to the type of function in which it appears. Flowing off the end of a function is equivalent to a return with no returned value.

# goto **Statement**

Control may be transferred unconditionally by means of the statement

**goto** *identifier* ;

The identifier must be a label (see "Labeled Statement") located in the current function.

# **Labeled Statement**

Any statement may be preceded by label prefixes of the form

*identifier* :

which serve to declare the identifier as a label. The only use of a label is as a target of a **goto**. The scope of a label is the current function, excluding any subblocks in which the same identifier has been redeclared. See "Scope Rules."

# **Null Statement**

The null statement has the form

;

A null statement is useful to carry a label just before the } of a compound statement or to supply a null body to a looping statement such as **while**.

# External Definitions

A C program consists of a sequence of external definitions. An external definition declares an identifier to have storage class **extern** (by default) or perhaps **static**, and a specified type. The type-specifier (see "Type Specifiers" in "Declarations") may also be empty, in which case the type is taken to be **int**. The scope of external definitions persists to the end of the file in which they are declared just as the effect of declarations persists to the end of a block. The syntax of external definitions is the same as that of all declarations except that only at this level may the code for functions be given.

## External Function Definitions

Function definitions have the form

> *function-definition:*
>  *decl-specifiers*$_{opt}$ *function-declarator function-body*

The only sc-specifiers allowed among the decl-specifiers are **extern** or **static**; see "Scope of Externals" in "Scope Rules" for the distinction between them. A function declarator is similar to a declarator for a "function returning ..." except that it lists the formal parameters of the function being defined.

> *function-declarator:*
>  *declarator ( parameter-list*$_{opt}$ *)*

> *parameter-list:*
>  *identifier*
>  *identifier , parameter-list*

The function-body has the form

> *function-body:*
>  *declaration-list*$_{opt}$ *compound-statement*

The identifiers in the parameter list, and only those identifiers, may be declared in the declaration list. Any identifiers whose type is not given are taken to be **int**. The only storage class that may be specified is **register**; if it is specified, the corresponding actual parameter will be copied, if possible, into a register at the outset of the function.

A simple example of a complete function definition is

```
int max(a, b, c)
        int a, b, c;
{
        int m;

        m = (a > b) ? a : b;
        return((m > c) ? m : c);
}
```

Here **int** is the type-specifier; **max(a, b, c)** is the function-declarator;
**int a, b, c;** is the declaration-list for the formal parameters; { ... } is the block
giving the code for the statement.

The C program converts all **float** actual parameters to **double**, so formal
parameters declared **float** have their declaration adjusted to read **double**. All
**char** and **short** formal parameter declarations are similarly adjusted to read
**int**. Also, since a reference to an array in any context (in particular as an
actual parameter) is taken to mean a pointer to the first element of the array,
declarations of formal parameters declared "array of ..." are adjusted to read
"pointer to ...."

## External Data Definitions

An external data definition has the form

*data-definition:*
    *declaration*

The storage class of such data may be **extern** (which is the default) or **static**,
but not **auto** or **register**.

# Scope Rules

A C program need not all be compiled at the same time. The source text of the program may be kept in several files, and precompiled routines may be loaded from libraries. Communication among the functions of a program may be carried out both through explicit calls and through manipulation of external data.

Therefore, there are two kinds of scopes to consider: first, what may be called the lexical scope of an identifier, which is essentially the region of a program during which it may be used without drawing "undefined identifier" diagnostics; and second, the scope associated with external identifiers, which is characterized by the rule that references to the same external identifier are references to the same object.

## Lexical Scope

The lexical scope of identifiers declared in external definitions persists from the definition through the end of the source file in which they appear. The lexical scope of identifiers that are formal parameters persists through the function with which they are associated. The lexical scope of identifiers declared at the head of a block persists until the end of the block. The lexical scope of labels is the whole of the function in which they appear.

In all cases, however, if an identifier is explicitly declared at the head of a block, including the block constituting a function, any declaration of that identifier outside the block is suspended until the end of the block.

Remember also (see "Structure, Union, and Enumeration Declarations" in "Declarations") that tags, identifiers associated with ordinary variables, and identities associated with structure and union members form three disjoint classes which do not conflict. Members and tags follow the same scope rules as other identifiers. The **enum** constants are in the same class as ordinary variables and follow the same scope rules. The **typedef** names are in the same class as ordinary identifiers. They may be redeclared in inner blocks, but an explicit type must be given in the inner declaration:

```
typedef float distance;
...
{
     int distance;
     ...
```

The **int** must be present in the second declaration, or it would be taken to be a declaration with no declarators and type **distance**.

## Scope of Externals

If a function refers to an identifier declared to be **extern**, then somewhere among the files or libraries constituting the complete program there must be at least one external definition for the identifier. All functions in a given program that refer to the same external identifier refer to the same object, so care must be taken that the type and size specified in the definition are compatible with those specified by each function that references the data.

It is illegal to explicitly initialize any external identifier more than once in the set of files and libraries comprising a multi-file program. It is legal to have more than one data definition for any external non-function identifier; explicit use of **extern** does not change the meaning of an external declaration.

In restricted environments, the use of the **extern** storage class takes on an additional meaning. In these environments, the explicit appearance of the **extern** keyword in external data declarations of identities without initialization indicates that the storage for the identifiers is allocated elsewhere, either in this file or another file. It is required that there be exactly one definition of each external identifier (without **extern**) in the set of files and libraries comprising a mult-file program.

Identifiers declared **static** at the top level in external definitions are not visible in other files. Functions may be declared **static**.

# Compiler Control Lines

The C compilation system contains a preprocessor capable of macro substitution, conditional compilation, and inclusion of named files. Lines beginning with **#** communicate with this preprocessor. There may be any number of blanks and horizontal tabs between the **#** and the directive, but no additional material (such as comments) is permitted. These lines have syntax independent of the rest of the language; they may appear anywhere and have effect that lasts (independent of scope) until the end of the source program file.

## Token Replacement

A control line of the form

> **#define** *identifier token-string*$_{opt}$

causes the preprocessor to replace subsequent instances of the identifier with the given string of tokens. Semicolons in or at the end of the token-string are part of that string. A line of the form

> **#define** *identifier(identifier, ... ) token-string*$_{opt}$

where there is no space between the first identifier and the **(**, is a macro definition with arguments. There may be zero or more formal parameters. Subsequent instances of the first identifier followed by a **(**, a sequence of tokens delimited by commas, and a **)** are replaced by the token string in the definition. Each occurrence of an identifier mentioned in the formal parameter list of the definition is replaced by the corresponding token string from the call. The actual arguments in the call are token strings separated by commas; however, commas in quoted strings or protected by parentheses do not separate arguments. The number of formal and actual parameters must be the same. Strings and character constants in the token-string are scanned for formal parameters, but strings and character constants in the rest of the program are not scanned for defined identifiers to replace.

In both forms the replacement string is rescanned for more defined identifiers. In both forms a long definition may be continued on another line by writing \ at the end of the line to be continued. This facility is most valuable for definition of "manifest constants," as in

```
#define TABSIZE 100

int table[TABSIZE];
```

A control line of the form

**#undef** *identifier*

causes the identifier's preprocessor definition (if any) to be forgotten.

If a **#define**d identifier is the subject of a subsequent **#define** with no intervening **#undef**, then the two token-strings are compared textually. If the two token-strings are not identical (all white space is considered as equivalent), then the identifier is considered to be redefined.

## File Inclusion

A control line of the form

**#include** *"filename"*

causes the replacement of that line by the entire contents of the file *filename*. The named file is searched for first in the directory of the file containing the **#include**, and then in a sequence of specified or standard places. Alternatively, a control line of the form

**#include** *<filename>*

searches only the specified or standard places and not the directory of the **#include**. (How the places are specified is not part of the language. See **cpp**(1) for a description of how to specify additional libraries.)

**#include**s may be nested.

# Conditional Compilation

A compiler control line of the form

**#if** *restricted-constant-expression*

checks whether the restricted-constant expression evaluates to nonzero. (Constant expressions are discussed in "Constant Expressions"; the following additional restrictions apply here: the constant expression may not contain **sizeof**, casts, or an enumeration constant.)

A restricted-constant expression may also contain the additional unary expression

**defined** *identifier*

or

**defined** (*identifier*)

which evaluates to one if the identifier is currently defined in the preprocessor and zero if it is not.

All currently defined identifiers in restricted-constant-expressions are replaced by their token-strings (except those identifiers modified by **defined**) just as in normal text. The restricted-constant expression will be evaluated only after all expressions have finished. During this evaluation, all undefined (to the procedure) identifiers evaluate to zero.

A control line of the form

**#ifdef** *identifier*

checks whether the identifier is currently defined in the preprocessor; i.e., whether it has been the subject of a **#define** control line. It is equivalent to **#if defined** (*identifier*).

A control line of the form

**#ifndef** *identifier*

checks whether the identifier is currently undefined in the preprocessor. It is equivalent to **#if !defined** (*identifier*).

All three forms are followed by an arbitrary number of lines, possibly containing a control line

#### #else

and then by a control line

#### #endif

If the checked condition is true, then any lines between **#else** and **#endif** are ignored. If the checked condition is false, then any lines between the test and a **#else** or, lacking a **#else**, the **#endif** are ignored.

Another control directive is

#### #elif *restricted-constant-expression*

An arbitrary number of **#elif** directives can be included between **#if**, **#ifdef**, or **#ifndef** and **#else**, or **#endif** directives. These constructions may be nested.

## Line Control

For the benefit of other preprocessors that generate C programs, a line of the form

#### #line *constant* *"filename"*

causes the compiler to believe, for purposes of error diagnostics, that the line number of the next source line is given by the constant and the current input file is named by *"filename"*. If *"filename"* is absent, the remembered file name does not change.

## Version Control

This capability, known as *S-lists*, helps administer version control information. A line of the form

#### #ident *"version"*

puts any arbitrary string in the **.comment** section of the **a.out** file. It is usually used for version control. It is worth remembering that **.comment** sections are not loaded into memory when the **a.out** file is executed.

# Types Revisited

This part summarizes the operations that can be performed on objects of certain types.

## Structures and Unions

Structures and unions may be assigned, passed as arguments to functions, and returned by functions. Other plausible operators, such as equality comparison and structure casts, are not implemented.

In a reference to a structure or union member, the name on the right of the $->$ or the . must specify a member of the aggregate named or pointed to by the expression on the left. In general, a member of a union may not be inspected unless the value of the union has been assigned using that same member. However, one special guarantee is made by the language in order to simplify the use of unions: if a union contains several structures that share a common initial sequence and if the union currently contains one of these structures, it is permitted to inspect the common initial part of any of the contained structures. For example, the following is a legal fragment:

```
union
{
        struct
        {
                int        type;
        } n;
        struct
        {
                int        type;
                int        intnode;
        } ni;
        struct
        {
                int        type;
                float      floatnode;
        } nf;
} u;
...
u.nf.type = FLOAT;
u.nf.floatnode = 3.14;
...
if (u.n.type == FLOAT)
        ... sin(u.nf.floatnode) ...
```

# Functions

There are only two things that can be done with a function: call it or take its address. If the name of a function appears in an expression not in the function-name position of a call, a pointer to the function is generated. Thus, to pass one function to another, one might say

```
int f();
...
g(f);
```

Then the definition of **g** might read

```
g(funcp)
        int (*funcp)();
{
        ...
        (*funcp)();
        ...
}
```

Notice that **f** must be declared explicitly in the calling routine since its appearance in **g(f)** was not followed by **(**.

## Arrays, Pointers, and Subscripting

Every time an identifier of array type appears in an expression, it is converted into a pointer to the first member of the array. Because of this conversion, arrays are not lvalues. By definition, the subscript operator **[]** is interpreted in such a way that **E1[E2]** is identical to **\*((E1)+(E2))**. Because of the conversion rules that apply to **+**, if **E1** is an array and **E2** an integer, then **E1[E2]** refers to the **E2 -th** member of **E1**. Therefore, despite its asymmetric appearance, subscripting is a commutative operation.

A consistent rule is followed in the case of multidimensional arrays. If **E** is an $n$-dimensional array of rank i×j×...×k, then **E** appearing in an expression is converted to a pointer to an (n−1)-dimensional array with rank j×...×k. If the * operator, either explicitly or implicitly as a result of subscripting, is applied to this pointer, the result is the pointed-to (n−1)-dimensional array, which itself is immediately converted into a pointer.

For example, consider **int x[3][5];** Here **x** is a 3×5 array of integers. When **x** appears in an expression, it is converted to a pointer to (the first of three) 5-membered arrays of integers. In the expression **x[i]**, which is equivalent to **\*(x+i)**, **x** is first converted to a pointer as described; then **i** is converted to the type of **x**, which involves multiplying **i** by the length the object to which the pointer points, namely 5-integer objects. The results are added and indirection applied to yield an array (of five integers) which in turn is converted to a pointer to the first of the integers. If there is another subscript, the same argument applies again; this time the result is an integer.

Arrays in C are stored row-wise (last subscript varies fastest) and the first subscript in the declaration helps determine the amount of storage consumed by an array. Arrays play no other part in subscript calculations.

## Explicit Pointer Conversions

Certain conversions involving pointers are permitted but have implementation-dependent aspects. They are all specified by means of an explicit type-conversion operator, see "Unary Operators" under "Expressions" and "Type Names" under "Declarations."

A pointer may be converted to any of the integral types large enough to hold it. Whether an **int** or **long** is required is machine dependent. The mapping function is also machine dependent but is intended to be unsurprising to those who know the addressing structure of the machine.

An object of integral type may be explicitly converted to a pointer. The mapping always carries an integer converted from a pointer back to the same pointer but is otherwise machine dependent.

A pointer to one type may be converted to a pointer to another type. The resulting pointer may cause addressing exceptions upon use if the subject pointer does not refer to an object suitably aligned in storage. It is guaranteed that a pointer to an object of a given size may be converted to a pointer to an object of a smaller size and back again without change.

For example, a storage-allocation routine might accept a size (in bytes) of an object to allocate, and return a **char** pointer; it might be used in this way.

```
extern char *alloc();
double *dp;

dp = (double *) alloc(sizeof(double));
*dp = 22.0 / 7.0;
```

The **alloc** must ensure (in a machine-dependent way) that its return value is suitable for conversion to a pointer to **double**; then the use of the function is portable.

# Constant Expressions

In several places C requires expressions that evaluate to a constant: after **case**, as array bounds, and in initializers. In the first two cases, the expression can involve only integer constants, character constants, casts to integral types, enumeration constants, and **sizeof** expressions, possibly connected by the binary operators

$$+ - * / \% \& | \char`\^ \ll \gg == != < > <= >= \&\& |$$

or by the unary operators

$$- \sim$$

or by the ternary operator

$$?:$$

Parentheses can be used for grouping but not for function calls.

More latitude is permitted for initializers; besides constant expressions as discussed above, one can also use floating constants and arbitrary casts and can also apply the unary **&** operator to external or static objects and to external or static arrays subscripted with a constant expression. The unary **&** can also be applied implicitly by appearance of unsubscripted arrays and functions. The basic rule is that initializers must evaluate either to a constant or to the address of a previously declared external or static object plus or minus a constant.

# Portability Considerations

Certain parts of C are inherently machine dependent. The following list of potential trouble spots is not meant to be all-inclusive but to point out the main ones.

Purely hardware issues like word size and the properties of floating point arithmetic and integer division have proven in practice to be not much of a problem. Other facets of the hardware are reflected in differing implementations. Some of these, particularly sign extension (converting a negative character into a negative integer) and the order in which bytes are placed in a word, are nuisances that must be carefully watched. Most of the others are only minor problems.

The number of **register** variables that can actually be placed in registers varies from machine to machine as does the set of valid types. Nonetheless, the compilers all do things properly for their own machine; excess or invalid **register** declarations are ignored.

The order of evaluation of function arguments is not specified by the language. The order in which side effects take place is also unspecified.

Since character constants are really objects of type **int**, multicharacter character constants may be permitted. The specific implementation is very machine dependent because the order in which characters are assigned to a word varies from one machine to another.

Fields are assigned to words and characters to integers right to left on some machines and left to right on other machines. These differences are invisible to isolated programs that do not indulge in type punning (e.g., by converting an **int** pointer to a **char** pointer and inspecting the pointed-to storage) but must be accounted for when conforming to externally-imposed storage layouts.

# Syntax Summary

This summary of C syntax is intended more for aiding comprehension than as an exact statement of the language.

## Expressions

The basic expressions are:

*expression:*
    *primary*
    * *expression*
    & *lvalue*
    − *expression*
    ! *expression*
    ~ *expression*
    ++ *lvalue*
    −− *lvalue*
    *lvalue* ++
    *lvalue* −−
    **sizeof** *expression*
    **sizeof (***type-name***)**
    ( *type-name* ) *expression*
    *expression binop expression*
    *expression ? expression : expression*
    *lvalue asgnop expression*
    *expression , expression*

*primary:*
    *identifier*
    *constant*
    *string literal*
    ( *expression* )
    *primary ( expression-list* $_{opt}$ *)*
    *primary [ expression ]*
    *primary . identifier*
    *primary* −> *identifier*

*lvalue:*
>    *identifier*
>    *primary [ expression ]*
>    *lvalue . identifier*
>    *primary* −> *identifier*
>    *∗ expression*
>    *( lvalue )*

The primary-expression operators

>    () [] . −>

have highest priority and group left to right. The unary operators

>    ∗ & − ! ~ ++ −− **sizeof** *( type-name )*

have priority below the primary operators but higher than any binary operator and group right to left. Binary operators group left to right; they have priority decreasing as indicated below.

*binop:*
>    ∗   /   %
>    +   −
>    >>   <<
>    <   >   <=   >=
>    ==   !=
>    &
>    ^
>    |
>    &&
>    |

The conditional operator groups right to left.

Assignment operators all have the same priority and all group right to left.

*asgnop:*
>    =   +=   −=   ∗=   /=   %=   >>=   <<=   &=   ^=   |=

The comma operator has the lowest priority and groups left to right.

# Declarations

*declaration:*
    *decl-specifiers init-declarator-list$_{opt}$ ;*

*decl-specifiers:*
    *type-specifier decl-specifiers$_{opt}$*
    *sc-specifier decl-specifiers$_{opt}$*

*sc-specifier:*
    **auto**
    **static**
    **extern**
    **register**
    **typedef**

*type-specifier:*
    *struct-or-union-specifier*
    *typedef-name*
    *enum-specifier*

*basic-type-specifier:*
    *basic-type*
    *basic-type basic-type-specifiers*

*basic-type:*
    **char**
    **short**
    **int**
    **long**
    **unsigned**
    **float**
    **double**
    **void**

*enum-specifier:*
    **enum** { *enum-list* }
    **enum** *identifier* { *enum-list* }
    **enum** *identifier*


*enum-list:*
    *enumerator*
    *enum-list , enumerator*

*enumerator:*
    *identifier*
    *identifier = constant-expression*

*init-declarator-list:*
    *init-declarator*
    *init-declarator , init-declarator-list*

*init-declarator:*
    *declarator initializer*$_{opt}$

*declarator:*
    *identifier*
    *( declarator )*
    *\* declarator*
    *declarator ()*
    *declarator [ constant-expression*$_{opt}$ *]*

*struct-or-union-specifier:*
    **struct** { *struct-decl-list* }
    **struct** *identifier* { *struct-decl-list* }
    **struct** *identifier*
    **union** { *struct-decl-list* }
    **union** *identifier* { *struct-decl-list* }
    **union** *identifier*

*struct-decl-list:*
    *struct-declaration*
    *struct-declaration struct-decl-list*

*struct-declaration:*
      *type-specifier struct-declarator-list ;*

*struct-declarator-list:*
      *struct-declarator*
      *struct-declarator , struct-declarator-list*

*struct-declarator:*
      *declarator*
      *declarator : constant-expression*
      *: constant-expression*

*initializer:*
      *= expression*
      *= { initializer-list }*
      *= { initializer-list , }*

*initializer-list:*
      *expression*
      *initializer-list , initializer-list*
      *{ initializer-list }*
      *{ initializer-list , }*

*type-name:*
      *type-specifier abstract-declarator*

*abstract-declarator:*
      *empty*
      *( abstract-declarator )*
      *\* abstract-declarator*
      *abstract-declarator ()*
      *abstract-declarator [ constant-expression$_{opt}$ ]*

*typedef-name:*
      *identifier*

# Statements

*compound-statement:*
    { *declaration-list*$_{opt}$ *statement-list*$_{opt}$ }

*declaration-list:*
    *declaration*
    *declaration declaration-list*

*statement-list:*
    *statement*
    *statement statement-list*

*statement:*
    *compound-statement*
    *expression* ;
    **if** ( *expression* ) *statement*
    **if** ( *expression* ) *statement* **else** *statement*
    **while** ( *expression* ) *statement*
    **do** *statement* **while** ( *expression* ) ;
    **for** ( *exp*$_{opt}$;*exp*$_{opt}$;*exp*$_{opt}$ ) *statement*
    **switch** ( *expression* ) *statement*
    **case** *constant-expression* : *statement*
    **default** : *statement*
    **break** ;
    **continue** ;
    **return** ;
    **return** *expression* ;
    **goto** *identifier* ;
    *identifier* : *statement*
    ;

# External Definitions

*program:*
      *external-definition*
      *external-definition program*

*external-definition:*
      *function-definition*
      *data-definition*

*function-definition:*
      *decl-specifier$_{opt}$ function-declarator function-body*

*function-declarator:*
      *declarator ( parameter-list$_{opt}$ )*

*parameter-list:*
      *identifier*
      *identifier , parameter-list*

*function-body:*
      *declaration-list$_{opt}$ compound-statement*

*data-definition:*
      **extern** *declaration ;*
      **static** *declaration ;*

# Preprocessor

**#define** *identifier token-string$_{opt}$*
**#define** *identifier(identifier,...)token-string$_{opt}$*
**#undef** *identifier*
**#include** *"filename"*
**#include** *<filename>*
**#if** *restricted-constant-expression*
**#ifdef** *identifier*
**#ifndef** *identifier*
**#elif** *restricted-constant-expression*
**#else**
**#endif**
**#line** *constant "filename"*
**#ident** *"version"*

# Appendix A: Index to Utilities

Throughout the text of this guide, commands are discussed without identifying the package to which the command belongs. The assumption has been that all command packages are present on the machine on which you are working.

If some commands seem to produce only a *not found* message on your computer, it may be that the package to which the command belongs has not been installed. If that happens, check with the administrator of your system.

## ■ Editing Utilities

## ■ Essential Utilities

## ■ FORTRAN Programming Language Utilities

## ■ Graphics Utilities

■ **Terminal Filters Utilities**

■ **Terminal Information Utilities**

■ **User Environment Utilities**

# Glossary

Ada

Named after the Countess of Lovelace, the nineteenth century mathematician and computer pioneer, Ada is a high-level general-purpose programming language developed under the sponsorship of the U.S. Department of Defense. Ada was developed to provide consistency among programs originating in different branches of the military. Ada features include packages that make data objects visible only to the modules that need them, task objects that facilitate parallel processing, and an exception handling mechanism that encourages well-structured error processing.

ANSI standard

ANSI is the acronym for the American National Standards Institute. ANSI establishes guidelines in the computing industry, from the definition of ASCII to the determination of overall datacom system performance. ANSI standards have been established for both the Ada and FORTRAN programming languages, and a standard for C has been proposed.

a.out file

**a.out** is the default file name used by the link editor when it outputs a successfully compiled, executable file. **a.out** contains object files that are combined to create a complete working program. Object file format is described in Chapter 11, "The Common Object File Format," and in **a.out**(4) in the *Programmer's Reference Manual*.

application program

An application program is a working program in a system. Such programs are usually unique to one type of users' work, although some application programs can be used in a variety of business situations. An accounting application, for example, may well be applicable to many different businesses.

archive

An archive file or archive library is a collection of data gathered from several files. Each of the files within an archive is called a member. The command **ar**(1) collects data for use as a library.

argument

An argument is additional information that is passed to a command or a function. On a command line, an argument is a character string or number that follows the command name and is separated from it by a space. There are two types of command-line arguments: options and operands. Options are immediately preceded by a minus sign (−) and change the execution or output of the command. Some options can themselves take arguments. Operands are preceded by a space and specify files or directories that will be operated on by the command. For example, in the command

**pr −t −h Heading file**

all of the elements after the **pr** are arguments. −**t** and −**h** are options, **Heading** is an argument to the −**h** option, and **file** is an operand.

For a function, arguments are enclosed within a pair of parentheses immediately following the function name. The number of arguments can be zero or more; if more than two are present they are separated by commas and the whole list enclosed by the parentheses. The formal definition of a function, such as might be found on a page in Section 3 of the *Programmer's Reference Manual*, describes the number and data type of argument(s) expected by the function.

ASCII

ASCII is an acronym for American Standard Code for Information Interchange, a standard for data representation that is followed in the UNIX system. ASCII code represents alphanumeric characters as binary numbers. The code includes 128 upper- and lower-case letters, numerals, and special characters. Each alphanumeric and special character has an ASCII code (binary) equivalent that is one byte long.

| | |
|---|---|
| assembler | The assembler is a translating program that accepts instructions written in the assembly language of the computer and translates them into the binary representation of machine instructions. In many cases, the assembly language instructions map 1 to 1 with the binary machine instructions. |
| assembly language | A programming language that uses the instruction set that applies to a particular computer. |
| BASIC | BASIC is a high-level conversational programming language that allows a computer to be used much like a complex electronic calculating machine. The name is an acronym for Beginner's All-purpose Symbolic Instruction Code. |
| branch table | A branch table is an implementation technique for fixing the addresses of text symbols, without forfeiting the ability to update code. Instead of being directly associated with function code, text symbols label jump instructions that transfer control to the real code. Branch table addresses do not change, even when one changes the code of a routine. Jump table is another name for branch table. |
| buffer | A buffer is a storage space in computer memory where data are stored temporarily into convenient units for system operations. Buffers are often used by programs, such as editors, that access and alter text or data frequently. When you edit a file, a copy of its contents are read into a buffer where you make changes to the text. For the changes to become part of the permanent file, you must write the buffer contents back into the permanent file. This replaces the contents of the file with the contents of the buffer. When you quit the editor, the contents of the buffer are flushed. |
| byte | A byte is a unit of storage in the computer. On many UNIX systems, a byte is eight bits (binary digits), the equivalent of one character of text. |

| | |
|---|---|
| byte order | Byte order refers to the order in which data are stored in computer memory. |
| C | The C programming language is a general-purpose programming language that features economy of expression, control flow, data structures, and a variety of operators. It can be used to perform both high-level and low-level tasks. Although it has been called a system programming language, because it is useful for writing operating systems, it has been used equally effectively to write major numerical, text-processing, and data base programs. The C programming language was designed for and implemented on the UNIX system; however, the language is not limited to any one operating system or machine. |
| C compiler | The C compiler converts C programs into assembly language programs that are eventually translated into object files by the assembler. |
| C preprocessor | The C preprocessor is a component of the C Compilation System. In C source code, statements preceded with a pound sign (#) are directives to the preprocessor. Command line options of the **cc**(1) command may also be used to control the actions of the preprocessor. The main work of the preprocessor is to perform file inclusions and macro substitution. |
| CCS | CCS is an acronym for C Compilation System, which is a set of programming language utilities used to produce object code from C source code. The major components of a C Compilation System are a C preprocessor, C compiler, assembler, and link editor. The C preprocessor accepts C source code as input, performs any preprocessing required, then passes the processed code to the C compiler, which produces assembly language code that it passes to the assembler. The assembler in turn produces object code that can be linked to other object files by the link editor. The object files produced are in the Common Object File Format (COFF). Other components of CCS include a symbolic debugger, an optimizer that makes the code produced as efficient as possible, productivity tools, |

tools used to read and manipulate object files, and libraries that provide runtime support, access to system calls, input/output, string manipulation, mathematical functions, and other code processing functions.

COBOL

COBOL is an acronym for COmmon Business Oriented Language. COBOL is a high-level programming language designed for business and commercial applications. The English-language statements of COBOL provide a relatively machine-independent method of expressing a business-oriented problem to the computer.

COFF

COFF is an acronym for Common Object File Format. COFF refers to the format of the output file produced on some UNIX systems by the assembler and the link editor. This format is also used by other operating systems. The following are some of its key features:

☐ Applications may add system-dependent information to the object file without causing access utilities to become obsolete.

☐ Space is provided for symbolic information used by debuggers and other applications.

☐ Users may make some modifications in the object file construction at compile time.

command

A command is the term commonly used to refer to an instruction that a user types at a computer terminal keyboard. It can be the name of a file that contains an executable program or a shell script that can be processed or executed by the computer on request. A command is composed of a word or string of letters and/or special characters that can continue for several (terminal) lines, up to 256 characters. A command name is sometimes used interchangeably with a program name.

command line

A command line is composed of the command name followed by any argument(s) required by the command or optionally included by the user. The manual page for a command includes a command line synopsis in a notation designed to show the correct way to type in a command, with or without options and arguments.

compiler

A compiler transforms the high-level language instructions in a program (the source code) into object code or assembly language. Assembly language code may then be passed to the assembler for further translation into machine instructions.

core

Core is a (mostly archaic) synonym for primary memory.

core file

A core file is an image of a terminated process saved for debugging. A core file is created under the name "core" in the current directory of the process when an abnormal event occurs resulting in the process' termination. A list of these events is found in the **signal**(2) manual page in section 2 of the *Programmer's Reference Manual*.

core image

Core image is a copy of all the segments of a running or terminated program. The copy may exist in main storage, in the swap area. or in a core file.

curses

**curses**(3X) is a library of C routines that are designed to handle input, output, and other operations in screen management programs. The name **curses** comes from the cursor optimization that the routines provide. When a screen management program is run, cursor optimization minimizes the amount of time a cursor has to move about a screen to update its contents. The program refers to the **terminfo**(4) data base at run time to obtain the information that it needs about the screen (terminal) being used. See **terminfo**(4) in the *Programmer's Reference Manual*.

data symbol      A data symbol names a variable that may or may not be initialized. Normally, these variables reside in read/write memory during execution. See text symbol.

data base      A data base is a bank of information on a particular subject or subjects. On-line data bases are designed so that by using subject headings, key words, or key phrases you can search for, analyze, update, and print out data.

debug      Debugging is the process of locating and correcting errors in computer programs.

default      A default is the way a computer will perform a task in the absence of other instructions.

delimiter      A delimiter is an initial character that identifies the next character or character string as a particular kind of argument. Delimiters are typically used for option names on a command line; they identify the associated word as an option (or as a string of several options if the options are bundled). In the UNIX system command syntax, a minus sign (−) is most often the delimiter for option names, for example, −s or −n, although some commands also use a plus sign (+).

directory      A directory is a type of file used to group and organize other files or directories. A directory consists of entries that specify further files (including directories) and constitutes a node of the file system. A subdirectory is a directory that is pointed to by a directory one level above it in the file system organization.

     The **ls**(1) command is used to list the contents of a directory. When you first log onto the system, you are in your home directory ($HOME). You can move to another directory by using the **cd**(1) command and you can print the name of the current directory by using the **pwd**(1) command. You can also create new directories with the **mkdir**(1) command and remove empty directories with **rmdir**(1).

A directory name is a string of characters that identifies a directory. It can be a simple directory name, the relative path name or the full path name of a directory.

dynamic linking

Dynamic linking refers to the ability to resolve symbolic references at run time. Systems that use dynamic linking can execute processes without resolving unused references. See static linking.

environment

An environment is a collection of resources used to support a function. In the UNIX system, the shell environment is composed of variables whose values define the way you interact with the system. For example, your environment includes your shell prompt string, specifics for backspace and erase characters, and commands for sending output from your terminal to the computer.

An environment variable is a shell variable such as $HOME (which stands for your login directory) or $PATH (which is a list of directories the shell will search through for executable commands) that is part of your environment. When you log in, the system executes programs that create most of the environmental variables that you need for the commands to work. These variables come from **/etc/profile**, a file that defines a general working environment for all users when they log onto a system. In addition, you can define and set variables in your personal **.profile** file, which you create in your login directory to tailor your own working environment. You can also temporarily set variables at the shell level.

executable file

An executable file is a file that can be processed or executed by the computer without any further translation. That is, when you type in the file name, the commands in the file are executed. An object file that is ready to run (ready to be copied into the address space of a process to run as the code of that process) is an executable file. Files containing shell commands are also executable. A file may be given execute permission by using the **chmod**(1) command. In addition to being ready to run, a file in the UNIX system needs to have execute permission.

exit
: A specific system call that causes the termination of a process. The **exit**(2) call will close any open files and clean up most other information and memory which was used by the process.

exit status: return code
: An exit status or return code is a code number returned to the shell when a command is terminated that indicates the cause of termination.

exported symbol
: A symbol that a shared library defines and makes available outside the library. See imported symbol.

expression
: An expression is a mathematical or logical symbol or meaningful combination of symbols. See regular expression.

file
: A file is an identifiable collection of information that, in the UNIX system, is a member of a file system. A file is known to the UNIX system as an inode plus the information the inode contains that tells whether the file is a plain file, a special file, or a directory. A plain file may contain text, data, programs or other information that forms a coherent unit. A special file is a hardware device or portion thereof, such as a disk partition. A directory is a type of file that contains the names and inode addresses of other plain, special or directory files.

file and record locking
: The phrase "file and record locking" refers to software that protects records in a data file against the possibility of being changed by two users at the same time. Records (or the entire file) may be locked by one authorized user while changes are made. Other users are thus prevented from working with the same record until the changes are completed.

| file descriptor | A file descriptor is a number assigned by the operating system to a file when the file is opened by a process. File descriptors 0, 1, and 2 are reserved; file descriptor 0 is reserved for standard input (**stdin**), 1 is reserved for standard output (**stdout**), and 2 is reserved for standard error output (**stderr**). |
| --- | --- |
| file system | A UNIX file system is a hierarchical collection of directories and other files that are organized in a tree structure. The base of the structure is the root (/) directory; other directories, all subordinate to the root, are branches. The collection of files can be mounted on a block special file. Each file of a file system appears exactly once in the inode list of the file system and is accessible via a single, unique path from the root directory of the file system. |
| filter | A filter is a program that reads information from standard input, acts on it in some way, and sends its results to standard output. It is called a filter because it can be used as a data transformer in a pipeline. Filters are different from editors and other commands because filters do not change the contents of a file. Examples of filters are **grep**(1) and **tail**(1), which select and output part of the input; **sort**(1), which sorts the input; and **wc**(1), which counts the number of words, characters, and lines in the input. **sed**(1) and **awk**(1) are also filters but they are called programmable filters or data transformers because a program must be supplied as input in addition to the data to be transformed. |
| flag | A flag or option is used on a command line to signal a specific condition to a command or to request particular processing. UNIX system flags are usually indicated by a leading hyphen (−). The word option is sometimes used interchangeably with flag. Flag is also used as a verb to mean to point out or to draw attention to. See option. |

fork

**fork**(2) is a system call that divides a new process into two, the parent and child processes, with separate, but initially identical, text, data, and stack segments. After the duplication, the child (created) process is given a return code of 0 and the parent is given the process id of the newly created child as the return code.

FORTRAN

FORTRAN is an acronym for FORmula TRANslator. FORTRAN is a high-level programming language originally designed for scientific and engineering calculations but now also widely adapted for many business uses.

function

A function is a task done by a computer. In most modern programming languages, programs are made up of functions and procedures which perform small parts of the total job to be done.

header file

A header file is used in programming and in document formatting. In a programming context, a header file is a file that usually contains shared data declarations that are to be copied into source programs as they are compiled. A header file includes symbolic names for constants, macro definitions, external variable references and inclusion of other header files. The name of a header file customarily ends with '.h' (dot-h). Similarly, in a document formatting context, header files contain general formatting macros that describe a common document type and can be used with many different document bodies.

high-level language

A high-level language is a computer programming language such as C, FORTRAN, COBOL, or PASCAL that uses symbols and command statements representing actions the computer is to perform, the exact steps for a machine to follow. A high-level language must be translated into machine language by a compilation system before a computer can execute it. A characteristic of a high-level language is that each statement usually translates into a series of machine language instructions. The low-level details of the computer's internal organization are left to the compilation system.

host machine
    A host machine is the machine on which an **a.out** file is built.

imported symbol
    A symbol used but not defined by a shared library. See exported symbol.

interpreted language
    An interpreted language is a high-level language that is not translated by a compilation system and stored in an executable object file. The statements of a program in an interpreted language are translated each time the program is executed.

Interprocess Communication
    Interprocess Communication describes software that enables independent processes running at the same time, to exchange information through messages, semaphores, or shared memory.

interrupt
    An interrupt is a break in the normal flow of a system or program. Interrupts are initiated by signals that are generated by a hardware condition or a peripheral device indicating that a certain event has happened. When the interrupt is recognized by the hardware, an interrupt handling routine is executed. An interrupt character is a character (normally ASCII) that, when typed on a terminal, causes an interrupt. You can usually interrupt UNIX programs by pressing the delete or break keys, by typing Control-d, or by using the **kill**(1) command.

I/O (Input/Output)
    I/O is the process by which information enters (input) and leaves (output) the computer system.

kernel
    The kernel (comprising 5 to 10 percent of the operating system software) is the basic resident software on which the UNIX system relies. It is responsible for most operating system functions. It schedules and manages the work done by the computer and maintains the file system. The kernel has its own text, data, and stack areas.

lexical analysis

Lexical analysis is the process by which a stream of characters (often comprising a source program) is subdivided into its elementary words and symbols (called tokens). The tokens include the reserved words of the language, its identifiers and constants, and special symbols such as =, :=, and ;. Lexical analysis enables you to recognize, for example, that the stream of characters 'print("hello, universe")' is to be analyzed into a series of tokens beginning with the word 'print' and not with, say, the string 'print("h.' In compilers, a lexical analyzer is often called by the compiler's syntactic analyzer or parser, which determines the statements of the program (that is, the proper arrangements of its tokens).

library

A library is an archive file that contains object code and/or files for programs that perform common tasks. The library provides a common source for object code, thus saving space by providing one copy of the code instead of requiring every program that wants to incorporate the functions in the code to have its own copy. The link editor may select functions and data as needed.

link editor

A link editor, or loader, collects and merges separately compiled object files by linking together object files and the libraries that are referenced into executable load modules. The result is an **a.out** file. Link editing may be done automatically when you use the compilation system to process your programs on the UNIX system, but you can also link edit previously compiled files by using the **ld**(1) command.

magic number

The magic number is contained in the header of an **a.out** file. It indicates what the type of the file is, whether shared or non-shared text, and on which processor the file is executable.

makefile

A makefile is a file that lists dependencies among the source code files of a software product and methods for updating them, usually by recompilation. The **make**(1) command uses the makefile to maintain self-consistent software.

| | |
|---|---|
| manual page | A manual page, or "man page" in UNIX system jargon, is the repository for the detailed description of a command, a system call, subroutine or other UNIX system component. |
| null pointer | A null pointer is a C pointer with a value of 0. |
| object code | Object code is executable machine-language code produced from source code or from other object files by an assembler or a compilation system. An object file is a file of object code and associated data. An object file that is ready to run is an executable file. |
| optimizer | An optimizer, an optional step in the compilation process, improves the efficiency of the assembly language code. The optimizer reduces the space used by and speeds the execution time of the code. |
| option | An option is an argument used in a command line to modify program output by modifying the execution of a command. An option is usually one character preceded by a hyphen (−). When you do not specify any options, the command will execute according to its default options. For example, in the command line |

**ls −a −l directory**

−**a** and −l are the options that modify the **ls**(1) command to list all **directory** entries, including entries whose names begin with a period (.), in the long format (including permissions, size, and date).

| | |
|---|---|
| parent process | A parent process occurs when a process is split into two, a parent process and a child process, with separate, but initially identical text, data, and stack segments. |
| parse | To parse is to analyze a sentence in order identify its components and to determine their grammatical relationship. In computer terminology the word has a similar meaning, but instead of sentences, program statements or commands are analyzed. |

PASCAL

PASCAL is a multipurpose high-level programming language often used to teach programming. It is based on the ALGOL programming language and emphasizes structured programming.

path name

A path name is a way of designating the exact location of a file in a file system. It is made up of a series of directory names that proceed down the hierarchical path of the file system. The directory names are separated by a slash character (/). The last name in the path is either a file or another directory. If the path name begins with a slash, it is called a full path name; the initial slash means that the path begins at the **root** directory.

A path name that does not begin with a slash is known as a relative path name, meaning relative to the present working directory. A relative path name may begin either with a directory name or with two dots followed by a slash (../). One that begins with a directory name indicates that the ultimate file or directory is below the present working directory in the hierarchy. One that begins with ../ indicates that the path first proceeds up the hierarchy; ../ is the parent of the present working directory.

permissions

Permissions are a means of defining a right to access a file or directory in the UNIX file system. Permissions are granted separately to you, the owner of the file or directory, your group, and all others. There are three basic permissions:

☐  Read permission (r) includes permission to cat, pg, lp, and **cp** a file.

☐  Write permission (w) is the permission to change a file.

☐  Execute permission (x) is the permission to run an executable file.

Permissions can be changed with the UNIX system **chmod**(1) command.

pipe

A pipe causes the output of one command to be used as the input for the next command so that the two run in sequence. You can do this by preceding each command after the first command with the pipe symbol ( | ), which indicates that the output from the process on the left should be routed to the process on the right. For example, in the command

**who | wc −l,**

the output from the **who**(1) command, which lists the users who are logged on to the system, is used as input for the word-count command, **wc**(1), with the **l** option. The result of this pipeline (succession of commands connected by pipes) is the number of people who are currently logged on to the system.

portable

Portability describes the degree of ease with which a program or a library can be moved or ported from one system to another. Portability is desirable because once a program is developed it is used on many systems. If the program writer must change the program in many different ways before it can be distributed to the other systems, time is wasted, and each modification increases the chances for an error.

preprocessor

Preprocessor is a generic name for a program that prepares an input file for another program. For example, **neqn**(1) and **tbl**(1) are preprocessors for **nroff**(1). **grap**(1) is a preprocessor for **pic**(1). **cpp**(1) is a preprocessor for the C compiler.

process

A process is a program that is at some stage of execution. In the UNIX system, it also refers to the execution of a computer environment, including contents of memory, register values, name of the current working directory, status of files, information recorded at login time, etc. Every time you type the name of a file that contains an executable program, you initiate a new process. Shell programs can cause the initiation of many processes because they can contain many command lines.

The process id is a unique system-wide identification number that identifies an active process. The process status command, **ps**(1), prints the process ids of the processes that belong to you.

program
: A program is a sequence of instructions or commands that cause the computer to perform a specific task, for example, changing text, making a calculation, or reporting on the status of the system. A subprogram is part of a larger program and can be compiled independently.

regular expression
: A regular expression is a string of alphanumeric characters and special characters that describe a character string. It is a shorthand way of describing a pattern to be searched for in a file. The pattern-matching functions of **ed**(1) and **grep**(1), for example, use regular expressions.

routine
: A routine is a discrete section of a program to accomplish a set of related tasks

semaphore
: In the UNIX system, a semaphore is a sharable short unsigned integer maintained through a family of system calls which include calls for increasing the value of the semaphore, setting its value, and for blocking waiting for its value to reach some value. Semaphores are part of the UNIX system IPC facility.

shared library
: Shared libraries include object modules that may be shared among several processes at execution time.

shared memory
: Shared memory is an IPC (interprocess communication) facility in which two or more processes can share the same data space.

shell
: The shell is the UNIX system program—**sh**(1)— responsible for handling all interaction between you and the system. It is a command language interpreter that understands your commands and causes the computer to act on them. The shell also establishes the

environment at your terminal.  A shell normally is started for you as part of the login process.  Three shells, the Bourne shell, the Korn shell and the C shell, are popular.  The shell can also be used as a programming language to write procedures for a variety of tasks.

signal:  signal number

A signal is a message that you send to processes or processes send to one another.  The most common signals you might send to a process are ones that would cause the process to stop: for example, interrupt, quit, or kill.  A signal sent by a running process is usually a sign of an an exceptional occurrence that has caused the process to terminate or divert from the normal flow of control.

source code

Source code is the programming-language version of a program.  Before the computer can execute the program, the source code must be translated to machine language by a compilation system or an interpreter.

standard error

Standard error is an output stream from a program.  It is normally used to convey error messages.  In the UNIX system, the default case is to associate standard error with the user's terminal.

standard input

Standard input is an input stream to a program.  In the UNIX system, the default case is to associate standard input with the user's terminal.

standard output

Standard output is an output stream from a program.  In the UNIX system, the default case is to associate standard output with the user's terminal.

stdio:  standard input-output

**stdio**(3S) is a collection of functions for formatted and character-by-character input-output at a higher level than the basic read, write, and open operations.

static linking

Static linking refers to the requirement that symbolic references be resolved before run time.  See dynamic linking.

stream

    ☐    A stream is an open file with buffering provided by the stdio package.

    ☐    A stream is a full duplex, processing and data transfer path in the kernel. It implements a connection between a driver in kernel space and a process in user space, providing a general character input/output interface for the user processes.

string

A string is a contiguous sequence of characters treated as a unit. Strings are normally bounded by white space(s), tab(s), or a character designated as a separator. A string value is a specified group of characters symbolized to the shell by a variable.

strip

**strip**(1) is a command that removes the symbol table and relocation bits from an executable file.

subroutine

A subroutine is a program that defines desired operations and may be used in another program to produce the desired operations. A subroutine can be arranged so that control may be transferred to it from a master routine and so that, at the conclusion of the subroutine, control reverts to the master routine. Such a subroutine is usually called a closed subroutine. A single routine may be simultaneously a subroutine with respect to another routine and a master routine with respect to a third.

symbol table

A symbol table describes information in an object file about the names and functions in that file. The symbol table and relocation bits are used by the link editor and by the debuggers.

symbol value

The value of a symbol, typically its virtual address, used to resolve references.

syntax

    ☐    Command syntax is the order in which command names, options, option arguments, and operands are put together to form a command on the command line. The command name is first, followed by options and operands. The order of the options and the operands varies from command to command.

☐ Language syntax is the set of rules that describe how the elements of a programming language may legally be used.

**system call**
A system call is a request by an active process for a service performed by the UNIX system kernel, such as I/O, process creation, etc. All system operations are allocated, initiated, monitored, manipulated, and terminated through system calls. System calls allow you to request the operating system to do some work that the program would not normally be able to do. For example, the **getuid**(2) system call allows you to inspect information that is not normally available since it resides in the operating system's address space.

**target machine**
A target machine is the machine on which an **a.out** file is run. While it may be the same machine on which the **a.out** file was produced, the term implies that it may be a different machine.

**TCP/IP (Transmission Control Protocol/Internetwork Protocol)**
TCP/IP is a connection-oriented, end-to-end reliable protocol designed to fit into a layered hierarchy of protocols that support multi-network applications. It is the Department of Defense standard in packet networks.

**terminal definition**
A terminal definition is an entry in the **terminfo**(4) data base that describes the characteristics of a terminal. See **terminfo**(4) and **curses**(3X) in the *Programmer's Reference Manual*.

**terminfo**

☐ a group of routines within the curses library that handle certain terminal capabilities. For example, if your terminal has programmable function keys, you can use these routines to program the keys.

☐    a data base containing the compiled descriptions of many terminals that can be used with **curses**(3X) screen management programs. These descriptions specify the capabilities of a terminal and how it performs various operations — for example, how many lines and columns it has and how its control characters are interpreted. A **curses**(3X) program refers to the data base at run time to obtain the information that it needs about the terminal being used.

See **curses**(3X) in the *Programmer's Reference Manual*. **terminfo**(4) routines can be used in shell programs, as well as C programs.

text symbol

A text symbol is a symbol, usually a function name, that is defined in the **.text** portion of an **a.out** file.

tool

A tool is a program, or package of programs, that performs a given task.

trap

A trap is a condition caused by an error where a process state transition occurs and a signal is sent to the currently running process.

UNIX operating system

The UNIX operating system is a general-purpose, multiuser, interactive, time-sharing operating system developed by ˙AT&T. An operating system is the software on the computer under which all other software runs. The UNIX operating system has two basic parts:

☐    The kernel is the program that is responsible for most operating system functions. It schedules and manages all the work done by the computer and maintains the file system. It is always running and is invisible to users.

☐    The shell is the program responsible for handling all interaction between users and the computer. It includes a powerful command language called shell language.

The utility programs or UNIX system commands are executed using the shell, and allow users to communicate with each other, edit and manipulate files, and write and execute programs in several programming languages.

**userid**

A userid is an integer value, usually associated with a login name, used by the system to identify owners of files and directories. The userid of a process becomes the owner of files created by the process and descendent (forked) processes.

**utility**

A utility is a standard, permanently available program used to perform routine functions or to assist a programmer in the diagnosis of hardware and software errors, for example, a loader, editor, debugging, or diagnostics package.

**variable**

□ A variable in a computer program is an object whose value may change during the execution of the program, or from one execution to the next.

□ A variable in the shell is a name representing a string of characters (a string value).

□ A variable normally set only on a command line is called a parameter (positional parameter and keyword parameter).

□ A variable may be simply a name to which the user (user-defined variable) or the shell itself may assign string values.

**white space**

White space is one or more spaces, tabs, or newline characters. White space is normally used to separate strings of characters, and is required to separate the command from its arguments on a command line.

**window**

A window is a screen within your terminal screen that is set off from the rest of the screen. If you have two windows on your screen, they are independent of each other and the rest of the screen.

The most common way to create windows on a UNIX system is by using the layers capability of the TELE-TYPE 5620 Dot-Mapped Display. Each window you create with this program has a separate shell running it. Each one of these shells is called a layer.

If you do not have this facility, the **shl**(1) command, which stands for shell layer, offers a function similar to the layers program. You cannot create windows using **shl**(1), but you can start different shells that are independent of each other. Each of the shells you create with **shl**(1) is called a layer.

word

A word is a unit of storage in a computer that is composed of bytes of information. The number of bytes in a word depends on the computer you are using. The AT&T 3B Computers, for example, have 32 bits or 4 bytes per word, and 16 bits or 2 bytes per half word.

# Index

# TEAR OUT THIS PAGE TO ORDER ADDITIONAL COPIES OF THIS TITLE AS WELL AS COPIES OF THE OTHER VOLUMES IN THE PRENTICE HALL/AT&T UNIX® SYSTEM V RELEASE 3.0 SERIES

| QUANTITY | TITLE/AUTHOR | ISBN | PRICE | TOTAL |
|---|---|---|---|---|
| _____ | UNIX® System V Utilities Release Notes, AT&T | 013-940552-6 | $21.95 | _____ |
| _____ | UNIX® System V Programmer's Reference Manual, AT&T | 013-940479-1 | $34.95 | _____ |
| _____ | UNIX® System V Network Programmer's Guide, AT&T | 013-940461-9 | $24.95 | _____ |
| _____ | UNIX® System V Streams Programmer's Guide, AT&T | 013-940537-2 | $24.95 | _____ |
| _____ | UNIX® System V Streams Primer, AT&T | 013-940529-1 | $21.95 | _____ |
| _____ | UNIX® System V User's Reference Manual, AT&T | 013-940487-2 | $34.95 | _____ |
| _____ | UNIX® System V User's Guide, 2nd Ed., AT&T | 013-940545-3 | $24.95 | _____ |
| _____ | UNIX® System V Programmer's Guide, AT&T | 013-940438-4 | $34.95 | _____ |

TOTAL $_____
— DISCOUNT (IF APPROPRIATE) _____
NEW TOTAL $_____

## AND TAKE ADVANTAGE OF THESE SPECIAL OFFERS!

When ordering 3 or 4 copies (of the same or different titles) take 10% off the total list price.

When ordering 5 to 20 copies (of the same or different titles) take 15% off the total list price.

To receive a greater discount when ordering more than 20 copies, call or write: Special Sales Department, College Marketing, Prentice Hall, Englewood Cliffs, N.J. 07632 (201-592-2406).

## SAVE!

If payment accompanies order, plus your state's sales tax where applicable, Prentice Hall pays postage and handling charges. Same return privilege refund guaranteed. Please do not mail in cash.

☐ **PAYMENT ENCLOSED**—shipping and handling to be paid by publisher (please include your state's tax where applicable).

☐ **SEND BOOKS ON 15-DAY TRIAL BASIS** & bill me (with small charge for shipping and handling).

Name _____

Address _____

City _____ State _____ Zip _____
I prefer to charge my  ☐ Visa      ☐ MasterCard
Card Number _____ Expiration Date _____

Signature _____
*All prices listed are subject to change without notice.*
*OFFER NOT VALID OUTSIDE U.S.*

**MAIL YOUR ORDER TO:** Prentice Hall Book Distribution Center, Route 59 at Brook Hill Drive, West Nyack, NY 10994

**DEPT. 1**                                                                D–JSAR–RO(3)